Steve Rubin

C

# Designing and Using Tools for Educational Assessment

**Madhabi Chatterji**

*Teachers College, Columbia University*

Boston • New York • San Francisco
Mexico City • Montreal • Toronto • London • Madrid • Munich • Paris
Hong Kong • Singapore • Tokyo • Cape Town • Sydney

*In memory of my Father*

**Series Editor:**  *Arnis Burvikovs*
**Editorial Assistant:**  *Christine Lyons*
**Marketing Manager:**  *Tara Whorf*
**Production Editor:**  *Kathy Smith*
**Editorial-Production Service:**  *Chestnut Hill Enterprises*
**Composition Buyer:**  *Linda Cox*
**Manufacturing Buyer:**  *JoAnne Sweeney*
**Cover Administrator:**  *Kristina Mose-Libon*
**Electronic Composition:**  *Achorn Graphics*

For related titles and support materials, visit our online catalog at www.ablongman.com.

Between the time Website information is gathered and then published, it is not unusual for some sites to have closed. Also, the transcription of URLs can result in unintended typographical errors. The publisher would appreciate notification where these occur so that they may be corrected in subsequent editions.

**Library of Congress Cataloging-in-Publication Data**

Chatterji, Madhabi.
  Designing and using tools for educational assessment / Madhabi Chatterji.
    p. cm.
  Includes bibliographical references and index.
  ISBN 0-205-29928-8
  1. Educational tests and measurements—Methodology.  I. Title.

  LB3051 .C453   2003
  371.26′2—dc21

                                                                2002026170

Printed in the United States of America

10  9  8  7  6  5  4  3  2  1      08  07  06  04  03  02

# C O N T E N T S

Preface    ix

## 1 Assessing Educational Constructs: Basic Concepts    1

Overview    1

1.1 What Is Educational Assessment?    2

1.2 Elements of a Useful Assessment Procedure    6

1.3 Operational Definitions of Constructs    9

1.4 Constructs and Variables    11

1.5 Assessment, Measurement, and Evaluation    12

1.6 Role of Assessment in Education    13

Summary    19

## 2 Purposes for Educational Assessment    22

Overview    22

2.1 The Need for Clear Assessment Purposes    22

2.2 A Typology of Assessment Uses in Education    25

2.3 User Path 1: Assessment for Teaching and Learning    27

2.4 User Path 2: Assessment for Program Planning, Evaluation, and Policy Contexts    33

2.5 User Path 3: Assessment for Screening and Diagnosis of Exceptionalities    39

2.6 User Path 4: Assessment for Guidance and Counseling    43

2.7 User Path 5: Assessment for Admissions, Licensure, Scholarships, and Awards    46

2.8 User Path 6: Assessment for Educational Research and Development    48

2.9 Crossover across User Groups    48

2.10 Responsibilities for Appropriate Assessment Use    49

Summary    50

## 3 Quality of Assessment Results: Validity, Reliability, and Utility   53

Overview   53

3.1 Validity   54

3.2 Validation and Types of Validity Evidence   58

3.3 Validation: When Should We Do It and How Far Should We Go?   65

3.4 Reliability   67

3.5 Utility   70

3.6 Prioritizing among Validity, Reliability, and Utility   73

Summary   74

## 4 Types of Assessment Tools   78

Overview   78

4.1 Traditional, Alternative, Authentic, and Performance Assessments   79

4.2 Other Ways of Classifying Assessments   83

4.3 Types of Assessments Based on Mode of Response   87

4.4 Advantages and Disadvantages of Different Assessment Methods   95

Summary   100

## 5 A Process Model for Designing, Selecting, and Validating Assessment Tools   103

Overview   103

5.1 Need for a General Process Model   104

5.2 Components of a Process Model for Assessment Design/Selection and Validation   105

5.3 A Case Study in Using the Process Model   111

5.4 The Importance of Following a Systematic Process   117

Summary   119

# 6 Specifying the Construct Domain     121

Overview     121

6.1 Specifying the Domain for Constructs in User Path 1     122

6.2 Taxonomies of Learning Outcomes     137

6.3 Specifying the Domain for Constructs in User Paths 2–6     142

Summary     149

# 7 Designing or Selecting Written Structured-Response Assessment Tools     152

Overview     152

7.1 Why Use Written Structured-Response Assessment Tools?     153

7.2 The Process Model Applied to W-SR Assessment Design or Selection     155

7.3 Developing Assessment Specifications for W-SR Tools     158

7.4 Guidelines for Item Construction for Different Types of W-SR Items     165

7.5 Complex Interpretive W-SR Exercises     187

7.6 The Last Word on Clues     190

7.7 Choosing the Best W-SR Item Format     190

7.8 W-SR Test Assembly     191

7.9 Content Validation     193

7.10 Bias During W-SR Assessment Design     195

Summary     196

# 8 Designing or Selecting Performance Assessments     200

Overview     200

8.1 Why Use Performance Assessments?     201

8.2 Justifying Performance Assessment Methods We Choose     202

8.3 Applying the Process Model with Performance Assessments     206

8.4   Designing Different Types of Performance Assessments     215

8.5   Scoring Rubrics and How to Develop Them     234

8.6   Specifications for Performance Assessments     239

8.7   Assembling and Content-Validating Performance Assessments     243

8.8   Using Rubrics: Sources of Random and Systematic Error     244

Summary     247


**9   Designing or Selecting Affective, Social-Emotional, Personality, and Behavioral Assessments     250**

Overview     250

9.1   Applying the Process Model in User Paths 2–6     251

9.2   The Nature of Constructs in Paths 2–6     262

9.3   Designing Self-Report Instruments     263

9.4   Designing Structured Observation Forms     277

9.5   Naturalistic and Anecdotal Observations     279

9.6   Selecting Assessment Tools Using Specifications     282

9.7   Classical Examples of Instrument Design in Paths 2–6     284

Summary     286


**10   Analyzing Data from Assessments     289**

Overview     289

10.1   Scales of Measurement     290

10.2   Continuous and Discontinuous Variables     294

10.3   Organizing Data     295

10.4   Measures of Central Tendency     301

10.5   Measures of Variability     309

10.6   Graphical Displays of Distributions     312

10.7   Normal Distribution and Its Applications     318

10.8   Skewness and Kurtosis in Distributions     320

10.9  Measures of Relative Position      322

10.10 Correlation Coefficients and Their Applications      328

Summary      338

# 11  Decision-Making Applications in Different User Paths      342

Overview      342

11.1  Setting Standards      343

11.2  Report Card Marking      353

11.3  Domain-Referenced Mastery Analysis      364

11.4  Mapping Long-Term Trends on Measured Constructs      371

11.5  Using Assessment Results for Planning, Determining Needs, or Evaluating Programs/Services      376

Summary      381

# 12  Quantitative Item Analysis      383

Overview      383

12.1  Purposes for Item Analysis      384

12.2  Item Analysis Indices      384

12.3  Differences between NRT and CRT Item Analysis      387

12.4  Application of Item Analysis for NRTs      388

12.5  Application of Item Analysis for CRTs      394

12.6  Item Descriptive Statistics      400

12.7  Limitations of Item Analysis Studies      403

Summary      404

# 13  Quantitative Evaluation of Validity and Reliability      407

Overview      407

13.1  Empirical Validation Methods      408

13.2  Empirical Estimation of Reliability      427

13.3  Reliability in Criterion-Referenced Measurements    441

Summary    443

# 14 Selecting and Using Standardized Assessment Tools    445

Overview    445

14.1  Distinguishing Characteristics of Standardized Tools    446

14.2  Standardized Tools in Use in Education    448

14.3  Norms, Norm-Referenced Scores, and Score Profiles    464

14.4  Evaluating Standards-Based Assessments    477

14.5  Resources for Finding Published Assessment Tools    480

Summary    484


Bibliography    486


Index    493

# PREFACE

As this book goes into production, a National Research Council publication recommends that educational practitioners be included in future assessment design efforts (Pellegrino, Chudowski, & Glaser, 2001). The lead article in *Educational Measurement: Issues and Practice* underscores the need to raise assessment literacy levels in educators (Stiggins, 2001). The aim of this textbook is to address the documented need to enhance measurement knowledge and skills in educators and professionals who develop, select, and use tests and assessments in their day-to-day work.

## Main Themes

The main theme of this book and accompanying computer module is the design, validation, and use of instruments in educational settings. The book and module attempt to address five main questions about assessment that practitioners typically confront in their daily work:

1. How can we design or select traditional and non-traditional assessment tools to best serve our needs?
2. How can the information produced through assessments be appropriately employed in decision-making?
3. What procedures can help ensure that the quality of information resulting from assessment tools is adequate for our needs?
4. Which guidelines and standards can help us evaluate the quality of assessment tools and the information they yield?
5. How can we ensure that our assessment practices are ethical?

## Target Audience

In the United States, the majority of the audience for this book consists of practicing teachers, administrators, and on-site specialists in curriculum, instruction, or assessment who work closely with instructors, including counselors, social workers, psychologists, health professionals, and technology/media specialists. This diverse group of professionals are typically not majors in measurement, but are enrolled in master's or advanced graduate programs where measurement/assessment courses serve as a core requirement or elective. Students in doctoral programs, who need to design instruments for research purposes, also fall into this group.

## Philosophy

Prior efforts in raising assessment literacy in educators and other professionals, including my own, have often been guided by the belief that practitioner audiences find the measurement material dry and uninteresting. Thus, there is a need to water down the concepts, even avoid technical terms, to make the material more palatable to them.

In writing this book, I abandoned that belief. The book unabashedly uses both measurement theory and "jargon" to make the applied work of instrument development and validation meaningful to its readers. Expanded understandings of validity and validation, performance assessment, and contributions of cognitive psychology to test theory are only a few changes we have witnessed in the past decade. The book attempts to help readers integrate these important developments with current assessment theory and practice. It draws their attention to the latest published *Standards* in educational and psychological testing.

In sum, the materials stand on the premise that theoretical knowledge is fundamental to sound practice. To promote sound assessment practices, professionals outside the field of measurement need to be *included,* rather than excluded, as the field evolves and changes.

# What's New

With every new textbook, the question: *Does it have anything new to say?* must be answered. This book offers the following to the reader/learner:

1. A procedural model—the *Process Model*—for designing, validating, and using assessment tools, in particular *User Paths* or decision-making contexts (Chapters 2, 5–9);
2. An integrated treatment of validity and reliability, with an emphasis on validity as the overriding concern in assessment development and use (Chapters 3, 13);
3. Integration of the latest *Standards* (AERA, APA, and NCME, 1999) throughout the chapters.

The *Process Model* and *User Paths* serve as the core organizing themes for material presented in the book, particularly the mid-section. Procedures that may strike seasoned readers as new or different are mostly grounded in older ideas (see citations), and were tested by me through projects conducted in U.S. school districts, the Florida department of education, and other government and nongovernment agencies between 1989–2000. Practitioners with various specializations participated in these assessment projects. Interactions with them helped shape my own professional growth over the years, and led to many of the examples I have included in the book.

The book draws mainly on ideas from classical test theory, emphasizing norm-referenced and criterion-referenced applications. This selective emphasis is based on the rationale that a sound knowledge of classical psychometrics is a necessary first step in appreciating a vast number of applications and instruments that are in use today. Interested readers wishing to pursue more recent developments and applications will need the classical framework from which to begin. The book presents some old, some new, and some adapted concepts (such as, a "functional" taxonomy of learning outcomes in Chapter 6 or modified-Ebel method for standard-setting in Chapter 11).

# Organization of Chapters

There are three main sections in the book. The first section, Chapters 1–5, deals with foundational concepts relevant to assessment design, selection, validation, and use. Chapter 2 identifies six main types of assessment use in education and introduces broad *User Paths*. Chapter 3 provides an integrated treatment of validity, reliability, and utility. Chapter 4 discusses different types of assessments applied in education. Chapter 5 introduces the *Process Model*.

The mid-section of the book includes procedural chapters that show how the *Process Model* can be applied to design, select, and validate different types of assessments tied to different *User Paths*. Chapters 6–9 are oriented toward audiences who need to develop their own tools for classroom, local decision-making, or research purposes.

The final section is geared for audiences interested in adopting existing instruments, both standardized and nonstandardized, and for analyzing/using assessment results. Chapters 10–11 present statistical procedures for analyzing data from assessments, and feeding the results into decisions tied to different User Paths. Chapters 12–13 provide information on methods for evaluating the psychometric quality of items and assessment tools. Standardized tests are treated in Chapter 14.

# Suggested Courses

To answer the question: *What are some courses for which the book might prove useful?*, I will draw on suggestions made by reviewers of earlier versions of this manuscript. The materials are intended for two types of *graduate courses* for students who are *not* majoring in measurement. A limited selection of chapters may also be used to teach classroom assessment courses for preservice teachers.

| Course Type | Suggested Chapter Selections |
|---|---|
| 1. Introductory measurement or assessment course for students in *master's degree* program. <br> <u>Student characteristics:</u> Majors can vary, including curriculum and instruction, educational psychology, educational leadership, counseling, school psychology, and recertification courses for inservice teachers. | Chapters 1–9, 11 (selected sections), and 14 <br><br> For reference: Chapter 10, 12, 13 (In my courses, I supplement the book with a copy of the *Standards*.) |

| Course Type | Suggested Chapter Selections |
|---|---|
| 2. Specialized research seminars/ practicum courses in instrument design and validation. Student characteristics: Students in *educational specialist (Ed.S) or doctoral programs* who need to develop and validate instruments as a part of their major project/thesis. | Chapters 1, 5–9, 10, 12, 13  For reference: Chapters 2–3, 11, 14 (Supplementary readings, including statistical analysis software, may need to be added for such courses.) |
| 3. Professional development workshops on testing or various assessment topics. Audience characteristics: Professionals in educational, health, or corporate organizations. | Selected sections. |

At the time of printing, I will have used the materials with all three of the above audiences at Columbia University in New York. I have used earlier versions of the materials regularly to teach a master's level measurement course at the University of South Florida (USF). My workshop/seminar audiences have thus far included professionals from school district, corporate, and higher education settings.

## End-of Chapter Exercises and Computer Module

The textbook comes accompanied with a computer module that may be useful in independent study or distance-learning courses. I am indebted to the Center for Teaching Enhancement (CTE), USF and its director, Dr. James Eison, for supporting the development of a prototype module. This book emerged as a result of that CTE grant-funded project. The current version of the module is available both on CD and website.

The end-of-chapter discussion exercises and more structured exercises in the module were intended to be an integral part of the book. They are meant to reinforce and facilitate application of concepts by students. The answers are provided to help students evaluate their own progress. Acceptable answers to many of the open-ended exercises may vary; they were intended to stimulate class discussions. The structured exercises for each chapter in the module provide learners with immediate feedback. The instructor's manual provides further information on various features of the module, including an option for instructors to modify or expand the item bank for each chapter.

## Acknowledgments

As of this printing, the full manuscript has undergone two rounds of review and revision. It has been field-tested with three classes at Teachers College, Columbia University. Every review and tryout has necessitated some changes. I close this phase of the work with the hope that any remaining errors are minor and will not pose major obstacles to readers and users of the materials.

There are numerous people to acknowledge as this endeavor draws to an end. First and foremost, I must acknowledge my debt to professors from USF who, in addition to facilitating my doctoral education, instilled in me the values to serve the field of educational practice. They were: Professors Bruce W. Hall, Joseph L. Mazur, and Douglas E. Stone. My debt is indirect, but deep, to other measurement scholars with whom I did not have the opportunity to study or work, but whose writings influenced my thinking and development. Their works are cited throughout the document (any errors in the presentations, of course, are mine). I am most grateful to all the reviewers of early drafts of the book, including Ronald A. Berk. Their honest and constructive criticisms have greatly improved the book.

I must acknowledge Pat Freda from Florida, who created a large number of the Figures and Tables, and designed the prototypes and present computer module that accompanies the book. Pat's patient and steady participation in a project that changed its shape and form over four years is more appreciated than he knows. My thanks are also due to Laura Paczosa and Tao Xin of the Measurement, Evaluation and Statistics Program at Teachers College. Laura proofread the chapters before each review, and did the painstaking work in securing permissions to use materials from external sources. Tao reviewed and checked the answers to all the exercises in the module and chapters. Their timely and thorough work was most appreciated.

I am very grateful to Nancy Forsyth, Paul Smith, and Arnis Burvikovs of Allyn and Bacon for offering me the chance to write my first book, and for supporting me all the way to the end. Their production staff are expert and flexible. I thank them all for their help.

In addition, the insightful comments of the following reviewers have been most helpful: Suzanne E. Cortez, Northern Kentucky University; Alan Davis, University of Colorado—Denver; Boyd Dressler, Montana State University; Jim Flaitz, University of Louisiana at Lafayette; Betty E. Gridley, Ball State University; Carl Huberty, University of Georgia; George Ladd, Boston College; Pat Pokay, Eastern Michigan University; Judith L. Speed, University of California—Davis; Cindy Walker, University of Washington; and Jon Walther, Chapman University.

Finally, I offer the book and module to practitioners and professionals, but I dedicate the work to the memory of my late father, Dr. Sambhunath Chatterji. Without his encouragement and moral support I would not have made the journey to the U.S., nor pursued a career in measurement and evaluation. I close by thanking my daughters, Raka and Ruma Banerji, and my mother, Deepti Chatterji, for the important roles they have played in my life.

M.C.
Teachers College, Columbia University

# 1 Assessing Educational Constructs: Basic Concepts

## Overview

Individuals differ with respect to what they learn, how fast they learn, and how much they learn. How large or small are these differences? How well can we assess these differences and the factors that affect them? What are the educational, social, and practical implications of these differences? *Educational Assessment,* a term used interchangeably in this book with *Educational Measurement,* is concerned with assessing characteristics of people, objects, or processes that are relevant to teaching and learning.

We begin the first chapter by formulating a working definition and building an understanding of the key elements of the assessment process. To do this, we draw upon a historical definition of measurement and examine how well that definition applies to educational asessment today. Since the 1990s, the terms *assessment, measurement,* and *evaluation* have had multiple connotations in the field. To avoid confusions in subsequent chapters, we look at definitions of salient terms as they appear in the rest of the book/module. We examine how educational assessments have been utilized in the past, and in the more recent context of educational reforms in the United States. Educational trends in the past decade have influenced assessment practices and redefined the roles and responsibilities of practitioners. We end the chapter by considering why it is more important today that educators be competent assessment practitioners.

## CHAPTER 1 OBJECTIVES

After studying this chapter and completing the structured exercises in the computer module, you should be able to:

1. Identify the philosophical and theoretical bases of methods used in educational assessment today
2. Analyze a historical definition of measurement and show its relationship to current understandings of the assessment process
3. Define key terms associated with assessment processes: *instrument, scale, construct, variable, population, assessment purposes, operational definition, measurement, assessment,* and *evaluation*
4. Describe the historical and current functions of assessment in education
5. Evaluate current trends in education and their influences on assessment practices and responsibilities of practitioners.

## 1.1   What Is Educational Assessment?

"Whatever exists at all exists in some amount. To know it thoroughly involves knowing its quantity as well as its quality."

Edward L. Thorndike (1918)[1]

**Educational assessment** deals with the measurement of characteristics integral to the educational process. We will refer to these characteristics as "constructs." Some constructs that interest educators are a person's aptitude to learn something, motivation to achieve in school, self-concept, achievement level in a scholastic area, and the environmental factors that affect how much a person learns. Not all constructs are attributes that are always directly or physically observable to us. It therefore becomes necessary for us to use indirect signs and indicators to make inferences about their existence.

Just as we measure physically observable characteristics, such as a person's height, we attempt to assess educational constructs with some form of systematic procedure, traditionally referred to as an "instrument." Let us consider examples of three rather different-looking instruments used in education, displayed in Figures 1.1 through 1.3. The issue that we must initially come to terms with is whether we are prepared to recognize *all* of these procedures as "measuring" instruments, and what the defining characteristics are of a useful assessment procedure.

The excerpted instrument in Figure 1.1 is a part of the Reading battery of the *Stanford Achievement Test Series: Ninth Edition* (Harcourt Brace Educational Measurement, 1997a). It represents what most people would typically call a "test." The two items measure different dimensions of the construct "reading," with the help of multiple choice items. In this test, item responses are scored as correct or incorrect. Responses to a series of such items are totaled to yield a quantitative score, such as 20 correct. The higher the score for an individual, the more proficient we consider that person to be in reading.

The instrument in Figure 1.2, "a product-based assessment," will appear different from what we commonly call a "test." For one thing, it is not a traditional, paper and pencil tool where items can be scored as clearly correct or incorrect. The assessment outcome depends on individuals' products (in this case, artwork) rather than a response they select from a preselected set of items with structured answer options. A *rating scale* is used for judging the underlying construct, "artistic ability." The criteria on the rating form relate to skills and techniques in the Cubism genre of art (Dake & Weinkein, 1997).

In determining the quality of the artwork in Figure 1.2, we would anticipate considerably more human involvement and subjectivity to influence the rating, because the

---

1. Excerpted from the chapter written by Edward L. Thorndike, entitled "The Nature, Purposes, and General Methods of Measurement of Educational Products" for the *Seventeenth Yearbook of the National Society for the Study of Education,* Part II (Bloomington, Illinois: Public School Publishing Company, 1918).

---

**Word Study Skills**

Find the word that is made up of two words and mark the space under it.

☻  teacher

☻  picture

☻  anywhere

---

**Reading Vocabulary**

Mark next to the word that means the same, or nearly the same, as the underlined word.

Someone who is glad is _____.

☻  tall

☻  proud

☻  happy

☻  alone

---

**FIGURE 1.1  Two Items from an Achievement Test Yielding Quantitative Scores**

*Source: Stanford Achievement Test: Ninth Edition.* Copyright © 1997a by Harcourt, Inc. Reproduced by permission. All rights reserved.

rater must render an overall judgment of its quality using the different dimensions listed in the rating form. If we called the numeric ratings (ranging from 0–10) "scores," we can see that they would be derived quite differently from the scores on the reading test in Figure 1.1, because there is no indisputable, single correct "product" in this assessment exercise. Although numbers are used, the ratings denote ordered categories, rather than a summed total score. The higher the assigned rating, the better the judged quality of the work.

Now let us review yet another instrument in Figure 1.3. This tool represents what psychologists refer to as an *attitude scale*. This instrument attempts to measure the attitude of educators towards a testing and assessment course, the underlying construct. Attitude scales can also be considered to be very subjective, since they depend on what people are willing to say about their feelings towards something. Yet, we see that there appears to be a built-in procedure for quantifying a person's attitude on the scale in Figure 1.3. People who respond must indicate their level of agreement or disagreement to a series of statements about the tests and assessment course, their responses can be recorded on the supplied rating scales, and summed to obtain a total attitudinal score.

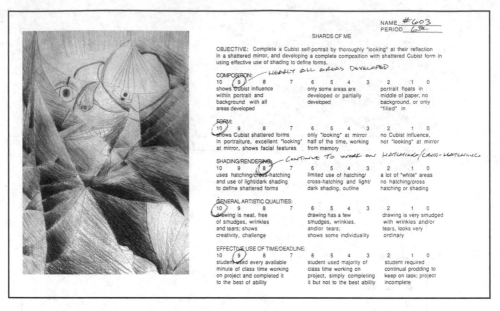

**FIGURE 1.2    A Product-based Assessment Yielding Qualitative Ratings**

*Source:* New Arts Basics Project. Reprinted with permission from the *Handbook of Classroom Assessment* by Gary Phye (Ed.), Academic Press, 1997.

---

**Key Concepts**

- Educational assessment, or educational measurement, is a process for measuring constructs in educational settings.
- Constructs are characteristics that we attempt to measure with an assessment procedure or instrument.
- Assessment procedures can vary greatly in form, structure, type of constructs measured, and methods by which they yield information on the constructs.

---

Are all three procedures illustrated in Figures 1.1–1.3 examples of useful measuring instruments? Because of the different degrees of subjective involvement of the assessor, some of us might be inclined to accept the reading test as an example of "measurement." The art exercise, on the other hand, might give us some doubts. The attitudinal tool may produce yet another reaction from us.

Let us begin with the premise that all three procedures could serve as legitimate measuring instruments, provided we employ a disciplined approach in the methods we use to arrive at the numbers which measure the constructs. *Disciplined inquiry* refers to an effort to consciously use a careful, methodical approach that will facilitate observations and conclusions with as little error as possible (after Cronbach & Suppes, 1969; Shulman, 1997). Adopting a disciplined approach in assessment design, selection, and use will help us make appropriate inferences from the results of an assessment procedure, whether they are more traditional (such as shown in Figures 1.1 and 1.3) or nontraditional, newer tools

**DIRECTIONS:**
Indicate the extent to which you agree or disagree with the statement by entering your selected response to the left of each statement. Use these response options.

| Strongly Disagree | Disagree | Uncertain | Agree | Strongly Agree |
|---|---|---|---|---|
| SD | D | U | A | SA |

_____ 1. This course should be required for all educators.
_____ 2. The course readings put me to sleep.
_____ 3. I want to learn how to design portfolio assessments.
_____ 4. I make it a point to attend class regularly.
_____ 5. My mind wanders during this class.
_____ 6. I want to learn how to write multiple choice test items.
_____ 7. I avoid coming to this class.
_____ 8. This course is critical for my professional growth.

**FIGURE 1.3    An Attitude Scale Yielding Quantitative Scores: Assessing Attitudes of Educators Towards a Measurement Course**

(Figure 1.2). We will employ two major criteria to decide whether or not an assessment procedure is "disciplined": first, the extent to which it employs careful and systematic methods in attending to various sources of error; and second, the usefulness of the assessment outcomes for the purposes at hand, whether in making practical decisions or in expanding our knowledge and scientific understandings of the targeted construct.

We saw in the three assessment examples that irrespective of whether the results they yield are in the form of numeric scores or qualitative ratings, each procedure could be designed with either a haphazard or a more controlled set of procedures. However, what if the results of the assessment shown in Figure 1.2 were intended for making pass/fail decisions for students taking an art class in high school? Our professional responsibility would then be to ensure that the tool was adequate to support such an application. Assuming that we developed, selected, and employed the assessment using disciplined methods, we could make such pragmatic decisions with assessment data in a more dependable and accurate manner. At the very least, we could defend the way in which we arrived at the results and any decisions tied to those results.

To summarize, traditional methodology in educational measurement is based on the methods of systematic observation and analysis employed in the physical and biological sciences. This book and module present the principles and methods of educational assessment using the basic assumptions that stem from the tradition of disciplined inquiry. In our approach, educational assessment will include procedures that aim to arrive at quantitative descriptions of characteristics that we study, such as procedures resulting in a score, as on the traditional test shown in Figure 1.1. Additionally, it will include procedures similar to product-based qualitative ratings shown in Figure 1.2. In the following sections and chapters, the term *assessments* will be broadly used to refer to a wide range of tools used in education, labeled variously as tests, rating scales, observation forms, checklists, performance assessments, portfolios, or, simply, measuring instruments.

---

**Key Concepts**

■ Educational assessments can yield both quantitative or qualitative information on constructs measured.

■ Using a disciplined approach to educational assessment means that we pay attention to various sources of error when we develop, select, or use assessment tools.

---

## 1.2   Elements of a Useful Assessment Procedure

"Education is concerned with changes in human beings . . . known to us only by the products produced from it—things made, words spoken, acts performed, and the like . . . To measure (the) product well means so to define its amount, that competent persons will know how large it is, with some precision, and that this knowledge may be conveniently recorded and used."

E. L. Thorndike (1918)

In the above quote from his chapter in the *Seventeenth Yearbook of the National Society for the Study of Education,* Professor Edward L. Thorndike recognized that evidence of the educational process can be found through a broad array of verbal and nonverbal products generated by students, not simply through written tests. He also pointed out that attempts to measure educational constructs need to be both convenient and useful for likely users.

To set up a useful assessment system, we must begin with a clear notion of what to measure, whom to measure, and an understanding of why we want to measure in the first place. Only then will it be possible for us to devise the best possible way to capture the construct so as to fulfill our purposes and needs.

The elements of a useful assessment procedure were suggested in a historical definition of measurement given by Stevens (1946). The definition stated that "measurement is a process for assigning numerals to particular characteristics of a class of people, objects, or events, according to specified rules (adapted from S. S. Stevens, 1946). Stevens's original definition appeared in the journal *Science,* and was intended to apply to constructs measured in various disciplines, including the pure sciences. On closer examination, that definition clarifies some essential aspects of the measurement process that continue to apply to educational assessments today.

### 1.2.1   "What" and "Whom" to Assess

The first important idea is that in order to assess, we need to focus on a particular *construct* (attribute, characteristic, or property) in members belonging to a well-defined *class* of people, objects, or events. When we assess, it is not an entire object or person that is the focus of the procedure, but rather a particular attribute of that object or person. Thus, we might assess the length of a table or the short-term memory span of a person, or the intelligence of a student. Further, from the definition we see that the person or object that is assessed usually belongs in a well-defined class of similar objects, referred to as the

**TABLE 1.1  Identifying "What" and "Whom" to Assess**

| Constructs | Class or Population |
|---|---|
| Weight | in a group of adults (people) |
| Physical strength | in a group of adolescents (people) |
| Readability | of measurement textbooks (objects) |
| Wind speed | in storm system (event) |

"population." A population is based on some common characteristic that is shared by all members of a bounded group, such as all fifth-grade students in a school or all adults in a particular ethnic community.

Table 1.1 illustrates some examples of constructs that could be the focus of assessment and corresponding classes of objects, people, or events—the "what" and "whom" to be assessed in each scenario. In the first example in Table 1.1, the class of interest is an adult population, and the construct to be assessed is the weight of each member. We see that the classes in the remaining examples consist of adolescents (people), textbooks (objects), and storm systems (events), respectively, each with different constructs that we could target for assessment. In education, a teacher's delivery of a series of lessons might be considered as a class of events; constructs to be measured in such "events" could be a teacher's "classroom communication skills" or "ability to engage students."

We could also exercise higher levels of specificity in defining the class. In thinking of textbooks, we could specify just biology textbooks for ninth-grade students with limited English proficiency. Why is it useful to set a clear boundary around the class of objects before we begin assessment? Such specificity usually enhances our ability to design or select assessment procedures that will be best suited for the population of interest, thus enabling us to control both the quality of the information generated and inferences made from the measurements. For example, if we know beforehand that an assessment is going to be used to make decisions on textbooks for students with limited English proficiency, it is possible for us to make conscious decisions as we select or design assessments that will help generate the most accurate and dependable information possible for that population and purpose.

## 1.2.2  Numerals Denoting Degrees of the Underlying Construct

Another concept embedded in the historical definition of measurement is that it is a process for assigning *numerals* to constructs. This part of the definition implies that the end result of the assessment process is generally, although not always, expressed in *numeric* terms. A numeral can be a symbol, as in a Roman numeral. Alternatively, it can be an integer from a number line. In both cases, numerals help to either classify differences or denote the degrees to which something exists—or "how much" of an attribute is present. Some authorities would characterize this last part of the measurement process as "scaling"—as it typically yields a scale of some sort, depending on the way in which the numerals are assigned and their resulting arithmetic properties (Brennan, 1998).

An important characteristic of a useful assessment procedure is that it ultimately yields information on the construct that is represented by numerals. If derived systematically, numerals from assessments are useful because they tend to communicate meanings about the underlying construct in more precise language, thus allowing more staightforward interpretations.

### 1.2.3 "Rules" for Assigning Numerals

Stevens's definition also suggested that a useful assessment process is rule-driven, not haphazard. Measurement involves *systematic* procedures. The "rules" are reflected in the instruments which provide the system for generating the numerals. The more carefully we draw the rules, the more meaningful and consistent the resulting information is likely to be. The notion of rules gets us back to the concept that we need to exercise some discipline during the design and application of assessment procedures.

### 1.2.4 Needs of Users

Finally, a useful assessment procedure must be responsive to the needs of the users. To begin the assessment design or selection process, we should ask ourselves: Why are we assessing? How will we use the results of the assessment? It is imperative that both designers and users have clear understandings of how the results of the assessment will be used, before they take any decisive actions on which assessment tool to use. The level of quality and precision needed in the assessment information can be controlled by developers and users, depending on their specific needs. For example, physiological measurements that impact critical diagnoses of health conditions in people would demand very high levels of accuracy and precision in the data. In other situations, such as in the assessment of day-to-day student learning in a classroom, differences expressed in decimal points may not be that crucial.

Some authors have suggested that the measurement process can be broken down into three essential parts: observation, differentiation, and quantification (Hopkins, 1998; Hopkins, Stanley, & Hopkins, 1990). From this alternate perspective, a useful assessment system should first help us observe and identify how an attribute differs among members in a class; then it should help us quantify those differences with enough accuracy and consistency to meet our needs.

---

**Key Concepts**

- To set up a useful assessment system we should pay attention to the following:
    1. the construct to be assessed
    2. the targeted population
    3. the purposes of assessment
- A useful assessment system is developed systematically and typically yields data in the form of numerals.

## 1.3    Operational Definitions of Constructs

Being able to articulate "what" is observed and measured in observable terms is the first hurdle of sound assessment design and interpretation. We began by acknowledging that most human attributes of interest in education and the social/behavioral sciences are unobservable, intangible traits that we *think* people possess. We used the term "construct" to refer to such attributes. Constructs are labeled as such because they are *mentally constructed* ideas of human traits. Scientists or observers interested in particular attributes hypothesize that they exist. They then give shape and definition to these unobservable constructs through the operations they use to measure them in their assessment procedures. The test or assessment then becomes the *operational definition* of the construct.

For example, a teacher might be curious about whether her students vary with regard to their "motivation to learn"—an unobservable construct. To examine this unobservable characteristic, she has to start with a mental image of what "motivation to learn" means in terms of actual student behaviors. Her notions of school motivation might lead her to choose the following behavioral indicators:

- The degree to which a student regularly attends class
- Whether a student asks thoughtful questions in class
- How often a student completes required school work on time

The teacher has now *operationally defined* the construct, "motivation to learn," with the three behaviors she selected. Observing these three behaviors in her students would allow the teacher to make justifiable differentiations between more- or less-motivated students. She can now use these indicators to develop a more formal assessment tool if she so chooses.

Operational definitions specifically outline the actual responses, actions, tasks, or behaviors that will serve as observable evidence of a construct. The operational definition of a construct lies at the crux of any assessment process. As the example on "motivation for school" illustrates, most educational constructs are often not directly observable and must therefore be inferred *indirectly* from a sample of indicators that can be observed. As stated earlier, an assessment procedure ultimately becomes the operational definition of a particular construct.

According to the most recently published *Standards for Educational and Psychological Testing* (APA, AERA & NCME, 1999) the term *construct* refers to all measured characteristics from which any meanings might be deduced, when directly or indirectly inferred from a set of actual occurrences, tasks, actions, behaviors, or responses.

### 1.3.1    Operational Definitions of the Same Attribute Can Vary

How a construct is operationally defined could vary from one observer to the next, even when different observers supposedly want to measure the same characteristic. Consider two teachers' different operational definitions of the construct "first-grade mathematics achievement" (Case Study 1.1). The teachers in Case Study 1.1 are making inferences about the same attribute, mathematics achievement in first-grade students, but from very different sets of operations and conditions. Each teacher's assessment results, whether in the form of a traditional test score, a qualitative rating, or some other index, will consequently convey very different meanings. What do the assessment results in the two first-grade classrooms tell us about the construct "mathematics achievement"?

## Case Study 1.1   The Meaning of Mathematics Achievement

**Teacher 1:** In my classes, I like to use the chapter tests in the first grade textbook. At the end of first grade, I expect students to be able to write and solve addition and subtraction problems with one- and two-digit numbers. I present the problems in vertical or horizontal format. The children don't regroup numbers, but they should be able to add and subtract correctly. They should also be able to work independently and finish all the problems in the time given.

**Teacher 2:** To test my children's knowledge of mathematics, I have them demonstrate that they can add and subtract with manipulatives and concrete objects. I test them one at a time using blocks or counters. I pose the problems verbally. They have to demonstrate their solution and show me how they check their answers before they write them down. If their answer is wrong, I encourage them to think again by saying "Are you sure?" or "Why is that the right answer?" They must begin to reason mathematically, even when they are in first grade.

### 1.3.2   Defending the Operational Definition and Construct Meanings

As we see in Case Study 1.1, what a construct means will be determined by its operational definition. When we measure constructs, we give our assessments particular labels and expect their results to carry particular meanings. The defensibility of our construct definition in terms of actual tasks, actions, and behaviors depends on how well it is grounded in established, formal knowledge about the characteristic in question, and the consensus of opinion among experts about its occurence in actual contexts. For instance, to measure "mathematics achievement" in a credible way, the teachers in the Case Study 1.1 should draw from current research, theory, and consensus among expert educators about what first graders are developmentally equipped to do, and about the mathematics curriculum that is typical in first grade.

**Key Concepts**

- To assess an unobservable construct, we must first define it in operational terms.
- Operational definitions consist of the observable responses, actions, tasks, or behaviors that will serve as evidence of a construct.
- In order to be justifiable, operational definitions should be based on agreed-upon and documented knowledge about the construct in question.

## 1.4 Constructs and Variables

In any given population, members typically differ on particular characteristics or measured constructs. For example, if we take a group of 20-year-olds and measure them on a physical attribute such as weight, we will find that the weights of different individuals will usually vary. *Variables* are characteristics of persons, objects, or phenomena that take on different values in members of the population. When assessed, variables yield a range of numerical values, showing the differences among members of a group.

The term "variable" is probably encountered most often in research contexts. Manipulating "experimental variables" or controlling for "extraneous variables" are standard components of scientific experimentation. The opposite of a variable is a *constant*. Constancy implies uniformity, while variability implies the existence of a characteristic that changes (that is, varies) in the group observed. Traditionally, educational measurement has been used to uncover individual differences, or variables, in human populations.

Whether or not a measured characteristic is a variable depends first on how one operationally defines the construct through the assessment process, and second on how the population (or class) is defined. To evaluate this proposition, assume that all the students who are attending a university-offered graduate course is a population, and then answer the following questions about them.

> Is *height* a variable in that population?
> Is their *interest in the course* a variable?
> Is their *educational major* a variable?
> Is their *university membership* a variable?
> Is their *status as graduate students* a variable?

Your answers to the questions posed might have been a "yes" or a "no," depending on the way in which you operationally defined each of the constructs and the population in your mind. For example, if *university membership* was defined to include only degree-seeking students, and the class in your mind only had enrollees from degree programs, the characteristic *university membership* would *not* be a variable in that scenario. On the other hand, if your definition of *university membership* were broadened to include non-degree-seeking students as well, and the class you envisioned had people enrolled in *and* outside degree programs, the same characteristic would now manifest as a variable.

**Key Concepts**

- Measured constructs that vary in members of a given population are called variables.
- To demonstrate how a targeted variable manifests itself, the construct (characteristic) must be defined and measured with an assessment procedure.

## 1.5   Assessment, Measurement, and Evaluation

Today, several terms found in the educational literature have meanings similar or closely related to the term "assessment." This book and module uses the terms *measurement* and *assessment* synonymously. Before we proceed any further, it is necessary to provide a rationale for this usage and to establish the distinction between it and another related term, *evaluation.*

In comparison to the term "measurement," "assessment" appears to be more broadly accepted among educators today. A current use of the term "assessments" encompasses a wide variety of assessment methods applied to educationally relevant constructs, and includes essay tests, multiple choice tests, performance assessments, and portfolios. The term "measurement," on the other hand, tends to conjure up visions of traditional, standardized achievement tests of the multiple choice variety only. While some researchers make a distinction between the processes of "assessment" and "measurement" (see Calfee, 1994; Linn & Gronlund, 2000), others use the term "assessments" to refer to different assessment procedures or instruments (see Shepard, 1989a; Cizek, 1997). This book subscribes to the latter convention in order to help the reader accept that both traditional and nontraditional tools are assessments, and all assessment procedures must conform with professionally established standards of quality if they are to yield useful information.

In particular contexts of use, the term *assessment* is used here to refer to a systematic device for generating information on a construct. When used to refer to the *assessment process,* activities included under assessment are:

- Writing items or designing an assessment tool
- Making observations or gathering data using an assessment tool
- Scoring responses from an assessment tool
- Developing a scale with specified properties
- Administering an instrument using prescribed guidelines

However, this book/module distinguishes between "assessment" and "measurement," on the one hand, and "evaluation" on the other. *Evaluation* is a process that comes *after* measurement is completed. It involves making a value judgment or interpretation of the resulting data in a decision-making context (after Hopkins, 1998). If a person receives a score of 40 on an assessment, evaluation would involve a judgment about whether that score of 40 was "good" or "bad." Evaluation often involves integration of information from several sources, including tests and other assessments. Evaluation also calls for greater degrees of subjective judgment. Examples of evaluation activities are:

- Comparing student test scores with a prescribed standard of mastery so one can make a pass/fail decision
- Assigning A–F marks or grades in a course, using results from a variety of assessments on students
- Deciding whether classroom instruction was effective based on the results from an array of assessments

- Deciding on the appropriateness of services based on assessed needs of clients
- Deciding on the worthwhileness of a program or service area based on compiled assessment data

---

### "Test" versus "Assessment": What the Most Recent Standards (1999) Say and Where This Book/Module Stands

This book/module has attempted to stay true to the latest standards in the measurement field. The 1999 *Standards for Educational and Psychological Testing* provides two ways in which the term *assessment* can be used. The Glossary of the *Standards* gives a definition of *assessment* that appears to be consistent with the way we will use the same term in this book/module. It states that assessment is "any systematic method of obtaining information (from tests and other sources used) to draw inferences about characteristics of people, objects, or programs" (p. 172, parentheses added). In another section of the *Standards* narrative that describes tests and test uses, there is some language that might confuse readers of this book/module. The *Standards* (p. 3) states:

> A distinction is sometimes made between *test* and *assessment. Assessment* is a broader term, referring to a process that integrates test information with information from other sources (e.g., information from the individual's social, educational, employment, or psychological history).

In this last-cited statement the usage of the term *assessment* is closer to what we call *evaluation,* with the qualification that judgment is used when combining information from many different sources to arrive at particular decisions about individuals, objects, or programs in particular decision-making contexts.

---

### Key Concepts

- The assessment (or measurement) process yields information on the measured construct.
- Evaluation involves decision-making and interpretation of the information obtained through one or more assessments.

## 1.6 Role of Assessment in Education

Now that you have been introduced to some key concepts, terms, and applications in educational assessment, it is important to review how assessment has been employed in historical and more recent educational contexts.

Assessment serves as a basic mechanism for generating data that support evaluative decisions and policies at the various levels of educational institutions in the United States. Assessments are employed in both public or private institutions. If we think in concrete organizational terms, information from assessments is used at the classroom, school, and district levels in pre-K through grade-12 institutions, and at the classroom, department, college, and university levels in higher education institutions. Accountability—the responsibility of educators (and educational institutions) to demonstrate that schooling is yielding the expected results in terms of student performance—is an integral part of how public education systems operate. Taxpayers and other public sponsors demand to know how their schools are doing. Decisions about accountability depend on assessment, thus necessitating a sound understanding of the measurement procedures in educational professionals.

Aside from accountability, educators employ assessment information in other ways as well. For example, educational measurement is applied in:

- Classroom teaching and decision-making
- Diagnosing needs of special populations
- Planning appropriate interventions for mainstream and special populations
- Setting graduation requirements
- Evaluating how well programs and services are functioning
- Admitting individuals to special programs
- Providing access or opportunities in selective programs
- Licencing and credentialing educational professionals

As is true in any field of practice, sometimes assessment functions are carried out well. At other times, these practices suffer, leading to mixed consequences for the individuals or institutions that are assessed. The need for educational professionals to be competent assessment practitioners, thus, cannot—and should not—be overlooked.

### 1.6.1   Recent and Historical Assessment Trends in the United States

To appreciate the shifts in educational assessment trends in the last three decades, let us review the information in Table 1.2, which illustrates what occurred in the state of Florida, as societal value systems on what matters in K–12 education and in educational assessment changed over time. In the left-hand column in Table 1.2, we see examples of some basic competencies represented in the test domain for Florida's *High School Competency Test* that was administered during the 1970s and 80s. In the right-hand column of Table 1.2, we see examples of standards and benchmarks targeted by the state's newly developed tests—the *Florida Comprehensive Assessment Tests* (FCAT). The FCAT have been employed in Florida since 1996.

During the 1970s, the "back to basics" educational movement led to widespread use of multiple choice tests tied to minimum competency requirements. Learning outcomes most valued by American educators at the time were very specific skills in reading, writing, and arithmetic, referred to as "behavioral objectives" or "minimum competency skills." Typically, these outcomes were narrowly stated, as Table 1.2 illustrates, and they were assessed with highly structured items on paper and pencil tests. Basic skills, similar to those illustrated, were emphasized in both curriculum and testing materials published by textbook companies for K–12 systems. The materials were eventually disseminated to teachers through school districts or state-mandated testing programs, and were soon used on a nationwide scale. Parallel trends were also evident in higher education and profes-

**TABLE 1.2   Comparing Learning Outcomes Valued by Society: 1970s to the 1990s**

| 1970s Educational Outcomes*<br>Grade 11 | 1990s Educational Outcomes**<br>Grade 10 |
| --- | --- |
| **Standard:**<br>Communications/Reading | **Strand:**<br>Reading |
| **Skill 8:**<br>The student will obtain appropriate information from pictures, maps, or signs | **Standard:**<br>*The student:*<br>Constructs meanings from a wide range of texts. |
| **Skill 8 Clarification:**<br><br>The student will identify a response indicating the correct interpretation of a picture, map, or sign. | **Benchmark (LA.A. 1.4.2):**<br>*The student:*<br>Selects and uses strategies to understand words and text, and to make and confirm inferences from what is read, including interpreting diagrams, graphs, and statistical illustrations. |
| *Assessed with a context-based multiple choice item* | *Assessed with multiple choice and open-ended, short response tasks* |

*Note:* Italicized information added for clarification purposes.

* High School Competency Test (HSCT): Reading Item Specifications

** Florida Comprehensive Assessment Tests (FCAT): Reading Test Item and Performance Task Specifications.

*Source:* Used by permission of the Florida Department of Education. All rights reserved.

sional testing programs, with standardized multiple choice tests serving as a primary vehicle by which to certify competence in teaching and other professions.

Basic skills tests dominated the 1970s era of testing, and persisted through the late 1980s. Marzano, Pickering, and McTighe (1993) have characterized this basic skill testing trend as one that emphasized "low-level functional skills" in U.S. education.

The publication of the report *A Nation at Risk,* which implied that loose standards in U.S. schools had placed the nation at a disadvantage for worldwide economic competition (National Commission of Excellence in Education, 1983), instigated numerous large-scale educational reform initiatives in the early 1990s. Pressures of worldwide competition spurred educators and politicians to move the assessment of student achievement to the forefront of educational agendas. As educators began to restructure school curricula in significant ways, there were widespread discussions of revamped local, state, national, and international testing programs.

The *America 2000* proposal, developed during the Bush administration in 1991 and continued through the Clinton presidency, outlined an ambitious set of goals for students who would achieve "world class standards" in academic subjects. To respond to this initiative, national subject area associations began developing national curriculum standards to describe what students should know and be able to do in each of the content areas before they graduated from high school. These national efforts culminated in the publication of several "Standards" documents, such as those published by the National Council of Teachers in Mathematics (NCTM, 1989; 1995). The new curriculum standards eventually permeated school district curricula, often endorsed by state departments of education.

A simultaneous curriculum development effort of the 1990s, initiated by the U.S. Department of Labor, identified an array of skills required by high school graduates when they entered the modern workplace. A report published by the Secretary's Commission for Achieving Necessary Skills (SCANS, 1991) highlighted the following outcomes for high school graduates:

- Decision-making
- Problem solving
- Communication
- Mathematical applications
- Learning how to learn
- Cooperative teamwork
- Leadership
- Self-management

As may be obvious, the above competency areas (now called the SCANS competencies) did not have a subject area focus. Consequently, they led to lengthy and controversial debates about the importance of "content" versus "process" skills in educational curricula.

The formulation of broader and more challenging standards in academic disciplines, coupled with the incorporation of lifelong learning skills within curricula, led many states to begin redesigning their assessment programs in significant ways. Leading states which delved into the standards-based assessment movement were California, Maryland, Kentucky, Maine, Minnesota, Pennsylvania, and Vermont. Educators recognized that the new "standards" of the 1990s were substantively and qualitatively different from the "basic skills" of the 1970s. Higher forms of cognition and learning reflected in the standards, such as decision-making and problem solving, could not always be satisfactorily exhibited and assessed with multiple choice tests. The realization that more complex curriculum standards would demand different and more complex forms of assessment led educators to call for the use of "alternative" or "authentic" forms of assessment. New knowledge about how learning occurs, offered by cognitive psychologists, also led to dramatically different approaches to conceptualizing assessment. Results from several of such large-scale assessment experiments are available for public scrutiny today.

Debates between proponents of alternative assessment and traditional testing spanned an entire decade, particularly the early 90s (see Marzano et al., 1993; Mehrens, 1992; Resnick & Resnick, 1992; Shepard, 1989a; Stiggins, 1991; Wiggins, 1989; Wolf, Bixby, Glenn, & Gardner, 1991). A few voices even protested the use of any testing at all in education. In the end, measurement specialists along with the larger educational community appeared to collectively agree that three major areas needed alteration in future assessment programs.

- Assessment methods used in education needed to be extended beyond the predominant assessment method of the previous era, namely, the multiple choice, paper and pencil test.
- The quality and usefulness of "alternate" or "authentic" assessment methods in various educational contexts needed to be carefully and systematically explored, investigated, and evaluated.
- Educators needed training to keep up with new assessment initiatives.

### 1.6.2  International Assessment Comparisons

In the new millennium, educators continue to struggle with questions regarding what helps students achieve; and politicians and legislators continue to consider what should and should not be mandated in schools so students can attain "world class standards." International assessment initiatives, such as the *Second International Mathematics and Science Study* (SIMSS) and the *Third International Mathematics and Science Study* (TIMSS), are routinely conducted today. These studies are designed to evaluate how the United States fares in worldwide competition, and their results are often used to spur public educators to improve schooling processes and student achievement outcomes. Consider Case Study 1.2.

## Case Study 1.2    Is the Educational Crisis in the United States Manufactured? Assessment in International Comparisons

How do American students compare in performance with students in other developed nations? Two visible international assessment programs of the 1990s were the Second International Mathematics and Science Study (SIMSS) and the Second International Assessment of Educational Progress (IAEP-2). Soon after the publication of the SIMSS and IAEP-2 results in 1992, a headline in *Newsweek* magazine pronounced that the United States had received "An 'F' in World Competition" (1992, February 17, *Newsweek,* p. 57).

The SIMSS results for 12th graders had shown that U.S. students were ranked 14th out of 15 nations in college algebra, 12th of 15 in geometry, and 12th out of 15 in calculus. On the IAEP-2, which tested nine- and 13-year-olds in mathematics, the United States was ranked 13th out of 15 nations, and 14th out of 15 nations, respectively. The media had a field day with these reports.

In response to such conclusions, Gerald Bracey (1996), conducted a reanalysis of the same results. Bracey's report showed that the apparently large differences in the rank-ordering of nations clouded the actual level of performance of U.S. students on the IAEP-2 tests. The U.S. average was only five percentage points below the international mean for nine-year-olds and three percentage points below the mean for 14-year-olds! He also identified important factors, such as differences in the extent to which students had opportunities to learn in school, that needed to be considered in making more "fair" comparisons of test performance across nations. Researchers today continue to reevaluate and reanalyze the SIMSS and TIMSS databases.

### 1.6.3   Assessment Responsibilities of Educators

What factors should we take into account if we want to interpret results of international, comparative assessment reports such as the SIMSS or IAEP fairly and accurately? In an environment driven by international competition and accountability, all educators shoulder the responsibility for employing assessments properly, whether they are classroom teachers, administrators, counselors, school psychologists, or measurement and research specialists. This is a formidable responsibility, as misperceptions and frustrations with testing practices are pervasive among the media, the public, and even within the educational community.

Repeated episodes of assessment misuse within the current social–political milieu (Millman, 1992) have led professional organizations, government agencies, and others concerned with the promotion of sound and ethical assessment practices, to publish standards for test development and use (Joint Committee of the American Educational Research Association, American Psychological Association, and the National Council on Measurement in Education; AERA, APA, & NCME, 1999).

Influential voices in the recent educational reform movement have pointed out that educational assessments should first meet "pedagogical standards and educator needs," with psychometric standards of quality given secondary importance (Wiggins, 1998, p. 21). *Psychometrics* is the science of measuring psychophysical phenomena, and includes the measurement of constructs relevant to education and psychology. Psychometric analyses involve various logical and statistical evaluations of an assessment's content, scale properties, item characteristics, and the validity of an assessment's results, in particular contexts of use. Wiggins's comment appeared as a part of a debate with a measurement specialist, J. S. Terwilliger. In it, Wiggins strongly advocated the use of "authentic" assessment methods for teachers and schools, emphasizing that assessments should be used as the means to define and raise performance standards in education. Certainly, educational assessments should be designed to augment, not harm, the educational process, and communicate standards and expectations for student performance. But should educators overlook the psychometric quality of assessments altogether?

This book takes the following position: Assessments should be designed or selected to meet both educational needs and psychometric standards befitting particular situations. To judge the extent to which an assessment tool is suited for a particular purpose or population, educators require an understanding of accepted standards of assessment practice *and* an adequate psychometric base from which to work.

A solid base of knowledge in assessment lies at the heart of appropriate assessment use. Educators trained in assessment methodology are in a far better position to evaluate assessment tools developed by others and the quality of information that they provide. They also should be capable of designing defensible assessment tools themselves, when they so need. Appropriately trained professionals are in a much stronger position to educate and caution laypersons (parents, lawmakers, politicians, the media, and the general public) about information contained in assessment reports. Professionals who prepare and interpret assessment reports, as many of you do (or will), need to convey the limitations of assessment results to clients. In an ideal world, decisions tied to assessment results should not lead to undesirable consequences for individuals or institutions that are assessed.

Are educators equipped with the necessary skills and knowledge that will make them confident, competent professionals in the assessment arena in the new millennium? Recent studies suggested that most educators, particularly teachers, are not (Plake, Impara, & Fager, 1993; Stiggins & Conklin, 1992). Stiggins (1991) described the state of affairs in K–12 schools as one where measurement functions are traditionally performed by "assessment" or "measurement" people, while the business of educating is done by those who "teach" but maintain a safe distance from those who "assess." The rift between educators at large on the one hand, and psychometricians on the other, is widened by the apparent discomfort and fear that people who are not measurement professionals harbor about the more complex, technical aspects of measurement.

An increasing number of studies today are documenting the need for educational practitioners to become more skillful in measurement. More recently, Impara and Plake (1996) studied assessment training needs of educational administrators. This study identified several administrative tasks that called for competence in measurement. These included evaluating student, teacher, and administrator performance, grouping and placing students, developing intervention procedures, evaluating school and program effectiveness, and training teachers in developing and using tests. A main purpose of this book is to bridge this documented gap between the practice of measurement and the practice of education by educators.

---

### Key Concepts

■ Traditionally, assessment data have been used to make a wide variety of decisions in educational institutions in the United States.
■ Current trends in assessment require educators to be proficient in assessment methodology.

## Summary

Educational assessment, used interchangeably with educational measurement in this book/module, deals with the procedures we use for measuring characteristics important to education. The principles and methods of educational assessment, as given in this book and module, are drawn from the tradition of disciplined inquiry. Characteristics that are of central interest to education, such as reading achievement, are referred to as constructs. The assessment process yields quantitative or qualitative descriptions of the constructs we target, in the group of individuals who are measured. Assessment tools can be of various types, and include written tests, product rating scales, observation checklists, or portfolios.

The first chapter used a historical definition of measurement to elaborate the parts of a well-functioning assessment system. Before we begin the assessment design or selection process, it is necessary for us to have a clear notion of the construct to be measured, the assessment purpose(s), and the population that will be the focus of the measurement. An early step in assessment design requires us to provide an operational definition of the construct. Next, we devise a procedure which will yield dependable and meaningful information on the construct, in the population of interest. The assessment tools we design or select must be both technically defensible as well as serve our practical needs.

Most constructs we measure are variables. Educational measurement was traditionally used to describe variables in human populations. A main purpose of this book/module is to illustrate methods for designing/selecting effective assessment tools that will help us gather information on variables with the desired levels of precision and accuracy. Data generated from assessments are used to support a wide variety of decisions and for evaluation purposes.

The most significant recent changes in educational assessment practices in the United States were triggered by the 1983 *Nation at Risk* document, which called for higher standards in education. Following that publication, we saw a shift in emphasis from basic skills and minimum competency testing to standards-based assessments. Most of the new instruments were alternative assessments or authentic assessments. Currently, educators are experimenting with standards-based assessment programs at the state, national, and international levels.

All educators bear the responsibility for constructing and using educational assessments appropriately, whether they are classroom teachers, administrators, counselors, psychologists, or measurement and research specialists. Technical and practical guidelines for us to follow during assessment design, administration, interpretation, and use can be found in the most recent technical standards published by the joint committees of the American Educational Research Association, American Psychological Association, and the National Council on Measurement in Education (1999).

# QUESTIONS FOR CLASS DISCUSSION

1. Identify three attributes that you (or other educators) might want to measure in your work context. What operational indicators would you use to define these constructs? What sources would you use to defend your operational definitions?

2. List four examples of educational assessments with which you are familiar. Identify the constructs measured (labels given by their authors). What are their operational definitions? Be specific in describing the tasks, behaviors, responses that are used to infer meanings about the construct.

3. Review 4 or 5 articles from recently published professional literature in your area of specialization (journals in your field). Identify scenarios in which assessments were used. Identify the purpose(s) for assessment, the population assessed, the construct(s) measured, and the operational definitions of the construct(s).

4. Think of the operational definition of the construct "driving ability" based on the following assessment procedures:
   i. A written test of road rules.
   ii. An actual driving test on a road.
   What are the observable indicators or "operations" that define the construct in each case?

5. The list below is a partially complete list of some commonly measured educational characteristics and the populations of interest. Continue the list by filling in the blanks. Evaluate whether the attributes are manifested as variables or constants in the circumscribed groups. Explain your answers.

| What to Assess (Construct) | Whom to Assess (Population) | Is it a Variable? Explain. |
|---|---|---|
| i. Athletic ability | A sixth-grade class | _____ |
| ii. Classroom management skills | Teachers | _____ |
| iii. Mathematical reasoning | Undergraduate students | _____ |
| iv. Poverty index | Schools | _____ |

NOTE: More structured exercises with immediate feedback for answers are available on the computer module.

# 2 Purposes for Educational Assessment

## Overview

This second chapter aims to facilitate thinking on why it is necessary for us to specify a clear purpose *before* we begin the assessment design or selection process. As we saw in Chapter 1, a large number of decisions in education rely on assessments. This chapter identifies the main groups of users of assessment in education and describes the decision-making contexts in which they use assessment results. Six "User Paths" are introduced in this chapter. Each describes the kinds of decisions made with assessment results in different work settings; in forthcoming chapters, you will find references to the same paths.

## CHAPTER 2 OBJECTIVES

After studying this chapter and completing the structured exercises in the module, you should be able to:

1. Describe the major purposes for which assessment is used in education

2. Identify the major assessment user groups, contexts of assessment use, and recognize situations where their roles overlap

3. Distinguish among different types of decisions which can be informed with data from assessments—instructional decisions, formative and summative decisions; program and policy-oriented decisions; high and low stakes decisions; guidance and counseling decisions; and screening and diagnostic decisions

4. Analyze case studies involving assessment applications by different user groups (identify purposes, decisions made, issues related to appropriate assessment practice)

5. Identify the relationship between assessment purposes and the processes of assessment design, selection, and use

6. Identify the responsibilities borne by users to ensure appropriate assessment use in different contexts

## 2.1 The Need for Clear Assessment Purposes

It is important to have a clearly articulated assessment purpose before we begin to design, select, or use assessments. The same instruments can rarely fit needs of users in different contexts. An assessment tool that a teacher might use to observe citizenship behaviors of students in the classroom cannot simultaneously be used by a clinician to diagnose a special learning need such as an attention deficit. Not only would the two users be concerned with different constructs; they would also be making qualitatively different decisions that have different consequences for the students assessed. To make each application defensible, their assessment procedures would need to meet very different technical standards. Using one in place of the other is not a reasonable option, since an assessment tool can be designed to yield only certain types of information, limited for use with certain populations, settings, and purposes.

In practice, the preceding, apparently straightforward principle is often violated. All too often assessment purposes are addressed too late in the assessment design or selection process, are treated perfunctorily, or are completely overlooked. Assessments developed to serve school accountability purposes are used for classroom assessment— or worse, to evaluate principal or teacher competence! Such oversights have led to improper assessment use and numerous legal and public battles, resulting in a generalized impression among many educators that "all assessments are bad" or that "testing should be banned" (Hopkins, 1998). The most vocal critics of assessment are often protesting inappropriate assessment use in particular contexts. Unfortunately, their criticisms are often warranted (most frequently, standardized achievement tests are the misused instruments). You might find Case Study 2.1, presented in the next box, to be an interesting story.

## Case Study 2.1  The Lake Wobegon Effect: Bad Tests or Poor Test Use?

In 1987–88, a physician by the name of John Jacob Cannell, representing a public organization called Friends for Education, collected extensive evidence showing that most states, school districts, and schools in the United States were scoring above average on nationally normed elementary achievement tests. Cannell claimed that such data were misleading and the tests flawed. "These tests . . . . allow 90% of the school districts in the United States to claim to be above average. As many as 70% of the students tested nationwide are told they are performing above average" (Canell, 1988, p. 6). Paradoxically, Cannell reported that he found many of the same states that were ranked above average on the standardized tests were ranked below the national average on other indicators of educational excellence, such as graduation rates and performance on college entrance examinations. It appeared that in states where all other educational indicators were suggesting poor educational performance, the elementary level standardized test scores were looking rather good.

Cannell suspected that the initial norms for the tests adopted or selected by states/districts were inaccurate. In addition, he pointed out that the spuriously high norm-referenced scores could be caused by teachers "teaching to the test," because "in states where steps have been taken to prevent the teaching of tests, dramatic yearly gains have not been found." Because of the statistical procedures used to develop norms in standardized achievement tests, only 50% of students should theoretically perform above average. The scores from the national comparison group that test-makers use, the norm group, are forced to take the shape of a bell curve.

*(continued)*

## Case Study 2.1    Continued

Cannell's observations came to be called the "Lake Wobegon Effect," after the mythical town of Lake Wobegon in Minnesota where "all the women are strong, all the men good-looking, and all the children are above average" (taken from Garrison Kiellor's radio program, *A Prairie Home Companion*). Several norm-referenced achievement tests published by well-known testing corporations were called into question by Cannell's findings. Were the tests really bad?

In responding to Cannell's challenge, several representatives of testing companies acknowledged that the Lake Wobegon problem could indeed be caused by outdated norms (see Williams, 1988). The facts were that the norms of most major national achievement tests were *not* based on the current year, but on the year when the tests were originally normed during test development (usually 3–10 years before the tests were actually used by school districts and states). This procedural reality was not fully appreciated by schools and districts—or was overlooked. Other measurement observers (Shepard, 1989a) commented that the tests were being used to make high stakes decisions locally, in environments which encouraged teaching to the test. A combination of these two practices—the adoption and use of norm-referenced tests with old norms and the narrowing of classroom teaching to cover only what was on the national tests, led to test score increases that were not accompanied by real student learning!

Shepard described the harsh assessment conditions that prevailed at the time in the following statement (1989a, p. 4): ". . . (S)tandardized tests are running amok. Newspapers rank districts by their test scores. Real estate agents use test scores to identify the "best" schools as selling points for expensive housing. Superintendents can be fired for low scores, and teachers can receive merit pay for high scores. Superintendents exhort principals and principals admonish teachers to raise test scores—rather than to increase learning." Sadly, some of the same practices are still in effect today.

*Note:* Full-length articles on the Lake Wobegon Effect were published in *Educational Measurement: Issues and Practice* (Volume 7) in the summer and winter of 1988.

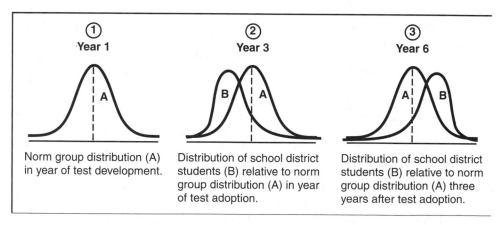

| ① Year 1 | ② Year 3 | ③ Year 6 |
| --- | --- | --- |
| Norm group distribution (A) in year of test development. | Distribution of school district students (B) relative to norm group distribution (A) in year of test adoption. | Distribution of school district students (B) relative to norm group distribution (A) three years after test adoption. |

**Lake Wobegon Effects in Testing**

Case Study 2.1 gives us some food for thought on appropriate uses of standardized achievement tests on the one hand, and classroom assessments on the other. It also forces us to think about the responsibilities borne by both test developers and users of assessments. Nationally norm-referenced achievement batteries are not designed to reflect the local curriculum. They are designed for use in large-scale accountability programs for checking whether students have mastered the basic content and skills common in most curricula across the nation. Teaching to such tests in individual schools and classrooms leads to a "dumbing down" of a potentially rich classroom curriculum—an inappropriate classroom practice.

In the same vein, norms for norm-referenced tests should be periodically updated and the new norms tables published by test-makers. National testing corporations, that develop and sell the tests, bear the responsibility of educating their users on the limitations of standardized tests for classroom applications, and particularly, on the importance of having recently normed tests in circumstances where users depend on the norm-referenced scores for information. Prior to test adoption, informed consumers of the tests have the option to demand that the assessments have up-to-date norms. To prevent future misuses, the Lake Wobegon controversy led many of the testing corporations to be more timely in producing new norms tables to accompany their tests.

Standardized achievement test applications are only one of many situations where assessments are employed for educational decision-making. Each situation presents different opportunities for potential misuses of assessments. Assessments to gauge reading interest in schoolchildren would need certain properties, while tools used to diagnose personality disorders in adults would call for different standards. Assessments used for school accountability would be required to meet one set of technical criteria, while instruments for evaluating teacher effectiveness would demand other characteristics. It is thus important that we obtain an understanding of the major user contexts where assessments play a part in education in order to appreciate the need for different kinds of assessments.

---

**Key Concepts**

■ To avoid misuses, a clear sense of purpose should influence how we develop, select, or use assessments and their results in different decision-making contexts in education.

■ Assessments for different User Paths differ in content, form, and technical characteristics.

## 2.2   A Typology of Assessment Uses in Education

Several authorities have devised classification systems to categorize the predominant purposes for which assessment is used in education. In an article published in 1951, entitled *"The Functions of Measurement in Improving Instruction,"* Ralph Tyler identified four uses of assessment in teaching. These were:

■ Selecting instructional objectives
■ Selecting content to be taught, learning experiences, and procedures for instruction

- Organizing learning experiences
- As an aid in the administration and supervision of instruction

Airasian (1991) and Nitko (1996) offered subsequent classifications focusing on particular groups of educators, such as classroom teachers. Others, such as Millman and Greene (1989) devised classifications of assessment purposes centering on instruments that measure particular constructs, such as tests of achievement and ability.

Table 2.1 presents a slightly broader typology, intended for a more diverse group of educators. It lists six major decision-making contexts, referred to as "User Paths," in which assessments are typically used in education. These are:

1. Assessment for teaching and learning
2. Assessment for program planning, evaluation, and policy contexts
3. Assessment for screening and diagnosis of exceptionalities
4. Assessment for guidance and counseling
5. Assessment for admissions, placement, scholarships, and awards
6. Assessment in educational research

Let us now consider each of the six broad categories of assessment users in detail, with more emphasis on the first five categories, under which a vast majority of practitioner applications fall.

**TABLE 2.1    Purposes for Assessment in Education**

| Assessment Purposes and Decision-Making Contexts | Users of Assessment Information | Specific Examples of Assessment Use |
|---|---|---|
| **User Path 1.** Teaching and learning | Classroom teachers, students, parents | Assigning marks, instructional planning, identifying student needs |
| **User Path 2.** Program planning, evaluation, and policy contexts | Program developers or managers, administrators, policy-makers | Improving programs and services, meeting accountability needs, conducting needs assessments |
| **User Path 3.** Screening and diagnosis of exceptionalities | Psychologists, counselors, social workers, (teachers, parents, students) | Identifying special needs, providing intervention for special populations |
| **User Path 4.** Guidance and counseling | Counselors, students, and parents | Choosing educational or career paths |
| **User Path 5.** Admissions, certification, recognitions, and awards | Awarding agencies, institutional committees and boards (and participants) | Admitting persons to programs, granting awards and scholarships, certifying professionals |
| **User Path 6.** Research and development | Researchers, social-behavioral scientists, practitioners, policy-makers | Developing theories, expanding knowledge about educational phenomena and practices |

## 2.3 User Path 1: Assessment for Teaching and Learning

Effective use of classroom assessment by teachers can facilitate various aspects of the teaching and learning process and ultimately help to answer the question: How much did my students learn? Instructors make a wide variety of classroom decisions with formal and informal assessments. *Achievement,* defined as the extent to which students can demonstrate mastery of a scholastic curriculum, is the most frequently assessed construct in the classroom. Student *readiness for learning, attitudes towards a subject area,* and *classroom conduct and behavior* also rank high on a teacher's list of classroom assessment priorities. Consider the examples of classroom decisions that Mr. Cruz, a high school science teacher, made during the planning and delivering of a unit of instruction (presented in Table 2.2).

### 2.3.1 Formative and Summative Classroom Decisions

Teachers make instructional decisions that fall under two broad categories, as illustrated in Mr. Cruz's examples. The first type, called *formative decisions,* are represented in Decisions 1, 2, 3, and 4 in Table 2.2. In all these cases, Mr. Cruz uses assessments to inform several instructional actions he takes in the classroom.

- Decision 1 has to do with identifying student readiness levels before a new unit of instruction is begun; the classwork exercise serves as a "pretest" that enables the teacher to "size up" his class (Airasian, 1991); the teacher identifies strengths and weaknesses of particular students, and obtains a picture of the range and diversity of student needs in the class.
- Decision 2 is an instructional planning decision where the teacher uses assessment data to create optimal conditions for accomplishing his instructional goals. Based on the teacher's judgment regarding the prerequisite skills needed for the unit and his desire to use cooperative learning methods, preexisting scores from formal assessments in mathematics are used to assign students to groups.
- In Decisions 3 and 4 the teacher uses ongoing informal observations as assessments to evaluate and alter his instructional approaches; he responds to new needs that arise as the unit progresses.

Note that all the formative decisions are not made to decide whether the students have fully learned the material taught in the new unit, but rather to help in shaping the instructional design and delivery processes, or in planning and revising instruction. Note also that the assessments used by the teacher range from formal tests to less structured homework and classwork exercises to some relatively informal classroom observations. Mr. Cruz conducts all the formative assessments either prior to instruction or during the instructional cycle, with the primary goal of managing the quality of the instructional process.

In contrast, Mr. Cruz' Decisions 5 and 6 exemplify *summative decisions* in classroom contexts. Here, the teacher uses three "final" assessments to determine how much learning has occurred and to decide whether students have made sufficient progress to merit graduation to the next level of instruction. Summative decisions "sum up" the effects

**TABLE 2.2   Assessment for Teaching and Learning: Examples of Formative and Summative Classroom Decisions**

| Decision-Making Scenario | Specific Type of Decision |
| --- | --- |
| 1. Based on a classwork exercise he gave to his new chemistry students at the first class meeting, Mr. Cruz decided that about a third of his class required some more instruction on the previous unit dealing with the Periodic Table. | Formative: Identifying student needs |
| 2. A major focus of Mr. Cruz's new unit was learning to balance chemical equations. Mr. Cruz believed that cooperative group work would facilitate teaching of this somewhat complex unit. He was also keenly aware that students needed certain prerequisite skills in mathematics to really master that material. Before he started to teach the new content, Mr. Cruz asked Ms. Turner, his students' mathematics teacher, for their mathematics score profiles. He reviewed the mathematics test scores carefully, and then assigned students to small groups for cooperative assignments, making sure that at least one student in each group had a strong background in mathematical applications. | Formative: Selecting strategies; planning delivery methods |
| 3. Once he began the new unit, Mr. Cruz's informal observations of some students' conduct and productivity led him to reallocate seats to three students. He had private conversations with each one, making a mental note to contact their family members if behavioral infractions recurred. | Formative: Managing effectiveness of instruction |
| 4. Classwork and homework exercises given during the unit showed Mr. Cruz that the cooperative group work resulted in certain misconceptions and gaps in what the students had been able to grasp. He decided to provide an added lecture to reinforce some essential concepts, followed by one-on-one tutoring of particular students. | Formative: Identifying strengths and weaknesses: managing instruction |
| 5. At the end of the 9-week unit of instruction, Mr. Cruz administered a final examination. Students also made an oral presentation and did a laboratory assignment for their unit grade (final marks). Mr. Cruz was pleased to discover that a vast majority of his class received A or B grades on the final assessments, suggesting that his instructional strategies had been effective. | Summative: Assigning marks |
| 6. At the end of the year, the principal asked Mr. Cruz to make a recommendation regarding the promotion or retention of each student based on his/her year-round performance in his chemistry class. | Summative: Retention or promotion of individuals. |

of the instructional process in terms of student learning outcomes. Such decisions should ideally be made after students have had adequate time to learn, practice, and reflect on the material taught, with assessment conducted at the end of an instructional unit, course, or program of study. Summative instructional decisions should describe the status of student achievement on material taught in a given time frame.

### 2.3.2   Are Classroom Decisions High or Low Stakes Decisions?

In most cases, the results of classroom assessments are not associated with serious consequences for particular students, teachers, or members of the school's staff. That is, decisions based on classroom assessments are low stakes decisions and, if controversial, can be reversed. However, if we compare Decision 6 in Table 2.2 to Decision 1, it will be obvious that the gravity of the consequences varies based on whether a teacher's assessment purposes are formative or summative.

In the summative Decision 6, Mr. Cruz is trying to answer the question: "Who in this group is ready to be promoted to the next grade level?" while in the formative Decision 1 he asks: "What is the best place for me to begin instruction with this group?" The stakes (or consequences) are usually much higher for individual students when a summative decision is in the making, as fairly serious actions (promotion or retention, for example) can hinge on the assessment results. Parents and students can and often do contest marks or promotion decisions made by teachers. Assessments used for summative purposes should thus be of a defensible quality; they should also be administered only at a time when students have had enough exposure to the material taught.

While assessments used for formative purposes generally are of much less consequence to the individual student (hence, they are referred to as "low stakes" decisions), we should make sure that their design or selection is consistent with the specific decision-making needs of the situation, or they will not give us adequately useful information.

### 2.3.3   Classroom Decision-Making with an Outcome-Driven Model

Mr. Cruz's decision-making approach to assessment data follows the basic principles of an *outcome-driven model* of classroom instruction and assessment. Figure 2.1 illustrates how an idealized cycle of formative and summative decision-making would occur in the classroom with an outcome-driven model (See Tyler, 1951; Nitko, 1989).

The diagram makes certain assumptions about how effective classroom instructors work. First, instructors must have a sound sense of the long- and short-term expectations they have of their students. Their expected outcomes are fashioned as statements of instructional goals and objectives. Second, they must be able to clearly formulate the short-term learning outcomes that they wish to address through units of instruction, so that these ultimately lead to accomplishment of the long-term outcomes. Third, and most importantly, when delivering instructional units, they must be able to closely link their instructional and assessment activities directly with the short-term outcomes, and indi-

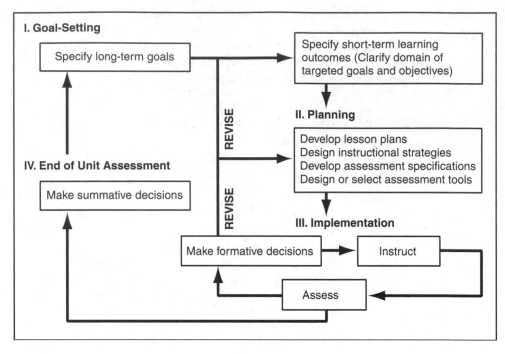

**FIGURE 2.1    An Outcome-Driven Model for Classroom Instruction, Assessment, and Decision-Making**

rectly with their long-term goals. The phases in employing the outcome-driven approach are illustrated in the diagram and are detailed in the text that follows.

***I.   Goal-Setting: Specifying Long- and Short-Term Outcomes.***    If a teacher were to follow the outcome-driven model, the first phase of an instructional cycle for a unit would begin with *goal-setting,* or the identification of long- and short-term goals of instruction. A major responsibility of the classroom teacher is to articulate clearly what the student is expected to learn in a unit *before instruction actually begins.* These expected outcomes clarify specific targets the teacher sets for the student to accomplish in terms of knowledge, skills/cognitive processes, attitudes, behaviors, or tasks. These targets serve as the framework around which classroom assessments are designed or selected. They form the beginning of the operational definition of "achievement" in a particular instructional cycle in a teacher's classroom.

***II.   Planning.***    The next phase is *planning.* The outcome-driven model suggests that a clear vision of the expected learning outcomes should ideally drive both classroom instruction and assessment. During the planning phase, teachers should develop plans for both instruction and assessment simultaneously, guided by an explicit definition of the desired learning outcomes for students. Just as the expected learning outcomes dictate the design of particular strategies for instruction, so should they guide the development and/or selection of assessments. This integration of instructional and assessment planning ultimately serves to enhance the accuracy of inferences we make about student achievement using the results of classroom assessments.

Prior planning of classroom assessments also gives teachers ample opportunity to communicate to students exactly what is expected of them. Clear communication of expectations is an excellent motivator for student learning. Awareness of academic expectations promotes more active involvement of learners in the learning process. It provides them with the information they need to monitor and control their own progress.

***III. Implementation.*** The *implementation* or "doing" phase follows planning, and involves the actual delivery of instruction and use of assessments for formative decision-making. Teachers should use ongoing assessments during the instructional delivery phase—similar to the actions 1 through 4 taken by Mr. Cruz in his chemistry unit—to continually improve their instructional effectiveness. Effective teachers use the results of formative assessments to strategically improve both their own instruction and student learning levels. By habit, they make modifications to their targeted outcomes, instructional strategies, and assessments as they move through the instructional unit. They develop skills in providing focused feedback to help individual students make achievement gains.

***IV. End-of-Unit Assessment.*** The last phase of the instructional cycle is the *end-of unit assessment*. This is the time to conduct assessments for summative decision-making (see Mr. Cruz's action 5 in Table 2.2). These assessments often count towards a student's final marks or course grades. Timely and appropriately conducted summative decision-making generally leads to the successful completion of a unit, followed by a class's or student's progression to the next unit of instruction.

### 2.3.4 Improving Classroom Assessment Practices with the Outcome-Driven Model

If the outcome-driven model is followed, most students should be proficient on the targeted learning outcomes by the end of an instructional cycle. Teachers would communicate their expectations to students early in the instructional unit; they would withhold summative assessment and decision-making until all the opportunities that students need to learn the material have been provided; and assessments for summative purposes would be developed more carefully and thoroughly than formative assessments.

Instructor practices in schools, however, rarely conform with pedagogical ideals. Review Case Studies 2.2 and 2.3. They describe common practices of instructors, as documented by Canady and Hotchkiss (1989), and help us distinguish between appropriate and inappropriate assessment applications in the classroom.

## Case Study 2.2    "Gotcha" Teaching

Mr. Telly recently had a conference with his son's English teacher. Mr. Telly's son, John, had been an above-average, hard-working student prior to taking this English course. Even though he took copious notes in class and studied them diligently, John was making Cs and Ds on assignments and tests. Mr. Telly explained that John seemed to have difficulty discerning what was important in the lectures. The teacher explained that he always paused briefly before discussing the topics that would appear on tests. *"John must learn to read those pauses"* said the teacher.

Excerpted with permission from: *It's a Good Score! Just a Bad Grade* by R. L. Canady and P. R. Hotchkiss in *Phi Delta Kappan,* September, 1989, pp. 70–71.

## Case Study 2.3    Grading First Efforts

In an elementary classroom, students were given their first shot at writing a composition as a classwork exercise. The teacher later decided to grade that attempt and incorporate those scores with the children's final semester marks (report card grade).

. . . Students in Tom's fifth-grade classroom were told to write an essay on the person they most admired. Tom wrote an eloquent essay on his older brother, Rob. He painted a vivid picture of his brother's free spirit. The paper was returned with a grade of F. Spelling and punctuation errors accounted for the points deducted. Yet mechanics had not been discussed as a factor to be graded (in class). No comments appeared on Tom's paper regarding its excellent content.

Excerpted with permission from: *It's a Good Score! Just a Bad Grade* by R. L. Canady and P. R. Hotchkiss in *Phi Delta Kappan,* September, 1989, pp. 70–71 (Parentheses and introduction added).

The last two cases suggest that the teachers were unclear about their own instructional goals and objectives, a prerequisite for sound classroom assessment practice within the framework of the outcome-driven model. Thus, they were unable to communicate their expected learning outcomes to their students. Canady and Hotchkiss (1989) contend that teachers who master the practice of "gotcha" teaching (their label) actually work at keeping the objectives of their classes a secret from students! This, they state, is a foolproof way for them to lower students' grade point averages.

The second case also illustrates a confounding of formative and summative decision-making in the classroom. A student's final grade was based in part on his early efforts. The assignment was given so early in the unit that the teacher had not yet addressed most of the valued objectives of his writing curriculum, particularly, a new objective dealing with essay writing. The learning process had barely begun, but a summative decision had already been made. Untimely or premature summative decision-making with assessments happens frequently, but is an inappropriate practice. Teachers who take such actions are not necessarily being deliberately cruel or punitive. However, their actions compromise the accuracy of conclusions they make about student achievement.

---

Key Concepts

- In User Path 1, classroom teachers make formative and summative decisions with assessments.
- Classroom assessments can be both informal or formal tools.
- The outcome-driven model can guide instructors in making appropriate uses of classroom assessment results.

---

## 2.4 User Path 2: Assessment for Program Planning, Evaluation, and Policy Contexts

In programs and larger institutional systems, assessments are used to make decisions for:

1. Planning of programs and services
2. Identifying needs for services to be delivered
3. Judging the effectiveness of programs and services
4. Making or revising institutional policy
5. Evaluating staff or employee performance

Scriven (1967) classified program-level or institutional decisions as either formative or summative. These terms have the very same meanings at the program level as they do in the classroom. In fact, writers applied the terms "formative" and "summative" to program evaluations *before* they were used to refer to classroom decision-making. In the above list of decisions, the first two represent formative program decisions, while the third is an example of a summative decision at the program level.

Let us turn to Table 2.3, which illustrates how assessment might be conducted at the program or institutional level to make formative and summative decisions. The table depicts programmatic assessments and decisions that might occur in any institution, public school, or other organization. The fictitious site in the table, Urban High School, is located in the World Class school district in the state of Utopia. The backdrop for the scenarios is the current environment of national educational reforms in the United States.

### 2.4.1 Program-Level Assessments and Decisions

***Formative Program Decisions***   Formative decisions employ assessment data to identify needs, devise plans, and monitor or improve the quality of services and products. Decisions 1 and 2 in Table 2.3 are examples of formative decisions. In Decision 1, staff members use information from the initial testing of all 12th graders for future planning and delivery of the school's instructional program in mathematics. This type of pre-program assessment is called a "needs assessment"—the school staff used the results to identify needs for an entire program. Similarly, Decision 2 deals with another needs assessment. Here, the staff used the survey information to identify a need for tutoring services for students. As the tutoring program was being operated, they continue to use assessments to follow up, monitor, and make improvements to the services delivered.

Like formative decisions in the classroom, the school staff conducted all of the

**TABLE 2.3   Examples of Formative versus Summative Decisions in Programs and Institutions**

| Decision-Making Scenario | Specic   Type of Decision |
|---|---|
| 1. Influenced by the national reform movement in mathematics, the state of Utopia has developed a new exiting assessment in mathematics that will be a high school graduation requirement for all 12th graders in two years time. To prepare for the forthcoming state assessment, the principal at Urban High asked a team of his instructional leaders to develop and administer a similar test to all the students in 9th, 10th, and 11th grades. The staff reviewed the results of the local test to set priorities for the school's mathematics program in the next year. | Formative Program Decision: Identifying instructional needs for the school's mathematics program. |
| 2. Simultaneously, a school committee conducted a survey of teachers, students, and parents to determine the need for an after-school tutorial program in mathematics. The survey data suggested a strong consensus among the three groups surveyed regarding the need for student tutoring. The principal and the committee used the survey results to develop an action plan to seek funds to institute a tutoring program. As the program was put in place, they continued to monitor the progress of participants. When problems surfaced, they made suggestions for making improvements. | Formative Program Decision: Identifying program needs; Monitoring and improving services. |
| 3. The World Class district supervisor in mathematics recognized the need for teacher training on the subject area standards that would be the focus of the new state test. To help prepare his teachers, he brought in national experts to provide several training sessions to all high school mathematics instructors in the district. The year after the training, an evaluation team was hired to examine whether the training had an impact on teacher practices. Classroom observations, lesson plans, and teacher surveys showed that the effects of the training, although uneven, were beginning to take hold. | Summative Program Decision: Determining effectiveness of teacher training programs. |
| 4. When the first statewide assessment occurred, the students of Urban High were found to obtain very high scores relative to the other schools in the district. The district superintendent commended the principal and leaders for their success. A district committee began to review the school's results to weigh the pros and cons of a rewards policy for other schools showing similar successes in the future. | Formative Decision: Formulation of reward and recognition policies using results. |

formative assessments either *before* the program was implemented or *during the delivery* of the program or service. The assessment purposes were to yield information for formulating new plans or for making ongoing improvements to the program/services. Unlike classroom assessments, which focus on individual students or a classroom, here the staff made decisions that were programwide; they aggregated data for the *entire school,* or system, to make decisions. Thus, in Decision 2, the assessments focused on *all* the 9th- and 10th-grade students receiving tutoring services in the school; the school staff drew conclusions about the *program as a whole* to make any subsequent alterations.

***Summative Program Decisions***   What distinguishes Decisions 1 and 2 from Decision 3 in the scenarios in Table 2.3? Decision 3 is a summative decision. Summative program decisions are usually conducted at the end of a program or service delivery to provide consumers with a final judgment of its effectiveness and worth. Scenario 3 illustrates a summative evaluation focusing on the quality of a teacher training program. Here, the district wanted information on whether their teacher training efforts to facilitate implementation of reforms had resulted in differences in teacher performance in classrooms. Summative evaluations typically lead to decisions on program continuation, termination, expansion or in the allocation/withdrawal of funds to support programs and services (Worthen, Sanders, & Fitzpatrick, 1997; Patton, 1986). In some cases, institutional members might use summative assessment data to review or institute new policies, as illustrated in the scenario for Decision 4.

***Differences between User Paths 1 and 2***   Refer to Table 2.2 as we review Table 2.3 to compare the assessment purposes that apply in User Paths 1 and 2. The first category (classroom assessment users) serves the needs of teachers in individual classrooms; they involve decisions on a much smaller scale with far lower stakes for an institution or individuals who run them. The second category of users (program participants, administrators, policymakers, and other stakeholders of programs and institutions) often make low stakes, formative decisions as well. However, many more of their assessment uses involve high stakes decisions potentially affecting institutions, programs, and various players in them.

## 2.4.2   Appropriate Use of Program-Level Assessments

***Accountability, Large-Scale Assessments, and High Stakes Decisions in Programs***
One of the most visible uses of assessment at the program level deals with assessments for accountability. In education, *accountability* refers to the responsibility of individuals providing educational services to demonstrate that the goals of the institution are being accomplished. *Stakeholders,* or individuals with a vested interest in the institution, typically ask the question: Is the program or institution providing the results we seek? Schoolwide, districtwide, and statewide accountability programs are summative evaluations of program effectiveness. They involve high stakes applications of tests and assessments, as the future of an institution and individual staff members is often dependent on the results. Funding may be discontinued, an institution's management might be replaced, or individual teachers or administrators may or may not receive merit recognitions and rewards.

The term *large-scale assessments* refers to systemwide use of assessments with large groups of students, teachers, or parents serving as subjects. Stakeholders use results of large-scale program assessments to make summative decisions involving accountability.

*Quality Control in Program-Level Assessments*    Like assessments in the classroom, well-designed assessment systems in programs and institutions should also be linked to the goals and objectives of an institution. Most institutions are organized as hierarchical systems. Assessments should ideally be linked to the goals operative at each level of an organization's hierarchy. The concept of an organizational hierarchy and multilevel application of assessments is illustrated in Figure 2.2 using the example of a K–12 public education system.

Alignment of assessment procedures with the goals and desired outcomes at different levels of the system influence the validity of results. The design/selection of assessments in an institution must take into account the extent to which variabilities can be expected in the implementation of goals at different levels of the hierarchy. A well-developed system of institutional assessment and decision-making would be synchronized with the overall mission and goals of the organization across various levels of the hierarchy, including different divisions within a given level. The tightness of the links may vary from loose to very tight as we move from decentralized to more centralized systems, but there should be some integration of the organizational mission/goals across and within levels of a system; such interdependencies in goals facilitate the functioning of the institution as a unified system.

If an institution allows freedom of activity at the microsystem levels through poli-

---

**National Goal of Schooling\*:**

By the year 2000, American students will leave grades four, eight, and twelve having demonstrated competency in challenging subject matter.

**State Curriculum Goal in Mathematics (a State Standard)\*\*:**

Students use numeric operations and concepts to describe, analyze, disaggregate, communicate, and synthesize numeric data, and to analyze and solve problems.

**District High School Program Goal in Mathematics:**

Students use technology to enhance mathematical analysis.

**Teacher's Instructional Goals and Objectives in a 10th-grade Precalculus Class**

    <u>Instructional Goal:</u> Students will graph data using selected computer software.

    <u>Objective:</u> With a graphing calculator, students will graph trigonometric functions.

---

**FIGURE 2.2    Integrated System of Goals and Assessments in the Organizational Hierarchy of a Public School System**

*Sources:* \*Excerpted with permission from document published by the National Education Goals Panel.

\*\*Adapted with permission from the Florida Department of Education (1997). All rights reserved.

cies such as site-based decision-making, assessments should be aligned to the more specific goals and objectives that are most likely to be operative at individual sites. To evaluate the quality of the programs at a district or statewide level, the assessments used should be aligned with the general goals that are common across schools rather than on very specific areas that may or may not be the focus of individual school programs or classrooms. For example, at a given point in time, we cannot use an assessment matched to specific objectives in an eighth-grade classroom to make conclusions about how well a districtwide or statewide science program is working. Only a very narrow portion of the system's science curriculum will very likely be evident in one classroom. Such assessment practices would compromise the quality of conclusions we draw about the program based on the assessment results.

*Instruments Used at the Program Level*   The choice of assessment procedures for different kinds of program-level assessments should not be arbitrary (prone to the influences of various participants, interest groups, and stakeholders), but systematic (yielding information on the system that is trustworthy). Many educational institutions tend to rely heavily on a single standardized achievement test to determine not only a scholastic program's effectiveness, but a host of other decisions, including those on individual teacher and staff competence. Consider the examples of assessment application in Case Study 2.4.

## Case Study 2.4   Consequences of High Stakes Assessment Reforms

The *St. Petersburg Times* (May 11, 1999) published a front-page article on the pressures of tough, high-stakes, statewide testing associated with current educational reform initiatives. Specifically, it raised the possibility that schools might "cheat" to raise scores on the new test. In states where the state's standardized test put reputations, jobs, and money on the line, the article said, "cheating by teachers and administrators is inevitable." It reported stories from Texas, Connecticut, New York, and Florida where:

A deputy superintendent was indicted on charges of tampering with test results to boost her district's test scores

A principal and several teachers were asked to resign amid allegations that someone changed a student's answers to a test

Teachers and entire school systems were under investigation for essays in which spelling errors were corrected in adult handwriting

*Source:* Used with permission from the *St. Petersburg Times.*

Historically, politicians and educational reformers have used high stakes, externally imposed assessment programs to drive large-scale educational change in schools. Is it right to reward or punish teachers and school superintendents based on the scores of a single test? Can scores on high stakes tests go up or down for reasons other than student achievement? Do political pressures associated with inappropriate use of standardized tests for accountability result in undesirable practices in schools and districts? What can we, as educators, do to inform our political leaders and the public on such matters?

Lorrie Shepard (1989a) brought to light several ethical issues surrounding such high stakes uses of standardized achievement tests for accountability and reform. Rather than encouraging better educational practice, she pointed out that attaching high stakes to particular tests tended to promote unsound teaching practices in classrooms, such as repetitive drilling on narrowed curricula. Because of the tremendous external pressures that schools are under to raise test scores, she recommended that rewards and incentives for schools and individual staff be untied from the results of large-scale accountability testing, and that census testing (where every pupil in every school and classroom is assessed), the common practice, be replaced with sampling methods.

Sampling is a strategy that would prevent individuals in positions of power from using assessment data to exert pressure upon or punish individual teachers or school leaders when test scores drop. Careful and judicious evaluation of the causes for low test scores might reveal that other factors, such as shifts in the population demographics, were the cause for temporary lapses in achievement scores in a given system.

Assessment practices illustrated in Case Study 2.4, although not widespread, are certainly inappropriate, and perhaps illegal. As we saw in the Lake Wobegon case, standardized achievement tests have several limitations. Combining achievement test results with data from other assessments, such as surveys, observations, self-studies, visits by external accreditation teams, personnel assessments, and content analyses of instructional materials, would help institutions obtain a far more comprehensive and valid understanding of the quality of their programs and services while revealing areas of need. Because of the many-faceted and complex structure of most educational programs and institutions, the Joint Committee on Standards for Educational and Psychological Testing recommended the use of multiple and varied assessments rather than overreliance on the results of a single assessment battery or test score (AERA, APA, & NCME, 1999).

Although a major focus in the preceding discussion has been the use of assessments in institutional/program evaluation and accountability contexts, we should remember that several other assessment functions fall within the purview of educational administrators/leaders. Impara and Plake (1996) identified as many as 24 capacity-building areas that were necessary for assessment users in Path 2. In the list, they included the following.

1. Developing Individualized Educational Plans (IEPs) for students based on assessment results
2. Using scores to decide on special program eligibility
3. Monitoring and evaluating student performance
4. Conducting observations of teachers when they conduct assessment functions
5. Placing or grouping students
6. Evaluating the school or system assessment program
7. Evaluating teacher/administrator performance

8. Developing interventions for students and teachers
9. Training teachers to develop or use tests
10. Conducting professional development programs for teachers/staff on assessment
11. Interpreting and using test scores

Some of these functions fall under User Paths 3, 4, or 5, and are discussed in the forthcoming sections of this chapter.

---

**Key Concepts**

■ In User Path 2, a wide variety of assessments can be used to make formative and summative decisions at the program level.
■ Appropriate assessment use at the program level requires that we attend to the multilevel structure of institutions and employ a wide array of assessments suited to the specific decision-making needs at different levels of an organization.

---

## 2.5 User Path 3: Assessment for Screening and Diagnosis of Exceptionalities

The term "clinician" applies to professionals in educational settings responsible for assessing special populations. This user group includes counseling psychologists, special educators, school psychologists, speech therapists, school nurses, and social workers (Sattler, 1988). Clinicians use a variety of clinical and psychoeducational assessments to:

1. Screen individuals for special needs, such as a hearing disability or intellectual giftedness
2. Diagnose particular conditions in individuals, such as a speech impairment
3. Determine a person's eligibility for therapeutic or special intervention services, such as treatment for learning disorders
4. Chronicle the progress and change of individuals with special needs during intervention

Clinicians use assessments of mental, pychosocial, behavioral, physical, or physiological constructs. Their assessment procedures range from records of their own observations, to behavioral ratings that they gather from parents, teachers, or subjects themselves, to very formal administrations of standardized assessment batteries. Both current and historical information may be gathered by clinicians to make informed judgments of a person's needs. Clinicians who make diagnostic decisions must be professionally trained to select, administer, interpret, evaluate, and write reports using data from assessments (Sattler, 1988). For screenings and observations, users in this path often employ assessments that they design or validate themselves; however, most of their assessment tools are standardized and commercially marketed instruments.

### 2.5.1   Assessment Uses by Clinicians

To obtain a sense of how data-based decisions made by clinicians differ from the first two categories of users, let us review the sequence of episodes for Mary, a six-year-old child, presented in Table 2.4. This example is adapted from *Assessment for Special Populations, Second Edition* (Salvia & Ysseldyke, 1981, p. 10).

**TABLE 2.4   Examples of Clinical Decisions for a Student with Special Needs**

| Assessment Events | Specific Decision and Decision-Makers |
| --- | --- |
| 1. At the end of her kindergarten year, Mary's scores on the reading readiness test administered by her classroom teacher were high. Consequently, the teacher recommended that Mary be promoted to first grade. | Summative classroom decision: Kindergarten teacher |
| 2. In first grade, however, the new teacher noticed that Mary was rapidly falling behind in reading. Mary was not fully attentive or engaged in class. The teacher requested assistance from a counselor. The counselor, working with the school psychologist and school nurse, found that Mary had been absent for a total of 31 days in January and February. On making informal observations, the clinical team found she could not associate letters with sounds, and appeared to have difficulties listening. | Identifying special needs: First-grade teacher, counselor, school psychologist, school nurse |
| 3. The clinicians then conducted a preliminary hearing examination. The test suggested that Mary was suffering from a moderate hearing loss that was likely to affect her progress in phonics. They conducted an interview of Mary's mother and found that the child had suffered from ear infections that past winter. They also gathered information on Mary's academic history from school records. Based on a review of all the data, they concluded that Mary's hearing was probably affected by the prolonged ear inammation, recommending that Mary see a doctor immediately. | Screening for hearing impairment, Gathering historical data: Clinicians |
| 4. The doctors (medical specialists) confirmed a middle ear infection following additional tests. They prescribed antibiotics to treat Mary's condition, asking for frequent follow-ups during the next two months. | Diagnosis of middle ear infection and treatment: Medical doctors |
| 5. When Mary returned to school, the counselor continued to make periodic observations of her classroom behaviors. The teacher planned special reading intervention activities for Mary until she was completely recovered. Gradually, Mary began to show progress in reading on classroom assessments. | Classroom intervention and follow-up: First-grade teacher and clinicians |

In the case shown, we see that a team of educational professionals work collaboratively to solve a problem that surfaced with one child in school. The team consists of past and present teachers, a school psychologist, a school nurse, and a counselor. Different members of the team, each of whom has a specialized responsibility, integrate information from various assessments. Current and past observations, test scores, and physical screenings are combined to make a careful analysis of the child's schooling and physical needs. Following a screening and recommendation by the educational clinicians, a medical practitioner prescribes treatment based on more formal diagnostic tests. Once the condition is diagnosed as a health-related problem, educational practitioners begin appropriate interventions and follow-up in school, taking into account the special need. Clinicians continue to use some of their own assessments to monitor the child's progress after the prescribed treatment begins.

Unlike Mary, whose condition was treatable and, happily, transient, a small proportion of students attending public schools are routinely identified by suitably trained educators with conditions that demand sustained care by specialists. These are children with disorders such as learning disabilities (LD), emotional disturbances (ED), or cognitive disabilities. On the other end of the spectrum are students classified as exceptional due to their extreme intellectual "giftedness" which must be "treated" with a suitably challenging and well-rounded curriculum.

The processes of identification, placement, and entitlement to educational services for special populations are governed by extensive legislation. Public Law (PL) 94-142, or The Education for All Handicapped Children Act of 1974, and the subsequent amendments to the same law as given in PL 94-457 and PL 105-17 (IDEA-97), are the key legislative mandates associated with assessment use in User Path 3. Although the details and content of the legislation lies outside the scope of this section, it is important for us to recognize that assessment errors with special needs populations can be very serious because of the legal restrictions and mandates.

## 2.5.2 Issues and Consequences Related to Assessing Students with Special Needs

Clinical assessments differ from classroom or program-level assessments in their focus on the individual child, who are referred for testing by their parents or school staff for identification of a disability or exceptional condition. Clinicians identify special needs using a medical model where screening is followed by in-depth diagnostic assessments. Professional teams including teachers and certified diagnostic specialists carry out such assessment functions.

Diagnosis of special conditions is an attempt to answer the question: Does the student have the condition or disability as we understand it? The accuracy with which special needs are diagnosed is a function of the scientific credibility of construct definitions of the disorder or condition being measured. Complex constructs involving disabling conditions often have definitions that are ambiguous, making their measurement error-prone. Although most tests used for clinical purposes are standardized, Shepard (1989b) pointed out that the measurement of the postulated constructs is often less than perfect because:

the underlying scientific understandings are incomplete and because the observable signs are limited proxies for the full concepts. . . . Because neither the (underlying) theory nor the measures are complete and exact, their mutual validity evolves slowly as evidence accumulates. To counteract the fallibility of a single measure, we seek confirmation from several indicators that have the concept in common, but have different sources of error (Shepard, 1989b, p. 547).

Good practice, in other words, demands that clinical practitioners use more than one assessment or data source to confirm findings, and attempt continuous validation to verify the meaning of the results from particular assessments. Validation involves ongoing, systematic research with the results (scores) of particular assessments to better understand and verify what they mean with respect to the underlying construct.

At least three issues concerning the use of clinical assessments have engendered heated discussions over time. First, people tend to view the identification of special needs and intervention that follows as an automatic consequence of assessment use. In actuality, governmental and legislative constraints determine entitlement to services, not just the results of testing. A tension exists in practice between the scientific measurement of a special needs condition and the government policies and regulations that control a child's placement within a program of special education services. The legal definitions are often influenced by the availability and allocation of government dollars to support the prescribed intervention program in the United States.

Second, because of the fallibility of commonly used testing procedures, there is often misidentification or overidentification of normal students as disabled or handicapped. Studies have shown that of students identified as having LD, as many as half may be wrongly classified because of predictive validity problems associated with the diagnostic instruments (Shepard, 1989b). Lack of predictive validity implies that the test scores simply do not have the properties to adequately forecast future behaviors, a factor that contributes to a test's poor classification accuracy rates. A negative consequence of misclassification is the mislabeling and possible stigmatizing of otherwise normal children as disabled or "deviants" from the mainstream.

Thirdly, special needs identification has traditionally depended heavily on IQ tests. Studies have shown that IQ tests developed in North American or other English-speaking countries tend to have a bias against linguistic minorities (non-English speakers), resulting in their misidentification as "disabled." Often, the needs of the non-English-speaking subpopulation are related to a language or a culture barrier, rather than a mental or learning disability. Overrepresentation of wrongly classified minorities in special education classes has been documented as a negative consequence of special needs assessments (Shepard, 1989b).

In terms of consequences of assessment use for a student, then, the practitioner must heed the following issues. If the special services are proven to be truly beneficial for a child, accurate identification and placement is, naturally, a positive and desirable educational consequence of clinical assessment use. On the other hand, the consequences of clinical testing could be viewed as negative when:

■ The assessments used are found to be technically deficient for the purposes at hand

■ Test administration and interpretation are conducted by untrained individuals
■ The intervention tied to assessment results is documented to have only marginal, mixed, or harmful results for the children identified with a "special need"

For those who see the labeling of individuals as "disabled" as detrimental in and of itself, the very act of making a referral for clinical assessment may be interpreted as a "negative consequence" associated with testing.

---

**Key  Concepts**

■ Clinicians use assessment results to screen, classify, place, and provide individualized intervention for students with special needs.
■ Clinical assessment tools are typically associated with high stakes decisions for individuals assessed, and must have adequate psychometric credibility.
■ Clinical assessments should be conducted by trained professionals, as these are governed by tight legislative requirements in the United States.

---

The case of *Daniel Hoffman v. the Board of Education of the City of New York* illustrates some of the consequences and issues related to assessment use in User Path 3, and is discussed in detail in Sattler (1988, pp. 2–3). The case underscores the important role that testing and psychological reports play in people's lives. The report in this case contained a recommendation for retesting the subject's intelligence that was ignored by school administrators. Years later when the case was tried, the failure to follow the recommendation and correctly diagnose a speech impairment (versus mental retardation), became a key issue. Sattler's analysis of the case included these generalizations.

1. Psychological reports prepared by trained professionals matter and their details should not be ignored by users.
2. Words can be misinterpreted in user contexts.
3. Measured intelligence can change over time.
4. Different tests and assessments may provide different results. Interpretations must be done carefully.
5. Placement decisions must be based on more than one assessment approach.
6. The instruments used must be appropriate.
7. Previous findings must be reviewed before high stakes decisions are made.

## 2.6   User Path 4: Assessment for Guidance and Counseling

Guidance counselors employ assessments to determine intellectual, emotional, and attitudinal readiness of their clients to make educational, vocational, and personal decisions in their lives (Harmon, 1989). A client is the recipient of guidance or counseling services. In a college or school setting, a counselor's primary clients are students. To conduct their functions well, counselors need a background in both psychology and measurement.

The guidance function of counselors centers around the problem of indecisiveness of their clients in making personal, career, or life-related plans at the expected developmental stage, time, or situation (as set by societal conventions). The indecisiveness may be related to self-doubt or anxiety about the future. It may be rooted in a lack of focus or confusion about one's strengths, weaknesses, interests, and aptitudes relative to choices available. It may also be related to a lack of drive, motivation, or other distracting factors in their lives. Through systematic use and interpretation of an array of carefully selected assessments, a guidance counselor can lead a person through an in-depth self-analysis, culminating in a decision that is satisfying to the individual. In sum, counselors use assessment techniques to help their clients explore educational plans, career plans, and/or life plans, thereby facilitating their personal growth and development.

There are situations under which the task of a guidance counselor can become difficult: first, where the client is considering an educational or career option that is not supported by the results of the assessments; and second, where there is "too much good news"—or too many directions and possibilities for future success that confuse the client.

### 2.6.1 Examples of Assessment in Guidance

Consider the example of an educational planning case in Table 2.5. Here, a high school student is facing difficulties in making future plans. She is systematically guided by a counselor towards a path that is a compromise between her two strongest areas. The counselor uses an array of evidence from aptitude, interest, personality, and other assessments. The process starts with an informal screening and interview. This is followed by the administration of a series of more formal assessment batteries and further interviewing. The final decision is made based on a review of the assessment data *and* a consideration of the goals, desires, and values of the student and her family. As in User Path 3, guidance and counseling applications of assessments also have an individual client focus.

### 2.6.2 Assessment Issues in Guidance and Counseling

Given that counselors use assessments that are well-developed and validated, the decision-making process would appear to be fairly straightforward in User Path 4. However, as in other contexts, the problems of inadequately defined constructs, insufficient validity evidence, and culturally biased assumptions underlying tests all affect assessment use for guidance as well. As with other practitioners who employ assessments as a part of their professional practices, counselors must also apply measurement principles in selecting, using, and interpreting assessments appropriately in guidance contexts. Harmon (1989) endorses that counselors need to be firmly grounded in applied psychometrics to make the right choices in work settings. According to him, tests cannot be misused in counseling unless a counselor abuses them. Inadequate measures should not be used, he states, and adequate measures should not be used for the wrong purposes or with the wrong populations (Harmon, 1989, p. 535).

Unlike clinicians, counselors can operate with very few legal constraints in their use

**TABLE 2.5   Examples of Guidance and Counseling Decisions**

| Assessment Events | Specific Decision and Decision-Maker |
|---|---|
| 1. Roberta, a high school senior, was referred to the guidance counselor by her teacher for help with her future planning. Her mother was concerned that Roberta wanted to avoid college although she had a strong academic record. "She seems confused, anxious, and unhappy about her future. Can you help her?" The counselor had an informal interview with Roberta to get an initial understanding of her needs. Then she scheduled some formal testing sessions to learn more about her interests, aptitudes, self-concept, personality traits, and values. | Informal screening of client needs: Guidance counselor |
| 2. Following testing, the counselor compiled the results of the assessments with Roberta's school records to put together a complete file. Roberta had strong inclinations and aptitudes for academic as well as fine arts careers. Her unhappiness and anxiety were rooted in questions about her possible success in the latter arena, to which she was currently drawn. In a one-on-one conference, the counselor explained that her client had many options open based on her diverse aptitudes and interests. However, the long-range implications of each path must be evaluated taking into account her personal needs and values. Prompted by the counselor's questioning, Roberta then considered each path, and narrowed down her future educational options to a program that was a compromise between the two. | Use of formal test batteries to obtain a profile of client traits; Use of assessment data to evaluate future options: Guidance counselor and client |
| 3. In a final interview with her parents present, the counselor made a recommendation for Roberta to explore both educational paths in an interdisciplinary college program, indicating that she was likely to succeed in both arenas. Roberta postponed a final decision on a career until she completed the recommended college program. | Final recommendation for client: Guidance counselor, client, client's family |

of assessments. Harmon (1989) emphasizes that in guidance contexts, client problems have to be explored in depth from emotional, cognitive, and behavioral perspectives before solutions are attempted by counselors. The information from assessments provides only a small part of the whole picture needed to form conclusions for individuals.

### 2.6.3   Other Assessment Applications by Counselors

Counselors in educational institutions, often teamed with social workers and psychologists, also provide clients with personal counseling and skill-based training programs in behavioral management. Such curricula focus on personal, social, and emotional areas of development, such as coping with stress, conflict resolution, dealing with personal or family crises, anger, or problems at home, work, and school. In any skill-based training context, counselors would employ assessments in much the same way as classroom teachers—i.e., to develop and deliver instructional strategies, identify student needs, and evaluate learning outcomes of their clients. This second type of assessment usage by counselors runs parallel to assessment used for instructional purposes (User Path 1). As with classroom teachers, counselors working in such contexts need to develop skills in classroom assessment design, selection, validation, and use.

**Key Concepts**

■ Guidance counselors use assessment results to help individual clients choose educational or career paths.
■ Guidance assessments are not legally regulated.

## 2.7  User Path 5: Assessment for Admissions, Licensure, Scholarships, and Awards

Another category of educational decisions made using assessment scores has to do with admission, licensure, promotion, and/or recognition of individuals in an institution, program, or profession. This category of assessment use is influenced by institutional policy on matters such as certification, admission, and reward systems. Testing corporations or private contractors formally develop and standardize most instruments used in such decision-making contexts. In the area of collegiate admissions, for example, the College Board is well known for tests such as the Scholastic Assessment Tests I and II (SAT I, SAT II). The Graduate Record Examination (GRE), the Law Schools Admissions Test (LSAT) and many others are used by admissions boards in undergraduate, graduate, and professional schools. The American College Testing Program (ACT) is another organization devoted to test development efforts to meet user needs in the fifth category. In the area of teacher certification and licencing, the Educational Testing Service (ETS) has developed the Praxis I and II tests that have now been adopted in teacher certification programs in several states in the United States. Table 2.6 illustrates the types of applications found in the fifth category (see Whitney, 1989).

### 2.7.1  Issues in Assessment for Admissions, Licensure, Scholarships, and Awards

Although there are public perceptions to the contrary, most institutions tend to use a variety of nontest indicators such as prior grades, interviews, actual performance in particular settings, and writing samples along with test scores to make admissions, licensing, or recognition decisions on individual candidates. The reasons for this practice are obvious—decisions in this category are high stakes decisions for individuals involved. Legal

**TABLE 2.6  Examples of Assessments Used for Admissions, Placement, Scholarships, and Awards**

| Assessment Used | Type of Decision/Application |
| --- | --- |
| 1. *Law School Admissions Tests* (LSAT) | Granting admission into law school |
| 2. *Graduate Management Admissions Test* (GMAT) | Granting admissions to graduate-level business management programs |
| 3. *Graduate Record Examination* (GRE) | Granting admission to graduate school; Awarding assistantships and fellowships to meritorious graduate students |
| 4. *Advanced Placement Program Tests* at the high school level, offered by the College Entrance and Examination Board (CEEB) | Placement of high school graduates in advanced, college-level courses |
| 5. *Praxis I* and *II* Examinations | Developed by Educational Testing Service for certifying teachers in specialized areas. Used in several northeastern states of the United States |

implications of assessment misuse in this category can be serious. Use of many and varied sources of information is, thus, far more prudent in such circumstances than dependency on any one measured indicator.

Developers, practitioners, and users must be able to demonstrate the technical defensibility of scores used for decisions in the fifth category in at least three areas. First, if the admission or placement hinges on assumptions of future performance of individuals in particular settings, the *predictive validity,* in particular, the predictive accuracy of scores used is an important factor. Predictive validity evidence, discussed in greater detail in Chapters 3 and 13, would provide justification that scores from the assessment are adequately correlated with future performance indicators that are relevant to the population. For example, users of the SAT should be interested in whether the SAT scores of high school graduates actually correlate with their later performance in undergraduate programs.

Second, evidence should exist that the assessment data agencies use are free from possible *selection biases* towards particular gender, ethnic, or minority groups. Issues of discrimination and fairness arise when subgroups are systematically denied (or offered) opportunities for recognition/licencing/admission based on particular test scores while others with similar abilities are not.

Third, the standards or cut-scores used in making selections, admissions, or recognitions should be both reasonable and psychometrically defensible. *Cut-scores* represent criterion levels of performance on the selected test score continuum that might grant particular individuals entry or recognition, for example the requirement of a score of 600 on the GRE-Verbal battery for a scholarship in a graduate program. Users should not set cut-scores arbitrarily, but after due consideration of statistical and other evidence that the required score is reasonable for the population or subpopulation of interest. In Chapter 11 we look at some methods for setting cut-scores for applications in User Path 5. For informed practices to occur in User Path 5, a sound grounding in the appropriate psychometric applications is necessary for practitioners.

### Key Concepts

- User Path 5 involves the use of assessment data for making decisions on licencing, certifications, admissions, placement, or recognition.
- These assessment applications involve high stakes decisions.
- To support the use of particular scores in User Path 5, the tests and assessments should have the necessary psychometric evidence.

## 2.8 User Path 6: Assessment for Educational Research and Development

Last but not least, construct assessments are needed when we conduct theoretical and applied research in education. Researchers interested in understanding and describing how the larger educational process works are also interested in measuring variables that are central to their research questions. Assessment in research contexts focuses on diverse attributes ranging from student demographics, to achievement, to affective, instructional, and environmental factors. The primary users of assessments in this category are quantitative theorists, researchers and scholars. Further details on assessment applications in User Path 6 can be found in textbooks of research design and methodology, and in research journals in education. In keeping with the practitioner focus of this book and module, this area will not be treated any further here.

### Key Concepts

- User Path 6 involves the use of assessment data in educational research endeavors.
- The quantitative tradition of educational research requires the use of valid and reliable measures.

## 2.9 Crossover across User Groups

The user groups treated in our typology in Table 2.1 are not mutually exclusive groups. Their roles often overlap in the world of practice. This is particularly true when professionals work in cross-functional teams to address an educational problem. You obtained a glimpse of this in the assessment scenario with Mary, the 6-year-old, where teachers and clinicians worked together to arrive at a solution (Table 2.4). If you have a sound grasp of measurement applications across a wide range of decision-making contexts, it is likely to make you a more effective professional.

Classroom teachers must be proficient in the design and selection of assessments for classroom decisions, but it is also necessary for them to make judicious interpretations of standardized test scores employed for programmatic decisions involving accountability or strategic planning at an organizational level. Similarly, administrators should be knowledgeable about the limitations and advantages of assessments used for accountability, program evaluation, and employee evaluation purposes. At the same time, they should be able to evaluate the quality of classroom assessment practices used by teachers and their impact on instructional services offered in their schools.

The movement towards full inclusion of severely challenged students in mainstream classrooms requires that public school teachers be cognizant about assessment practices used for special populations today, particularly in the diagnosis of special needs. Counselors, social workers, school psychologists, and media specialists/technologists are now required to serve as instructional support personnel in schools, making it necessary for them to be well versed in classroom assessment methodology. The first five user groups, consisting primarily of practitioners, rarely function in isolated islands in educational settings. They should thus be prepared to carry out assessment functions across the gamut of the applied contexts listed in Table 2.1.

## 2.10 Responsibilities for Appropriate Assessment Use

No matter what your primary User Path might be, we could draw certain generalizations from the assessment application scenarios and case studies we have reviewed in the five practitioner paths (excluding Path 6). These generalizations could serve as "rules" to help us guard against inappropriate practices (after Messick, 1989; 1994).

*Rule 1*   We should use careful judgment in the design or choice of assessments for particular purposes, keeping in mind the psychometric defensibility of the results for particular uses, and the stakes likely to be tied to the assessment results.

*Rule 2*   Needs of assessment users are different in various decision-making contexts. Assessments used for program-level decisions differ in purpose, content, form, and technical characteristics from assessments designed for other purposes, such as clinical diagnosis or classroom decisions. We should be cautious when substituting assessments across user contexts, as there is the potential of misusing instruments and the information that they yield.

*Rule 3*   Prior to using assessments, we should evaluate who might be affected by the results, and the extent to which the decisions made with the results are likely to have serious consequences for the assessors, various users and stakeholders, and those assessed. We should implement assessments after weighing all possible social, legal, and practical consequences of their use, both deliberate and inadvertent.

# Summary

In Chapter 1 we learned that any work with assessments should begin with a clear awareness of the construct, the population and the assessment purposes. Pinpointing the assessment purpose(s), the major focus of Chapter 2, is important for the designer as well as the user of assessments. To ensure that an instrument will indeed be able to serve its intended purposes, it helps to start with a clear articulation of purposes, and then to let the purposes guide us during the assessment design, selection, and validation processes.

This chapter recognized six major decision-making contexts, referred to as User Paths, in which educational measurements typically play a part. These are classroom assessment (User Path 1); assessment for program evaluation, planning, or policymaking (User Path 2); assessment for screening or diagnosis of exceptionalities (User Path 3); assessment for guidance and counseling (User Path 4); assessment for admissions, placement, recognitions and awards (User Path 5); and finally, assessment in educational research (User Path 6). In practice, these user contexts are not mutually exclusive; assessment users often cross the context boundaries. The purposes, or specific usages of data from assessments in the different contexts, however, differ.

Ideally, the assessment purposes should guide specific decisions we make during the construction or selection of an assessment tool, and ultimately the inferences we make with the assessment results. Early decisions that would be influenced by the decision-making context are factors such as the content of a test, the format of the tasks or items, the type of scaling, the degree of precision we need for particular score ranges, and the amount of error that we can tolerate in the results. We would then need to gather psychometric evidence to verify that the assessment tool generates information that is of adequate quality to support our inferences and specific decisions (this work is called validation). This chapter provided some examples of different types of validation evidence that might be needed for assessment tools used for different purposes. For example, predictive validity, reliability, or the dependability of cut-scores serves as important supporting evidence in assessments used for placement decisions (User Path 5). In sum, both assessment design and validation should be dictated by the needs of a specific situation. Later chapters in this book/module present a process model to help integrate the work related to assessment design/selection, validation, and use, keeping in mind the assessment purposes in given User Paths.

# QUESTIONS FOR CLASS DISCUSSION

1. Consider the headings in the list that follows showing an example of an assessment user in the medical profession. Continue the list by identifying different attributes that are of interest to the educational user groups, such as teachers, counselors, psychologists, media specialists, and so on, and describe the types of decisions they make with assessment information. *Be specific.*

| User Group | Whom to Assess? (Population) | What to Assess? (Constructs) | Decisions Made (Uses) |
|---|---|---|---|
| Physicians | Patients | Physiological characteristics (e.g., blood sugar levels, cholesterol levels) | Disease diagnosis Intervention |

2. The College Board's Scholastic Assessment Test (SAT) was designed to be used as a part of a college admissions testing program and is usually administered to 10th, 11th, and 12th grade students in high school. The SAT score scale ranges from 200 to 800, with a mean of 500. During the period extending from the mid-1960s to the early 1980s, the average SAT score was found to steadily decline. Declines in the SAT Verbal scores were found to be in the order of 50 points. In the Mathematics area, research reports showed a drop of about 35 points. Soon after, a number of publications from concerned members of the educational and general community concluded that the decline in scores reflected a failure of the U.S. public education system.

(a) What category of assessment use and user group is represented in this case?

(b) Identify the type of decision being made by the "concerned individuals" with the SAT scores.

(c) Describe why their conclusions could be erroneous. What factors could have contributed to the drop in test scores? What types of information needed to be sought in order to make appropriate interpretations of the observed SAT score decline?

3. In an attempt to cover the material in the biology textbook before the spring term ended, Mr. Slepp asked his two honors classes to read a difficult chapter on their own on Monday night. On Tuesday, he administered a True/False test on that chapter, and scored and recorded the students' grades that same night. On Wednesday, he communicated the results of the assessment to the students. Most of the class had received Cs, Ds or Fs. Both the students and the teacher were very disappointed. The teacher discussed the test and the material covered on it in detail for the remainder of the class period on Wednesday (adapted from Canady and Hotchkiss, 1989, with permission).

(a) Identify the type of assessment use and decisions made in the above scenario.

(b) Evaluate Mr. Slepp's classroom assessment practices with reference to the outcome-driven model of classroom instruction and assessment presented in this chapter. To maximize learning in his students, what could he have done differently?

4. During the 1980s, several school systems in the United States began to use a commercially marketed, early childhood test to identify developmental delays in kindergartners. Based on the recommendations of the test-makers, children who were identified as delayed were then held for two years in developmental or transitional kindergartens. This practice of "kindergarten retention" became rather controversial. Available documentation on the properties of the test scores was very limited, and suggested that the test had characteristics similar to that of a screening test, but not one that could be used for accurate diagnosis and classification of developmental delays.

(a) Identify the assessment user and category of test use illustrated above using the typology in Table 2.1.

(b) Evaluate the appropriateness of the assessment practices in the above scenario.

(c) What should the assessment users have done prior to using the test in the manner that they did? What could test developers have done to promote appropriate practices? What could be the social and practical consequences of the above application of testing in schools?

5. Review some recent articles in the professional literature in your area of specialization that involve assessment applications. Identify case(s) where an assessment was misused due to inadequate understanding by users of the assessment purposes. Present a description of the case(s) in class. Explain why you believe the problem was caused by ambiguity in assessment purposes.

NOTE: More structured exercises with immediate feedback for answers are available on the computer module.

# 3 Quality of Assessment Results: Validity, Reliability, and Utility

## Overview

As a practitioner, you will be designing or selecting assessments to meet numerous needs (some of which we examined in Chapter 2). An assessment system that performs well should generate information possessing three qualities: validity, reliability, and utility. The purpose of this chapter is to help you see how current understandings of validity, reliability, and utility relate to practical decisions made during assessment design, selection, validation, and use. This chapter's aim is to lay the foundation for Chapters 5 through 9, which provide a "how to" process for developing and selecting assessments tied to different decision-making paths. The intent of this chapter is to communicate the essential theoretical concepts that you will need to take the assessment design/selection process as far as a step that is called "content validation" in this book. Statistical applications used when investigating validity and reliability are briefly mentioned here and treated in more detail in Chapters 10 and 13. To illustrate the concepts in concrete terms, the chapter provides several examples and case studies.

The concepts introduced in this chapter might seem complex at first. Should you find that to be true, a second review, with attention to the tables, examples, case studies, and the summary, might help. Note that the chapter uses the term "measure" to refer to both the instrument used to measure a construct as well as to the score that it generates. This usage is consistent with that found in the literature.

## CHAPTER 3 OBJECTIVES

After studying this chapter and completing the structured exercises in the module, you should be able to:

1. Define the concepts of validity and systematic measurement error

2. Analyze the predominant sources of systematic error affecting the validity of assessment results in specific examples

3. Describe the concept of validation and different methods for gathering validity evidence

4. Relate different methods for gathering validity evidence to validation questions and assessment purposes

5. Define the concepts of reliability and random measurement error

6. Analyze the predominant sources of random error that could influence reliability of assessment results in specific examples

7. Identify factors that affect assessment utility in particular applications

8. Identify steps and actions that can be taken during assessment design and selection to enhance validity, reliability, and utility of an assessment tool and its results.

# 3.1   Validity

Validity refers to the accuracy of inferences and interpretations we make from the results or "scores" of an assessment tool. Validity is concerned with the question: What do the results tell us about the meaning of the underlying construct, as represented by the items or tasks that make up the assessment tool? Validity is affected when we inadvertently let *systematic error* cloud the meaning of "what" is measured because of the way we create an instrument or because of the way we use it. Validity should be the most important consideration guiding our assessment development and selection efforts, and has been identified by the AERA, APA, & NCME (1999) standards committee as the foremost factor affecting the quality of assessment results. Consider Case Study 3.1 for an example of a systematic source of error in measurement.

## Case Study 3.1   How Systematic Errors Affect Validity of Our Inferences from Scores

Suppose an assessment developer designs a science examination to measure science knowledge and abilities with a population of fluent English speakers in mind. The results of the assessment would be valid if it gave us accurate information on a student's science knowledge and abilities in as pure a form as possible. Suppose also that, without the assessment designer's intent or the test user's conscious decision, the assessment is administered to a group of students with rather poor English language skills. Now we have a situation where these students' weakness in English could interfere with the assessment results, giving us invalid information on their science abilities. The "science score" could now also partially be an "English language score," but to what degree? To the extent that the students' language deficiency affected the science score, it would be a source of systematic error affecting the validity of our inferences about their science abilities. Unless the students' English language skills changed significantly from one assessment occasion to the next, the individuals would be likely to obtain the same low scores each time the same test was given, predictably and consistently. Hence, we refer to the language interference as a "systematic source of error."

The presence of systematic interfering factors that prevents the assessment or interpretation of a measured construct in its "pure" form causes invalidity in results. Table 3.1 presents more specific examples to illustrate why assessment results are often low in validity and the associated source of systematic error that could potentially influence our inferences about the construct. You will no doubt be able to expand the list in Table 3.1 with examples from your own assessment experiences.

- In Example 1, we see that systematic errors can result from a few items or tasks on an assessment that fail to *match the construct* well. In the example, the presence of the items dealing with science affect how the examinees perform in arithmetic and may provide us with misleading information on their arithmetic abilities. Such items should be detected during assessment development, and revised or deleted from the assessment tool to improve validity.
- Example 2 makes assumptions about the prior preparation levels of the *population* assessed when measuring achievement related to a specific curriculum. To measure achievement in geometry in a valid way, all the students should have received the geometry curriculum; otherwise our inferences about their achievement levels will be invalid. Examples 3, 4, and 7 are similar in that the assessment designers make assumptions about the cultural or other background characteristics of the targeted population. When the assessment is used, however, the assumptions are violated. Violations such as the one in Example 7 give us a *biased* result, where some subgroups obtain systematically lower (or in some cases, higher) scores due to factors that are unrelated to the construct of interest.
- Example 4 shows us that sometimes the *conditions of assessment* can affect how students perform and give us a distorted picture of where they stand on a measured construct. Here, the reading levels and other assessment conditions fail to take into account the developmental level of the examinees, which systematically interferes with the assessment results.
- Example 5, where writing skills are measured with selected response items, has to do with the assessment designer's choice of an *inappropriate assessment method* and conditions. The multiple choice format is so far removed from the true nature of the targeted construct, that it serves as a systematic interference.
- Finally, in Example 8, we see a disregard for the original *assessment purposes* that threatens the validity of conclusions that the user makes about the construct, a speech disability.

To summarize, the validity of our inferences from assessment results is adversely affected if the items, tasks, and conditions that make up an instrument fail to match the construct that we initially set out to assess. Validity is also lowered in instances where the populations or subpopulations assessed with an instrument are not a good match with the populations for whom the instrument was originally intended. Finally, validity is diminished when the purposes for which the assessment results ultimately are used fail to match the original purposes for which the instrument was designed.

As we can see, it is not the assessment tool that can be characterized as valid or invalid, but the *inferences* that we make from the scores that can be valid or invalid. In the

**TABLE 3.1  Why Assessment Results Are Often Low in Validity: Some Common Sources of Systematic Error**

| Source of Systematic Error | Example |
| --- | --- |
| 1. Items or tasks that do not truly reflect the construct | An arithmetic assessment includes a few problems that assume the students know concepts from the elementary science curriculum. |
| 2. Respondents or examinees lacking the opportunity to learn the content* | A required state assessment is administered with the assumption that all high school students have taken an advanced geometry course. In fact, only students in the honors track took that course. |
| 3. Language or cultural barriers for particular sub-populations assessed | Students from different cultural backgrounds take an assessment including problems that assume they live in an urban environment in North America. |
| 4. Assessment conditions that pose barriers to the respondents or examinees | The vocabulary and length of sentences on an elementary assessment makes it difficult for the typical student to understand the questions. Further, assessment instructions require that students take the assessment independently, without receiving any outside help. |
| 5. Assessment format or conditions that interfere with how the construct is known to be manifested | Writing skills are measured with only multiple choice items. |
| 6. Inappropriate developmental levels of content or format of tasks or items | Young children (age 5–6 years) are expected to bubble in their responses to multiple choice items on a scan form of a standardized achievement test. |
| 7. Bias in the items or assessment content | An assessment includes word problems based on baseball, a game played mostly by boys. This causes girls to get systematically lower scores. |
| 8. Assessment is used for a purpose for which it was not designed | Diagnosis of a speech disability is done with a teacher-made classroom assessment focusing on oral reading skills. |

*Applies when assessing scholastic achievement.

final analysis, validity has to do with the *meaningfulness* of an assessment's results for particular constructs, given the purposes for which the assessment is used and populations relevant to the assessment context. When we approach assessment design, selection, or use, the question we should ask is not: "Are these assessment results valid or not?" but rather:

- To what degree are these results a valid reflection of the construct we want to measure?
- To what degree are these results valid for the purposes we want to fulfill?
- To what degree are these results valid for the population of interest?

We cannot evaluate validity in absolute terms. As we saw in the case studies in Chapter 2, validity of scores in one context does not automatically guarantee their validity in others. If we are aware of the systematic errors that could potentially threaten validity in an assessment application, we can take steps to prevent or control for these interferences when we develop, select, or use assessments.

---

Key Concepts

- Validity has to do with the meaningfulness of the information we obtain about a measured construct.
- Validity is affected by systematic errors in the assessment situation.
- Systematic errors are predictable and can come from different sources.
- To improve validity of results, it helps to pin down the construct targeted for assessment, the purposes for assessment, and population.

---

### 3.1.1 Validity, Fairness, and Bias in Assessments

An unfair assessment procedure yields invalid results. A well-constructed assessment tool should not yield scores that have biases towards any of the individuals assessed. However, Examples 2, 3, 4, and 7 in Table 3.1 all portray different ways in which the *use* of an assessment can result in unfairness or bias towards one or more subgroups tested. The diversity of the examples tells us that unfairness can be caused by several factors. Thus, there is no single, technical definition of a "fair test." Individual items or questions might cause two groups of equal ability to perform differently (Example 7); this is known as "differential item functioning (DIF)." In other circumstances, some individuals or subgroups might be differentially treated during the assessment administration or scoring process, with lopsided results that fail to reflect their true abilities. In achievement testing, we assume that everyone tested has had equal opportunities to learn what we assess; violation of this assumption leads to biased outcomes. Tests used for admissions or certification should predict equally well how individuals of similar ability will perform in future work or educational settings, irrespective of differences in gender, ethnicity, and language spoken. However, interfering factors often mar the predictive validity of such inferences. The degree to which such interferences could affect assessment results need to be systematically checked out. The procedures we employ to ensure that an assessment tool will yield valid results are collectively called *validation procedures,* the topic of the following section.

## 3.2    Validation and Types of Validity Evidence

Once an assessment tool is developed, good practice demands that we evaluate the extent to which it actually yields meaningful results *in context* by gathering evidence of validity. *Validation* is the collection of logical and empirical evidence to support inferences we wish to make with the results of an assessment tool. *Logical* evidence of validity is gathered through reviews of the assessment tool and its results by suitable experts. Logical reviews are based on opinions of the reviewers and yields qualitative evidence of validity. *Empirical* evidence of validity is gathered through actual tryouts and data collection with an assessment tool, followed by appropriate forms of analyses. Empirical evidence is usually quantitative. Validity evidence could also include data from preexisting studies, perhaps conducted by the original developers or other interested researchers. At other times, validation may require that we gather new or additional evidence to support a local application that departs from the original purpose of an assessment. Both assessment developers and users must be able to support their assessment applications with evidence of validity (AERA, APA & NCME, 1999). This section will introduce you to the different kinds of validity evidence, methods for gathering the evidence, and the assessment purposes that drive the collection of each type of evidence. In Chapter 13, you will find more detailed information on empirical validation methods.

The most recent *Standards* document (AERA, APA, & NCME, 1999) recognizes five major types of evidence that we could use to support validity of the most common uses made with results of educational and psychological assessments. In Table 3.2, we see the various types of validity evidence linked to questions we might ask about what the construct means, the assessment's purposes, and the most typical methods of data collection and analysis. Let us consider each situation in some detail.

### 3.2.1    Content-Based Evidence of Validity

The first criterion for determining validity is based on the extent to which the assessment results faithfully reflect the theoretical construct in terms of *content*. This aspect of validity was traditionally labeled *content validity,* or *content-related validity* (AERA, APA & NCME, 1985). Messick (1989, 1994) pointed out that to gather content-based validity evidence, it is necessary for us to attend to two things during assessment design or selection: (1) content representativeness, and (2) content relevance.

A critical early step in designing or selecting an assessment tool is specifying the *domain* of observable indicators or behaviors that represent the construct we wish to measure. Specifying the domain is the first step in operationally defining a construct (see Chapter 1). The term "domain" refers to the entire gamut of all possible items or tasks by which a theoretical construct can be represented. For instance, to assess "mathematics achievement in first grade," our domain would include every possible category of mathematics problem that can be written to match a first-grade curriculum. An assessment tool measuring that construct would be made up of only a sample of the items/tasks from the larger domain.

**TABLE 3.2  Validation Questions Linked to Validity Evidence and Methods**

| Questions to Be Answered during Validation | Validity Evidence Needed | Validation Method: How Evidence Is Typically Collected and Analyzed |
| --- | --- | --- |
| 1. Does the assessment tool contain only the behaviors, skills, knowledge, attitudes, and/or tasks that match the theoretical definition of the construct? Is the content of the assessment relevant to the specified domain? Are the items or tasks weighted appropriately? | ■ Content-based validity evidence<br>■ Judgment of content relevance and representativeness<br><br>(*Traditional label:* Content validity or content-related validity) | Validity is established through logical reviews of the content, format, scoring and administration procedures of an assessment by knowledgeable experts. |
| 2. Do the response, administration, and scoring processes agree with the underlying assumptions about the construct? | ■ Evidence of validity in processes used by respondents and scorers<br><br>(*Traditional label:* Construct validity) | Validity is established through direct questioning of respondents or observation of scoring and recording patterns. |
| 3. Do the items and components of the assessment intercorrelate in a manner consistent with theoretical hypotheses about the construct? Does the internal structure support the proposed interpretations of results/scores? | ■ Evidence of internal structure<br><br>(*Traditional label:* Construct validity) | Validity is established through empirical correlations of item to total scores, factor analyses, evaluations of scale or subscale dimensionality. |
| 4. Do the assessment results interrelate with external variables in a manner consistent with theory? Do the scores converge with measures of similar constructs and diverge from measures of dissimilar constructs? | ■ Evidence of convergent and discriminant validity<br>■ Evidence of group or subgroup differences<br><br>(*Traditional label:* Construct validity: convergent and discriminant validity) | Validity is established through empirical correlations of scores with data from similar and dissimilar measures or various subgroup analyses. |
| 5. Do the assessment results predict future behaviors or performances, as hypothesized? Do the scores concur with scores of other measures taken at the same time, as hypothesized? | ■ Evidence of criterion-related validity<br><br>(*Traditional label:* Criterion-related validity; concurrent validity; predictive validity) | Validity is established through empirical correlations of scores with data from criterion variables gathered at a future time (predictive validity) or at the same time (concurrent validity). |

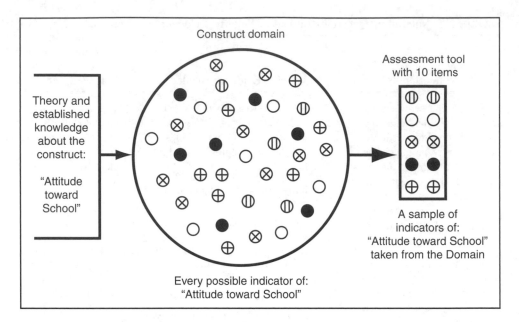

**FIGURE 3.1** Sampling Indicators from a Construct Domain to Ensure Content Relevance and Content Representativeness

To create an instrument that has *content relevance,* we would have to ensure that all the different types of behaviors (or mathematics problems) in the domain are included in the sample of items or tasks that make up the assessment. If there are two major types of behaviors in the domain, dealing with number concepts and operations, a content-relevant assessment would include items that match both these areas of the domain. For the instrument to have *content representativeness,* we would need to *proportionately* sample each different type of behavior (or mathematics problem). If the number concepts and operations were equally distributed in the domain, a content-representative test would need to have equal numbers of items of each kind.

In Figure 3.1, we see an illustration of how content-based validity can be achieved using a theoretical domain for the construct "attitude toward school." Here, we see that the domain contains five different types of attitudinal behaviors, represented with solid circles, empty circles, circles with crosses, and so forth. An attitude scale that has content relevance would include items with all four types of behaviors in the domain. If it has content representativeness, it would also have equal distributions of each type of behavior, thus mirroring the distribution we find in the theoretically specified domain—that is, 20% of the items on the assessment tool would match each of the four different types of attitudinal behaviors in the domain.

Content relevance, then, deals with the relevance of the content of the items in the assessment with regard to the proposed interpretations to be made with assessment results. We determine content relevance by answering the question: "Do the assessment tasks, behaviors, and questions, *substantively* reflect the construct that we want to assess?" Content representativeness has to do with proportionate sampling and weighting of the questions, tasks, or behaviors on an assessment tool so that they closely reflect the distribution in the domain.

***How to Gather Evidence of Content-Based Validity.*** We establish content-based validity of an assessment by asking knowledgeable experts to systematically review and verify that an assessment's items or "operations" match the domain and its theoretical underpinnings. The operations of an assessment include the content of the items or tasks, their structure and format, and the conditions under which the assessment is administered and scored (for example, how the directions are given, whether the assessment is an open-book or closed-book test, and so forth).

Who are "knowledgeable experts" qualified to content-validate assessment tools? Expert reviewers would vary depending on the assessments and constructs in question. For example, classroom teachers might ask peer teachers to review assessments tied to particular curricula; reading teachers and language arts specialists would be the best reviewers for a reading assessment; psychologists with appropriate specializations would be suitable for reviewing particular psychological assessments such as attitude scales; and banking professionals should conduct the content reviews of a test of finance or banking concepts. Assessment development in formal settings also involves reviews by test development experts, who screen the items/tasks, directions, layout, scoring, and administration procedures to certify that they adhere to rules for test construction. Chapters 7 through 9 illustrate how poor item construction and scoring can affect both the validity and reliability (discussed in the next section) of results. Screening for gender, ethnic, or culture biases should also be done with assessments used for high stakes decisions. Bias reviews are typically conducted by individuals who have studied gender, linguistic, and cultural issues and are sensitive to likely problems.

***Is Content-Validity Evidence Necessary for All Assessments?*** We should attempt to establish content-based validity of all assessments as a part of the development process, that is, before their use. Ideally, even classroom and other locally made assessments should be content-validated, whether we design them from scratch or select them from available resources. Often, content-based evidence is the only validity evidence that we can feasibly gather to support interpretations made from classroom assessment results. Chapters 5 through 9 provide further details of content-validation procedures and questions to ask during the review process, situated in specific assessment design contexts. Assessments used in high stakes contexts have to meet higher standards for gathering content-based evidence than instruments used in low stakes contexts.

### 3.2.2 Evidence of Validity in Processes Used by Respondents, Observers, and Scorers

Some performance assessments, such as open-ended reasoning tasks scored by human judges, rest on theoretical assumptions about cognitive processes that examinees will use to arrive at a solution. Others are based on beliefs that the scorers will be focusing on particular aspects of examinee behaviors or responses when awarding points. How can we be sure that the scores truly reflect the cognitive processes that examinees were expected to employ? Case Study 3.2 illustrates an episode where evidence of validity in response or scoring processes becomes important.

---

### Case Study 3.2    When Is Evidence of Response and Scoring Processes Critical to Making Valid Inferences about a Construct?

In a southern state, the developers of the state-mandated timed essay-writing examination intended to use the scores for making inferences about the writing skills of fourth graders. Soon after, the state began to use the test's scores to identify "critically low-performing" schools. Around that time, newspaper reporters found that teachers and school staff were drilling students in composing paragraphs with the help of memorized, fill-in-the-blank "props." These props were prewritten paragraphs set up with an introduction, a body, and conclusion—requirements that they expected would yield a passing score (or better) on the essays. School staff systematically coached their students to fill in the blanks with the words related to an expected range of essay topics for particular grade-level examinations. Students soon learned to complete the essays with the help of the props that they were reciting from memory. In a couple of years, newspapers reported gains in writing scores of initially low-ranking schools on the state's writing test.

Putting the ethics of high stakes testing aside for a minute, we could consider some validity issues that surface through occurrences such as the above. For example:

- Could the writing scores of students who were drilled with props be interpreted as accurate evidence of cognitive skills and processes needed to compose original essays in a timed setting?
- How might the test developers and users gather evidence showing the extent to which the scores reflected a student's ability to actually write?

---

*Gathering Evidence of Validity of Response/Scoring Processes.*   In cases like the one described in Case Study 3.2, inferences made from particular examinees' scores can only be justified if the assessment developer or user is certain that the responses/scores from the task genuinely reflect the anticipated levels of cognitive functioning. For this, they must gather evidence proving that the assumptions underlying their assessments are met during administration and scoring. Methods for gathering validity evidence about response or scoring processes involve direct questioning of respondents, observers, or scorers using focus group interviews and survey methods. We could also gather such data through direct observations and critical analysis of response patterns in answer papers.

### 3.2.3   Validity Evidence of Internal Structure

This third category of validity evidence pertains to whether the relationships among responses to individual items, tasks, or sections of an assessment are consistent with the designer's hypotheses regarding the *structure* of the underlying construct. Evidence of a test's internal structure is generally quantitative in nature, and calls for the use of particular statistical procedures after data are gathered with the assessment. Chapters 10 and 13 deal with statistical applications and examples of validation of internal structure in more detail. Here, we will look at the logic that drives this method of validation.

When we develop assessments based on theoretical concepts, we have particular notions in our minds about how the internal parts of the assessment, as reflected in the scores, are likely to interrelate. For example, suppose a writing assessment has five parts, each scored separately, as follows:

|       |             |         |
|-------|-------------|---------|
| **I.**   | Ideas       | Score 1 |
| **II.**  | Logic       | Score 2 |
| **III.** | Originality | Score 3 |
| **IV.**  | Grammar     | Score 4 |
| **V.**   | Punctuation | Score 5 |

The developer of the above assessment might reasonably hypothesize that while all the scores from different sections would have some relationship, scores in the Ideas, Logic, and Originality sections will be more highly correlated with each other than with scores in the Grammar and Punctuation sections. Another hypothesis might be that the Grammar and Punctuation scores will be highly related with each other because they deal with mechanics. Such expectations about possible interrelationships point to an *internal structure* of an assessment that can be tested with empirical data. Like all the forms of evidence listed in Table 3.2, validity of the hypothesized internal structure is a form of construct-validity evidence that becomes important when particular subscores of an assessment will be taken seriously in user contexts.

### 3.2.4 Evidence of Relationships with Other Constructs

Another important source of validity evidence deals with the relationship of an assessment's scores with scores of other pertinent variables. To build credibility, assessment designers would expect that scores from a newly developed instrument would overlap sufficiently with scores from other measures of similar constructs. Conversely, they would hope that scores from the new tool would not correlate with measures of dissimilar constructs. However, such theoretical expectations need to be validated with real data. How would such studies be conducted and what is the logic that would guide the design of such studies?

Suppose you have just developed a new reading skills assessment, and you now wish to validate what the scores mean. To lend credence to the reading scores generated, you would need to conduct a series of empirical studies to demonstrate how the scores relate to other relevant variables. For example, you should be able to demonstrate that the reading scores correlate positively and substantially with scores of similar, established measures of verbal or reading ability. This first category of evidence would support the *convergent validity* of your measure, because it would help confirm the congruence between scores from your tool and an alternate instrument that taps the same construct (Campbell & Fiske, 1959). Simultaneously, you should also be able to illustrate that scores from your reading test do *not* correlate with measures of other established but different constructs, such as, say, a test of physical strength. This second type of evidence supports the *discriminant validity* of your results, as it would affirm the postulated differences between two unlike construct measures (Campbell & Fiske, 1959). To further establish credibility of your assessment and its scores, you may wish to test additional hypotheses, such as the assumption that girls tend to be better readers than boys. This last hypothesis would require studies of group or subgroup differences, specifically, examining of gender differences in reading test score distributions (Angoff, 1988). By compiling a body of such evidence you would soon be in a position to verify the extent to which the construct measured by your new tool was performing in a manner consistent with other measures of reading skills.

In gathering evidence of relationships with other constructs, it is important to choose variables that are *reasonable and consistent* with the theory underlying the "what" being assessed (that is, the construct measure being validated). The quality of the assessments used to measure the other variables will also influence the meaningfulness of the validity evidence that such studies yield. More specific and detailed information on validity studies is provided in Chapter 13.

### 3.2.5   Evidence of Relationships with External Criterion Variables

This last source of validity evidence is associated with the following question: To what extent can claims that an assessment's results will overlap with or predict performance on other measures be verified? The assessment under investigation is typically called the predictor, and the external instrument, the "standard" against which the predictor is evaluated, is called the criterion measure. We establish criterion-related validity, the traditional label for such evidence, through statistical procedures such as correlation and regression. Here we will only become familiar with the rationale that guides this approach to validation and examine the statistical applications in Chapter 13.

An example of an assessment requiring evidence of criterion-related validity is a placement or admissions test, such as the *Graduate Record Examination* (GRE) test. Here, the test-makers claim that scores on the GRE, administered *prior to* admitting or placing students in a graduate degree program, will tell us how successful that person is likely to be once he or she is actually in graduate school. To verify such a claim, we would need to correlate the predictor, the GRE scores, with appropriate criterion measures. Several indicators of success in graduate school, such as test scores in particular semester examinations, the cumulative grade point average at the end of a degree, or completion of a graduate program, could serve as the criterion variables in studies to verify criterion-related validity of GRE scores. Because the validation of GRE scores would call for a longitudinal follow-up and verification that the scores could predict future performance of examinees, this form of criterion-related evidence is called "predictive validity" evidence.

A second form of criterion-related validity evidence is called "concurrent validity" evidence. Here, we would collect data on the predictor and criterion at the same time. Validation of scores from a new version of a test against an earlier version would call for a concurrent validity study. For example, the authors of the *Vineland Adaptive Behavior Scales* (VABS) gathered and reported concurrent validity evidence when they wanted to convince their users that the new version of the VABS assessment yielded information similar to the earlier edition of the VABS.

Whether a test developer or user who is gathering criterion-related evidence uses the predictive or concurrent approach would depend on the purposes for an assessment. As we saw, in a longitudinal predictive design the goal of the developer or user would be to gather evidence that the assessment results can be used to predict some future criterion. In the concurrent design, the aim is usually to replace or substitute the use of one test with another, comparable instrument that might have some advantages over the one being replaced.

---

**Key  Concepts**

- To support inferences we wish to make with the results of an assessment, we should collect logical and empirical evidence of validity.
- There are five major kinds of validity evidence.
- Whether we need to gather one or more kinds of validity evidence will depend on how we use the assessment.

## 3.3   Validation: When Should We Do It and How Far Should We Go?

At what point should we begin our validation efforts? In situations where a new assessment tool is constructed, content validation processes should be conducted soon after the design process is completed. Assessment developers should begin the content validation when they have a first draft of the instrument. The goal of content validation, as with all validation efforts, is to obtain information that will help the designer make improvements to the tool. Following the content-based reviews, you might refine the wording, content, number of items, layout of items, the directions, supporting materials, scoring procedures, and/or the conditions of assessment. The next step would be to conduct some form of empirical tryouts and analyses, *if* the specified assessment purposes so demand.

How extensive do the empirical validation studies need to be for practitioners? Should we be held responsible for every kind of evidence listed in Table 3.2? At this time, you are likely to be overwhelmed with how much work validation entails and how complicated it can soon become. In most situations involving an existing instrument, practitioners may not actually need to conduct empirical validation studies themselves. However, you need to be informed about what kinds of validity evidence to seek in making your selection decisions. Further, you should also be able to interpret and evaluate existing validity evidence found in manuals that accompany commercially published assessments.

**TABLE 3.3    Validation Demands and Stakes Tied to the Decision**

**More convincing validity evidence is needed when:**

| | *Example* |
|---|---|
| ■ Decisions are final | ■ Diagnosis of a clinical condition |
| ■ Decisions are irreversible | ■ College admissions |
| ■ Decisions have lasting consequences for individuals or institutions | ■ Accountability |
| ■ Decisions are based on constructs that are not well understood | |
| ■ Decisions depend heavily on results of one assessment tool | |

**More limited validity evidence is sufficient when:**

| | *Example* |
|---|---|
| ■ Decisions are reversible | ■ Reteaching a lesson |
| ■ Decisions are less important for individuals | ■ Improving strategies |
| ■ Decisions have temporary effects for individuals or institutions | ■ Revising assessments |
| ■ Decisions can be confirmed with other data sources | ■ Quizzing in the classroom |

If you or your colleagues develop an assessment locally, you should make an attempt to gather and evaluate enough validity evidence to support your needs and purposes. How much would depend on the decisions you wish to make with the assessment results and will be a matter of judgment. You will need more convincing evidence for irreversible, high stakes decisions; less will suffice for decisions that have lighter consequences.

Table 3.3 provides some guidelines on how to seek validation information. Depending on the purposes of the assessment, the validation methods can vary in formality and extensiveness. For *all* assessments, you should at least conduct a content validation. For high stakes assessments, such as a test used for admission, licensure, or promotion, validation will be more involved, requiring extensive reviews, data collection, and statistical analyses tied to complex research designs. When assessments are designed for purposes with less serious consequences, such as classroom assessments for day-to-day decisions, an adequate validation process might involve content reviews by your peers. Validation of response processes might be useful if you are developing performance assessments. For multiple choice assessments, item analysis techniques can help you in refining your originally developed pool of items. (Procedures for quantitative item analysis are presented in Chapter 12.)

---

**Key Concepts**

■ The seriousness of decisions made with assessment results will dictate how much and what kinds of validity evidence are necessary to support inferences from those results.
■ At the very least, all assessments should be content-validated prior to their use.

## 3.4 Reliability

Reliability refers to the consistency of an assessment's results under different conditions. Suppose you were asked to perform a given assessment task repeatedly, such as the typing of a letter. Assuming that the assessment was valid, the likelihood is that your performances would still vary across the several occasions, even though your inherent typing ability or speed remained constant. Such variations, caused by *random* factors in the assessment situation (rather than by systematic factors), affect the "reliability" of an assessment's results. *Random error* refers to unsystematic, unforeseen, and uncontrollable fluctuations in the person being measured or some aspect of the assessment procedure or environment that influences the results. Even in situations where an assessment might be designed to control for all or most systematic interferences, presumably providing the maximum possible levels of validity in results, random error can affect the assessment outcome, causing some degree of unreliability. In this section, we will examine the logic and conceptual basis for reliability. Formal procedures for obtaining quantitative estimates of reliability will be addressed in more detail in Chapter 13.

The fact that unreliability in results is caused by *random measurement error* (Stanley, 1971) in the assessment situation can be illustrated through many case study examples. Like systematic errors, random errors can come from different sources. Hence, in theory, there could be as many different estimates of reliability as there are sources of random error. Read Case Study 3.3 carefully and attempt to identify the source of random fluctuations that affect the resulting scores.

## Case Study 3.3    Random Errors in Essay Scores

An instructor gave an essay test to his students. During the following week he maintained a schedule to make sure that he completed grading the papers in seven days. Everyday, he scored some of his students' papers in the morning, before he left for work. Then, he scored others at the end of the work day, sometimes working rather late into the night. About a month later, he had a chance to inspect his ratings when he was entering the scores into his grade book.

To his surprise, he found that the students' whose papers were scored in the evening were spread all over the rating scale, irrespective of the quality of their work. In comparison, the scores on the papers that he graded in the morning appeared to be far more consistent with his memory of what the students had actually produced.

Case Study 3.3 illustrates a situation where rater fatigue at the end of the day affected the scoring process, making the scores less reliable. The source of random error was the rater, or more specifically, rater fatigue. The rating errors that affected the student papers scored in the evening were random, unpredictable events; this is why the evening ratings were highly variable and unrelated to the students' performance.

## 3.4.1    Sources of Random Error in Assessment Situations

Random errors can also come from the individuals being assessed, as their concentration, motivation, fatigue, or interest in the assessment activity fluctuates during the assessment process. Random errors can be rooted in a poorly constructed tool, where items or behaviors are sampled in a limited manner from the domain, thereby yielding an inconsistent score. Badly written directions or uncontrolled assessment conditions are other sources of random measurement error.

If we are aware of the common sources of random error, we can make decisions to keep such errors down to a minimum during assessment design, administration, and scoring. This entails taking a "common sense" approach to tightening the assessment procedure, keeping in mind two general principles:

1.  Obtaining an adequate sample of behaviors from the construct domain
2.  Controlling random errors that could potentially arise from the assessment procedure, conditions, or environment.

Let us see what each of these principles mean in practice.

***Obtaining an Adequate Sample of Behaviors***    If you are trying to obtain a reliable assessment of a person's ability to add, would you be able to depend more on the results if the score was based on two addition problems or on 20? Naturally, 20 problems would considerably reduce the possibility that the respondent got the answers correct merely by chance (or due to random factors). A key principle in enhancing reliability of assessment results is to obtain an adequate sample of behaviors on the attribute measured. "Adequate sample" here refers to the number of items, tasks, observations, or behavior samples, taken of the *same person(s)* from the *same domain.* As a general rule, the greater the numbers of observations, items, or tasks in an assessment, the greater the dependability of the results, and the higher the quantitative estimates of reliability.

***Controlling Errors in Assessment Conditions***    All assessments are vulnerable to random error from different sources, including those from an unfavorable assessment environment. Consider Case Study 3.4. It provides an example of error resulting from distracting factors in the environment. If the timing for or environment in which the assessment is conducted distracts test-takers, random fluctuations in performance unrelated to the trait being measured can result. In such circumstances, it makes sense to alter the time or conditions of test administration to improve reliability of results. Unreliability in results can be tied to factors like sudden changes in the temperature in the room, sounds in the environment, the mental state or metabolism (lowered blood sugar) of the respondents, or inadequacies in directions or materials provided by teachers, observers, or proctors.

---

## Case Study 3.4    Environmental Distractions Affect Reliability of Results

A teacher once complained that she simply could not understand why one of her best writers was producing rather shabby pieces of writing when she asked him to write compositions in class. She *knew* the child was a better writer. On some days and for various reasons, the student was unable to concentrate when he wrote the compositions. His hurried writing, indicating a lower level of performance, had little to do with his innate writing ability. On other days, however, his work lived up to his teacher's expectations. Moving the time of the writing exercise to an earlier period in the day resulted in remarkable changes in the consistency of his performance. The teacher later discovered that she had been administering the exercise during the class period just before the lunch break and recess!

---

Other examples of assessment systems vulnerable to random error are those that incorporate human observers or scorers within the assessment system, as in most performance-based assessments. As we saw in Case Study 3.3, we need to control the scoring procedures to counter the fact that human beings are fallible and inconsistent. Controlling random fluctuations in scoring or recording of observations, particularly with high stakes assessments, involves instituting systems with observation and scoring guidelines (called "rubrics") and by using trained raters or observers.

Table 3.4 summarizes some commonly acknowledged sources of random error (also referred to as "measurement error") that cause low reliability in assessment results. Note

### TABLE 3.4   Causes for Low Reliability: Some Sources of Random Measurement Error

- Too few items, tasks, or behavior samples are collected to obtain a consistent reading of where a person stands on a construct domain.

- Misleading or inadequate directions cause inconsistencies in how respondents react to the items.

- Inadequate time is allocated for assessing all or most of the examinees.

- Distractions or poor conditions in the assessment environment cause respondents to fluctuate in their concentration or focus.

- Subjectivity or random biases of raters or observers affect the consistency of the results.

- Persons who take the assessment behave inconsistently during the process due to random causes outside the control of the assessor (e.g., feeling sick).

again that the factors affecting reliability are different from the systematic factors that affect validity. The influence of random factors on the assessment results are not always the same; that is why they are *not predictable* errors. An inadequate sampling of items could either inflate or deflate a person's score; because the influences are random, we would not be able to predict the direction in which it will affect the results. Behaviors of raters that lead to unreliable ratings are similarly random; sometimes they will make the score higher, at other times the score will be lowered.

---

**Key  Concepts**

- Reliability has to do with the consistency of an assessment's results under different conditions.
- Reliability is affected by random measurement errors in the assessment situation.
- If we become sensitive to the sources of random errors, we can control them during assessment design, selection, and use.

### 3.4.3   Quantitative Estimates of Reliability

Once an assessment is constructed, developers should conduct formal tryouts and studies to quantitatively estimate the extent to which the assessment results are indeed reliable. There are two major quantitative indices of score reliability, as given by classical test theory: the Standard Error of Measurement (SEM) and the Reliability Coefficient. These statistics are theoretically related but in the reverse direction. When the estimated SEM is high, the reliability coefficient is low; conversely, when the estimated error is low, reliability is high. Chapter 13 will describe these and other statistics that yield information on the dependability of assessment results with more conceptual and methodological details.

## 3.5   Utility

Time and resources available for conducting assessments is almost always in competition with other professional responsibilities that assessment users carry. *Utility* or usability deals with the practicality of using an assessment in particular circumstances. This book will submit that usability/utility of assessments is not as important a consideration in designing, selecting, or applying assessments as validity or reliability. However, practical factors define the needs and constraints within which teachers, administrators, scorers, and other users of assessments work. Thus, to build a well-functioning assessment procedure, utility has to be carefully balanced against the two other properties that we examined in this chapter.

Gronlund (1981) pointed out that assessment usability could be affected by several factors, including the administration conditions, time, costs, procedures for scoring, and ease with which results can be applied. Overlooking assessment utility could result in compromises with regard to the ultimate validity and/or reliability of results. The next section elaborates on four major utility factors and is followed by a list of issues pertinent to the utility of instruments.

### 3.5.1   Administration Conditions

Ease of administration deals with the simplicity and directness of instructions, the length of time needed to administer the assessment, the availability of materials needed for the assessment, and the ease with which it can be set up and conducted. We should design or select assessments to optimize administration conditions for the user.

An assessment tool with high utility in administration conditions is one that relatively untrained or inexperienced individuals can conduct with little or no obvious errors. A long, cumbersome assessment, needing complicated materials and instructions, is not only low on utility, but can adversely affect the validity and reliability of results. By the same token, time-consuming, individually administered assessments have lower utility than those that can be more efficiently administered to large groups in shorter testing times. Similarly, assessments with several subtests and which need many separate sessions to administer, are lower in utility than those that can be administered in a single, relatively short session.

### 3.5.2   Human and Material Costs

Traditional paper and pencil testing, such as the use of multiple choice tests, was relatively inexpensive, making the cost of such tests an unimportant consideration during assessment design and selection. As we have begun to use performance assessments in education, it has become necessary for us to weigh validity and reliability factors against utility.

Teacher-made performance assessments make great demands on teacher time, as do performance assessments used in high stakes assessment programs. Material resources needed for such assessments are often high. Training programs for proctors and scorers are also costly to deliver. Furthermore, once trained, individuals serving as raters or proctors have to be continually paid for their time and services for the program to be maintained. Other assessments, such as licencing examinations in medicine, are known to require costly equipment and expendable supplies that need to be replenished from time to time. Such factors increase the cost of the assessment procedure, affecting its utility. They must be borne in mind during assessment design and selection.

### 3.5.3   Scoring Procedures

One of the most burdensome and tedious chores associated with assessing is the matter of scoring. Developments such as machine scoring, stencil keys, separate answer sheets, and improved directions for scoring have significantly contributed to raising the utility of structured-response tests. The need for human scorers or judges in alternative assessment applications, however, presents a serious challenge to users. As a rule, we should prefer assessment designs that offer both ease and speed without sacrificing accuracy of scores. Assessments should be designed or selected with provisions made for maximizing scoring utility.

### 3.5.4   Ease of Interpretation and Use

Finally, how easily and accurately the assessment results can be used in particular decision-making contexts is of paramount importance. The success or failure of an assessment procedure is a direct function of the use made with the results. Information on what the scores or results mean should be clear and unambiguous to both professional and non-professional users of the results. For example, standardized, norm-referenced assessments should be accompanied with technical manuals and norms tables guiding users on how to interpret scores correctly. Such data should be presented in a complete and user-friendly manner that promotes accurate interpretations of results.

To conclude, review Case Study 3.5. It illustrates how practical constraints in context of test use resulted in changes to item format of a large-scale, national assessment program (NAEP), and altered the validity of information that the tests provided. As you review the shifts documented in the type of items that the NAEP tests included in the past as compared to the present, consider the following utility issues.

- How might the developers of the NAEP have attended to utility factors during development stages, so that validity of inferences remained unaffected as the tests were implemented?
- Is it OK for utility factors to override validity factors as circumstances of test use change?

---

**Case Study 3.5    Can Utility Factors Affect Validity or Reliability? The History of the National Assessment of Educational Progress (NAEP) in the United States**

The National Assessment of Educational Progress (NAEP) tests were designed in the 1960s to obtain periodic assessments of student achievement at three levels of the U.S. public education system, grades 4, 8, and 10. Initially, the specifications for the assessments called for open-ended tasks, measuring higher-order learning outcomes. As the test was implemented over time, however, the test questions changed in format to multiple choice items in order to improve the efficiency of large-scale administration and scoring. The changed item format affected the substantive nature of the construct domain tested—items began to tap skills at a lower cognitive level than was originally intended by the developers of the open-ended tasks. The shift in item format was influenced primarily by utility considerations. Currently, the assessments look rather different from the versions developed according to the original test specifications.

*Source:* Adapted from L. V. Jones (1997). A History of the National Assessment of Educational Progress and Some Questions about its Future. *Educational Researcher, 25* (7), 15–22.

---

Although the NAEP example is that of a large-scale assessment program, practical factors must be considered even when we are designing or selecting assessments for local applications. Some of the more important utility questions that could shape our decisions during the assessment development or selection process follow:

- Are the materials for the assessment likely to be available and accessible to most users of the assessment?
- Is the time required for assessment reasonable for prospective users?
- Is the time required for scoring reasonable for users?
- Do the assessment materials facilitate the ease of administration, scoring, and use?
- Do the directions facilitate proper administration of the assessment?
- Are the users likely to be able to use the key or scoring systems? Are adequate instructions provided to train scorers, if needed?
- Are the prospective users of the assessment likely to have the resources, time and staff to use the assessment as designed?

## Key Concepts

- Utility deals with practical factors, such as time, cost, and resource availability that affect use of an assessment in particular circumstances.
- A sound assessment system should have adequate utility without compromising the validity and reliability of results.

# 3.6    Prioritizing among Validity, Reliability, and Utility

Should we prioritize validity over reliability, or vice versa? Although we have attempted to distinguish between the two using the notions of systematic and random error, conceptually, reliability can be seen as a component of validity. If your assessment is tightly controlled to ensure validity, chances are high that you will also have reliability. The reverse, however, is not necessarily true. That is, if you have high reliability in the results, you cannot be certain that they are also valid. It could be that you are assessing something unrelated to what you intended but your assessment procedure is highly consistent and replicable (i.e., reliable), yielding the same results each time you use it. An example of high reliability with no validity would be if you wanted to measure the width of a room, but repeatedly and unknowingly measured its length instead. If your measuring tape was precise and dependable, you would get very reliable results. However, the results would be completely invalid.

We should also remember that utility can be very high in an assessment procedure, without yielding much validity or reliability. For example, we may use a very short (5 items) multiple choice assessment with grammar and punctuation items to make inferences about a student's writing ability. The test would be extremely time-efficient, but poor in content relevance and representativeness. Because of the low sampling of items, the score would be very unreliable too.

Which factor of the three, validity, reliability, and utility, should matter the most in an assessment development or selection situation? This chapter has leaned towards placing greater emphasis on validity and reliability, rather than on assessment utility. The rationale for this bias is the documentation of instances, such as the NAEP case, where the developers or users lost sight of the targeted construct and rejected appropriate assessment methods in favor of less appropriate ones to save money, time, or resources. Having said this, we should bear in mind that assessment utility affects the user. Thus, there is not much point in designing a complex assessment that is highly valid but impossible to use. Practicality is a factor that we should not set aside in our deliberations. In the view of this author, the most important criterion is and should be validity, followed closely by reliability. Utility, although important, should be ranked after the first two criteria. There will no doubt be situations where you will need to make some compromises to these guidelines to accommodate different demands.

# Summary

Chapter 3 highlighted three criteria for evaluating the quality of an assessment tool and the results it yields in given contexts: validity, reliability, and utility. Effective design and use of assessment tools requires that we have a thorough understanding of factors that could affect the quality of the results and interpretations that we wish to make with those results. Such an awareness makes it possible for us to control and attend to various interferences during the development of an instrument or in subsequent applications with it (see Chapter 2).

Validity refers to the accuracy of inferences we make from an assessment's results. In theory, our inferences will be perfectly valid when all systematic errors in the responses are caused by actual differences on the measured construct, and not by any other external interference. Cultural biases in the questions that might give a particular group of respondents an advantage/disadvantage when taking a test is an example of a systematic error that would affect validity. We determine the validity of inferences by verifying the extent to which we are successful in keeping systematic, external interferences out of an assessment tool and its results. This work is called validation.

Both assessment developers and users share the responsibility for conducting some validation work with instruments they design or choose to use, before they actually use them. Validation is necessary to support particular interpretations of an assessment's results in given populations and decision-making contexts. The five major types of evidence that we could use to get affirmation of validity are:

- Evidence of content-based validity (content relevance and content representativeness)
- Evidence of validity in response/scoring processes
- Evidence of validity of internal structure
- Evidence of convergent and discriminant validity
- Evidence of criterion-related validity (concurrent validity and predictive validity).

In particular applications, we might need only one, some, or several kind(s) of evidence to defend the assessment use. For this reason, validation studies vary in design, formality, and extensiveness.

Reliability is another important criterion for evaluating measurement quality. Unreliability in assessment results is caused by random error(s) in the assessment situation. The common sources of random error are unpredictable changes in the assessment environment, the persons assessed, the assessors/observers, the occasion of the assessment, or the form of the assessment tool used. Quantitative estimates of reliability are obtained through two related statistics: the Standard Error of Measurement (SEM) and the Reliability Coefficient. As in validation research, designs for gathering and evaluating reliability evidence can vary, and are discussed in more detail in Chapter 13.

Practical considerations that affect the ultimate usefulness of an assessment tool in actual user contexts, such as its costs and efficiency during administration, are relevant to its utility. Utility factors should be kept in mind by assessment developers or users during assessment design and selection. The utility of an assessment tool eventually affects how it gets implemented in practice, which in turn can influence the validity and reliability of the assessment results.

# QUESTIONS FOR CLASS DISCUSSION

1. Attempt to answer the following questions for each of the scenarios, A–D.
   - Is this a valid assessment application?
   - If not, what is/are the source(s) of systematic error?

   A.   An assessment is designed to measure writing skills. In the first administration, students are asked to write essays on current topics they are expected to be familiar with at their level. When the results are analyzed, we find that examinees with a stronger background in current affairs receive higher writing scores than those with less knowledge of the same.

   B.   In the beginning of the year, a biology teacher informally asked her students to write a paragraph describing what they knew about cells. The information from the exercise helped her plan her units. Later in the semester, she ran out of time and could not administer a scheduled examination. So, she decided to grade that first assignment and include the grade in the students' semester report cards.

   C.   To comply with a new legislative requirement, an assessment originally intended to measure job performance of teachers in the classroom was used by state officials for conducting performance evaluations of administrative staff. Several administrators who were out of touch with classroom management duties were cited for poor performance.

   D.   A team of psychologists gathered literature on Attention Deficit Disorder (ADD) to develop a screening checklist for adolescents in school. However, new research showed that many of the behavioral symptoms on the instrument were actually indicators of sleep disorders.

2. How would you make sure that an assessment you design is (a) content relevant and (b) content representative in the following scenarios.

*Scenario* A.    To assess mathematics skills in second graders attending a school where the curriculum emphasizes number concepts, addition, and subtraction operations equally.

*Scenario* B.    To assess an area of job performance for a particular grade of employees in the finance industry. (Professional manuals provide job descriptions, requisite skills, and standards of performance for the employee group, and place the most emphasis on executive decision-making.)

*Scenario* C.    To design an assessment to match a reading curriculum that emphasized the development of reading comprehension and critical thinking skills, with three times more emphasis on the latter.

3. Report a case study of an assessment application (For example, use of a scale in selecting candidates for a job in your school; the use of a classroom assessment; applications with a screening instrument; or a parent survey). How well were issues of validity, reliability, and utility evaluated and addressed in that application? Identify the possible sources of systematic error and random error that could have affected the results in that application. What were the consequences of assessment use?

4. Suppose you have to make a presentation to a group of your professional peers on the importance of validity, reliability, and utility in assessment applications. Select and summarize the most important ideas tied to these concepts. Give examples to illustrate your points.

5. Prepare a checklist that you could use to ensure that validity, reliability, and utility factors were addressed in designing an assessment tool of your choice. Be specific in your answer.

6. Consider the assessment scenarios below. Identify the type(s) of validity evidence you would gather to support the stated uses of assessment results. Provide a justification for your answers.
   (a) A teacher developed a test to help her identify the best mathematicians in her class for a state competition.
   (b) A psychologist wanted to use the Slosson intelligence test instead of the Stanford-Binet test (S-B) to test a client. The S-B is an individually-administered test, which takes a much longer time to administer.
   (c) A researcher developed a self-concept instrument for adults and made claims that it would relate positively to several variables, such as a Happiness scale, a Success at Work scale, and so on.
   (d) A technology specialist developed a training program on using internet browsers. He designed an assessment to determine the proficiency levels of his trainees when they completed the training.
   (e) An art teacher developed a set of assessments to recognize the "best artist" in her class.

7. Consider the assessment scenarios below to identify the possible sources of random error that could affect the results: person, environment, scorer, instrument/assessment system. Describe briefly how you could control for them in your design.
   (a) Students were taking the SAT test when a loud bang from outside startled them.
   (b) Performance assessments of employees were done based on observations made by their supervisors.
   (c) An instrument was used to certify female nursing students while they were in the midst of a grueling semester in the nursing program.

(d) Two students who lived in the teacher's neighborhood were found to receive the highest scores in class on their projects.

(e) A technician used a metal tape to measure length of objects in summer. The measurements he made on the same objects were found to vary depending on whether he measured them in the early morning when it was cooler, or in the mid-afternoon when it was much warmer.

(f) An administrator of the teacher certification examination, *Praxis I* and *II*, overlooked some important directions during an assessment session. Some of the examinees figured it out and made adjustments, others did not.

NOTE: More structured exercises with immediate feedback and answers are included in the computer module.

# 4 Types of Assessment Tools

## Overview

Assessment devices can be classified variously based on constructs they measure, how they are administered and scored, how their results are interpreted, the formats in which they are presented, and the modes in which subjects respond to them. This chapter introduces you to different types of assessment tools, beginning with a discussion of traditional, performance, authentic, and alternative assessments. The chapter gives particular attention to a classification scheme that identifies five different assessment methods based on the subjects' response mode. The chapter recommends that selection of particular assessment methods (referring here to the assessment format) during the design process should be guided by considerations of validity, reliability, and utility.

## CHAPTER 4 OBJECTIVES

After studying this chapter and completing the structured exercises in the module, you should be able to:

1. Classify different types of assessment devices used in education. For example,
   - Instruments measuring cognitive, affective, and personal–social constructs
   - Standardized and unstandardized assessment tools
   - Norm-referenced and criterion-referenced tools
   - Speed and power tests
   - Different types of assessment tools based on response mode

2. Differentiate among five assessment methods based on the response modes of individuals assessed

3. Compare the advantages and disadvantages of each of the five assessment methods in measuring cognitive, affective, social and behavioral constructs in particular educational contexts

4. Evaluate how the choice of a particular assessment method during assessment design affects the validity, reliability, and/or utility of the resulting assessment tool and its results.

# 4.1 Traditional, Alternative, Authentic, and Performance Assessments

To begin our discussion on types of assessments, a few terms, such as "authentic assessment" or "alternative assessment," need clarification. These terms were first mentioned in Chapter 1. To support the initial discussion on assessment types, this section will ask you to briefly examine information provided in Tables 4.1 through 4.8. The same tables will be further explained in later sections of the chapter.

Review the following quotes excerpted from the literature on recent educational assessment reforms to examine how the terms traditional, alternative, authentic, and performance have been used as descriptors of particular forms of assessments. All the quotes that we examine deal with classroom or large-scale assessment of scholastic achievement.

> Assessment is the cornerstone of education reform in the '90s. . . . (T)his heightened emphasis on assessment comes at a time of growing dissatisfaction with *traditional,* multiple choice forms of testing. The result is an explosion of interest in *alternative forms of assessment* . . . (Herman, Aschbacher & Winters, 1992, p. 1, italics added).

> *Authentic,* performance-based testing is a reality, not a romantic vision. . . . *Authentic* tests have four basic characteristics in common. First, they are designed to be truly representative of performance in the field. . . . Second, far greater attention is paid to teaching and learning of the criteria to be used in the assessment. . . . Third, self-assessment plays a much greater role than in conventional testing. And, fourth, the students are often expected to present their work and defend themselves publicly and orally to ensure that their apparent mastery is genuine (Wiggins, 1989, p. 45, italics added).

> What is meant by *authentic?* . . . Authentic to what? An authentic reflection of classroom work or an authentic representation of ability to read in real life? One must come to grips with this issue before even beginning to discuss authentic tasks (Arter & Spandel, 1992, p. 38, italics in original).

> ". . . . *(P)erformance* assessment has reemerged in recent years with a new and flashier look that has caught the eye of educators everywhere. Witness the exploding popularity of portfolios, exhibitions, demonstrations, direct writing assessments, science fairs . . . etc. (Stiggins, 1991, p. 264, italics added).

The term "traditional" is commonly used to refer to the multiple choice assessments, as evidenced in the first quote. Other writers have used the term to refer to standardized, norm-referenced, multiple choice achievement tests (see Shepard, 1989a). More broadly, a traditional test can be thought of as the traditionally popular, structured-response, written test (Table 4.1 provides definitions; Table 4.2 shows item examples).

The second term, "alternative" assessment, distinguishes itself from "traditional" in its open-ended response format. Alternative assessments offer alternative modes of response to respondents; in this sense they serve as alternatives to the traditional, highly structured items. As described in the quote, all free-response exercises, using interviews, products, or behavioral observations, can be classified as examples of alternative assessments (see

**TABLE 4.1  Types for Assessments Based on Different Classification Criteria**

| Classification Criteria | Assessment Type and Common Definitions | Examples |
|---|---|---|
| **1.0** Construct assessed | **1.1 Achievement tests**<br>Assessments measuring mastery of a defined body of knowledge and skills. | ■ *Stanford Achievement Test Series (STA)*<br>■ *Iowa Tests of Basic Skills (ITBS)*<br>■ *Comprehensive Tests of Basic Skills (CTBS)*<br>■ Classroom assessments |
| | **1.2 Intelligence and aptitude tests**<br>Assessments of potential to learn, problem-solve, and adapt in a new environment. | ■ *Wechsler Adult Intelligence Scale (WAIS)*<br>■ *Scholastic Assessment Test (SAT)* |
| | **1.3 Affective, behavioral, interest, and personality inventories**<br>Assessments of attitudinal, social, personal, and behavioral traits. | ■ *The Strong-Campbell Interest Inventory (S-CII)*<br>■ *The Vineland Adaptive Behavior Scales (VABS)*<br>■ *The Minnesota Teacher Attitude Inventory (MTAI)*<br>■ Locally-made behavioral screening tests |
| **2.0** Conditions of assessment | **2.1 Standardized tests**<br>Assessments that are administered and scored under tightly controlled and uniform conditions. | ■ *Stanford Achievement Test Series*<br>■ *Wechsler Adult Intelligence Scale*<br>■ *Scholastic Assessment Test*<br>■ *Graduate Record Examination (GRE)* |
| | **2.2 Unstandardized tests**<br>Assessments that are administered and scored under relatively unstructured conditions; could include informal assessments. | ■ Classroom assessments<br>■ Locally-developed instruments |
| | **2.3 Speed tests**<br>Assessments that impose strict time limits on respondents. Usually the speedness is relevant to the construct measured. | ■ A timed typing test<br>■ Timed tests of clerical skills |
| | **2.4 Power tests**<br>Assessments that provide ample time to respondents to finish, with items usually organized by dificulty. | Many classroom assessments are power tests |

**2.5 Subjective versus objectively scored assessments**
Assessments that are scored by human judges or raters as opposed to using a right/wrong answer key that keeps human judgment out of the scoring procedure.

- Essay (Subjective)
- Multiple choice (Objective)

**3.0** Methods of score interpretation and use

**3.1 Norm-referenced tests** (NRT)
Assessments that are designed to describe an individual's ranking relative to that of a known, comparison group on the attribute measured. The comparison group is called the norm group.

- *Stanford Achievement Test Series*
- *Wechsler Adult Intelligence Scale*
- *Graduate Record Examination*
- Classroom Assessments that "grade on a curve"

**3.2 Criterion-referenced tests** (CRT)
Assessments that are designed to describe an individual's performance relative to a preset standard linked to a clearly defined domain of knowledge and skills. (Also called domain-referenced, mastery, objective-referenced, or competency tests).

- *High School Competency Test* (Florida)
- Most classroom assessments are CRTs.

**4.0** Developer of the assessment

**4.1 Teacher-made and locally-made assessments**
Assessments that are designed locally and are implemented on a small scale.

- Classroom assessments
- Surveys
- Inventories

**4.2 Commercially developed and marketed assessments**
Assessments that are designed for large-scale distribution and/or are marketed by commercial agencies, testing corporations, and textbook publishing companies.

- *Stanford Achievement Test Series*

**5.0** Mode of presentation or mode of response.

**5.1 Mode of presentation**
Assessments that vary with respect to how they are presented to respondents, such as in verbal, nonverbal, audio-visual, or computer-based modes of presentation.

- GRE administered as a paper and pencil versus a computer-delivered assessment

**5.2 Mode of response**
- Written assessments, structured-response or open-ended
- Behavior-based assessments
- Product-based assessments
- Interview-based assessments
- Portfolio-based assessments

- Essay or multiple choice assessment
- Driving test (road test)
- Laboratory report
- One-on-one conference
- Artist's portfolio

Tables 4.3–4.7 for examples). Unlike traditional assessments that depend on answer keys, most alternative assessments call for the use of *scoring rubrics,* or a set of guidelines/ criteria intended to keep judgments and observations free from personal biases or errors from raters. We will look at rubrics and how they are developed in greater detail in Chapter 8, where we focus on the designing guidelines for alternative assessments.

The term *authentic* is not as easily clarified as the first two, as it enjoys multiple and varied usages. Wiggins, a strong advocate for using authentic assessments, views them as tools for raising standards and expectations of schooling. His example of an authentic oral history project (Wiggins, 1989) required students to gather historical data from sources using interviews and other methods, and compile the information in a paper that they defended to an external panel. Scoring standards in Wiggins' assessments would not be on a "curve," but rather based on explicit and demanding performance criteria. Likewise, the California Assessment Program (CAP) used "authentic assessments" in their statewide accountability program in the early 1990s. The CAP assessments used portfolio and performance-based assessments in writing, mathematics, and science that focused on key "process" skills such as observing, comparing, communicating, organizing, relating and applying. Although subsequent political shifts drastically changed the state assessment program in California, that state was one of the first to embrace the concept of "authentic assessments" for large scale use. Both models of authentic assessment described were influenced by assessment practices in educational programs in Great Britain and New Zealand.

From a measurement perspective, it is appealing to think of authenticity as equivalent to validity. If an assessment of school achievement, irrespective of format, is a genuine reflection of what is taught and valued in the classroom, it could be considered authentic. This makes "authentic" a twin of the term "valid." Such a use of the term, however, is less common than the connotation "realistic"—i.e., situated in actual settings, requiring demonstrations that meet real life, and often rather challenging expectations of performance (Wiggins, 1989). While a road test in driving would be "authentic" by the latter definition, a paper and pencil test on road rules would not. An interesting issue for debate might be phrased as follows: Can the more "authentic" road test replace a "traditional" written test of road rules, or are both necessary to enable valid inferences of the construct of "driving proficiency"?

In theory, we could devise most assessments (other than perhaps multiple choice tests) so that they are situated in actual, simulated, or semisimulated settings—giving them degrees of authenticity with respect to context. Thus, we could assess a person's job performance through written tests (a simulated setting), role-play exercises (a semisimulated setting), or by directly observing on-the-job performance (an actual field setting). Similarly, performance requirements set to certify proficiency could fit real world standards of the expected behaviors or skills. For example, the writing of business letters for job applications could be a simulated classroom assessment. Alternatively, the task would be even more "authentic" if the letters were assessed by prospective employers, using criteria from the world of work.

Lastly, let us consider the term "performance" assessment. As used in the quote shown earlier, performance assessment appears to be synonymous with alternative assessment, and reflects a rather broad use of the term. In other usages (Berk, 1986a), a performance assessment is equivalent mainly with direct observations of behavior.

What terminology shall we employ here? We will use the term "performance assessments" to refer to a wide array of nontraditional assessments with response formats that are alternatives to the highly structured, written test (such as a multiple choice test). Performance assessments will include written-, product-, and behavior-based assessments. A vast majority of such performance assessments will require respondents to give open-ended responses. The book will, thus, equate the terms *alternative assessment* and *performance assessment*. The preference for the term "performance assessment" over "alternative assessment" is simply to avoid any inadvertent suggestion that the latter represent alternatives to the "real thing," and that traditional assessments are somehow superior simply by virtue of their historical tradition of development. When used, the term *authentic assessment* will refer only to assessment exercises that integrate actual or "real world" settings and criteria.

Some writers have characterized alternative assessments as those that engage the learner and promote better teaching and learning while traditional assessments have been portrayed as the "evil enemies" of education, assessing "passive knowledge" and leading to drill-based instruction (Mitchell, 1992). Remember, that both traditional and performance assessments can be designed well or poorly; they can both be employed appropriately or abused in practical contexts. As we saw in the case studies in Chapters 2 and 3, in high stakes contexts, both forms have been found to lead to less than desirable instructional methods.

It is important for us to keep in perspective that how we choose to label an assessment device does not automatically instill within it all the properties that we desire. As practitioners, we are responsible for ensuring that an assessment is designed or selected to have qualities we seek. A basic premise that we will work from will be that *all assessments,* irrespective of their format, should meet the highest possible standards of technical quality within particular contexts of use.

**Key Concepts**

- Performance assessments employ a wide variety of response formats but are typically open-ended.
- A particular type of assessment tool is not necessarily superior to another. We should design, validate, or select assessment devices to ensure that they have the qualities we specify in given contexts of use.

## 4.2 Other Ways of Classifying Assessments

Let us turn our attention to Table 4.1. The table presents five broad classes of assessments with commonly accepted definitions and examples of instruments within each category. Some of the examples in the table represent formally titled and published tests that have been used for years; other examples reflect general classes of tools that local developers might construct in less formal circumstances.

Classifications of assessments differ based on the criteria used for categorization. Assessment "types" vary depending on the basis for classification. Typologies have used various criteria to distinguish among classes of assessments. As Table 4.1 shows, these include:

- The constructs being measured (Classification Criterion 1.0)
- The level of control in the administration and scoring conditions (Classification Criterion 2.0)
- How their results are intended to be interpreted (Classification Criterion 3.0)
- Who bears responsibility for developing, standardizing, and/or distributing them (Classification Criterion 4.0)
- The formats in which they are presented to subjects (Classification Criterion 5.0)
- The modes in which subjects respond to them (Classification Criterion 5.0)

### 4.2.1 Assessments of Different Constructs

The first categorization scheme (1.0) recognizes that instruments can be differentiated on the basis of "what" they assess. *Achievement* tests, irrespective of their format or other characteristics, aim to measure the extent of knowledge or skill gained by examinees in a content domain in which they have already received instruction. Achievement tests can be both teacher-made classroom assessments and standardized tools, such as the STA, ITBS, and CTBS.

*Intelligence, ability,* and *aptitude* tests, on the other hand, are typically instruments that target current levels of functioning (intelligence or ability) or future potential (aptitude) in some defined cognitive, neuropsychological, psychomotor, or physical domain. The WAIS is a widely used standardized intelligence test for adults. Its corresponding version for children, offered by the same publisher, the Psychological Corporation, is called the *Wechsler Preschool and Primary Scale of Intelligence-Revised* (WPPSI-R, The Psychological Corp., 1996).

*Affective, behavioral,* and *personality* inventories include tools that attempt to assess particular psychological attributes of individuals or their interpersonal proclivities. These latter instruments may also be standardized or otherwise. The three examples in the table, S-CII, VABS, and the MTAI, are all published tools supported with varying degrees of formal psychometric data and standardization procedures.

### 4.2.2 Conditions of Assessment

In the second categorization scheme (2.0), assessments are distinguished based on the conditions in which they are *administered* and *scored.* The first set of subcategorizations here, separating *standardized* and *nonstandardized assessments* (2.1 and 2.2), is based on the degree of control deliberately imposed on the assessment conditions by the developer. Standardized assessments (WAIS, SAT, STA) employ a very tight structure as compared to the less formal, unstandardized assessments (classroom assessments).

Under 2.0, another subcategorization can be made with respect to the speed limits associated with the assessment (2.3 and 2.4). Speed tests utilize strict time limits. An example is a timed test of typing skills. Power tests are typically untimed. The time constraint built into an instrument should preferably be relevant to the nature of the construct measured; otherwise it may lead to varying degrees of mismeasurement. For example, achievement, ability, and aptitude tests should ideally be constructed as *power* tests, or the resulting scores might be unduly influenced by whether or not respondents can finish on time.

Yet another way of differentiating assessments by condition is based on whether the assessments are subjectively or objectively scored (2.5). The essay examination, for example, is far more subjectively scored relative to a multiple choice test. In the latter case, once a key has been set, the scoring could be done by a machine.

### 4.2.3 Methods of Score Interpretation

The third categorization scheme (3.0) is based on methods of score interpretation and properties built into the design of the assessment to support the proposed interpretations. A *norm-referenced assessment* (3.1) gives meaning to a score by comparing it with the scores of a well-defined comparison group of respondents, the *norm group*. A *criterion-referenced assessment* (3.2), on the other hand, gives meaning to a score by comparing it with a previously set standard, called the passing *criterion* or a *cut score,* tied to a defined domain of knowledge and skills. Criterion-referencing, therefore, is not concerned with how an individual's performance compares with that of similar test-takers, but rather with how well an individual has mastered a domain of information and skills. Criterion-referencing, for this reason, is associated primarily with achievement or proficiency testing.

If you have taken norm-referenced admissions tests such as the *Graduate Record Examination* (GRE), you might be familiar with the *percentile rank,* a well-known norm-referenced score. The percentile rank (PR) indicates the proportion of students in a carefully selected comparison group, the norm group, who receive scores lower than a given person's test score. If you obtain a PR of 88, your score on the test places you above 88% of the scores in the norm group. On the other hand, if you take a professional certification test and received a Pass, it signifies that your score was equal to or above the *cut-score* set as the passing standard on a criterion-referenced test designed for certification purposes.

Teacher-made assessments of achievement can be either norm-referenced or criterion-referenced. Some teachers like to "grade on a curve," the colloquial label for the norm-referenced testing (NRT approach). Use of this practice suggests that the teacher is more interested in the assessments that show where each student stands relative to his or her peers, irrespective of their level of proficiency on the domain tested. Other teachers prefer criterion-referenced tests (CRT approach). When criterion-referencing, a teacher would be explicitly interested in a student's degree of mastery of the domain, rather than where he or she was ranked in comparison to the rest of the class or another group of students. Teachers who value criterion-referencing tend to set performance criteria to determine mastery, such as a score of 80% items correct on the overall test or parts of a test. Because of its consistency with the basic mission of teaching, namely, to make students proficient on a defined set of curricular outcomes, this author admits to a bias towards the criterion-referenced approach in classroom contexts.

Another method of score interpretation, not presented in Table 4.1, is *ipsative.* In the ipsative approach, which is difficult to apply in practice, a person's performance is compared to how he or she fared previously on the same or comparable assessment system.

### 4.2.4    Assessment Developer

A fourth way to differentiate among assessments is on the basis of the developer (4.0). Two broad distinctions are recognized depending on whether the tools are made by teachers or local educational practitioners (4.1) or by commercial testing companies or developers (4.2). The former are likely to more richly reflect the local curriculum; the latter, national or state-mandated standards.

### 4.2.5    Presentation Mode or Response Mode

Finally, a fifth method of categorization of assessments is based on the mode of presentation of the items or tasks (5.1) or mode of response by respondents (5.2).

Presentation modes today go far beyond the traditional paper and pencil stimulus. Test items can be presented through video or audio format or through actual demonstrations. A recent development in the field of measurement is the *computer-based assessment*. Here, the test is administered by the computer. The items and graphics appear in a computer-produced display, and the respondent indicates their answers with the help of a computer-based device, such as a keyboard or a mouse.

With respect to response mode of subjects (5.2), this book and module will recognize five major *assessment methods*. These are:

Written assessments (structured-response or open-ended assessments)
Behavior-based assessments
Product-based assessments
Interview-based assessments
Portfolio-based assessments

In Section 4.3, we will treat each of these types in detail and review their characteristics with reference to Tables 4.2 through 4.7.

### 4.2.6    An Assessment Can Belong in More Than One Category

The categories in Table 4.1 are not mutually exclusive. In this sense, the typologies here are akin to the classification of assessment purposes in Chapter 2 (see Table 2.1). They simply provide us with a language to describe critical characteristics of an assessment procedure. As illustrated by the examples in Table 4.1, numerous assessments of cognitive, affective, and personal-social constructs are both norm-referenced and standardized.

For example, several achievement tests, such as the STA and the ITBS, fall simultaneously into more than one category. Both the STA and ITBS are standardized assessments because of the tight controls built into their design. They are timed and proctored examinations, where the administrators follow a prepared script. At the same time, the STA and ITBS are norm-referenced tests that come with norm-referenced reports for users. The latter information enables a test-taker or user to interpret his or her placement relative to that of a relevant comparison group. The STA and the ITBS series also provide criterion-referenced reports for users. The criterion-referenced information is skill-referenced (or objective-referenced), showing test-takers and users the levels of proficiency on individual skills or skill areas within the larger domain. All the above tests are commercially developed.

In sum, if we had to use the descriptors in Table 4.1 to characterize assessments like the STA or ITBS, the description would go something like this:

Tests in the Stanford Achievement Test Series (STA) are *commercially developed, standardized, achievement* tests that provide both *norm-referenced* and *criterion-referenced* information on an examinee's performance. The items are *verbally presented,* and the predominant response mode is a *written, structured-response* format. The tests are *objectively scored* with an answer key.

---

**Key Concepts**

- Assessment typologies are classification systems that use different criteria to categorize different types of assessments.
- Each classification system provides us with a language to describe and distinguish among different types of assessments.

---

## 4.3 Types of Assessments Based on Mode of Response

We now turn to an elaboration of the classification scheme (Type 5.2) that focuses only on the nature of the responses made by respondents to identify five different assessment methods. The same scheme will be used when we delve deeper into assessment design, validation, and selection in later chapters. Specifically, Chapters 7 through 9 will address procedures for constructing the different types of assessments as classified by response mode. Let us, therefore, review some concrete descriptions and examples of each method.

### 4.3.1 Written Assessments

*Written assessments* include all assessments to which subjects respond using a paper and pencil format or, as is common today, on a computer using a word processor. The distinctive feature of assessment methods in this category is their written or verbal mode of response. Examples include essay, multiple choice, or fill-in-the blank tests.

A further breakdown of this broad category is useful. Paper and pencil assessments can be of two kinds based on the degree of structure in the response: structured or open-ended. As indicated before, a structured-response assessment is made up of questions which require highly structured responses from respondents. Thus, the respondent may select an answer from several answer options provided, or he or she may fill in one or a series of blank(s) with answer(s). All items in structured-response assessments have only one possible or correct response, making it easy to objectively score them; scanning machines are often used. Tests using multiple choice, true/false, completion (fill-in-the-blank), and matching items are all examples of written, structured-response assessments. For fill-in-the blank tests, typical answers are brief, made up of single words or phrases. Historically, numerous educational constructs, ranging from achievement to attitudes, were primarily assessed with the written, structured response format.

**TABLE 4.2    Sample Items from Written Assessments with a Highly Structured Response Format**

**Example 1    True/False**

| *Item* | *Response Options* |
|---|---|
| *Directions: Indicate whether (T)rue or (F)alse by circling the best/correct answer.* | |
| According to exercise scientists, one should consume water during an exercise routine. | A. True<br>B. False |

**Example 2    Multiple Choice Item for Measuring Achievement/Aptitudes**

| *Item* | *Response Options* |
|---|---|
| *Directions: Select the best/correct answer from the options given.* | |
| Which of the following is an example of a food in the *carbohydrate* food group? | A. Bread<br>B. Chicken<br>C. Spinach<br>D. Water |

**Example 3    Likert Scaled Item for Measuring Opinions/Attitudes**

| *Item* | *Response Options* |
|---|---|
| *Directions: Circle the answer that applies to you the most.* | |
| The government should allocate a bulk of its funds towards health care services. | A. Strongly Agree<br>B. Agree<br>C. Uncertain<br>D. Disagree<br>E. Strongly Disagree |

**Example 4    Portion of a Cloze Test**

*Complete the following paragraph by filling in the missing words.*

The Salvador Dali Museum _____ home to the world's _____ comprehensive collection of works _____ the late Spanish surrealist, _____ Dali. This is a place _____ time flows easily and _____ are not quite what they _____.

Every fifth word deleted.

Answers in sequence: is, most, by, Salvador, where, things, seem.

Written, open-ended assessments include those where respondents construct their own answers using a free-response format. Here, both the length and content of the response is generally determined by the respondent. Two common examples are essay and short answer tests. Creative writing ability is an example of a construct that lends itself to measurement with the written, open-ended assessment format. Open-ended assessments are also called "free-response" or "constructed response" tests.

Consider the items shown in Tables 4.2 and 4.3. In Table 4.2, Examples 1 and 2 are items from an achievement test in health education. Example 3 is an attitudinal item that attempts to capture personal opinions and values about health care, using a five-point scale named after its original developer, Rensis Likert. All three items use a highly structured response format in that respondents must choose only one of several response options provided to them—they cannot supply their own answers.

You will find numerous variations of the structured response formats in the testing literature. A *Cloze* test, also shown in Table 4.2, is one such variation of the "fill-in-the-blanks" variety. Cloze tests are generally used to measure reading comprehension, where the respondent receives narrative text on a topic with key words deleted in a specified order (for example, every third word). The examinee must then fill in the blanks with the correct terms to demonstrate understanding of the material.

The examples in Table 4.3 illustrate the use of an open-ended, written format. The item in Example 1 is excerpted from a survey questionnaire intended to measure values about health care in adults. Example 2 utilizes a combination of two methods, structured response for part (A) and open-ended for part (B). All examples shown in Tables 4.2 and 4.3 fall under the broad category of written assessments.

**TABLE 4.3  Sample Items from Written Assessments with Open-Ended Response**

**Example 1  Open-Ended: Short Answer**

*Item*

| | |
|---|---|
| *Directions: Answer in 3–5 sentences.* | *Expected Response* |
| At this time in your life, what actions do you take to care for your health? | Unstructured |
| If you had the chance, what actions would you take to improve your personal health care program? | Unstructured |

**Example 2  Combination: True/False and Short Answer**

| | |
|---|---|
| *Item* | *Expected Response* |
| *Directions: (A) Indicate whether (T)rue or (F)alse. (B) Give two reasons to justify your chosen answer.* | |
| (A) If properly followed, diets produce permanent results. | A. True |
| | B. False |
| (B) Explanation | Unstructured |

### 4.3.2  Behavior-Based Assessments

The second type of assessment method is labeled the *behavior-based assessment*. This assessment method requires respondents to demonstrate behaviors or processes that must be directly observed. The distinctive feature of assessments in this category is that actual behaviors, performances, and demonstrations have to be assessed as they are occurring. Motor behaviors, on-the-job performance, and social skills are examples of attributes that lend themselves to measurement with behavior-based assessments. Other examples include assessments of speeches, debates, dancing or diving performances, or demonstrations of behaviors and skills in actual settings (e.g., measures of driving proficiency).

Most behavior-based assessments use an open-ended response format, allowing the respondent to freely generate answers. Depending on the way they are administered, however, behavior-based assessments might be *structured observations* or *naturalistic obser-*

**Table 4.4  Behavior-Based Assessments**

**Example 1  A Structured Observation Record**

Teacher or counselor checks categories based on observations of children in classroom settings.

| Behaviors Observed | Observation Record # | Not at all (pts. 0) | Some of the time (pts. 1) | Most of the time (pts. 2) |
|---|---|---|---|---|
| 1. Participates in group activities | 1 _____ | √ | | |
| | 2 _____ | | √ | |
| | 3 _____ | √ | | |
| | Score = | | | |
| 2. Demonstrates "Sharing" behaviors— e.g., trades toys with peers. | 1 _____ | | √ | |
| | 2 _____ | | | √ |
| | 3 _____ | | | √ |
| | Score = | | | |
| 3. Waits for turn during group activities | 1 _____ | | √ | |
| | 2 _____ | | √ | |
| | 3 _____ | | | √ |
| | Score = | | | |

**Example 2  An Anecdotal Record**

Record 3            5.18.92 9:00 AM In class            Subject: Johnny

Johnny was 15 minutes late. He explained his tardiness by saying that he was delayed in the cafeteria eating breakfast. He took out his books and began his class work. He completed 5 of the 8 math problems that the class was doing, then put his head down. He appeared to fall asleep in a few minutes.

*vations.* We could view the level of structure in various behavior-based assessmen methods as a continuum. On one end of this hypothetical continuum, we would locate highly structured observations, while completely unstructured observations would lie at the other end. If observers exercise little or no control in the methods for making observations and recording of responses, the observations would be unstructured. "Naturalistic observations" are unstructured observations of behaviors that we make in actual or real-life settings, with little or no intrusion of the observer and few external constraints. Observations for behavior-based assessments can be either timed or untimed.

Table 4.4 provides illustrations of a structured and an unstructured behavior-based assessment. In Example 1, social behaviors of young children are observed by their teachers or counselors in a classroom setting. Three observations are possible on each behavioral indicator, and categories checked can be quantitatively summarized to obtain a score on each indicator or a total score on the overall scale.

Relative to the previous example, Example 2 represents unstructured notes describing a teacher's observations of a specific behavioral incident of a student. Such *anecdotal records* are a special case of unstructured, behavior-based assessments, as they are descriptions of episodes in a natural setting. A collection of anecdotal records suggests behavioral patterns of the subject observed. Conventions exist for recording "good" anecdotal observations. When properly done, anecdotal observations should be brief, factual descriptions; inferences, opinions, or judgments of the observer should not be evident in a record; the record should describe critical incidents involving the subject; and multiple observations must be recorded before patterns are discerned (Mehrens & Lehman, 1984). However, the conditions, methods of observation, and scoring procedures are far less rigid in Example 2 than in Example 1. The observer has far greater latitude in how records are made, summarized, and interpreted.

### 4.3.3 Product-Based Assessments

*Product-based assessment* requires the respondents to create or construct a product, which then serves as the basis for measurement. Examples of product-based assessments are journals, term papers, laboratory reports, science projects, books, or artwork. Attributes such as artistic abilities, culinary skills, scientific scholarship, and skills related to specialized trades or crafts are often assessed using product-based assessments. Product-based assessments generally have generous time allotments for completion and often include take-home exercises. The distinctive feature of this assessment method is that the product created by the respondent serves as evidence of the underlying construct.

Product-based assessments are usually open-ended, where respondents have the freedom to create their own product with only a few given parameters. An exception would be a case where all respondents are assessed by means of a fixed product. For example, to measure typing expertise, all examinees are asked to type the contents of the same business manual. Table 4.5 gives an example of a product-based assessment intended to measure science achievement outcomes in elementary students. The product assessed is the report produced by the students on planets; examinees have freedom in choosing the planets they investigate, as well as in how they compile the report, within some guidelines and scoring criteria given.

**TABLE 4.5  Product-Based Assessments**

**Example 1    A Fifth-Grade Science Report**

*Directions to Students from Teacher:*

Write a report comparing any two of the nine planets in our Solar System. Be sure to discuss the following in your comparison: names of the planets, time needed by each planet to rotate on its axis, time needed to revolve around the sun, two facts about each planet's moon(s), average temperature, size of the planets, average distance from the sun, the planet's nickname, and whether or not the planet can support life as we know it. Make sure you separate your opinions from the facts. Give reasons to support any opinions given. The paper should be accurate, clear, and two pages long.

You will be given 3 class periods (one hour each) to gather information on your planets and write the report. You may use resources in the classroom, the Media Center, or from home for your research. All your work must be done during the time allocated at school. Your work will be collected at the end of each class period.

The report will have 50% weight in your total grade. I will use the criteria provided on the attached checklist to score your reports. Please check them as you prepare your report.

| Scoring Criteria (Excerpted) | | Check Yes or No (1 point for each "Yes") | |
|---|---|:---:|:---:|
| | | Yes | No |
| Planets identified by name. | Present: | ✓ | |
| | Accurate: | ✓ | |
| Planet sizes given. | Present: | | ✓ |
| | Accurate: | | ✓ |
| Average temperatures given. | Present: | ✓ | |
| | Accurate: | ✓ | |
| Remaining portion of scoring criteria not shown. | | | |

## 4.3.4  Interview-Based Assessments

*Interview-based assessments* require the respondents to make spoken responses in an interview situation. What makes this assessment method distinct is its dependence on orally articulated responses. Interviewee responses are usually open-ended, but like behavior-based assessments, interviews can be presented and scored in highly structured or unstructured ways. Similarly, they can be timed or untimed. Interviews provide a means for the respondent to explain responses given in written or other formats, and thus are advantageous from a validity perspective when reasoning and explanation skills are in the domain.

Examples of interview-based assessments are *viva voce* examinations—oral examinations used in scientific disciplines to supplement written or laboratory examinations.

**Table 4.6  Interview-Based Assessments**

**Example 1  One-on-One Interview to Measure Locus of Control**

| *Interview Question* | *"Look Fors" in Responses* | *Scoring of "Look Fors"* |
|---|---|---|
| 1. Think of a project that you just finished at home. | It met my own standards of quality; my time line; my goals. | Internal Locus of Control (Code 1) |
| How did you decide that you have *successfully completed* the project? | Others (e.g., my mother) said nice things. | External Locus of Control (Code 2) |
| *Interview Probe for Question 1:* Did you feel a sense of accomplishment? Why were you satisfied with the results? | "They" liked the work. | |

Most tests of language usage or conversation skills employ interviews, such as the *Test of Spoken English*. Certain personality, attitudinal, and psychological variables have also been measured successfully with interviews.

Table 4.6 illustrates the use of an interview to measure "locus of control." Attribution theorists identify locus of control, a personality characteristic, as a determinant of human behavior. The hypothesis is that locus of control drives the extent to which an individual's actions are controlled by internal or external factors. Those who are more intrinsically motivated tend to link their actions, feelings, and reactions about phenomena to their own inner abilities, needs, and drives—that is, an internal locus of control. Externally controlled individuals, on the other hand, tend to attribute their behaviors and feelings to factors that lie outside themselves. In the example shown, the interviewer looks for particular indicators in the responses made by the interviewee. Coding of "look fors" is a structured process guided by the psychological theory underlying the construct. The "look fors" are intended to control for error during assessment administration and scoring.

### 4.3.5  Portfolio-Based Assessments

*Portfolio-based assessments* are purposeful collections of work or behavioral records that together provide a comprehensive picture of proficiencies in a broad area. Traditionally, occupations such as art, photography, and architecture made routine use of portfolios to showcase products and portray processes used to develop products. Educators have recently found applicability of portfolio-based assessments in measuring scholastic constructs such as writing development, in particular to chronicle development over time in a particular area, or to demonstrate skills in a specialized subject, craft, or trade.

The portfolio is often promoted as the best means for comprehensive documentation of evolving skills and knowledge in a particular area. For example, teacher education programs are now using portfolios to assess emerging pedagogical skills of preservice teachers by including items such as lesson plans, teacher-made assessments, and video-tapes of classroom teaching, in their performance portfolios.

Portfolios have some unique features, and so we will treat them in an independent category. A definition given by Arter and Spandel (1992), adapted from several sources, highlights some of these special characteristics. It states:

> A portfolio is a purposeful collection of student work that tells the story of a student's efforts, progress, or achievement in (a) given area(s). This collection must include student participation in selection of portfolio contents; the guidelines for selection; the criteria for judging merit; and evidence of student self-reflection (Arter & Spandel, 1992, p. 36).

The portfolio can serve not only as an effective tool for integrating instruction and assessment in educational contexts, it can also be used to *engage the learner* in learning and assessment processes. When portfolios utilize work samples, they may be considered a special case of product-based assessments or written assessments. As in the teacher portfolio using videotapes of teacher performance, we could also include behavior-based assessments. Portfolios are also unique in their incorporation of self-reflection, or an introspective analysis of the collection of work by the individuals being assessed.

Table 4.7 provides an example of a portfolio-based assessment that a teacher used to measure achievement outcomes in a high school English class. Specifically, the teacher uses a collection of poems, documentation of the processes used to develop the poems, and self-reflection, as the basis for measuring a range of complex learning outcomes. A product-based assessment may not have adequately captured the full scope and complexity of the domain, making the portfolio a better assessment method in this case.

**TABLE 4.7  Portfolio-Based Assessments**

**Example 1 A Portfolio for Students in a High School English Class (Excerpted)**

*Directions to students from teacher:*

I would like you to include one original poem in each of the following categories in your portfolio.

1. Limerick        2. Haiku        3. Cinquain        4. Diamantes        5. Bio Poem

The poems should reflect use of the following poetic devices: personification, onomatopoeia, similies, metaphors, and rhyme. Show the process you followed to draft, edit, revise and create the poems in publishable form. Include *all* your work in the portfolio.

To complete your portfolio, write a reflective essay (about 2 pages long, double spaced). In this essay:

  a) identify where you used various poetic devices and why,
  b) describe what you learned from this exercise, and
  c) which parts of the work were the most difficult or rewarding for you.

Your score will be determined based on the scoring rubric handed out in class.

> **Key Concepts**
>
> ■ Based on the response mode of the examinees or respondents, five main assessment methods were identified in this chapter.
> ■ The classification system based on response mode will be used in subsequent chapters.

## 4.4 Advantages and Disadvantages of Different Assessment Methods

Of the five assessment methods identified based on response mode, no single method is the "best" for all situations, functions, or needs. Table 4.8 (adapted from Banerji et al., 1997) ties the assessment methods with a list of the measurement-related advantages and disadvantages of each. A careful review of the list will help you make balanced decisions as to the most appropriate method(s) for particular attributes, purposes, and populations. Sometimes your needs will be best served by one particular method. At other times, you may want to combine several methods to meet your needs. The guiding criteria for making selections should be validity, reliability, and utility of the resulting application and its results (see Chapter 3).

### 4.4.1 Advantages and Disadvantages of Written Structured-Response (W-SR) Assessments

The W-SR format (1a in Table 4.8) has several advantages. It allows us to cover a wide range of material in a limited testing time, it is easy to administer to large groups, and it can be scored quickly and objectively with a key. More questions enable a better representation of the construct domain, enhancing validity. In addition, formats such as the multiple choice item have been shown to be very versatile in tapping cognitive behaviors ranging from recall of facts to higher-order thinking (Hopkins, 1998; Mehrens, 1992; Mitchell, 1992). If the domain includes behaviors and skills that can be tapped with the structured format, we could use the format to get both validity and high levels of utility.

Furthermore, we could include more items or questions in a given time frame, thus improving reliability of the results with a larger sampling of behaviors. A large number of questions enables us to evaluate if respondents are answering in a consistent manner when given repeated opportunities to do so. Because there is only one possible or correct response to each question, it is possible to keep human involvement or error from human judges completely out of the scoring process, another advantage in the area of reliability. Assuming that the answer key used is accurately prepared, machine scorability is another factor that adds to the utility.

It is not difficult to see why the W-SR tests, in particular the multiple choice format, has been a traditional favorite with commercial test developers and large-scale test users. W-SR tests have also been well represented in textbooks and teacher-made classroom assessments. But what about their disadvantages?

TABLE 4.8 Advantages and Disadvantages of Assessment Methods

| Assessment Method | Description | Advantages | Disadvantages |
|---|---|---|---|
| **1a Written structured-response assessments** | Usually timed, fixed or selected response, written exercises | ■ More content can be sampled in short testing time<br>■ Can measure a range of cognitive skills/behaviors<br>■ Objective to score<br>■ Efficient to score<br>■ Can be designed to have high internal consistency<br>■ Efficient to administer to large groups | ■ Guessing is a source of error<br>■ Difficult to construct technically effective items<br>■ Cannot be adapted to measure some behaviors (social behaviors, procedural knowledge)<br>■ Only one correct answer possible<br>■ Items typically measure discrete concepts rather than integrated knowledge and skills<br>■ Partial credit cannot be given |
| **1b Written open-ended assessments** | Usually timed, constructed response, written exercises | ■ Can measure complex thinking and processes (organization, problem-solving, creativity, integrated skills)<br>■ Partial credit can be given to answers<br>■ Allows analytic or holistic scoring<br>■ More than one correct answer possible<br>■ Efficient to administer to large groups | ■ Less content can be sampled in a given testing time<br>■ Bluffing causes error<br>■ Subjective to score without clear criteria<br>■ Scorer consistency needed<br>■ Time consuming to score<br>■ Cannot be used for nonwriters<br>■ Human scorers needed<br>■ Scorer training may be needed |
| **2 Behavior-based assessments** | Behaviors or demonstrations exhibited in natural or structured settings | ■ Can measure complex performances and behaviors in group and individual settings<br>■ Requires actual demonstration and direct observation<br>■ More than one correct response possible<br>■ Allows analytic or holistic scoring<br>■ Partial credit can be awarded | ■ Time consuming to make observations<br>■ Time consuming to score<br>■ Subjective to score without clear criteria<br>■ Less content can be sampled in a given time<br>■ Scorer consistency needed<br>■ Scorer training may be needed<br>■ Cannot be done with large groups |

| | | |
|---|---|---|
| | | ■ Cannot be done with large groups<br>■ Human observers and scorers needed |
| **3 Product-based assessments** | Products, reports, or items created in structured or unstructured situations | ■ Can measure complex thinking and processes (organization, problem-solving, creativity)<br>■ Partial credit can be given to answers<br>■ Allows analytic or holistic scoring<br>■ More than one correct answer possible<br>■ Efficient to administer to large groups<br>■ Requires actual production<br>■ Requires application of product development skills<br>■ Can be untimed take-home exercises | ■ Time consuming to score<br>■ Less content can be sampled in a given time<br>■ Limited to processes that result in products<br>■ Subjective to score without clear criteria<br>■ Scorer consistency needed<br>■ Human scorers needed<br>■ Respondents can get outside help unless structured tightly<br>■ Scorer training may be needed |
| **4 Interview-based assessments** | One-on-one verbal (oral) interaction in structured or unstructured situations | ■ Needed when oral communication is the focus (language learning)<br>■ Preferred format for very young or special populations<br>■ Can measure a range of cognitive, personal-social, and effective behaviors<br>■ More than one correct answer possible<br>■ Partial credit possible<br>■ Allows analytical or holistic scoring | ■ Time consuming to administer<br>■ Time consuming to score<br>■ Less content can be sampled in a given time<br>■ Limited to processes that need human interaction<br>■ Human interviewers needed<br>■ Interviewer training and structure may be needed<br>■ Subjective to score without clear criteria<br>■ Scorer consistency needed<br>■ Human scorers needed<br>■ Scorer training may be needed |

*(continued)*

TABLE 4.8 Continued

| Assessment Method | Description | Advantages | Disadvantages |
|---|---|---|---|
| **5 Portfolios** | Purposeful collections of behaviors of work samples made over time | ■ Can be designed to measure growth over time or periodic, summative evaluations<br>■ Can be easily integrated with instruction<br>■ Can measure complex outcomes or behaviors<br>■ Possible to individualize or adapt to groups<br>■ Can measure complex thinking and processes (organization, problem-solving, creativity)<br>■ Partial credit possible<br>■ Allows analytic or holistic scoring<br>■ More than one correct answer possible<br>■ Efficient to administer to large groups<br>■ Requires production of actual samples<br>■ Requires application of product development skills<br>■ Can be untimed and have take-home exercises | ■ Requires proper content sampling<br>■ Requires adequate number of samples<br>■ Limited to processes or behaviors that can be included in a portfolio<br>■ Subjective to score without clear criteria<br>■ Scorer consistency needed<br>■ Human scorers needed<br>■ Respondents can get outside help<br>■ Scorer training may be needed |

*Source*: Adapted from the original by M. Banerji and Design Team, Pasco County School System (1997), published by the Bureau of Curriculum, Instruction, and Assessment, Florida Department of Education. Excerpted with permission from the Florida Department of Education. All rights reserved.

Table 4.8 shows some of the commonly-faced limitations of the W-SR format. In particular, for items where the respondent must select from given responses, there is always a chance that the answer was *guessed*. A two-option item has a 1 in 2 chance of being right when guessing. A five-option item provides a 1 in 5 chance for guessing. Assuming that guessing is a random rather than a systematic event, it would affect the reliability of the results.

Furthermore, good W-SR items are difficult to construct. Ambiguous or poorly written items can lead to systematic and unsystematic errors—potential threats to both the validity and reliability of resulting scores. Numerous rules must be followed to construct technically defensible items (as you will discover in Chapter 7). Because their construction demands technical skills and time, this format will affect utility concerns of assessment developers.

If the content domain contains behaviors that cannot be captured by the high level of structure in the response, W-SR items will fail to yield valid information. Only one, usually brief, response can be made in this format. Several important learning outcomes in today's curricula, such as application of complex processes, writing skills, originality, organizational abilities, logical thinking, social behaviors, and many others simply cannot be measured directly with a W-SR assessment. Important parts of the domain might thus be overlooked if assessment design and selection is restricted to this format, compromising validity.

### 4.4.2 Advantages and Disadvantages of the Written Open-Ended (W-OE) Format

The W-OE assessment method has lower utility and scoring reliability than the W-SR method, but for complex learning outcomes it provides us with advantages. Since the 1990s, several state testing programs have mandated essay examinations. In making the shift from the S-R to the essay format, language arts specialists working with test developers have placed a greater value on the skills tapped by the more direct assessment method. This trend has resulted in the adoption of the less utilitarian essay format in writing assessment programs in public education. Traditionally used indirect methods, such as multiple choice tests in language mechanics, provided rather different information on writing proficiency. To control for possible unreliability introduced by human raters of the essays, state programs have invested in costly training and scoring programs. When we opt for the open-ended assessment method, we are placing greater emphasis on validity of results, despite some losses in the areas of utility and reliability.

### 4.4.3 Advantages and Disadvantages of Other Performance Assessments

If we continue to evaluate the advantages and disadvantages of the remaining assessment methods in Table 4.8, we see that our decision to design or select a tool demanding a particular response mode by subjects will impact validity, reliability, and utility of the assessment and its results. Direct methods of assessment, such as behavior-based assessments, may be the more valid choice for certain constructs. However, in making that choice, one might have to forsake some utility. All performance assessments are costly in terms of their need for time and human resources. For those that require direct assessments by human judges, observers, or interviewers, inconsistency of judges poses a threat to the reliability of results. Steps can be taken to combat various anticipated errors, but it usually involves a cost with respect to time and resources.

### 4.4.4    Why Is It Useful to Weigh the Advantages and Disadvantages of Different Assessment Methods?

In practice, we develop or select assessments to fulfill purposes specified in different User Paths (Chapter 2). During planning, we have to grapple with psychometric and usability issues when choosing the best assessment method(s) to fulfill our needs and the targeted construct as best as we can. As pointed out in Chapter 3, we should keep the stakes tied to assessment results in mind during this work. The "driving proficiency" construct, measured to certify proficient automobile drivers, is an instance where two assessment methods, W-SR and behavior-based, are usually considered better than either one individually. In Chapter 5, we begin to look in depth at the step-by-step procedures for developing or selecting assessments in different user contexts. Irrespective of the User Paths (i.e., whether you are a classroom teacher, counselor, administrator, or a large-scale assessment developer), decisions on the best-fitting assessment method for the construct of interest must be tackled. Inevitably, some compromises will have to be made based on the constraints of the assessment context. As a general rule, the most important criterion for selecting assessment methods when we evaluate particular constructs and populations for given purposes should be validity. Reliability and utility considerations should follow after.

### Key Concepts

- The nature of the response mode gives us five types of assessment methods, each with its advantages and disadvantages in different situations.
- The advantages and disadvantages we get with each assessment method in a given circumstance are related to validity, reliability, and utility.

## Summary

Chapter 4 provided various classification systems for different types of assessments used in education. It began with a discussion of popular usages and references to traditional, performance, authentic, and alternative assessments. We then looked at a classification system based on constructs measured, as in tests of achievement, intelligence, and aptitude, or inventories focusing on attitude, behavioral, interest and personality variables. The degree of control in assessment conditions yielded another classification, recognizing standardized and unstandardized instruments. Time constraints in the design helps us differentiate between speed and power tests. The kinds of interpretations we make with the scores/results helps us distinguish between norm-referenced and criterion-referenced tools. Classification by developer yield teacher-made tests and commercially developed assessments. The modes in which the items or tasks are presented to the respondents or examinees enables distinctions between verbal and nonverbal assessments. Finally, the modes in which the subjects or examinees respond yields yet another classification scheme.

Chapter 4 recognized six types of assessment methods based on the modes in which the subjects or examinees respond. During assessment design or selection, we will have to choose from these six assessment options. The six assessment methods are:

- Written, structured-response assessments (W-SR)
- Written, open-ended assessments (W-OE)
- Behavior-based assessments (BB)
- Product-based assessments (PB)
- Interview-based assessments (IB)
- Portfolio-based assessments

Relatively speaking, all but the W-SR type are subjectively scored assessments, and need scoring rubrics. W-SR assessments are objectively scored tools.

The chapter demonstrated how we could evaluate the advantages and disadvantages of each assessment method from a measurement perspective. Our choice of assessment method must be done keeping in mind the assessment purposes, the targeted population, and the substantive nature of the construct to be assessed. The chapter recommended that both developers and users evaluate the pros and cons of employing one assessment method over another, or of combining more than one assessment method in particular testing situations. Such decisions would affect the validity, reliability and utility of an assessment and its application. Justification of the assessment method during assessment design is detailed in later chapters as a part of the process model for assessment design/selection, validation, and use.

## QUESTIONS FOR CLASS DISCUSSION

1. Find an example of each of the following types of assessment in your field of work, based on the definitions in Chapter 4. Explain why you would place them in these categories.
   (a) Authentic assessment
   (b) Traditional assessment
   (c) Alternative assessment
   (d) Performance assessment

2. Some advocates of authentic assessments claim that a good assessment serves as a good teaching activity, and teaching to an authentic test promotes learning. Make arguments for or against this claim, with support from your own experiences. (Refer to the definition of an authentic assessment provided by Wiggins earlier in this chapter if you need to.)

3. Review descriptions of assessment tools in your state's assessment and accountability program for public schools.

   (a) Using the language from classification schemes given in Table 4.1, describe the *types of assessments* that are targeted for the program.

   (b) Evaluate the assessment methods with regard to how they will influence validity, reliability, and utility.

4. Review the literature in your field to identify two major assessments, standardized or otherwise, that professionals employ in different decision-making contexts. Use the descriptors for different types of assessments given in Table 4.1 to describe the characteristics of the assessments.

   Example of an answer (from chapter):

   Tests in the Stanford Achievement Test Series (STA) are *commercially developed, standardized, achievement* tests that provide both *norm-referenced* and *criterion-referenced* information on an examinee's performance. The items are *verbally presented,* and the predominant response mode is a *written, structured-response* format. The tests are *objectively scored* with an answer key.

5. Describe an assessment need that you are likely to face at work. In general terms, identify:

   The assessment purposes

   The population

   The construct you will assess

   Using the classification scheme based on response modes, select the best assessment method(s) that will give you the desired levels of validity, reliability, and utility for the construct. Justify your selection with three reasons that relate to measurement quality (Table 4.8).

**NOTE:** More structured exercises with immediate feedback for anwers are available on the computer module.

# 5 A Process Model for Designing, Selecting, and Validating Assessment Tools

## Overview

So far, we have examined several foundational concepts in assessment methodology. We have studied the theoretical and philosophical underpinnings of the assessment process (Chapter 1); how assessment tools are used in education (Chapter 2); the qualities of a sound assessment procedure (Chapter 3); and various ways in which assessment devices are classified (Chapter 4). In building that foundation, the aim was to provide you with conceptual tools that you will need to serve in the role of a competent assessment designer. The focus of the next few chapters is on the "how to" process of assessment development and validation.

The present chapter, intended as a preamble to Chapters 6–9, introduces you to a process model for assessment design, selection, and validation. The model serves as the organizing framework around which Section I of this book is built. A key purpose of Chapter 5 is to demonstrate that the process for designing, selecting, and/or validating assessments is generalizable across different User Paths, constructs, assessment methods, and populations. The chapter demonstrates with a case study how the *same process*—that is, the same phases or steps in the work—apply in designing two different types of tools, traditional and performance assessments in User Path 1, the classroom decision-making path. Although the case study happens to be from User Path 1 and focuses on two secondary-level assessments, keep in mind that the phases in implementing the process model would be applied in the *same way* in User Paths 2–5, and with populations at different levels—primary, elementary, or adult. More examples across different levels and User Paths are provided in the chapters that follow.

## CHAPTER 5 OBJECTIVES

After studying this chapter and completing the structured exercises in the module, you should be able to:

1. Describe the rationale for the four-phase process model for assessment design, selection, validation, and use

2. Analyze the components of the process model and identify the interdependencies in procedures and work involved in the different phases

3. Define key terms related to the process model (construct domain, assessment specification, table of specifications, test blueprint, content validation, empirical validation)

4. Evaluate case study applications of the process model for assessment design, selection, validation, and use, starting with a case in User Path 1 (designing tools for classroom assessment)

## 5.1    Need for a General Process Model

The most visible recent change in the assessment practices of educators has been their use of a wide variety of assessment methods. (Here, we are using the term *assessment methods* as we did in Chapter 4, to refer to different types of assessment tools based on the mode of response of the examinees or respondents.) It was during the 1990s that the language of "performance assessments," "alternative assessments," and "authentic assessments" became popular in education. Portfolios, behavior-based, product-based, and interview-based assessments were soon added to the list of assessment options, a list that had been previously dominated by the multiple choice test. The broadening of assessment options for educators reflected a shift in values about "what" is important to assess in education. It also reflected a change in values regarding "how" to assess important educational constructs.

Simultaneously, a sizable portion of published literature of the 1990s suggested that with the changes in assessment options, traditional theory and practices in measurement were no longer applicable, and needed to be discarded. There was much talk about "revamping assessments" and "redesigning" assessment practices. This raised several questions in the minds of educators and measurement specialists alike. Today, despite the publication of an expanded and updated set of standards for educational and psychological measurement (AERA, APA, & NCME, 1999) that incorporate changes to show how time-tested principles would continue to apply to a wide array of assessments, doubts remain. Educational practitioners and measurement professionals have not received complete and definitive answers to many questions dealing with the basic issues of assessment development.

For example, if we choose to develop a performance assessment, will the process that we follow be substantially different from the process that would apply for written, structured-response assessments? Will we need to work from different understandings of validity, reliability, and utility? If the user of assessment information changed from a classroom teacher to an administrator or to a counselor, should the individual go about designing or selecting assessment tools to meet their different needs in a markedly different manner? Will our work process be different when instruments are designed or selected for different populations? Condensed into a single question, the critical issue is: Will the essential process of assessment design/selection and validation remain the same as factors in the assessment context change?

The premise of this chapter is that the essential process does *not* change; that the basic principles of validity, reliability, and utility will apply in *all* assessment design and selection situations; that we will follow the same phases or steps in our work.

The *process model,* the central theme of this chapter, provides us with the four essential phases of work that are necessary when we attempt to design/select and validate assessment tools for different purposes. Specific details of our actions will vary within each phase when we attempt to assess substantively different constructs, or build different types of assessments to serve different ends, but the general phases of the model will remain constant irrespective of these differences.

You should not view the process model as a cookbook "recipe" that you can blindly follow to create good assessments. This chapter aims to sensitize you to the many complex decisions that you will need to make during the process. Each evaluative action that you take during various phases of the design/selection process will define the characteristics and limitations of the assessment tool that results.

## 5.2 Components of a Process Model for Assessment Design/Selection and Validation

Let us now examine the parts of the Process Model in depth. As we proceed, a few relatively new (or not so new) concepts and terms will be incorporated in the description as they are an intrinsic part of the model. These are:

- Domain, construct domain, performance domain
- Assessment specification, table of specifications, test blueprint
- Content validation
- Empirical validation

All these terms will be defined again in the narrative and reinforced in the Key Concepts boxes located close by; they will be repeated over and over again and elaborated with concrete examples in the following sections and chapters.

Figure 5.1 displays a flow-chart with the critical components of the *process model.* According to the model, there are four major phases in the assessment design and validation process, Phases I–IV. If a user does not wish to develop an assessment tool, the same phases would also apply for the systematic selection and validation of preexisting instruments that are intended for use in similar or different settings. Phase I involves planning decisions that require us to take into account three important factors in the assessment context—the *construct,* the *population,* and the *purposes for assessment.* Phases II and III indicate two products to be generated (or selected) through the process. Respectively, they are the assessment plan that guides design or selection of assessment tool(s), called the *assessment specification* (Phase II), and the actual *assessment tool(s)* or instruments to measure the construct (Phase III). Phase IV involves validation decisions and actions linked to contextual factors we identify in Phase I.

Decisions we make in Phase I will drive our work in Phase II, and subsequently in Phase III. Similarly, decisions we make on validation and the types of validity evidence

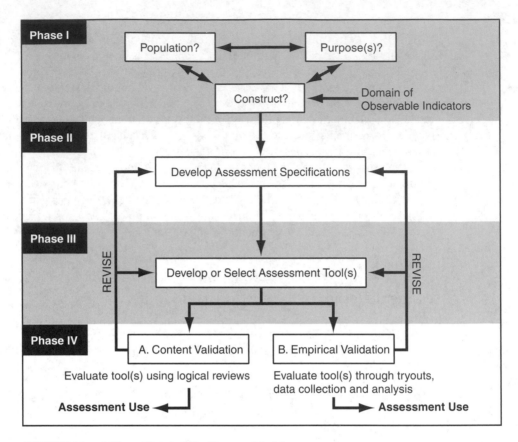

**FIGURE 5.1    A Flow Chart of the Process Model**

that will be necessary in Phase IV, will similarly be guided by our planning decisions in Phase I. For example, identification of formal, high stakes assessment purposes in Phase I would demand that we gather greater amounts of and/or particular kinds of validity evidence in Phase IV to support the proposed applications. Specification of informal assessment purposes and contexts of use in Phase I, on the other hand, might lead us to take different actions in Phases II, III, and IV. If we recognize these links among the work involved in the four phases, we will be able to make use of the model to produce assessments that are better aligned with not just the construct, but also with the targeted population and our specific needs.

## 5.2.1    Phase I of the Process Model

The first phase of assessment design and validation (Phase I) requires us to identify and begin definition of the construct and contextual elements within which the assessment tool is most likely to be used. The three elements in Phase I are linked with arrows to illustrate that we need to consider them together. They all affect the quality of products in Phases II and III.

***Construct.*** "What" are we assessing? The construct needs to be identified by us with a label in Phase I, for example, "attitude toward school," "science achievement," or "hearing loss." More important, however, we begin to define the *domain* for the construct by identifying some *operational indicators* that are reasonably supported by the theory and established knowledge about the construct. In Chapter 1, you were introduced to the role of an operational definition in measurement. When discussing content-based validity, Chapter 3 first presented the idea of specifying the domain of observable behaviors or indicators. For example, we know that teachers would use their targeted learning outcomes in a unit of instruction to specify their achievement domain.

The specification of the domain is the first step in operationally defining the construct. In Figure 5.1, the arrow pointing to the construct from the domain of "observable indicators" tells us that we need to begin to operationally define the construct, here, in the first phase.

***Population.*** Whom are we assessing? What are their defining characteristics? Chapter 1 addressed the usefulness of identifying the population to be assessed (Table 1.1). Chapter 3 gave you examples of systematic errors that result from using instruments on the wrong populations (Table 3.1). To help us design or select an instrument that will help generate the most accurate information on the group or individuals you wish to assess, it is useful to specify the characteristics of the population at the start.

***Purposes for Assessment.*** How will the information resulting from the assessment tool be interpreted and used? What meanings are to be inferred from the results or "scores," and in what contexts? Early specification of purposes is necessary to avoid invalid assessment uses and interpretations later on. The case studies in Chapter 2 attempted to drive this point home. The assessment purposes drive our validation work in Phase IV. In Chapter 3, we saw that particular usages of scores and the stakes tied to the results of assessments call for particular kinds of validity evidence. Our work of instrument design and validation will become much more efficient if we clarify our assessment purposes from the beginning.

### Key Concepts

- The domain is made up of a defined list of observable behaviors or indicators that assessment designers use as the first operational definition of the construct they want to measure. They then use the domain to develop the final assessment tool. In the literature, the domain is also called the "construct domain," "content domain," "content universe," or "performance domain."
- The process of identifying and clarifying the observable behaviors or indicators for a construct is called "specifying the domain." This book recommends that assessment designers specify the domain in Phase I of the Process Model.
- The operational indicators are the observable behaviors of the construct we want to assess.

### 5.2.2    Phase II of the Process Model

Our initial work in Phase I becomes incorporated into a concrete assessment plan in Phase II. Stated in another way, the second phase involves the development of a formal plan that will guide the design or selection of assessment(s) in Phase III. The plan is called the *assessment specification.* In the measurement literature, synonyms for this term are a "table of specifications" and "test blueprint." Both are typically used for written, structured-response (W-SR) tests. The term *assessment specification* is used here to broaden the application of specifications to an array of different assessment methods.

The information from Phase I feeds into Phase II. A fully developed assessment specification includes information from the three elements from the first phase (purpose, population, construct domain). Additionally, it specifies other critical dimensions of the assessment to be developed or selected. For example, we could specify how the actual tasks or questions should look, or detail the procedures for administration and scoring of the tasks or questions. Plans for more technical characteristics of the final instrument could also be delineated in the assessment specification document. For example, what will the scale look like? How much weight will be allocated to different questions or tasks? If we are planning for a norm-referenced tool, how will the norming occur and what kinds of norm-referenced scores will be incorporated into reports?

What we must remember is that the details of the assessment specification should be dictated by the definition of the construct, the assessment purposes, and the population. Some constructs will be best measured by particular assessment methods (see Chapter 4), just as some purposes will be best served with particular types of scores properties. For example, if we are developing a norm-referenced instrument, we should plan for the norming thoughtfully, keeping in mind the population we specified in Phase I. You will soon begin to appreciate such interdependencies as we review a concrete case study in this chapter.

---

**Key Concepts**

- Assessment specifications serve as the guiding blueprint for designing or selecting an assessment tool. They are put together in Phase II of the Process Model.
- A Table of Specifications is formatted in table form, and is traditionally used for designing structured-response tests.
- A test blueprint is another name for a Table of Specifications.

### 5.2.3    Phase III of the Process Model

Once we have developed an assessment specification in Phase II, we could either produce or select assessments to fit the requirements outlined in them. As indicated, the specifications form the blueprint through which the "construct" becomes fully operationalized as a test or assessment tool. Multiple assessments could be produced to match the same set of assessment specifications, as in parallel forms of a test or task. This is useful from a practical standpoint. For example, a teacher who delivers a particular unit of instruction repeatedly can carefully develop assessment specifications to match the domain of learning outcomes. Then, the teacher could develop several assessments to match those specifications. Such preparation will provide teachers with many optional assessment tools when they need to make formative or summative decisions in the classroom. At the same time some of the instruments can be kept secure.

Existing assessment devices could also be identified to match the specifications we generate. Should the assessment users (for example, teachers) not want to create new assessments, a prepared set of assessment specifications can serve as a useful guide to help them select assessments from existing resources—such as textbook materials, curriculum guides, or commercial test catalogs—to serve their specified needs. In sum, the assessment specifications could dictate our selection of assessment(s) from existing sources.

If we choose to develop instruments ourselves, Phase III requires that we become proficient in applying established rules and guidelines for writing different types of items and tasks. For example, what are rules that we can follow to construct multiple choice items of defensible quality? What are the rules that will help us in designing sound performance assessments with appropriate scoring rubrics (criteria for scoring)? What rules can guide us in developing items for an attitudinal scale? Chapters 7–9 provide these guidelines in detail.

### 5.2.4   Phase IV of the Process Model

The last phase (Phase IV) entails an evaluation of the quality of the assessments constructed or selected, prior to their use in actual situations. Validation can be a logical review (Phase IVA); or it can involve empirical work (Phase IVB). In most assessment applications, we will need to do a bit of both.

The first part of validation, Phase IVA, involves *content validation* (AERA, APA, & NCME, 1985; 1999). As we saw in Chapter 3, content validation is a logical, evaluative review conducted by peers or external experts to determine the extent to which the items and assessment as a whole are indeed aligned to the specifications and theoretical underpinnings of the construct. The content-validation procedure also helps in affirming that the questions or tasks are constructed in such a way that they are not vulnerable to potential sources of error that could lower both the validity or reliability of the results. As Chapter 3 indicated, it is at this stage that we evaluate the assessments for *content relevance* and *representativeness*. If the assessment shows a satisfactory "fit" with the construct (as specified in the domain), purposes, and populations of interest, it is ready for use. If it fails to pass the review, we make revisions to the tool. Thus, Phase IVA leads to arrows with feedback loops. In the case study that follows, Case Study 5.1, we will see how teachers used a checklist to content-validate and revise their tools.

Content validation should be the first action that we undertake in the overall validation process (Phase IVA). Historically, when tests were developed mainly for prediction of future behaviors of respondents, test developers often bypassed or devalued the content validation phase. Sound construction requires that we content-validate all assessments, irrespective of their purposes. Phase IVA yields the first body of validity evidence to support interpretations of the construct (AERA, APA, & NCME, 1999).

The second part of the evaluation, *empirical validation* occurs in Phase IVB. The term "empirical" implies actual data collection, observations, and analysis of data generated by the instrument devised, followed by evaluations of the psychometric quality of the results. Phase IVB typically involves field tryouts of the test or items. The question we try to answer here is: Is the information produced by the assessment adequately free of error, free enough to be useful for the purposes and populations identified?

In Chapter 3, we were introduced to various approaches to validation and gathering of quantitative forms of validity evidence. Obtaining quantitative reliability estimates also falls under the work in Phase IVB. In Chapter 13, we will see more details of these procedures. Here, we need to appreciate that

1. The empirical validation work occurs in Phase IVB
2. The results are used to supplement findings of Phase IVA
3. The results help the designer to continually revise and improve the instrument until the targeted levels of quality are achieved

In combination, the logical and empirical analyses will typically reveal areas in which the instrument can be improved. As needed, Phase IV should ideally be followed by adaptations, revisions, and/or complete redesigning of an assessment or its parts *before* it is employed in practical decision-making situations. As Chapter 3 indicated, the depth with which you conduct the Phase IV studies will be a function of the assessment purposes and the seriousness of consequences tied to the assessment results. In formal test development projects, Phase IVB can involve technical investigations dealing with item analysis, validity, reliability, scaling, standard-setting, and norming.

In summary, the Process Model involves systematic steps in planning (Phases I and II), designing or selecting instruments (Phase III), and finally, evaluating and improving the instruments (Phase IVA and B) prior to using them in decision-making contexts. Arrows leading back from the later to the earlier phases of the model in Figure 5.1 attempt to make clear that the process of assessment design, selection, and validation is cyclic and iterative. Theoretically, it could never end. In the practical world, of course, it becomes prudent for us to conclude the process as soon as *the desired levels of meaningfulness, precision, and utility are obtained* from the results.

---

**K e y   C o n c e p t s**

■ Content validation is a procedure for logically reviewing and screening an instrument and its items. Checklists help in conducting such reviews.

■ Empirical validation refers to a variety of procedures that involve field-testing and data collection with the instrument under development, for the purposes of investigating item quality, validity, reliability, and various other psychometric properties of scores.

■ Depending on the purposes for an assessment, the extent of the validation investigations can vary.

## 5.3 A Case Study in Using the Process Model

Let us now shift our attention to an application of the Process Model for classroom decision-making. In Case Study 5.1, high school teachers devise two classroom assessments for a unit of instruction emphasizing critical thinking skills. They follow the four-phase Process Model for designing both a traditional and a performance assessment. As you review the case study, you will encounter terms that were introduced in previous chapters, such as scoring rubrics, weighting, criterion-referenced testing, validity, and reliability coefficients. Refer back to those chapters if you have difficulty following the text. The terms are further elaborated in subsequent chapters.

---

### Case Study 5.1    Using the Process Model for the Development and Validation of Classroom Assessments in User Path 1

***Background.***    Two ninth-grade teachers decided to integrate the teaching of critical thinking skills within their subject area units. In studying the research literature on the topic, they found that while psychologists did not always agree on what constitutes critical thinking, there was a fair degree of consensus on some of the cognitive abilities underlying the attribute (Norris & Ennis, 1989; Nitko, 1996; Woolfolk, 1995). Particularly, the research literature suggested that *critical thinkers* should be able to:

- Deal in an orderly manner with parts of a total problem (a complex whole)
- Seek precise information about problems from credible sources
- Evaluate the accuracy of information
- Take positions and argue with supporting reasons and evidence
- Give good reasons for conclusions they make

Satisfied with their findings, they developed plans to incorporate critical thinking within a language arts unit focusing on nonfiction and humorous writing. Tables 5.1 through 5.4 illustrate the results of their planning and assessment design efforts using the Process Model.

***Phase I:    Identifying Purpose, Population, and Construct.***    In Phase I, the teachers identified their assessment purposes to be *summative-decision-making* at the end of their unit. In particular, they wanted to assign grades to students once the quarter ended. They agreed that they wanted to make *criterion-referenced interpretations* of student performance with the results, not being concerned about how the students stacked up against one another, but rather on their level of proficiency on the critical thinking domain. Their population consisted of all three sections of *ninth graders* whom they were teaching that quarter. The construct they were assessing was, of course, *critical thinking skills.* (Keep in mind that simultaneously they were also developing instructional plans, along with day-to-day lesson plans—although this aspect of their work is not of direct concern to us here.)

*(continued)*

## Case Study 5.1    Continued

*Phase II:  Developing the Assessment Specifications.*    Table 5.1 shows you the full-blown *Assessment Specifications* that the teachers developed. They not only specified the purpose, population, and construct (from their work in Phase I), but also the domain. The *domain specification,* which shows us a list of observable indicators of the construct (critical thinking), helped the teachers begin to operationally define what critical thinking meant to them. You will notice that the indicators in the domain are organized from fairly general to more specific terms. Also, you will find that the indicators are substantively coordinated with the theoretical definition of critical thinking that the teachers discovered through their study of the theoretical literature. In instructional contexts, the *domain* actually consists of the general goals and specific objectives of the targeted curriculum (also called "learning outcomes").

The assessment specifications also show us that the teachers had a very clear vision of the exact types of assessment methods that would help them capture the cognitive skills and processes in the performance domain. They combined the *written, structured-response* (W-SR) and *open-ended* (W-OE, essay) formats. They allocated equal *weight* to each part—indicated by the "50%" next to their chosen assessment method. If tools are designed to match their weighting specifications, the scores from each part will have equal points.

They specified scoring procedures that were appropriate for each assessment method that they chose, with the use of a dichotomous (right/wrong) *key* for the W-SR part and an analytic *rubric* for the W-OE sections of the assessment. To meet their summative decision-making needs, they specified that the assessments would be conducted and *scored by teachers,* rather than, say, by student peers. Finally, they specified that their assessments would be *individually scored* (as opposed to awarding scores to a group or small groups of students).

At the bottom of the Assessment Specification we see a table. This is a *Table of Specification.* It is used to specify exactly how many items will be used to measure the specific indicators in the domain. The number of items reflects the weight allocated to particular sections of the domain. (How many items we specify in the table is a matter of professional judgment. In designing classroom assessments, we would attempt to align the degree of emphasis we place on particular objectives during instruction, with the weights we specify to domain indicators in the assessment specification.)

The Table of Specifications in Table 5.1 depicts the teachers' vision of a 10-item W-SR test with one essay. The weighting that they allocated to the different items varied, and was adjusted by multiplying by different weighting constants, such that each indicator (objective) in the domain was equally weighted.

*Phase III:  Developing or Selecting Assessments.*    Tables 5.2 and 5.3 illustrate a sample set of assessments that fit the requirements set forth in the Assessment Specification that we reviewed in Table 5.1. To provide a context for students to demonstrate critical thinking, the teachers used a humorous article called *HELP!* This selection was synchronized with their emphases in writing instruction, which the teachers incorporated with the teaching of critical thinking skills. Test A illustrates a sample of four W-SR items (of the total of 10) and one essay item that teachers designed to match the specifications. Table 5.4 shows the analytic *rubric* to score the essay.

*Phase IVA:  Logical Reviews.*    Once the assessments were developed, the teachers called on two colleagues to conduct a content validation of the assessments. To help their colleagues in this endeavor, they gave them the assessment specifications, drafts of their assessment tools with

**TABLE 5.1  Assessment Specifications for Critical Thinking Skills Unit with**
*HELP!* **Article**

| | |
|---|---|
| Assessment Purposes: | To make criterion-referenced interpretations of performance tied to the domain; end-or-quarter summative decision-making |
| Population: | Ninth-grade students |
| Construct: | Critical thinking skills |

Domain:

*General Indicator (Instructional Goal)*

1.0  Given documentary information (with or without humorous content), students will conduct a critical analysis and evaluation of the information.

*Specic   Indicators (Objectives)*

The students will:

1.1  Restate/paraphrase key concepts and facts presented in article with accuracy (*Cognitive level: Factual knowledge*).

1.2  Evaluate the contents of the article with respect to credibility, completeness, logical consistency and coherence (*Cognitive level: Higher-order thinking*).

1.3  Take a position for or against the theme of the article, and justify/defend position with clarity and logic (*Cognitive level: Higher-order thinking*).

Assessment Methods(s) and Weight Desired:

1.1             Written, structured-response assessment (50%)

1.2 and 1.3  Written, open-ended assessment–essay (50%, equally distributed by indicator)

Scoring Methods:

1.1             Answer key

1.2 and 1.3  Analytic rubric

Group/Individual Assessment: Individual

Who Assesses:                  Teacher

Sample Assessment:          See Test A with *HELP!* Article

1.1             (Items 1–4)

1 1 and 1 3 (Item 1)

## Table of Specifications

| Domain-Specific Indictors | Cognitive Level | | Weight | Weighted Points |
|---|---|---|---|---|
| | *Factual Knowledge* | *Higher-Order Thinking* | | |
| 1.1 | 10 (W-SR) | | ×1 | 10 |
| 1.2 and 1.3 | | 1 (W-OE) | ×10 | 10 |
| Weighted Points | 10 | 10 | | 20 |

*(continued)*

## Case Study 5.1    Continued

**TABLE 5.2**  *HELP!* **Article: Assessment of Critical Thinking Skills**

### HELP!

We have run across some absolutely irrefutable statistics that show exactly why you are tired. And, brother, it's no wonder you're tired. There aren't as many people working as you may have thought, at least not according to a survey recently completed.

The population of this country is 200 million with 84 million over 60 years of age, which leaves 116 million to do the work.

People under 20 years of age total 75 million, which leaves 41 million to do the work.

There are 22 million employed by the government, which leaves 19 million to do the work.

Four million are in the armed forces, which leaves 15 million to do the work.

Deduct 14,800,000—the number in state and county offices—leaving 200,000 to do the work (except schools and school systems).

There are 188,000 in hospitals, insane asylums, etc., so that leaves 12,000 to do the work.

Now it may interest you to know that there are 11,998 people in jail, so that leaves just TWO PEOPLE to carry the load.

That's you and me—and brother, I'm getting tired of doing everything myself!

answer keys and scoring criteria, and a screening checklist. The checklist assisted the reviewers in looking for *content-relevance* and *representativeness,* as well as a logical screening to check for *reliability* and *utility.*

### A) Content-Based Validity Questions

- Do the learning outcomes (domain indicators) reflect the definition of "critical thinking" found in the theoretical literature?
- Do the items on the assessment, Test A, reflect the cognitive processes specified in the "critical thinking" domain?
- Are the items on Test A distributed to properly represent different parts of the domain specified?
- Is the answer key accurate? Does the scoring rubric for the essay match the domain?
- Do the items match the indicators of the domain?
- Are the items at an appropriate reading and difficulty level for ninth graders?
- Will the assessment results support the intended summative decisions?

### B) Reliability Questions

- Are there enough items in the assessment to get a reliable assessment of the students' critical thinking skills?
- Are there misleading or ambiguous directions that might lead to inconsistent student responses?

**TABLE 5.3  A Few Items from the Sample Assessment (Test A) on Critical Thinking with *HELP!***

---

*Test A*

*Directions:* Read the article *HELP!* and then answer the questions.

The following test contains ten objective type items and one essay item. Read each question carefully before you answer. This test is untimed. However, the average time taken to complete it is 30 minutes. Items 1–4 are worth 1 point each. The essay item is worth 50 points.

For items 1 and 2 choose the best answer.

1. According to the article, the population of the country is:
    a. 200 million
    b. 240 million
    c. 260 million
    d. 300 million

2. Given that 84 million people out of 200 million are above 60 years of age, what percent of the population is left to do the work?
    a. 30%
    b. 36%
    c. 42%
    d. 58%

3. Fill in the blank.
    According to the article, the number of people in the armed forces is
    _____ million.

4. Based on the article, is the following statement True (T) or False (F)?
    There are 11,998 in jail. _____

*Directions for essay:*

The following item is an essay item that requires you to organize your thoughts and knowledge before you present it in a logical, coherent manner. Your score on the item will depend on the clarity and logic of your presentation.

5. Is the rationale given in the article requiring that you don't are third living. What factors were omitted in the article? What are the flaws in the logic? What populations were not accounted for?

[space provided]

---

- Are the conditions of assessment likely to lead to inconsistent student responses?
- Will the rubric help to control for subjectivity of teachers who score the essay?

**C) Utility Questions**
- Will we be able to find materials (e.g., informational articles) easily for the assessments?
- Is the time required for scoring reasonable?

*(continued)*

## Case Study 5.1    Continued

**TABLE 5.4    Rubric for Open-Ended Assessment on Critical Thinking Skills**

Analytic Rating Scale for Essay Item on *HELP!*—Test A

**Subdomain 1. Ability to evaluate content of an article (6 points)**

| | | | |
|---|---|---|---|
| Accuracy of Facts | 0<br>No Facts Accurate | 1 | 2<br>All Facts Accurate |
| Completeness of Answer | 0<br>No Gaps/Logical<br>Inconsistencies<br>Identified | 1 | 2<br>All Gaps Identified |
| Logic and Coherence of Answer | 0<br>Unreasonable,<br>Incoherent Analysis | 1 | 2<br>Highly Coherent,<br>Logical Analysis |

**Subdomain 2. Ability to take and defend position on article with clarity and logic (4 points)**

| | | | |
|---|---|---|---|
| Statement for/against Article | 0<br>Statement Missing/<br>Unclear | 1 | 2<br>Clear Position Taken in<br>Statement |
| Logical Defense of Position | 0<br>Illogical, Poor Defense | 1 | 2<br>Logical, Strong Defense |

**Total Score** (Maximum = 10):

- Do the directions facilitate proper administration of the assessment?
- Are the key and scoring systems easy to use?

*Results of the Logical Review.*    The teachers received valuable information from their peers on the quality of the assessments that they had designed. They discovered some substantive problems that needed to be addressed.

For example, did the 60–40 weights specified on the rubric agree with the weighting the authors wanted to allocate to (Outcomes 1.2 and 1.3)? Further, Item 2 appeared to require computation skills that fell outside the listed domain of skills. Other minor editing errors also needed attention; for example, the true-false Item 4 needed a question mark following the directions. Based on the feedback, the teachers made several revisions to Test A.

*Phase IVB:   Empirical Validation.*    For the empirical phase of the work, the teachers decided to consult with the school district's Research and Evaluation department after they had used the assessments for a few semesters. In particular, they asked for assistance in checking the quality of the items for criterion-referencing, the reliability of the scores, and some convergent validity

---

**TABLE 5.5  Steps in Assessment Design/Selection and Validation**

---

Phase I.
    1. Identify "whom" to assess—the population.
    2. Identify "what" you are assessing—the construct.
    3. Identify "why" you are assessing—the assessment purposes.
    4. Specify the construct domain with observable indicators.

Phase II.
    5. Prepare a more detailed set of assessment specifications.

Phase III.
    6. Develop or select assessment tools to match specifications.
    7. Write or select items/tasks.
    8. Develop or select supporting materials, directions, prompts.
    9. Develop or select scoring key or rubric.
    10. Assemble the tool.

Phase IV.
    11. Conduct a content validation of the instrument.
    12. Conduct empirical validation studies needed to support use of scores in the context of use.
    13. Revise the tool to meet specifications and assessment context (Phase 1). Use the tool in decision-making or research contexts.

---

evidence to evaluate whether the scores from their assessments reflected what other test developers claimed was "critical thinking." They felt that such information would help them use the results of the assessments for other purposes in the future. One of their aims was to disseminate the assessments to other teachers who taught the same curriculum in the school district. The consultants selected only the validation methods that best served the needs of the teachers.

*Assessment Use.*   The teachers are now using the assessments regularly. Some revisions were needed to their assessment tools based on the validation results. The information that the teachers currently have convince them that their assessments are functioning well enough to satisfy their classroom needs. They have also developed a set of similar assessments that tap the same domain, tied to the same specifications. Other teachers in the school who teach critical thinking are now able to use the assessment bank containing their specifications and the collection of assessments, making modifications to meet their purposes and populations. Table 5.5 summarizes the sequence of steps that the teachers followed in the assessment development and validation process.

## 5.4  The Importance of Following a Systematic Process

Why is the Process Model beneficial? If used to our advantage, the Process Model can serve as a safeguard in keeping our design and validation work focused on the purposes, populations, and the construct of interest, thus making the entire effort more efficient and manageable.

One advantage in following the Process Model is that the assessment design is guided by the specifications, leading us to a focus on the behaviors relevant to the construct. In Case Study 5.1, you might have noticed the connections in the content and cognitive processes in the domain on one hand, and in the items to which students were expected to respond on Test A on the other. The tasks in Test A also matched the conditions specified in the domain, in that an informational article with some humorous content was used, maintaining congruence with the overall emphasis in the language arts unit. As required, *HELP!* contained the documentary types of information that students could evaluate to demonstrate their critical thinking abilities. Similarly, the rubric also reflected indicators in the domain.

Such correspondences are necessary for establishing content-based validity, and can be assured if we start with thoughtful planning and tie the assessment design or selection to the specifications. If we dive directly into assessment construction without a guiding plan—the specifications—we might hit or miss the important indicators in the domain. You might refer back to the outcome-driven model of instruction, assessment, and decision-making (in Chapter 2) to see the overlap in the process model to assessment construction and validation, and the outcome-driven approach in classroom practices.

Assessment specifications in Phase II can help us create multiple, parallel assessments that capture generalizable sets of behaviors. Notice that Test A in Case Study 5.1 is only one of several assessments that could be designed to match the specifications in Figure 5.2. Instead of the *HELP!* article, the teachers could have used a newspaper article to measure the same domain of skills, in much the same way. The questions and scoring criteria would still capture the same set of critical thinking skills. This highlights a basic measurement principle; namely, that while individual assessments reflect a sample of specific items or tasks from the domain, *specifications reflect much broader, generalizable domains* of skills and performance. The use of specifications helps in keeping our focus on the larger domain, and thus we are not sidetracked into measuring narrow, task-specific knowledge or skills that are unlikely to transfer elsewhere.

Assessment specifications can be used flexibly by users to either design or select assessment tools. Notice that once the specifications are developed, the users could either select assessments from existing collections that fit the specifications, or design new assessments to match them. In this sense, assessment specifications are analogous in function to an architect's blueprint for designing buildings. Likewise, one could think of specifications as being analogous to the DNA code in a human genome. The human DNA code contains instructions to assemble only human beings—no other animal form could result from those instructions. Well-designed specifications also lead to either the construction or selection of a series of similar assessments tools with similar properties. By linking planning with the production and validation phases, the Process Model gives us a method for controlling assessment quality.

The validation phase of the Process Model is also important for ensuring quality. Assessments developed for one purpose often get employed for other purposes (see Chapter 2). Both logical and empirical evaluations are necessary, but these must be guided by *the purposes and contexts* of assessment use. It is easy to forget this. Evidence of content-based validity alone may not be sufficient to support all the conclusions we wish to make from classroom assessment results. On the other hand, validity evidence from every possible source may not be practical or necessary for every assessment situation.

## Summary

In Chapter 5, we examined a four-phase model, involving a series of tasks that we would perform to develop or select, and then validate assessments tied to particular decision-making contexts (User Paths). The Process Model stipulates a cyclic process, involving planning (Phases I and II), the work of actually designing or selecting the assessment tools (Phase III), content validation of the tools we generate (Phase IVA), and empirical validation of the same tools (Phase IVB). Two products generated in the course of the process are the:

- Assessment specifications (in Phases I–II)
- The assessment tools, linked to the assessment specifications (in Phase III)

The assessment tools usually undergo revisions following validation (in Phase IV), until a level of quality is obtained that meets the demands of the decision-making context. Then the tool is ready for use. Validation, then, is a quality-control process.

Assessment specifications are necessary planning tools that set the design parameters for the instruments that we wish to create or select. For example, a Table of Specifications (also called a test blueprint) is used for designing written, structured-response achievement tests. Such specifications would identify the number of questions that would have to be written to measure particular learning outcomes in the achievement domain. Specifications guide the detailed work of generating the actual assessment tools. Chapters 6 through 9 elaborate the rules and guidelines to follow when we actually construct the items and assemble tools in User Paths 1–6 (Phase III of the Process Model). A well-prepared set of specifications will usually lead to the construction of better assessments.

The Process Model is *iterative*. The feedback loops in Figure 5.1 show that we continue the design, validation, and revision cycle until we get the level of quality we want. Sound evaluative judgment plays an important part in our decisions about quality. To keep the process manageable, we continuously ask ourselves: Is the instrument a good match for the construct and population we originally specified? Will the quality of the information likely to be generated by the tool be a good match for our assessment purposes? Affirmative responses to these questions help us stop the work at an appropriate time.

The Process Model is *generalizable*. That means it can be applied by us to design or select assessments tied to *any* User Path (assessment purpose), to measure *any* construct, to serve the needs of *any* assessment development project—from very formal to relatively informal, or to design any type of assessment tool, from traditional assessments to performance assessments to portfolios. There will be *only minor variations* in the phases of work involved in different situations.

The Process Model is *integrative*. It helps us link the user context with assessment design and validation work. As designers, it helps us to consider the decision-making context when taking actions on assessment design and validation. As users, it helps us consider the context of assessment design and evidence from validation studies before we put an instrument to use. Such integrative links help us in avoiding misuses of assessment tools and promote better assessment practices.

## QUESTIONS FOR CLASS DISCUSSION

1.  Describe an assessment development or selection activity in which you have participated. Compare and contrast the steps you took with the recommended phases of the process model in Chapter 5. As a practitioner in your field of work, evaluate the advantages and disadvantages you see in applying each approach (yours versus the Process Model).

2.  In your own words, describe the parts of the Process Model for assessment design, selection, and validation. What might go wrong in terms of assessment practice if a practitioner were to skip Phases I and II (planning), and go directly to Phase III (developing assessment tools) of the Process Model? List some of the problems you foresee.

3.  What is the purpose of Phase IV (validation) in the Process Model? What might go wrong in terms of assessment practice, if a designer/practitioner chooses to overlook Phase IV and begin using an assessment tool directly after Phase III (design/selection)?

4.  Review some standardized test manuals and popular textbook materials used in teaching different subjects. Find examples of test plans (Assessment Specifications, Tables of Specifications, Test Blueprints) used in (a) a standardized assessment development project, and (b) a nonstandardized assessment development project. What information do they contain? How are they formatted? Compare the usefulness of the plans you find with the one illustrated in Case Study 5.1.

**NOTE:** More structured response exercises with immediate feedback for answers are available on the computer module.

# 6 Specifying the Construct Domain

## Overview

Chapter 6 marks the beginning of Part Two, which deals with procedures for designing or selecting different types of assessment devices using the four-phase Process Model that was introduced to you in Chapter 5. As the objectives for this chapter illustrate, we have now shifted from foundational concepts to procedural skills in educational assessment.

The sixth chapter aims to demonstrate how to specify the *domain* for a construct as we apply the Process Model. How well we specify the domain will directly affect content-based validity of inferences that we subsequently make from the assessment results. Specifying the domain is a necessary step in developing the plan for an assessment tool, which we call the *assessment specifications*. You will recall that in using the Process Model, the two products that the assessment design or selection process will yield are the (1) assessment specifications in Phase II, and the (2) assessment tools in Phase III. Once the domain is specified, it will guide us as we put together a complete set of assessment specifications.

To maintain consistency with prior themes introduced in this book and module, the chapter discusses the Process Model linked to different decision-making paths (User Paths 1–6). The five User Paths applicable to practitioners are:

*User Path 1.* Assessment for teaching and learning
*User Path 2.* Assessment for program planning, evaluation, and policymaking
*User Path 3.* Assessment for screening and diagnosis of exceptionalities
*User Path 4.* Assessment for guidance and counseling
*User Path 5.* Assessment for admissions, certification, scholarships, or awards

The chapter will first deal with procedures for specifying the domain for constructs typically measured in User Path 1. Next, it will illustrate how to specify the domain when assessing attributes in User Paths 2–5.

## CHAPTER 6 OBJECTIVES

After studying this chapter and completing the structured exercises in the module, you should be able to:

1. Distinguish between the concepts of learning and achievement as they apply to User Path 1

2. Given an assessment need in a particular User Path, identify the construct to assess

3. Apply recommended guidelines when specifying the domain for a construct in User Paths 1–6

4. Given a construct to assess, write and organize indicator statements in the domain

5. Evaluate the quality of a domain specification from a measurement perspective

6. Use taxonomies to clarify the nature and levels of learning outcomes in achievement domains (User Path 1)


# 6.1    SPECIFYING THE DOMAIN FOR CONSTRUCTS IN USER PATH 1

## 6.1.1    Distinctions between Learning and Achievement

Teachers in User Path 1 design curriculum-based assessment tools. "What" teachers teach and "what" they assess (the constructs) through formal or informal tools, should ideally be linked. Teachers measure constructs dealing with the desired *learning outcomes,* or what they expect students to have learned through a formally delivered curriculum in school. But, is the targeted construct in classroom teaching contexts *achievement?* Or is it *learning?*

So far, the terms "learning" and "achievement" have not been differentiated in any systematic way in our discussion. To begin the work on specifying domains in User Path 1, we need to pay some attention to whether these two commonly heard labels for constructs measured in Path 1 are one and the same in the view of learning psychologists and theorists.

Drawing from recent literature on cognitive psychology, Cizek (1997) made a distinction between the terms "learning" and "achievement." He defined *learning* as a change that occurs as a result of an individual's experience and the active construction of knowledge and processing of information that is not the simple result of maturation or development of an individual (p. 3). Learning is an internal cognitive process that could be instigated both by external experiences or internal reorganizations of our knowledge structures. External influences that result in learning could include anything other than our biological development, including a formal course of study delivered through school. Internal influences include events occurring within a person's mind, such as thinking, reflection, and a reorganization of cognitive structures to make new connections (called *schemas* by cognitive psychologists). In particular circumstances, learning could result from some combination of both internal and external factors.

Most definitions of *achievement* differ from current understandings of learning. Achievement refers to "knowledge gained or skills developed in the school subjects, usually designated by test scores or by marks assigned by teachers, or both" (Good, 1973, p. 7). This definition of achievement presupposes a match between the curriculum delivered and the assessments teachers design or use. It tells us that if we could glean the body of skills and concepts embedded in a subject area curriculum, it could well serve as the "construct domain" from which we could design classroom assessment tools.

Based on distinctions made by learning theorists, then, do we measure "learning" or "achievement" when we engage in assessment design as classroom teachers? Here are some conclusions suggested by Cizek's discussion.

- Assessments related to a defined curriculum are better called "achievement tests" rather than measures of learning, because they tend to be indirect and fallible assessments of learning. Learning involves internal cognitive reorganizations that are not directly visible and often incidental in their occurrence. For this reason, learning (as psychologists now view it) is very difficult, if not impossible to capture completely through assessment tools we design. We could view achievement as an *index* of learning, but must recognize that it is often a somewhat limited one.
- *Achievement* requires a performance or a demonstration by the student, related to a defined set of curriculum outcomes. In fact, it is described by Good & Brophy (1986) as the "performance potential of learning." However, learning is not a necessary condition for achievement to be demonstrated. This means that achievement, as indexed by assessment results, can be high even when learning is low. This would happen when a person gets a high score due to prior exposure to similar assessment tasks outside the delivery of the curriculum or simply by luck in guessing. Similarly, learning can be high, but achievement low. The last situation would arise when what is learned by an individual remains untapped by the demonstration required by an assessment exercise.

The above theoretical distinction between learning and achievement is important to bear in mind. It will remind us that when we use the common label of "achievement" to refer to domains tapped with curriculum-based assessments (as we will do in this chapter), inferences we make with the results will be a direct function of the learning outcomes that we specify in the construct domain. The links we can establish between the assessment items or tasks and the outcomes listed in the domain will depend on the clarity of the domain specification. Inferences of actual "learning" could also be limited by the format of the assessment items or tasks we employ as indicators of the different learning outcomes. Choice of an appropriate assessment method for substantially different outcomes will improve the validity of our inferences about the underlying construct.

## 6.1.2 Processes and Products of Learning

In User Path 1, then, our main mission is to assess what students attain through exposure to formal instruction in a scholastic setting. Advances in cognitive psychology have suggested new models for teaching, learning, and assessment in school (Herman et al., 1992; Marzano et al., 1993; Resnick & Resnick, 1992; Wolf et al., 1991). The constructivist movement in cognitive psychology, concerned with how a learner actively constructs meanings about this world, holds that it is beneficial to assess both the *processes* and *products* of learning through applied activities. Thus, to begin the domain specification exercise, we must first recognize that the "achievement" domain could be made up of two kinds of learning outcomes—*process* and *product outcomes*.

Process outcomes deal with *how* an individual completes a task or solves a problem.

They involve cognitive or other multi-step procedures that students employ to find solutions. Using a scientific method to conduct a research study is an example of a process outcome. An example of a process outcome in sports would be: "The student will use the correct technique to execute a golf swing." In the second example, the subject or examinee has to demonstrate a technique (a process) taught by the coach. Emphasis on following a prescribed set of procedures is the hallmark of a process outcome.

Product outcomes, on the other hand, focus on the final *result* or solution to a task. Calculating the area of a room, or writing a book report are examples of product outcomes, where we would place greater importance on the student getting the "correct" answer/solution, irrespective of the process followed by them. Product outcomes emphasize whether or not the learner can deliver the right response, result, or product.

In some tasks, we could emphasize both process and product outcomes during assessment, such as in the "use of a writing process (process outcome) to compose a story (product outcome)." In the event that both the process and product are valued parts of the curriculum, we may have to make a decision as to whether we wish to assess both or just one of the two targeted outcomes.

**Key Concepts**

- In User Path 1, teachers measure the construct: "achievement." The achievement domain is made up of the learning outcomes that teachers expect students to master.
- "Learning" and "achievement" are not interchangeable concepts.
- The targeted outcomes of learning can either be process or product outcomes.

### 6.1.3   The Achievement Domain in User Path 1

The procedures for specifying the achievement domain for assessment purposes run parallel to the procedures for developing a teachable curriculum. The only difference is that for assessment design or selection we need higher levels of clarity and specificity in the outcome statements. Metaphorically speaking, we could think of the *achievement domain* in User Path 1 as the entire expanse or territory of knowledge, cognitive skills, attitudes, or behaviors that is targeted for learning in an educational program or course. The content and structure of this territory would depend on the subject area or discipline of focus. As we saw in Chapter 1, the construct to be measured, achievement, can take on very different meanings when it is operationally defined by different instructors for given units, semesters, or courses. This is because individual instructors draw what they want to teach from the existing knowledge base in their curricular areas, using their professional judgment.

The long-term outcomes of an educational program are typically addressed by teachers through more manageable segments that take the form of time-bound instructional units or courses of study. These units focus on learning outcomes that are more limited in scope, and represent what teachers can realistically expect of their students in shorter time periods. Over many years and instructors, as the instructional units build on one another, we expect them to cumulatively lead to the accomplishment of the broader, more complex goals of a long-term educational program. What guidelines exist to guide instructors in the domain specification exercise for individual units of instruction?

***National Trends in the Organization of Achievement Domains.*** There is no single "correct" method for specifying an achievement domain in Path 1. Strong differences in viewpoints are apparent as we move from one discipline to the next, but national subject-area associations provide us with some useful designs to follow. In most nationally published curricular domains, the learning outcomes are organized from very broad areas to gradually narrower parts arranged in a hierarchy (see Figures 6.1–6.3). Modern curricula use the terms, *standards* or *strands,* to refer to the broadest categories of knowledge, processes, and skills within a discipline. The building blocks of the broader outcomes, or the component information and skills, are variously called *outcomes, benchmarks, competencies, targets,* or *grade-level expectations,* depending on the level of specificity at which they are broken down. The traditional terminology of *goals* for broad outcomes, and *objectives* for more narrow statements, is rarely encountered in curriculum documents developed by national subject area experts today. However, they carry the very same meaning in terms of their place in the hierarchy of curriculum design. Because of their association with narrowly defined, highly specific behavioral objectives and the basic skills testing movement of the 1970s , "goals" and "objectives" have been eliminated from many educators' vocabularies today.

Figure 6.1 provides an idea of the implied leveling or hierarchical structure found in the *National Standards for United States History* (National Center for History in Schools, NCHS, 1994). This example of a content domain spans grade levels 5–12, and distinguishes between *historical thinking standards* (process outcomes) and *historical content standards* (product outcomes focusing on knowledge and comprehension of historical facts). The five major, broadly stated thinking "Standards" are to the left of the diagram in Figure 6.1. Each of these standards, such as the one labeled as "Historical Analysis and Interpretation," is then broken down further into component thinking skills and abilities, called "Benchmarks." The "content standards" in history (not shown in the figure) deal with ten major eras in U.S. history starting with the 1620s through to modern times (1970 to the present) and are similarly broken down into smaller elements. Such hierarchal arrangements, from general to greater levels of specificity, or from higher to lower levels of complexity, are also evident in published national standards for science (National Research Council, NRC, 1996) and mathematics (National Council of Teachers of Mathematics, NCTM, 1989, 1995).

In contrast, the document on *Standards for English Language Arts* (1996)—published jointly by the National Council of Teachers of English (NCTE) and the International Reading Association (IRA)—lists 12 broadly articulated standards (see Figure 6.2 for an excerpt). The NCTE and IRA don't identify specific skills and information subsumed under these standards, and they don't authorize reprinting of the standards without their accompanying text, which discourages further analysis or breakdown of their content domain. The language arts organizations have taken the position that dissecting the standards into their component elements will destroy the holistic nature of language learning and communication (NCTE & IRA, 1996). Marzano & Kendall (1996) noted that the

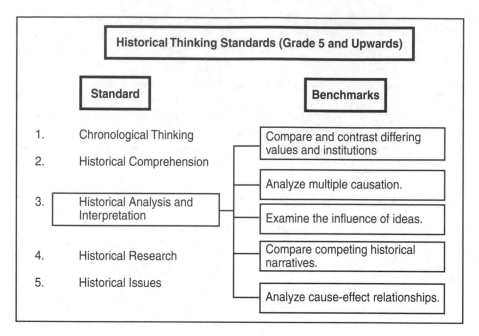

**FIGURE 6.1    An Achievement Domain in History**

*Source:* Excerpted with permission from the *National Standards for United States History: Exploring the American Experience* (1994).

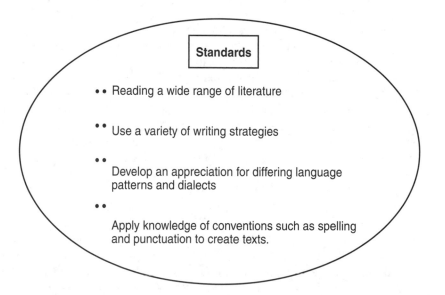

**FIGURE 6.2    An Achievement Domain in Language Arts**

*Source:* Excerpted with permission from *Standards for the English Language Arts* (1996), developed and published by the National Council of Teachers of English (NCTE) and the International Reading Association (IRA).

NCTE/IRA position has not met with universal acceptance, possibly leading to a discontinuation of federal funding for their standards development project.

***What Procedures and Language Shall We Use?*** As we begin to select and articulate the learning outcomes for the domain we wish to assess, however, we need an agreed-upon method and language to use. Figure 6.3 shows a working model, called a "tree-diagram," for use in the analysis and organization of achievement domains. We will use a tree-diagram approach to specify the domain of learning outcomes in User Path 1. The contrasting philosophies reflected in the manner in which different subject-area domains have been organized highlight the fact that procedures for specifying the domain vary across disciplines.

Tree diagrams assume that most subject areas can be organized in some graduated or hierarchical format. This approach is similar to those employed by NCHS, NRC, and NCTM (see tree in Figure 6.1). A tree illustrates pictorially how a generally stated, complex, and often vague standard or outcome can be broken down into its building blocks. These blocks, in turn, can be broken down into smaller and smaller elements. Analyzing the achievement domain, as shown in Fig. 6.1, helps us to bring the broader outcomes of learning into sharper focus, much like bringing a camera lens to clearly focus on a picture we wish to take, so that the achievement targets can be "hit" accurately with the assessment and instructional strategies that we design.

The breaking down of broad outcomes into component skills might superficially appear to be a throwback to older and outdated behaviorist learning theories which assume that learning occurs sequentially in little pieces that are linked together like a chain. It is this fear that prevented organizations such as NCTE from breaking down broad language arts strands into their component elements (see Figure 6.2). Using a tree diagram need not suggest that our teaching or assessment will focus individually on the narrow elements only. Nor does it mean that we reject the constructivist view of learning and assessment, which posits that learning is holistic and involves building of complex cognitive schema. The tree organization does not dictate the sequence in which instructional delivery should occur; nor is it intended to portray how schema become organized or reorganized in individuals' minds during the learning process. The tree diagram is simply a way to organize the expected learning outcomes in a way that clarifies the processes and products of learning that we will target during assessment design.

To properly assess something that is undefined, it is necessary for us to identify all its relevant parts and facets in as clear terms as possible. Once we have the domain clearly specified, we have a choice as to whether we assess each outcome individually or target clusters of outcomes in integrated, whole tasks that we situate in "real" contexts. Both options become open to us and possible only after we have the domain of targeted outcomes clearly outlined and defined in observable terms.

As we identify and differentiate the "big concepts" from their smaller components with the tree-diagramming method, we need consistent terminology to refer to the general and specific levels of outcomes in the hierarchy. When it comes to specifying the domain with outcome statements, there are multiple terms in educational documents that serve as synonyms. Some of these terms, such as *objectives, benchmarks, outcomes,* and *competencies,* were mentioned earlier. Table 6.1 attempts to group and clarify the meanings of some common labels for learning outcomes. The italicized terms there are the ones that

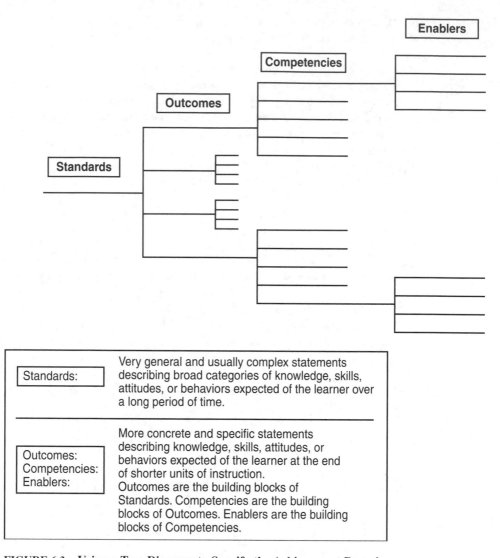

FIGURE 6.3    Using a Tree Diagram to Specify the Achievement Domain

you will find used in this book and module, namely, outcomes (general indicators), competencies (more specific indicators), and enablers (most specific indicators).

***Steps in Specifying an Achievement Domain.***    When planning, teachers would specify the achievement domain by listing and organizing the targeted learning outcomes for a given unit, course, or program of study in the form of a tree diagram (see Box 6.1). The full range of content, skills, cognitive processes, behaviors and/or attitudes to be taught and assessed become the domain to be assessed in User Path 1. Examine the example of a mathematics

**TABLE 6.1  Domain Specification in User Path 1: Synonymous Terms**

| Level of Generality in Outcome Description | Synonymous Labels* |
|---|---|
| 1. Broadest statements of expected learning outcomes | ■ strands<br>■ key concepts<br>■ standards |
| 2. Somewhat more specific statements of expected learning outcomes** | ■ *outcomes*<br>■ *instructional goals*<br>■ general achievement<br>■ targets<br>■ learning targets<br>■ *general indicators*<br>■ benchmarks |
| 3. Even narrower statements of expected learning outcomes** | ■ *objectives*<br>■ *competencies*<br>■ *enabling competencies*<br>■ *enablers*<br>■ specific learning targets<br>■ *specific indicators*<br>■ grade-level expectations |

\* Italicized terms are used in this book.

\*\* Levels at which teachers or instructors typically operate.

B O X  **6.1**

## Steps in Domain Specification for User Path 1

**Step 1**   Review appropriate source documents in the subject area, such as textbook materials and curriculum guides. Identify all the targeted topics and skills to teach and assess. Set a perimeter around this "domain." Label the construct so that you can begin to define the boundaries of the achievement domain more clearly.

**Step 2**   Visualize competent *exiting* learners, and brainstorm what they should know and/or be able to do *at the end of the course/unit of instruction* if they were masters of the domain. As you brainstorm, begin to separate the *content* to be assessed from the *behavior,* and the *conditions* of performance. Similarly, separate *process outcomes* from *product outcomes*.

**Step 3**   Make sure that the outcome statements focus on *end results* of instruction, not on instructional activities that could potentially lead to learning. Outcome statements should be written in terms of student learning, not teacher activities.

*(continued)*

# 6.1  Continued

**Step 4**   Formulate the targeted learning outcomes so that they are clear, unambiguous statements. Use Guidelines A through D in Table 6.3 to write crisp and clear statements of targeted outcomes.

**Step 5**   Maintain the substantive links of the outcome statements to the source documents (see Step 1). Ensure that the domain is as complete as it can be.

**Step 6**   Organize the statements in the form of a "tree," so that the simpler, more specific outcomes are subsumed under the broader, more complex ones. Cluster outcome statements that appear to be related in content or processes within the domain in a way that makes logical sense, either from a teaching/learning perspective or from a theoretical one.

**Step 7**   Use a *taxonomy of learning behaviors* to identify the levels of cognitive, affective, or motor processing in the outcomes listed in the achievement domain.

---

**TABLE 6.2   A Mathematics Achievement Domain**

---

**Construct:**        **Math Achievement in a Unit for First Graders**

Outcome 1:

1.0   The student will correctly add single digit numbers without regrouping and evaluate/revise answers as needed. (*Higher-Order Thinking*)

   **Competencies:**

   1.1   Add sets of numbers from 0–9, without regrouping, using concrete objects or pictures. (*Application*)
   1.2   Add sets of numbers from 0–9, without regrouping, presented in vertical or horizontal notation on paper. (*Application*)
   1.3   Check/revise answers by representing sets added in pictures (*dots, houses, stick figures*). (*Complex Procedural Skills*)

Outcome 2:

2.0   The student will correctly subtract single digit numbers, 0–9, without regrouping and will evaluate/ revise answers as needed. (*Higher-Order Thinking*)

   **Competencies:**

   2.1   Subtract sets of numbers from 0–9, without regrouping, with the help of concrete objects or pictures. (*Application*)
   2.2   Subtract sets of numbers from 0–9, without regrouping, presented in vertical or horizontal notation on paper. (*Application*)
   2.3   Check/revise answers by representing subtraction problem in pictures (*dots, houses, stick figures*). (*Complex Procedural Skills*)

**Prerequisite Competencies:**

   Recognize numbers 0–9 by name and symbol. (*Factual Knowledge*)
   Demonstrate number sense for sets (0–9), using concrete objects. (*Factual Knowledge*)
   Represent numbers 0–9 in writing. (*Application and Motor Skills*)

achievement domain for a first-grade unit shown in Table 6.2, with reference to the seven major steps for specifying the domain. Table 6.3 elaborates on these steps.

*Step 1. Sources for the Achievement Domain.*   The sources for the outcome statements can include relevant curriculum resources such as textbooks, curriculum guides, manuals, and other appropriate professional literature and materials. Selection of the information for a domain must ultimately be left to the professional judgment of the teacher or assessment developers. The process begins by setting a perimeter around topics for a given unit of instruction, and then bringing the domain into sharper focus by articulating the outcomes representing the construct in progressively more specific terms.

You might face some frustration in coming up with authoritative documents that indisputably define the domain in which you are interested. Use sources that are defensible from a theoretical standpoint and relevant to the setting in which you work. Useful sources include:

- Curriculum documents published by state or national subject area associations
- The mission/goals of your local institution or school district programs
- Current textbooks adopted by your district or institution for a particular level
- Professional literature

From the reference materials you select, you will then need to specify in further detail the outcome statements as they apply to your own instructional setting in particular units.

*Steps 2–4. Bringing the Domain into Sharper Focus.*   Guidelines on how to write the outcome statements with clarity are given in Table 6.3, and illustrated with examples taken from mathematics domains, language arts domains, and other subject areas, including a professional training course for IBM sales trainees. The variety of examples is intended to demonstrate that the procedures generalize across most disciplines. Each outcome statement should identify the *content* and *behavior* dimension. Additionally, in some cases, you might want to add the *condition,* or even a *performance criterion* to the statement. The outcomes must be gradually honed down from general, somewhat vague statements to ones that are more and more clear, concrete, and specific.

The refined version of the domain in Table 6.2 might actually arise from a teacher's early brainstormed ideas about a proficient learner shown in Figure 6.4. Although the notes in Figure 6.4 appear disorganized, you can see that the teacher successfully identified the most important dimensions of the learning outcomes in the earliest stages of domain specification, namely, the *behaviors* (e.g., add), *content* (numbers 0–9), and *conditions* of performance (with concrete objects or using a horizontal written format). In the domain that emerged, none of the statements reflected learning activities that the teacher or students might use to attain the outcomes.

Note that there are some important differences between statements of learning *outcomes* versus teaching/learning *activities.* In a language arts class, reading or listening to a novel that is read aloud is an activity; but identifying the characters and main plot of the novel is an outcome of that teaching/learning activity. Likewise, in a biology class, viewing plant tissue under a microscope is an activity; distinguishing different cell and tissue types is a learning outcome that results from that activity. During assessment design, it is the learning outcomes that we use to specify the achievement domain in User Path 1.

**TABLE 6.3   Specifying an Achievement Domain: STEP 4—Clarifying Outcome Statements in Terms of Content, Behavior, Conditions, and Criterion Levels**

A. Outcome statements should at least clarify the CONTENT and the BEHAVIOR to be assessed. Distinguish between product and process outcomes.

*Examples of Product Outcomes*

| BEHAVIOR | CONTENT |
|---|---|
| The students/trainees will . . . | |
| A.1. Define . . . | the term "metaphor." |
| A.2. Provide examples to distinguish between . . . | "metaphors" and "similes." |
| A.3. Describe . . . | the benets  of an IBM network to a customer. |
| A.4. Deduce . . . | a geometric proof using the Pythagorean Theorem. |

*Examples of Process Outcomes*

| | |
|---|---|
| A.5. Use systematic questioning techniques to determine . . . | patient health histories. |
| A.6. Follow rules while driving . . . | a standard vehicle in a large city thoroughfare. |

B. If relevant to what is to be learned, also clarify the CONDITIONS under which the knowledge, skill, or behaviors will be demonstrated.

*Examples of Outcomes with Conditions Specified*

(CONDITIONS)
B.1. *Given a graphing calculator,* the student will . . .

| (BEHAVIOR) | (CONTENT) |
|---|---|
| graph . . . | a trigonometric function. |

(CONDITIONS)
B.2. *Given specifications for file size and number of copies to transmit,* the IBM sales representative will . . .

| (BEHAVIOR) | (CONTENT) |
|---|---|
| calculate . . . | the standard fee for sending a file via the IBM file transfer system. |

(CONDITION)
B.3. *Given the length and the width,* the student will . . .

| (BEHAVIOR) | (CONTENT) |
|---|---|
| calculate . . . | the area of a room. |

(CONDITION)
B.4. *Given a selection of sonnets by Shakespeare,* the student will . . .

| (BEHAVIOR) | (CONTENT) |
|---|---|
| identify and analyze . . . | literary devices used. |

**TABLE 6.3    Continued**

*A Poor Example of Specifying the Condition:*

(CONDITION)
B.5. *Given a paper and pencil,* the student will . . .

| (BEHAVIOR) | (CONTENT) |
|---|---|
| identify and analyze . . . | literary devices. |

C. When designing or selecting an assessment for criterion-referencing, it is often necessary to add a CRITERION LEVEL OF PERFORMANCE, or the STANDARD that the teacher will use to decide on student mastery of the outcome.

*Examples*

C.1. Given specifications for file size and number of copies to transmit, the sales representative will calculate the standard fee for sending a file via the IBM file transfer services *with 80% accuracy.*
(CRITERION LEVEL OF PROFICIENCY)

C.2. Given an excerpt from the emergent level literature series, the student will read the passage aloud *with 90% word recognition.*
(CRITERION LEVEL OF PROFICIENCY)

D. General outcomes (i.e., standards statements in a subject area domain) might be very broad and relatively ambiguous, but their building blocks should be more clearly and explicitly stated. Use OBSERVABLE *action* verbs or words to add clarity to behaviors in outcome statements at the specific level.

*Examples of Observable Action Verbs*

D.1a. Know the definition of the term "metaphor."
*Poor! Know* is not an observable, action verb.

D.1b. Identify examples of metaphors used in a passage.
*Better!!*

D.2a. Understand the use of "metaphors."
*Poor! Understand* is not an observable, action verb.

D.2b. Use "metaphors" and "similes" to enhance written descriptions.
*Better!!*

---

The *conditions* in outcome statements must be *relevant* to a learner's demonstration of proficiency on the behaviors and content specified, whether it is a product or a process outcome. In Example B.5 (Table 6.3), we see an example where the condition specified concerns "using a paper and pencil" in an outcome dealing with analyzing literary devices. Although "using a paper and pencil" would be the most likely condition under which responses will be made by students here, it is an irrelevant condition to specify for assessing a person's ability to analyze literary devices, the content focus of the outcome. In B.4, however, the condition requiring a student to work with a particular body of literary works (sonnets) adds both substantive meaning and clarity to the achievement that is targeted by the teacher.

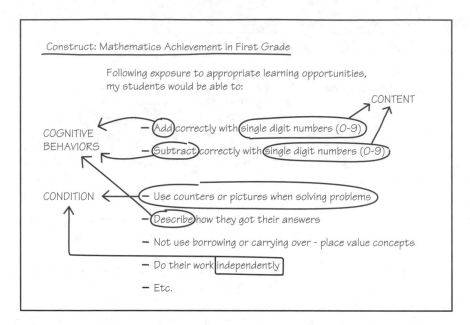

**FIGURE 6.4   Specifying an Achievement Domain: Brainstorming Outcomes**

*Step 5. Review the Defined Achievement Domain*   Once your domain is defined with general and specific outcomes, check back to make sure that the connections are intact in terms of content, processes, behaviors, and conditions highlighted in the original source documents. Just as we do not want to go beyond what the theoretically accepted definition of the domain might be, nor do we want to have major gaps in the domain that we define.

For example, if the domain in Table 6.2, *Mathematics Achievement in First Grade,* included an outcome on multiplication, it would go beyond what most first grade mathematics curriculum documents would include as a developmentally appropriate task for students of this age. In a similar vein, if the condition that first graders add using concrete objects was omitted from the outcome statements, that could be seen as an "omission" in the domain specified. Recent publications of NCTM (1995) emphasize the use of hands-on approaches while assessing mathematics learning in younger children.

*Step 6. "Tree" Organization and Grouping.*   Organization of the outcome statements within the domain should make both practical and theoretical sense to the teacher or assessment designer. In Table 6.2, we see that there is one broad "addition" outcome with a few competencies subsumed beneath it. These are in a separate cluster from those involving "subtraction" skills. Such an organization of outcome statements suggests that the teacher is likely to teach addition and subtraction in separate lessons, attending to the former set of skills before the latter. The prerequisite skills, deemed by the teacher to be common requirements for developing addition and subtraction skills, are in a group by themselves. A "tree-like" organization is implied in the outcome arrangement.

*Step 7. Classify Learning Behaviors.* A taxonomic analysis of the outcomes in the Mathematics Achievement in First Grade domain adds further to their meaning and clarity. In Table 6.2 we see parenthetic information on the teacher's analysis of the levels of cognition targeted for the learner—Higher-Order Thinking, Application, or Factual Knowledge. Such analyses are done using a taxonomy of learning behaviors and outcomes.

The taxonomy used in Table 6.2 is an adaptation of Bloom's taxonomy (Bloom et al., 1956), and indicates the nature and complexity of cognitive processing required by a student to perform the expected tasks. Labeled as the Functional Taxonomy, it is further elaborated in Table 6.5 and later in this chapter. The taxonomic analysis reveals that a prerequisite skill, such as "recognize numbers from 0–9," requires a student to simply demonstrate knowledge of numbers by recall, and is classified by the teacher as a Factual Knowledge outcome. The adding and subtracting competencies (1.1 and 2.1) are at the Application level, as the teacher will expect the student to apply some rules or a step-by-step procedure taught in class to come up with a solution. The evaluation and checking of answers is a Complex Procedural Skill, a *process outcome,* where the child will not only have to apply the multistep procedure to get to the right answer, but another to verify it, with some judgment involved in the process. If a child is expected to employ all of the competencies in a holistic task (all of Outcome 1.0, for instance), the teacher would classify that level of performance as a Higher-Order Thinking outcome, as it would call for complex levels of cognitive functioning and integration of multiple skills and abilities.

## 6.1.4 A Language Arts Domain

Another example of a finished domain specification for User Path 1 is illustrated in Table 6.4. The construct is labeled "Reading Aloud with Comprehension." The tree-diagram method is again employed to clarify and break down the domain of targeted outcomes. There are two major outcomes—oral reading fluency and reading comprehension, respectively. This particular domain is also drawn from a first-grade curriculum. As is evident, the broad outcome, 1.0, requires students to recognize words fluently while reading aloud, using certain reading skills to strategically cue themselves or sound out words. There is a *performance criterion* set by the teacher or assessment designer on Outcome 1.0 (90% word accuracy), suggesting that a criterion-referenced assessment would be designed. Three of the competencies, 1.2–1.4, are classified at Application levels of the taxonomy. Outcome 2.0 has a different focus, dealing with comprehension of what is read; the competencies 2.1–2.5 spell out observable behaviors that the teacher will use as indicators of "comprehension."

A teacher or assessment designer could choose to design or select an assessment tool to assess both the outcomes together in an integrated manner. They could also simply focus on selected portions of the domain at particular times, using a different assessment method for each portion of the domain. The higher the clarity in outcome statements of the domain specified, the easier it will be for you to make a sound selection of the best assessment method(s) to fit your domain.

**TABLE 6.4    Example of an Achievement Domain in Reading/Language Arts**

**Construct:          Reading Aloud with Comprehension (6–7 year olds)**

Outcome 1:

1.0   When reading aloud, students will recognize 90% of words in passages selected from the 1st- and 2nd-grade, literature-based reading list *(complex procedural skills)*.

    **Competencies:**

    1.1   Read words by sight *(factual knowledge)*.
    1.2   Use semantic cues, pictorial cues, and context cues to read words and text *(application)*.
    1.3   Apply phonics skills to sound out unknown words *(application)*.
    1.4   Read with appropriate pauses and expression to convey meaning *(application)*.

Outcome 2:

2.0   Students will summarize passages they read by synthesizing the main ideas, plot, sequence of events and characters in stories selected from the 1st- and 2nd-grade literature series.

    **Competencies:**

    2.1   Identify main ideas in passages *(factual knowledge)*.
    2.2   Describe the main characters and events *(factual knowledge)*.
    2.3   Retell the order of events in story *(factual knowledge)*.
    2.4   Synthesize the plot, setting and characters *(higher-order thinking)*.
    2.5   Write 5 complete sentences to summarize plot, setting and characters of story *(higher-order thinking)*.

## 6.1.5    Other Ways to Specify the Domain: Concept-Mapping

Although the tree-diagramming approach is the method employed in this book and module, you may have seen other methods that attempt to achieve similar ends. Our aim is basically to clarify the content, behaviors, and cognitive or other processes that are embedded in a curriculum, and that will be targeted through the instructional and assessment design processes that we (teachers) employ. An alternate way to specify the domain is in the format of a concept map (Greeno, 1976). Concept maps show a breakdown and interrelationships among the content elements of a defined curriculum, focusing on a theme, such as Cultures in social studies, or Sound in science. Such maps show a subject area expert's representation of critical parts of a construct domain and how they are expected to relate to one another during learning. For example, one could begin with a definition of what the concept "culture" means in designing a thematic unit on "Cultures." From that primary concept, we could think of two main idea strands; how cultures are common and how cultures are different. From these secondary concepts, many other ideas could branch out, leading to a network of schematic relationships that the teacher could use as the framework for both instruction and assessment design. (See Valencia, Paerson, Peters, & Wixson, 1989 for an example of a concept map on a "cultures" theme.)

---

**Key Concepts**

- Achievement domains in User Path 1 can be specified by following a 7-step procedure.
- A tree diagram is one approach to specifying the domain for a construct we wish to measure.

---

# 6.2   Taxonomies of Learning Outcomes

The domain specification examples made use of a *functional taxonomy* to clarify the targeted learning outcomes in the construct domains. A *learning taxonomy* is a classification system that teachers and assessment developers can use to analyze and obtain a deeper understanding of the types of behaviors or levels of cognitive complexity that will be targeted for assessment. Classifying outcomes in the domain by taxonomic category helps in the selection of assessment methods that are the best "fit" for the parts of the domain in which we are most interested. Memorization of facts can be appropriately assessed by a structured-response format; reasoning and critical thinking, on the other hand, could call for an open-ended assessment method; attitudes and social behaviors might require a different assessment method altogether.

How we classify the outcomes will depend on the taxonomy we use. We have several learning taxonomies to choose from as we go about the work of assessment design, each with different degrees of usefulness with different domains. This section of the chapter will address three alternative taxonomies: Bloom's taxonomy; the Dimensions of Learning taxonomy; and a Functional Taxonomy.

## 6.2.1   Bloom's Taxonomy

The most prominent learning taxonomy in use in education is the classic *Taxonomy of Educational Objectives* (Bloom et al., 1956), better known as Bloom's taxonomy. In this system, learning outcomes can be classified into three major areas or "domains." (Do not confuse his "domains" with our use of the term "construct or achievement domain.") These are broadly construed areas of cognitive, affective, and psychomotor learning. Bloom's *cognitive domain* includes educational objectives dealing with the development of intellectual skills and understandings. The *affective domain* deals with objectives focusing on the development of attitudes, values, and appreciations. The *psychomotor domain* includes all objectives dealing with physical and motor skill development.

In an early analysis, Krathwohl et al. (1964) determined that the biggest percent of educational objectives tend to fall under Bloom's Cognitive Domain. An excellent elaboration of Bloom's taxonomy with illustrative objectives in each of the three major Domains and their subcategories was prepared by Gronlund (2000). Gronlund's work can serve as a useful resource for us as we proceed with assessment design activities.

Bloom's *cognitive domain* can be further broken down into a hierarchical system with six categories that cumulatively build on each other, as follows. For learners to perform at a higher level (say, the application level), they would have to incorporate all the lower taxonomic levels of functioning, such as knowledge and comprehension.

- **Knowledge**        Requiring only remembering by the learner (lowest level)
- **Comprehension**    Requiring basic understanding of the material
- **Application**      Requiring use of information or skill in a new setting
- **Analysis**         Requiring break down, differentiation, and analysis of material
- **Synthesis**        Requiring compiling, composing, or creation of material
- **Evaluation**       Requiring comparing, contrasting, judgment, or criticism of material (highest level)

Research has shown that in assessment development contexts, experts in curriculum and testing have successfully used the "knowledge" and "comprehension" categories of Bloom's cognitive taxonomy to classify both educational objectives and test items. The distinction of the "application" level from the remaining cognitive categories has also held up in applied settings. When it comes to the "analysis," "synthesis," and "evaluation" categories, however, expert consensus has been hard to reach, leading authors such as Hopkins (1998) to comment that "agreement is the exception, rather than the rule" among experts who attempt applications with the higher categories of Bloom's taxonomy (p. 175).

### 6.2.2   Dimensions of Learning

A need for alternate taxonomic tools emerged as curricular domains changed in content and complexity in recent years. The Dimensions of Learning model, offered by Marzano, Pickering, and McTighe (1993) recognizes five major categories of learning that we could assess. The authors of the Dimensions of Learning model (see Box 6.2) state that effective learning results from interaction among the five dimensions. Each of their five dimensions are elaborated next with an example of a task aimed at assessing Dimension 3.

We can see from the example of the Error Analysis task that if the targeted outcomes of schooling are judged to fall under Dimension 3, we will have to think in significantly different ways with respect to both how we deliver the curriculum and in how we design assessments to tap achievement. Complex types of thinking are expected of the learner and the emphasis is on integrated use of such cognitive processes. Often the tasks deal with real world problems. Like the one shown, many other examples of Dimensions of Learning tasks require problem-solving in groups.

---

BOX **6.2**

## Assessment Using the Dimensions of Learning Model

**Dimension 1: Positive Attitudes and Perceptions about Learning**
This dimension has to do with developing affective dispositions related to learning. The authors contend that whether learners are motivated, enthused, anxious, or fearful about what they will learn is a determinant of how successful the learning will be.

**Dimension 2: Acquiring and Integrating Knowledge**

This dimension includes tasks that show knowledge and understanding of information learned.

**Dimension 3: Extending and Refining Knowledge**

This dimension includes tasks requiring comparing, classifying, inducing and deducing, analyzing errors, analyzing perspectives, and abstracting what was learned.

**Dimension 4: Using Knowledge Meaningfully**

This dimension has to do with using learned skills and knowledge to perform purposeful "real-life" tasks. It includes tasks requiring decision-making, investigation, experimental inquiry, problem-solving, and invention.

**Dimension 5: Productive Habits of Mind**

The last dimension requires the demonstration of habits found in critical, creative, and self-regulated thinkers.

*Assessing Dimension 3: An Example of An Error Analysis Task.* Identify a recent disaster that local newspapers and television stations have been reporting on. Your task is to work with a partner to determine how the media convey information about the disaster and identify specific examples of inaccurate information. Determine a way to present your findings to a member of the media, record that person's response, and share it with members of the class.

*Source:* Adapted by permission of MCREL from *Assessing Student Outcomes*, by Marzano, Pickering, and McTighe © 1993. Published by MCREL. All rights reserved.

## 6.2.3   A Functional Taxonomy

Most curricula that we presently deal with include a mix of outcomes that can best be classified by some of the old and some of new taxonomic schemes. The taxonomy that this book and module will use (and that you have already seen employed in Tables 6.2 and 6.4) attempts to synthesize Bloom's categories with the newer taxonomies available, such as the Dimensions of Learning model. This *functional taxonomy* was developed by the author of this book, and has been tested successfully by expert teacher teams in local, state, and district-related assessment development projects.

Review the categorization scheme of the Functional Taxonomy offered in Table 6.5 with definitions and examples of outcome statements that fall under each category. The Functional Taxonomy recognizes five major categories of cognitive learning: factual knowledge, application, complex procedural skills, and higher-order thinking, which includes Bloom's analysis, synthesis, and evaluation categories. Additionally, it offers separate categories for classifying attitudinal outcomes, social behaviors, and motor outcomes.

Unlike Bloom's taxonomy, there are no implied dependencies as one works with the different categories of the Functional Taxonomy. *Each category is intended to stand alone.* Thus, if you choose to classify an outcome at the application level, it signifies that the assessment design (and instruction) will focus on application skills as defined in the Functional Taxonomy only. Even if a student requires factual knowledge to demonstrate the application level of cognitive functioning, it will not be the primary focus of the assessment. Thus, valid assessment design would call for us to have a clear categorization of the taxonomic level of the outcome in mind, and to identify the best assessment method to gather evidence of *that level of learning.*

*Why Taxonomies Are Useful.*   The instructional and assessment value of taxonomies lies in the fact that they raise the consciousness of teachers or assessment designers with regard to the range and complexity of processes and behaviors that are represented in the domain. The biggest criticism we hear against traditional, structured response assessments center on their almost singular focus on *factual knowledge,* or at best, *application* levels of learning. Taxonomic analyses of the achievement domain help us guard against a narrowed focus on low level, easy-to-teach and easy-to-assess outcomes. After a taxonomic analysis, we can flag the most valued taxonomic categories, then deliberately design our instructional and assessment strategies to attack them—even if it means making use of more than one assessment method.

**TABLE 6.5   A Functional Taxonomy of Knowledge, Skills, and Behaviors**

---

1. **Factual Knowledge**

   Reproduce information such as facts, terms, denitions,  formulas, and concepts in the same form as it was presented. Alternatively,  reproduce information in a different form than it was originally presented.

   Typical behaviors: State, dene,   restate, describe, illustrate, translate, paraphrase, recall, give examples, and non-examples.

   Examples of learning outcomes:
   *Describe the parts of a ower.*
   *Provide examples of each part of speech.*
   *State Newton's third law of motion with an example of an application.*

2. **Application**

   Use a principle, one- or two-step rule, algorithm, or procedure to nd   a solution to a problem.
   Typical behaviors: Use, apply, solve, write, calculate, make, demonstrate.

   Examples of learning outcomes:
   *Count in 2s and 3s.*
   *Calculate the area of a room when given length and width.*
   *Write sentences with subject and verb agreement.*
   *Apply Boyle's law to solve quantitative problems.*

3. **Complex Procedural Skills**

   Use multistep procedures—often involving hypothesizing, reasoning, applying specialized techniques or instruments, or making judgments or decisions along the way—to solve a complex problem or complete a complex task. The emphasis is on implementation of the process rather than on the products generated. The steps in the complex procedure are often the accepted standard in the discipline or eld.

**TABLE 6.5    Continued**

Typical behaviors: Employ a procedure, demonstrate a procedure, document use of standard operating procedures.

Examples of learning outcomes:
*Use a scientific method to investigate hypotheses about physical or social phenomena.*
*Use standard procedures to develop a project action plan and budget.*
*Use a writing process (planning, drafting, editing, revising, publishing) to compose a story.*
*Using processes taught in class, develop a thesis statement for a research paper.*
*Conduct a task analysis to determine resources needed to complete a job.*
*Use the "plan, solve, check, and revise" strategy to solve problems.*

4.  **Higher-Order Thinking and Problem-Solving**
    Identify problems and possible strategies or principles for solutions. Might involve some combination of analysis (breaking down the problem into parts), synthesis (compiling or putting together the parts) and/or evaluation (making a judgment of merit or worth). Depending on the task, multiple behaviors and cognitive skills could apply, including the development of products.

    Examples of learning outcomes:
    *Given information sources about a current (environmental) problem,*
    *   *synthesize the information provided*
    *   *formulate a problem statement*
    *   *devise and justify a solution strategy*
    *Create a design for space and facilities needed for a project.*
    *Given available service options and a needs analysis, develop a proposal to meet customer needs.*
    *Create a self-portrait reflecting an early 20th-century style (e.g., Cubist).*
    *Compare literary devices used by two 20th-century poets and evaluate their style of expression.*
    *Contrast two theories on why dinosaurs are extinct.*

5.  **Attitudes and Values**
    Express and/or take actions based on feelings, opinions, and personal beliefs regarding people, objects, and events.

    Example of learning outcomes:
    *Show respect for the property, rights, and views of others.*
    *Accept diversity in cultural practices.*

6.  **Social Behaviors**
    Demonstrate behaviors that conform with social conventions in informal and formal group settings.

    Examples of outcomes:
    *Perform assigned roles in cooperative group tasks at school.*
    *Communicate ideas that facilitate group functions.*

7.  **Motor Skills**
    Demonstrate coordination, strength, control, and skills related to physical tasks/sports.

    Examples of outcomes:
    *Run a mile on a flat terrain in less than 10 minutes.*
    *Demonstrate keyboarding proficiency (typing).*

***Disputes in Taxonomic Categorizations.***   Disagreements on taxonomic categorizations often occur because of semantic differences in outcome interpretations. Your interpretation of the same words used in outcome statements may not be the same as mine. How do we get around this dilemma? As indicated before, for the purpose of assessment design, it is not as important that your taxonomic classification of an outcome agrees with mine; but rather that your ultimate choice of the appropriate *assessment method is consistent with your own taxonomic categorization of the outcomes.* If you can identify the desired taxonomic levels of your outcomes and select assessment methods that are the best fit for those taxonomic categories, a major criterion for obtaining validity will be satisfied. On the other hand, if we start with only a very vague notion of what we are attempting to assess in terms of taxonomic category, chances are that we will select assessment methods or item formats that require more, less, or very different kinds of processing or behaviors from respondents—leading to invalid results and interpretations.

***Which Taxonomy to Use.***   You need to use your own professional judgment in selecting a taxonomy that will work well with the outcome statements in your discipline. Bloom's taxonomy is a reputable resource and one with which almost every educator today is familiar. Despite its broad utility, a disadvantage might be that the taxonomy was designed for curricula that predominated in the 1960s. The introduction of constructivist approaches in education has led to the inclusion of broader, more complex skill areas. Such integrated areas of performance cannot be indisputably classified with Bloom's taxonomic categories. The Marzano, Pickering, & McTighe (1993) dimensions are more current, and best-suited for curricula that are heavily laden with complex, performance-based outcomes. This book and module will use the Functional Taxonomy in its illustrations, because it provides a pragmatic balance between the two. The Functional Taxonomy has been tested in recent assessment development projects and found to be applicable to a range of curricula and subject areas targeting a mix of broad and more narrow outcomes. As will probably be clear to most readers, it draws (with gratitude) on ideas from both the above sources.

**Key Concepts**

- Taxonomies assist us in clarifying the levels of cognitive processing or behaviors in statements of learning outcomes.
- Choice of a taxonomy by assessment designers should be guided by the nature of outcomes in a given subject or curriculum.

## 6.3   Specifying the Domain for Constructs in User Paths 2–6

### 6.3.1   Constructs Assessed in User Paths 2–6

As in User Path 1, defining the domain for constructs in other User Paths would entail use of similar procedures and steps. A major difference, though, is that we will no longer be dealing with *achievement*. The constructs in Paths 2–6 would now focus on *typically or naturally occurring characteristics* of people, objects, or institutions in the population of interest.

How shall we label the constructs measured in User Paths 2–6? In User Path 2, dealing with assessment for program planning, evaluation, and policymaking, many of the constructs will be broadly titled, such as "program or service needs," "program or service quality," "program effectiveness," or "staff or employee satisfaction." The term "program" might need to be narrowed in particular cases to refer to specific program or particular service areas. In User Path 3, dealing with assessment of exceptionalities in individuals, constructs would deal with various exceptional conditions, including social–emotional or behavioral variables, such as social maladjustment, learning disability, or hearing loss. In User Path 4, dealing with guidance and counseling, constructs would include attitudes, interests, or aptitudes useful in counseling individuals in different personal, educational, and vocational areas (e.g., vocational interests). In User Path 5, dealing with assessments for certification, licensure, or recognition, constructs would include broad areas of expertise, knowledge, and skill in particular professional or educational tracks (e.g., certification of proficient accountants). In User Path 6, concerned with assessments used in educational research contexts, a wide variety of constructs could be measured, each with labels relevant to the research problem.

In every case, however, specification of the domain would be a necessary step in beginning to operationally define the constructs. As before, we will again attempt to make the construct observable by identifying the general and specific indicators that best represent it. The literature and reference documents from which we will draw the indicators of the construct would now be far more diversified. If the established, formal knowledge on the construct to be assessed is scant, we will need to use other data sources to formulate the domain.

Note again that we cannot refer to indicators of constructs measured in User Paths 2–6 as "learning outcomes" any longer. Note also that because we are now out of the arena of scholastic curricula, we can dispense with Step 6 in the Guidelines for Specifying a Domain for User Path 1, dealing with taxonomic analysis of learning outcomes.

### 6.3.2 Domain Specification Guidelines in User Paths 2–6

In this section, we will use as an example the construct "effective classroom teaching" to see how the step-by-step domain specification process would be applied in User Path 2. Effective classroom teaching could be measured by school program leaders or managers in User Path 2 for administrative decision-making purposes; by users in Path 5 for making certification decisions; or by users in Path 6 for incorporation in research-related analyses. Notice that the five steps applicable to Paths 2–6, shown next, are only slightly modified from the seven steps we used in Path 1 (see Box 6.3).

B O X **6.3**

## Domain Specification Guidelines for User Paths 2–6

**Step 1**  Review appropriate source documents or data on the construct (e.g., effective classroom teaching). Identify the construct with a label and define the boundaries for the domain, keeping the population in mind (e.g., skills needed for effective K–12 public school teachers).

*(continued)*

# 6.3    Continued

**Step 2**    Visualize a "typical" member of the population and brainstorm general and specific indicators of such individuals, using the literature and source documents as a guide (e.g., What are the characteristics of an effective classroom teacher?). If programs/institutions (rather than individuals) serve as the unit of measurement, think of the general and specific indicators of a "typical" institution (e.g., What are the characteristics of public schools that have effective teachers?). Begin to identify the *conditions* under which indicators might be observed (e.g., classroom, community).

**Step 3**    Formulate the general and specific indicators so that they are as clear, explicit, and unambiguous as possible. Make specific indicators *observable*.

**Step 4**    Maintain the substantive links of the list of general and specific indicators with the data sources/documents. Ensure that the domain is as complete as it can be.

**Step 5**    Cluster indicator statements that appear to be related within the domain in a way that makes logical and/or theoretical sense. Organize the statements so that the specifically stated indicators or behaviors are subsumed under the broader, more general ones (in the form of a "tree diagram").

---

*Steps 1–2*    As in the User Path 1, we must search for relevant, reliable, and recent literature to obtain an understanding of the characteristic in question, in this case, effective classroom teaching. Recency is important because theoretical and conceptual models of constructs such as "effective teaching" can change drastically over time.

In working through Steps 1–2 for the example in Table 6.6, research on teaching might give us insights into the relationships between teacher behavior and student outcomes, how student behaviors and learning are interrelated, how skilled teachers manage classroom processes, and the factors that affect their cognitions about how the teaching-

---

**TABLE 6.6    Domain Specified for Assessing "Effective Classroom Teaching": Results of Step 3**

*General Indicator*
    1.0    Effective teachers possess specific knowledge relevant to their profession.

*Specific Indicators*
    1.1    Teachers demonstrate a thorough understanding and knowledge of their students, inside and outside the classroom.
        1.1.1    Teachers demonstrate knowledge and understanding of how students learn and develop.
        1.1.2    Teachers demonstrate knowledge of how their students' background factors affect learning in the classroom.
        1.1.3    Teachers understand how individual students differ in their approaches to learning.
    1.2    Teachers demonstrate a thorough understanding and knowledge of their subject area.
        1.2.1    Teachers demonstrate proficiency in the central concepts, skills, tools of inquiry, and structures of the disciplines they teach.

**TABLE 6.6  Continued**

1.2.2  Teachers demonstrate proficiency in the general areas of reading, writing, and mathematics.

1.3  Teachers demonstrate a thorough understanding and knowledge of pedagogical principles.

1.3.1  Teachers demonstrate knowledge of principles of curriculum, instructional design and delivery, and classroom assessment.

*General Indicator*

2.0  Effective teachers apply their knowledge (see 1.0) continuously in the classroom.

*Specific Indicators*

2.1  Teachers demonstrate proficiency in classroom planning.

2.1.1  Teachers plan instruction based on knowledge of their students, subject matter, curriculum, principles of learning and instructional design, and community influences.

2.1.2  Teachers create or select learning opportunities that are meaningful and facilitate learning.

2.2  Teachers instruct in a creative, flexible, and adaptive manner.

2.2.1  Teachers create a positive learning environment by maintaining appropriate standards of classroom behavior/conduct.

2.2.2  Teachers create learning opportunities that support a student's academic, personal, and social development.

2.2.3  Teachers create instructional opportunities to foster critical thinking and skill building.

2.2.4  Teachers use effective verbal, nonverbal, and media communication techniques to foster individual and collaborative inquiry.

2.3  Teachers demonstrate proficiency in designing and using assessments effectively.

2.3.1  Teachers design, select, and use appropriate assessment techniques to assess and evaluate student learning.

2.3.2  Teachers use assessment results to provide timely feedback and coaching to students.

2.3.3  Teachers use assessments to appropriately modify and adjust instruction.

2.3.4  Teachers can make appropriate interpretations of the results of standardized assessments designed for different purposes.

*General Indicator*

3.0  Effective teachers are committed professionals and community leaders.

*Specific Indicators*

3.1  Effective teachers observe ethical standards of practice.

3.1.1  Teachers comply with professional codes of ethics.

3.1.2  Teachers take responsibility for student well-being and growth.

3.2  Effective teachers reflect upon and continuously evaluate their learning/performance.

3.2.1  Teachers are introspective and evaluative of their own teaching.

3.2.2  Teachers seek out and participate in professional growth opportunities.

3.3  Effective teachers serve as leaders in the community.

3.3.1  Teachers demonstrate leadership qualities in various school and community projects.

3.3.2  Teachers are committed to improving their profession.

*Sources Used:* State of Connecticut's Common Core of Teaching (Foundational Skills and Competencies).
NCATE 2000
State of Florida's Accomplished Practices for the Teaching Professions.
Research articles: Darling-Hammond (1998); Noddings (1996); Shulman (1987); Stiggins & Conklin (1992).

learning process is progressing (Shulman, 1987). Such reviews might guide us to the finding that effective teachers base their instructional decisions on a sound knowledge of student characteristics (Stiggins & Conklin, 1992); or that the stronger their content knowledge in the discipline that they teach, the better they are able to reach their students (Shulman, 1987; Darling-Hammond, 1998; Noddings, 1996). Other supplementary sources we use could include journals and books on teacher education, documents from national associations that accredit teacher education programs or K–12 schools, or material published by state agencies that certify teachers. Through such a synthesis, we might arrive at the brain-stormed general structure as follows. Effective teachers:

- Have a sound knowledge of their students, both inside and ouside the classroom, their subject area, and pedagogical practices (how best to design and deliver instruction)
- Can effectively apply their knowledge in the classroom; they are flexible and can effectively adapt their classroom methods to meet students needs
- Are true professionals (that is, they commit themselves to ongoing reflection, improvement, and growth, often serving as leaders in the community)

*Steps 3–5*    By following Steps 3–5, we would progressively refine the domain until it resembled the final version shown in Table 6.6. The general and specific indicators can be broken down more and more *to reach a level of clarity and functionality for particular measurement purposes*. For instance, if the version in Table 6.6 still looks too broad and vague to allow assessment design for performance evaluations of early childhood teachers in Path 2, a further level of breakdown might be warranted. Thus, the indicator 1.1.1 could be further specified as follows:

> 1.1.1    Teachers demonstrate knowledge and understanding of how students learn and develop.
> 1.1.1.1    Teachers identify the major stages of Piaget's theory of cognitive development.
> 1.1.1.2    Teachers use the major stages of Piaget's theory of cognitive development to develop instructional and assessment strategies.

Once specified, we could use the domain to design a host of assessments to serve different purposes (not necessarily within the same User Path), such as instruments for conducting teacher evaluations, tools for determining needs for teacher training, or instruments for evaluating the quality of instructional programs with a measure of teacher competence. Depending on the assessment purposes specified (Phase I of the Process Model), our assessment design and validation efforts would be appropriately varied (Phase IV).

### 6.3.3    Seeking Other Data Sources for Defining Construct Domains

With some constructs, very little formal information might exist in the literature for us to draw from, making it necessary for us to seek other data sources to develop the domain. Recently, this dilemma was faced by a graduate student who was attempting to design an instrument to help identify students most likely to be successful with Web-based courses. Because distance learning is such a new phenomenon, she found very little information in the literature on the characteristics of "Web-savvy" learners. Thus, to begin the domain specification work, she conducted interviews of relevant groups of "experts" who might have insights on her targeted population and construct. These groups included students who had been exposed to Web-based (or distance learning) learning environments, instructors who taught such courses, technologists who designed software, and authors of educational materials for such courses.

The interview data were rich with suggestions for her to begin to specify a domain to represent a "successful Web-learner." Her records of the specific types of competencies, attitudes, and other characteristics provided the general and specific indicators she could then use to list indicators for the domain, labeled as "Characteristics of successful Web-based learners." She then supplemented her interview findings with as much relevant literature on technology-based learner characteristics as she could access.

When attempting to measure clinical or personality constructs, such as mental depression, psychologists have traditionally defined a construct by making observations of symptoms exhibited by mentally ill or special populations. Some early work on the *Minnesota Multiphasic Personality Inventory* (MMPI), for example, was conducted in this manner. To develop items on the depression subscale (D Scale), psychologists observed individuals who had been medically diagnosed as depressed and contrasted their behaviors with those exhibited by individuals from normal populations. Another related technique for identifying behavioral indicators for relatively unstudied constructs is the *critical incident technique*. Here, one would record observations of extreme behavioral episodes of individuals, such as the peak activity periods of manic depressives. Construct indicators would subsequently be derived from recorded observations of symptomatic behaviors.

**Key Concept**

■ The construct domain in User Paths 2–6 can be specified using a five-step procedure. These steps are similar to the steps followed in User Path 1.

## 6.3.4 Specifying the Domain for the Construct

*"Subjective Well-Being" in User Paths 3–4.* The last example of a domain for us to examine is shown in Table 6.7. This domain focuses on the trait "subjective well-being" of individuals, or a person's subjective assessment of their quality of life. This construct could be the focus of instruments developed in User Path 3 for therapy or clinical diagnosis purposes, in User Path 4 for counseling, intervention, and coaching purposes, or User Path 6 for research purposes.

*Steps 1–2* Bender (1997) suggests that self-assessments of subjective well-being are made by people using both their affective faculties, which clue them into how *happy* they feel they are, as well as their cognitive–judgmental areas, which help them analyze how well their life is going and their *satisfaction with life*. If we accepted Bender's theoretical assumptions about "subjective well-being" (construct label) when designing an instrument to measure that construct for adolescents (population specified), we would start with two subdomains—"happiness" (subdomain 1) and "life satisfaction" (subdomain 2)—within the overall domain of "subjective well-being." If on further research we were to find that life satisfaction could be viewed as a global construct, then by generating one index, we would seek a set of observable indicators that falls under this single generalized area. On the other hand, if the predominant body of literature suggested that life satisfaction is multidimensional (made up of different components, such as satisfaction with family, satisfaction with school/work, satisfaction with friends/relatives, satisfaction with income), the domain would reflect this partitioned structure (after Andrews & Robinson, 1991; Bender, 1997; Lewinsohn, Redner & Seeley, 1991). Our interpretations of construct meanings would, of course, directly emerge from the specified structure of the domain, whether unidimensional or multidimensional, as drawn from the theoretical literature and established knowledge about the construct.

*Steps 3–5* In Table 6.7, you can view possible results of the domain specification exercise, assuming that we took a multidimensional theoretical approach to measuring "subjective well-being" in adolescents. Happiness here is defined by both positive and negative affect (feelings) that an individual might have towards different aspects of life. Depressed teens would tend to have more negative than positive affect on a "happiness" scale that we develop based on this domain; happy adolescents would be likely to have low levels of

---

**TABLE 6.7  Domain Specified for Assessing the "Subjective Well-Being" of Adolescents**

The person expresses . . .

| *General Indicator:* | 1.0 Happiness (positive and negative affect towards life) |
|---|---|
| *Specific Indicators* | *Behavioral/response indicators* |
| 1.1 Positive Affect | *Makes or Agrees with statements such as:* <br> I feel good about my relationship with my mother. <br> I feel good about being part of my family. |
| 1.2 Negative Affect | I feel resentful towards my brother/sister. <br> I feel down when I am in school. |
| *General Indicator:* | 2.0 Life Satisfaction |
| *Specific Indicators* | *Behavioral/response indicators* |
| | *Makes or Agrees with statements such as:* |
| 2.1 Satisfaction with self | I like the way I look. |
| 2.2 Satisfaction with friends/relatives/social life | I like spending time with my friends in school. |
| 2.3 Satisfaction with home life | I like doing things with my mom/dad. |
| 2.4 Satisfaction with school | I like going to school. |
| 2.5 Satisfaction with work | I am comfortable with the work that my employer asks me to do. |
| 2.6 Satisfaction with income | I usually have enough spending money. |

*Sources Used:* Andrews & Robinson, 1991; Bender, 1997; Lewinsohn, Redner, & Seeley, 1991.

negative affect, and also frequently associate themselves with the positive affect indicators.

In the "life satisfaction" subdomain, we would expect adolescents who are generally satisfied with life to respond positively to all or most of the specific indicators listed. The multidimensional domain structure would enable us to design tools that discriminate between those who were experiencing low levels of satisfaction in some areas (e.g., school life) but not in others (e.g., family life).

---

**BOX 6.4**

## What the 1999 *Standards* for Testing Say on Specifying the Domain

To help ensure that the assessment purposes, assessment specifications, and items/tasks that make up an assessment and scoring criteria are all linked together, two standards, Standard 3.2 and Standard 3.11, particularly highlight the importance of a well-specified domain for assessment designers and users. Here they are.

> Standard 3.2: The purpose(s) of the test, definition of the domain, and the test specifications should be stated clearly so that judgments can be made about the appropriateness of the defined domain for the stated purpose(s). . . . and about the relation of the items to the dimensions of the domain they are intended to represent.

> Standard 3.11: Test developers should document the extent to which the content domain of a test represents the defined domain and test specifications.

*Source: Standards for Educational and Psychological Testing.* Copyright © 1999 by the AERA, APA, and NCME. Reproduced with permission. All rights reserved.

---

## Summary

Chapters 6–9 deal with design and validation of assessment tools using the Process Model. Chapter 6 dealt with procedures for specifying the domain for a construct that we might want to measure. The *domain* (or *domain specification*) forms a part of the assessment specification. If we follow the Process Model (see Chapter 5), we would specify the domain in Phase 1. Poorly specified domains obstruct the writing of items or tasks tied to the targeted construct. Chapter 6 provided several guidelines for specifying the domain in order to enhance measurement quality.

We started the chapter by focusing on a domain specification exercise in User Path 1. Then, we examined slightly modified guidelines for constructs that we might measure in User Paths 2–6. Table 6.8 summarizes the essential ideas in Chapter 6 in the form of a checklist.

We made a distinction between "learning" and "achievement" in User Path 1. Learning can vary in different individuals and may or may not be inferred directly from the evidence that an assessment procedure yields. Provided that we begin with a clear definition of the *achievement domain,* achievement is a more measurable construct in User Path 1.

By stating the targeted learning outcomes in clear terms, teachers specify the achievement domain for a given unit or course of study. Vague statements of outcomes must be clarified for measurement purposes. Achievement domains could be made up of both *product outcomes* and *process outcomes.* We applied the tree diagram approach to organize outcomes in achievement domains. In a tree diagram, there are three levels of generality in outcome statements: *outcomes, competencies,* and *enablers.* A taxonomy of learning outcomes is useful in analyzing the *types of behaviors* or *levels of cognitive complexity* embedded in outcomes in an achievement domain. We reviewed three alternate taxonomies that might be useful during assessment design.

Specifying the domain for constructs in User Paths 2–6 requires procedures similar to those in User Path 1. Unlike achievement in Path 1, constructs in these paths are *typically or naturally occurring characteristics.* The domain specification process was modified to a five-step process for constructs in User Paths 2–6. Here, we would identify the *general* and *specific indicators* of the construct (as opposed to outcomes, competencies, and enablers). Depending on the construct we target, the literature, reference documents, and data sources from which we would draw the indicators could be diverse.

To conclude this chapter, we must remember that specifying the domain is only the first important step in operationally defining the construct. The actual instrument or assessment tool still has not been developed! Chapters 7 and 8 show you how the domain that is specified in Path 1 can be incorporated within an assessment specifications document, which, in turn, can assist us in actual construction of achievement tests and other

---

**TABLE 6.8   A Checklist to Evaluate How Well a Domain Is Specified for any User Path**

---

*Coverage and Substance*

❑    1. Does the domain adequately cover the knowledge, skills, abilities, processes, behaviors, or dispositions expected in a
   ■ competent, exiting learner in User Path 1?
   ■ a typical member of the population in User Paths 2–6?

❑    2. Does the domain have any missing elements or major gaps?

❑    3. Does the domain include any redundancies?

❑    4. Are data sources used credible and documented?

*Organization*

❑    5. Are indicators organized from complex to simple or in some logical way?

❑    6. Is there adequate breakdown of broad indicators into more clear, measurable ones?

*Application of Guidelines*

❑    7. Are the statements clear, concrete, and explicit?

❑    8. Are observable, "action" verbs used where appropriate?

❑    9. Are conditions of observation made explicit where appropriate?

❑   10. Are performance criteria specified where relevant?

assessments used by classroom teachers. Chapter 9 will demonstrate how domains similar to the "effective teaching" and "subjective well-being" domains can be used to develop a complete set of specifications, leading up to the design/selection of tools to meet particular purposes in Paths 2–6.

## QUESTIONS FOR CLASS DISCUSSION

1. Consider the domain specified below (Construct: Proficiency in using a sewing machine). Critique its quality from a measurement perspective using the guidelines given in Chapter 6 (Table 6.8). What revisions would you make, if any?

---

Assessment Purpose: Summative decision-making (to advance students to next level).
User Path 1
Population:       Adolescents/Adults

Construct:  Proficiency in using a sewing machine
Domain:
Outcome 1.0   The student will understand the workings of a sewing machine (complex procedural skills).
Competencies:
    1.1   Know the basic parts of a sewing machine.
    1.2   What are the functions of the parts of a sewing machine?
    1.3   Follow step-by-step procedures for operating a sewing machine.
    1.4   Given sewing problems during operation, analyze and solve the problem (higher-order thinking).
        1.4.1   Check tension settings.
        1.4.2   Skipped stitches.
        1.4.3   Broken needles.
    1.5   Safe procedures (application).
    1.6   Given instructions, operate a sewing machine to create a stitched product.

Revisions:

Reasons for Revisions:

---

2. Specify the domain for a construct of your choice using a tabular or tree format shown in Chapter 6. Evaluate its quality using the checklist in Table 6.8.

3. Evaluate the advantages and disadvantages of the three learning taxonomies presented in this chapter for designing assessments for curricula in User Path 1.

4. What are the major similarities and differences in the steps followed for domain specification for constructs in User Path 1 versus Paths 2–6?

5. Specify the domain for the construct "Art Appreciation" using a tabular or tree format. Identify the sources you used for the specification process. Evaluate its quality using the checklist in Table 6.8.

# 7 Designing or Selecting Written Structured-Response Assessment Tools

## Overview

The seventh chapter aims to demonstrate how to apply the Process Model, introduced in Chapter 5, to design or select written, structured-response (W-SR) assessment tools to meet needs of users in Path 1. In User Path 1, assessment for teaching and learning, primary users of assessment information are teachers and instructional personnel who support classroom teaching, along with students and others interested in the results. Note that we have also used the term "traditional tests" to refer to different types of written, structured-response (W-SR) tools in earlier chapters.

The concepts in this chapter logically follow those presented in Chapters 5 and 6. The chapter picks up where we left off in Chapter 6, after a prospective assessment designer or user has identified the construct and specified an achievement domain in User Path 1. It attempts to detail the tasks we need to accomplish in each phase of the Process Model as applicable to W-SR assessment tools, beginning with the development of the assessment specification, and ending in the final assembly and content validation of the tool. We examine the applicability of four major types of W-SR item formats—matching, true-false, multiple choice, and completion—and illustrations of how to apply specific item-writing guidelines or "rules" for each item type.

There are textbooks that provide as many as 40 different rules for particular item types, such as multiple choice items. This chapter has extracted what this author considers to be the most essential rules for each item type that would assist assessment designers in the mechanics of item-writing. Readers are encouraged to pursue more extensive treatments if they so need. Examples of good and bad items, spanning levels from elementary to higher education and a variety of disciplines, illustrate how the skills can be integrated in a complete test design or selection effort for classroom assessment purposes. Because the subject matter of this chapter consists of procedural skills, you will find sections highlighting "Rules" for item-writing instead of "Key Concepts." The chapter concludes by presenting a checklist summarizing the general and more specific rules for designing W-SR instruments (Table 7.5).

## CHAPTER 7 OBJECTIVES

After studying this chapter and completing the structured exercises in the module, you should be able to:

1. Describe the main components of assessment specifications needed to design or select written, structured-response (W-SR) assessment tools

2. Select W-SR item formats that are best suited to measure learning outcomes represented in the achievement domain

3. Develop assessment specifications, including a table of specifications, to guide the development or selection of items for a W-SR assessment tool

4. Apply rules for writing different types of W-SR items, namely, matching, fill-in-the blank, true/false, and multiple choice items

5. Evaluate the quality of W-SR items constructed to match particular specifications

6. Assemble (or select) W-SR assessment tools to meet specifications

7. Conduct a content validation followed by revision of W-SR items and the overall assessment tool.

## 7.1 Why Use Written Structured-Response Assessment Tools?

Design of assessments to support teaching and learning should be viewed in the larger context of planning, development, delivery, and evaluation of an instructional unit or educational program designed to promote student learning. If the intent is to determine whether the student has acquired particular skills or specific knowledge delivered through a program, assessment design should be closely coordinated with curriculum and instruction. Thus, as we think about classroom functions, keeping a framework such as the outcome-driven model (Figure 2.2, Chapter 2) in mind, will facilitate our endeavors in designing curriculum-based assessments.

Despite the influence of alternate perspectives and advances in modern learning theory on assessment design methodology, the written, structured-response (W-SR) item format has continued to have a significant place in recent assessment programs. The advantages of the W-SR item formats, in particular the multiple choice items, lie in their versatility in capturing different levels of the cognitive taxonomy, their amenability to objective scoring methods, and their high utility in testing large numbers of students. Assuming that the W-SR method of assessment is the best fit for the purposes, population, and learning outcomes in the domain, Table 7.1 summarizes how the four phases of the Process Model would play out when we construct a W-SR assessment tool.

**TABLE 7.1  Tasks in the Process Model as Applied to the Design/Selection and Validation of W-SR Assessments**

Phase I. Specification of Population, Assessment Purpose, and Construct Domain

| | |
|---|---|
| 1. Identify "whom" to assess. | For example, *Title 1 students in grade 5,* students enrolled in an undergraduate course, trainees in a corporate training program. |
| 2. Identify "why" you are assessing. | For example for a *formative decision* (to aid in identifying student weaknesses, goal-setting, planning, or improving your instruction); for making a *summative decision;* for a *norm-referenced or a criterion-referenced decision;* for ongoing *documentation of growth.* |
| 3. Identify "what" to assess. | Identify the *construct,* for example, achievement in a particular subject area, at a particular level; proficiency in cognitive skills and processes (such as critical thinking). |
| 4. Specify the *construct domain.* | Write and organize descriptive statements of indicators (learning outcomes) that represent the construct domain. |

Phase II.

| | |
|---|---|
| 5. Prepare Assessment Specifications, including a Table of Specifications. | The assessment specifications should specify the: *population, assessment purpose, construct domain, assessment methods* selected, *conditions* of assessment, *administration* procedures, *scoring* procedures, and a *table of specifications* showing item breakdown by outcome/taxonomic level, and *weights* to be allocated to different indicators in the domain. |

Phase III.

| | |
|---|---|
| 6. Develop or select W-SR items matched to Assessment Specifications. | Write or select items using item-writing rules. Develop or select supporting materials, directions, prompts. Develop or select scoring key. Assemble the test. |

Part IV.

| | |
|---|---|
| 7. Evaluate the quality of the W-SR items and overall assessment tool. | Phase IV A. Conduct content validation of items and overall instrument by external reviewers. Revise items and assessment tool, as needed. Phase IV B. Conduct empirical tryouts and validation studies as appropriate to purposes. For example: Conduct item analysis studies. Conduct reliability studies. Conduct empirical construct-validation studies. Conduct norming, scaling, or standard-setting studies Revise items and assessment tool as needed. |

**Prepare to use W-SR assessment tool in actual contexts.**

## 7.2 The Process Model Applied to W-SR Assessment Design or Selection

### 7.2.1 Tasks in Phase I

The first task in Phase 1 would be to specify the *population* (whom to assess), *assessment purposes* (why we are assessing), and *construct* to be assessed (what we want to assess). As you are now aware, these three pieces of information are incorporated into the *assessment specification* document (plan) for designing or selecting the W-SR tool in Phase II.

***Specifying the Population.*** Because primary assessment users in Path 1 are individuals who develop or use assessments for classroom decision-making, students in their classes would serve as the population to be assessed. One example in Table 7.1 consists of a population of Title 1 students from fifth grade. That example assumes that the primary decision-maker interested in the assessment information is a teacher of a fifth-grade Title 1 class. In this particular example, the assessment design or selection procedures would be coordinated with the needs and confines of the Title 1 group specified.

***Specifying the Assessment Purposes.*** The next task is to specify the assessment purposes in some detail. To accomplish this, the instructor or assessment designer must be able to answer the question: How will the results of the W-SR assessment tool be used? What specific decisions will I or others make with the information that the assessment yields? Staying with the example of the fifth-grade Title 1 class, monitoring student achievement changes during the instructional cycle and identifying areas that need further instruction (both formative decisions) could be a reasonable purpose for a teacher dealing with a Title 1 population. It is important for us to specify exactly what *type of formative decisions* are to be made, and the exact nature of the *summative decisions* in which developer/users are likely to be interested.

In Table 7.2, we see a more specific listing of some common reasons for which different users depend on classroom assessment in User Path 1. Note that some of the purposes we see listed are formative (e.g., grade level or team planning), while others are summative (e.g., assigning grades). As Table 7.2 points out, the users of the information could vary depending on the number and nature of decisions that we identify as relevant. For some decisions, administrators might be involved along with teachers and parents in examining assessment data.

As Tables 7.1 and 7.2 illustrate, it is also relevant to clarify whether the results will be interpreted in a *criterion-referenced* or *norm-referenced* manner when specifying the assessment purpose in User Path 1. Depending on whether your intent is to design a criterion-referenced (CRT) or a norm-referenced tool (NRT), the subsequent design specifications and empirical validation steps will vary. The present and forthcoming chapters (particularly, Chapters 12 and 13) will make clear to you what some of these differences could be in terms of concrete actions.

***Specifying the Construct Domain.*** Domain specification, a key exercise in Phase 1, requires us to identify the construct to be assessed, and to specify its domain of opera-

TABLE 7.2 **Specific Purposes and Audiences for Classroom Assessment: User Path 1**

| *Why are you assessing?* | *Who is most likely to use the information?* |
|---|---|
| 1. To identify student needs prior to beginning instruction | __ Teacher(s)/Instructor(s) |
| 2. To set instructional goals* | __ Student(s) |
| 3. To plan or improve instructional strategies* | __ Parent(s) |
| 4. To place students in temporary instructional groups* | __ Team or Department |
| 5. To track student growth | __ School Administrators/Leaders |
| 6. To communicate expectations to students, to motivate students | __ Other *Explain:* |
| 7. To diagnose student strengths and weaknesses* | |
| 8. To provide coaching and feedback to students* | |
| 9. To provide a basis for grading/marking involving**: | |

a. a criterion-referenced approach

b. a norm-referenced approach

c. a combination of the two.

10. To communicate student progress to parents

11. To make decisions on student retention or promotion**

12. To generate data for teaching evaluations***

13. To generate data for teacher team/department planning*

14. To generate data for program evaluations (e.g., grade-level programs)***

15. **Other:**

---

*Formative Decision

**Summative Decision

***Could be either formative or summative decision

tional indicators. As we saw in Chapter 6, there are some fairly clear-cut guidelines for us to follow in specifying the indicators of the achievement domain to be assessed. To better understand the exact nature of the indicators in the domain, we need to employ a taxonomy of learning behaviors to classify them. Assessment designers can choose from an array of available taxonomies to perform this task.

As assessment designers, we should not take the task of domain specification lightly, as it will impact the content-based validity of inferences we ultimately draw from the results of the W-SR assessment. The substance and clarity of the general learning outcomes (instructional goals) and more specific competencies (objectives) in the domain will impact the quality of resulting W-SR items that we write.

## 7.2.2    Tasks in Phase II

In Phase II, the first responsibility is to prepare the Assessment Specifications document that will guide the design or selection of the W-SR assessment tool. In W-SR design, this document is often called a "table of specification" or a "test blueprint." There is no single way to develop an assessment specification; a useful one would outline the critical structural components of the tool that will be the best fit for the purposes, population, and construct domain. This chapter will provide examples of traditional assessment specifications (FORMS I and III); simultaneously, it will introduce a form of W-SR specification that has some proven functionality with recent standards-based curricula (FORM II).

## 7.2.3    Tasks in Phase III

The major task in Phase III is to decide on the W-SR item formats that will be the best match for particular competencies or objectives in the domain, and to follow item-writing rules to develop or select them. The item format we choose should be suitable for tapping the desired level of cognitive, affective, or psychomotor processing revealed by the taxonomic analysis—such as factual knowledge, application, or higher-order thinking. This chapter will devote an extensive section to guidelines for writing W-SR items, showing examples of poorly and well-constructed items of each different format.

The final task in Phase III is to assemble the tool. This step requires us to develop supporting materials, such as graphics or tables, directions for examinees and users, and an answer key for scoring.

## 7.2.4    Tasks in Phase IV

Our work in Phase IVA would begin with a verification of content validity of the individual items and overall assessment tools by external, expert reviewers. Preferably, the content validators would be other teachers or professionals who were not involved in the assessment design or selection process, so that they can provide us with a fresh perspective on test and item quality. Revisions to items or the overall test will follow. We could opt to use the assessment at this stage. Preferably, however, we would conduct some empirical evaluations.

In Phase IVB, we would gather empirical evidence of score validity, keeping in mind the assessment purposes that we specified in Phase I. More and varied forms of evidence would be necessary for high stakes applications than for low stakes classroom decisions (see Chapter 3). Evidence would also vary for criterion-referenced versus norm-referenced decisions. For example, if a CRT is being designed, our analytic procedures in Phase IVB would have to be appropriate for evaluation of CRTs. Thus, we would include methods of item analysis, reliability estimation, and standard-setting that are most applicable to CRT development. If we were designing or selecting an NRT, our item analysis procedures would have to be altered to suit NRT development, along with checks on the quality of the norms and any norm-referenced score scales that we choose to develop or eventually use. Chapters 10 through 14 will provide you with more technical details of such procedures. More revisions to the tool will probably occur after our work in Phase IVB is over. Then, the assessment will be ready for use.

Let us now shift our attention to the procedural details of each of the tasks in Phases I–IVA of the Process Model, assuming that you have decided that a W-SR assessment is the most suitable method for your targeted construct, population, and purposes. The chapter now treats the following topics in sequence.

Development of assessment specifications for W-SR instruments (Phases I–II)
Characteristics of different types of W-SR item formats and rules for item construction (Phase III):

- matching items
- fill-in-the-blank or completion items
- true/false items
- multiple choice items
- complex, interpretive exercises

W-SR test assembly (Phase III)
Conducting a content validation for W-SR assessments (Phase IVA)

Again, keep in mind that in Phase IV, our focus in this chapter will be limited to *content-validation* procedures only. This narrow focus is to facilitate the instructional purposes of this book and module; it does not mean that Phase IVB is irrelevant to the construction of W-SR tools. Empirical methods for checking W-SR test quality, Phase IVB, are treated in Chapters 10–14.

## 7.3   Developing Assessment Specifications for W-SR Tools

Sound assessment specifications provide assessment developers and users with a comprehensive set of guidelines for developing the items and the overall assessment tool. When applied to W-SR tests, the assessment specifications are a set of detailed blueprints which specify the characteristics, content parameters, taxonomic levels, item weightings, and formats of individual items, as well as the structure and organization of the test as a whole. Specifications for writing individual items—called item specifications—provide item writers with directions regarding the item content, conceptual difficulty, characteristics of the *stimulus,* another name for the question or prompt that helps frame the question, and characteristics of the *responses* (the answer options provided to the test-taker). If graphic displays or text material are used to present the stimulus, well-prepared specifications should guide item writers as to their exact nature and contents. Three examples of assessment specifications follow, FORMS I, II, and III.

### 7.3.1   Form I: A Table of Specifications

A Table of Specifications is the most common, traditionally used form of a W-SR test blueprint. Table 7.3 provides an example of a Table of Specifications used to develop a traditional W-SR instrument. The test to be designed is for a unit on classroom assessment excerpted from an undergraduate teacher education curriculum. The table has two dimensions. The vertical dimension (the first column), called the "content" dimension, contains statements of specific learning outcomes taken from the achievement domain. The horizontal dimension (columns 2 through 4), labeled "taxonomic level," specifies the taxonomic categorization of each learning outcome that will be assessed and its weight. In this particular illustration, we are using the Functional Taxonomy introduced to you in Chapter 6. The *cells* inside the table contain the number of items, or questions, to be constructed to measure each learning outcome at the specified taxonomic level.

Assuming that each item is worth one point, the numbers of items in the cells signify the weights to be allocated to the different outcomes and taxonomic levels on the test. For instance, the distribution of item numbers in Table 7.3 suggests that the test would have about half the questions ($4 + 4 + 3 + 3 = 14$ out of 30 items) tied to learning outcomes numbered 1.2, 2.2, 2.3, and 2.4, classified at the *higher-order thinking* level. Thus, the test score would be weighted 47% at the higher-order thinking level.

The totals in Columns 2–4 provide an overall look at the weights to be reflected on the test. In Table 7.3, we see that the *factual knowledge* outcomes, 1.1 and 2.1, added together would be devoted a weight of 33% of the total test score (10/30), the *higher-order learning* outcomes, added together, would account for 47% of the total test score (14/30), and *application* items (1.3 only) would be allocated only 20% weight (6/30).

The taxonomic classifications in a Table of Specifications dictate the level of conceptual difficulty at which the items must be written. An outcome classified at the application level would call for an item requiring the examinee to apply rules or principles in a unique problem setting. This calls for a more complex level of performance than the factual knowledge level, which requires mere recollection or interpretation of a principle or rule, but a level of performance that is less complex than an item calling for higher-order thinking skills.

As will probably be clear to you by now, to effectively use a Table of Specifications during test construction and planning, two assumptions need to be met: first, individual learning outcomes represented in the *content* dimension must be narrow or specific enough in scope to be classified at *one and only one* taxonomic level; and second, each learning outcome has to be measurable with one of the W-SR item formats, such as fill-in-the-blank or multiple choice. Further details can be specified in the table to guide item construction and selection. Such additional information is optional. Notice the parenthetic information included with the numbers in the cells in Table 7.3; these details indicate the exact format of the W-SR items that will be developed (for example, multiple choice, true/false, or fill-in-the-blank). We could also indicate in the table the exact test items, indexed by number, that would be linked to particular outcomes and taxonomic levels (for example, Item 10–15 in the *Application* column of Table 7.3). Whether or not such added details will improve test construction are decisions that individual assessment designers and teachers must weigh on a case-by-case basis.

**TABLE 7.3   FORM I: A Table of Specifications for a Written-Structured Response Test**

Unit Title:     **Classroom Assessment (from a Teacher Education Curriculum)**

| Content | Factual Knowledge | Application | Higher-Order | Total (Weights) |
|---|---|---|---|---|
| The student-teacher will . . . | | | | |
| **1.0   Specify the domain to assess.** | | | | |
| 1.1   Define technical terms such as *domain, learning outcomes, taxonomic levels.* | 5 (true/false) | — | — | 5 (17%) |
| 1.2   Given a general outcome, select specific outcomes that would help clarify the domain. | — | — | 4 (matching) | 4 (13%) |
| 1.3   Classify outcome statements at the appropriate taxonomic level. | — | 6 (multiple choice) | — | 6 (20%) |
| **2.0   Construct written, structured-response items.** | | | | |
| 2.1   Identify the major item-writing rules to follow during item construction. | 5 | — | — | 5 (17%) |
| 2.2   Identify items that match conditions, content, and/or behaviors specified in outcome statements. | — | — | 4 | 4 (13%) |
| 2.3   Identify reasons why a particular item is poorly written. | — | — | 3 | 3 (10%) |
| 2.4   Evaluate the quality of items and violations of item-writing rules. | — | — | 3 | 3 (10%) |
| **Total Items:** | **10** | **6** | **14** | **30** |
| **(Weight):** | **33%** | **20%** | **47%** | |

The Table of Specifications can be useful to both developers and subsequent users of the assessment tool. If you are an assessment designer and item writer, the table will guide you with regard to how many items you need to measure particular learning outcomes, taxonomic levels, and topics in the domain in order to obtain optimal levels of *content relevance* and *content representativeness*. If you are an assessment user who is selecting a W-SR instrument from another source, a Table of Specifications could guide the test selection process. The table can help in evaluating whether the test you choose reflects the emphases (weights) that you will place during instruction on particular sections of the domain, and whether all of the important learning outcomes in your desired domain will be assessed with the emphasis you want.

## 7.3.2   Form II: Assessment Specifications

The next form of an assessment specification is more generalized in that it does not have a built-in assumption that *all* learning outcomes specified in the achievement domain will be best measured by W-SR items only (although a portion of the domain might be). FORM II was illustrated in Chapter 5, through Case Study 5.1, and it will be used in subsequent achievement test construction exercises illustrated in this book and module.

A second example of FORM II is shown in Table 7.4. For ease of communication, we will continue to use a unit on classroom assessment excerpted from an undergraduate teacher education curriculum as a specific instance for FORM II, where the construct to be measured deals with test construction skills for preservice teachers. The assessment designers have specified the domain with six competencies, representing the specific learning outcomes or indicators of the construct. Three of the competencies will be measured with W-SR items, accounting for 30% of the total score, while the remaining three outcomes will be measured with open-ended assessments, the latter accounting for 70% of the total score (see Assessment Methods and Weights desired).

---

**TABLE 7.4   FORM II: Assessment Specification for Test Construction Unit**

---

**Assessment Purposes:**  To make criterion-reference interpretations of performance tied to the domain; end-of-unit summative decision-making.

**Population:**  Preservice teachers (undergraduate seniors)

**Construct:**  Test construction

**Domain:**

*General Indicator* (Learning Outcome):

**1.0   The students will develop written, structured response tests to serve classroom decision-making needs.**

*Specific Indicators* (Competencies):

The students will:

1.1   Restate/paraphrase key concepts and terms relevant to test construction (e.g., domain, learning outcomes, taxonomy, test specifications, structured response items). (*Cognitive level: factual knowledge*)

**TABLE 7.4    Continued**                                                                  rs

1.2    Given a general outcome, write specific outcomes to clarify the domain.
       (*Cognitive level: higher-order thinking*)

1.3    Given outcome statements, classify them at the appropriate taxonomic level.
       (*Cognitive level: application*)

1.4    State the major item-writing rules to follow during item construction.
       (*Cognitive level: factual knowledge*)

1.5    Construct items that match conditions, content, and/or behaviors specified in outcome
       statements.
       (*Cognitive level: higher-order thinking*)

1.6    Given item samples, make necessary revisions to items that violate relevant item-
       writing rules.
       (*Cognitive level: higher-order thinking*)

**Assessment Method(s) and Weights Desired:**

Indicators 1.1, 1.3, 1.4      Written, structured-response test (30%)
Indicators 1.2, 1.5, 1.6      Written, open-ended assessment (70%)

**Scording Methods:**

Indicators 1.1, 1.3, 1.4      Written, structured-response assessment (30%)      Answer key
Indicators 1.2, 1.5, 1.6      Written, open-ended assessment (70%)              Analytic rubric

**Group/Individual Assessment:**      Individual

**Who Assesses:**      Instructor

### Table of Specifications for W-SR Portion of Assessment

| Content | Taxonomic Level | | Weight | Weighted Points |
| | *Factual Knowledge* | *Application* | *Weight* | *(Total)* |
|---|---|---|---|---|
| **Specific Indicators** | | | | |
| 1.1    Restate/paraphrase key concepts and terms relevant to text construction. | 10 (matching, true/false) | — | x1 | 10 |
| 1.3    Given outcome statements, classify them at the appropriate taxonomic level. | — | 6 (multiple choice) | x2 | 12 |
| 1.4    State the major item-writing rules to follow during test construction. | 8 (ll-in-blanks) | — | x1 | 8 |
| **Weighted Points** | **18** | **12** | | **30** |
| **(Total)** | | | | |

FORM II specifies the structural pieces of the desired assessment tool(s) as follows:

- Assessment purpose
- Population
- Construct, with a detailed Domain represented with a list of general and specific outcomes
- Assessment methods
- Weights
- Scoring methods
- Scorers
- A Table of Specifications showing item distributions desired for the W-SR component of the assessment at the bottom of the form

A new element illustrated in the Form II Table of Specifications is the use of a *weighting constant,* by which different item sets are multiplied, yielding a differentiated weighting allocation to the final score. In the example (Table 7.4), the resulting emphasis on the application level items is double that placed on factual knowledge items.

FORM II has high utility in planning, designing, or selecting assessment tools that might employ a mixture of assessment methods, either when combining traditional (W-SR) with performance assessments, or when using more than one performance assessment method. It provides a comprehensive set of specifications for designing the critical dimensions of assessments. Most achievement domains emphasized in curricula today require that we employ more than one assessment method to achieve adequate levels of validity.

### 7.3.3   Form III: Item-Level Specifications

Another type of test specification, illustrated in Form III, focuses on individual item development. *Item specifications* were originally created for large-scale testing programs by commercial test developers. Item specifications provide a very tight set of guidelines to build replicas of a particular item type. Item writers, who might be working independently can use item-level specifications to generate a large pool of items matched to the same set of design criteria (see Popham, 1984). Each item thus produced is in a sense a clone of the others that are developed to match the same design parameters. Large-scale assessment developers often utilize very detailed item specifications as a quality-control device.

An example of an Item Specification used to design criterion-referenced test items for a Grade 1 Communications domain is shown in Figure 7.1 (FORM III). FORM III provides a high degree of structure and guidance to the item writer. It specifies the general skill (the "objective") and specific skill (the "skill clarification") to be measured by each item, directions to accompany the item, characteristics of the stimulus and characteristics of the response options. It also provides a sample item from a hypothetical pool to illustrate to writers what a typical item might look like. FORM III does *not* specify what the overall assessment tool might look like, nor does it provide any insight regarding the larger domain within which the particular item or skill belongs. The specifications for

**Objective:** The student will visually discriminate between letters, words, phrases, and sentences.

**Skill Clarification:** The student will perceive likenesses and differences in up to 6 randomly ordered letters.

**Item Structure**

Directions should be read by the examiner for each item.

Options should be presented horizontally.

**Stimulus Characteristics**

1) Oral Directions: "I am going to hold up a card. Look at your paper and find the picture of the star. Put your finger on the star. Then look at the letters beside the star. Mark an 'X' on the letter that looks most like the letter on the card."

or

2) "Look at your paper and find the picture of the star. Put your finger on the star. Then look at the letters beside the star. Mark an 'X' on the letter that looks different from all the others."

**Option Characteristics**

1) Students should be presented with no more than six (6) options.

2) Letters should be arranged randomly.

3) There should be one and only one correct response.

**Sample Item**

1) The examiner reads: "I am going to hold up a card. Look at your paper and find the picture of the star. Put your finger on the star. Then look at the letters beside the star. Mark an 'X' on the letter that looks most like the letter on the card."

Cue Card:

Printed in test booklet:

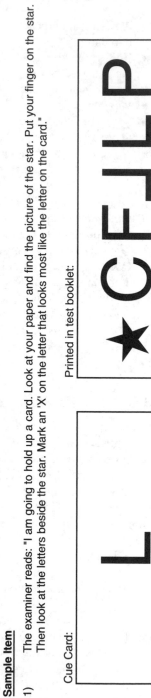

**FIGURE 7.1 Form III: Specifications for Grade 1 Communications Skill**

the overall test are separate, and are typically a variant of Form I. To create criterion-referenced tests at different times, developers draw random samples of items from the item pool according to the overall test specifications.

Useful ideas from large-scale testing projects, such as the FORM III item specifications can easily be transferred to local item-development efforts that will facilitate day-to-day tasks in the classroom. Classroom teachers can use item specifications similar to FORM III to create item banks that they can store in computer databases or websites. Such item banks can be shared among instructors who teach the same curricula across institutions or school districts.

# 7.4 Guidelines for Item Construction with Different Types of W-SR Items

There are four major W-SR item formats: matching, fill-in-the-blanks or completion, true/false, and multiple choice, with several possible variations from these basic forms. We should construct items for all W-SR formats to comply with *four* cardinal rules. These are:

1. Each item must be designed to measure *only the selected outcome* from the domain.
2. Items must elicit the desired performances in *as direct a manner* as possible.
3. Each item should deal with *a single question* or concept with *one clearly correct* or *best answer.*
4. Items should *not provide clues,* grammatical or otherwise, to the respondent.

Tricky items are *not* desirable. Wordy items with intricate or confusing language are similarly problematic. The aim is *not* to trip the examinee, but rather to elicit information on the knowledge, skill, or behavior in as clean a manner as possible, without extraneous interference. A good W-SR test item would help you determine who is proficient and knowledgeable on the skill/knowledge tested and who is less so.

## 7.4.1 Matching Exercises

In its typical form, a matching exercise is comprised of two adjacent columns of information that must be matched by the examinee through simple association. Column A presents the item prompts or *premises,* while Column B lists the *response* options. Review Example A1.1 that follows. The topic deals with terms and definitions of descriptive statistics from a high school statistics curriculum. Example A1.2 illustrates another matching exercise from an elementary science curriculum. In the first example, the examinee must associate the terms with their correct definitions. Items are numbered. Answer options are identified with letters. In the second, the test taker matches the parts of a green plant with their primary function.

When learning outcomes require students to identify associations among two things, the matching exercise is a useful item format. The taxonomic level most typically measured is, thus, *factual knowledge.*

---

**EXAMPLE A1.1   A Matching Exercise from a High School Statistics Curriculum**

---

<u>Learning Outcome</u>: The student will identify definitions of descriptive statistical terms (*factual knowledge*):

Items 1–8

Directions: Match the statistical <u>terms</u> listed in Column B with their <u>definitions</u> in Column A by entering the *letter* of the term in the blank space to the left of each definition. A LETTER response can be used once, more than once, or not at all.

Column A (Definitions)                                                          Column B (Terms)

E   1. The difference between the highest and lowest score in        A. frequency
       a distribution.                                               B. mean
C   2. The score value that is found at the mid-point of a           C. median
       distribution of data.                                        D. mode
D   3. The score(s) in a distribution with the highest              E. range
       frequency.                                                   F. deviation
I   4. The point in a distribution below which lie a quarter of     G. standard
       the scores.                                                  H. percentile
F   5. The distance of a score from the mean in a distribution.     I. 25th percentile
A   6. The number of times a score appears in a distribution.
B   7. The sum of the scores divided by their number
       deviation.
C   8. Another name for the 50th percentile.

---

**EXAMPLE A1.2   A Matching Exercise from an Elementary Science Curriculum**

---

<u>Learning Outcome</u>:

The student will match the parts of a green, seed-bearing plant with their primary functions (*factual knowledge*).

Items 1–5

Directions: Match the <u>parts of a plant</u> listed in Column A with the <u>work that each part does</u> in Column B. Enter the *letter* of the term in the blank space to the left of each definition. A response can be used only once.

Column A                                          Column B
(Parts of a plant)                                (Work that the part does)

C   1. Carries water and food to other parts      A. flower
G   2. Grows into an adult plant                   B. leaf
B   3. Makes food using the sun's light            C. stem
F   4. Protects the seed                           D. root
D   5. Draws in water and minerals for the         E. pollen
       plant                                       F. fruit
                                                   G. seed

Topics that can be tested through a matching exercise are (after Gronlund, 1981):

| Years/dates | - | Historical events | Persons | - | Achievements |
| Terms | - | Definitions | Principles | - | Illustrations |
| Inventors | - | Inventions | Parts | - | Functions |
| Quotations | - | Authors | Rules | - | Examples |

Creative item writers could explore the usability of the matching format to measure *application* or *higher-order thinking* in item sets similar to the ones below.

| Problems | - Answers (e.g., in mathematics) |
| Problem scenarios | - Solution strategies |
| Scientific theories | - Applications |
| Quotations | - Translations/interpretations |

There are seven rules to help us in constructing effective matching exercises.

## Matching Exercises

*Rule 1*    The matching exercise should be aligned to the content, behavior, condition, and taxonomic level specified in the selected learning outcome.

The first rule should guide *all* item-writing tasks and is the key to establishing content-based validity at the item level. Item writers should review available specifications and sample items with care before undertaking the item-writing task. This will help them ensure that all items get at the essential content or skill that they were intended to measure. The item set in Example A1.1 shows a satisfactory match with the outcome listed above it. Both the outcome and the items focus on factual knowledge, dealing with definitions in descriptive statistics.

In contrast, consider the two items in Example A2.0 shown next, which were also designed to measure the outcome listed with A1.1. The A2.0 item set focuses on *compu-*

**EXAMPLE A2.0   Poor Content-Based Validity!**

Learning Outcome:

The student will identify definitions of descriptive statistical terms. (*factual knowledge*)

Directions:    Match the *answers* listed in Column B with the *problems* in Column A by entering the letter in the blank space to the left of each item. Each letter response can be used only once.

Column A                                                                                              Column B

_____ 1. The range of the following set of numbers is: 4, 8, 8, 3, 10, 15            A. 5
_____ 2. The median for the following set of numbers is: 4, 7, 8, 3, 9, 12           B. 12
                                                                                                                       C. 8

*tation of descriptive statistics* at the *application level,* rather than on identification of definitions. Its departure from the defined boundaries of the behavior to be tested (computation versus identifying definitions), and the taxonomic category of focus (application level rather than factual knowledge), weakens its content validity. Item-writers bear the responsibility of making sure that items match all the dimensions specified in the outcome: *condition, content, behavior,* and *taxonomic category.*

Matching Exercises

*Rule 2*   Information contained in the matching exercise should be homogeneous in content.

In Example A1.1, we saw that all the items and responses focus on a common topic (descriptive statistics) yielding a *homogeneous* set of matching items. Example A1.2 similarly deals only with parts of green plants, another homogeneous set of items. This is desirable. A heterogeneous matching exercise might look like Example A3.0 (next).

In A3.0, we see that the terms "assessment," "reliability," and "learning outcome," although taken from a course in classroom assessment, do not exactly belong with the terms C–F, which deal with descriptive statistics. A person who is "test wise," but has limited knowledge of the material, could possibly identify the correct answers from fewer number of dissimilar-appearing options. Even greater heterogeneity could be introduced by mixing item sets from completely different courses, units, or topics, basically by mixing apples with oranges! The result would be that the exercise becomes less and less difficult for a canny examinee.

**EXAMPLE A3.0   A Heterogeneous Item Set**

Directions:   Match the terms listed in Column B with their definitions in Column A by entering the letter of the TERM in the blank space to the left of each DEFINITION. Each letter response can be used only once.

Column A (Definitions)

___ 1.   The difference between the highest and lowest score in a distribution.
___ 2.   The score value that is found at the mid-point of a distribution of data.
___ 3.   The score in a distribution with the highest frequency.
___ 4.   Whether a test's results stay consistent.
___ 5.   Another word for a learning objective.

Column B (Terms)

A.   learning outcome
B.   assessment
C.   median
D.   mode
E.   range
F.   reliability

A heterogeneous set of matching items provides unnecessary clues to the respondent. Responses pertinent to one topic might appear as obviously implausible options for other items, encouraging the examinee to respond by guessing or by elimination of unreasonable response options. This impedes valid measurement of the skill or knowledge targeted in the learning outcome.

---

## Matching Exercises

*Rule 3* Longer statements should be used for items (prompts or premises), and placed in the left-hand column (Column A). Response options should be shorter, and placed in the right-hand column (Column B).

As was shown in Examples A1.1 and A1.2, we should place the heavier reading load in the items in Column A, which will help us to frame the question or pose the problem better. The answer options in a matching exercise should ideally be short, succinct, and direct, and placed in Column B.

---

## Matching Exercises

*Rule 4* There should be more response options than items in a matching exercise.

This strategy will reduce chances of examinees simply guessing the right answers to some questions, once they have been able to match up a few of the other items. It will also raise the difficulty level of the exercise, provided that the distracters used are all plausible. (An exception to this rule would apply to an exercise where the same options could be used more than once.)

---

## Matching Exercises

*Rule 5* Directions should very explicitly focus the examinees on the basis for matching, and should indicate clearly whether answer options can be used only once, more than once, or not at all.

Too often, we find matching exercises with less than adequate directions, such as "Match the Columns A and B." Clear and detailed directions protect examinees from misunderstanding the matching task, and control for irrelevant factors in the measurement process. If the task is constructed such that the same answer options could apply to more than one item, this should be pointed out to examinees in the directions given.

Matching Exercises

*Rule 6*   Answer options should be arranged in a logical order.

It is always good to have some logical ordering system in mind when one creates response options for all W-SR items. This rule is especially important for matching exercises. Commonly, we use an alphabetical ordering system for answer options (see Example A4.0). With historical content, one could use a chronological system for arranging dates or years. When the content matter is numeric, items could be arranged in an ascending or descending order. The key for the item writer is to employ the chosen system *in a consistent manner* in all items throughout the test. Again, this strategy guards against providing clues to the examinee. The next example employs an alphabetical arrangement of response options (A4.0).

**EXAMPLE A4.0   Alphabetical Arrangement of Response Options**

Directions:   Match the statistical <u>terms</u> listed in Column B with their <u>definitions</u> in Column A by entering the letter of the TERM in the blank space to the left of each DEFINITION. Each response can be used only once.

| Column A (Definitions) | Column B (Terms) |
|---|---|
| ___ 1. The difference between the highest and lowest score in a distribution. | A. frequency |
| ___ 2. The score value that is found at the midpoint of a distribution of data. | B. mean |
| | C. median |
| ___ 3. The score in a distribution with the highest frequency. | D. mode |
| | E. range |
| ___ 4. The number of times a score appears in a distribution. | F. standard deviation |

Matching Exercises

*Rule 7*   Keep a matching exercise limited to one page. The number of premises should be more than two (2) but less than 15.

This rule is intended to facilitate readability of a matching exercise by keeping all items together on the same page. Barriers to a straightforward presentation of the exercise can introduce both random or systematic errors to the measurement process. Too few premises (two or less) would defeat the advantages of constructing a matching exercise—an alternate format, such as completion or true/false could be considered. Similarly, the item set should not be excessively long. A general rule of thumb is to keep the list below 15 and above 2 items (Hopkins, 1998).

### 7.4.2 Completion or Fill-in-the-Blank Items

The completion or fill-in-the-blank item is another W-SR format that is relatively easy to construct. It is different from the selected-response variety, such as a matching exercise, in that examinees must *supply* an answer on their own. The response is usually required in a single word, short phrase, a number, symbol, or formula. The common presentation formats are (a) the incomplete sentence, (b) a direct question, or (c) a statement of the problem in a complete sentence, each followed by the blank(s).

The *supply* format opens up the possibility of examinees coming up with a range of answers that might be partially correct or nearly correct, but not a perfect match with the response in the answer key. This introduces potential ambiguity and possible errors in objective scoring of the completion items. Consider the item shown in the next example, originally provided by Nitko (1996, p. 127; reproduced with permission).

> Completion Item: Who is the author of the book: "Alice in Wonderland"? _____.
>
> Keyed Answer: Lewis Carroll.
>
> Possible Answers: Lewis Carroll (correct); Louis Carol (correct but misspelled); Charles Dodgeson (correct, as Lewis Caroll was Charles Dodgeson's pen name, but does not match answer key); Charles Dickens (incorrect response).

In the four responses given to the "Alice in Wonderland" question, the first one is clearly correct while the last one is clearly incorrect. However, the two other answers could pose a thorny problem to the scorer. The student who writes "Louis Carol" appears to have knowledge of the answer although the response shows inattentiveness to accurate spelling, a factor that a teacher might or might not value. The student who writes in "Charles Dodgeson" is showing an awareness of the author's actual name, although the expected answer is the author's pen name. In summary, it is important that item writers specify the *exact range of answers that they consider to be fully correct,* as opposed to partially or completely incorrect, when a completion item is conceived. Such information should ideally be included in the specifications for the assessment or item before the items are constructed, so that future items can be written to meet those criteria.

What taxonomic levels are best measured by the completion format? Examples B1.0 through B3.0 illustrate that the completion format is clearly suitable for measuring factual knowledge levels of the taxonomy, whether the performance calls for simple recall or somewhat deeper comprehension of information. This format has also been used effectively in application level items involving basic numeric manipulations or the use of algorithms or rules. Most such usages, however, involve only a few steps of calculations or interpretations. The examples illustrate applications from curricula at the elementary, middle, high school, and possibly higher education levels. The subject areas include statistics, geography, mathematics, and chemistry. After you review Examples B1.0 through B3.0, consider the seven major rules for constructing completion items that follow.

## EXAMPLES B1.0–B3.0    Completion Items

Directions: Complete the following statements by filling in the missing blanks.

B1.0    Learning Outcome: The student will state definitions of statistical terms (*factual knowledge*).

1.    The difference between the highest and lowest score in a distribution is called the _____.
(Answer: *range*)

2.    The score value that is found at the mid-point of a distribution of data is the _____.
(Answer: *median*)

3.    What is the score in a distribution with the highest frequency called? _____.
(Answer: *mode*)

B2.0    Learning Outcome: The student will demonstrate knowledge of selected historical and geographical facts on Florida (*factual knowledge*).

1.    Based on the 1980 census, the population of the city of Tampa, Florida was _____.
(Answer: *800,000*)

2.    The capital city of Florida is _____.
(Answer: *Tallahassee*).

B3.0    Learning Outcome: Given relevant information, the student will use the appropriate rules, formulas, or algorithms to find solutions (*application*).

1.    What digit is in the tens place in the number 521? _____
(Answer: *2*)

2.    The following score distribution was obtained following the administration of a test to 15 students:

    10, 12, 12, 17, 18, 19, 19, 19, 20, 21, 22, 23, 24, 24, 25.

Calculate the mean.                      A. Answer: _____        B. Formula used: _____
Calculate the standard deviation.        C. Answer: _____        D. Formula used: _____

3.    The length of a room is 12 feet. Its width is 8 feet. Use this information to answer the questions below.

    A. What is the area of the room? _____.
    B. What formula did you use in A? _____.

4.    Examine the chemical reaction below. Balance the chemical equation using rules of valency.

    __$CaCo_3$ + __$HCl$ = __$CaCl_2$ + __$H_2O$ + __$CO_2$

## Completion Items

*Rule 1*   The completion items should match the content, behavior, condition, and taxonomic level specified in the selected learning outcome.

To help understand this important principle with completion items, review item sets B1.0 through B3.0, tied to different learning outcomes. The B1.0 set focuses on identification of statistical terms and definitions at the *factual knowledge* level and matches the specified outcome, satisfying the criterion for content validity. B2.0 items are also *factual knowledge* items. To have content validity, they must not only match the taxonomic level, but also show a match with the specified historical/geographic *content* in the outcome.

The B3.0 outcome statement specifies the *conditions* (given relevant information), *behavior* (use the appropriate rules, formulas, or algorithms to find solutions), and *taxonomic level* (application) quite clearly. All the B3.0 items appear to match these three specifications, showing content validity. The B3.0 outcome leaves the content unspecified. As the examples illustrate, it can thus be adapted to different subject areas requiring application of rules, algorithms, or formulas.

## Completion Items

*Rule 2*   Use the direct question form rather than the incomplete statement form when writing completion items.

The direct question format is recommended by most authorities because it is more straightforward, clear, and less subject to ambiguous interpretation by examinees (Nitko, 1996; Linn & Gronlund, 2000). Variations of the question or problem format are illustrated in Examples B1.0 and B3.0. Most incomplete statements can be rewritten in question form, as the next example demonstrates (based on B2.0).

The capital city of the state of Florida is: _____ (Tallahassee) (Incomplete statement)

What is the capital of the state of Florida? _____ (Tallahassee) (Question)

## Completion Items

*Rule 3*   Do NOT use statements that are excerpted verbatim from the text or reading materials with which examinees are likely to be familiar.

When framing questions, verbatim extraction of text encourages a very low level of cognitive functioning, namely, simple association by recall, scaffolded with textbook language. We could measure a deeper level of concept comprehension by the use of different language and sentence structures. We could tap application levels by using novel situations in creating the questions (see the examples in B3.0).

---

## Completion Items

*Rule 4*    Use blanks for key words, concepts, ideas, or principles that are directly relevant to the specifications in the learning outcome.

Focus the statement or question on the specific knowledge sought. Consider the following items, based on the example set in B1.0.

The score in a distribution _____ the highest frequency is the mode. (Answer: *with*) *Poor!*

The score in a _____ with the highest frequency is the mode. (Answer: *distribution*) *Still weak!*

The score in a distribution with the highest frequency is the _____. (Answer: *mode*) *Much better!*

Since the specifications in the learning outcome for the preceding items call for knowledge of definitions of descriptive statistics, the first example, where the word "with" is deleted, is completely irrelevant to what was intended to be measured in the first place. This results in an item with poor content validity. The term deleted in the second example, "distribution" is a statistical term that is related, but somewhat tangentially to the central concept that the item is attempting to measure, knowledge of particular descriptive statistics, such as the "mode." The last item does the best job of capturing a key concept in the outcome.

---

## Completion Items

*Rule 5*    Do NOT use multiple blanks in a given question or statement.

The meaning and purpose of a completion question or statement can be destroyed or distorted by deleting too many words. The consequence is that statement will no longer communicate to the examinee what the item writer had originally hoped it would. To avoid miscommunication, multiple blanks should be avoided. The following item example, based on B1.0, shows alternate, but reasonable responses to an item with multiple blanks that completely contradicts the objective of the item.

The _____ in a _____ with the highest _____ is the _____. (Expected answers: *score, distribution, frequency, mode*)

The <u>senior</u> in a <u>high school</u> with the highest <u>GPA</u> is the <u>valedictorian.</u> *(Answer received from one examinee!)*

## Completion Items

*Rule 6*  Ideally blanks should be placed at the end of the statement, unless the targeted skill or knowledge requires the blank to be inserted earlier.

Rule 6 enables the item writer to pose the problem more completely and clearly, before the examinee is asked to fill in the blank. Keeping all the blanks at the end or to the right also facilitates ease of scoring, keeping the scorer focused on one side of the paper only. The utility of this rule is illustrated in examples B1.0–B3.0. On occasion, you will need to make an exception to this rule, as the next item on correct grammatical usage illustrates.

> Fill in the blank with the correct form of the verb.
> The flowers ———— so lovely! *(Answer: are)*

## Completion Items

*Rule 7*  Blanks should be used for words or phrases of approximately equal length.

This rule is intended to guard against providing clues to examinees through the physical size of the blank inserted in the statement or question, such as shown below.

> *Joining words* used in sentences are called ————, while *naming words* are called ————.
> (Expected answers: *conjunctions,* long word; *nouns,* short word)

***A "Clozing" Note on Variations of the Completion Format.***  Chapter 4 provided an example of a Cloze exercise. Rules 5–7 for completion items need to be modified if Cloze exercises are the item format chosen by the designer. When invented, *Cloze* exercises were intended to assess readability and reading comprehension (Taylor, 1953). In their original form, words from a body of running text would be deleted at fixed intervals by the designer. For instance, every fifth word in a sentence would be a blank, irrespective of its content, length, or relevance to the main theme of the text. Respondents filled in the missing words, and based on the accuracy of their responses, inferences could be made of their ability to comprehend the overall gist of the text. Cloze tests have been effectively employed in foreign language assessments. Cloze exercises can be made more effective by deleting key words rather than words at particular intervals.

The end-of-chapter Comprehension Checks inserted in the computer module accompanying this textbook are examples of modified Cloze exercises. In the versions found for Chapters 1 through 5, only key terms are deleted. Further, a clue is provided in the immediate vicinity of the blank to help the respondents find the answer through sematic cueing. Because they were designed to be formative in their purposes, the semantic scaffolding was deliberately built into the Cloze exercises as a learning support system. The end-of-chapter Comprehension Checks are meant to serve a three-way function: first, to help students identify their own gaps in understanding of basic concepts, second, to serve as a reinforcing, instructional aid that facilitates further learning of material that was still somewhat new; and third, to relieve frustration in the early stages of learning new material. An excerpt from the Chapter 1 Comprehension Check is shown below to illustrate the specific characteristics of the adapted versions of the Cloze exercises.

### Illustration of a Modified Cloze Exercise

During assessment, we measure ____ (1) ____ or characteristics of objects, people, or events. Human traits such as intelligence are called ____ (2) ____ as they are given shape and form by the assessor using operational indicators.

Acceptable answers:   (1)    traits, constructs, variables         Clue: characteristics of objects, people, or events

Acceptable answers:   (2)    constructs                           Clues: given shape and form by the assessor, operational indicators

Excerpted from Chapter 1 Comprehension Check

## 7.4.3   True/False Items

The true/false format is another popular form of selected response item. A typical item of this type consists of a propositional statement that the examinee must affirm or negate with a *yes* or *no*, a *true* or *false,* or a *right* or *wrong* response. The statement can be posed in question form or as a direct statement. Typically, one finds a series of 5 to 15 true/false propositions clustered on a test—a design strategy that helps in providing common directions for the entire item set.

True/false items can be modified to include an explanation or justification component, where the examinees must defend the response they choose. Such additions serve to raise the cognitive demands of the items. The item writers' competence in designing sound true/false items is contingent on their ability to identify propositional material in the content domain.

Like most W-SR item formats, true/false tests have been predominantly used to measure *factual knowledge* outcomes. However, many authors have concluded that the true/false format can be used by skilled item writers to test performances requiring generalizations, comparisons, causal relationships, evaluations, as well as computational skills (Ebel, 1971; Nitko, 1996). There are eight critical rules that we should follow when writing true/false statements. Consider the examples in C1.0–C4.0.

C1.0   Learning Outcome: The student will identify definitions of terms (*factual knowledge*).

Directions:
Indicate in the space provided to the left of each item whether the following statements are True or False.

Subject: Statistics
(Answer: *false*)              _____ 1. The difference between the highest and lowest score in a distribution is called the frequency.

(Answer: *true*)              _____ 2. The score value that is found at the midpoint of a distribution of data is the median.

(Answer: *true*)              _____ 3. The score in a distribution with the highest frequency is called the mode.

Subject: Parts and Functions of a Flower
(Answer: *true*) T F      _____ 2. After fertilization, the ovary of a flower becomes the fruit.

C2.0   Learning Outcome: Given relevant information, the student will apply the appropriate rules, formulas, or algorithms to check mathematical solutions (*application*).

Directions: Indicate in the space provided to the left of each item whether the following statements are Correct or Incorrect.

*Incorrect*              _____ 1. The digit in the tens place in the number 18563 is 5.
*Correct*              _____ 2. The median in the following score distribution is 19.
                         10, 12, 12, 17, 18, 19, 19, 19, 20, 21, 22, 23, 24, 24, 25.
*Incorrect*              _____ 3. The shape of the following score distribution can be described as normal.
                         10, 12, 12, 17, 18, 19, 19, 19, 20, 21, 22, 23, 24, 25

C3.0   Learning Outcome: The student will evaluate the correctness of applied propositions, taken from a given subject area or topic (*higher order-thinking*).

Directions: Indicate in the space provided to the left of each item whether the following statements are (T)rue or (F)alse.

Subject: Statistics
(Answer: *true*)              _____ 1. Together, the mean and range are useful in describing the shape of a distribution.

Subject: Classroom Assessment
(Answer: *false*)              _____ 3. Increasing the number of items on a short response test from 20 to 30 will improve the content validity of results.

(Answer: *false*)              _____ 4. Reliability is improved by making sure that an item is written to match the content specified in a learning outcome.

C4.0   Learning Outcome: The student will evaluate the correctness of propositions in a problem situation taken from a given subject area or topic (*higher-order thinking*).

Directions:
Indicate in the space provided to the left of each item whether the following statements are (T)rue or (F)alse. Provide an explanation for your answer.

_____ 1. The following multiple choice item measures the *application* level of Bloom's taxonomy.

   *Circle the sign below that means add.*
   *a)* +
   *b)* ×
   *c)* −

Answer:              False
Explanation:         *It is false because the item requires only association of the symbol with the addition operation, but not the actual adding of numbers.*

True or False

*Rule 1*    True/false items should match the content, behavior, condition, and taxonomic level specified in the selected learning outcome.

This important rule applies to the true/false item for the same reasons that it does for the other item formats—to ensure content-based validity during item construction. Evaluate the match of the items in examples C1.0–C4.0 with the learning outcomes above each item set. Using the statistics examples, do the items matched to Outcome C1.0 measure only factual knowledge? Do the items matched to C.2.0 measure application? Does the item requiring the examinee to consider the quality of a multiple choice item call for evaluation level skills? To what extent does each item have content-based validity?

True or False

*Rule 2*    Focus on one idea in each proposition. Avoid double-barreled items.

Incorporation of more than one idea raises the chances of creating an item that is partly true and partly false. It also makes the item confusing to the reader, as the item below illustrates.

*Indicate whether True or False*
T/F. 1. Tallahassee is the capital city with the largest population in Florida.

In the previous item, the writer includes two separate concepts: 1) capital city of Florida and 2) city with the largest population in Florida. The part of the item that states that Tallahassee is the capital of Florida is true. However, the part stating that it is the city with the largest population in Florida is untrue. This dual proposition is impossible to affirm or negate with a categorical response, making it problematic for a true/false item.

True or False

*Rule 3*    Focus on important ideas, NOT trivia or common knowledge in each proposition.

Avoid measuring trivial topics or common sense ideas, as this makes the assessment process inefficient. The answer to items should not be obvious to uninstructed groups.
    For example:

*Indicate whether True or False*
T/F 1. Teachers use tests.                                   *Relatively obvious and trivial!*
T/F 2. Teacher-made tests should be designed to have high content validity. *Better!*

### True or False

*Rule 4*   Do NOT use statements that are excerpted verbatim from the text or from reading materials with which examinees are likely to be familiar.

Restate statements from the text or reading materials so that somewhat higher mental demands are made on the examinee. Use of verbatim statements encourages testing for memorization rather than conceptual understanding.

### True or False

*Rule 5*   Do NOT use double negatives in statements.

More than one negatively stated word leads to ambiguity in a propositional statement. This makes it difficult for the examinee to make a singular judgment about its accuracy. For example:

> *Indicate whether (T)rue or (F)alse*
> T/F   1. It is *not* desirable that scores from classroom assessments have *no* content validity.
>     *Ambiguous!*
> T/F   2. Results from classroom assessments should have high content validity.
>     *Better!*

Preferably, true/false items should be stated positively. If negative terms are used, they should be limited to only one and should be highlighted. For example:

> *Indicate whether True or False*
> T/F   1. Content-based validity is *not* important in classroom assessments.
>     *Acceptable!*

### True or False

*Rule 6*   Make sure the statement used is indisputably true or false.

Items based on opinions can rarely be defended as indisputably true or false. Avoid the use of opinions, unless you cite the source. Also avoid the use of material that is conditionally true. For example:

> T/F Norming is an important step during assessment design.
>     *Poor!*

As stated, the above item might pose a problem, as the proposition would hold true only when applied to developing norm-referenced tests. The statement would be false if a criterion-referenced assessment was being designed. This makes the statement condition-ally true, and therefore unsuitable material for true/false items.

A revised and improved version of the previous item might focus on a principle that would be universally true under most or all conditions, such as the concept of validation in assessment design.

> T/F According to Jones (1995), validation is necessary before assessments are used in particular contexts.
> *Better!*

---

True or False

*Rule 7*   Keep true and false statements of approximately equal length, distribute them randomly, and have approximately equal numbers of true or false answers on the test.

Item writers must guard against falling into predictable patterns when developing true/false item sets so that test-savvy students are not clued into finding the correct answers without mastery of the material. Some of these patterns could include inadver-tently making all the true statements longer sentences than the false ones, having more true items than false ones, or falling into a fixed arrangement of the items on the test, such as TTFFTT, TTTFTTTF, or TFTFTF.

---

True or False

*Rule 8*   Avoid using words such as "always," "never," "usually," or "generally" in statements.

Finally, absolutes such as "always" or "never" are usually found in statements where the item writer attempted to make the statement completely true or completely false, and serve as a clue to the test-wise! Item writers tend to use catchall terms such as "usually" or "generally" for the same purposes. Such specific determiners serve as semantic clues to verbally adept students, giving us reason to avoid their use when constructing items.

### 7.4.4   Multiple Choice Items

The multiple choice item (D1.0–D3.0) is the most widely applied selected response item format. In its basic form, it consists of a *stem*, which presents the problem or question, fol-lowed by a number of *response choices*, of which only one is the best or correct answer. Incorrect response options are called *distracters* or *foils*. The number of answer options usually varies from three to five, with the probability of simply guessing the answer by chance decreasing from 33% to 20% as the number of alternatives increase.

The basic multiple choice format (see D1.0, Item 1) uses an incomplete statement in the stem, and can be enhanced with several modifications. Consider the other examples in D1.0–D3.0. The second item in the D1.0 set uses the *analogy* form. Another notable variation is the *context-dependent* item, in which a reading passage, scenario, data, and/or graph precedes a series of multiple choice questions (see the D2.0 set). The examinee is required to use the information provided to determine the correct responses.

The popular perception (and one that is well-supported by common practice) that W-SR tests tend to measure only low levels of learning can be dispelled by skilled and creative use of the multiple choice format. Multiple choice items are more versatile than the other formats in their ability to tap a wide variety of cognitive levels, ranging from simple recall to more in-depth interpretation, application, complex generalization, or problem-solving skills. The examples in D1.0–D3.0 attempt to illustrate applications covering a range of cognitive levels. The nine most important rules for writing multiple choice items run parallel to the guidelines for the other item formats.

Multiple Choice

*Rule 1*   Multiple choice items should match the content, behavior, condition, and taxonomic level specified in the selected learning outcome.

To ensure content-based validity, we must heed this important rule when designing multiple choice items as well. You are now familiar with the steps for conducting such an item evaluation. To reiterate, they are:

1. Identify the specific content, behavior, condition, and taxonomic level in the learning outcome to be tested.
2. Check to see that the item is written within the confines of these specifications.

Application of this rule is illustrated in the examples in D1.0–D3.0. For example, items 1 and 2 (D1.0) measure the *factual knowledge* outcome dealing with definitions of statistical terms, showing a match with the intended outcome. The D2.0 item set, on the other hand, requires the examinee to apply some rules, formulas, or processes with data provided to determine the correct answer, making them *application* level items that are consistent with the outcome specifications.

The taxonomic level of the outcome and the specific content, behavior, and condition embedded in the outcome are often interdependent. Violating one leads to the violation of one or more of the others, thus lowering content validity. Consider the following item, written to measure the *application*-level learning outcome in example D2.0:

> *Outcome:* Given relevant information, the student will apply the appropriate rules, formulas, or algorithms to check mathematical solutions.
>
> *Item:*     Thirty minutes is equal to:
>
> A.   a quarter of an hour
> B.   *a half of an hour*
> C.   a full hour.

## EXAMPLES D1.0–D3.0   Multiple Choice Items

D1.0   Learning Outcome: The student will identify definitions of statistical terms (*factual knowledge*).

Directions: In items 1–2, select the best answer from the choices given.

(Incomplete statement as stem)

    1.   The difference between the highest and lowest score in a distribution is called the:
       A.   frequency
       B.   mean
       C.   median
       D.   *range*
       E.   standard deviation

(Analogy form)

    2.   Mean is to central tendency as Standard deviation is to:
       A.   correlation
       B.   distribution
       C.   histogram
       D.   range
       E.   *variability*

D2.0   Learning Outcome: Given relevant information, the student will apply the appropriate rules, formulas, or algorithms to evaluate mathematical solutions (*higher-order thinking*).

Directions: Select the best or correct answer from the choices given.

(Question as stem)

    3.   What is the digit in the tens place in the number 18563?
       A.   1
       B.   3
       C.   5
       D.   *6*
       E.   8

Directions: Plot the following data in a frequency polygon and then answer question 4.
10, 12, 12, 18, 19, 19, 19, 19, 19, 21, 22, 24, 24, 25

(Context-dependent item)

    4.   The best descriptor of the shape of the distribution is:
       A.   Bimodal, symmetrical
       B.   Unimodal, approximately normal
       C.   Unimodal, positively skewed
       D.   *Unimodal, negatively skewed*
       E.   Multimodal, nonnormal

D3.0   Learning Outcome: The student will evaluate generalizations and cause and effect relationships in science (*higher-order thinking*).

Directions: Look at the time on the clock to the right to answer question 5.

(Context-dependent)

    5.   The time on the clock is:
       A.   1:40
       B.   1:45
       C.   a quarter hour before 2:00
       D.   three-quarter hours after 1:00

In the preceding item, the *condition* appears to be violated, and in doing so, the taxonomic level that is captured is *factual knowledge*. Will a student need to read the time on the clock to answer the item, as specified in the outcome? Clearly not. Without being forced to use that information, the student will very likely simply recall the response from memory. If the item elicits memorization rather than application of the rule for reading time on an analog clock (as intended in the outcome), it would weaken its content-based validity. The mismatch could be fixed by altering the item as follows:

> *Directions:* Look at the time on the clock to the right to answer the next question. If the small hand points to the number shown and the big hand on the clock is pointing to 12, as in the picture, what time would it be?
>
> A.   1:00
> *B.   2:00*
> C.   3:00

Multiple Choice

*Rule 2*   The stem should be longer than the response options.

Application of Rule 2 is illustrated in all the examples in D1.0–D3.0. The reading load in the stem gives the writer the opportunity to state the question more clearly and completely. It can also help you avoid wordiness and redundancies in the response options. This simple strategy controls error in communication of the question to the examinee, as illustrated below:

> A tomato is:                                   *Poor!*
> A.   the part of the plant called the root.
> B.   the part of the plant called the fruit.
> C.   the part of the plant called the stem.
> D.   the part of the plant called the flower.
>
> What part of the plant is the tomato?         *Better!*
> A.   flower
> B.   fruit
> C.   root
> D.   stem

Multiple Choice

*Rule 3*   The stem should NOT be repeated in the response options.

Avoid redundancies in your use of language as it makes the item confusing. The next item would be much improved if the phrase *"Paul spent"* was retained in the stem to say *"Altogether, Paul spent:"* , and deleted from the answer options. In the example shown earlier, the phrase *"is the part of the plant called"* should not be repeated, but moved to the stem to say: *"What part of the plant is the tomato?"*, followed by response options such as, *"the root," "the stem," and "the fruit."*

Paul bought a dozen eggs for $1.29 and bread for $1.99. Altogether:

A.  Paul spent $3.28                              *Poor!* Delete repeated phrases.
B.  Paul spent $2.18
C.  Paul spent $0.79

A tomato:                                         *Poor!* Delete repeated phrases.

A.  is the part of the plant called the root.
B.  is the part of the plant called the fruit.
C.  is the part of the plant called the stem.
D.  is *not* a vegetable.

---

Multiple Choice

*Rule 4*   The incorrect response options, or distracters, should be plausible and of approximately equal difficulty.

Implausible options are usually answers unrelated to the topic in the outcome measured. They provide opportunities for the test-wise student to use processes of elimination to discern the answer. A *plausible* response, in contrast, is one that will look like the right answer to examinees with partial knowledge of the material, or to those that may have some conceptual misunderstandings.

In the following item, the correct response (option A) is balanced by two distracters that tap common errors made by elementary students (failing to regroup numbers from one column to the next, as in options B, C), or choosing the wrong operation to solve the problem (subtraction, as in option D). Implausible response options here might have been a *$0.0, $100.0,* or *All of the above,* answer. Notice also that the use of plausible distracters puts all the options on similar levels of difficulty.

Paul bought a dozen eggs for $1.29 and bread for $1.99. Altogether, *Paul spent:*

*A.*   $3.28
B.   $3.18
C.   $2.18
D.   $0.79

---

Multiple Choice

*Rule 5*   The incorrect response options, or distracters, should be parallel in structure, content, and length with the correct option.

The rationale for Rule 5 is to keep the item distracters homogeneous with the correct answer—thus reducing the chances of providing unwarranted clues to the test-wise.

We must guard against making the correct answer the longest one! We should avoid inconsistencies in grammatical or syntax structure, as they make us vulnerable to providing clues. All answers should be homogeneous with respect to the topic, as this increases the difficulty of the item. To appreciate why the homogeneity rule is important, examine a distorted version of the example of Item 2 below (D1.0) and compare it to the original.

2. *Mean* is to central tendency as *Standard Deviation* is to:
   A. a lesson plan
   B. norm-referenced test development and validation
   C. calculating averages
   D. the school reform movement
   E. *variability*

*Problems:* Answers not parallel in content, grammatical form (lack of consistency in use of articles *a* and *the*) or length. *Poor!*

The lack of homogeneous content makes options a, b, and d obviously wrong answers to individuals who exercise some common sense when taking the test. Only options c and e deal with statistics, making the item relatively easy. In terms of language usage for direct communication, the lack of parallelness also results in unnecessary ambiguity that can lead to unreliable responses from examinees.

Multiple Choice

*Rule 6*   The response options should be listed vertically and follow a logical arrangement or ordering scheme.

Most authorities recommend the vertical presentation of answer options. This makes for a less cluttered and confusing presentation. The rationale for using a logically driven order in presenting the answer options (whether alphabetical, increasing numbers, or decreasing numbers) is consistent with that given for matching items. The idea is to prevent ourselves from providing inadvertent clues. We should decide on an ordering scheme for an entire W-SR test and apply it consistently for the whole instrument.

Multiple Choice

*Rule 7*   In a list of questions, the correct answer position should vary.

Random distribution of the correct answer options, in terms of their location on the test, will ward off the test-wise from finding patterns. Assessment designers should make a deliberate attempt to randomly vary the correct answer position after a test has been constructed.

Multiple Choice

*Rule 8*    Options like "All of the above" and "None of the above" should be used with judgment.

Multiple choice item writers feel some pressure to generate distracters! Often the third or fourth distracter is very difficult to create—an easy standby is the "all of the above" or "none of the above" option. However, *it is better to have fewer distracters than implausible or ineffective ones.* "All of the above" or "none of the above" options should thus be used sparingly and judiciously. Consider the next multiple choice item, which has a definite correct answer.

Paul bought a dozen eggs for $1.29 and bread for $1.99. Altogether, Paul spent:
A.   *$3.28*
B.   $3.18
C.   $2.18
D.   $0.79
E.   All of the above

Here, option E, clearly is an impossible answer, and one that the item writer appears to have used unthinkingly in order to find a fifth distracter. An improved version might have used "none of the above" instead, where the student would be forced to do the calculations to decide whether the right answer is included among the options.

Multiple Choice

*Rule 9*    Items should be stated positively. If the negative form is used, the negative words should be underlined or highlighted.

Consider the following item (Example D2.0, Item 5). It is a context-dependent item, where the student must refer to the picture of the clock to respond; additionally it is stated in negative form. The word "not" is enlarged in order to get the attention of the respondent, thus preventing potential misunderstandings. Rule 9 should be followed in every instance of W-SR item construction where the negative form is used.

Look at the time on the clock to the right to answer questions 5 and 6.
5.   The time on the clock is NOT:
  A.   forty minutes after 1:00
  B.   fifteen minutes before 2:00
  C.   three-quarter hours after 1:00
  D.   a quarter hour before 2:00

## 7.5 Complex Interpretive W-SR Exercises

### 7.5.1 What Are Complex Interpretive Exercises and When Are They Useful?

A complex, interpretive exercise is a context-dependent set of W-SR items that functions as a whole, and is specifically designed to capture higher-order thinking abilities. Interpretive exercises consist of a written, tabular, or graphic presentation, followed by a series of items. The contextual material can be an informational passage, such as a newspaper article; a literary passage, such as a poem or story; quantitative material, like an excerpt of a data table or graph from a technical report; or a piece of art, like a musical score or painting. Typically, each item set targets a complex-level learning outcome, under which is included a cluster of more specific skills and mental abilities. The questions could call for comparing and contrasting, determining relevance, finding inaccuracies or gaps, or drawing generalizations and inferences from the information provided.

Linn & Gronlund (2000) identify the following as suitable learning outcomes to test with an interpretive W-SR exercise:

- Recognizing valid conclusions and inferences from information given
- Interpreting relationships in verbal or quantitative data, as displayed in tables and graphs
- Recognizing the relevance of information for a purpose
- Evaluating arguments.

### 7.5.2 Examples of Complex Interpretive Exercises

Two examples of interpretive exercises that employ multiple choice and modified true/false formats are excerpted from other sources to facilitate our understandings of this particular approach to assessing complex learning outcomes (see Figures 7.2 A-B). Let us consider each one in turn.

In Figure 7.2 (A, excerpted with permission from Linn & Gronlund, 2000, pp. 220–221), we see an elementary level example dealing with evaluating relevance of information to solve a problem. The contextual information for the item is provided in a scenario that precedes seven relevant/irrelevant pieces of information needed to solve a problem that is posed. The items require students to read and interpret the passage accurately, determine the kinds of information that would be relevant to solving the problem, and evaluate the information given in Items 1–7 to determine its pertinence for generating a solution. Items employ a modified true-false format (yes versus no). As a whole, the item set demands several levels of cognition, including high levels of functioning.

How can we make meaningful inferences about levels of cognition from the response patterns of examinees (a validity issue)? Further, how can we design the inter-

EXAMPLE      Bill lost his boot on the way to school.  He wanted to put a notice on the
bulletin board so that the other children could help him find it.  Which of the
following sentences tell something that would help children find the boot?

**Directions:**  Underline YES if it would help, NO if it would not help.

<u>Yes</u>   No      1. The boot was black.
Yes   <u>No</u>      2. It was very warm.
<u>Yes</u>   No      3. It was for his right foot.
Yes   <u>No</u>      4. It was a Christmas present.
Yes   <u>No</u>      5. It was nice looking.
<u>Yes</u>   No      6. It had a zipper.
<u>Yes</u>   No      7. It had a gray lining.

**FIGURE 7.2    Complex Interpretive W-SR Exercise (A)**
Reprinted from *Measurement and Assessment in Teaching* by Linn/Gronlund © 2000, by permission of Pearson Education, Inc., Upper Saddle River, NJ 07458.

pretive exercise to control for differences that are caused by unintended interferences (say, prior knowledge of examinees), unrelated to the higher levels of cognition that we are targeting here? In the example in Figure 7.2, we see that the items are not directly related to any subject area. It would be rare if a few students *knew* some of the answers beforehand. Thus, we can safely assume that while different students may employ cognitive processes in different ways and to different degrees to arrive at their responses, they will probably be using higher order thinking processes to respond to the exercise as a whole. By controlling for subject-area dependence when we design the item, we can thus enhance the validity of our inferences from responses.

For assessment designers, then, an issue for serious deliberation is whether we want the interpretive exercise to be *content-free* or *content-dependent*. If there is a built-in expectation that students have prior knowledge of terms and concepts relevant to the problem scenario, students who are more familiar with the content matter or have been *taught to think* in particular ways with the material will have an advantage. A good start would be to clarify the *content* and *cognitive behaviors* in the learning outcomes that we target for measurement with an interpretative exercise. Next, we need to make a decision regarding whether we wish to have the exercise dependent on prior knowledge at all. If we do, we need to ask to what degree we can assume prior knowledge of the topic in a typical group of examinees? Selection of appropriate contextual material for the population we are assessing is a crucial design decision for interpretive exercises.

In Figure 7.2 (B, also excerpted with permission from Linn & Gronlund, 2000, pp. 220–221), we see another example that targets learning outcomes similar to that in example (A). This item set is intended for an older population and another relatively content-free item set. Very few adults would likely be familiar with the statistical data embedded in the scenario.

EXAMPLE    Percentage of population between the ages of 25 and 34 who have completed secondary and higher education, by gender, for large industrialized countries: 1995.

| | Males | | Females | |
|---|---|---|---|---|
| Country | Secondary Education | Higher Education | Secondary Education | Higher Education |
| Canada | 82.4 | 19.2 | 85.4 | 19.7 |
| France | 87.3 | 13.7 | 83.8 | 14.3 |
| Germany | 91.0 | 13.7 | 86.7 | 11.3 |
| Italy | 46.9 | 7.8 | 51.2 | 8.6 |
| Japan | 89.3 | 34.2 | 91.8 | 11.5 |
| United Kingdom | 87.5 | 16.3 | 84.7 | 13.1 |
| United States | 86.1 | 25.1 | 88.2 | 24.9 |

(Source: Data from "The Condition of Education 1998," Washington, D.C.: National Center for Educational Statistics, U.S. Department of Education, 1998. Available online at http://nces.ed.gov/pubs98/conditio0n98/index.html)

**Directions:** The following statements refer to the data in the table above. Read each statement and mark your answer according to the following key.
Circle –
   **S** if the statement is supported by the data in the table.
   **R** if the statement is refuted by the data in the table.
   **N** if the statement is neither supported nor refuted by the data.

| | | | |
|---|---|---|---|
| *S* | R | N | 1. The United States has a smaller discrepancy in percentage completion of higher education for males and females between the ages of 25 and 34 than any of the other countries listed. |
| S | R | *N* | 2. College admissions policies give preferential treatment to male applicants over female applicants. |
| Ŝ | R | *N* | 3. It is more difficult to get into college in Germany than in Japan. |
| S | *R* | N | 4. When males and females are combined, the U.S. has the highest secondary school completion percentage for young adults between the ages of 25 and 34. |

**FIGURE 7.2    Complex Interpretive W-SR Exercise (B)**
      Reprinted from *Measurement and Assessment in Teaching* by Linn/Gronlund © 2000, by permission of Pearson Education, Inc., Upper Saddle River, NJ 07458.

## 7.5.3   Rules for Writing Complex Interpretive Exercises

All the rules for writing specific W-SR items would still apply when we design W-SR exercises that call for complex levels of interpretation based on a given passage or contextual material. However, the issues raised about the level of content-dependency when measuring higher-level thinking should be borne in mind. Linn and Gronlund (2000) suggest that we follow these added guidelines to the previously listed rules. Among their suggestions are the following:

- Select contextual material that is new to the student, but appropriate and meaningful for the curriculum outcomes and developmental level of examinees. For example, a graph from a news digest, or a newspaper cartoon appropriate for the age group, could be good sources.
- Keep the contextual information clear and easy to read. The reading level should be kept low; pictures, graphs, and tables should be uncluttered and easy to read.
- Frame the questions so as to require higher levels of analysis and interpretation of the material.
- Keep all the items dependent on the contextual information.
- Keep the list of questions approximately equal in length with the body of contextual information.
- Make sure that knowledgeable experts on the content area and typical examinee group can agree with your answer key.

Further information on interpretive exercises is available in Wesman (1971). In designing such exercises, we should remember that they are difficult to develop and some of the targeted learning outcomes may be better measured with open-ended or performance assessments (Oosterhof, 1999).

## 7.6   The Last Word on Clues

Clues for the correct answer in W-SR items help narrow down choices for test-wise examinees, thus giving the answer away. They can be caused by five major factors:

| | |
|---|---|
| 1. Grammatical or sentence structure: | Where the use of an article or verb gives away the answer |
| 2. Lack of parallel form, content, or length: | Where the correct answer stands out from the other options because of its length, form, or contents |
| 3. Clang associations: | Where a prefix, word, or phrase in the stem is also repeated in the correct answer, suggesting an association |
| 4. Nonsensical options: | Where a distracter is so unreasonable that it can easily be eliminated |
| 5. Verbatim use of textbook language: | Where familiar language association rather than the skill to be measured helps the respondent find the right answer |

## 7.7   Choosing the Best W-SR Item Format

Of the four major W-SR formats, how would you decide on the best one for a particular assessment design situation? If one thinks of advantages and disadvantages of the individual item types, matching and completion are possibly the best for measurement of *factual knowledge* (knowledge and comprehension in Bloom's taxonomy). They are easier to construct without flaws. With large type, pictorial, or other adaptations, they are well suited for young or special needs populations.

True/false items are better for propositional material. As shown, they can also be modified for complex interpretive exercises. However, because there are only two options for each item, they provide a 50% chance of examinees guessing the right answer.

Multiple choice formats and their variations, when well constructed, reduce the chances of guessing the correct answer. Research has shown them to yield high reliability and usability across multiple taxonomic levels, particularly the higher ones. Thus, this last format continues to be a favorite among test developers.

True/false and multiple choice formats are better for older examinees. Directions for complex item sets can appear demanding for individuals uninitiated in W-SR test taking. To be valid, both true/false and multiple choice items demand greater skills from item writers, but both formats lend themselves better to the measurement of higher-level skills than matching and completion.

## 7.8  W-SR Test Assembly

With experience, you will be able to generate a pool of items for each cell in a table of specifications, from which you can randomly select the required number to assemble a test. Alternatively, you might select the required number of items from textbook or other curricular materials to match your assessment specifications. The final assembly of an achievement test entails the following tasks:

- Providing a succinct title that identifies the test purpose and topic
- Organizing/arranging the items on the test by section or subdomain
- Preparing directions for the overall test and for groups of items that require specific instructions
- Inserting graphs, tables, pictures, or passages according to the specifications
- Developing an answer key that is accurate/reasonable
- Conducting a content validation followed by necessary revisions of the tool

### 7.8.1  Directions

Examine the sample set of test directions shown in Figure 7.3. Test directions should stand out and be very clear to examinees. Occasionally, you might need additional directions for the test administrator or proctor. At other times instructions may have to be read aloud to students. All such requirements should be specified in the Assessment Specifications document.

### 7.8.2  Layout

The layout and arrangement of items on a test should ideally be aesthetic and uncluttered. Different sections and items should be spaced appropriately. The print should be clear and

---

**Examination Unit 1**
**Fall, 1999**
**Part One**
**Directions**

1. Your examination has two parts.
   Part 1 is closed book. When you
   finish Part 1, turn in your booklet and
   answer sheet. Then, you will be given
   Part 2 of the examination.

2. Make sure that there are 60 items on
   Part 1 of the test.

3. All items are multiple choice with 3-5
   answer options. For each item,
   indicate the best or correct answer by
   marking the appropriate space on the
   separate answer sheet. Select only
   one answer per item. There is no
   penalty for guessing, so attempt all
   items. Use a No. 2 soft lead pencil to
   bubble in your answers.

4. Carefully read specific directions
   given for a particular group of items.

5. The test is untimed.

6. If you have questions while taking the
   test, please raise your hand.

---

**FIGURE 7.3    A Set of Directions for W-SR Assessment Tool**

legible. Item numbering must be sequential and accurate. Supporting materials, such as pictures or passages, should be large enough, appropriately labeled, and easy to read. Clustering of items by type—such as all true/false items together, followed by all matching items, and so on—enables the designer to develop common sets of directions for each subset. Such arrangements are also very likely to help respondents adjust to format changes as the test progresses.

If *criterion-referenced* test use is indicated in the specification, the test items should be organized on the test by subdomains tied to specific learning outcomes (or objectives) in the larger domain. This will facilitate analyses of student mastery levels by outcome with the results (discussed in Chapter 11). Outcome-based coaching, feedback, and remediation can follow for individual or subgroups of examinees. Different sections of the test should have appropriate subheadings to facilitate the examinees in making the transitions during test-taking.

With *norm-referenced* tests, items are usually organized from easy to more difficult—this is typical in power tests (Hopkins, 1998). The psychometric consequence of alternative item arrangements has been found by most researchers to be negligible, unless the test is a speeded one (Hambleton & Traub, 1974; Sax & Carr, 1962). Arranging the items from easy to difficult can naturally be more reassuring to examinees from a psychological standpoint, as their self-confidence is likely to build with every item that appears familiar.

### 7.8.3 Answer Key

Preparation of an accurate answer key is often taken for granted by test developers with W-SR tests. The answers keyed as correct should be arrived at by consensus among individuals knowledgeable about the domain, such as the test developer, as well as others who teach the same subject at the same level. If the correct answer involves assumptions regarding the examinees' prior experience or exposure to the material, developers should make sure that the population specified will have the necessary background.

## 7.9 Content Validation

Content validation helps us control for common pitfalls that we face during item and test construction. Examine Table 7.5, which provides a checklist for conducting a systematic, logical review or content validation of a drafted W-SR assessment. The checklist encapsulates and reiterates the major W-SR test construction rules with which you are now familiar. In formal W-SR test development settings, these reviews are three-dimensional and consist of:

- Reviews by subject area experts who teach at the same level (other teachers)
- Reviews by measurement experts who can evaluate the items with criteria such as validity and reliability in mind
- Reviews by experts who are qualified to screen the items for possible inclusion of biased content or language that might work against special needs populations or those in different cultural, linguistic, and gender groups

The first level of review should be done in classroom situations. You could seek the help of knowledgeable reviewers who were preferably not involved in the item or test development process for this purpose. The reviewers would juxtapose the drafted test against the specifications, and use a checklist similar to Table 7.5 to identify weak areas in the tool constructed. If the review is done conscientiously, areas that need revision or deletion should become apparent right away.

Typically, other teachers from similar classrooms would be the best "peer reviewers" or content experts to perform the content validation. It would be advantageous if the persons also had some expertise in assessment methodology. An introductory training in measurement, as you are gaining through this course, will help peers screen the items for content validity, clues, and potential sources of extraneous error with greater levels of comfort.

**TABLE 7.5   Content-Validation Checklist for Written Structured Response (W-SR) Assessment Tool**

*Quality of the W-SR Assessment Specification:*

1. Is the assessment purpose clear?
2. Is the population identified with adequate detail?
3. Is the construct domain clarified with general and specific indicators?

   a. As applicable, do individual indicators clearly specify the content, behavior, conditions, and performance criterion?

   b. Are the indicators classified by taxonomic level?

4. Is there a Table of Specification indicating the number of items to be allocated to different indicators and taxonomic levels?
5. Is all the information on FORM II complete?

*Overall Check of the W-SR Assessment Tool:*

1. Does the overall test/instrument match the Table of Specifications (check number of items by indicator and taxonomic level)?
2. Does the assessment tool match other specifications outlined in FORM II?
   - Conditions of testing?
   - Developmental level, age, and other specifications for the intended population?
   - Assessment purposes?
   - Adaptations or modifications for special populations?
3. Are vocabulary and reading level appropriate?
4. Is the test title clear?
5. Are the directions clear?
6. If sections are present, are the directions clear for the separate sections?
7. Is the item layout and spacing good? (Does it enhance easy reading and interpretation of the items)?
8. If applicable, are charts, graphs, pictures, and passages clear and appropriate?
9. Is the total time for testing and scoring procedure clearly defined for examinees?
10. Is the type or writing legible?
11. Is the scoring key accurate and reasonable?
12. Is the test free of any biased and inflammatory language or pictures?

13. If used as specified, is the test likely to be free from an "opportunity to learn" bias?

*Checks for Individual W-SR Items:*

1. Does the item match the content, behavior, condition, and taxonomic level in the targeted outcome?
2. Does the item have correct grammar, punctuation, and spelling?
3. Does the item have only *one* clear best or correct answer?
4. Is intricate or confusing language avoided?
5. Is the item free of any clues?
6. Is the item stated positively? If negative words are used, are they highlighted?

*Additional Checks for Matching Items:*

1. Are directions for the matching set clear?
2. Are the item groups homogeneous?
3. Are there >2 and <15 items in a set?
4. Are items to the left and answers to the right?
5. Are there more response options than items?
6. Are items and responses arranged using a logical system?

*Additional Checks for Completion Items:*

1. Are blanks placed at the end of the statement (unless the outcome requires a different placement)?
2. Are the blanks for key words only?
3. Are multiple blanks avoided?
4. Are blanks of approximately equal length?
5. Are statements from the text rephrased (no statements are picked verbatim from the text)?

*Additional Checks for True-False Items:*

1. Is the statement clearly true or clearly false?
2. Are double negatives avoided?
3. Are true and false statements about equal in length?
4. Are there approximately equal numbers of true and false statements in a set?
5. Are the true and false statements randomly distributed in a set?
6. Are statements from the text rephrased (no statements are picked verbatim from the text)?

**TABLE 7.5  Continued**

*Additional Checks for Multiple Choice Items:*

1. Is there only one question or idea in the stem?
2. Are the responses parallel in form and content?
3. Are responses about equal in length?
4. Are "All of the above" or "None of the above" used sparingly and with judgment?
5. Does the correct answer position vary in a list of items?
6. Are responses to items listed in some logical order?
7. Are response options listed vertically?
8. Are response options to an item of about equal difficulty?

9. Are the distracters plausible? Do they reflect common errors or misunderstandings in typical examinees?

*Additional Checks for Interpretive Exercises:*

1. Is the contextual material likely to be NEW to the student?
2. Is the information clear and easy to read?
3. Do the questions require higher levels of analysis and interpretation?
4. Are items dependent on the contextual information?
5. Is the list of questions of appropriate length?
6. Is the answer key reasonable?

### 7.9.1  Key Flaws in W-SR Assessment Development

What are some key flaws in putting together W-SR tests? Table 7.5 tells us that these would include:

- Losing sight of the assessment purposes during test construction
- Forgetting who is in the targeted population
- Improper or inadequate specification of the domain
- Too many or too few items for particular domain indicators or learning outcomes (not using a table of specifications can lead to this problem)
- Writing items that fail to closely match the domain indicators or learning outcomes
- Writing items that are ambiguous, flawed, or written without adequate attention to rules
- Poor formatting and presentation of the overall instrument
- Introduction of biases in the language or content of the test or items.

Biases can be introduced in W-SR tests when we do not control for the reading level of the items, use words or material that might offend or confuse particular segments of the population in a systematic way, or include material that may not be taught through the curriculum that is typically provided to targeted examinees. The next section provides a discussion of factors that lead to biases during W-SR test design.

## 7.10  Bias during W-SR Assessment Design

### 7.10.1  Bias Due to Readability

During content validation, assessment developers should also screen the test and items for possible sources of bias. The first of these would be a systematic bias due to the reading level of the test being too high for examinees. Unless reading ability is part of the outcome being assessed or an integral part of the construct, the rule to follow is to *keep the reading level low* by using simple vocabulary and sentence structure.

There are quantitative methods to check for *readability,* or the measurement of the reading difficulty level of a test. However, the most straightforward procedure for practitioners would be to pretest the instrument on a small group of individuals from the population of interest. A compilation and analysis of their reactions to the wording will indicate whether the test's language is posing a systematic barrier in measuring the construct.

### 7.10.2   Inflammatory Bias or Appearance of Bias

In certain circumstances, an item might be mechanically acceptable (follow rules, measure the skill), and yet might contain language or material that is objectionable to a particular subgroup of examinees—such as females, a specific ethnic group, or individuals with a special need. Such material could take on many forms in a test—such as stereotypic portrayals of a particular group, use of debasing language, or showing some groups to be more deficient than others—and is categorized as *inflammatory bias* in the test. Because it can provoke emotional responses or anger in particular examinees, inflammatory bias has the potential to serve as an irrelevant, interfering factor during testing. Words or phrases detected by validators during content validation as sources of inflammatory biases should be eliminated before the W-SR test is used in formal settings.

### 7.10.3   Bias Due to Lack of Opportunity to Learn

On most achievement tests, bias can arise if the developers are not in tune with the exact nature of instructional exposure and classroom experiences of all the individuals tested— a factor that results in an *opportunity-to-learn* bias in the assessment. Such systematic biases should not occur if the classroom teacher is also the assessment designer. However, it has been known to happen!

In a typical case, the designer works from the assumption that learning opportunities have been provided, but some examinees do not in fact receive adequate instruction on parts of the curriculum relevant to the assessment. This results in systematically lower scores for examinees underexposed to the material tested—a serious validity issue. Questions 3, 12, and 13 on the validation checklist (Table 7.5) are intended as guards against the three major sources of bias during assessment design.

## Summary

As teachers' assessment philosophies, needs, and purposes vary, specific decisions they make while implementing the Process Model to design W-SR assessment tools for classroom use will also vary. Despite these differences, however, the core set of tasks involved in the assessment design/selection process remain the same (illustrated in Table 7.1). The basic process is invariant across different constructs, assessment methods, users, user paths, and assessment development situations; teachers should follow the same model that assessment developers do in more formal test development settings.

Table 7.2 listed the common decision-making needs of members in User Path 1, comprised of teachers, instructional support personnel, and students. Specific types of formative or summative classroom decisions were illustrated with examples. Identifying whether the W-SR test will be used for norm-referencing or criterion-referencing can also influence how the test is designed.

Phase II of the process model involves the development of assessment specifications. This chapter presented three alternative formats for W-SR assessment specifications. These were FORM I, the Table of Specifications; FORM II, a more general assessment specification format; and FORM III, Item-level Specifications. The chapter discussed the pros and cons of using each form in different assessment situations, and recommended the use of FORM II for most current classroom applications, where the W-SR test is typically one component of the larger assessment plan.

Well-constructed W-SR test items help the user/designer reliably discriminate between masters and non-masters of targeted learning outcomes in the domain. The chapter detailed the guidelines for constructing four major types of W-SR items: matching, completion, true/false, and multiple choice. These four basic item types can be modified in various ways, but item writers should make every attempt to ensure that the items:

1. Measure important learning outcomes
2. Elicit the desired performances in a straightforward manner
3. Pose *a single* question or problem with *only one* clearly correct or best answer
4. Do not provide clues to test-wise examinees
5. Follow specific guidelines applicable to the chosen W-SR format

With appropriate attention to item-writing mechanics, all four W-SR formats could be employed by creative item writers to measure higher levels of learning. Interpretive, W-SR exercises are especially useful in assessing complex outcomes. Table 7.5 provided a checklist for conducting a systematic content validation of a drafted W-SR assessment. The best reviewers for classroom assessment tools are peer teachers with some measurement expertise, or individuals likely to be sensitive to the nuances of the validation exercise (as given in the checklist). During content validation, reviewers should check for three possible sources of bias in the W-SR assessment tool: readability bias, inflammatory bias and opportunity to learn bias.

## QUESTIONS FOR CLASS DISCUSSION

1. Prepare an Assessment Specification (FORM II) for constructing a W-SR test in a subject area of your choice. In the specification, make sure that you:

   - Include a Table of Specifications.
   - Include learning outcomes at three different levels of a learning taxonomy, including a higher-level outcome.
   - Indicate the chosen W-SR format to test different outcomes with a rationale for your choice.
   - Show number of items and weights to be allocated to different outcomes.

   Ask your peers to review the specifications (use Table 7.5 as a guide). Could you select an existing test or test items from existing materials to match your specifications? Why or Why not?

2. Construct items to match the specifications you developed in Question 1. Attempt to construct each of the following types of items:

- A matching exercise
- True/false items
- Completion items
- Multiple choice items
- A context-dependent, interpretive exercise

Ask a peer to conduct a content validation of your items using Table 7.5 as a guide. How well did you do?

3. Identify learning outcomes in your curriculum that will be best measured with a W-SR item format. Explain why you would choose a particular W-SR format with reasons that address validity, reliability, and utility issues (revisit Chapters 3 and 4 for reference).

4. From your experiences and readings, find examples of each of these biases in operation in a W-SR testing environment:

- Readability bias
- Inflammatory bias
- Opportunity-to-learn bias

5. Refer back to Chapter 5 for assessment specifications for the *HELP!* problem to complete this next exercise. Examine the simulated test and items that follow, designed by an individual untrained in measurement. Revise and rewrite each of the W-SR items so that they comply with the rules given in Chapter 7.

### Simulated Test on *HELP!* Article

The following test contains five objective items and one essay item. Read each question carefully before you answer. This is a timed test. You have exactly two minutes to complete it. Each item is worth five points:

i. Fill in the blanks.

There are _____ as _____ _____ working as you _____ _____ thought _____ _____ _____ _____ to a _____ recently _____.

ii. Choose the right answer.
The population in this country is 200 million.
A. True
B. False
C. Partly true
D. Partly false
E. More true than false

iii. The reason why there are only two people (you and me) to do the work is that:
A. There are 180,000 in hospitals and insane asylums and we are not there
B. There are 11,988 people in jail and we are not there
C. Both A and B are correct
D. A and C but not B
E. A and B but not C
F. All of the above

iv. Say whether True or False.
The population in this country is 200 million, at least it was in 1980.
A. True
B. False

v. According to the article, there are 11,988 people in jail of which some proportion could be related to us.
   A. True
   B. False

vi. The main reason why you and I are tired today is: _____.

**6.** Clues in W-SR items can be caused by five major factors:
   **a.** Grammatical or sentence structure
   **b.** Lack of parallel form, content, or length
   **c.** Clang associations
   **d.** Nonsensical options
   **e.** Verbatim use of textbook language

Review the items that follow closely. Which clue(s) are evident in them?

**I.**    Based on your reading, Tom's favorite choice of a fruit for snacks is a(n):

   **a.** orange
   **b.** grapes
   **c.** apple
   **d.** pear

**II.**   Look at the line segment below. How long is it in inches?
   _____ (An approximately 2 in. long line segment is provided)

   **a.** 2 inches
   **b.** 3 inches
   **c.** 4 inches
   **d.** both a and b
   **e.** both b and c

**III.**  Read the sentence below and choose the best definition for the underlined word.

   *When my father realized he was lost, he <u>reexamined</u> the map.*

   **a.** put away
   **b.** moved
   **c.** reviewed
   **d.** found
   **e.** folded

**IV.**   Read the passage and answer the question.

   *Paul heard a siren. He saw a fire truck racing down his street. Then he saw flames coming from his neighbor's home. What did Paul hear?*

   **a.** a gun shot
   **b.** birds
   **c.** sounds from his neighbor's house
   **d.** He heard a siren from a fire truck racing down his street

# 8 Designing or Selecting Performance Assessments

## Overview

Chapter 8 demonstrates how the four-phase Process Model would apply when we design or select *performance assessments* in User Path 1, dealing with classroom decision-making. All classroom assessments should be closely aligned with curriculum and instruction. Thus, the assessments discussed in this chapter could be called *curriculum-based assessments*.

We defined performance assessments as exercises that utilize open-ended response formats, requiring human judges to directly observe or score them (see Chapter 4). Under the broad category of *performance assessments,* we recognized five different assessment methods:

- Written, open-ended assessments
- Behavior-based assessments
- Product-based assessments
- Interview-based assessments
- Portfolio-based assessments

Chapter 4 compared the five different assessment methods by evaluating their advantages and disadvantages from a measurement angle (Table 4.8).

Chapter 8 begins by briefly revisiting the question: Why use performance assessments at all in educational contexts? This discussion is followed by an overview of the core tasks in the four-phase Process Model as they would apply in the design or selection of performance assessments. The chapter then provides "rules" that we can follow when designing different types of tools in this category. Embedded throughout are examples of performance assessments designed for curricula in a single discipline, such as mathematics, as well as interdisciplinary curricula, where the targeted learning outcomes are from more than one subject-area curriculum. The chapter uses examples to illustrate the functions of a set of assessment specifications in constructing performance assessments. As in the previous chapters, examples attempt to span elementary and higher levels, and cross various disciplines. In addition to "Key Concept" boxes, here you will encounter boxes with rules for developing performance assessments and short checklists to help you evaluate the quality of different performance assessment tools that you construct.

# CHAPTER 8 OBJECTIVES

After studying this chapter and completing the structured exercises in the module, you should be able to:

1. Apply the Process Model to design or select sound performance assessment tools in User Path 1

2. Select performance assessment methods that are best suited for measuring particular learning outcomes (use validity, reliability, and utility criteria to guide choice of assessment methods)

3. Develop assessment specifications (FORM II) to guide the development or selection of performance assessment tools

4. Construct or select different types of performance assessment tools to meet specifications and accepted guidelines

   - Written, open-ended assessments
   - Behavior-based assessments
   - Product-based assessments
   - Interview-based assessments
   - Portfolio-based assessments

5. Distinguish between different types of scoring rubrics, identifying their advantages and disadvantages in particular circumstances

6. Use recommended procedures to design valid and reliable scoring rubrics

7. When using performance assessment tools, identify the major sources of rater/observer error and strategies for controlling them

8. Conduct a content validation of a performance assessment tool

# 8.1   Why Use Performance Assessments?

Performance assessments were an integral part of standards-based reforms in the 1990s, when educators faced the need to measure complex outcomes and integrated performances (see Chapter 1). With the advent of curriculum reforms, it was no longer sufficient to be able to measure discrete elements of knowledge or skills, one item at a time, with structured response tests. Procedural knowledge (process outcomes) and higher-order outcomes occupied a prominent place in new educational curricula. Other areas stressed in standards-based reforms were the development of social habits, skills needed for cooperative teamwork, and decision-making behaviors. All of these latter outcomes called for assessment methods that involved direct assessments, including observations.

Such changes stimulated educators and learning psychologists to begin an exploration of assessment formats that were alternatives to the written, structured-response (W-SR) test. National subject-area associations and other proponents of educational reforms questioned (and sometimes strongly opposed) the use of the traditional W-SR format to tap the critical educational outcomes in the new or revamped subject area curricula (Marzano, Pickering, & McTighe, 1993; Mitchell, 1992; NCTE, 1996; NCTM,

1995; Stiggins, 1991; Wiggins, 1989). Advocates of performance assessments were calling for tools with certain properties. Specifically, they asked that tools:

- Were designed to foster thought, persistence, construction of meaning, and deepening of understanding in students
- Could potentially have an instructional value and could be easily integrated with instruction
- Assessed "big ideas" in a curriculum by focusing on broad clusters of outcomes and competencies
- Would foster application of concepts and principles to the real world, even if they were not always situated in real-life settings.

Several of the arguments in support of performance assessments were indeed both reasonable and compelling. Supporters of performance assessments generally viewed *metacognition,* or the abilities with which learners reflect upon, evaluate, and monitor their own learning processes, as a necessary condition for learning and intellectual development. Constructivists claimed that performance assessments were better tools for describing the thought processes and metacognitive strategies used by a learner (Herman, Aschbacher, & Winters, 1992; O'Connor & Gifford, 1992; Resnick & Resnick, 1992). The open-ended format could potentially reveal multiple avenues used by students to arrive at solutions to problems. It also opened up the possibility of rewarding multiple correct answers.

Simultaneously, however, we saw evidence in the literature of W-SR test "bashing" by certain advocates of performance assessments. In opting to use alternative formats during assessment design, we should not be influenced by the reasoning that performance assessment approaches are better because they are "in vogue"; nor because their use would be a good way to undermine supporters of traditional W-SR tests. Nitko (1996) cautions us with the following words:

> Performance assessments can and should be justified in their own right rather than by "bashing" other assessment tools and formats. Teachers should not be fooled by spurious arguments. They should demand that advocates of any assessment technique justify the technique in their own right (p. 259).

## 8.2   Justifying Performance Assessment Methods We Choose

The two assessment design case studies that follow, Case Studies 8.1 and 8.2, illustrate how assessment designers might justify their choice for particular performance assessment methods by weighing the pros and cons from a measurement perspective. Table 4.8 (Chapter 4), which summarizes the advantages and disadvantages of each major type of performance assessment method, will be a useful reference as we review the cases.

---

## Case Study 8.1  Assessment Design (A)

Population:  Elementary students (3rd–5th grade)

Purposes:  Formative, ongoing, informal

Construct:  Responsible behaviors in school

Domain:  The student will:

> General Indicator:
> Demonstrate responsibility in completing school-related tasks *(Taxonomic classification: social behaviors).*
>
> Specific Indicators:
> - Set goals for school-related tasks
> - Stay focused on assigned tasks in school (in classroom, lunchroom, recess, field trips)
> - Make behavioral changes based on feedback received from teachers/counselors/peers
> - Use strategies to complete tasks in a timely manner (e.g., checklists, calendars)
> - Respond to praise and criticism in a manner accepted by teacher
> - Fulfill obligations in a timely manner

Assessment Method:  Product-based assessment, a biweekly journal

Self-assessments of students based on periodic summaries of journal entries

Justification provided by teacher:
In my classroom, I keep my behavioral expectations posted on the wall to help students remember them. Every second Friday, we have a journal hour when the students write about how they met those expectations in the past two weeks by providing anecdotes. At the end of each semester, they identify where they did well and where they need to grow or change. We share journal entries during class discussions. By keeping the indicators visible to all, I make sure we don't stray from the expectations during the self-assessments. This helps maintain the *validity* of the exercise. Journals are high in *utility* for me because students conduct their own assessments. Plus, I can combine my instruction with the assessment. Because we make repeated journal entries, I am able to follow the growth of particular students over time. Simultaneously, my conclusions about individual children are more *reliable.*

---

We should be able to justify the selection of specific performance assessment method(s) using validity, reliability, and/or utility reasons. To ensure valid inferences, the performance assessment method we choose should be suitable—the *best* in that circumstance—for tapping the desired levels of cognitive, affective, behavioral, or motor behaviors in the targeted construct domain. The assessment method should also be the best fit for the purposes and the population to be assessed. We now know that all performance formats are vulnerable to subjective errors during scoring, which challenges the reliability of results. We should therefore sensitize ourselves to the major sources of error and attempt to build in constraints that will help us generate more reliable results. Another challenge with performance assessments is their utility. Here, we must work at creating or selecting tools that are not overly resource-dependent or burdensome for ourselves or other users.

The thinking demonstrated by the two teachers in Case Studies 8.1 and 8.2 shows that they both incorporated measurement principles in the earliest stages of the assessment design/selection process. The teachers in both cases are dealing with the same *construct domain* and *population*. However, their assessment *purposes* vary. This discrepancy leads them to select very different methods of assessment (product-based and behavior-based methods, respectively). Each teacher defends the chosen assessment method(s) with reasonable arguments that attend to validity, reliability, and utility concerns.

## Case Study 8.2   Assessment Design (B)

Population:   Elementary students (3rd–5th grade)

Purposes:    Summative, midyear "conduct" grade for report card

Construct:   Responsible behaviors in school

Domain:    The student will:

General Indicator:
Demonstrate responsibility in completing school-related tasks *(Taxonomic classification: social behaviors)*

Specific Indicators:
- Set goals for school-related tasks
- Stay focused on assigned tasks in school (in classroom, lunchroom, recess, field trips)
- Make behavioral changes based on feedback received from teachers/counselors/peers
- Use strategies to complete tasks in a timely manner (e.g., checklists, calendars)
- Respond to praise and criticism in a manner accepted by teacher
- Fulfill obligations in a timely manner

Assessment Method:    Behavior-based assessment

Two structured observations and anecdotal records of critical incidents

Justification provided by teacher:
Here's how I would design the assessment. First, I would tell my students what I expect from them in the beginning of the year. Then, to ensure *validity,* I would develop a structured form

based on the behavioral indicators in the domain. I would make 2–4 records of each student based on the behaviors I see in class/school, in the beginning, middle, and at the end of the term. I will use their behavior in class, the lunchroom, library, classwork, and homework as evidence. My form would have three rating categories for each indicator, similar to these:

> Little or no evidence of this behavior (1 point)
> Some evidence of this behavior (2 points)
> Consistent evidence of this behavior (3 points)

There will be a box where I can describe the evidence I have seen in abbreviated form. In between, I will keep 1–3 anecdotal notes of any "great moments" or "not so great moments" for individuals. I expect to have enough observations combined to make a *reliable* judgment around mid-year. Although *utility* will be somewhat lessened because of the time I will need for recording, I will feel better if I can document the basis for student grades in conduct.

---

Several of the teachers' actions in the cases suggest well-reasoned and optimal conditions for using performance assessments in the classroom. The construct was classified by both teachers as a "social behavior" using the functional taxonomy—better measured through direct observation when the stakes are high. Although the two teachers opt for different assessment methods, both attempt to capture the full range of indicators that represent their construct, "responsible behaviors," thus maximizing the advantages of using a performance assessment approach. They gather the assessment data on students' behaviors in real school settings, a possibility that can be realized when we use performance assessment formats.

The self-assessment procedure that the first teacher in Case Study 8.1 chooses is consistent with the informal, formative purposes of the assessment, and does not compromise the validity of the resulting information. The same teacher also embeds the assessments closely within his day-to-day instruction, thus providing a seamlessness in the classroom activities dealing with instruction and assessment. In Case Study 8.2, the purposes involve summative decision-making. To have some back-up evidence to bolster her observations with the behavior-based method, the second teacher employs anecdotal observations. Both teachers communicate to their students what they expect of them, giving the children opportunities to employ metacognitive strategies. Such communications faciltate student engagement in their own development in the targeted area.

## Key Concepts

- We should choose performance assessment methods to meet our assessment needs where appropriate, with justification for that choice.
- Some learning outcomes, assessment purposes, and populations lend themselves better to performance assessments than to traditional W-SR assessment methods.

## 8.3    Applying the Process Model with Performance Assessments

Justifying why we opt for a particular assessment approach is a good way to ensure that we are not using performance assessments simply for the sake of using something novel. Assuming that performance assessments are the best fit for the needs of an assessment situation, let us now examine the main tasks in the assessment design or selection process. Continuing with the theme introduced in Chapters 5 through 7, this chapter also argues that to design or select performance assessments of optimal quality, we need to follow the core process involving Phases I–IV. The process is just as applicable for our local, small-scale assessment development projects as it is for large-scale testing applications. The methodology and underlying measurement principles for us to follow are common across various user contexts and applications.

Table 8.1 gives us the phases of the Process Model that we could apply to develop performance assessments. It uses an example of an open-ended graphing exercise for middle schoolers to illustrate the essential tasks we need to perform. The graphing exercise is made up of "short answer" items, which permit different students to come up with different but equally acceptable answers to the same problems. Although the items require a more restricted response than an essay, they would be classified as written, open-ended assessments (W-OE) in the classification scheme we used in Chapter 4.

Table 8.2 shows us the specifications produced in Phases I–II of the process. A graphing item developed to match the specifications is attached at the bottom of Table 8.2, and labeled as a "sample assessment." It was generated in Phase III of the process.

Performance assessments need special scoring procedures, called *rubrics*. Table 8.3 illustrates what an *analytic rubric* for the graphing domain might look like; Table 8.4 illustrates a *holistic rubric* for the same domain. These terms will be described in further detail soon. Examinee responses can potentially be scored with either one of the two rubrics shown (Table 8.3 and 8.4).

### 8.3.1    Tasks in Phase I

To develop the graphing assessment, we would begin by specifying the population, assessment purposes, and the construct to be assessed. This information is incorporated into the assessment specifications for designing or selecting a performance tool in Phase II.

*Specifying the Population*    Table 8.1 provides the example of a population of sixth- through eighth-grade students in a general education program. A general program is distinguished from a special education curriculum because it serves students who are in mainstream classes. The assessment design or selection procedures here, therefore, would have to be aligned to the developmental needs and mathematics expectations appropriate for middle schoolers receiving a mainstream curriculum.

*Specifying the Purposes*    The next step would be to specify the assessment purposes. Here, we should attempt to identify both the *specific purposes for assessment,* as

**TABLE 8.1   Tasks in the Process Model as Applied to the Design/Selection and Validation of Performance Assessments**

Phase I.  Specification of Population, Assessment Purposes, and Construct Domain

| | |
|---|---|
| 1. Identify the target population or "whom" to assess. | For example: Mainstream students in 6th, 7th, or 8th grade. |
| 2. Identify the assessment purpose or "why" you are assessing. | For example: To plan and improve instructional strategies. To provide coaching and feedback to students. |
| 3. Identify the construct | For example, Graphing Skills |
| 4. Specify the construct domain. | Use your own knowledge and curriculum guides, textbooks, training manuals, and the research and professional literature to identify general and specific indicators of the construct. |

Phase II.

| | |
|---|---|
| 5. Prepare Assessment Specifications. | The assessment specification (or assessment plan) should specify the: *population, assessment purpose, construct domain, assessment methods* selected, *conditions* of assessment, *administration* procedures, *scoring* procedures, and *weights* to be allocated to different indicators in the domain. |

Phase III.

| | |
|---|---|
| 6. Develop or select assessments matched to Assessment Specifications. | Create or select tasks using appropriate rules. Develop or select supporting materials, directions, prompts. Develop or select scoring rubrics. Identify scoring anchors. Assemble the tool. |

Phase IV.

| | |
|---|---|
| 7. Evaluate the quality of the overall assessment. | Phase IV A: Conduct content validation of the assessment tool by external reviewers. Revise assessment tool as needed. |
| | Phase IV B: Conduct empirical tryouts and validation studies, as appropriate to purposes. Revise tasks and overall assessment as needed. |

Prepare to use assessment in actual contexts.

well as persons *most likely to use the assessment information.* (Revisit Table 7.2 in Chapter 7; it should help you identify the assessment needs in User Path 1 with the necessary level of detail.)

In the example used in Table 8.1, we see that the designers aimed to develop a criterion-referenced assessment to serve predominantly formative purposes, implying a

TABLE 8.2   FORM II: Assessment Specification for Middle Level Graphing Skills

**Assessment Purposes:**   To make criterion-referenced interpretations of performance tied to the domain; formative or summative decision-making. To provide feedback and coaching.

**Population:**   Middle school students in general mathematics courses (grades 6–8)

**Construct:**   Constructing and interpreting line graphs

**Domain:**

*General Indicator* (General Learning Outcome):
**1.0 Given a real data set, students will construct a line graph.**
*(Cognitive level: complex procedural skills)*

*Specific Indicators* (Competencies):
The students will:

1.1   Given a data-based problem situation, decide when it is appropriate to construct a line graph (versus a bar or circle graph).
*(Cognitive level: application)*

1.2   Select appropriate axes for variables given.
*(Cognitive level: application)*

1.3   Based on ranges of values, identify reasonable scale units for variables.
*(Cognitive level: application)*

1.4   Label, graph, axes, scale units neatly.
*(Cognitive level: factual knowledge)*

1.5   Plot at least 10 X, Y coordinates accurately.
*(Cognitive level: application)*

1.6   Connected plotted against accurately and neatly to depict data trend.
*(Cognitive level: application)*

*General Indicator* (Learning Outcome):
**2.0 Given a line graph, students will correctly interpret data trends.**
*(Cognitive level: higher-order thinking)*

*Specific Indicators* (Competencies):
The students will:

2.1   Describe changes in data points plotted (recognize similarities and differences over time).
*(Cognitive level: factual knowledge)*

2.2 Use mathematical language to analyze trends (e.g., higher, lower, hotter, cooler, change).
(*Cognitive level: higher-order thinking*)

**Assessment Method(s):** Written, open-ended assessment; short answer context-dependent tasks; data and problem scenario provided.

Four (4) tasks will make up the assessment. Each task should measure both outcomes 1.0 (Indicators 1.1–1.6) and 2.0 (Indicators 2.1–2.2) in an integrated way.

**Weights Desired:**

| | *Weight* |
|---|---|
| Outcome 1.0 | ×3 (75% of total points) |
| Outcome 2.0 | ×1 (25% of total points) |

**Scoring Methods:** Analytic rubric
(For summative decisions, use total score)

**Group/Individual Assessment:** Individual

**Who Assesses:** Instructor

**Assessment Conditions:** This is a closed book assessment. Following some instruction, it should take students approximately 60 minutes to complete. Estimated time needed for individual tasks is 15 minutes.

**Sample Assessment Task:**

Starting on Sunday, the average daily temperatures in degrees Fahrenheit were recorded for 14 consecutive days. The data are as follows:

| Days: | 1 | 2 | 3 | 4 | 5 | 6 | 7 | 8 | 9 |
|---|---|---|---|---|---|---|---|---|---|
| Temperature in degrees: | 56 | 58 | 57 | 60 | 61 | 75 | 72 | 71 | 77 |
| Days: | 10 | 11 | 12 | 13 | 14 | | | | |
| Temperature in degrees: | 55 | 56 | 54 | 56 | 58 | | | | |

A. Make a graph to show how the temperature changes from Day 1 to Day 7, and then from Day 8 to Day 14.

B. Describe in your own words how the temperature looked in Days 1–7 as compared to Days 8–14.

C. What type of graph did you use (bar, circle, or line graph) and why?

**TABLE 8.3  Analytic Scoring Rubric for Line Graphing Assessment**

Directions to Raters:
- This rubric is designed to meet the assessment specifications outlined in Table 8.2.
- The total rubric is designed for an integrated task measuring both outcomes, 1.0 and 2.0. Portions of the rubric can be used selectively for tasks focusing on individual outcomes.
- The analytic framework is intended to provide teachers/users with a profile of student strengths and weaknesses to support student coaching and feedback. The summated total score (max. 20) could be used to make summative decisions at appropriate times. Raters are encouraged to practice scoring with sample answers before using the rubric for summative purposes.
- MAXIMUM SCORE = 80 POINTS ON ASSESSMENT WITH 4 TASKS (20 POINTS PER TASK)

*OUTCOME 1.0*
*16 points*

  *Analytic checklist:*
  The student:

|  |  | *Yes* | *No* |
|---|---|---|---|
| 1.1 Selected/defended a line graph to depict data. | | 1 | 0 |
| 1.3 Identified appropriate scale units for: | X axis: | 1 | 0 |
| | Y axis: | 1 | 0 |
| 1.4 Labeled graph accurately: | Title: | 1 | 0 |
| | X variable: | 1 | 0 |
| | Y variable: | 1 | 0 |
| | Scale units: | 1 | 0 |
| | Neatness: | 1 | 0 |

*Analytic Rating Scale*

|  |  | *None* | *One* | *Both* |
|---|---|---|---|---|
| 1.2 Selected appropriate axes for variables. | | 0 | 1 | 2 |

|  | *None* | *1 to 5* | *6–9* | *10–14* |
|---|---|---|---|---|
| 1.5 Plotted all X, Y coordinates accordingly. | 0 | 1 | 2 | 3 |
| 1.6 Connected plotted points accurately. | 0 | 1 | 2 | 3 |

*OUTCOME 2.0*
*4 points*

|  | *Absent/ Many Errors* | *1–2 missing or inaccurate ideas* | *Accurate & complete answer* |
|---|---|---|---|
| 2.1 Describe changes in data points. | 0 | 1 | 2 |
| 2.2 Used appropriate language to analyze trends. | 0 | 1 | 2 |

**TABLE 8.4  Example of a 5-Point Holistic Rubric for Graphing Assessment**

| Rating | Description of Performance |
|---|---|
| 4 | Opted for and appropriately defended use of a line graph. Identified appropriate scale units. Selected appropriate axes for variables. Labeled graph completely, accurately, and clearly. Plotted and connected 10–14 data points correctly. Used appropriate language to accurately describe data trends. Neat and coherent presentation. |
| 3 | Opted for but did not defend use of a line graph. Plotted and connected 10–14 data points correctly. Used appropriate language to accurately describe data trends. *Minor errors in:* identifying scale units *or* selecting axes for variables *or* labeling graph, *or* presenting information neatly and coherently. |
| 2 | Opted for but did not defend use of a line graph. Plotted and connected 6–9 data points correctly OR made *minor errors* in describing data trends. *There could also be minor errors in:* identifying scale units *or* selecting axes for variables *or* labeling graph, *or* presenting information neatly and coherently. Did not defend graph. |
| 1 | Opted for a line graph. Plotted and connected at least 1–5 data points correctly BUT omitted or made *major errors* in describing data trends. *There could also be minor errors in:* identifying scale units *or* selecting axes for variables *or* labeling graph, *or* presenting information neatly and coherently. Did not defend graph. |
| 0 | Opted for circle graph (pie chart) or other inappropriate graphing technique, with incoherent presentation of information. |

low stakes assessment situation. The primary decision-makers would be middle school mathematics teachers. The designers (who were probably teachers) also specify a need for using the assessment results to coach students. When delineating purposes in FORM II (the assessment specification document; see Table 8.2), such details help in focusing the designer on the type of assessment exercise and scoring framework that might best serve the articulated assessment needs.

**Specifying the Construct Domain**  The next job for us is to specify the *construct* to assess. To clarify the *domain of operational indicators,* assessment designers should comply with guidelines for specifying achievement domains given in Chapter 6. Case studies 8.1 and 8.2 provided an example of a domain for a "social behavior" construct, which was also developed following the guidelines in Chapter 6.

In the middle school example illustrated in Table 8.2, the construct label is "constructing and interpreting line graphs." The indicators in this achievement domain, thus, consist of learning outcomes that emphasize the skills and knowledge relevant to line graphing. Once specified, the domain is inserted in FORM II (see Table 8.2).

### 8.3.2  Tasks in Phase II

Preparing the assessment specification that will guide the design or selection of the performance assessment comes next. Table 8.2 illustrates the use of FORM II for the graphing assessment. The important structural parts of the ultimate performance assessment tool become evident to us through the specifications. The different parts of FORM II are similar to that shown in Chapter 7 (Table 7.4).

When designing performance assessments, the assessment method(s) we specify in Phase II must be able to capture several competencies or learning outcomes as an inter-connected group of skills/abilities. Performance assessment approaches permit us to gather evidence of a construct through exercises that simultaneously integrate a number of skills/abilities. This is a format-related advantage that we should capitalize upon when designing a performance assessment tool. In fact, it is this feature that sets the process of performance assessment design clearly apart from the processes we employ for con-structing structured-response tests. In the latter, you will recall, we typically attempt to tar-get single outcomes/competencies that are relatively narrow in their scope with individual items (see Chapter 7).

A new dimension added to FORM II, relevant to the design of performance assessments, is the "Assessment Conditions." To make performance assessments as tight and error-free as possible, more details need to be specified with regard to *conditions* under which performances tied to the domain will be observed or documented. To help outline conditions in adequate detail, we must attempt to answer questions such as the following:

- Will it be an individual or group that will be the focus of the assessment?
- Will the students be timed or untimed?
- Will students be directly observed or videotaped?
- Will students be allowed any help from the examiners or teachers?
- Will students be provided with any materials or equipment?

You may recall that for structured-response item construction (Chapter 7), conditions were specified *within* the individual learning outcome or competency statements, and could be varied from item to item. When designing performance assessments, we would typically specify the conditions for the exercise *as a whole*.

### 8.3.3    Tasks in Phase III

The key task for us in Phase III would be to actually design and assemble the tool, guided by the specifications. This work would require us to actually design the items and assessment setting; select or compile supporting materials; write directions for examinees, observers, scorers, or other users; and develop scoring rubrics for the assessment.

The specifications in Table 8.2 indicate that the overall graphing assessment would be comprised of four short answer tasks, each of which would provide a separate data set to examinees and require them to employ the skills and mental abilities listed in the domain. You will note that the specifications can be used by the teacher to design or select similar items from textbook or other resources. As long as they fit the specified dimen-sions, the same rubric could be applied to score all of the items we design or select from a given set of specifications.

### 8.3.4 Tasks in Phase IV

The work in Phase IV would begin with a content validation of the individual items, the entire assessment tool with all supporting materials, and is conducted by reviewers. In formal test development settings, content validation involves constructive criticisms by subject-area specialists, measurement experts, and individuals who are qualified to screen the tool for biases against special populations or different cultural, linguistic and gender groups. In less formal environments such as a classroom, it is advantageous if peer teachers or co-workers who serve as reviewers have the necessary subject-area specializations and some measurement skills to help improve the tool. Throughout the sections of this

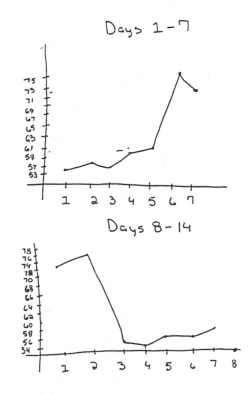

In days 1-7 the temperature remains within a 6° difference for the majority of the days until a drastic 14° change on the sixth day. The temperature remains in the high 70's until about day 9. By day 10, the temperature has once again lowered to the 50's and stays relatively constant. The most relevant change occurred between days 6 and 9 for the most part.

**FIGURE 8.1   Student Response (A) to Line Graphing Task**

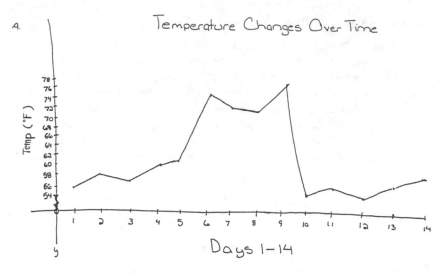

A.

Temperature Changes Over Time

B.    The temperature from days one to seven generally increases, with the steepest incline occuring between days five and six. Days seven and eight seem to be a stabilizing period. Days eight to fourteen generally show a decline in temperature, where the steepest decline occurs on day ten and is followed by smaller drops.

C.    I used a line graph to illustrate the rises and falls in temperature over a period of time. A line graph clearly shows the relationship between each day's temperature and the day proceeding it.

**FIGURE 8.2    Student Response (B) to Line Graphing Task**

chapter, there are checklists that can guide us during content validation. Once content validation is over, we should make alterations to those sections of the instrument that the reviewers judged as deficient.

We could opt to employ the assessment tool following a thorough content validation and revision. However, to evaluate the quality of the data it generates more completely, empirical studies should be conducted soon after we complete the content validation procedure. Empirical efforts in Phase IV B, should be guided by the assessment purposes, and conducted in a unified manner.

For example, the graphing assessment presented in Tables 8.2–8.4 is a *criterion-referenced* assessment. If we assume that the assessment results will be used for passing students to the next grade, what empirical evidence of validity might we seek to support such inferences? Some of our empirical work could be guided by the following questions pertaining to validity and reliability issues, respectively.

Validity of Passing Standard:    How will we set a passing score on the overall assessment that will help us distinguish between proficient and nonproficient students in a fair and valid way?

Rater Consistency:     Can different raters use the rubric and accompanying directions to give the same or similar scores to student papers of comparable quality?

Empirical validation procedures are treated in further detail in Section III of this book. Such work may reveal that other areas of the instrument need to be improved. Ideally, we would make all the needed modifications before the tool is applied for data gathering and decision-making purposes.

---

**Key Concepts**

- When designing or selecting performance assessment tools, the four phases of the Process Model apply as they did in the case of W-SR test design.
- The Form II Assessment Specification is recommended when designing or selecting performance assessments in User Path 1.

---

## 8.4  Designing Different Types of Performance Assessments

Let us now turn our attention to some rules that can guide us when we develop assessment tools with one or more of the five performance assessment methods identified in Chapter 4. These were:

1. Written open-ended assessments (short response and essay)
2. Behavior-based assessments
3. Product-based assessments
4. Interview-based assessments
5. Portfolio-based assessments

### 8.4.1  Designing Written Open-Ended (Essay and Short Response) Items

The *written open-ended* (W-OE) format, such as *short response tasks* or *essays,* requires the assessment designer to provide a written prompt. The examinees are generally provided with an answer booklet in which they supply a response to that prompt. Typically, the essay requires a lengthier response than a short response task; however, both formats are well-suited for measuring higher levels of thinking and problem-solving. Today, both formats can be adapted for computer-based delivery. Because it assumes that respondents are capable of written expression, the W-OE assessment method is not suitable for young children or special populations of nonwriters.

The W-OE format is a highly desirable format for some assessment purposes; it is also vulnerable to several sources of error. Following are some rules to keep in mind for the design/selection of essays and short-response tasks.

---

Essay and Short Response Items

*Rule 1*   We should choose written, open-ended items to measure those learning outcomes that *cannot* be adequately measured with W-SR formats or with other performance assessment methods.

Essays or short response items should involve thought-provoking tasks. The following types of learning outcomes would be well measured with W-OE formats:

- Process outcomes, typified as *complex procedural skills* in the functional taxonomy, such as the use of a multistep problem-solving procedure in mathematics
- Broad outcomes that include several indicators, all of which *need to be measured as a whole,* such as the writing of a letter, or construction and interpretation of a graph (Table 8.4)
- Outcomes that involve skills in reasoning, defending, justifying, or explaining of a problem or issue, such as an essay on an environmental issue
- Other outcomes that combine the *synthesis, analysis,* and/or *evaluation* levels of Bloom's cognitive taxonomy or *higher-order thinking* and *problem-solving* in the functional taxonomy.

---

Essay and Short Response Items

*Rule 2*   The prompts and directions must define the task clearly for examinees.

Vague essay prompts do a poor job of focusing the respondents on the expected performance and generate responses that are difficult to grade with any kind of consistency. Consider the following essay prompt, which led secondary students to provide a wide range of responses.

*Example of a Vague Essay Prompt*

*Directions:* Explain the Boston Tea Party.

Answers obtained:

A list of major facts (on the Boston Tea Party)

A description of some facts

An explanation of the major facts with supporting details

A brief analysis of possible causes and effects

A well-written, lengthy argument for cause-effect relationships among events

A combination of the above, plus/minus errors!

To improve the design of the prompt, we must thus ask: *What were we looking for as evidence of achievement?* If the targeted learning outcomes are explicitly stated in the domain, referring back to them will help us delimit the exercise. Examine the content and cognitive behaviors closely and align the directions to narrow down the exercise for examinees. They might look something like this for a secondary school essay:

*Example: Delimiting the Essay Exercise*

Targeted learning outcomes:

- Student can analyze causes and effects of historical events (e.g., the Boston Tea Party).
- Student can provide supporting details to justify cause and effect relationships.

*Directions:* Write a 2- to 3-paragraph essay on the following historical topic. You will be graded based on your ability to link causes with effects and on justification of your answer with historical facts and sources. Points will be awarded for accuracy of events, dates, names of people, organizations, and legislative acts that you cite. You will have 90 minutes to complete the essay. This is a closed book test.

*Topic:* Identify the key events that led to the Boston Tea Party. Which groups were most affected by the Boston Tea Party and how? Justify your answer.

Notice that the *length* of the expected answer, the *scoring criteria,* the *expected contents* of the essay, and *conditions* (e.g., time limits, closed book) under which the student must respond, are all defined for the examinee in the directions. Inclusion of the actual *scoring rubric* could further focus the examinee on the performances we expect. Structuring of the exercise in the manner shown will control for likely errors from both the examinees when they respond, as well as the scorers when they rate the essays.

## Essay and Short Response Items

*Rule 3*   To attain reliability, an adequate number of items (tasks) should be incorporated within the assessment exercise.

Essays and short response items need much more response time than W-SR items. It is difficult to specify the exact number needed to obtain an "adequate" sample of tasks. In classroom or local design efforts, we must use our best judgments to make such decisions. Economy of time needed for administration and scoring must be balanced against an ideal number that will fit the assessment purposes.

In an assessment such as the graphing example (Tables 8.2–8.4), relying on one item would be too tenuous for a *reliable* decision. Using 20 items, on the other hand, could seriously affect *utility* of the assessment. Thus, to meet the combined formative and summative decision-making needs specified, the designer settled on four items. In large-scale testing situations, designers often have the resources to empirically estimate the reliability advantages obtained by adding more items or more raters to a performance assessment situation before they make a decision on the number of items to sample from the domain. In local applications, we are left to our best judgments.

Essay and Short Response Items

*Rule 4*   We should develop well-designed scoring rubrics and anchor papers as an integral part of the assessment procedure.

More will be said about rubric design in the next section, but we should bear in mind that well-prepared scoring rubrics must accompany all W-OE items, and preferably be shared with students prior to assessment. Validity in rubrics is determined by the extent to which they match the targeted outcomes/indicators of the construct domain in terms of their content. For example, in the line graphing assessment, a valid rubric would focus on labeling, titling, plotting of points, and interpretation of a line graph—the indicators listed in the construct domain. To facilitate reliable scoring by raters, rubrics should be clear and unambiguous; the scale points should allow raters to consistently rate tasks/essays of varying quality. The ease with which rubrics can be used by raters will determine their utility.

*Anchor papers* are sample answers that represent different levels of performance on a task, such as responses that qualify for a score of 1 versus a 3 or a 4. Two anchor papers are provided on the graphing assessment (see Figures 8.1–8.2). During scoring, anchors serve as concrete references for scorers and can significantly cut down rating errors. They should be included as a part of the design of W-OE items.

Essay and Short Response Items

*Rule 5*   If applicable, the assessment should be accompanied by all necessary directions for scorers, proctors, and other users.

This last rule would apply when you are designing the assessment for someone else to use, administer, or score. It attends to the needs of those who conduct or implement the assessment.

In classroom settings, the same teacher typically serves in all three roles—designer, proctor, and scorer. In other situations, such as an institution-wide essay contest, other teachers or staff are likely to be involved in the assessment process. In designing assessments for such purposes, we should develop guidelines to adequately structure the assessment conditions to help individuals serving in the roles of proctor and/or rater perform with as little variation as possible. The scoring rubrics should come accompanied with clear directions for other users/scorers.

The following checklist summarizes the key factors we should keep in mind when selecting or designing essays or short response tasks. It could be a useful resource during the content-validation phase of our work in Phase IV A of the Process Model.

## A Checklist for Designing Essay and Short Response Tasks

❏   **1.**   Do the short response or essay items show a logical match with targeted learning outcomes?

❏   **2.**   Do the items match the developmental level, age, and other characteristics of the population?

❏   **3.**   Does the design of the items, rubrics, and materials support the assessment purposes?

❏   **4.**   Is the number of questions reasonable for the assessment purposes (test not too long or too short)?

❏   **5.**   Do the prompts clearly delimit the tasks for examinees?

❏   **6.**   Are the directions adequate and clear for examinees?

❏   **7.**   Is the rubric:
- clear?
- easy to use?

❏   **8.**   If applicable, are the raters or test administrators given clear and adequate instructions?

❏   **9.**   Is adequate time built in for examinees to complete the tasks?

❏   **10.**   Is enough response space provided in the answer booklet?

❏   **11.**   Are the rubrics aligned to indicators in the domain?

❏   **12.**   Are the rubrics accompanied with anchor papers to guide scorers?

### 8.4.2   Designing Behavior-Based Assessments

In Case Study 8.2, we saw an example of a construct domain that lends itself to a behavior-based assessment. Table 8.5 provides a structured recording form designed to match the domain specified in Case 8.2. This instrument was intended for documenting social behaviors of elementary students in a natural school setting. The form also allows for some relatively unstructured observations to be noted with teacher anecdotes (see bottom).

Behavior-based assessments utilize direct observations of behaviors *in situ* or in simulated contexts. They require human resources for both observation and scoring. In this section, we focus on the design of structured or semistructured, behavior-based assessments only. Rules to keep in mind when designing assessments requiring direct observations are as follows.

**TABLE 8.5  Responsible Behaviors in School Settings: Observation Recording Form**

| Name of Student:        Grade:                                School: | | | |
|---|---|---|---|
| Ratings:    1   Little or no evidence of this behavior<br>          2   Some evidence of this behavior<br>          3   Consistent evidence of this behavior<br>       N/A Not applicable/student has no opportunity to demonstrate<br>            this behavior | | | |
| | Week 1–4 | Week 5–8 | Week 9–12 | Week 13–16 |
| a. Set goals for school-related tasks.<br><br>Areas (List): | | | | |
| b. Stayed focused on assigned tasks in:<br><br>Classroom<br>Media center<br>Recess/lunchroom<br>Field trips | | | | |
| c. Made changes in behavior based on criticism/feedback from:<br><br>Teachers<br>Counselors<br>Peers | | | | |
| d. Used strategies to complete tasks on time.<br><br>Checklists<br>Calendars<br>Other (explain): | | | | |
| Anecdotal Notes: | | | | |

## Behavior-Based Assessments

*Rule 1*    The behavior-based method should be a justifiable match for the targeted content, behaviors, and conditions in the domain.

Applied skills and outcomes, such as speech-making, acting, driving, or use of equipment or machinery that must be observed directly in order to obtain evidence of competence demand the use of behavior-based assessments. Affective and social behaviors, such as cooperative group behaviors and leadership skills, are also best measured by direct observation with behavior-based assessments. Other reasons for selecting this format could have to do with the population you have in mind—for example, the students might be too young for a paper and pencil test, making it necessary for us to select a behavior-based approach. Alternatively, they might belong to a special needs population, requiring us to actually observe their performance.

## Behavior-Based Assessments

*Rule 2*    The setting, assessment conditions, prompts, and directions must elicit the behaviors to be observed from examinees and allow for direct observations to be made by examiners.

We should design appropriate prompts, conditions, and directions to guide the respondents towards the task at hand and help the examiner make the records. For example, in an effort to define the expected performance to third-grade examinees, a teacher prepared the following directions: "Read a passage aloud to convey meaning." While the student read, she used a structured form to rate reading behaviors represented in her domain. A much better set of directions follows.

*Example: Delimiting a Behavior-Based Assessment*

*Directions* (Spoken aloud by teacher): Read the first page of this story aloud to me. Read it in a way that I can understand what is happening in the story just by listening to you. Remember to pause at the right places and use expression as you read. You may start now.

## Behavior-Based Assessments

*Rule 3*    To attain reliability, an adequate number of observations should be made by observers or recorders.

Another critical decision deals with how we should sample the behaviors to observe. How many observations would provide us with enough reliability, while keeping the assessment process feasible? In what locations should we make the observations to obtain a complete picture? How frequently should we record our observations? In Table 8.5, we see that the teacher chose to observe the students in multiple, preselected locales. Four quarterly records were to be documented on the form, with anecdotal notes to support them. The assessment purposes were summative. Such factors should be carefully considered when we design a behavior-based assessment. Be sure to keep in mind the purposes to be served by the assessment results during design, as well.

---

Behavior-Based Assessments

*Rule 4*   Well-designed scoring rubrics must accompany structured behavior-based assessments.

A sound rubric helps to reduce errors during coding. What criteria will we use to categorize different levels of performance on the indicators? Designers must start by using their professional judgment to set these parameters beforehand, so that the assessment tool can be used in a consistent manner when observations are eventually recorded.

In the example in Table 8.5, a three-point rating scale was devised to distinguish among different levels of performance. The teacher recognized that all of the indicators may not apply to every student; this led her to include a N/A coding category on her form. A recognition of the variabilities in behaviors to observe helped her to design an appropriate scoring procedure.

---

Behavior-Based Assessments

*Rule 5*   If the assessment requires the use of special materials/equipment, design the assessment environment in a clear, easy-to-follow format, with necessary supporting directions and prompts.

Many observational assessments call for the use of equipment or special materials. For example, in science experiments, the use of slides, microscopes, or other laboratory equipment might be necessary. In such circumstances, students should be able to read or hear the directions and make the connections between the materials and the expected performances. To set up the assessment environment, the designer could take the following steps:

1. Make a list of all the materials and information that students will need to complete the exercise.
2. Draw a diagram to show how the supporting materials will be arranged in the assessment environment.
3. Assemble or create the materials, directions, and prompts necessary for the exercise.
4. Make sure that the materials and equipment are:
   - Easily accessible to students
   - Labeled clearly
   - In sound working condition

The validation checklist that follows is intended to help us ask some necessary questions to keep errors down to a tolerable level when designing behavior-based assessments. (Note: Rules for making anecdotal observations will be addressed in Chapter 9.)

---

## A Checklist for Designing Structured Behavior-Based Assessments

❏   **1.**   Is the behavior-based method a logical match for targeted learning outcomes?

❏   **2.**   Is the method suited to the characteristics of the population?

❏   **3.**   Does the design of the tool support the assessment purposes?

❏   **4.**   Are the number of observations reasonable for the assessment purposes?

❏   **5.**   Do the prompts clearly delimit the tasks for examinees?

❏   **6.**   Are the directions adequate and clear for examinees?

❏   **7.**   Is the rubric easy to use?

❏   **8.**   If applicable, are the other observers or test administrators given clear and adequate instructions?

❏   **9.**   Does the tool make clear the:
- Settings for observations?
- Timing and frequency of observations?

❏  **10.**   If applicable, are there clear instructions for other raters to use the observation form and rubric?

❏  **11.**   Is the rubric aligned to indicators in the domain?

❏  **12.**   If special equipment and materials are used, are they working soundly?

---

### 8.4.3   Designing Product-Based Assessments

A product-based assessment is one where examinees create a *work sample* or a *product* utilizing the skills/abilities embedded in the learning outcomes of a curriculum. Product-based assessments are different from W-OE assessments in that they are *untimed*. They can include take-home projects, papers, and reports.

For example, in a master's level measurement course for professionals-in-training, this author requires students to develop a traditional W-SR tool and a performance assessment, both product-based assessments, that demonstrate a student's skills in instrument design and validation. Through the products, the author obtains evidence of the students' ability to:

- Apply the phases of the Process Model
- Follow the specific rules of item or instrument development
- Generate content-validated products that they can use for actual decision-making at work

All these are learning outcomes of the measurement curriculum. The targeted construct is "proficiency in assessment design," and the outcomes represent the indicators in the construct domain. The rules for designing product-based assessments overlap considerably with several of the guidelines for preceding kinds of performance assessments. There are a few exceptions. Consider the following recommendations when developing product-based tools.

---

## Product-Based Assessments

*Rule 1*    The product-based method should be a justifiable match for the targeted content, behaviors, and conditions in the domain.

Most product-generation tasks require students to employ multiple levels of behavior from the cognitive, motor, or other domains of Bloom's taxonomy. Use product-based assessments to measure learning outcomes that require the use of complex procedural skills and techniques for generating products, but where direct observations of the process are unnecessary in obtaining evidence of achievement. Direct observations are time-consuming and dependent on human observers. Product-based assessments eliminate the need for observations, while giving the assessor the same information on student performance.

For example, a laboratory report (a product) will provide evidence of a student's ability to employ a scientific method, without a teacher having to observe a student actually conduct the experiment. An assessment tool developed by a student teacher (a product) will show how well the student teacher used of the complex procedures of test design, without the instructor having to directly observe his or her work during the developmental phases.

Some outcomes that include a cluster of specific indicators, all of which need to be measured together, may also call for product-based assessments. Examples include creating a short story or a poem, developing a piece of art, or building a tool in shop class.

---

## Product-Based Assessments

*Rule 2*    The assessment conditions, prompts, and directions must clearly define the product expected of examinees.

This rule applies to product-based assessments just as it did with the previous types of performance assessments. Clear directions are necessary for product development. Reasonable time frames must be given to students to create the products. Assistance and materials allowed must be clearly outlined.

In school settings, products are often developed by students as extended homework exercises. Potential threats to valid measurement with student products are the opportunities they may have for outside help. The availability of resources through the internet can make certain product-development tasks much easier today. In such cases, the assessment designer/teacher needs to clearly define the task and structure the assessment conditions so that students are aware when they are to create original products.

Product-Based Assessments

*Rule 3*   To achieve reliability, an adequate number of products or work samples should be gathered.

This standard rule for sound assessment design must be adapted to product-based assessments as well. It is unreasonable for us to expect large numbers of products from examinees when products involve huge time commitments. Scoring burdens on the assessor also build up with increased numbers of products. However, in some instances, there may be opportunities for students to generate several work samples over time. For example, students could produce several written products in the course of a semester. With the preceding example of a measurement curriculum for master's students, this author requires students to develop two instruments in a 16-week semester. Having more than one product improves the reliability of the inferences. In other instances, we might combine results of more than one assessment method, such as a written test with product-based assessments. This last approach will strengthen both content validity and reliability.

Product-Based Assessments

*Rule 4*   Well-designed scoring rubrics must accompany product-based assessments.

As with all performance assessments, products have to be assessed with well-structured rubrics. The characteristics of sound rubrics are addressed in the next section of this chapter. Rubrics that serve formative purposes have different characteristics when compared to rubrics designed for summative needs.

As in the previous examples, we end this section with a validation checklist to evaluate the quality of a product-based tool.

## A Checklist for Designing Product-Based Assessments

❑   **1.**   Is the product-based method a logical match for targeted learning outcomes?

❑   **2.**   Is the assessment suited to the characteristics of the population?

❑   **3.**   Does the design of the tool support the assessment purposes?

❑   **4.**   Will the number of products/work samples provide adequate reliability?

❑   **5.**   Do the directions clearly set the conditions for product development?

❑   **6.**   Is adequate time provided for examinees to complete the products?

❑   **7.**   Is the rubric easy to use?

❑   **8.**   Does the design control for the possibility of students getting outside assistance?

❑   **9.**   If applicable, are there clear instructions for other raters to rate the products?

❑ **10.**   Is the rubric aligned to indicators in the domain?

### 8.4.4   Designing Interview-Based Assessments

An interview-based assessment is one where examinees respond in a one-to-one conference setting with the examiner. They demonstrate their mastery of the skills/abilities valued in a curriculum through their responses to interview questions posed by the teacher or examiner. For example, kindergarten children might be interviewed by a teacher to determine their "print concepts" prior to beginning formal reading instruction. To gain insights into a child's reading readiness, a teacher might employ an interview to answer questions such as:

- Does the child know that words and sentences are read from left to right?
- Does the child show understandings of how stories are printed in books?

The interview demands that we not only develop interview questions, but prompts for probing students when they provide us with inadequate or incomplete answers. *Probes* are questions related to the original query that the examiner asks to help focus the examinee on the task when they stray from the target. Probes give us an opportunity to verify how deeply a student understands particular concepts.

*Example: Print Concepts Interview*

*Interview Question:*  Tell me how would you hold this book if you wanted to read it?

*Probes:*          (If child does not respond)
Would you hold it this way? (Hold with print sideways)
Would you hold it this way? (Hold with print upside down)
Would you hold it this way? (Hold with print right side up)
Are you sure?

A challenge in designing interviews is the coding of the open-ended responses obtained, leading to a systematically derived "score." This method requires that we allocate time for questioning students individually, as well as time for scoring their responses.

The general rules for interview-based assessment design are no different from other performance assessments. Specifically, we need to attend to the level of structure we desire in the interview format, the probes allowed or disallowed, the response coding criteria, and scoring method.

---

Interview-Based Assessments

*Rule 1*   The interview-based method should be a justifiable match for the targeted content, behaviors, and conditions in the domain, as well as the purposes and populations.

Because interviews demand a lot of time from the designer, interviewer, and scorer (usually the same individual in local settings), we should select this method when it is the best fit for our learning outcomes, purposes, and populations. Curricula involving conversational language skills are best measured with interviews. High-level performances, where examiners want to check for deep understandings and reasoning processes, such as the defense of a doctoral thesis, also lend themselves well to an interview. Generally, it does not make good sense to use the interview to measure factual knowledge or low-level application skills in school populations.

Informal interviews are particularly well suited for *formative* assessment purposes. In such applications, teachers might wish to embed one-on-one questioning of students with their day-to-day instruction. Interviews generate valuable information on individual student misunderstandings that can be easily overlooked in large group settings.

Young children and special populations are best assessed with interviews. In fact, several standardized intelligence tests employ a one-on-one interview format for young children.

---

Interview-Based Assessments

*Rule 2* The interview conditions must be structured to fit the assessment purposes.

During design, we need to make a decision on the level of structure necessary for the purposes to be served. Naturally, informal, formative purposes would have far less structure. With high stakes decisions, it is necessary to consider factors such as the following.

- What instructions should we give the examinee to help him or her understand what we expect?
- Once a question is asked, how much time should we allow before we move on to the next question?
- How many probes will be allowed after each prompt?
- What is an acceptable probe?
- If the interviewee rambles, what methods will we use to code responses?

In Chapter 4, we saw an example of an interview assessment where the assessor could "look for" particular words or themes in the responses to code them in particular scoring categories. For example, in the "print concepts" interview for kindergartners, a teacher could use the following "look fors" to differentiate among students who have more or less mastery of the domain. In summative assessments using the interview, we should be careful that the probes do not give the answer away to respondents.

*Example: Print Concept mastery*

"Look for" words and themes in responses that would be coded as 1 to denote that a child has mastered the print concepts.

*The child:*

- Conveys how to hold book right side up.
- Talks about looking at words or sentences from left to right.
- Conveys that words tell us something about the pictures in a book.

Interview-Based Assessments

*Rule 3*    To achieve reliability, an adequate number of questions that are linked to particular outcomes should be asked.

For each outcome or indicator targeted, we should have two or three interview questions that can help us make reliable conclusions about the interviewee. In interview-based tools, the probes count as added questions and generally help to improve reliability.

Interview-Based Assessments

*Rule 4*    Well-designed questions, probes, coding guidelines, and scoring rubrics must accompany interview-based assessments.

Rules for writing questions and probes with clarity are similar to those we considered in Chapter 7. The problem must be posed to the student in a clear, straightforward manner, with no tricks or confusing language. The questions should be linked to the targeted indicators with respect to content and behavior. We should thoughtfully decide on coding methods and appropriate guidelines before we use the tool. The following checklist highlights the major design criteria that we could use when developing interview-based tools.

## A Checklist for Designing Interview-Based Assessments

❑  **1.**   Is the interview-based method a logical match for targeted learning outcomes?

❑  **2.**   Is the method suitable for the population?

❑  **3.**   Does the design of the following support the assessment purposes?
- Questions
- Probes
- Coding criteria
- Rubric

❑  **4.**   Are interview questions clear and unambiguous?

❑  **5.**   Are individual interview questions linked to targeted outcomes in the domain?

❑  **6.**   Are the number of interview questions reasonable for the assessment purposes?

❑  **7.**   Do the directions clearly set the conditions for the interviewee?

❑  **8.**   Do instructions for interviewers or recorders clarify:
- The time allowed for each prompt?
- The probes allowed for each prompt?
- The method and degree of structure in coding responses?

❑  **9.**   If present, is the rubric easy to use?

### 8.4.5 Designing Portfolio-Based Assessments

Portfolios are a unique assessment procedure in several respects. They require collections of student work or behavior samples that are systematically gathered to serve many different educational purposes.

Portfolio-based assessment became a "buzz word" in education during the reform movement of the 1990s because it was viewed as another tool that could potentially assess learning outcomes which were poorly captured with traditional W-SR formats. Their particular advantages adapted from Arter and Spandel (1992), are as follows.

1. Portfolios can provide a documentation of the *processes* that students employ to develop *products*. For instance, when students develop written products, we could collect samples of their early drafts and outlines in a portfolio to make a more comprehensive assessment of their proficiency on targeted learning outcomes.
2. Portfolios are unique tools for *chronicling growth* over time in particular skill areas. For example, by compiling ongoing writing samples in a portfolio, we could see how a student's skills developed and changed with continuing instruction.
3. Portfolios can be easily *integrated with instruction* in the classroom, so that the assessment is not a one-time procedure, but an *ongoing event*.
4. Portfolios can deliberately be designed with *student participation and reflection*.

In summary, the purposes best served by portfolios are to provide evidence of a student's best work; to document change or growth over time in particular areas; to measure both the processes and products of learning, and, finally, to involve the student in the assessment process through self-reflection, selection of portfolio items, self-assessment, or other metacognitive exercises.

In Table 8.6a, we see an example of a language arts portfolio for K–2 students. At the top, the designers have outlined their instructional goals (learning outcomes). Their purpose was to map growth of students over time in language expression skills, editing skills, and hand-writing skills. At the end of each year, the student would select what they thought were their best pieces for the summative evaluation. They would also write a letter to their next teacher and parents summarizing how they had grown in writing (the metacognitive piece).

A separate rubric is needed for each different outcome or area targeted in a portfolio. In Table 8.6b, we see the scoring rubric/recording form that the teacher used for assessing the childrens' handwriting development. This is a behavior-based assessment combined with a written component. Two records were made by the teachers on each child based on all the writing exercises they completed in a year. Note that in this example, the handwriting rubric cannot be used to score the writing pieces on a child's language development skills.

Although there is considerable overlap with the other types of performance assessments, the rules for designing portfolios are a little different. They are summarized next.

Portfolio-Based Assessments

*Rule 1*    We should be clear about the purposes for using portfolio-based assessments.

Clarity of purposes, whether to assess growth over time, or to showcase best products or behavior samples, is essential for methodical assessment design. The *uses,* whether high stakes or low stakes, should be clear to the designers as the procedures are made final. The users of the results should similarly be identified. Portfolios for college admissions will need much tighter procedures than portfolios for daily classroom use.

---

Portfolio-Based Assessments

*Rule 2*    The portfolio-based procedure should be the best fit for the populations, purposes, and the targeted learning outcomes.

The portfolio procedures should be the best match for the assessment purposes, populations, and learning outcomes. If a short answer assessment can provide the same information to us, there is no need to pursue the portfolio-based approach. There has to be a compelling reason for us to opt for this method.

---

Portfolio-Based Assessments

*Rule 3*    The portfolio assessment conditions should be clear with respect to:

- Who will participate in the assessment design?
- Who will participate in the selection of work or behavior samples?
- Who will score the work or behavior samples?
- Under what conditions will the student samples be generated?

The conditions for portfolio assessment demand that we attend to several details. The involvement of students (and others) is one of the defining characteristics of the portfolio assessment approach. Thus, we need to structure the level of involvement that would be appropriate for the purposes.

Would students, other teachers, and parents/community members participate in the design of the procedures? What criteria will be used to include particular pieces in the portfolio? Where would the students *do the work* that serves as a portfolio sample? What kinds of *support* will they be allowed? Would the sample be scored by students, their teachers, peer students, or external examiners? Answers to all these question must be sought before the portfolio procedures are implemented. Many of the answers will be guided by the assessment purposes that you identify.

Portfolio-Based Assessments

*Rule 4* Sufficient student samples should be collected to ensure reliability.

As with other performance assessments, reliability needs must be addressed by gathering multiple work samples in a portfolio. Here, again, a sound designer would keep in mind the assessment purposes to decide on the number of products and samples.

---

**TABLE 8.6a An Example of a Portfolio-Based Assessment**

---

### Language Arts Portfolio: Cover Page

**Directions**

To the Teacher and Parent(s):

**Purpose:**

The contents of this portfolio are designed to assess the following goals for grade levels K–2 in Project CHILD.

L 1.0 Compose descriptive, narrative, and practical pieces in writing.

L 2.0 Edit using language conventions of punctuation, sentence structure, capitalization, and paragraphing.

L 3.0 Demonstrate manuscript handwriting skills.

**Portfolio Contents**

1. Writing Samples

   At least four writing samples, two from each quarter (4 per semester), must be included, with at least one sample in each of these categories:
   - Descriptive writing (e.g., personal experience)
   - Narrative writing (e.g., a story)
   - Practical writing (e.g., a letter)

   Samples may include final drafts or works in progress. Samples will be selected by students with teacher participation as best examples of his/her work for that semester. Samples may be drawn from journal entries, original stories, retold stories, letters, poems, or rhymes.

2. Language Expression Development Summary (Attachment 1)

   Checked by teacher once every semester with comments. This is a summary record.

3. Handwriting Samples—4 per semester

   These may be the same as the Writing Samples.

4. Handwriting Development Summary (Attachment 2 [see Table 8.6b])

   Checked by the teacher once every semester. This is a summary record.

5. Cover Letter Written by Student at the End of School Year

   This letter will be the student's reflection and self-evaluation of what he/she has learned during the past year. In it, the student will justify why the pieces in the portfolio were chosen as the best pieces of his/her work for that year.

**Suggestions:**

Kindergarten–2nd-Grade Students: The letter may be written to parent(s) or to the new teacher of the following grade. It could be used as a goal-setting activity for individual children for the following year.

**TABLE 8.6b  Scoring Rubric and Recording Form for Mapping Handwriting Growth in Students**

Language Arts Portfolio: Handwriting Development Summary

Name: _____     Grade: _____

Codes:

√ = Consistent Evidence of This     E = Early Signs of This     N = No Evidence Yet     U = Unable to Determine

| Sample Description (Letter, Manuscript, Practice) | Date Reviewed | Teacher Comments |
| --- | --- | --- |
| 1. | | |
| 2. | | |

1. Holds pencil properly
2. Shows left to right directionality
3. Has correct posture when writing
4. Has correct paper position when writing
5. Identifies uppercase letters (How many?)
6. Forms uppercase letters correctly (How many?)
7. Identifies lowercase letters (How many?)
8. Prints lowercase letters correctly (How many?)
9. Spaces correctly between words in a sentence
10. Demonstrates mastery of uppercase alphabet in writing
11. Demonstrates mastery of lowercase alphabet in writing
12. Prints legibly
13. Writes legibly in cursive
14. Other indicators:
    Neatness

| Date produced | Semester 1 | Semester 2 |
| --- | --- | --- |
| | | |

Please fill in this section based on discussion with student and parents.

What can we work on next?

Note to the Teacher:
*This instrument must be filled in by the teacher based on observations made of the child in class as well as examination of handwriting samples produced. Share with parents at appropriate times.*

Portfolio-Based Assessments

*Rule 5* Different types of products/samples in a portfolio should have separately designed rubrics.

Finally, portfolios can include multiple and varied samples of student work, each tied to different areas of the curriculum. We need to have appropriately designed rubrics to score the various samples. All of the preceding information suggests that portfolios are very time-consuming assessment devices; however, they are not necessarily so. When appropriately integrated with instruction, they can be very useful assessment tools.

## A Checklist for Designing Portfolio-Based Assessments

❑ **1.** Are the portfolio purposes clear? For example:
Is it to assess growth over time?
Is it to showcase best products or behavior samples?
Is it for other purposes?

❑ **2.** Is the portfolio the best match for the learning outcomes and population?

❑ **3.** Are adequate work or behavior samples included for purposes specified (not too many nor too few)?

❑ **4.** Are criteria for inclusion of work or behavior samples clear?

❑ **5.** Is adequate time provided for examinees to complete the work samples?

❑ **6.** Does the design control for the possibility of students getting outside assistance?

❑ **7.** Do the directions clearly set the conditions for the students/examinees?

❑ **8.** Are there separate rubrics for different work samples to be included in the portfolio?

❑ **9.** Are the rubrics:
■ Easy to use?
■ Aligned to outcomes?
■ Clear and unambiguous?

❑ **10.** Is the frequency with which work samples must be scored clear?

❑ **11.** Is the level of involvement of students and other participants in the design and use of the portfolio clear?

To close our discussion on different performance assessments, we should bear in mind that such tools can have an "interdisciplinary" focus. An *interdisciplinary assessment* attempts to assess proficiency on selected outcomes taken from *more than one subject area curriculum*. Interdisciplinary tools are necessary when teachers organize their instructional planning and delivery around integrated, multidisciplinary themes. If several outcomes need to be assessed in unison, it often make sense to opt for performance assessment approaches that are interdisciplinary. For example, an instructor wanting to measure mathematics, science and writing learning outcomes together might decide to design a product-based assessment tool, such as a report describing an experiment that gives evidence of mastery on all three domains.

---

**Key Concepts**

■ There are five different assessment methods that we could employ when we design performance assessments in User Path 1.

■ Depending on the assessment method we choose, specific rules for designing performance assessment tools can vary.

■ Performance assessments can focus on learning outcomes drawn from particular disciplines or from multidisciplinary curricula.

---

## 8.5    Scoring Rubrics and How to Develop Them

As we have seen, a critical structural component of a performance assessment is its scoring system. Scoring systems for open-ended assessments are referred to as "rubrics" or "scoring criteria." Rubrics are guidelines that we use to ensure that our judgments of open-ended responses are accurate, consistent, and fair. They should accompany all performance assessment methods where we anticipate *degrees of correctness or acceptability* in responses, such as short answer items (e.g., the graphing task in Table 8.2), essays, products (e.g., a book report), or behavior-based exercises (e.g., a diving contest). Without rubrics, the assessment tool is only partially developed. Rubrics provide us with a means to make finer discriminations in performances that vary in degrees of quality.

To understand rubrics in detail, we will refer back to the line-graphing assessment in Tables 8.2, 8.3, 8.4, and Figures 8.1 and 8.2. There are two main types of rubrics—*analytic* and *holistic*.

### 8.5.1    Types of Rubrics

*Analytic Rubrics*    In an analytic scoring system, the response is *broken down into relevant parts,* and each part is assessed separately and assigned a separate score. The number of scores or ratings produced from an analytic rubric is equal to the number of parts we separately assess. Often, a student may show a strong performance on some indicators of a construct, but much weaker performance on others. For example, we might be very good at writing original stories, but relatively weak in spelling. An analytic rubric will be able to pick up such differences in the quality of the performance on different indicators of a construct.

Refer to the analytic rubric for the line graphing task illustrated in Table 8.3. Notice that each indicator can be scored separately, with the rubric yielding a profile of scores for a student. There are separate scores for labeling/identifying scale units, other scores for plotting the data points, and still others for interpretation of the graph. While it is possible to sum ratings across all the indicators to obtain a total score out of 20, it is the property of describing *differential performance on different indicators* that gives the rubric its analytic character.

The student who produced the response in Figure 8.1 might receive a total score of 15 on the task (see Table 8.1). The summary score, however, does not provide any insights about his/her weaknesses on specific areas of the domain. To coach and help the student make specific improvements, the teacher could use the analytic profile of scores on individual indicators. As is evident in the Figure 8.1 response, this particular student appeared to have been negligent in the areas of labeling and selection of scale units. The response fails to justify the graphing technique. The rest of the graphing task appears to have been completed as expected.

*Holistic Rubrics* In a holistic scoring system in contrast to an analytic approach, the response is judged more or less as a whole by the scorer/rater, resulting in an overall rating of its quality. A *single score* or *rating* is generated from a holistic rubric. Table 8.4 provided an example of a holistic rubric for the graphing task. Holistic scoring is also called *global scoring,* because of its focus on the whole response rather than its parts.

Compare the sample answers shown in Figures 8.1 and 8.2 again with reference to the holistic rubric in Table 8.4. Figure 8.1 received a score of 3 on the holistic rubric. The rating indicated that while the response was generally acceptable, it had some imperfections. It did not reveal the exact areas in which the student made mistakes. What holistic rating would you give to Figure 8.2?

*Combining Analytic and Holistic Rubrics* It is possible to have a performance exercise that is scored both analytically and holistically. For example, consider an assessment requiring students to both develop and present a research report in social studies. The report could be scored analytically, while the oral presentation in class may be given an overall holistic score. Decisions on whether an analytic approach would be more useful should be prompted by our assessment purposes and the task.

## 8.5.2 Deciding Whether to Use a Holistic or Analytic Rubric

To decide whether or not a holistic or analytic system would be appropriate, keep in mind the purposes for assessment. Is it to obtain an overall, summative judgment at the end of a course or unit of instruction? Is expeditious scoring necessary? If answers to these questions are in the affirmative, a holistic approach is indicated. Several large-scale assessment programs incorporating performance assessments opt for the holistic approach to serve the needs listed above. The holistic rubric, however, cannot be easily adapted for diagnostic applications.

If our purpose is to diagnose strengths or weaknesses in pupils, or to facilitate formative decision-making, we would lean towards an analytic approach. An analytic profile of ratings on indicators, as seen in Table 8.3 for the line graphing task, naturally, would be better suited for feedback and coaching purposes. Additionally, the analytic rubric could serve both formative and summative purposes. The analytic breakdown of scores can be used to diagnose student needs, while the total score summed across indicators could provide a picture of performance on the overall task.

## 8.5.3 Deciding on the Type of Scale

Once a decision is made about whether or not to use a holistic or analytic scoring rubric (or some combination of the two) the next decision in developing a rubric deals with the type of point-allocation scheme or "scale" we will use. Depending on the task and degrees of variability that can be reasonably expected in the responses, we could use either a checklist or a rating scale to score the responses. Checklists have a 2-point range. Rating scales can be 3-point, 4-point, 5-point, 7-point, or of even greater width.

Let us consider their definitions.

**1.** Checklist—Typically, a checklist is linked to the indicators in the construct domain, and allows for a dichotomous classification of quality based on each indicator. Each scoring category checked is associated with a numeric value. In the analytic rubric shown in Table 8.3, we see a checklist used for Indicators 1.1, 1.3, and 1.4.

> *Checklist examples:*    Yes = 1, No = 0;
>
> Present = 1, Absent = 0,
>
> Observed = 1, Not observed = 0

**2.** Rating Scales—A set of ordered categories denoting different degrees of quality is called a "rating scale." In Table 8.3, a rating scale is provided to rate students on Indicators 1.2, 1.5, 1.6, and 2.1 and 2.2.

> *Example of a 4-point rating scale:*
> 0 = Not observed,
>
> 1 = Observed some of the time,
>
> 2 = Observed most of the time,
>
> 3 = Observed consistently and very frequently.

***Choosing the Best Scoring Scale***    How do we decide on the best method for allocating points? Let us consider the graphing example again. In Table 8.3, Indicator 1.4, which deals with labeling the graph, could only have two possible student responses: a student could have labeled the graph, and we would check "present" (score = 1); or a student could have omitted the label, and we would check the "absent" category (score = 0). On Indicator 1.4, therefore, it is sensible for us to use a dichotomous checklist for describing the variabilities in student performance.

For the plotting of data points (Indicator 1.5), however, there could be far greater variation in possible answers. For example, one student might consistently miss all or most of them, another might get all or most of them correct, while still others might get 5, 6, 8, or 10 correct. How many levels of performance should we differentiate? Here, the teacher/assessment designer would be astute in actually examining some samples of student responses to make a professional determination of the number of rating categories that would best describe the range in responses from typical examinees.

***Operationally Defining Scale Points***    To enable consistent scoring by different raters or observers, it is important to operationally define the scale points with observable indicators of performance that will be evidenced in typical responses. Consider the examples of rating scales that are very popular in education, but extremely difficult to implement reliably, because the category descriptors are vague and not directly observable:

### Rating Scales without Clearly Observable Descriptors

Indicator on rubric: Plotted X, Y coordinates accurately

| Rating scale 1: | 0 = Poor | 1 = Satisfactory | 2 = Good | 3 = Excellent |
|---|---|---|---|---|
| Rating scale 2: | 0 = Below Average | 1 = Average | 2 = Above Average | 3 = Outstanding |

Problem in both scales: Descriptors like "Good" and "Excellent" are too broad and can have different meanings to different raters.

Improvements on the descriptors tied to scale points could be made by using typical errors and omissions found in sample answers. For example, for the graphing task (Indicator 1.5), use of *observable descriptors* might generate a four-point scale like this:

### A Rating Scale That Uses Observable Descriptors

Indicator on rubric:  Plotted X, Y coordinates accurately

| Rating Scale: | 0 = None | 1 = 1–5 points | 2 = 6–9 points | 3 = 10–14 points |
|---|---|---|---|---|

The above rating scheme would rest on the empirical finding (by the assessment designer) that there were at least four *distinguishable* levels of performance in typical student answers based on the number of points that they could accurately plot.

On occasions when we use a *checklist* for scoring, there is a likelihood of rater errors if the indicator statements to be checked off are too broad, vague, or unreasonable for the expected responses. For example, in the graphing exercise, the following checklist would probably cause rating problems.

### A Checklist without Clearly Observable Descriptors

| | Indicate by circling (Y)es or (N)o. | Points: | 0 | 1 |
|---|---|---|---|---|
| Indicator: | Plotted X, Y coordinates accurately: | | Y | N |

In the preceding example, every one who failed to plot *all 14 points* in the line graph correctly should receive a 0 on that indicator, a rather harsh and inaccurate description of proficiency for students who produced seven or more accurately plotted points. While using the scale, raters who disagreed with the scoring scheme would introduce their individual judgments to provide a fairer score, causing variability and rater unreliability in the results. A possible improvement to the above checklist follows.

### A Modified Checklist That Uses Observable Descriptors

Check the descriptor that applies to the response.

| | | CHECK (1 point) | | Weight | Points |
|---|---|---|---|---|---|
| Plotted X, Y coordinates accurately. | | | | | |
| | 0–5 points: | _____ | | (×1) = | ❑ |
| | 6–10 points: | _____ | | (×2) = | ❑ |
| | 11–14 points: | _____ | | (×3) = | ❑ |

### 8.5.4   Steps in Constructing a Rubric

The steps we would take in designing the rubrics for performance assessment would start with actions taken during planning (or while developing the specifications) and end with the finished assessment task and rubric, as listed next.

In the specifications:

1. Identify and justify the best assessment method by which to gather evidence of proficiency on outcomes/behaviors in the domain. (A product? An observation of actual behaviors or demonstrations? An essay? A portfolio?)
2. Specify whether an analytic or holistic scoring rubric will be used, or some combination of the two.
3. Specify the scoring scheme or point-allocation scale to be used. Checklist, rating scale, or both?
4. Identify weights in terms of point values to be allocated to different components. This step is particularly relevant for analytic rubrics.

Then:

5. Design an exercise to capture the specified outcomes and behaviors in the domain. Write the the instructions and prompts to elicit responses; set the context/conditions; provide instructions for assessors.
6. Develop a draft of a scoring rubric to score the responses. Use *observable* descriptors to define the quality of a response at different levels of acceptability. Try to operationally define each scale point.
7. Try out the task on a sample of typical respondents. (Or, alternatively, perform the task yourself.) Observe or gather data on the possible range of responses to the task(s).
8. List common errors, omissions, or inaccuracies that you find in typical responses. Based on an error analysis, revise the descriptors of scale points on your rubric. Use the actual responses to tighten and clarify observable indicators at different levels of quality.
9. Attempt scoring actual responses using the revised rubric. Evaluate the extent to which the rubrics facilitate consistent scoring by different, but knowledgeable, raters.
10. Check back to make sure that rubric matches with indicators originally specified in the domain, as this will ensure content-based validity of the results.
11. Hold on to some sample answers at each score point to use as "anchor papers" during scoring. This will enhance reliability by controlling scorer errors.

---

**Key  Concepts**

- Performance assessment tools are incomplete if they have no scoring rubrics.
- Scoring rubrics can be analytic, holistic, or a combination of the two.
- Scoring schemes we employ in rubrics (the point-allocation scale) can be dichotomous (0,1), polytomous (0,1,2), or a combination of the two.

## 8.6    Specifications for Performance Assessments

Assessment specifications are guiding "blueprints" that help us design or select assessments that are the best fit for a particular situation. The validity of the resulting performance items or assessment as a whole will be influenced by the extent to which we are able to stay within the boundaries that were specified in the blueprint.

You might find yourself in situations where you do not have the time or inclination to design an instrument yourself, but would like to gather a set of assessments suited to your needs from available resources. In such circumstances, assessment specifications can be especially useful. Adaptation of assessment tools can be done easily using existing specifications and sample assessments as the starting point, and making any needed modifications. To maximize validity in local settings, classroom assessments should be adapted by individual teachers to fit particular assessment conditions within their own classrooms.

In Table 8.2, we saw an application using FORM II, the general assessment specification form, to devise the graphing assessment items. Another specification form, illustrated in Figure 8.3, could also help us to plan for or develop performance assessments. This form was originally intended for producing large numbers of similar assessment tasks for a state testing program. However, it provides us with useful ideas for local applications. Let us briefly review its components.

### 8.6.1    FCAT Assessment Specifications

Figure 8.3 illustrates an assessment specification form that was used for designing the fifth-grade mathematics component of the *Florida Comprehensive Assessment Test* (FCAT) Program in 1996–97. The FCAT tasks were intended for statewide accountability testing. The specifications were intended to guide item writers in developing a large pool of tasks from which the Florida department of education could randomly draw samples for use during testing in different years. This is a common strategy that testing program managers use to keep their assessments secure from year to year.

In the FCAT form, the *strand, standard,* and *benchmark* information begins to define the domain to be tapped; the Content Limits, Item Clarification, and Stimulus Attributes sections further specify the content, behaviors, and conditions in the domain. The domain deals with the "Geometry and Spatial Sense" strand. The specification indicates that two Item Types could be constructed to measure the domain specified: MC (multiple choice) or SR (short response). Samples of SR item type and rubrics are attached to the specifications in Figure 8.3.

### 8.6.2    How Useful Are the Assessment Specifications?

With assessment specifications, the "proof of the pudding" lies in their usefulness in producing replicas of the same class of items or tasks, with comparably high levels of quality. To test the merits of the specifications in Figure 8.3, for example, you could attempt to develop some additional items to match them. Do the specifications provide adequate guidelines for you to comfortably design new items, or did you have to stop and look for

# Florida Comprehensive Assessment Test (FCAT)

Mathematics Test Item and Performance Task Specifications
Grade 5

Strand C    Geometry and Spatial Sense

Standard 2    The student visualizes and illustrates ways in which shapes can be combined, subdivided, and changed.

Benchmark    MA.C2.2.1 The student understands the concepts of spatial relationships, symmetry, reflections, congruency, and similarity.

Item Type    This benchmark will be assessed using multiple-choice (MC) items and short-response (SR) items.

Clarification    MC Items The student identifies or classifies figures and/or solves a problem using the concepts of spatial relationships, including reflections, symmetry, congruency, or similarity.

SR Items The student classifies, illustrates, and/or explains the concepts of spatial relationships, including symmetry, reflections, congruency, or similarity.

Content Limits    Items should use only two-dimensional shapes: three-dimensional shapes will not be assessed under this benchmark.

Items may assess spatial relationships such as seeing figures upside down or in other different positions. Other content limits are specified in the "Content Limits by Grade Level" section of the Mathematics General Test Item and Performance Task Specifications.

Grade 5 C2.2.1

## Sample SR Item

Look at the picture of the button drawn below. On the grid, draw another button that is congruent to the one shown.

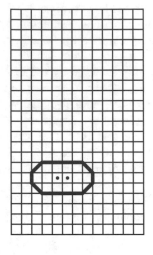

On the lines below, explain why the button you drew is congruent to the first button on the grid.

_____

Item Context: Mathematics

Grade 5 C2.2.1

**Correct and Complete Response**

A correct and complete response includes a correct drawing and an explanation.

• Congruent button drawn (the two buttonholes must be present)

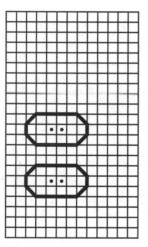

• OR drawing of a congruent button with another orientation

AND

• An explanation similar to the following:

The button I drew is the same shape and the same size as the first button.

**Scoring Rubric**

2 points    A score of two indicates that the student has demonstrated a thorough understanding of the mathematics concepts and/or procedures embodied in the task. The student has completed the task correctly, in a mathematically sound manner. When required, student explanations and/or interpretations are clear and complete.

1 point    A score of one indicates that the student has provided a response that is only partially correct. For example, the student may provide a correct solution, but may demonstrate some misunderstanding of the underlying mathematical concepts or procedures. Conversely, a student may provide a computationally incorrect solution but could have applied appropriate and mathematically sound procedures, or the student's explanation could indicate an understanding of the task, even in light of the error.

0 points    A score of zero indicates that the student has provided a completely incorrect or uninterpretable response, or no response at all.

Grade 5 C2.2.1

**FIGURE 8.3 Assessment Specification and Sample Tasks for FCAT Mathematics Assessment**

*Source:* Used by permission of the Florida Department of Education. All rights reserved.

further information and clarification? It is the answer to this question that will help you decide whether the blueprint for a performance assessment is helpful from a design standpoint.

In the top panel of Table 8.7, which is provided to help you during content validation, we see some criteria for ensuring that the specifications were well thought out *before* we begin writing or selecting the assessments or items to match them. According to the

---

**TABLE 8.7   A Content-Validation Checklist for Performance Assessment Tools**

---

*Quality of the Assessment Specification (FORM II)*

1.  Is the assessment purpose identified with adequate detail?
2.  Is the population identified?
3.  Is the construct domain clarified with general and specific indicators (goals and objectives)?
4.  Are the domain indicators stated in clear terms?
5.  Are the intended taxonomic levels specified?
6.  Are the chosen assessment method(s) justified?
7.  Does the specification indicate the weights to be allocated to different indicators?
8.  Is the scoring method clearly specified?
9.  Are the assessment conditions clearly specified?

*Overall Check of the Performance Assessment Tool*

1.  Does the assessment show a logical match with the:
    - Targeted indicators of the domain specified?
    - Intended population?
    - Assessment purposes?
2.  Is the expected performance clearly defined for examinees?
3.  As applicable, are appropriate materials, pictorials, models provided, accompanied with clear, easy-to-follow labels or instructions? If any equipment is used, is it in working condition?
4.  Are instructions for other assessors/users clear?
5.  Are conditions clearly outlined in the instructions?
6.  Are the scoring rubrics:
    - Clear?
    - With operationally defined scale points?
    - Linked to targeted domain indicators?
    - Matched to weights specified?
    - Aligned with taxonomic levels?
    - Appropriate for the assessment purposes and population?
7.  Are anchor answers/samples provided to supplement the rubric?
8.  Are the assessment and rubric easy to use and practical?
9.  Will materials be easily available and inexpensive to set up in typical assessment environments (e.g., classrooms)?
10. Are enough observations or samples included to generate reliable results without hurting utility?
11. Does the assessment *appear to be* free of the following biases:
    - Readability bias
    - Inflammatory bias
    - Opportunity-to-learn bias
    - Conditions/materials bias

checklist, a useful specification for designing/selecting a performance assessment will give us clear instructions in the following areas.

- Assessment purpose(s)
- Population
- Construct domain
- Assessment method(s)
- Weighting plan
- Scoring procedures and criteria
- Assessment conditions
- The level of training needed for Scorers or Observers

## 8.7 Assembling and Content-Validating Performance Assessments

Performance assessments are complex tools. Each type has unique features and functions. To help summarize in more general terms what we need to do when designing or selecting performance assessments, this section outlines what the components of an assembled tool would be, and the general guidelines we could follow during content validation.

A fully assembled performance assessment tool should have the following components:

1. The assessment tasks/exercise
2. Instructions and prompts for examinees
3. Instructions for assessors to implement the assessment (if applicable):
   - Instructions for proctors/administrators
   - Instructions for interviewers
   - Instructions for observers and/or recorders
   - Instructions for raters/scorers
   - Instructions for score interpretation and use by other users
4. Materials and equipment needed to support the assessment (if applicable)
5. Scoring rubrics
6. Sample papers, products, or recorded behaviors that could serve as anchors for raters

While not all of the above might be necessary for everyday classroom assessments, a teacher or local designer would be well advised to include as many of them as might be needed to obtain valid and reliable results in given circumstances.

Table 8.7 summarizes in checklist form the key criteria for determining the quality of performance assessments. Note that these general criteria should be used in conjunction with the *specific checklists* for designing each different type of assessment. The criteria are consistent with the rules discussed previously. The checklist could serve as a guide to peer reviewers or formally trained external expert teams responsible for content validation in Phase IV A of the process model.

## 8.8    Using Rubrics: Sources of Random and Systematic Error

Human judges serve as an integral part of a performance assessment tool. Like all human beings, they are vulnerable to error during scoring. To help generate valid and reliable scores, good raters make themselves very familiar with the rubrics and expected responses from examinees. However, random errors in scoring occur even when there are well-designed rubrics to guide raters in their work. Large-scale assessment programs, as a result, invest in formal rater training programs and maintain "banks" of assessment raters who are likely to rate more consistently than others. In local assessment applications, we can take similar steps to ensure that human lapses in judging are not adverse influences on the ratings.

Based on research on rater errors applicable to essays, Hopkins (1998) placed common sources of rater error in five major categories. These errors could also apply to other forms of performance assessment, as the following examples illustrate. Five major sources of random rater error are the:

1. Halo effect
2. Item or task carry-over effect
3. Test or performance carry-over effect
4. Order effect
5. Writing/language mechanics effect

### 8.8.1    Halo Effect

The *halo effect,* a kind of subjective bias, is evident in circumstances where the observer/rater's impression of the the examinee or respondent on characteristics unrelated to the task/performance affects the rating/score. This influence is usually in a positive direction, although the reverse could also be true. In an Olympic figure-skating championship, we would conclude that the halo effect was contaminating the assessment environment if we found that the U.S. judge on the panel was awarding generally higher ratings to the U.S. skaters, irrespective of their actual performance, or that the German skaters were obtaining especially high ratings from the German judge, regardless of mistakes they made.

As teachers, we are vulnerable to the halo effect whenever we use open-ended assessments. A generally favorable impression we hold of particular students will tend to make us award correspondingly favorable ratings to these individuals, regardless of their performance. Conversely, if we have a very poor impression of a student's behavior in the classroom, we might be inclined to be particularly strict when rating the same student's academic work.

Controlling the halo effect in W-OE or product-based assessments is possible by keeping the scoring process anonymous. Ask students to place their names on the back of the answer booklet, product, or paper; not knowing student names will facilitate scoring without the influence of unrelated, confounding factors.

### 8.8.2 Item or Task Carry-Over Effects

This error is caused by the rater's judgment of the quality of the first item/performance carrying over to the next item for that same examinee. In a figure skating championship, if a rater's judgment of an ice skater's performance on the short program influenced the judgment of that skater's performance on the following long program, we would have an instance of an *item* or *task carry-over effect*. In a W-OE assessment, if the score on the first short response problem influenced the scores on the problems that followed next, we would see another example of an item or task carry-over effect. To counter such effects, we should rate the first item or task for all examinees before we moved to rating of the next one.

### 8.8.3 Test or Performance Carry-Over Effect

Educational researchers have found that essays of poor quality tend to be rated much higher when they are rated after two badly written essays, than when the two preceding essays are well-written papers (Hales & Tokar, 1975; Hughes, Keeling, & Tuck, 1980). This type of contamination is called a *test* or *performance carry-over effect,* because the judged performance level of one examinee carries over and influences the score on the next examinee's paper. With behavior-based assessments, a performance carry-over effect would occur if judgments of the first person's performance colored the rater's judgment of the performers that immediately followed. To combat the effects of the test or performance carry-over effect, we should periodically shuffle papers in a random order, or randomly distribute observations and rating sessions for individuals observed.

### 8.8.4 Order Effects

The order in which papers are read or individuals observed has also been found to result in inconsistent rating patterns. Prolonged observation, recording, or scoring has been found to lead to a gradual decline in the quality of ratings on papers at the bottom of the pile. This "slide effect" occurs because fatigue, resulting from the repetitive drudgery of the work, sets in with later observations.

   To reverse the impact of order, we should take breaks to rejuvenate ourselves during long scoring or observation sessions. A general rule to follow is to randomly observe or rate examinees to help counterbalance the order or "slide" effect.

### 8.8.5 Writing and Language Mechanics Effects

In written or product-based assessments, the skills of the writer in language usage often influences the score on the paper or product, even when the targeted learning outcome is not related to writing ability. Research shows that scorers can rarely stay focused on the *targeted content domain* of the assessment without being influenced by spelling, vocabulary, punctuation, grammar, length of the answer, neatness, or presentation—extraneous factors that confound the final assessment results. Test-wise students capitalize on this vulnerability of raters when they think they can "bluff" their way through essay examinations. If the influence of writing or language mechanics effects becomes systematic, it affects the validity of the results; when random, it alters the reliability of scores.

The solution here is to craft a tightly defined task and scoring rubric that are closely linked to the assessment specification and indicators in the domain. Instructions to the assessment should help direct the examinee to the expected response, where they understand that mastery of the content domain, *not* writing ability, will help them score well. In the same vein, raters should also have explicit scoring criteria tied to the valued indicators from the domain. Rubrics and accompanying instructions should be designed to help raters maintain validity during scoring.

Use of anchor papers, or sample responses/products that represent different levels of performance tied to the scoring rubric, are another useful way to keep scorers focused on expectations of performance. In the line graphing assessment shown earlier, for example, the response in Figure 8.2 could serve as an anchor paper for a score of 4 on the holistic rubric.

## 8.8.6   Systematic Biases during Scoring

As with W-SR achievement tests, we should attempt to reduce systematic biases from affecting results of performance assessments. The three sources of bias discussed in Chapter 7 also apply to performance assessments: *bias due to readability, inflammatory bias,* and *opportunity-to-learn bias.* Two additional sources of bias apply to performance assessments. The first, called a "conditions/materials bias" here, stems from a mismatch of the assessment conditions or materials used in the tasks with the targeted group of examinees. The second, referred to as "rater bias" here, would arise from individual raters being consistently strict or consistently lenient in their ratings. All of these errors are different from random rater fluctuations discussed in the preceding section, such as the halo effect, in that these errors tend to be systematic and predictable, thus affecting validity rather than reliability of results.

*Conditions/Materials Bias*   For valid inferences to be drawn from the results, the materials and operations expected of the examinees must be suited to their developmental level, age, or special needs status. For example, if respondents are expected to handle computer equipment in order to demonstrate particular skills, we must ask, is the hardware and software used to design the assessment reasonable for the targeted age, developmental stage, and any special needs that examinees might have? During content validation, we should screen the assessment materials to ensure a reasonable match of the conditions and materials with the population specified.

*Systematic Rater Bias*   Research scientists in agencies such as the Educational Testing Service have recently begun to use specialized psychometric techniques to calibrate how lenient or severe raters are on some of their better known assessments (e.g., *Test of Written English;* see Myford & Mislevy, 1995). The literature on rater severity or leniency is still rather sparse; however, it suggests that individual raters tend to score papers, products, or performances within particular ranges of a given rating scale. Severe raters tend to stay in the lower region of a rating scale, assigning low scores to everyone;

while lenient raters favor a range of scores that are relatively higher on the scale. These observations suggest that rater severity/leniency is a systematic biasing factor rather than an unpredictable chance factor. Individual rater bias is undesirable in high stakes uses of performance assessments because an examinee's score would depend on whether the paper happened to be scored by the more severe or lenient raters, or by raters who lie somewhere in between. Such research findings have led to the practice of reporting examinee scores adjusted for estimated levels of rater severity in some testing programs.

### Key Concepts

- Raters should make themselves aware of possible sources of random and systematic scoring errors when they use scoring rubrics that accompany performance assessments.
- To keep such errors down in high stakes testing situations, raters should receive training with rubrics, use anchors, or otherwise structure the scoring conditions.

## Summary

In User Path 1, performance assessment formats should be used when our curriculum aims and philosophy call for their use and they are the best means for capturing the targeted learning outcomes in a valid way for the assessment purposes and population. Performance formats are distinctly advantageous in three main ways:

1. They can be designed to assess bigger "chunks" of an achievement domain.
2. They can be easily integrated with instruction because they are activity-based.
3. They are well suited for measuring certain educational constructs—particularly reasoning, higher-order thinking, application of concepts and principles in real life settings, and social and motor behaviors.

The selection of a performance assessment method poses some unique challenges to the designer and users in the areas of reliability and utility. We should therefore take deliberate steps to sensitize ourselves to the sources of error or practical barriers that we are likely to face, and design the assessment tools to address the anticipated problems. Assessment designers should also practice justifying assessment methods that they select during the assessment design or selection process, using validity, reliability and utility criteria. Chapter 8 attempted to elaborate on such issues with case studies and examples.

Use of the Process Model to design or select performance assessments would involve the same general procedure illustrated in Chapters 5–7. These are:

1. Specifying the purpose, population, and construct domain in Phase I
2. Developing the specification in Phase II
3. Designing or selecting the assessment tasks and scoring rubrics in Phase III
4. Evaluating content-based validity of the assembled assessment tool (Phase IV A)

Chapter 8 touched on, but did not provide details of, empirical validation methods that might be pertinent to performance assessment development (Phase IV B).

The chapter illustrated how to use assessment specification forms for designing or selecting performance assessment tools. For each type of performance assessment method, the chapter provided guidelines (rules) for task and rubric design. During content validation of performance assessment tools, we should attend to specific criteria for quality that apply to each of the five performance assessment methods.

The chapter described two major types of rubrics: analytic and holistic. The purposes for assessment should guide the decision as to whether we use a holistic or analytic rubric. The scoring scheme can either be dichotomous (a checklist) or polytomous (a rating scale). In both cases, it is important to operationally define the scale points with observable indicators of performance likely to be evidenced in the responses of typical examinees. Checking that the rubric matches with indicators originally specified in the domain ensures content-based validity of the assessment results. Rater training with the rubrics and anchor papers helps reduce unreliability in the ratings produced.

This chapter also attempted to raise your awareness regarding different sources of error that apply to performance assessments. Random rater errors are typically caused by the halo effect, item or task carry-over effect, test or performance carry-over effect, order effect, and writing/language mechanics effects. Systematic biases in performance assessments can be caused by biases due to readability, inflammatory biases, opportunity-to-learn biases, conditions biases, or systematic rater biases.

## QUESTIONS FOR CLASS DISCUSSION

1. For a population and assessment purpose of your choice, identify a general learning outcome (or a set of learning outcomes) that is best measured by each of these assessment methods.
   - A behavior-based assessment
   - An essay/short answer items
   - Product-based assessment
   - An interview-based assessment

   Justify your decisions using validity, reliability and utility reasons.

2. Review the following learning outcome (elementary mathematics curriculum) and short response task. Then answer a–c.

   Outcome:
   Identify, continue and explain growing patterns involving beginning level arithmetic operations and number concepts (e.g., 1, 10, 100, 1000 . . .), using mathematical language.

   Sample Task:
   Continue this pattern of numbers: 10, 15, 20, 25, __, __, 40, __, __ .
   What rule did you use to fill in the blanks?
   What number would you expect after the last blank in the series?

   a. What is the taxonomic level of the outcome? Does the sample task have content validity?
   b. Design two more tasks to match the same outcome. Do your tasks have content validity?
   c. Design a holistic rubric for the tasks with 3–5 levels of performance.

3. Identify an assessment context (purpose, population, construct domain) which is best served using a performance assessment with an analytic rubric. Explain your selection.

4. Design a performance assessment and rubric for an assessment context (purpose, population, construct domain) of your choice. Ask a peer to content-validate your tool using the checklists in Chapter 8. How well did you do?

5. You are asked to lead the design of a portfolio-based assessment for certifying professionals in a field of your choice (for example, teachers, psychologists, counselors, or technology specialists). Outline the phases of your work and the design decisions you would make.

# 9 Designing or Selecting Affective, Social-Emotional, Personality, and Behavioral Assessments

## Overview

The focus of Chapter 9 is on assessment applications that typically fall outside User Path 1. In Chapter 2, we learned that User Paths 2–6 dealt with the following decision-making contexts:

*User Path 2.* Assessment for program planning, evaluation, and policymaking
*User Path 3.* Assessment for screening and diagnosis of exceptionalities
*User Path 4.* Assessment for guidance and counseling
*User Path 5.* Assessment for admissions, licensure, scholarships, or awards
*User Path 6.* Assessment in educational research and development

Across these rather diverse user contexts, we discovered that assessment tools could be employed to generate information to support inferences about programs or institutional units on a system-wide scale. In User Paths 2 and 6, for example, we could aggregate (or average) measurements on *groups* of participants or clients within a system when our intent is to make system-level inferences. Alternatively, in User Paths 3, 4, and 5, our assessments might involve in-depth examinations of *individuals*. Thus, we might use the results from one or more measured indices to support decisions on interventions, placement, certification, or admission of particular students or subjects. Depending on the application, *constructs* we measure in Paths 2–6 could span an extensive range of cognitive, affective, social-emotional, personality, and behavioral variables.

There are numerous occasions where professionals in Paths 2–6 face the need for designing their own instruments, or for making significant adaptations to existing ones to custom-fit them for particular conditions. The purpose of Chapter 9 is to illustrate in detail how we would design or select assessment tools to support decisions in Paths 2–6.

Chapter 9 begins with two case studies of assessment design/selection that employ the four-phase Process Model in Path 2, and Paths 3 and 4, respectively. The specific instrument types and methods on which the chapter provides guidelines are:

1. Self-report instruments
2. Structured observations
3. Anecdotal observation procedures

You will immediately notice that the primary users in the case studies are *not* teachers. This is because we are now examining applications in somewhat different decision-making realms. The rules for designing instruments, however, would not change in instances where teachers were a part of the primary user group.

Chapter 9 does not contain any information on standardized measures of achievement, mental aptitudes, or intelligence. Similarly, there is no discussion of standardized measures of affective or personality variables. Chapter 14 discusses standardized assessment batteries and their applications in detail. Chapter 9 will, however, illustrate how we could assemble a set of specifications in order to *select* standardized measures to serve assessment needs in Paths 2–6.

## CHAPTER 9 OBJECTIVES

After studying this chapter and completing the structured exercises in the module, you should be able to:

1. Describe the core tasks in the Process Model needed to design or select assessment tools to measure constructs in User Paths 2–6

2. Identify characteristics of particular assessment methods best suited to measure constructs in User Paths 2–6

3. Develop assessment specifications to guide the design or selection of instruments in User Paths 2–6

4. Apply guidelines for writing items for self-report questionnaires and interviews

5. Apply guidelines for constructing structured, behavior observation schedules

6. Apply guidelines for writing and interpreting anecdotal records

7. Identify the major threats to validity, reliability, and utility, and methods to control them in assessment procedures used in Paths 2–6

8. Design and assemble (or select) assessment tools to meet specifications and accepted guidelines in User Paths 2–6

9. Conduct a content validation of assessment tools in User Paths 2–6

## 9.1   Applying the Process Model in User Paths 2–6

A consistent theme in this book has been the application of a generalizable Process Model to design or select assessments in various User Paths. The book has attempted to demonstrate that by following the Process Model, we enhance the outcomes of the assessment process, both in terms of the quality of information we obtain as well as its efficiency. The core tasks of the Process Model remain invariant irrespective of the differences in constructs we measure, the type of assessment methods we choose, specific decision-making needs of users, or the levels of formality imposed in the instrument development situation. Let us examine two case studies in Paths 2–6 and compare them with those in User Path 1. New concepts introduced through these case studies, such as *self-report measures, subdomains, unidimensionality,* and *homogeneous item sets,* will be elaborated in subsequent sections.

## Case Study 9.1    Designing an Instrument to Determine Needs for Teacher Training in a School District (User Path 2)

*Background:*    A school district's central office appointed a staff development committee to create an instrument to assess training needs of teachers and instructional support staff. The district had recently hired a number of newly prepared teachers and staff from colleges of education. However, changes occurring in the state's teacher certification requirements and national/regional school accreditation policies placed new demands on what teachers and support staff were currently expected to know and be able to do in the classroom. In sum, the district office needed to conduct a "needs assessment" survey in all of their schools, and selected a broad-based committee to assist them with this task. The committee consisted of a school principal, an assistant principal, two experienced teachers, a reading specialist, two counselors, and a school psychologist. The instruments developed by the committee would be used to gather information to support decisions on future staff development programs.

The committee began their work by focusing first on an instrument to assess the training needs of classroom teachers. They collected and read the recently published documents on teacher education and discovered that as a consequence of national education reform movements, new and rather different directions for teacher training had been set by state and national bodies. Conceptions of "good" teaching had broadened to the point where previously designed instruments would not be useful in providing the information they now needed. Based on the advice of three of the committee members, they decided to design a "self-report" questionnaire. A *self-report* procedure would directly ask teachers to report on how prepared they *felt* on indicators of effective teaching that were relevant to recent educational reforms. They followed a four-phase Process Model for designing the tool.

*Tasks in Phase I:    Specifying the Population, Purposes, and the Construct Domain*    In Phase I, the committee specified the targeted population as all full-time classroom teachers who spent 70% or more of their time teaching in the classroom. They specified their assessment purposes as formative decision-making. Their intent was to use the information for decisions on training programs that could be offered at schools and the district as a whole. Thus, they wanted a description of training needs aggregated by the school and for the district.

The committee labeled the construct to be assessed "training needs for effective classroom teaching." The recent research and policy literature on teacher education provided them with some general and more specific indicators of "well-trained" teachers in an environment that encouraged teaching reforms. Once they located defensible sources, the committee members followed standard guidelines to specify the construct domain. Their initially operationalized domain looked as shown in the following box.

# Box 9.1
## Domain Specified for Assessing the Construct: "Training Needs for Effective Classroom Teaching"

*General Indicator*
1.0    Effective teachers can plan, instruct, and assess in the classroom using specific types of knowledge.

*Specific Indicators*
1.1    Teachers demonstrate proficiency in classroom planning.
       1.1.1    Teachers plan instruction based on knowledge of their students, subject matter, curriculum, principles of learning and instructional design, and community values/influences.
       1.1.2    Teachers create or select learning opportunities that are meaningful and facilitate learning.
1.2    Teachers instruct in a creative, flexible, and adaptive manner.
       1.2.1    Teachers create a positive learning environment by maintaining appropriate standards of classroom behavior/conduct.
       1.2.2    Teachers create learning opportunities that support a student's academic, personal, and social development.
       1.2.3    Teachers create instructional opportunities to foster critical thinking and skill building.
       1.2.4    Teachers use effective verbal, nonverbal, and media communications techniques to foster individual and collaborative inquiry.
1.3    Teachers design assessments and use their results effectively.
       1.3.1    Teachers design, select, and use appropriate assessment techniques to evaluate student learning.
       1.3.2    Teachers use assessment results to provide timely feedback and coaching to students.
       1.3.3    Teachers use assessments to appropriately modify and adjust instruction.
       1.3.4    Teachers make appropriate interpretations of the results of standardized assessments designed for different purposes.

*Sources Used:*   State of Connecticut's Common Core of Teaching (Foundational skills and competencies).
Policy document of the National Council for the Accreditation of Teacher Education institutions (NCATE, 2000).
State of Florida's Accomplished Practices for the Teaching Professions.
Research articles: Darling-Hammond (1998); Noddings, (1996); Shulman (1987); Stiggins & Conklin (1992).

*Tasks in Phase II:   Developing the Assessment Specifications*    The members recognized that without some structure in the instrument, the respondents might provide their own individual perceptions of training needs, which could fail to comply with directions for educational reform being set in their state or nation. Preparing the full set of assessment specifications to guide the design or selection of the instrument was, thus, the next task for the committee. In Table 9.1, we see an example of FORM IV, as developed by the committee. FORM IV is a version of an assessment specification that is formatted a bit differently from FORMS I and II.

*(continued)*

## Case Study 9.1 Continued

**TABLE 9.1 FORM IV: Assessment Specifications for Designing a Self-Report Instrument to Measure Teacher Training Needs**

I. Assessment Purpose: To use results for making formative decisions on staff development programs (User Path 2)
II. Population: Teachers with at least 70% assignment in classroom teaching
III. Construct: "Training needs for effective classroom teaching"
IV. Assessment method: Written, structured response (Likert-type scales)

| IV. DOMAIN INDICATORS | Number of Items | Content/Behavior Focus and Item Type |
|---|---|---|
| A. Background | 5 | One (1) item each on: Gender Grade Level(s) taught Subject(s) taught Ethnic background Years of experience *Item Type:* Multiple choice SAMPLE ITEM Indicate grade level(s) at which you teach. *A. Grade 4* *B. Grade 5* *C. Grade 6* *D. Mixed grade levels.* |
| B. General Indicator: 1.0 | | |
| Effective classroom teaching | 18–20 (total) | Four-point scales with ordinal response categories Each item asks for an experience-based response: *"Indicate the level of adequacy of your previous training in this area . . ."* |
| Specific Indicator 1.1 | 4–5 | |
| Specific Indicator 1.2 | 4–5 | |
| Specific Indicator 1.3 | 4–5 | |

SAMPLE ITEMS

Specific Indicator 1.1 Proficiency in classroom planning

*Indicate the level of adequacy of your previous training in this area:*

|  | RESPONSE CHOICES |
|---|---|
| *1. Planning using knowledge of how students learn* | *a---b---c---d* |
| *2. Planning using knowledge of subject matter* | *a---b---c---d* |
| *3. Planning using instructional design principles* | *a---b---c---d* |

*a. More than adequate*
*b. Adequate*
*c. Less than adequate*
*d. Not at all*

In Table 9.1, we see that the committee decided on a total set of 18–20 "self-report" items. Specifically, the items were expected to draw out teachers' perceptions regarding the adequacy of their training experiences in areas associated with current notions of good class-room teaching, the construct they wanted to measure. To attain reliability, they decided upon 4 or 5 items for each specific indicator in their domain. The overall *content* focus of their items had to do with "effective classroom teaching." Behaviorally, the items attempted to tap "affective" responses, because the teachers would be offering their perceptions. The committee opted for a four-point gradually increasing response scale with ordered catego-ries (as seen in Chapter 4). Five items asked for background information from the teach-ers that would help the committee in sorting their responses by grade level and field of specialization.

As would be true in all of the instrument development exercises, once the developers (in this case, the committee) had their specifications compiled, they had the option to write the items themselves or extract/adapt items from other instruments to meet their requirements. In this case, the committee chose to develop the instrument themselves.

***Tasks in Phase III: Developing the Assessment Tool.*** The key task in Phase III was to write the items according to specifications and item guidelines, and finally to assemble the tool with directions. The committee wanted a layout that would be easy to follow for teachers. They fol-lowed standard guidelines for writing items for self-report tools (presented later in this chapter). The results of their work is shown in Table 9.2, which presents the directions (top panel) along with an excerpt of their "training needs survey" (bottom panel).

***Tasks in Phase IV: Validating the Assessment Tool.*** The work in this phase (Phase IVA) began with a content validation of the assessment and supporting materials by two teachers who had not participated in the design work. The committee first administered the instrument to the "external" reviewers as if they were subjects of the training needs survey. Next, they completed an item-by-item review using a content-validation checklist that the committee provided for them to use as a guide. The validation checklist helped the reviewers screen the quality of the tool from four perspectives.

1. Did the individual items match the indicators listed in the domain?
2. Were all of the important rules for writing items for self-report instruments followed by the committee?
3. Did any of the items appear to have apparent biases against the teachers to be surveyed?
4. Did the instructions, layout, and language appear to be clear and easy to use?

With respect to content-based validity, the reviewers found that there were no items at all on three indicators that had been listed in the original domain specification. In other respects, the reviewers found the items and presentation to be clear, unbiased, and readable. The committee corrected the omission in the revised version of the instrument, which consisted of 32 items in its final version. Some of the language in the original items was also revised as a result of the reviews. Following the revisions, they were ready to implement the instrument in their own school. Because the immediate uses were to be formative, empirical validation efforts (Phase IV B) were planned by the committee, but not undertaken right away.

*(continued)*

## Case Study 9.1    Continued

**TABLE 9.2    Excerpt from a Self-Report Instrument**

A Training Needs Survey for Teachers

PURPOSE          State and national organizations have set new requirements for teacher training. The purpose of this survey is to gather information on training needs of teachers in our school and district based on these new requirements. The results will be used by the district office to develop teacher inservice programs. Please <u>do not</u> give us your name or identification number. The results will be averaged by school. Individual responses will be kept <u>completely confidential</u>. Your cooperation in filling out the survey honestly and completely is appreciated by the School Inservice Committee.

DIRECTIONS:    For the items listed (#1–20), you will be asked to *indicate the level of adequacy of your <u>previous</u> training in different areas of teaching. Your response choices for all the items are as follows.*

RESPONSE CHOICES:
        *a. More than adequate*
        *b. Adequate*
        *c. Less than adequate*
        *d. No training at all*

CIRCLE <u>ONE</u> OF THE RESPONSE CHOICES PROVIDED TO ANSWER EACH ITEM.
EXAMPLES:
*1. Planning using knowledge of how students learn*          a---ⓑ---c---d
*2. Planning using knowledge of subject matter*          a---ⓑ---c---d
*3. Planning using instructional design principles*          a---b---c---ⓓ

The last five items (#21–25) ask for information on your background.
CHOOSE ONE OF THE RESPONSE CHOICES PROVIDED TO EACH ITEM.
THANKS FOR YOUR TIME!

The listed items represent areas of proficiency for effective classroom teaching. Indicate the level of adequacy of your <u>previous</u> training in each area listed under "ITEMS."

| ITEMS | *RESPONSES* |
|---|---|
| 1.  Planning for instruction using knowledge of how students learn. | a---b---c---d |
| 2.  Planning for instruction using knowledge of subject matter. | a---b---c---d |
| 3.  Planning for instruction using instructional design principles. | a---b---c---d |
| 4.  Developing the curriculum using community values. | a---b---c---d |
| 5.  Using classroom assessment to plan and improve teaching. | a---b---c---d |
| 6.  Maintaining high standards of classroom conduct/behavior. | a---b---c---d |
| 7.  Designing activities that support academic growth. | a---b---c---d |
| 8.  Designing activities that develop students' interpersonal skills. | a---b---c---d |
| 9.  Designing activities that build students' critical thinking skills. | a---b---c---d |
| 10.  Developing activities that use modern media/technology. | a---b---c---d |

## Case Study 9.2     Applying the Process Model to Design or Select Assessments for Counseling and/or Intervention (User Paths 3 or 4)

*Background:*     At a dropout prevention school, a student's parents approached the counselor with concerns that their 16-year-old son was acting "very strange and withdrawn" at home. His close friend had recently been killed in a car crash; the parents suspected that that particular episode had brought on the present behaviors as the student was "just not the same any more." However, they were not sure if there was something else bothering him.

To follow up, the counselor decided to interview the student one-on-one, and screen his responses for symptoms of dissatisfaction with specific areas in his life that might suggest reasons for his withdrawn behavior. The results of this "screening" assessment would then be used to provide individual counseling. To fulfill this assessment purpose, she decided to develop an interview-based tool to gather data on the student's *subjective well-being,* a psychological construct that is formally defined as a person's subjective assessment of his or her quality of life (Bender, 1997; Deiner, 1994). To supplement the interview data, she asked the student's teachers to keep anecdotal observations of his behaviors in class.

*Tasks in Phase I:   Specifying the Population, Purposes, and the Construct Domain*     The counselor started the instrument design effort by identifying the population as one consisting of adolescents referred for counseling following a personal or family crisis; the assessment purpose as initial screening for symptoms of dissatisfaction with life; and the specific construct as a measure of "subjective well-being." The counselor was hesitant to screen for "mental depression" because of her uncertainty as to the seriousness of the problem. If signs of a more serious mental condition surfaced during the interview, she resolved to seek more specialized psychological consultation for the student. Her initial intent was to conduct a preliminary screening interview.

The counselor specified the domain with the indicators listed in the following box. As is evident, she conceptualized the domain as multidimensional, hypothesizing that a student's satisfaction levels might vary in several areas of his life, such as his social, work, or home life. Further, her understandings of the separate "dimensions" of the construct reflected that a student's feelings of satisfaction in one area need not generalize to his satisfaction in others, although the different dimensions might be related. Through a survey of related literature, the counselor collected a long list of observable, behavioral, or response indicators, and planned to use the latter to look for particular patterns in the student's responses during the interview.

*Tasks in Phase II:   Developing the Assessment Specifications*     Table 9.3 illustrates the details of the counselor's plan for the instrument using FORM IV. As is evident, she selected the interview-based assessment method as the best approach for a screening tool. This method would provide more opportunities for her to probe the student, while simultaneously allowing her to be sensitive to the subject's mental state. Her initial goal was to develop six to ten semistructured items linked with the Specific Indicators in her domain. Each item was to have a structured part (A), followed by an unstructured part (B). The structured part would have dichotomous response categories. Two probes were allowed per part, as illustrated in the sample item. She hypothesized that each dimension of her interview, representing a *subdomain* of the overall construct, would be internally *homogeneous.* In other words, her expectation was that, if her items were written in a

*(continued)*

**Case Study 9.2    Continued**

# Box 9.2
## Domain Specified for Assessing "Subjective Well-Being" of Adolescents

| | |
|---|---|
| *General Indicator:* | 1.0  The adolescent expresses satisfaction with different areas in his/her life. |
| *Specific Indicators* | *Behavioral/response indicators* |
| | *Makes or Agrees with statements such as:* |

| | |
|---|---|
| 1.1  Satisfaction with self | I like the way I look. |
| 1.2  Satisfaction with friends/relatives/social life. | I like spending time with my friends in school. |
| 1.3  Satisfaction with home life | I like doing things with my mom/dad. |
| 1.4  Satisfaction with school | I like going to school. |
| 1.5  Satisfaction with work | I am comfortable with the work that my employer asks me to do. |
| 1.6  Satisfaction with income | I usually have enough spending money. |

*Sources:* Andrews & Robinson, 1991; Bender, 1997; Lewinsohn, Redner, & Seeley, 1991.

valid way, a subject was likely to respond similarly to all items that were linked to a Specific Indicator (such as *Satisfaction with work*).

***Tasks in Phase III:   Developing the Assessment Tool***   An initial version of a tool is illustrated in Table 9.4. It is assembled with directions for interviewers other than the developer. It provides guidelines for conducting the interview, as well as for scoring the items following the interview. The item layout illustrates the physical appearance of the final instrument.

***Tasks in Phase IV:   Validating the Assessment Tool***   The counselor invited another colleague to content-validate the tool prior to its use. The same colleague then conducted the actual interview, as he had previously established a rapport with the student who was to be counseled. As in Case Study I, a content-validation checklist served as a guide to help the co-counselor review the draft instrument for content validity and item quality (Phase IVA). The co-counselor found a good overall match between the content and behaviors in the instrument with that in the specifications. The directions for the interview were found to be satisfactory. However, the reviewer thought that the consistency in item delivery during the interview would be enhanced if the specific probes applicable to each item were inserted in the instrument for interviewers to use. In addition, the item: "Are you satisfied with your friends/social life?" appeared to be asking two questions, instead of one—an item that would be dubbed as *double-barreled*. He recommended that the item be split it into two separate questions, as follows:

**TABLE 9.3  FORM IV:  Assessment Specifications for Designing a Screening Interview**

| | | |
|---|---|---|
| I. | Assessment purpose: | To use results to screen for signs of dissatisfaction with life; decisions on further counseling, intervention, or referrals |
| II. | Population: | Adolescents facing personal or family crises |
| III. | Construct: | "Subjective well-being" |
| IV. | Assessment method: | Interview-based assessment yielding a total score on construct |

| IV.  DOMAIN INDICATORS | Number of Items | Content/Behavior Focus and Item Type |
|---|---|---|
| A. Background | 4 | Stand-alone items<br>Structured-response, nominal scale<br>One (1) item each on:<br>Gender<br>Ethnic background<br>Age<br>Grade level<br><br>SAMPLE ITEM<br><br>Indicate your grade level.<br>*A. Grade 8*<br>*B. Grade 9*<br>*C. Grade 10*<br>*D. Grade 11*<br>*E. Grade 12* |
| B. General Indicator:<br><br>1.0 The adolescent expresses satisfaction with different areas in his/her life. | <br><br>12–18 (total) | Homogeneous subdomains and domain<br>Two-part items with probes to clarify negative and positive responses<br>Semistructured responses<br>Behavior focus of items: Feelings |
| Specific indicators (abbreviated):<br>1.1  Satisfaction with self<br>1.2  Satisfaction with friends/social life.<br>1.3  Satisfaction with home life.<br>1.4  Satisfaction with school<br>1.5  Satisfaction with work<br>1.6  Satisfaction with income | <br>3<br>3<br>3<br>3<br>3<br>3 | |

SAMPLE ITEM
   Specific Indicator 1.1, Satisfaction with self
   *A. At this time in life, how satisfied are you with how things are with* <u>*yourself*</u>*?* (Response Coding categories:)
   a. Satisfied
   b. Dissatisfied
   c. Cannot answer/No response
   *B. Explain why you think you feel this way:* (Note down answers)

| | | |
|---|---|---|
| Probes for A: | For example, | *With how you look?*<br>*With how you interact with or relate to others?*<br>*With your accomplishments?*<br>*With how you're coping with life?* |
| | Probes for B: | *Has anything happened to make you feel this way?* |

*(continued)*

**TABLE 9.4    Subjective Well-Being: Screening Interview for Adolescents\***

| | |
|---|---|
| *Directions for Interviewers:* | This one-on-one interview-based tool is intended for conducting a preliminary screening of adolescents if they have been referred to you. The construct, "subjective well-being," is based on recent psychological literature. |
| | Each item is accompanied by two probes. |
| | Make the subject comfortable during the interview. Build trust with subject through a preliminary conversation. |
| | "Heard you did well in gym class. . . . Do you mind if I ask you a few questions?" |
| | Assure the client that the purpose is to help. Offer thanks for cooperation during interview. If client is uncooperative, reschedule the interview for another day. |
| *How to Code a Sample Item:* | For all the items listed, you will first ask Part A of the question, and UNDERLINE the response given using ONE of the 3 coding categories given. For example: |
| | *A.   At this time in life, how satisfied are you with how things are with <u>yourself</u>?* |
| | *a. <u>Satisfied</u>* |
| | *b. Dissatisfied* |
| | *c. Cannot answer/No response* |
| | If no response is forthcoming, offer TWO Probes for A: For example, |
| | *With how you look?* |
| | *With how you interact with or relate to others?* |
| | *With your accomplishments?* |
| | *With how you're coping with life?* |
| | Next, present Part B of the question. |
| | *B.   Tell me why you feel this way.* |
| | Write down answers. |
| | If no response is forthcoming, offer TWO Probes for B: For example: |
| | *Has anything happened to make you feel this way?* |
| | *Do you know why you feel like this?* |
| | IF YOU RECEIVE NO RESPONSE AFTER TWO PROBES, SKIP TO THE NEXT ITEM. |
| *How to Score Responses:* | *PART A:* Total the frequency of *satisfied* versus *dissatisfied* responses of all items. Note particular areas of satisfaction/dissatisfaction for follow-up. |
| | *PART B:* Use the attached sheet of "Look for" indicators to code and categorize responses as *dissatisfied* versus *satisfied*. Tally the frequency with which you find negative (dissatisfaction) versus positive (satisfaction) comments in open-ended notes. Schedule a consultation with a professional team (e.g., teachers who observed the student, a school psychologist, another counselor) to verify interpretations. Plan follow-up activities/referrals. |

**TABLE 9.4   Continued**

Item 1.  A.  *At this time in life, how satisfied are you with how things are going generally for <u>you</u>?*

<u>Response</u>

*a. Satisfied*
*b. Dissatisfied*
*c. Cannot answer/No response*

B.  *Explain why you think you feel this way.*

Item 2.  A.  *At this time in life, how satisfied are you with <u>your friends and social life</u>?*

<u>Response</u>

*a. Satisfied*
*b. Dissatisfied*
*c. Cannot answer/No response*

B.  *Explain why you think you feel this way.*

Item 3.  A.  *At this time in life, how satisfied are you with how things are in <u>your home life</u>?*

<u>Response</u>

*a. Satisfied*
*b. Dissatisfied*
*c. Cannot answer/No response*

B.  *Explain why you think you feel this way.*

Item 4.  A.  *At this time in life, how satisfied are you with <u>your school life</u>?*

<u>Response</u>

*a. Satisfied*
*b. Dissatisfied*
*c. Cannot answer/No response*

B.  *Explain why you think you feel this way.*

Item 5.  A.  *At this time in life, how satisfied are you with how things are at <u>work</u>?*

<u>Response</u>

*a. Satisfied*
*b. Dissatisfied*
*c. Cannot answer/No response*
*d. Does not work*

B.  *Explain why you think you feel this way.*

Item 6.  A.  *At this time in life, how satisfied are you with how things are with <u>your income/spending money</u>?*

<u>Response</u>

*a. Satisfied*
*b. Dissatisfied*
*c. Cannot answer/No response*

B.  *Explain why you think you feel this way.*

\* Note: This tool is designed to meet specifications in Table 9.3.

*(continued)*

Are you satisfied with your relationships with close friends?

Are you satisfied with the way things are going with your bigger circle of friends and acquaintances?

To obtain a little more reliability in each subdomain, the co-counselor also recommended that at least three separate questions be asked for each specific indicator, making the instrument longer (18 items instead of the original six).

Informally, the counselors decided to verify the validity of the data from the interview-based assessment against the findings from the anecdotal records of teachers. Was there a convergence in results obtained from two different and independent assessment procedures? More formal work in Phase IVB was to be pursued after the revised instrument was tried out on a few more students who were referred for similar purposes—yielding an adequate sample size to begin statistical evaluations of the tool and its scores. Empirical validation would begin with investigations of score reliability and item quality. The counselors also agreed to examine the extent to which items in the overall domain and subdomains were indeed interrelated, allowing inferences about the construct using the total score as well as the subdomain scores.

## 9.2    The Nature of Constructs in Paths 2–6

The two case studies in this chapter should have brought a couple of points home. Compared to attributes targeted for assessment in Path 1, there are two significant differences in the nature of constructs we typically pursue in Paths 2–6. First, the constructs tend to be either *preexisting* or *naturally occurring* characteristics of the population. Second, the results serve as *descriptions* of things as they are in individuals or groups assessed; we could not employ an answer key or rubric here to check the responses of subjects as "correct" or "satisfactory."

The measurement of affective variables and natural behaviors, such as "attitude towards science," cannot be judged as right or wrong —it simply describes the *existing dispositions and tendencies* of an individual. Questions such as: "Should the United States devote a portion of its national budget towards space exploration?" or "What are your perceptions of the quality of your training in (an area)?" yield responses reflecting personal opinions, likes/dislikes, and values that are neither wrong or right, quite unlike the answer to a question like "Name the first man who walked on the moon." Here we find a distinctive feature of several characteristics in User Paths 2–6. Let us now turn to design principles for self-report instruments.

---

**Key Concepts**

- Affective and personality constructs that we commonly target for measurement in Paths 2–6 are either preexisting or naturally occurring characteristics of individuals.
- To measure naturally occurring constructs in a valid way, our instruments must capture "typical behaviors" of individuals rather than their "best" or maximum levels of performance.

■ The four-phase Process Model for design, validation, and use of assessment tools applies in Paths 2–6 in the same way that it did for constructs targeted in Path 1.

## 9.3 Designing Self-Report Instruments

For measurement of constructs such as a person's attitudes, interests, self-concept, or perceptions of satisfaction with something, the most direct and practical method for gathering data is to pose a series of relevant questions to appropriate individuals. Such questions are compiled in a *self-report inventory* or *questionnaire* (also called "survey instruments"). As we saw, in its typical form, self-report measures consist of *structured response* items, where the respondents select one of several response options when provided with a stimulus question or statement. They include Likert-scaled items or variations thereof (responses are on an *Agree-Disagree* continuum), dichotomously scaled items (as in a *Yes/No* questionnaire ), and other item forms with ordered rating scales (as in a *Frequently—Rarely—Not at all* response continuum). Open-ended items, as relevant to indicators in the construct domain, are also frequently used in self-report instruments. Depending on the user's needs, population being assessed, and resources available to the assessor, self-report measures could be administered as *interviews* or in *written* format (see Table 9.6). The development procedures are similar for both, although administration procedures for interviews demand considerably more directions and supporting prompts for assessors.

---

Self-Report Measures

*Rule 1*    Specify the construct domain and subdomains with indicators rooted in the literature or established knowledge on the construct.

The starting point in developing self-report measures is to specify a domain of *observable indicators* for the construct, using appropriate theoretical and empirical support. For example, to measure the construct, "attitude towards school," we might start with a relatively broad domain, represented by a General Indicator, "makes (or endorses) positive statements about school," as shown next. The general domain, in turn, could be comprised of six specific behavioral indicators, each having to do with different aspects of school, such as teachers, the academic curriculum, school clubs, and so forth. The indicators would all stem from existing theoretical or conventional knowledge about the construct, "attitudes toward school."

Attitude toward School—Domain Specification (Excerpt)

*General Indicator:*    1.0    Makes (or endorses) positive statements about school.

*Specific indicators:*    Makes (or endorses) positive statements about:
        1.1    Teachers.
        1.2    Academic curriculum.

     1.3 School clubs/activities.
     1.4 Classmates and school companions.
     1.5 Social environment/climate.
     1.6 Learning environment.

---

## Self-Report Measures

*Rule 2* Write items to match the content focus of the indicators.

The next step is to write a group of questions/statements tied to the indicators in the domain. The methodological literature stresses the need for *unidimensionality* in items from given construct domains and subdomains. This means that the items should be constructed to generate responses that "hang together" for particular individuals. In other words, items measuring "attitude towards academics in school" (Indicator 1.2 in the domain just shown) should *not* generate responses that indicate one's "attitude towards school clubs and activities" (Indicator 1.3 in the example). Even when the two subdomains are hypothesized to be related by the assessment designer, the items must be written to ensure that responses pertinent to one subdomain are not confounded by the subject's responses to another subdomain. Individual indices tied to subdomains should possess an internally *homogeneous* item structure.

To achieve homogeneity during item construction, we should attempt to keep the *content* of items tightly linked to the content specified in the general or specific indicators. Thus, all items written to match Specific Indicator 1.2 should concern academic activities only, while those constructed to assess Indicator 1.3 should deal with school clubs/ activities. The dimensionality of indices can subsequently be statistically checked and verified as a part of the empirical evaluation of the instrument.

A sample of items from the larger general domain (1.0) and one subdomain (1.1) might appear as shown next. A respondent would be asked to answer by using the response choices provided. With the Likert scale shown, they would select a category to indicate their level of agreement or disagreement with a statement.

### **Attitude toward School: Sample Items from Overall Domain and a Subdomain**

*Items from Overall Domain* (General Indicator 1.0 *Attitude toward School*)

Indicate your level of agreement with the following statements by circling your chosen response on the following scale:

  a. Strongly Agree (SA)
  b. Agree (A)
  c. Uncertain (U)
  d. Disagree (D)
  e. Strongly Disagree (SD)

| | | | | | |
|---|---|---|---|---|---|
| 1. I like going to school. | SA | A | U | D | SD |
| 2. I learn a lot in school. | SA | A | U | D | SD |
| 3. I have friends in school. | SA | A | U | D | SD |
| 4. I feel like a part of the school. | SA | A | U | D | SD |

*Items from one Subdomain* (Specific Indicator 1.1 *Attitude toward teachers*)

| | | | | | |
|---|---|---|---|---|---|
| 5. My teachers are helpful. | SA | A | U | D | SD |
| 6. My teachers are good listeners. | SA | A | U | D | SD |
| 7. I learn a lot from my teachers. | SA | A | U | D | SD |
| 8. My teachers are fair. | SA | A | U | D | SD |
| 9. My teachers teach well in the classroom. | SA | A | U | D | SD |

The *domain* consists of all the items that represent the General Indicator. A *subdomain* would consist of a cluster of items linked to each Specific Indicator. For example, Indicator 1.1 has been operationalized with five items, all of which probed into different aspects of a student's attitudes toward his/her teachers. The fully developed instrument that emerged from the overall domain, attitude toward school, could consist of a total of 30 items, with five items designed for each subdomain. A set of items on a self-report measure together yields a composite "score" of the underlying construct domain or subdomain.

---

## Self-Report Measures

*Rule 3*    Write items to target particular types of affective/perceptive behaviors in the indicators.

Another strategy for achieving unidimensionality is to write items that are homogeneous with respect to the specific *behaviors* we tap. Just as we targeted particular taxonomic levels (such as "application" or "factual knowledge") when designing achievement test items, assessment designers could similarly examine *affective behaviors* embedded in the indicator statements to construct affective items. Affective behaviors assessed through self-report measures can be roughly categorized as four types. They could involve a person's:

1. Feelings towards something.   An item example from the *Attitude toward School* scale reflecting feelings is: *I enjoy school.*
2. Opinions/Values about something.   An item example from the *Attitude toward School* scale reflecting opinions/values is: *Schooling is important for children.*
3. Experience-based perceptions.   An item example from the *Attitude toward School* scale reflecting subject's experiences is: *Last year, my teachers were fair.*

**4.** Perceptions of awareness about something.    An item example from the *Attitude toward School* scale reflecting awareness is: *I believe my teacher's job is to help me when I get into fights.*

To identify the type of affective behavior in item sets, attempt to answer the guiding questions (a) through (d) for the construct that you are trying to measure. For example, suppose you are measuring the construct, "perceptions of child abuse." During domain specification, try to identify the type of affective behaviors as follows.

*Guiding Questions for Identifying Affective Behaviors in Items:*

(a) If I want respondents to report on their *feelings* about child abuse, what would a sample item look like?

<u>Sample Item:</u>    I get angry when my parents/guardians raise their voice when speaking to me.
(Agree-Disagree response scale)

(b) If I want respondents to express their *values or opinions* about child abuse, what would a sample item look like?

<u>Sample Item:</u>    It is OK for parents /guardians to raise their voices when disciplining their children at home.
(Agree-Disagree response scale)

(c) If I want respondents to report on *experiences* they have had, what would a sample item look like?

<u>Sample Item:</u>    My parents/guardians raise their voice when they discipline me.
(Agree-Disagree response scale)

(d) If respondents report on their *awareness* of child abuse, what would a sample item look like?

<u>Sample Item:</u>    Child abuse is a criminal offense in our state.
(Agree-Disagree response scale)

---

Self-Report Measures

*Rule 4*    Make sure that the items are direct, concrete, and clear.

As in all other instrument design efforts, good writing skills and the ability to make appropriate word choices are essential qualifications for good item writers. All respondents in the targeted population should read and interpret the same item *in the same way* (Jaeger, 1997).

The concreteness in language used to write individual items will add to validity of data gathered with self-report items. A concretely stated item is clear because it provides a well-defined reference framework that a respondent can use to generate the response. Such a framework provides specific details of the context, such as a timeframe, location or a particular episode/experience.

Consider the following items (dealing again with the child abuse construct) that reflect degrees of concreteness in the item statements.

| *Item Statement* | *Is it concrete enough?* |
| --- | --- |
| My parents/guardians yell at me. | Vague! |
| My parents/guardians yell at me when I defy them. | Better! Item is situated within a concrete experience. |
| In the past month, my parents/guardians yelled at me each time I defied them. | Even better! Item is situated within a concrete experience and a timeframe. |

*Note:* Assume that an Agree-Disagree response scale is used for all items.

As is obvious, the clarity of the statement is enhanced with the addition of more and more concrete details, such as "in the past month" (a time frame) or "when I defied them" (specific experience).

Other strategies for improving clarity in your item-writing are the following.

***Use complete sentences or questions as much as possible.*** This strategy facilitates communication of the essential idea in an item. All the preceding examples in this chapter have attempted to comply with this rule. Thus, the item

> *I attend school regularly.*     *Agree     Uncertain     Disagree*

is *better* than one that is constructed as follows:

> *My school attendance record is:*     *Good     Average     Poor*

***Avoid jargon, technical or otherwise, in items.*** Consider the following item:

> *I frequently observe symptoms of attention deficit disorder in my child.*

Chances are that the technically loaded phrase "symptoms of attention deficit disorder" will carry little meaning for lay persons—leading to misinterpretations and invalid data. A better item would use simple language at a low reading level with reference to a concrete symptom, such as: "My child has trouble finishing tasks at home."

***Avoid abbreviations.*** An item using acronyms such as "The WHO condemns child abuse," hampers readability and direct communication. It makes the assumption that all respondents are aware that the abbreviation, WHO, refers to the World Health Organization. As a rule, we should spell out such labels.

***Avoid double- or triple-barreled items.*** Items that contain more than one idea or question are poor for measurement purposes. For example, the item, "I feel abused by my parents and teachers," is better split into two separate items. Otherwise, it will be ambiguous for individuals who feel in one way with regard to their teachers but in another with respect to their parents.

***Avoid leading questions.*** An item similar to the following: "Given the booming economy, do you think Bill Clinton did a good job during his term as president?" strongly suggests an answer to the respondent, and should be avoided. The item wording should not lead respondents in any direction.

## Self-Report Measures

*Rule 5*    Adequately sample items from the domain and subdomains.

The actual *number of items* constructed per subdomain and overall domain will influence the internal consistency reliability of results. There is no consensus among theorists regarding the number of items necessary for obtaining optimal reliability levels. Provided that the instrument does not become too long, a general rule of thumb is to develop between three and seven well-designed items per subdomain to build reliability into the design. A useful practice is to create a few more items per indicator than we will actually need. This will enable us to delete poorly functioning or redundant items after content validation and empirical evaluations are completed.

The principle of improving reliability by adding more items, naturally, will not apply to items on a self-report instrument that stand alone. On typical surveys, individual items focusing on demographic characteristics of respondents fall into this category. An example would be one that asks for the respondents' ethnic origins, yielding categorical responses such as Caucasian American, African American, Hispanic American, Native American, and so on. Such items may be necessary for the assessment purposes specified, but are not a part of a theoretically specified domain/subdomain.

## Self-Report Measures

*Rule 6*    Use judgment to choose between open-ended and structured-response item formats. The response options should be a good fit for the stem of particular structured-response items.

***Choosing Between Open-Ended and Structured-Response Items***    Not all items on self-report instruments need to be structured with only one possible response. Items calling for open-ended responses are less efficient for assessment designers and users. It takes longer both to gather as well as to code and compile the data, particularly when using one-on-one interviews. In some circumstances, however, open-ended items are very useful. Consider using them in the following circumstances:

1. When responses on the construct are likely to vary so greatly in the population that using a highly structured response format will result in a loss of information
2. When the measurement process is still exploratory, and response choices that will work are unknown to the designer (i.e., not enough is known about either the topic or the population for us to design structured-response items efficiently)
3. When we seek to probe deeply or clarify answers that respondents give to structured items (as we saw in the examples of interview-based items in this chapter)
4. When the respondents are too young or have special needs that are barriers to using a structured-response tool (e.g., if they cannot use a paper and pencil)
5. When time and resources available permit us to properly conduct and compile the results of an open-ended assessment

***Selecting the Best Response Choice***    Another design-related decision that affects the quality of the resulting instrument is the choice of the most suitable response scale for the structured-response items. In making our decision regarding response options, we should evaluate the degree to which the response scale categories are consistent with the content and behavioral focus of the indicator.

The Likert scale, designed to capture a person's level of agreement with statements that present a position, is most familiar to us. However, numerous modifications to that basic ordered scale have been used in the social sciences. Fink (1995) asks us to consider one of five categories of response choice options when designing self-report instruments.

<u>Endorsement:</u>    Strongly Agree, Agree, Uncertain, Disagree, Strongly Disagree
Definitely true, True, Don't Know, False, Definitely False
<u>Frequency:</u>    Always, Very Often, Sometimes, Rarely, Never

<u>Intensity:</u>    Mild, Moderate, Severe

<u>Comparison:</u>    More than last year, About the same as last year, Less than last year

Other variations of structured-response choices also exist, and are illustrated in Examples 1–6 that follow. The examples illustrate that response choices in self-report items should represent a *gradient,* moving progressively from negative to positive, or from low to high. A central point often serves as the neutral anchor, as in the Uncertain response in the Likert scale or the Not Sure response in Example 2. The response scale in Item 6 was employed for young elementary school children. Although all these examples are of 5-point scales, one could have fewer or more scale points.

---

**Self-Report Instruments: Examples of Stems and Response Choice Options**

*1. Stimulus:*    *To what <u>extent</u> did you . . . ?*
Responses:    a. To a great extent
b. To a moderate extent
c. To some extent
d. Very little
e. Not at all

*2. Stimulus:*    *Describe <u>how much</u> you <u>like</u> . . . ?*
Responses:    a. Like it a lot
b. Like it somewhat
c. Not sure
d. Dislike it somewhat
e. Dislike it a lot

*3. Stimulus:*    *How <u>often</u> (frequently) do you . . . ?*
Responses:    a. All the time
b. Most of the time
c. Some of the time
d. Rarely
e. Not at all.

*(continued)*

**Self-Report Instruments    Continued**

---

*4. Stimulus:*    *How highly would you rate the quality of . . . ?*
Responses:    a. Very high
              b. High
              c. Average
              d. Low
              e. Very low

*5. Stimulus:*    *Rate the quality of . . .*
Responses:    a. Very good
              b. Good
              c. Satisfactory
              d. Poor
              e. Very poor

*6. Stimulus:*    *How happy do you feel about . . . ?*
Responses:    (A) I feel:                    (B) I feel:
              a. Happy                        a. Happy
              b. Not sure/Don't know          b. Neither happy nor sad
              c. Unhappy                      c. Sad

                   Happy    Not Sure    Sad

*Note:* Pictorial excerpted from Hopkins (1998), with permission.

---

The wording of the response scale should be *logically and semantically consistent with the stimulus statement or question.* Such matches are illustrated in Examples 1–6 above. Thus, if the assessment designer is looking for the "extent to which" a person likes something, the response options should also deal with different levels or "extent" of their liking.

Often, the lack of concreteness and clarity in the language of the stem makes it difficult to find the right wording for response choices. The following example illustrates a less than ideal semantic match between the stimulus-response set.

A poor stimulus–response choice match:

*7. Stimulus:*    *How do you feel about . . . ?*

Responses:    a. High
              b. Satisfactory
              c. Low

"I feel low" might be acceptable colloquially, but it is too informal for instrument development purposes! A better match for the same stimulus-response set was seen in Example 6. How a person feels about something does not quite fit linguistically or logically with the *high, satisfactory,* or *low* response options provided. They could potentially generate subjects' responses from widely different behavioral angles.

One should also attempt to equally *balance the number of positive and negative response options* so as not to inadvertently suggest any directions for the respondent to take. The next example shows a heaver positive than negative loading on the response scale—an undesirable item feature. A heavier loading in one direction, as when we provide more positive response options, creates a built-in bias in the instrument.

An unbalanced stimulus-response scale (from Example 6):

*Stimulus:*      *How happy do you feel about. . . ?*

Responses:      a. Very happy
                b. Happy
                c. Indifferent
                d. Unhappy

---

## Self-Report Measures

*Rule 7*   Use judgment in choosing the number of response options (or scale points) in structured response items.

You have already reviewed examples of response scales with two to five options. The number of categories in the response scale can vary from two to as many as ten. The most commonly used number is five. On occasion, we might choose to drop the middle option, such as "unsure," to create a four-point scale that forces respondents to take a position. Literature in social sciences and health areas suggest that we stay with five to seven options for self-report tools (Babbie, 1990; Fink, 1995). For populations that do not have the attention span, time, or inclination to respond to demanding item structures, a three-point scale may be the best.

What are the advantages to having more scale anchors—say, six or more—as opposed to fewer? In theory, more scale points would potentially add more variability to response distributions, a property that improves the quality of the scale from a classical perspective. However, if the underlying construct being scaled is not properly mapped by all the scale points, respondents are likely to use only a narrow segment of the scale to respond. Additionally, having a large number of scale points may sometimes impede on the respondents' ability to satisfactorily discriminate among the different levels of the attribute. Response category usage in individual items should thus be empirically checked out through pilot tryouts, before the most useful number of scale points are set.

What about the values of the central "unsure" response in a five-point scale? The uncertain option has been historically used in Likert scaling, but subsequent work has suggested that it provides very little or no information on the underlying attribute. Some authors recommend dropping it altogether, forcing respondents to make a choice. The use of a "not applicable" or "no response" as a fifth option could yield more valid information in circumstances where segments of the targeted population may not have a position on the construct being scaled. Of course, the "not applicable" respondents would have to be separated from the others during scoring, particularly if inferences are to be made about the responding group on the construct measured.

Self-Report Measures

*Rule 8*   Mix positively and negatively oriented items. Avoid use of negatively oriented items or statements unless they are very clearly stated.

Negatively oriented items contain words such as "not." Alternatively, they are stated in ways that signify a negative position on the construct. For example, with "attitude toward school," the following are both negatively oriented items.

I do *not* like going to school.
I have more fun when I am absent from school.

The practice of mixing up positively and negatively oriented statements in self-report measures is a strategy we could use to guard against *fixed response sets* or *faking* by subjects (discussed in detail later). Recent studies, however, do not suggest any particular advantages to including negative items, provided other precautions are taken by users to control for "response sets" (Schumann & Presser, 1996). Unless they can be constructed with very high levels of clarity, negatively stated items tend to be easily misinterpreted or misunderstood by respondents, yielding inconsistent response patterns. This book therefore recommends that we avoid negatively oriented statements, except in circumstances where the assessment designer believes they have a specific purpose to serve (see also Babbie, 1990; Fink, 1995). As indicated, negatively oriented items were traditionally used to minimize acquiescence bias.

**Key Concepts**

■ There are eight major guidelines (rules) that we should follow when designing items for self-report instruments.
■ The rules represent the most essential factors to bear in mind during item construction.
■ The rules should be employed with thoughtful judgment.

## 9.3.2   Assembly of Self-Report Measures

As with all assessment methods, once items have been constructed to a designer's satisfaction, the final step concerns the assembly—involving the writing of directions for respondents and assessors, and finalizing the printed presentation format of the tool. The layout of all instruments should be clear and easy to follow for both users and respondents.

For written questionnaires, general directions are a must; in addition, some questions might require specific instructions, as when the response scale suddenly changes for a group of items, or the stem is common for a series of items. Questionnaires with many parts require separate instructions for each part.

The practice of using brief but descriptive titles or subtitles for sections of a questionnaire is also useful for orienting the respondent to what lies ahead. This strategy could enhance the validity of responses obtained. In some instances, however, titles are best avoided. An example would be the measurement of constructs dealing with a clinical condition (such as a phobia), where the use of a title might encourage faking or unconscious denials from respondents.

Interviews demand that we prepare instructions for both the interviewer and the scorers. If a highly standardized interview delivery is desired by the designers/users, the entire script (including questions, probes, and pauses allowed in between) should be prepared in advance for interviewers to follow verbatim (Babbie, 1990). Ideally, such a script would begin with a greeting, and end with an expression of thanks to the interviewee for their cooperation.

### 9.3.3    How to Score Self-Report Instruments

Scoring of data from self-report instruments is the first task to tackle after gathering your data. The procedures vary depending on whether the data are generated from highly structured or open-ended items. The following boxes illustrate how self-report data can be scored using the "attitude toward school" example. The step-by-step procedures shown for compiling quantitative data are widely accepted and used. For further details of methods for compiling and summarizing qualitative data from interviews and questionnaires, the reader should consult books on qualitative data analysis (for example, Miles & Huberman, 1994).

### 9.3.4    Measurement Problems with
###            Self-Report Measures

Although self-report measures are widely employed, they are treated rather dubiously by most users. Responses to self-report measures can be easily faked or influenced by factors that are completely irrelevant to the construct. Semantic ambiguities in items could lead to fluctuating, unexpected, and sometimes meaningless responses. All such factors threaten both the validity and reliability of the information. Let us briefly consider the most common measurement problems with self-report measures.

*Faking*    Most self-report measures can be falsified in both the positive or the negative direction by respondents. For example, one person might choose to say nice things about their home environment even when it is abusive; another might choose responses that make the home environment look more abusive than it actually is. There is no way for the assessor to check the truthfulness of the responses provided, nor to control for faking once the data are gathered.

# Box 9.3

**How to Score Self-Report Instruments with Structured-Response Items**

Data from *Attitude toward School Scale*
Answer options selected by one respondent, Carlos, are underlined and in italics.

| | | | | | |
|---|---|---|---|---|---|
| 1. I like going to school. | *SA* | A | U | D | SD |
| 2. I learn a lot in school. | SA | *A* | U | D | SD |
| 3. I feel lonely in school. | SA | A | U | *D* | SD |
| 4. Most of my teachers are helpful. | SA | *A* | U | D | SD |
| 5. I like being absent from school. | SA | A | *U* | D | SD |

Step 1. Separate negatively stated items from positively stated items.

In a positively stated item, the stronger their <u>agreement</u>, the more positive their attitude. E.g.,

| | | | | | |
|---|---|---|---|---|---|
| 1. I like going to school. | SA | A | U | D | SD |

In a negatively stated item, the stronger their <u>disagreement</u>, the more positive their attitude. E.g.,

| | | | | | |
|---|---|---|---|---|---|
| 5. I like being absent from school. | SA | A | U | D | SD |

Step 2. Allocate an increasing number weight to each response option in positive statements. Reverse the numbers on negatively stated items. E.g.,

| | | | | | |
|---|---|---|---|---|---|
| Number Weights: | 5 | 4 | 3 | 2 | 1 |
| 1. I like going to school. | SA | A | U | D | SD |
| 5. I like being absent from school. | SD | D | U | A | SA |

Step 3. Sum the numbers across all items in a subdomain or domain to obtain a total score.

Carlos's Scores

| | | Item Scores |
|---|---|---|
| 1. I like going to school. | *SA* | 5 |
| 2. I learn a lot in school. | *A* | 4 |
| 3. I feel lonely in school. | *D* | 4 |
| 4. Most of my teachers are helpful. | *A* | 4 |
| 5. I like being absent from school. | *U* | 3 |
| Total Score on 5-item scale | | 20 |
| Max. Score possible on 5-item scale: | | 25 |

***Social Desirability***    Responses often reflect the unconscious tendencies of people to say things that will meet with social approval, the "social desirability" factor. For example, if asked about whether we like going to school with people from different ethnic backgrounds, we might be inclined to say, "Of course!" without really thinking about where we personally stand on the issue. Socially desirable responses are culturally conditioned and make us say what we believe others want to hear.

# Box 9.4

## How to Compile and Analyze Data from Open-Ended Items

1. As you design items tied to domain indicators, list what to "look for" in open-ended answers that will denote a particular standing of the person on the attribute. The "look fors" should emerge out of the literature that you survey during domain specification.

For example, in the following item:

1.     A. Do you like going to school? ———.
        B. If Yes, give two reasons why: ———

"Look fors":     i. Responds with Yes. Gives two specific reasons that are clearly related to school.
        Such as *"I like my teacher." "I like my friends in school."*
        *"I like the math we do." "I like doing net searches in the media center."*

Interpretation: Positive attitude towards school   Code = 2

ii. Says Yes to (A) but is vague about reasons.
        Such as: *"Because." "Dunno—We do stuff." "Its OK."*

Interpretation: Indifferent to Average Attitude   Code = 1

iii. Says No to (A) and gives reasons that support the response.
        Such as: *"I don't like my teacher." "I dislike my friends in school." "Its boring." "Its too hard."*

Interpretation: Negative Attitude         Code = 0

2. Following administration of the assessment, use the previously identified "look fors" to code and classify responses obtained. For all the open items tied to the domain, compute the total frequency of responses in each code category for individuals (e.g., Johnny has 5 under Code 2, and 1 under Code 1).

3. The total counts in each coding category should enable you to make descriptive comments on the person's standing on the attribute. For instance:

*The open-ended responses suggest that the individual has a predominantly positive Attitude toward School. This inference is supported by the preponderance of remarks such as "I like my teacher," "I love my friends in school," "I like the math we do," "I loved the last field trip to the theater," in her responses to Items 5–8 (coded as 2). The total frequency of responses coded as 2 was 15.*

4. To aggregate the data across groups of respondents, again, you could compile frequencies in each coding category by group. A descriptive summary statement for a group might look like this.

*Aggregating results by gender groups suggests that more girls have a positive Attitude toward School than boys. This inference is supported by the preponderance of remarks such as "I like my teacher," "I love my friends in school," "I like the math we do," "I loved the last field trip to the theater," in responses to Items 5–8 (coded as 2) from girls. The total frequency of responses coded as 2 was 235 for girls compared to 129 for boys.*

5. Many remarks and comments will <u>fall outside</u> the "look for" boundaries. Use different colored highlighters to differentiate among different sounding written or spoken comments. Cluster similar sounding remarks in separate piles, obtain counts by pile, and use labels to describe the nature of remarks in each pile.

6. Verify and Summarize Comments that fall outside the "look fors." Ask a professional peer to read through each pile of comments with you. Come to a consensus on the number of separate categories evidenced in the data. Identify a descriptive label for each separate pile, such as:

Type of remark:   *I'm sure my teacher likes me. He always says "Hi." And he reads my answers to the class.*
Label:           *"Positive Self-Concept–School related"*
Count for Carlos (an individual student):    *3*

*Response Sets*    "Response sets" refer to the tendency, conscious or unconscious, to mark a particular response choice repeatedly without consideration of the content of the item. Thus, a person might demonstrate an "agree" response set; or an "uncertain" response set, when asked to fill out a questionnaire. Such a response pattern completely masks the true standing of a person on the construct, leading to invalid results.

*Semantic Ambiguity*    The risks for poor measurement due to semantic issues were suggested in the section on item-writing (see Rules 1–9). If the language in the items connotes various meanings to various people, responses can be inconsistent with the major thrust of the construct domain. Poor semantics can flaw the items from both a validity and reliability perspective.

*Strategies to Control for Errors*    Some early research (Edwards, 1957; Hopkins, Kretke & Averill, 1983–84) attempted to embed items that would gauge the level of integrity in responses within self-report measures. Hopkins (1998) later reported that with an Attitude toward School scale, only 7–8 percent of student responses had lowered levels of response integrity—a reassuring finding for educators who like self-report instruments. Other researchers, however, found contradictory results. Consider the following evidence.

> ". . . (In) a study . . . a group of industrial workers filled out identical health questionnaires under two conditions. One questionnaire was returned to the company's health department as a preliminary to a medical examination. The other was mailed directly to a research group at a university. Far more symptoms were indicated on the research questionnaire than on the company's." (Excerpted from Hopkins, 1998, p. 175 from the original by Cronbach, 1970)

Were the workers afraid to reveal illnesses on forms collected by the company in case it jeopardized their jobs? We can only speculate about the causes for the differential responses in the industrial scenario just presented. A general rule in designing and using self-report measures, however, is that we try to create conditions that do not make respondents anxious; nor should we inadvertently reward them for avoiding telling the truth. The design strategies discussed in this section, although not foolproof, will take us a long way towards obtaining information of better quality from self-report tools. Additional strategies that have been known to work in controlling for errors in data from self-report measures are:

1. *Assurance of Privacy and Confidentiality*—Communicating to respondents that results will not be shared with anyone other than a select group of individuals whom the respondents trust; making sure that the confidentiality is maintained

2. *Anonymity*—Asking respondents to conceal their identities, thereby erasing fears that how an individual responds can be linked to names, or perhaps, be used against them

3. *Obtaining Informed Consent*—Openly communicating to respondents the purposes for assessment and how the data will be used; asking for the cooperation and informed consent of respondents in gathering accurate data to fulfil the purposes

4. *Random Mixing of Negatively and Positively Stated Items*—preventing response sets if negative statements are used

## 9.4    Designing Structured Observation Forms

Another method for measuring affective, behavioral, or personal-social variables for applications in Paths 2–6 is with structured, behavior-based assessments. Procedures for developing behavior-based assessments for User Path 1 were discussed in Chapter 8. Methodologically, the same criteria would apply to design processes here. We are aware that behavior-based assessments can be variously constrained in terms of:

- Times and settings for making observations
- Types of behaviors we observe

## Box 9.5

### Attitude toward School

### Behavior Rating Schedule for Parents

### DIRECTIONS

Observe your child's behavior at home closely for the next week. Keep informal notes if he/she says or does anything related to school. After the period is over, complete this form by indicating how your child behaved in the areas numbered 1–5. Refer to any notes you might have made as you complete the form. Follow the example below to use the response scale.

**Response Scale**
a. *Every day this week*
b. *Most days this week*
c. *Some days this week*
d. *Not at all*

| **Example:** | **ITEM** | **RESPONSE** | **COMMENTS** |
|---|---|---|---|
| | 5. My child cried when I asked about school. | <u>d</u> | He likes school. |

| **ITEMS** | **RESPONSE** | **COMMENTS** |
|---|---|---|
| My child: | | |
| 1. talked about his day at school. | _____ | _____ |
| 2. talked about his classmates or school friends. | _____ | _____ |
| 3. was happy when talking about school. | _____ | _____ |
| 4. showed me his schoolwork. | _____ | _____ |
| 5. avoided answering when I asked about school. | _____ | _____ |

Note: Remaining items not shown.

- Frequency and number of observations we make
- Methods we use for recording observations
- Methods we use to summarize and score our observation records
- The training that we provide to observers and scorers

An example of a structured observation form is reproduced in the next box. The construct measured is attitude toward school. Here, parents serve as the observers in a relatively low stakes application. (A high stakes assessment might involve assessing an employee's on-the-job performance for a merit raise or the screening of a child for a clinical condition that would require treatment.) A time period and setting is given as a reference framework for noting observations. A four-point, ordered rating scale is provided to mark observations. The level of structure in the recording form is not very high.

### 9.4.1   Rules for Developing Structured Observation Forms

The procedures for developing structured observation forms for User Paths 2–6 run parallel to those outlined for designing self-report instruments, with only a few differences. You will also find commonalities with "rules" presented in Chapter 8 for the same assessment method. After we identify the assessment purpose and population, we should attempt to adhere to the following guidelines.

*Rule 1*    Specify the domain and subdomains for the construct with observable indicators.

*Rule 2*    Develop items for the observation form that are linked to the domain indicators.

*Rule 3*    Make sure observation items are concretely situated in time frames, episodes, experiences, and/or settings (e.g., at home, this week, related to school, as shown in the Attitude toward School example).

*Rule 4*    Select a response scale (in this case, "recording categories") that fits logically and semantically with the item statements. If the designer targets frequency of behaviors, coding categories should reflect how often the behaviors were observed, as shown in the Attitude toward School example.

*Rule 5*    Make sure we have item sets that are homogeneous with respect to the content and/or behavior focus of the domain or subdomain for the construct.

*Rule 6*    To attain reliability, include enough items per subdomain and overall domain that tap different dimensions (indicators) of the construct.

### 9.4.2   Measurement Problems with Structured Observations

From a utilitarian perspective, structured observations are disadvantageous because it takes much more time to make the observations, as well as to score them. One can only observe one individual at a time. Subjectivity and factors such as the halo effect during scoring or recording, threaten the reliability of data from behavior-based assessments (discussed in Chapter 8). Because they take a lot of time to execute, we can only have so many items on an observation form—allowing only small portions of the domain to be sampled at a time. This last limitation potentially inhibits the content-based validity of observations, due to incomplete representation of the domain.

The *Hawthorne effect* is another artificial factor associated with structured observations. This factor actually influences the subjects to *overperform* because they are conscious of being observed. The reverse effect, where the subjects become unduly anxious and underperform, is equally common. When conditions permit, the practice of videotaping performances or behaviors that can be scored later, is often employed to control for such interferences. The parent observation example shown in this chapter utilizes the strategy of keeping the subjects of the observation uninformed about the assessment to prevent the Hawthorne effect (or its opposite) from occurring.

Nevertheless, structured observations are the only way to measure some kinds of behaviors. For example, to evaluate an employee's work performance, the self-report technique is not a good option, as it is likely to encourage faking and inflated ratings. A structured observation is better, provided that enough structure is built into the conditions of observation and scoring. Structured observations are also preferred for nonwriters or special populations who do not respond well to group-administered, written assessments (see Chapter 4).

Observer and scorer training is necessary when important decisions depend on the results of behavior-based assessments. In formal assessment projects, training of observers and scorers is typically done by having them review a number of videotaped behaviors or actual performances of subjects. In a typical training routine, a structured recording or scoring form is provided to the rater under training, similar to that shown in the Attitude toward School example. The trainees study an "expert" observer's rating behaviors for each subject observed. The expert's ratings then serve as the standard against which the trainees' rating behaviors are compared.

---

**Key Concepts**

- The six guidelines (rules) to follow when designing structured observation forms parallel those for self-report instruments.
- Structured observations require that direct observations of behaviors be made by trained observers, using the form we design.

## 9.5   Naturalistic and Anecdotal Observations

*Naturalistic observation* is the direct observation of behaviors as they occur naturally and spontaneously in real-life settings. Unlike structured observations (where subjects may be aware that they are under observation), naturalistic observations are conducted by an external observer in an unobtrusive manner. In some cases, the observer might actually participate in the proceedings along with the subjects of the observation, thus becoming a *participant–observer*. Participant observation is a technique borrowed from ethnographic methods of inquiry used in fields like anthropology. Subjects in such applications are unaware that they are being watched.

Although the title suggests otherwise, record-taking with anecdotal observations is a systematic process. Only the *incident observed* is spontaneous and unstructured. For this reason, we cannot deliberately design naturalistic observations using assessment specifications or a previously thought-out plan, as we did with the more objective and structured procedures described thus far. In education, the most-used naturalistic observation technique is the *anecdotal record*.

### 9.5.1   What Is an Anecdotal Record?

Anecdotal records were originally conceived as a "critical incident" technique. Consider a scenario where Johnny starts the school year as a regular child in a teacher's class. The teacher does not find any of Johnny's behaviors—which fluctuate between the positive and negative—to be out of the ordinary. Then, one day Johnny comes to school late. Further, he does not appear to participate in class at all. Finally, he falls asleep before the second class period is over. A *critical incident* has occurred that sets Johnny's behavior apart from his own typical conduct, as well as that of the rest of the class. The episode signals the teacher to make an anecdotal record.

Anecdotal records are descriptions of specific incidents and behaviors in a natural setting. They are typically used to assess social behaviors and attitudes. A collection of anecdotal records suggests patterns of behavior from which inferences can be drawn about underlying constructs, such as *social maladjustment*. Well-made anecdotal records provide rich insights into the causes of particular behaviors, and can be used to compliment and verify data collected through more structured assessments (Linn & Gronlund, 2000).

### 9.5.2   How to Make a Good Anecdotal Record

Individual anecdotal records can be made on index cards. A good anecdotal record has the following characteristics. We could think of these as "rules."

*Rule 1*  Records should be brief, to-the-point, factual descriptions of events.
*Rule 2*  Each record should indicate who was observed, what happened, when and where it happened (date and time), and the circumstances under which it occurred.
*Rule 3*  Each record should describe a single incident.
*Rule 4*  Record-making should be instigated by critical incidents. Such episodes could be either positive or negative behaviors.
*Rule 5*  Multiple records should be reviewed to make judgments, interpretations, and conclusions about individuals observed.

**TABLE 9.5    Examples of Well-Written and Poorly Written Anecdotal Records**

**A Poor Record**

| RECORD 1A | 4/15/2002 | 9:00 AM |
|---|---|---|

Johnny showed up late again. I am tired of his bad attitude and behaviors. He came in dragging his book bag. Slouched in his seat. I could tell he was not attending in class. His lack of interest is bound to show up on his grades. He is a real burden to the teacher.

**A Better Record**

| RECORD 1B | 4/15/2002 | 9:00 AM |
|---|---|---|

Johnny was 10 minutes late for class. When asked for an explanation, he did not answer and went to his seat. He sat slumped in his seat, did not take out his books, or participate in class in any obvious way. Appeared to be nodding off after a while.

> *Rule 6* Individual records should not contain the observer's opinions, judgments, or explanations—nothing outside what was actually observed should be recorded.

Consider Anecdotal Record 1 shown in Table 9.5, with reference to the preceding guidelines. The table shows two records, A and B, of the same episode made by two different observers. How would we evaluate the quality of these records? Record 1A shows several violations of the rules we just reviewed. Obvious ones include the absence of information on time, setting, and circumstances, and the flagrant inclusion of opinions, inferences and judgments in the record. Record 1B is a considerably better record. However, it has information gaps related to the setting and circumstances of the event.

In Table 9.6, we see two more records on Johnny (Records 3 and 8), giving the observer a total of 8 episodes from which they may now make conclusions. Although we do not have access to all eight records, Records 1B, 3, and 8 together, allow us to draw very different, and *more reliable* conclusions about Johnny's behaviors than a consideration of only the first record. While the first might have suggested that Johnny has a poor attitude towards school, by the eighth record we are able to see that the child was probably facing difficulties at home—difficulties that caused him to come late to school, with no breakfast! Now, the teacher can plan meaningful interventions, including consultations with the school's social worker or counselor.

### 9.5.3    When to Use Anecdotal Records

Anecdotal records became a very popular means of assessment in educational programs in the 1990s, as a part of the alternative assessment movement in U.S. education. One

**TABLE 9.6    Continuing Anecdotal Records on One Student**

---

RECORD 3                                           4/18/2002                                        9:00 AM

Johnny was 15 minutes late. He gave an explanation today. He said he was delayed in the cafeteria eating breakfast. He took out his books and began his work. He completed 5 of the 8 math problems that the class was doing. Then, he put his head down.

---

RECORD 8                                           5/2/2002                                         9:00 AM

Johnny came into class as the bell rang. He went up to the teacher to say that Mrs. Smith in the cafeteria was helping him get to class on time. He said he is usually hungry and tired when he comes to school every morning. He tried and completed all 10 of his math problems today. He got 7 of them right.

---

commercially published preschool curriculum, *High Scope,* required the use of anecdotal records as the sole basis for documenting student growth and learning in multiple areas of their program—including academics. Because of the enormous investment of time needed to document and interpret findings skillfully, such practices place unrealistic demands on classroom teachers. Anecdotal records are better used as a critical incident technique (that is, to enhance, confirm, and supplement information obtained through other, more efficient and objective assessment procedures).

**Key Concepts**

- Naturalistic observations are unplanned, anecdotal records of critical incidents.
- Anecdotal records should be systematically made, following six major guidelines.

## 9.6    Selecting Assessment Tools in Paths 2–6 Using Specifications

Recall that for designing or selecting assessments in User Path 1, we examined the utility of having a plan, called the Assessment Specifications, or a Table of Specifications, to guide us in our work ( FORMS I–III in Chapters 5–8). Similarly, in designing or selecting tools in User Paths 2–6, Fink (1995) recommends that we use a plan to guide the process. She calls the plan an "Outline." An adaptation of her assessment plan was provided in Tables 9.1and 9.3 when discussing the two case study applications. This book presented a reformatted Assessment Specifications for Paths 2–6 as FORM IV.

Once you have grasped the information needed to make the most important assessment design/selection decisions for Paths 2–6, FORM IV will be easy to complete. FORM

**TABLE 9.7   Content Validation Checklist for Personality Affective or Behavioral Assessment Tools**

*Quality of the Assessment Specification (FORM IV)*
1. Is the assessment purpose and population identified with adequate detail?
2. Is the domain clarified with general and specific indicators?
3. Is the chosen assessment method (self-report or structured observation; interview vs. written), a logical fit for the purposes, population, and construct?
4. Does the specification indicate focus of items, item formats, and response or recording categories?
5. Is the scoring method clearly specified?

*Overall Check of the Assessment*
6. Do the assessment (items) show a match with the content and behaviors in:
   - targeted indicators of the domain?
   - developmental level, age, and other specifications of the intended population?
   - assessment purposes?
7. Are directions for respondents/assessors/observers clear?
8. Are conditions clearly outlined for assessors in the instructions?
9. Are the scoring procedures clear and unambiguous?
10. Are there enough observations or items to generate reliable results?
11. Does the assessment *appear to be* free of the following biases:
   - readability bias
   - inflammatory bias
   - conditions bias

*Additional Checks for Written Self-Report Instruments*
12. Are item statements clear and concrete?
13. Do response choices fit the item stem?
14. If used, are negatively oriented items clear and unambiguous?
15. Are items free of:
   - jargon (e.g., use of technical terms such as "affective" or "attention deficit")
   - abbreviations (e.g., ADD for Attention-Deficit Disorder, WHO for World Health Organization)
   - biased language or content (e.g., the suggestion that boys have Attention Deficit Disorder more than girls)
16. Are double- or triple-barreled items absent?

*Additional Checks for Structured Behavior-Based Assessment Tools*
17. Do instructions for observers/recorders clarify the degree of structure in
   - time(s) of observation?
   - duration?
   - setting?
   - frequency?
   - recording?
   - scoring of observations?

*Additional Checks for Interview-Based Assessment Tools*
18. Are interview questions provided?
19. Do instructions for interviewers/recorders clarify:
   - the time allowed for each prompt?
   - the probes allowed for each prompt?
   - the method and degree of structure in coding responses?

IV is particularly helpful in situations where our intent is not necessarily to create an entirely new instrument ourselves, but to *select* items as is from existing tools, or to *adapt* available items from another assessment design project, so as to meet new purposes, populations, or slightly altered construct definitions. Our goal should be to attempt to design/select a sound instrument within the contextual framework we define (using purpose and population).

In the two case study applications in the chapter, we found references to *content validation*. A content-validation checklist suited for the types of instruments introduced here is provided in Table 9.7. The checklist is deliberately designed to reflect the "rules" presented for designing self-report, observation, and interview-based assessments elaborated in the chapter.

## 9.7 Classical Examples of Instrument Design in Paths 2–6

The literature offers a rich array of formal studies undertaken by measurement theorists and researchers at different times in history to measure affective variables, some of which utilize the methods you have seen in Chapter 9. Not all of instrument development and validation efforts follow the "Likert-scaling" tradition that has been highlighted through the case studies and methodological sections of this chapter.

Likert scales, as we saw, have an Agree-Disagree type of response continuum, or some modified form of this basic structure. In addition, they are typically developed using a *domain-sampling method*. The domain-sampling tradition was started by Rensis Likert. In this approach, positively and negatively oriented item statements were sampled by designers from a hypothetical domain with all possible items. Because they were drawn from the same domain, the items were expected to perform as homogeneous, interrelated sets of behaviors that measured the same underlying attribute, as represented by the summated total score. Using the total score, it was possible to scale people with different degrees of the construct on a single continuum. Instruments with such scale properties could be validated using correlational statistical methods that checked for homogeneity of the item response distribution with that of the total score. (Domain sampling methods were also illustrated in Chapters 7 and 8 for designing achievement tests and performance scales in User Path 1.)

To obtain somewhat different perspectives of scale development, three areas of work are recommended to you for additional study. These are the works of L. L. Thurstone (Thurstone, 1959) in the area of attitude scaling; the work of Osgood (Osgood, Suci, & Tanner, 1957) in the assessment of meaning through semantic differential scales; and the more recent, combined work of R. Shavelson, B. Byrne, and H. W. Marsh in the measurement of student self-concept, particularly, academic self-concept (for examples, see Byrne, 1984; 1986; Marsh, Byrne & Shavelson, 1988; Marsh & Craven, 1997).

## 9.7.1   Thurstone's Attitude Measurement

Thurstone's approach to scale development was different from the domain sampling approach we employed. He attempted to design instruments composed of items that were ordered by *intensity* on a unidimensional continuum. Thurstone attempted to scale *items,* rather than people, on scales with equal-sized units, or at least "equal-appearing" intervals. In his "Attitude toward movies" scale, for example, the intensity values for three items located at different points on the scale continuum were as follows (Thurstone, 1959).

> *It is a sin to go to the movies.*                                      Intensity = 0
> Endorsing of this item would indicate a very negative attitude towards movies!
>
> *Sometimes I feel movies are desirable and sometimes I doubt it.*      Intensity = 2.4
> Endorsing of this item would indicate a middling attitude towards movies.
>
> *Movies are the most powerful influence for good in American life.*    Intensity = 4.7
> Endorsing of this item would indicate a very positive attitude towards movies!

Item intensities were determined based on ratings given by several hundred judges, and their level of consensus on individual items an agreement scale. In the final version of the instrument, of course, the item ordering was random rather than from low to high intensity, as just illustrated. Thurstone scales did not use titles or subtitles in the layout that might suggest item intensities to respondents, thereby possibly swaying their responses. Respondents used an agree-disagree-uncertain scale to respond. Their responses were eventually scored by weighting them with predetermined item intensity values. Thurstone's item-development process was extremely time-consuming and involved; however, it is considered the foundational method for scaling items, rather than people on a continuum, using human discrimination processes.

## 9.7.2   Semantic Differential Scales

Osgood's semantic differential scaling approach was developed to answer the question: What kinds of *meaning* do people attribute to different things? To answer this question, he developed a seven-point, bipolar rating scales that could be ranked from good to bad (the evaluation dimension); from strong to weak (the potency dimension); and from fast to slow (the activity dimension). Semantic differential scales are scored in ways similar to Likert scales, and offer an alternate technique for scaling people on a construct continuum.

Let us review an example. Suppose we wished to find out what "alternative assessment" meant to educators today. We could devise a semantic differential scale for this purpose as follows:

*Alternative Assessments*

1.  Good        — — — — — — —  Bad
2.  Fast        — — — — — — —  Slow
3.  Weak        — — — — — — —  Strong
4.  Effective — — — — — — —  Ineffective

Osgood's approach to scaling was readily applied by educators in more simplified form, where they focused only on the value of something, and basically treated the scale as unidimensional. Thus, they asked the question: What kinds of *value* do people attribute to something? Regarding Osgood's technique, Hopkins (1998) states "its chief value is ease of construction and administration. Its disadvantages include a lack of flexibility and greater ambiguity in interpretation" (p. 302).

### 9.7.3   Measurement of Self-Concept

Finally, the measurement of academic self-concept, which refers to a person's self-image related to their abilities in particular academic disciplines such as reading or math, was undertaken by R. Shavelson, B. Byrne, and H. W. Marsh, and other colleagues during the last two decades. Their comprehensive body of work is particularly interesting, since it shows the evolution of their collective understanding of self-concept as a generalized singular construct to a clearly differentiated, multidimensional trait tied to different disciplines. Their recent research examines the influence of academic self-concept on achievement. The Self-Description Questionnaire for primary school students (SDQI, see Marsh & Craven, 1997, p. 140–141) uses a five-point, true-false response continuum, and includes some of the following items.

> I am good at all school subjects.
> I have lots of friends.
> I get good marks in reading.
> I like reading,
> I'm good at reading.

As is evident, the first two items target more general impressions of a child's self-concept, while the last three focus specifically on the area of reading.

## Summary

Chapter 9 dealt with the design or selection of assessment tools for constructs measured in User Paths 2–6. Assuming we start with an appropriately specified construct domain, Chapter 9 reviewed the core tasks in the four-phase Process Model, using two case study examples (Case Studies 9.1 and 9.2). The case studies demonstrated instrument design tied to User Paths 2 and 3, repetively. Both applications were in low stakes decision-making contexts. Case Study 9.1 illustrated the procedures used to design a self-report survey for determining teacher training needs in User Path 2. Case Study 9.2 dealt with the design of an interview-based screening tool for assessing "subjective well-being" in adolescents in User Path 3 (or 4). Both applications illustratcd the use of the FORM IV Assessment Specification, during the planning phase of the Process Model.

We started by acknowledging that several constructs in Paths 2–6 are preexisting, naturally occurring characteristics of the population that cannot be scored as "correct" or "incorrect." Attitudes, social-emotional behaviors, perceptions, and similar affective variables are the common focus of assessment. Although cognitive variables, such as aptitudes and achievement are also assessed, the *particular uses* of results in Paths 2–6 make these assessment applications distinct from uses in User Path 1.

In turn, the chapter offered procedural guidelines for developing/selecting self-report instruments and structured observation tools, including guidelines for making and interpreting anecdotal records, a form of naturalistic observation. Self-report measures could consist of both structured-response and open-ended items. Response scales could take the form of Likert scales, dichotomous scales, or other ordered rating scales. Although the development procedures are similar for both interviews and written assessment methods, administration procedures vary considerably. The chapter presented detailed rules and examples on how to develop, assemble and score self-report tools. Threats to validity, reliability, and utility were also discussed with suggested methods of control.

Awareness of sources of error unique to structured observations, such as the Hawthorne effect and observer variability in the absence of training, are important to remember when high stakes uses are made with assessment results. Six guidelines were provided to help us make sound anecdotal records.

To conclude, the chapter recognized three classical examples of instrument design and validation for Paths 2–6. These were Thurstone scales, semantic differential scales, and self-concept measures in education.

## QUESTIONS FOR CLASS DISCUSSION

1. Identify two *Assessment Purposes* in each of the User Paths 2–6, and the *Constructs* to be assessed.

2. Use the domain specification below to develop (a) a complete set of assessment specifications (FORM IV), and (b) a structured observation form for school principals to assess teaching skills of beginning teachers. The principals would use the results to coach teachers in areas where they needed assistance. Ask a peer to content-validate your instrument using the checklist provided in this chapter. How well did you do?

   *General indicator*  Teachers instruct in a creative, flexible, and adaptive manner.
   *Specific indicators:*
   - Teachers create a positive learning environment by maintaining appropriate standards of classroom behavior/conduct.
   - Teachers create learning opportunities that support a student's academic, personal, and social development.
   - Teachers create instructional opportunities to foster critical thinking and skill building.
   - Teachers use effective verbal, nonverbal, and media communications techniques to foster individual and collaborative inquiry.

3. Now, use the domain specification below to develop (a) a complete set of assessment specifications (FORM IV), and (b) a self-report measure for beginning teachers to conduct a self-assessment of their performance in the classroom. Again, ask a peer to content-validate your instrument. How well did you do?

*General indicator*    Teachers instruct in a creative, flexible, and adaptive manner.
*Specific indicators:*

- Teachers create a positive learning environment by maintaining appropriate standards of classroom behavior/conduct.
- Teachers create learning opportunities that support a student's academic, personal, and social development.
- Teachers create instructional opportunities to foster critical thinking and skill building.
- Teachers use effective verbal, nonverbal, and media communications techniques to foster individual and collaborative inquiry.

4. Visit the classroom of a special educator in action with his or her pupils. Select one student to observe. Make an anecdotal record of your observations of that student during the first half hour of class. Share your record with your measurement classmates and allow them to give you feedback on the quality of your record. How well did you do?

# 10 Analyzing Data from Assessments

## Overview

Once we have gathered numeric data on constructs, how do we make sense of all that information? How can we systematically analyze the "numbers" to inform decisions in User Paths 1–6? Chapter 10 demonstrates how to analyze data with selected descriptive statistics and graphing techniques so as to facilitate data-based decision-making. A mastery of basic statistical vocabulary and procedures is necessary whether we prepare statistical reports and summaries ourselves or interpret statistical and psychometric reports prepared by others.

The primary focus of Chapter 10 is *descriptive statistics. Inferential statistics,* dealing with methods for drawing conclusions about parameters of some larger population using the statistics computed on samples from that population, lies outside the scope of the present book. Chapter 10 concentrates on procedures for organizing, summarizing, graphing, describing, and interpreting measurements on one or more variables.

The chapter is organized in ten major sections; each section presents definitions of key statistical concepts, formulas that apply, computational steps, and interpretive guidelines and uses.

To illustrate applications, two major data sets are used throughout the chapter. The computations are shown in boxes labeled as "Demonstrations." Key Concept boxes will reinforce definitions of new terms. Note that most of the calculations demonstrated can be done using computer software. The aim of this chapter is to make you thoroughly familiar with the formulas used, steps in the procedures, and interpretations of the statistics.

## CHAPTER 10 OBJECTIVES

After studying this chapter and completing the structured exercises in the module, you should be able to:

1. Distinguish among nominal, ordinal, interval, and ratio scales of measurement
2. Recognize differences in discrete and continuously distributed variables

3. Apply methods for tabulation and arrangement of data generated from assessments
   - Rank order distributions
   - Simple (ungrouped) frequency distributions
   - Grouped frequency distributions

4. Compute and interpret commonly used measures of central tendency and variability
   - Mean, median, mode
   - Standard deviation, range

5. Graph and interpret shapes of distributions
   - Histograms
   - Frequency polygons
   - Ogives

6. Describe mathematical properties of the normal distribution and its uses in measurement

7. Compute and interpret correlation coefficients
   - Pearson's $r$ and other correlation coefficients
   - Bivariate scatterplots

8. Demonstrate awareness of how regression and factor analysis is used to investigate measurement problems/issues

9. Compute and interpret measures of relative position in normal and non-normal distributions
   - $z$-scores, $T$-scores
   - Percentiles, percentile ranks

# 10.1    Scales of Measurement

Before beginning data analysis, we should recognize that different instruments incorporate different types of measurement scales and yield different kinds of numeric data. Identification of the level of scaling helps in making decisions on arithmetic manipulations and interpretations that are best suited to the data.

You will recall that during the design of assessments, we specified rules that determine how a construct will be operationally defined and numerically scaled. The rules become manifested through the assessment specifications, and subsequently, the items, scoring mechanisms, and conditions of the assessment. Depending on the way we assign numerals to constructs measured, we could generate one of four levels of measurement scales, ranging from the most primitive to gradually more sophisticated forms. In each scale type, the numbers carry different meanings and have different properties (Stevens, 1946). The four levels of measurement are:

1. Nominal scales (scale with most primitive properties)
2. Ordinal scales
3. Equal-interval scales
4. Ratio scales (scale with most advanced properties)

In Table 10.1 we find a synopsis of the four scales of measurement, their properties, interpretations allowed, and examples of each scale type.

## 10.1.1   Nominal Scales

The lowest level of measurement is the *nominal scale,* where the number has no meaning beyond serving as a label for mutually exclusive, but qualitatively different classes of individuals/objects on a construct. Nominal scaling is applied in education when we assess individuals on background characteristics, such as race, gender, or educational major. In all these applications we place individuals in different categories using numbers to label the different groups.

## 10.1.2   Ordinal Scales

Higher up in Stevens' scaling taxonomy is the *ordinal scale.* Here we see *ordered categories* with the absence of a meaningful zero. Ordinal scaling is found with most open-ended assessments where we score the responses with a rating scale. For example, if we use a rating form with 0–4 points to assess writing samples, we are employing an ordinal scale. Here, a zero would not indicate that the person receiving the score has no writing ability at all. Rather, it means that relative to others, the person's writing ability was ranked in the lowest category of the scale. On an ordinal scale the difference in writing ability of students receiving a 0 versus a 1 may be more or less than the difference between students receiving a 3 versus a 4. As categories on an ordinal scale only have the property of order, the differences between consecutive units of measurement can be unequal and remain unknown to users.

## 10.1.3   Interval Scales

At the next level of scaling, we see equal-sized units that correspond to equal increases in amounts of the underlying attribute. *Equal-interval scales* are more difficult to construct than the preceding two types of scale, as they call for a one-to-one correspondence between the increments of the underlying attribute and the units of measurement on the scale. This type of scale has an "arbitrary" zero; that is, we start measuring where it is most useful and convenient for the variable in question.

A Centigrade thermometer is an equal-interval scale. The freezing point of water corresponds to the arbitrary 0 on the Centigrade scale, a convenient starting point for measuring the construct "temperature." From that arbitrary origin, units increase in equal amounts, making it meaningful to add and subtract amounts of the attribute. The "true zero" here, denoting the total absence of heat, is really $-273$ degrees C (absolute zero on the Kelvin scale). Using a Centigrade scale we can say that 20 degrees C has 10 more units of heat than 10 degrees C. However, we cannot say that 20 degrees is twice as hot as 10 degrees on the scale. This is because the zero on the Centigrade scale is an arbitrary point with no true meaning with respect to temperature. On an absolute scale with a true zero it becomes clear that $(273 + 20 =)$ 293 degrees is *not* twice the value of $(273 + 10 =)$ 283 degrees. Figure 10.1 illustrates the logic underlying this interpretation.

**TABLE 10.1  Four Scales of Measurement**

| Type of Scale | Properties | Examples |
|---|---|---|
| **1. NOMINAL** | | |
| *Empirical Operations*: Involves placing objects or individuals into *different categories* based on observable differences on an attribute. | ▪ Numbers merely stand for names (hence, the descriptor "nominal") or labels of categories<br>▪ No true meaning of a zero<br>▪ No "more" or "less" value in numbers<br>▪ Numbers cannot be arithmetically manipulated meaningfully<br><br>*Interpretation:* Individuals assigned values of 1 are qualitatively different from individuals assigned values of 2 or those assigned values of 3, and so on. | ▪ Scaling people based on their *gender* with a "1" for males and "2" for females<br>▪ Scaling people based on their hair color with a "1" for blondes, a "2" for browns, a "3" for blacks, and a "4" for other colors |
| **2. ORDINAL** | | |
| *Empirical Operations*: Involves placing objects or individuals in *ordered categories* based on direct comparison of how much an attribute is present. | ▪ Numbers have a "more" or "less" value on an ordered continuum, but not equal-sized intervals<br>▪ Zero does not necessarily connote total absence of the attribute; just that there is less of it than in the next highest category, "1"<br>▪ Meaningful arithmetic manipulations are limited because of only transitive properties<br><br>*Interpretation:* Individuals with scores of 1 have less of the attribute than individuals assigned values of 2. Both 1 and 2 have less of the attribute than those with values of 3. However, with respect to the amount of the underlying attribute, the difference between 1 and 2 may not be the same as the difference between 2 and 3. | ▪ Ranking systems<br>▪ Marking systems (A, B, C, D, F)<br>▪ Rating scales, e.g., Likert scales |

**TABLE 10.1 Continued**

| Type of Scale | Properties | Examples |
| --- | --- | --- |
| **3. INTERVAL** | | |
| *Empirical Operations:* Involves placing objects or individuals in *ordered categories that are at equal distances from each other,* starting from an *arbitrary zero*. | ■ Numbers are on an ordered continuum, with equal-sized intervals that correspond with units of measurement<br>■ Zero is an arbitrary starting point for the scale; does not represent a true absence of the attribute<br>■ Meaningful arithmetic manipulations include adding and subtracting of scale units (cannot multiply or divide meaningfully because of arbitrary zero)<br><br>*Interpretation:* Individuals with a score of 12 on an interval scale have 6 more units of the attribute than those with a score of 6. However, those with scores of 12 *do not* have twice more of the attribute than those with 6, because the distance from the true zero to 12 is not twice that of the distance from zero to 6. | ■ Centigrade scale for temperature, where the zero is the freezing point of water, and each unit that follows is at equal intervals<br>■ Most standardized achievement tests, intelligence scales, and scales of psychological attributes |
| **4. RATIO** | | |
| *Empirical Operations:* Involves placing objects or individuals with different amounts of the attribute in *ordered, equally distanced units,* starting from a *true zero*. | ■ Numbers are on an ordered continuum, with equal-sized intervals that correspond with units of measurement<br>■ Zero is true; does denote a total absence of the attribute<br>■ Meaningful arithmetic manipulations include adding, subtracting, multiplying, and dividing<br><br>*Interpretation:* Individuals with a score of 12 on a ratio scale have twice more of the attribute than those with 6, because the true zero at the starting point. | Height, weight, speed of movement |

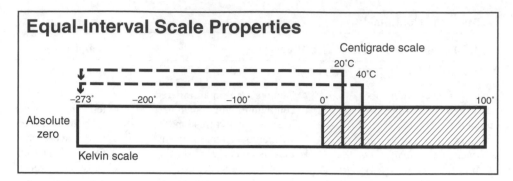

**FIGURE 10.1**    Relationships of units of the Centigrade scale to the absolute zero in measuring temperature

Most achievement, intelligence, and attitudinal scales are attempts at interval scaling. When using the domain-sampling approach to construct such tools, the arbitrary zero is set by the sample of items we write to represent the construct domain. On an achievement test, the lowest possible score on the instrument is usually a zero when a person gets all the items wrong. We cannot conclude that a 0 score derived thus denotes a total absence of the attribute. Rather, it stands for a convenient starting point for measuring that construct.

### 10.1.4   Ratio Scales

The highest level of measurement in Stevens' taxonomy is the *ratio scale*. In Table 10.1 we see that here, all the properties of the equal-interval scale hold true; but, now there is also a *true zero*. Ratio scaling is possible with physical and physiological variables that have directly observable indicators, and measurement can begin at a point where a true zero point is visible. Height, weight, blood pressure, and speed are examples of ratio-scaled variables. In all of these traits, the 0 on the instrument (e.g., a tape measure for height) indicates that there is truly an absence of the attribute at that point. Units are all equal-sized and match equal increments of the construct. Educational and psychological traits can rarely be measured on a ratio scale.

## 10.2   Continuous and Discontinuous Variables

Just as it is important for us to identify the level of scaling prior to beginning data analysis, it is also relevant to determine whether the variable is distributed in a *continuous* or *discrete* manner. Common observation will tell you that some variables, such as height, weight, intelligence, and achievement, naturally occur in a form that permits them to be scaled on a continuum. On all these constructs, objects or individuals can have some amount of it as well as every possible fractional amount in between. For example, persons can be 5.5, 5.56, 5.567, or 5.5679 feet in height. Similarly, distances can be measured as 10 meters (m), 10.2 m, 10.25 m or 10.2559 m. Both these are examples of *continuously distributed variables*. Continuously distributed variables are best measured with interval or ratio scales.

---

**Key Concept**

■ Continuous variables are those that can be measured with units increasing on a limitless continuum, where the units can be broken down into all possible intermediate values.

---

*Discontinuous* or *discrete variables* are those that are naturally distributed so that they vary or increase in increments of whole units, with intermediate values not possible or meaningful. Discretely distributed variables, such as gender, are usually scaled on nominal or ordinal scales, lending themselves better to categorical analysis and counting. Discrete variables can be unordered classes, as in gender, with 1 for males, and 2 for females. They can also be ordered classes, as in the variable, family size. Family size can grow from 1 (family with one individual) to 2, 3, and 4 (family with four individuals). We cannot talk about a family of 1.78 individuals, however, as the intermediate units have no meaningful values when variables are discrete.

---

**Key Concept**

■ Discontinuous or discrete variables cannot be measured on a continuum, as the units do not have meaningful intermediate values.

---

In the social and behavioral sciences, we strive to achieve measurements of continuous variables that are at least at the interval level. While there is debate as to whether educational and psychological assessments yield anything beyond ordinal data, most researchers and practitioners are willing to assume continuous, interval-level properties for their scales when employing various statistical procedures.

## 10.3 Organizing Data

Following measurement, we are faced with a set of data. We begin analysis by organizing the *data set* in ways that facilitate the application of particular statistical procedures. Appropriate organization of data helps us get a better understanding of the group of individuals measured on the construct.

Assume that we have administered a 10-item achievement test to a group of 20 individuals. We will treat the test as a continuous, interval scale. The number of individuals tested, *N,* is 20. The summed score derived from the total number of correctly answered items is referred to as the *raw score, X.* Each individual in the group tested, would have a raw score, yielding $X_1, X_2, X_3 \ldots X_{20}$ scores. The scores could be distributed on the scale as shown in Demonstration 10.1 with tallies. If the items are all dichotomously scored, we might have raw scores ranging from 2 to 10, denoting 2 correct or 10 correct.

---

**DEMONSTRATION  10.1**

**Organizing a Data Set**

$$X_1 \qquad\qquad\qquad\qquad X_{20}$$

People tested:    /  /  //  //  ///  /        ////  /
                                    //              ///
----------------0----1----2----3----4----5----6----7----8----9----10----------------

Achievement Scale

$X_1$, raw score for student 1 = 2
$X_{20}$, raw score for student 20 = 10
*N*, number of individuals tested = 20

---

The first task following data collection is to organize the data set. There are three major methods for tabulation and arrangement of data, each with advantages and disadvantages in particular situations. These are:

- Rank order distributions
- Simple (ungrouped) frequency distributions
- Grouped frequency distributions

### 10.3.1   Rank-Ordered Distribution

In the first method of arrangement, the *rank-ordered distribution,* we would simply place the scores in an ascending array from the lowest to the highest, as shown in Demonstration 10.2. Once displayed in a rank-ordered arrangement, we can discern the patterns suggesting how the group is distributed on the variable.

An advantage of the rank-ordered arrangement is that it gives us instant information on several characteristics of the group. In Demonstration 10.2, we immediately see that the *range (R)* of the scores, or the difference between the highest and lowest score, is 8. The *frequency (f)* of each score, or the number of times the same score appears in a distribution, is also obvious to us. We see that a raw score of 6 has a frequency of 5, while a score of 2 has a frequency of 1. Finally, we also get an idea of the *mode,* defined as the most frequently occurring score in the distribution. The mode in the distribution shown is 9, with a frequency of 7. As we will soon see, the mode is a rough measure of *central tendency* or a kind of "average" for a group.

---

### DEMONSTRATION 10.2
### A Rank-Ordered Distribution

$\underline{X}$

10
9
9
9
9
9
9       Range $(R) = X_{maximum} - X_{minimum}$
9       $R = 10 - 2 = 8$
7
6
6       Frequency $(f)$ of raw score of $6 = 5$
6
6
6       Mode (Mo) = most frequently
5       occurring raw score in a distribution
5       Mo = 9
4
4
3
2

$N = \overline{20}$

---

**Key Concept**

■ Rank-ordered distributions involve arranging of scores from low to high.

The disadvantage in using the rank-ordered arrangement becomes apparent when we have data sets with a large number of cases (individuals) and/or when the measurement scale is a long one (beyond the 10 operative points shown in the demonstration data set). One can envision the rank-ordered layout of a large data set that snakes its way off the page becoming cumbersome, and perhaps impossible to read.

## 10.3.2    Simple or Ungrouped Frequency Distribution

More commonly, we might choose to organize our data in a *frequency distribution*. If you have ever administered a test, recorded the numerical scores for individuals, and tallied how many students received a different score on your test, you have created a *simple* or *ungrouped frequency distribution.*

In a *simple frequency distribution,* the scores are treated as continuous units on an equal interval scale. Each scale unit is represented by an "interval" which ranges from half a unit below a score to half a unit above the score. Each score is not seen as a discrete point, but a *score interval* with a theoretical upper and lower limit. For example, for a score of 5, the score interval actually extends from half a unit below (4.5, the lower limit of the interval) to half a unit above a score (5.5, the upper limit of the interval). A score of 6, which follows next, is defined by an interval extending from 5.5, the lower limit, to 6.5, the upper limit of the score.

Demonstration 10.3 shows a data set organized as a simple frequency distribution. Here, the score interval for 9, extending from 8.5 to 9.5, has a frequency of 7; while the score interval of 8, extending from 7.5 to 8.5, has a frequency of 0. Although a continuous scale is unlimited from a theoretical standpoint, we typically depict only the operative part of the scale, or the range within which individuals actually obtain scores, when arranging the data in frequency distributions. By convention, it is acceptable to leave score intervals such as 8 out of the arrangement when their frequency is zero. Alternately, we can include them in the arrangement, as shown in Demonstration 10.3. Computationally, this decision will not make a difference in the statistics we calculate. Inclusion of all the scores is favored when we wish to obtain a complete picture of the group's distribution on the variable scale.

**Key Concepts**

- A *simple frequency distribution* involves arranging a group of scores to show how many individual scores fall within each interval on the measurement scale.
- A *score interval* is found in a simple frequency distribution. Each score interval has an upper and lower limit, extending from half a unit below to half a unit above a score.

The advantage of the simple frequency distribution lies in a more compact presentation of data without loss of any of the information from the rank-ordered arrangement. We still know the frequencies of each score, we can immediately identify the modal score interval of 9, and we can see that the range of the distribution is 8.

## 10.3.3    Grouped Frequency Distribution

A third alternative in data organization is the *grouped frequency distribution*. In a grouped frequency distribution, the interval includes *a cluster of scale units,* and is called a *class interval.* In Demonstration 10.4A, the class interval size is 3, and includes three scale units.

## DEMONSTRATION **10.3**
### A Simple or Ungrouped Frequency Distribution

| (Scale) | (People) | (Frequency) |
|---------|----------|-------------|
| $\underline{X}$ | <u>Tallies</u> | $\underline{f}$ |
| 10 | / | 1 |
| 9 | ⊬⊬ // | 7 |
| 8 | | 0 |
| 7 | / | 1 |
| 6 | ⊬⊬ | 5 |
| 5 | // | 2 |
| 4 | // | 2 |
| 3 | / | 1 |
| 2 | / | 1 |
| | | $N = \overline{20}$ |

*A Score Interval of 6 on a Continuous Scale*

Lower Limit      Upper Limit

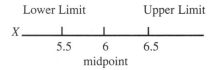

5.5    6    6.5
midpoint

---

Frequencies are tallied within the class intervals of specified size in Demonstration 10.4A. Using the exact upper and lower limits and a class interval size of 3, the first interval in our data set extends from 0.5 to 3.5, with 2 as the midpoint, as shown. That interval now has a frequency of 2, representing the 2 individuals who received scores within that range.

### Key Concepts

■ A grouped frequency distribution involves arranging a group of scores to show how many individual scores fall within each class interval on the measurement scale.
■ A class interval consists of a cluster of consecutive scale values with an upper and lower limit.

What are the conventions for deciding on the size of the class interval when using the grouped frequency distribution? Class interval sizes in grouped frequency distributions are usually 5, 10, 15, and 20. In the data set (Demonstration 10.4A), we have a rather short, 10-point scale that limits our ability to see the application of the conventions on interval size.

DEMONSTRATION   **10.4A**

## A Grouped Frequency Distribution

| (Scale) | (People) | (Frequency) |
|---|---|---|
| $X$ | Tallies | $f$ |
| 10–12 | / | 1 |
| 7–9 | $\cancel{HHH}$ /// | 8 |
| 4–6 | $\cancel{HHH}$ //// | 9 |
| 1–3 | // | 2 |
| | | $N = \overline{20}$ |

*A Class Interval on a Continuous Scale* (Class Interval Size = 3)

| Lower Limit | | Midpoint | | | Upper Limit | |
|---|---|---|---|---|---|---|

$$X \quad \underset{.5}{\llcorner} \quad \underset{1}{\lrcorner} \quad \underset{1.5}{\lrcorner} \quad \underset{2}{\lrcorner} \quad \underset{2.5}{\lrcorner} \quad \underset{3}{\lrcorner} \quad \underset{3.5}{\lrcorner}$$

Demonstration 10.4B, which follows, attempts to apply the interval conventions with a longer scale, where we do find an advantage with a grouped frequency arrangement. Let's say we administered a 100-point test to a group of 54 students, where the scores ranged from 46 to 98. To determine the class interval size suitable for that data set, we would typically use the calculated range and a specification for the number of classes we desire for presenting the data in a table format. The typically accepted number of classes in a frequency table is from 10 to 20. Here, since the

$$\text{Range } (R) = 98 - 46 = 52,$$

if we desire 10 classes in the distribution, our class interval size would be 5, based on the following calculation:

$$52/10 = 5.2 \text{ (rounded to 5)}$$

If we find that the range of scores in the distribution is too small (as it is in Demonstration 10.4A), using the grouped distribution will not give us much advantage over the ungrouped approach. We should then opt for the simple or ungrouped frequency distribution.

Notice that in grouping the scale points into class intervals in Demonstration 10.4A-B, some information is lost or distorted. For example, the exact range of the actual data is masked; as is the exact mode of the distribution. The modal interval appears to be 4–6, although the mode is actually located in the next interval of 7–9. The exact frequencies of individual scores is lost. In this instance, we pay a price for the convenience of a more compact arrangement of the data.

DEMONSTRATION **10.4B**

**Deciding on Class Interval Size for a Grouped Frequency Distribution**

| (Scale) | (Frequency) |
|---------|-------------|
| $X$ | $f$ |
| 95–99 | 4 |
| 90–94 | 0 |
| 85–89 | 3 |
| 80–84 | 10 |
| 75–79 | 11 |
| 70–74 | 5 |
| 65–69 | 2 |
| 60–64 | 1 |
| 55–59 | 8 |
| 50–54 | 8 |
| 45–49 | 2 |
| | $N = \overline{54}$ |

Range $= 98 - 46 = 52$
Desired number of classes $= 10$
Class interval size $= 52 \div 10 = 5.2$

Class Interval Size $= 5$ (rounded)

In the remaining parts of this chapter, computational formulas and examples will assume the use of a *simple* or *ungrouped frequency distribution,* since it yields the most accurate summaries while providing efficiency in organization. At the same time, variations of the same formulas that would apply to a rank-ordered distribution and grouped frequency tables are also provided. To follow the computations, read the frequency tables horizontally by row. Occasionally, formulas will call for summing of a vertical column of figures in a table.

## 10.4  Measures of Central Tendency

Once the scores have been organized, the next step is to seek a single numerical index that will represent *all* of them. If the data set consists of scores from an achievement test administered to sixth graders, we would like to summarize the general trend of performance in the group with a single number. The commonly used term "average" stands for a single number that reflects an entire group's performance; in statistical language, such indices are called *measures of central tendency.* The three measures of central tendency that this section will present are the *mode, arithmetic mean,* and the *median* (or *midpoint*).

### 10.4.1   Mode

The *mode,* which we have already encountered, is the score with the highest frequency in a distribution. It can be quickly derived by inspection of a distribution.

***Formulas***   There are no mathematical calculations needed for the mode; hence, no formulas! As shown earlier, the mode (Mo) becomess evident once the data are organized in a rank-ordered or simple frequency distribution format. In some cases, there may be more than one mode in the distribution. In such cases, both the modes are reported separated by a comma. Distributions with two modes are called *bimodal;* those with more than two modes are called *multimodal.*

***Steps in Computation***   No computations apply to the mode.

***Interpretations and Uses***   Because the mode does not involve complicated calculations, it is easy to undertand and interpret. It is a quick and easy method for evaluating a group's performance. The main disadvantage of the mode is that it is prone to sampling error. It does not have much stability from sample to sample drawn from a given population.

A bimodal distribution, such as the one shown in Demonstration 10.5, suggests that there are two distinct groups with respect to the measured variable, one with very high scores and the other with relatively low scores. To a teacher reviewing data from a classroom test, such a distribution would suggest that mastery levels of the domain are rather different in two subgroups of the class. Accordingly, the design of subsequent instruction should be varied for students bunching around the score of 4 versus those hovering around 11. For a counselor or program manager, a similar distribution of data from, say, a needs assessment survey, would suggest varying service needs for two distinct subgroups of clients.

---

**DEMONSTRATION 10.5**

## A Bimodal Distribution

| $X$ | Tallies | $f$ |
|-----|---------|-----|
| 12 | / | 1 |
| 11 | ⴙⴙⴙ /// | 8 |
| 10 | /// | 3 |
| 8 | // | 2 |
| 7 | / | 4 |
| 5 | // | 2 |
| 4 | ⴙⴙⴙ /// | 8 |
| 3 | // | 2 |
| | $N = \overline{30}$ | |

Mo = 4,11

> **Key Concepts**
>
> ■ The mode is the most frequently occurring score in a distribution.
> ■ There can be more than one mode in a distribution.

## 10.4.2 Arithmetic Mean

The *arithmetic mean* (or, *mean*) of a set of values (scores) is obtained by taking their sum and dividing by the total number of values. (We know this also as the *average*. The algebraic sum of the deviations (distances) of all the scores, weighted by their corresponding frequencies, from their arithmetic mean is always equal to 0. Thus, the mean is sometimes referred to as the center of gravity of a distribution.

***Formulas***   The formulas for calculation of the mean in a simple frequency distribution (1) versus a rank-ordered one (2) vary slightly because they assume different arrangements of the data set. They both yield the same result with the same data.

1.  When raw scores for a variable, *X*, are organized in a *simple frequency distribution,* the mean is represented by the symbol $\bar{X}$, and the formula is:

$$\bar{X} = \frac{\Sigma fX}{N} \text{, where}$$

   *fX* is the f(requency) times each raw score, *X*,
   $\Sigma fX$ is the sum of the product of *f* and *X* for all the scores, and
   *N* is the number of cases (or individuals) in the group.

2.  When raw scores for a variable, *X*, are organized in a *rank-ordered distribution,* the mean is represented by the same symbol $\bar{X}$, and the formula is:

$$\bar{X} = \frac{\Sigma X}{N} \text{, where}$$

   $\Sigma X$ is the sum of all raw scores, and
   *N* is the number of scores (or individuals) in the group.

***Steps in Computation***   To compute the mean in a *simple frequency distribution* (see Formula 1), follow these steps.

1.  Set up a *fX* column in the frequency table. Compute the product, *f* times *X*, for each score value that has a frequency greater than 0.
2.  Make a sum of the *fX* column. This should give you $\Sigma fX$, the numerator in the formula for the arithmetic mean.
3.  Divide the $\Sigma fX$ by the *N*. The *N* is the sum of the frequency column, and is the denominator in the formula.

The steps are shown in Demonstration 10.6A. The steps for calculating the mean in a *rank-ordered distribution* (see Formula 2) are illustrated directly after in 10.6B.

---

DEMONSTRATION **10.6A**

## Calculation of the Arithmetic Mean in a Simple Frequency Distribution

| $X$ | $f$ | $fX$ *(Step 1)* | | How Derived |
|-----|-----|-----|---|-----|
| 10 | 1 | 10 | $\Rightarrow$ | $10 \times 1 = 10$ *(Step 1)* |
| 9 | 7 | 63 | $\Rightarrow$ | $9 \times 7 = 63$ |
| 8 | 0 | 0 | | |
| 7 | 1 | 7 | | |
| 6 | 5 | 30 | | |
| 5 | 2 | 10 | | |
| 4 | 2 | 8 | | |
| 3 | 1 | 3 | | |
| 2 | 1 | 2 | | |

$$N = \overline{20} \qquad \Sigma fX = \overline{133} \quad \Rightarrow (10+63+0+7+30+10+8+3+2)$$
$$\textit{(Step 2)}$$

$$\overline{X} = \frac{\Sigma fX}{N} \text{ , or}$$

$$\overline{X} = 133 \div 20 = 6.65 \checkmark \textit{(Step 3)}$$

Note: To apply the above formula with a *grouped frequency distribution*, simply use the *midpoint of each class interval* as the $X$ value.

---

### Key Concept

■ The arithmetic mean of a set of values (scores) is their sum divided by their number.

---

***Interpretations and Uses***   Unlike the mode, the arithmetic mean is the most stable measure of central tendency. That is, the mean on any measured variable is likely to remain the same in different samples of individuals drawn from the same population. The mean is also very useful for computing other statistics on the group of interest. For example, the variance and standard deviation, both measures of variability, are computed using the mean as the reference point. Studies of group differences and effects, including associated inferential tests, are conducted using the mean as the starting statistic.

A disadvantage of the mean is that it is sensitive to outlying scores in the distribution. *Outliers* are score values that are extremely low or high compared to the majority of scores in a group. Because the mean is computed by taking into account every score in the

DEMONSTRATION **10.6B**
## Calculation of the Arithmetic Mean in a Rank-Ordered Distribution

$X$

10
9
9
9
9
9
9
9
7
6
6
6
6
6
5
5
4
4
3
2

Step 1: $\Sigma X = \overline{133}$

Step 2: $\overline{X} = \dfrac{\Sigma X}{N}$

$N = 20$
$\Sigma X = 133 \div 20 = 6.65$ ✓

distribution (weighted by its frequency), it is influenced by outlying scores, which distort the obtained measure of central tendency. If the outlying score is a very low value, the mean will be lower than the mean for the majority of scores in the group. It will be higher than the general distribution when the outlying scores are extremely high values.

A "trimmed" mean is more representative of a group that has outliers. To obtain a trimmed mean we delete the outlying scores and recompute the mean for the remaining scores. Choosing an alternate measure of central tendency, such as the *median,* provides another option for treating data sets with outliers.

### 10.4.3  Median

The *median* is the midpoint of a distribution of scores. Another name for the median is the *50th percentile.*

#### Formulas

  1. When raw scores for a variable, *X*, are organized in a *simple frequency distribution,* the median is represented by the symbol *Mdn,* and the computational formula is:

$$\text{Mdn} = \frac{L_{MI} + i\left(\dfrac{N}{2} - \text{Cum } f_{\text{below MI}}\right)}{f_{\text{in MI}}} \text{ , where}$$

MI = middle interval or the score interval within which the median is located

$L_{MI}$ = lower limit of the middle interval

$N/2$ = half of the total number of scores (individuals) in the group

$\text{Cum } f_{\text{below MI}}$ = cumulative frequency in the interval below MI

$f_{\text{in MI}}$ = frequency in the middle interval

$i$ = size of the interval (in a simple frequency distribution, this number is always 1).

2. When raw scores for a variable, $X$, are organized in a rank-ordered distribution and have no tied scores (i.e., every score has a $f = 1$), the median is simply the middle value on the scale that divides the number of scores into equal halves. If the number of cases is odd (say, $N = 7$), the median could be identified visually as the score located in the middle with three scores on either side. The median below is 4.

$$X: \quad 1 \quad 2 \quad 3 \quad \underline{4} \quad 5 \quad 6 \quad 7$$

When the number of cases is even ($N = 6$), the median is the midpoint, or arithmetic mean of the two middle scores (3 and 4).

$$X: \quad 1 \quad 2 \quad \underline{3} \mid \underline{4} \quad 5 \quad 6$$

$$3.5$$

Mdn = (3 + 4)/2 = 3.5

***Steps in Computation***   In a *simple frequency distribution,* follow these steps to compute the median. Demonstration 10.7 shows how to apply these steps.

1. Set up a Cumulative Frequency (Cum $f$) column by cumulatively adding the frequencies in the $f$ column from bottom upwards using this algorithm.

Cum $f = f$ in given interval $+$ Cum $f$ in previous interval

The running total should reach a value equal to $N$ when you reach the topmost interval.
2. Find $N/2$ or half of the total number of scores. This $N/2$ value will be used in the median formula.
3. Find the Middle Interval (MI). The MI is the interval within which the median is located. You will find MI by going from bottom upwards in the Cum $f$ column until you find the *first interval* where the cumulative frequency value equals $N/2$ or a value just higher than $N/2$. (In Demonstration 10.7, $N/2 = 10$, and the MI has a cumulative total of 11 scores.)

4. Mark the lower limit of the MI. This value is the $L_{MI}$ in the formula.
5. Go to the Cum $f$ column again and highlight the Cum $f$ value found in the interval just below the Middle Interval. This is the Cum $f_{below\,MI}$.
6. Now, go to the $f$ column and highlight the $f$ value found inside the middle interval (MI). This is the $f_{in\,MI}$.
7. Finally, plug in the values in the formula below and solve.

$$\text{Mdn} = \frac{L_{MI} + \left[ i\left( \dfrac{N}{2} - \text{Cum } f_{below\,MI} \right) \right]}{f_{in\,MI}}$$

---

**DEMONSTRATION 10.7**

## Calculation of the Median in a Simple Frequency Distribution

$N/2 = 20/2 = 10$ *(Step 1)*

| X | $f$ | Cum $f$ *(Step 2)* | How Derived |
|---|---|---|---|
| 10 | 1 | 20 $\Rightarrow$ | $1 + 19 = 20$ *(Step 2)* |
| 9 | 7 | 19 $\Rightarrow$ | cum $f = f +$ cum $f$ in previous interval |
| 8 | 0 | 12 | or $7 + 12 = 19$ |
| 7 | 1 | 12 | |

6.5 - - - - - - - - - - - - - - - - - - - - - - - - - - - - - - - - - - - - - - - -

| Middle Interval 6 | 5 | *11 (Step 3)* | |
|---|---|---|---|

5.5 - - - - - - - - - - - - - - - - - - - - - - - - - - - - - - - -

| *(Step 4)* 5 | 2 | 6 *(Step 5)* | |
|---|---|---|---|
| 4 | 2 | 4 | |
| 3 | 1 | 2 $\Rightarrow$ | cum $f = f +$ cum $f$ in previous interval |
| 2 | 1 | 1 | or $1 + 1 = 2$ |

$$N = \overline{20}$$

$$\text{Mdn} = \frac{L_{MI} + [i\,(N/2 - \text{Cum } f_{below\,MI})]}{f_{in\,MI}} \quad \textit{(Step 6)}$$

$N/2 = 10$
$L_{MI} = 5.5$
$\text{Cum } f_{below\,MI} = 6$
$f_{in\,MI} = 5$
$i = 1$

$\text{Mdn} = 5.5 + [1 \times (10 - 6) \div 5] = 6.3$

*Note:* To apply the above formula with a grouped frequency distribution, replace $i = 1$, with the actual size of the class interval in the distribution, for example, $i = 3$, or $i = 5$. The remaining calculations will be unchanged.

*Interpretations and Uses*    The median is the point on the scale above and below which *half* the scores in the distribution fall. Unlike the mean, the median is not influenced by magnitude of the scores on either side, but simply by their counts. Thus, even when there are one or more scores with extremely high or low values, the computed value of the median will tend to reflect the midpoint of the group. Consequently, the median is the preferred measure of central tendency in distributions with outliers. The median is also a stable measure of central tendency, although it does not have the precision and sampling stability of the mean.

---

**Key Concept**

■ The median of a set of values (scores) is the point on the underlying scale above which exactly 50% of the scores are distributed. Another name for the median is the "50th Percentile"

---

Why is the median called the "50th percentile?" *Percentiles* are points in a distribution below which certain percents of the total group fall. As we saw, because the median is a scale point below which 50 percent of the group tested falls, it is called the *50th percentile*. The *25th percentile* is the point below which a quarter of the group falls, and is also called the *first quartile*. Similarly, the *75th percentile* is the point below which three-quarters of the group tested falls, and is the *third quartile*. Although we will not be computing percentiles, it is easy to see they can be derived by modifying $N/2$ term in the formula for the median to reflect the proportion that corresponds to the desired percentile, and finding the appropriate interval. For the 25th percentile, the term should be $N/4$, and for the 75th percentile it is $3/4N$, as shown in the modified formulas below.

Computing the 25th percentile in a simple frequency distribution:

$$25\text{th Percentile} = L_{\text{Interval with first quartile}} + \left[ i \frac{\left( \dfrac{N}{4} - \text{Cum} f_{\text{below first quartile}} \right)}{f_{\text{in interval with first quartile}}} \right]$$

Computing the 75th percentile in a simple frequency distribution:

$$75\text{th Percentile} = L_{\text{Interval with third quartile}} + \left[ i \frac{\left( \dfrac{3N}{4} - \text{Cum} f_{\text{below third quartile}} \right)}{f_{\text{in interval with third quartile}}} \right]$$

## 10.5    Measures of Variability

Score distributions with exactly the same mean might end up having a very different "spread" on the measurement scale. Groups made up of individuals that are homogeneous on the attribute will tend to cluster closely around the mean, while those that are made up of dissimilar individuals will show a wide spread. Thus, while a measure of central tendency, like the mean, is an important first step in understanding how a group is distributed on a measured construct, one also needs to assess a group's *variability* or *dispersion*. This section will present two commonly used numerical indices of variability: the *range* and *standard deviation*.

### 10.5.1    Range

As we saw, close scrutiny of a frequency distribution gives away its range, especially when the two extreme scores, lowest and highest, can be located. The range, *R,* is the difference between the lowest and highest scores in a distribution, and denotes the number of scale units between the highest and lowest score in the distribution.

***Formulas***    We have seen that the range is calculated by the formula:

$R = X_{max} - X_{min}$, where
$R$ is the range,
$X_{max}$ is the highest obtained score, and
$X_{min}$ is the lowest obtained score.

Sometimes, the *inclusive range* is used, which denotes the total number of different scores represented within the range.

$R' = X_{max} - X_{min} + 1$

Of the two indices, most applied researchers prefer to use the simpler index, $R$.

***Steps in Computation***    Computation of the $R$ has already been illustrated. In the data set we are using, it is:

Range $(R) = X_{max} - X_{min}$
$R = 10 - 2 = 8$

***Interpretations and Uses***    The $R$ represents the number of scale units lying between the highest and lowest score in a distribution. Its greatest advantage is its ease of computation and interpretation. Its greatest disadvantage is its sampling instability. Because it relies only on the two extreme scores in a data set, the $R$ is prone to fluctuate from sample to sample. Sampling procedures can lead to the possible inclusion or exclusion of the most exceptional cases, which would affect the computed value of $R$ in different samples from the same population.

> **Key Concept**
>
> ■ The range, $R$, is the difference between the lowest and highest scores in a distribution.

## 10.5.2 Standard Deviation (and Variance)

The *standard deviation* is the principal measure of spread of a distribution, calculated by using the arithmetic mean as the central point of reference. The term "deviation" stands for the distance of any raw score, $X$, from the *arithmetic mean* of the distribution. The *standard deviation s* is the positive square root of the mean squared deviation of a set of scores from the arithmetic mean. The mean squared deviation, calculated in the second-to-last step in arriving at $s$, is called the *variance, $s^2$.*

*Formula*   The formula for the *standard deviation s* in a simple frequency distribution is:

$$s = \sqrt{\frac{\sum fx^2}{N}} \text{ , where}$$

$x = X - \overline{X}$, or the deviation of each raw score from the mean,
$x^2$ stands for the squared deviation scores,
$f x^2$ represents the product of the frequency times the squared deviation scores (needed because scores may have frequencies >1),
$(\sum f x^2)/N$ represents the mean squared deviation (variance or the sum of squared deviations divided by their number).

This formula is the *deviation score method* for computing $s$.

Formulas also exist to derive $s$ from raw scores (raw score methods). The computation of the standard deviation from raw scores that are arranged in a simple frequency distribution can be done with the following formula. Although this book will not present the derivations, the raw score formula can be derived mathematically from the deviation score formula for $s$.

Raw score formula for standard deviation:

$$s = \sqrt{\frac{\sum fX^2}{N} - \overline{X}^2}$$

***Steps in Computation***   The deviation score method will be demonstrated next. To start, the mean must be computed and the data set organized in a simple frequency arrangement. The standard deviation, $s$, is calculated by first obtaining the deviation scores, $x$, for all the raw scores in the data set. These deviations are then squared and averaged by taking their sum and dividing by $N$. This yields the variance, $s^2$, or mean squared deviation. The final step is to take a positive square root of the variance. In sequence, the steps are as follows.

1. Find the deviation score for each raw score using $x = X - \overline{X}$, and set up an x column.
2. Square the deviation scores for each raw score, to obtain an $x^2$ column. (Note that if you were to sum the deviation scores taking into account their frequencies, their sum would be zero. This happens because of the way the arithmetic mean is defined. We square the $x$ values to bypass this problem.)
3. Multiply the $x^2$ values with the $f$ values in the frequency column to set up a $fx^2$ column.
4. Sum the values in the $fx^2$ column and divide by $N$ to obtain $(\Sigma fx^2)/N$ or the variance.
5. Find the positive square root of the variance,

$$s = \sqrt{\frac{\Sigma fx^2}{N}}$$

In a *rank-ordered* distribution, the $f$ column would be absent, hence the same basic procedure would apply without Step 3. The formula would be:

$$s = \sqrt{\frac{\Sigma x^2}{N}}$$

In a *grouped frequency* distribution, the same steps would apply, except in Step 1, you would find the deviation of the *midpoint of each class interval* from the mean.

***Interpretations and Uses***   Conceptually, the standard deviation is a numeric index that describes how far away from the mean, on average, the scores in the distribution are located. This concept is best understood through the deviation score method that was just illustrated, which utilizes the distances of every score from the mean in the formula. A higher value of $s$ indicates a wider, more heterogeneous spread of raw scores on the scale. A lower value indicates a narrower, more homogeneous distribution. The standard deviation enjoys widespread use because it tends to display sampling stability. It is like the mean in that its computation demands the inclusion of every score in the distribution. It is the preferred statistic for variability because of its algebraic maneuverability.

DEMONSTRATION **10.8**

**Calculation of the Standard Deviation in a Simple Frequency Distribution Using the Deviation Score Method**

Start with: $=(\sum fX)/N = 133 \div 20 = 6.65$ ✓

Then:

| $X$ | $f$ | $x$ (Step 1) | $x^2$ (Step 2) | $fx^2$ (Step 3) |
|-----|-----|------|------|------|
| 10 | 1 | 3.35 (10 − 6.5 = 3.35) | 11.22 (3.35 × 3.35 = 11.22) | 11.22 (1 × 11.22) |
| 9 | 7 | 2.35 | 5.52 | 38.64 |
| 8 | 0 | 1.35 | 1.82 | 0.00 |
| 7 | 1 | 0.35 | 0.12 | 0.12 |
| 6 | 5 | −0.65 | 0.42 | 2.10 |
| 5 | 2 | −1.65 | 2.72 | 5.44 |
| 4 | 2 | −2.65 | 7.02 | 14.04 |
| 3 | 1 | −3.65 | 13.32 | 13.32 |
| 2 | 1 | −4.65 | 21.62 | 21.62 |

$N = 20$

$$\sum fx^2 = 106.5$$

$$s = \sqrt{\frac{\sum fx^2}{N}} \text{ or } \sqrt{(106.5)/20} = 2.30 \checkmark \quad \text{(Steps 4–5)}$$

**Key Concept**

■ The standard deviation, *s,* is the square root of the sum of the squared deviations of a set of scores from their mean.

## 10.6    Graphic Displays of Distributions

Graphing of frequency distributions facilitates visual interpretation of group performance. We can also compare shapes of empirical distributions with a mathematical model, namely, the *normal distribution,* or the familiar *bell curve.* Three common procedures for plotting frequency distributions are the frequency polygon, the histogram and the ogive. No matter which procedure we follow, all graphs should be clearly titled with appropriate labels for the *axes.* We will examine all three methods prior to reviewing the properties of the normal distribution.

## 10.6.1 Frequency Polygon

In a *frequency polygon*, the horizontal *x*-axis is represented by the scores on the scale. The vertical *y*-axis is represented by the frequencies. The frequencies are plotted *at the midpoints* of the score or class interval.

***Steps in Construction of a Frequency Polygon***   To construct a frequency polygon with the data set in Demonstration 10.8, follow these steps. Figure 10.2A shows the completed graph. We need to begin by deciding whether to organize the data in a simple frequency table.

If the range of scores is very high, say with scores of 22–95, $R = 73$, it might be better to opt for the *grouped frequency distribution* with class intervals of a suitable size. With scores in the 22–95 range, we could establish class intervals of size 10, with the two extreme intervals being 20.5–25.5 (midpoint = 23), and 95.5–100.5 (midpoint = 98). The procedures are similar for both arrangements.

1. Set up the *x*-axis for the graph with its origin at zero, and equal-sized units representing the raw score scale. If your data set has scores starting well beyond 0, ranging from say, 22–38, you would still begin with the 0 at the origin, include the first couple of units, then break the scale with two vertical slashes, and restart the scale with units close to the region where people scored, 21, say. Always end the scale a couple of units *beyond the observed R*. In Figure 10.2A, the *X scale* units are equal to 1.
2. Set up the vertical *y-axis,* always starting with a 0, and frequencies increasing in equal units on a continuum until you reach the highest frequency. If the *N* is small, your *y-axis* units can be 1. If the *N* is large, say 100, then it may be more practical to have *y-axis* units of 10, 20, 30 and so on. In Figure 10.2A, the *Y scale* units are equal to 1.
3. Plot and connect the *midpoints* of each score interval or class interval, against the frequencies, as recorded in your frequency table.
4. Anchor the polygon to the baseline by bringing the lines to the midpoints of the two intervals adjacent to intervals with the highest and lowest scores.

***Interpretations and Uses***   The frequency polygon is simply a line graph representation of data from a frequency table. Visually, polygons can be described in terms of their *symmetry, modality,* and *variability.*

In Figure 10.2A, we see that the distribution is *unimodal.* The *mode* of the distribution is depicted by the highest point or the peak of the polygon. However, although 9 is the mode, 6 is another score drawing a high frequency of students. The spread of the distribution is quite wide, suggesting heterogeneity (remember, there were only 10 test items). The range can also be visually picked up from the graph. The distribution suggests some *asymmetry.* The two individuals with scores of 2 and 3 can be called *outliers,* with a vast majority of the scores (70% exactly) hovering around scores 6–10, causing the lack of symmetry. Technically, a distribution is *symmetrical* if the mean and median have equal or close to equal values.

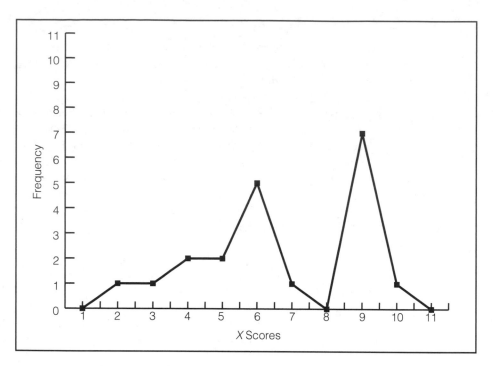

**FIGURE 10.2A    Frequency Polygon**

Let us now review the polygons in Figure 10.2B, which represent boys and girls assessed on an arithmetic test. If two groups with equal *N*s are assessed on the same instrument, the frequency polygon can be used to make comparisons between groups. This type of comparison is possible to make when the units on *x-* and *y-axes* for both distributions are comparable. The two score distributions suggest that boys have a slightly higher mode than the girls, and are distributed on a somewhat higher region of the scale than girls. In terms of the ranges, the distributions seem to have similar dispersions, although their maximum and minimum scores vary.

### 10.6.2    Histogram

The *histogram* is a *bar graph* of data from a frequency table. As in a frequency polygon, to construct a *histogram,* the horizontal *x*-axis is represented by the scores on the scale; the vertical *y*-axis is represented by the frequencies. However, in a histogram the frequencies are plotted as bars that extend over the exact upper and lower limits of each interval on the *x*-axis, with the midpoints at the center of each bar.

***Steps in Constructing a Histogram***    The construction of a histogram is shown in Figure 10.3, and uses these steps.

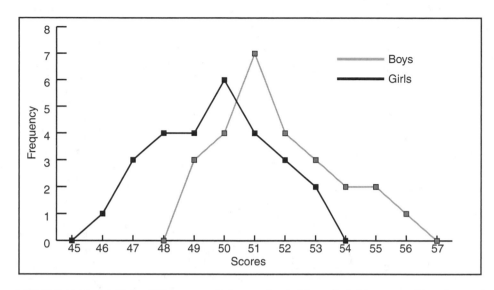

**FIGURE 10.2B    A Pair of Frequency Polygons for Arithmetic Achievement-Test Scores for Boys and Girls of a Sixth-Grade Class**

1. Organize your data in a simple or grouped frequency table.
2. Set up the *x*-axis for the graph with its origin at zero, and equal-sized units representing the raw score scale.
3. Set up the vertical *y*-axis, always starting with a 0, with frequencies increasing in equal units on a continuum until you reach *N*.
4. Plot a bar for each score interval or class interval, against the frequencies, as recorded in your frequency table, using the the *exact lower and upper limits of the intervals*. Thus for a score of 5, the bar in Figure 10.3 extends from 4.5 to 5.5. The midpoint of the bar should be 5.

***Interpretations and Uses***    The histogram is simply an alternate way to depict the data in a frequency table and yields much the same visual information as a frequency polygon. Interpretation of group performance is done using *modality, variability,* and *symmetry.* Comparison of two more groups, however, is not as effective with histograms as it is with the frequency polygon, as overlapping bars tend to cloud information and are difficult to read.

## 10.6.3   Ogive

An *ogive* is an *S*-shaped graph that shows cumulative proportions of students scoring at particular points of the *X* scale. To create an ogive, frequency distributions are graphed

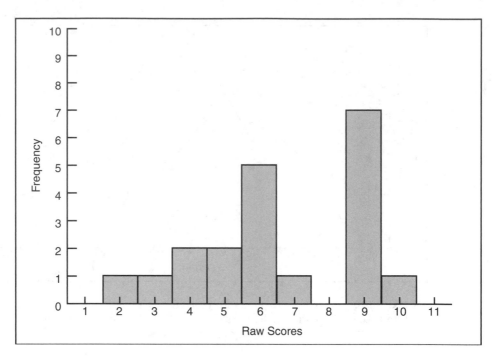

**FIGURE 10.3    Histogram of Scores on a 10-Item Test**

using *cumulative percents of the frequencies* in the *y*-axis instead of the actual frequencies, against *upper limits of units* on the *x*-axis. Ogives can be useful for comparing groups and also for deriving *approximate percentile ranks* corresponding with upper limits of particular score intervals.

***Steps in Constructing an Ogive***    To construct an *ogive,* one must begin with the addition of two columns to a simple or grouped frequency table: the Cumulative Frequency (Cum *f*) column, and the Cumulative Percent (Cum %) column. The Cum *f* column was used for computation of the median. The Cum % column is set up by dividing the Cum *f* value at each interval by *N,* as shown in Demonstration 9.

1. Set up a frequency table with a Cum % column.
2. Set up the *x*-axis for the graph with its origin at zero, and equal-sized units representing the raw score scale.
3. Set up the vertical *y*-axis with percents starting with 0 at the origin. The percents increase in equal units of 10 from 0 through 100.
4. Plot the *upper limits of each interval* on the *x*-axis against the Cum % on the *y*-axis. Connect the points with a line.

---

**DEMONSTRATION 10.9**

## Constructing an Ogive

Cum % at a given interval = Cum $f$ at that interval/$N$

| $X$ | $f$ | Cum $f$ | Cum % | | How Cum % is derived |
|---|---|---|---|---|---|
| 10 | 1 | 20 | 100 | $\Rightarrow$ | 20/20 $\times$ 100 = 100 |
| 9 | 7 | 19 | 95 | $\Rightarrow$ | 19/20 $\times$ 100 = 95 |
| 8 | 0 | 12 | 60 | | |
| 7 | 1 | 12 | 60 | | |
| 6 | 5 | 11 | 55 | | |
| 5 | 2 | 6 | 30 | | |
| 4 | 2 | 4 | 20 | $\Rightarrow$ | 4/20 $\times$ 100 = 20 |
| 3 | 1 | 2 | 10 | | |
| 2 | 1 | 1 | 5 | | |
| | $N = \overline{20}$ | | | | |

---

### Key Concepts

- A frequency polygon is a line graph depicting the frequencies of each score against the midpoints of the corresponding intervals on the $x$-axis.
- A histogram is a bar graph depicting the frequencies of each score against the exact upper and lower limits of the corresponding intervals on the $x$-axis.
- An ogive is an $s$-shaped graph depicting the cumulative frequencies of a distribution at the exact upper limits of each interval on the $x$-axis.

***Interpretations and Uses***   Ogives have several uses. They are useful for comparing the performance of two or more groups that have *different N*s but are measured on the same scale. If multiple measurements are made on the same group of individuals over time using the same instrument, the rightward movement of the ogives from Time 1, Time 2, to Time $t$, will illustrate the changes of the group on the measured construct. Such applications are discussed in detail in Chapter 11. Ogives can also be used for deriving *approximate* percentile ranks (PR) corresponding with upper limits of particular score intervals.

   *Percentile ranks* are derived for score intervals of 6 and 8 in the ogive in Figure 10.4. As you see, the score of 6 can be connected with a percentile rank of 55 by drawing straight lines from the axes to the graphed point, which indicates that individuals obtaining scores around that interval were ranked above 55% of the rest of the group. Similarly, a score of 9 had an approximate PR of 95, meaning that the student's score surpassed 95% of the comparison group. Using the ogive, we could also approximate the PR for a score of 8, although no one in the group received that particular score. Percentile ranks obtained in this manner are *approximations* because the percents correspond with the upper limits

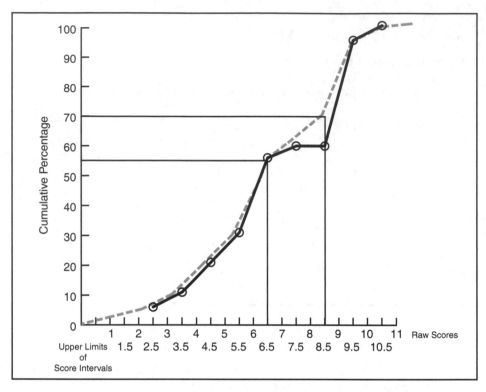

**FIGURE 10.4    Ogive Representing the Results of the Same 10-Item Test**

Note: A smoothed ogive is shown by the dotted line

of intervals rather than the actual location of the score within an interval. Precise computational procedures for PRs follow in a later section of this chapter.

## 10.7    Normal Distribution and Its Applications

The *normal distribution* is a symmetrical bell-shaped curve based on a mathematical function describing the distribution of a random normal variable. The standard normal distribution has a $\mu$ (mean) of 0, a $\sigma$ (standard deviation) of 1, and total area of 1.0 (100%). In a distribution that is perfectly normal, one can predict what the frequencies will be of all the scores on the X scale ranging from $+\infty$ to $-\infty$, by using the formula for the normal probability function. Figure 10.5 presents a graphic representation of the normal distribution. The important properties of the normal distribution can be summarized as follows.

1. The distribution is *unimodal*.
2. It is *bilaterally symmetrical*. The left side of the bell curve is a mirror image of the right side.

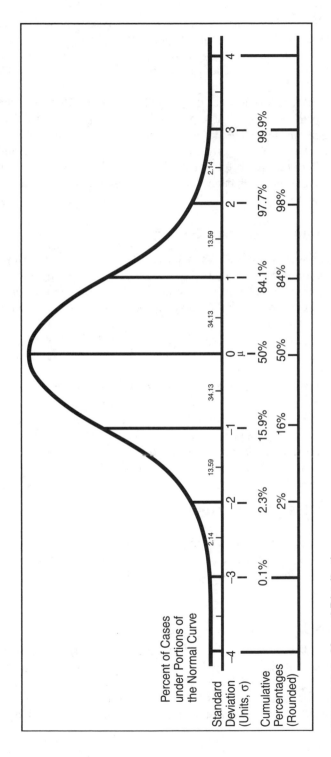

**FIGURE 10.5 Normal Distribution**

3. The mean, median, and mode have *equal values*. The mean is symbolized as $\mu$ in the theoretical distribution, and represents the population mean.

4. The scale on the *x*-axis is expressed in terms of the distance of each score value from $\mu$ in standard deviation units. These units are called $\sigma$ units (standard deviation units).

5. The mathematical function specifies the percent of area under the curve that will lie between given pairs of $\sigma$ units. These percents give the distribution its characteristic bell shape. Approximately 99.7% of the area under the curve lies between $-3.0$ $\sigma$ units and $+3.0$ $\sigma$ units; 95.4% of the area lies between $-2.0$ $\sigma$ units and $+2.0$ $\sigma$ units; and 68.3% of the area is found between $-1.0$ $\sigma$ units and $+1.0$ $\sigma$ units.

6. The tails of the curve approach but never touch the baseline. Theoretically, the *x*-axis extends from $+\infty$ to $-\infty$.

## Applications with the Normal Distribution

The normal curve is also called the Gaussian curve after one of its pioneering scholars, K. F. Gauss. Although originally studied from a theoretical standpoint by mathematicians in the seventeenth century, the value of the *normal distribution* in interpreting real world phenomena was discovered soon after. When systematic measurements were made using large numbers of individuals on several psychological, physiological, and physical/motor variables, many of the variables were found to be distributed normally in nature. When random samples were drawn from large populations, sampling errors were found to be distributed normally. Such findings were incorporated into work on hypothesis testing and inferential statistics. Errors of measurement, directly related to the concept of estimating the reliability of assessment results, were also found to distribute normally. Psychometricians found this third finding useful in formulating mathematical definitions of reliability. Developers of standardized tests capitalized on the bell-shaped distributions in large samples in developing test norms and norm-based scores. (The measurement applications mentioned here will be further clarified in Chapters 13 and 14.)

## 10.8   Skewness and Kurtosis in Distributions

We have talked about describing shapes of distributions in terms of their variability, symmetry and modality. The normal distribution provides us with a reference framework to describe shapes of empirical distributions using two additional concepts, *skewness* and *kurtosis*.

### 10.8.1   Skewness

*Skewness* is a measure of asymmetry in score distributions. In visibly skewed distributions, there is a pronounced "tail" in one direction, with the bulk of the scores lumped at the opposite end, as shown in Figure 10.6.

One way to determine skewness is by visually superimposing an imaginary normal curve over the frequency polygon (or histogram) of an empirical distribution. If the real

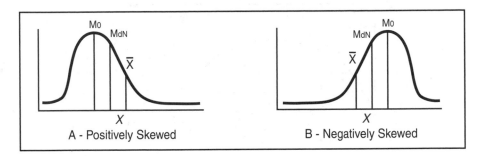

**FIGURE 10.6    Skewness in Distributions**

data distribution is *positively skewed,* a majority of scores will be concentrated at the lower end, with the tail of the curve overlapping the baseline of the normal distribution where the σ units are positive. In other words, in a positively skewed curve, there will be relatively few scores located in the "tail," or *above* the mean of the distribution (see Figure 10.6A). In a negatively skewed distribution, a reverse picture is obtained, with the tail of the curve over the baseline of the normal distribution where the σ units are negative. Now, there will be fewer scores located *below* the mean (see Figure 10.6B). Skewness can be calculated as the difference between the mean and the mode of a distribution in standard deviation units.

$$\text{Skewness} = (\mu - \text{Mo})/\sigma$$

Because of the low sampling stability of the mode, another formula for skewness uses the difference between the mean and the median (not shown here).

In skewed distributions, the mean, median and mode usually have predictable locations on the *X* scale. In a negatively skewed distribution, the mean is pulled towards the outliers at the low end of the scale, making the mean the lowest in value, followed by the median and the mode. The opposite pattern is usually found in positively skewed distributions, where the mean is pulled towards outliers at the high end of the scale, making the mean the highest in value, the median lower, and the mode the lowest value (see Figures 10.6). These predictable patterns tend to apply with unimodal distributions.

## 10.8.2    Kurtosis

*Kurtosis* is another measure of non-normality in a distribution, and refers to its flatness or peakedness (see Figure 10.7). If a distribution is narrow and sharply peaked relative to a normal distribution, it is called a *leptokurtic* distribution. When a distribution is flat and spread out, resembling a plateau, it is described as *platykurtic*. The normal (bell-shaped) distribution is described as *mesokurtic* in its shape, and lies somewhere in between a leptokurtic and platykurtic form.

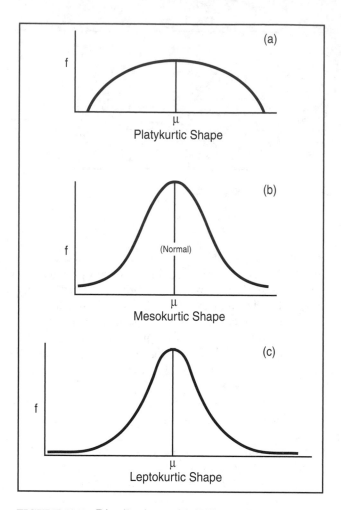

**FIGURE 10.7    Distributions with Different Degrees of Kurtosis**

**Key Concept**

■ The normal distribution is a bell-shaped curve based on the normal probability function.

## 10.9    Measures of Relative Position

It is often useful to interpret measurements in a comparative manner. For example, a little girl born today might weigh 6½ pounds—the *raw score* that we would read on the weighing scale. We might ask, Is 6½ lbs a good birthweight? How is her "score" compared to that of a typical newborn in the U.S.? A *measure of relative position* is helpful in answering such a question. If, by comparing the baby's birthweight to that of newborn children born in the last five years in the U.S., we found it to be below average, the value of $6\frac{1}{2}$ pounds would acquire new significance in our minds.

To make meaningful comparative interpretations, we would naturally require a "reference group" against which the comparison will be made. This is called the *comparison group,* or *norm group.* The norm group must be similar to the individual being compared on important variables. In the example on birthweight, if the norm group was from a country in the Far East or from a time that was decades past, the comparison would be rendered far less meaningful than if we had a group from the United States in the past 10 years.

Measures of relative position provide a means for "ranking" individuals in a given group. In this section, we will consider two measures of relative position that are most frequently used in the educational testing field. These are: (1) *standard scores,* specifically, *z-scores* and *T-scores,* and (2) *percentile ranks.*

---

**Key Concepts**

- Measures of relative position provide a way of comparing a person's score with scores from a specified reference group, referred to as the comparison group or norm group.
- Any score expressed in terms of its distance from the mean of the distribution in standard deviation units is called a standard score.

## 10.9.1   *z*-Scores

The most basic form of a standard score is the *z-score.*

***Computation of the z-score***   For a raw score on variable $X,$ the *z-score* would be computed with the formula:

$$z_X = (\overline{X} - \text{mean}_X) \div \text{standard deviation}_X$$

Similarly for a construct, $Y,$ the *z-scores* could be computed starting with raw scores for all individuals assessed on $Y,$ with the formula:

$$z_Y = (Y - \text{mean}_Y) \div \text{standard deviation}_Y$$

The utility of *z-scores* as a measure of relative position might be best understood through their computation in a data set. Computation of the *z-score* is shown in Demonstration 10.10. There we see raw scores for six students (A–F) from two assessments, Reading $(X),$ and Mathematics $(Y).$ The $X$ and $Y$ distributions, not shown in their entirety, each have a mean and standard deviation.

DEMONSTRATION **10.10**

## Steps in Computing z-Scores

1. Find the deviation of each score from the mean of the distribution. ($x = X -$ mean$_x$).

2. Divide the deviation score by the standard deviation of the distribution ($z = x/s$).

| Student | X | $z_x$ | Y | $z_y$ | | How Derived |
|---------|---|-------|---|-------|---|-------------|
| A | 9 | +1.0 | 24 | +3.0 | $\Rightarrow$ | (24–12) = 12 *(Step 1)* |
| | | | | | | 12/4 = +3.0 *(Step 2)* |
| B | 7 | 0.0 | 16 | +1.0 | | |
| C | 5 | −1.0 | 12 | 0.0 | | |
| D | 2 | −2.5 | 8 | −1.0 | | |
| E | 10 | +1.5 | 19 | +1.75 | | |
| F | 12 | +2.5 | 22 | +2.5 | | |

Mean$_X$ = 7, $s_x$ = 2
Mean$_Y$ = 12, $s_y$ = 4

---

*Interpretation of z-scores*    The z-score tells us how far a given raw score deviates from the mean of the reference distribution in standard deviation units. As is evident, z-scores can be positive or negative, depending on whether the score is located above or below the mean of the distribution. A *z-value* of +1.0 indicates that the student's raw score is located exactly one standard deviation above the mean of the distribution (see Student A's performance on X, and Student B's on Y). When the *z-score* is 0, as is the case with Student B on the X measure, the student's score score falls exactly on the mean of the distribution.

Keeping in mind that the means and standard deviations in the two distributions vary, one can make comparisons of performance on two different tests using a common z-score scale. Thus, we can say that Student B's performance on Test X is just about average ($z = 0$) relative to the rest of the group; however, the same student is placed one standard deviation above the mean in the Test Y distribution ($z = +1.0$). Student F's performance on both tests, on the other hand, places him two and a half standard deviation units above the mean of the X and Y distributions, respectively.

The z-scale is an equal-interval scale. A fact to remember is that *the shape* of the distribution remains *unchanged* after computation of z-scores; z-scores have a one-to-one, straight-line relationship with raw scores. If the original raw score distribution is skewed, the same shape will be replicated when we compute z-scores. Similarly, if the orginal distribution is normal, the z-scores will also retain that normal shape. This property becomes important when we use z-scores to derive percentile ranks, another measure of relative position.

## 10.9.2  *T*-Scores

The *T*-score, another standard score, is a linear transformation of the *z*-score. The *T*-score retains all the properties of the *z*-score but has the advantage of being free of negative values and decimals.

***Computing* T-*Scores***    The *T*-score is computed from a *z*-score using two constants, 10 and 50, incorporated in the formula as follows.

$$T = 10z + 50$$

If the *z* is +1.0, the *T* will thus be:

$$T = 10 (+1.0) + 50 = 60.$$

When the *z* is +2.5, the *T* will be:

$$T = 10 (+2.5) + 50 = 75.$$

---

**DEMONSTRATION  10.11**

**Mapping *z*- and *T*-Scores on a Common Scale**

The *z*- and *T*-scales can be mapped on a common scale, starting with a raw score distribution, as follows.

| X scale:<br>(Mean = 7, s = 2) | 1 | 3 | 5 | 7 | 9 | 11 | 13 | 15 | 17 |
|---|---|---|---|---|---|---|---|---|---|
| z-scale | −3.0 | 2.0 | −1.0 | 0.0 | +1.0 | +2.0 | +3.0 | +4.0 | +5.0 |
| T-scale | 20 | 30 | 40 | 50 | 60 | 70 | 80 | 90 | 100 |

---

The *T*-score scale is the preferred score for reports used by many standardized test-makers. Developers of tests like the SAT, GRE, and TOEFL use a modification of the *T*-scale. Standard scores are far more user-friendly in appearance than *z*-scores. Their interval properties allow straightforward interpretations of the units.

## 10.9.3  Percentile Ranks

The *z*-score is the basic building block for deriving a number of norm-referenced scores, including the *percentile rank*. We first encountered the concept of the percentile rank (PR) when dealing with ogives. The PR indicates the proportion of scores in a distribution that is surpassed by a paricular raw score (or *z*-score). Thus, if a raw score of 10 is located above 35% of the group tested, a student with a raw score of 10 would have a PR of 35.

---

**Key Concept**

- The percentile rank (PR) denotes the percent of individuals in the distribution who fall below a particular raw score or $z$-score.

---

The shape of the distribution, whether normal or non-normal, is particularly important in the determination of the PR. The shape of the distribution predicts the frequencies that particular scores on the scale will have. If we are dealing with an empirical distribution having a perfectly *normal* or *near-normal* shape, the percents of individuals who would fall below given $z$-values are predicted by the normal probability function. Recall that the relationship between $z$-units and percents of the area under the bell curve are mathematically specified in the normal distribution. We could use cumulative percent values in a normal curve (see Figure 10.5) to derive percentile ranks associated with particular $z$-values. When the distribution shape is non-normal, we would need to employ a formula that does not assume normality in the distribution of scores. Tables showing the relationship between given ranges of $z$-values and proportions of area under the normal distribution can be found in most introductory statistics textbooks. See Demonstration 10.12 and 10.13 next.

## DEMONSTRATION 10.12
### How to Determine Percentile Ranks from a Normal Curve Graph

| Student | $X$ | $z_x$ | PR | How derived |
|---------|-----|-------|-----|-------------|
| L | 9 | +1.0 | 84 | Read cumulative % below $z$-score in graph |
| M | 7 | 0.0 | 50 | |
| N | 5 | −1.0 | 16 | |

(Mean $= 7$, $s = 2$)

Assume that the scores of the six students above (L–N) were from a normal distribution.

Step 1    Convert raw scores to $z$-scores.

Step 2    Read the PR directly from the abscissa of the graph of a normal curve by obtaining the cumulative percent of scores lying below a $z$-score.

Example:    The cumulative percent of scores lying below a $z$ of $+1.0$ is 84%; hence, the PR of a person who obtains a $z$-score of $+1.0$ in a normal distribution is 84.

| $z$ | PR | |
|------|------|------|
| −3.0 | 0.1 | (rounded 0) |
| −2.0 | 2.3 | (rounded 2) |
| −1.0 | 15.9 | (rounded 16) |
| 0.0 | 50.0 | (rounded 50) |
| +1.0 | 84.1 | (rounded 84) |
| +2.0 | 97.7 | (rounded 98) |
| +3.0 | 99.9 | (rounded 100) |

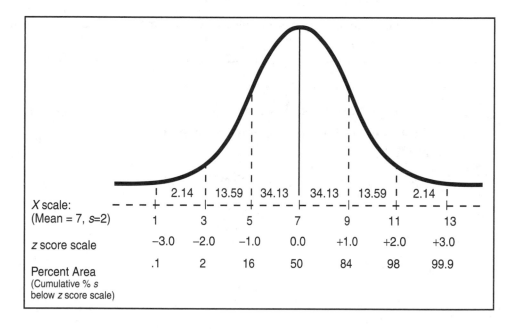

## Determining Percentile Ranks Irrespective of the Distribution Shape

With data from classroom or locally-administered assessments, we often obtain a *non-normal distribution* of scores (similar to the data set in Demonstration 10.1). In such a case, we would miscalculate the PR if we used a normal curve table/graph. To compute the PR, we use a formula that will first require us to organize the data in a simple or grouped frequency table. This method provides a more accurate percentile rank than the use of an ogive. It can be used for *both normal and non-normal* distributions. The formula is as follows:

$$PR = 100 \left[ \frac{\dfrac{f(X - \text{Lower limit of interval of } X)}{\text{interval size, } i} + \text{Cum} f_{\text{in interval below}}}{N} \right]$$

*(continued)*

# 10.12    Continued

where,

$X$ = raw score for which PR needs to be calculated

$f$ = frequency

$i$ = size of class or score interval (in a simple frequency distribution, this value is always 1)

Cum $f$ is cumulative frequency, and

$N$ is total number of cases.

Although the formula appears complicated on the surface, the substitutions can be easily made once the frequency table is set up.

---

## DEMONSTRATION 10.13

### Determining Percentile Ranks in a Non-Normal Distribution

| $X$ | $f$ | Cum $f$ | Cum % |
|-----|-----|---------|-------|
| 10 | 1 | 20 | 100 |
| 9 | 7 | 19 | 95 |
| 8 | 0 | 12 | 60 |
| 7 | 1 | 12 | 60 |
| 6 | 5 | 11 | 55 |
| 5 | 2 | 6 | 30 |
| 4 | 2 | 4 | 20 |
| 3 | 1 | 2 | 10 |
| 2 | 1 | 1 | 5 |
|  | $N = \overline{20}$ |  |  |

What is the PR for a raw score of 6?

$$PR = 100 \ [6 - 5.5) \div 1 \times (5) + (6)] \div 20$$
$$100 \ [.5/1 \times 5 + 6] \div 20$$
$$100 \times 8.5 \div 20 = 42.5$$

*Note:* Compare this result with the approximate PR of 55 at the upper limit of the same interval (6.5), derived using the ogive method (see Demonstration 10.9).

---

## 10.10    Correlation Coefficients and Their Applications

Two statistical concepts, *correlation* and *prediction,* can be applied to examine relationships among two or more variables. In this last section, we will consider mainly the concept of *correlation*. In education, correlations among variables are typically studied in populations of students, teachers, counselors, administrators, or parents and other clients. Scientists in virtually every field are interested in the degree to which different variables, say intelligence, *X,* and scholastic achievement, *Y,* relate to one another. Practitioners, also, often seek answers to similar correlational questions, such as:

- Is <u>student attendance</u> (<u>X</u>) related to <u>achievement</u> (<u>Y</u>)?
- Does <u>retention in early grades</u> (<u>X</u>) predict <u>dropout rates</u> of students (<u>Y</u>)?
- Is <u>time-spent doing homework</u> (<u>X</u>) associated with student <u>performance in school</u> (<u>Y</u>)?

Answers would become pertinent if a school district or institution was interested in formulating an attendance or homework policy. Elsewhere, this text has indicated that correlations are also used in psychometric research, particularly in evaluating the validity and reliability of scores representing constructs.

**Key Concept**

- Correlation coefficients are descriptive statistics that portray the manner in which two or more variables are associated.

To express how two variables are related in quantitative terms, one has to compute *correlation coefficients*. Correlation coefficients describe relationships in two ways. First, they tell us something about the *strength* or magnitude of the relationship, and second, they indicate the *direction* of the relationship between two or more variables. Although there is more than one type of correlation coefficient, they are all interpreted similarly. Common properties of all *correlation coefficients* are summarized in the box below.

## BOX **10.1**

## Common Properties of Correlation Coefficients

- All correlations utilize measurements on two or more variables made on the same group of individuals or objects.
- Correlation coefficients typically range in value from $-1.0$ to $+1.0$. Both these extremes reflect perfect relationships, one in the positive direction and the other in the negative direction. The middle value of 0 represents that there is no relationship between the variables concerned. (An exception is the phi coefficient—$\phi$—which ranges from 0 to $+1.0$).
- A positive correlation indicates that individuals with high values (scores) on one variable also tend to receive high values on the other, and vice versa. When the correlation is negative, those who receive high scores in one variable tend to obtain low scores on the other, and vice versa.
- The type of correlation coefficient that will apply in a given situation depends on the level of measurement of the variable scales (see Table 10.2).

**TABLE 10.2    Correlation Coefficients Using Two Variables**

| Correlation Coefficient | Symbol | Level of Measurement | |
|---|---|---|---|
| | | *Variable 1* | *Variable 2* |
| Pearson product moment correlation | $r$ | Interval or ratio | Interval or ratio |
| Spearman rank-order correlation | Rho or $r_S$ | Ordinal | Ordinal |
| Kendall's tau | $\tau$ | Ordinal | Ordinal |
| Point-biserial correlation | $r_{pb}$ | Nominal | Interval |
| Phi | $\phi$ | Nominal | Nominal |
| Contingency coefficient | $C$ | Nominal | Nominal |
| Tetrachoric | $r^t$ | Transformed nominal | Transformed nominal |
| Biserial | $r_{bis}$ | Interval | Transformed nominal |

When only two variables are correlated, the resulting relationship is called a *bivariate* correlation; and pairs of measurements on two constructs are used on the same individuals. If more than two variables are involved, the statistic is a *multiple correlation*. The aim of this section is to help build a conceptual basis for interpretation of correlational statistics in general, with details mainly on bivariate correlation coefficients.

Table 10.2 provides a summary of the major types of bivariate correlation coefficients and levels of scaling that are assumed for each variable. These are: Pearson's product-moment correlation, Spearman's rank order correlation, the point-biserial correlation, the phi coefficient, and the terachoric coefficient.

The computational procedure and interpretation of correlation coefficients is illustrated using the Pearson *product moment correlation, r,* as an example. "Pearson's *r*" is a widely used statistic in the educational measurement literature.

### 10.10.1    The Product Moment Correlation, *r*

Pearson's *r* indicates the degree to which the same individuals occupy the same relative position in distributions of two variables, in terms of their distance from the mean in standard deviation units. It is most appropriately used when both variables are measured on interval or ratio scales.

*Formula*    There are several algebraically equivalent methods for obtaining *r*. The "conceptual" formula for the Pearson's *r* for two variables, *X* and *Y*, is given by the *z-score method* for computing *r*.

$$r = \frac{\sum z_x z_y}{N} \text{ , where}$$

$z_x = (X - \bar{X})/s_x$, or the deviation of each raw score from the mean of *X*, expressed in standard deviation units of the *X* distribution (also called "*z*-scores for *X*"),

$zy = (Y - \bar{Y})/s_y$, or the deviation of each raw score from the mean of *Y*, expressed in standard deviation units of the *Y* distribution ("*z*-scores for *Y*"),

$z_x z_y$, the cross product of the $z$-scores for $X$ and $Y$

$(\Sigma\, z_x z_y)/N$ represents the sum of the cross products of $z$-scores divided by the number of individuals measured.

The corresponding "raw score" formula, which is a derivative of the $z$-score method, is as follows.

$$r = \frac{\Sigma XY - \dfrac{(\Sigma X)(\Sigma Y)}{N}}{\sqrt{\left[\Sigma X^2 - \dfrac{(\Sigma X)^2}{N}\right]\left[\Sigma Y^2 - \dfrac{(\Sigma Y)^2}{N}\right]}}$$

As is evident from the formulas and the calculations in the following demonstration data sets, the $z$-scores provide a method for assigning "ranks" to individuals within a distribution using its arithmetic mean and standard deviation. When the "ranks" or $z$-scores are in perfect agreement on both variables for every individual in the group, the computed $r$ value is 1.0.

As we previously noted, $z$-scores provide a common scale that have the *same meaning in distributions of different variables*. Take, for instance, student E in the demonstration data set. E has $z$-scores below $+1.0$ in both the $X$ and $Y$ distributions. The $z$ values indicate that his raw scores (10, 20) placed him one quarter to one half standard deviation above the mean of both the $X$ and $Y$ distributions, although each distribution has a different mean and standard deviation.

---

**DEMONSTRATION 10.14**

## Calculation of Pearson's *r*

Given: $\overline{X} = 9$, $s_x = 4$
$\overline{Y} = 16$, $s_y = 7$
$N = 8$

| People | X | $z_x$ *(Step 1)* | Y | $z_y$ *(Step 2)* | $z_x z_y$ *(Step 3)* |
|--------|---|------------------|---|------------------|----------------------|
| A | 2 | $-1.75$ | 4 | $-1.71$ | $+2.99$ |
| B | 4 | $-1.25$ | 8 | $-1.14$ | $+1.43$ |
| C | 6 | $-0.75$ | 10 | $-0.86$ | $+0.65$ |
| D | 8 | $-0.25$ | 18 | $+0.29$ | $-0.07$ |
| E | 10 | $+0.25$ | 20 | $+0.57$ | $+0.14$ |
| F | 12 | $+0.75$ | 18 | $+0.29$ | $+0.22$ |
| G | 14 | $+1.25$ | 8 | $-1.14$ | $-1.43$ |
| H | 16 | $+1.75$ | 28 | $+1.71$ | $+2.99$ |

$N = 8$                                                      $\Sigma\, z_x z_y = 6.92$ *(Step 4)*

$r = \dfrac{\Sigma z_x z_y}{N} = 6.92/8 = .865\ \checkmark$ *(Step 5)*

(continued)

## 10.14    Continued

**Steps in Computation of *r* with the mean deviation method**

Step 1    Compute z-scores for all the $X$ scores in the distribution using $z_x = (X - \overline{X})/s_x$.
In example, where $X = 2$, $z_x = (2 - 9)/4 = -1.75$

Step 2    Compute z-scores for all the $Y$ scores in the distribution using $z_y = (Y - \overline{Y})/s_y$.
In example, where $Y = 4$, $z_y = (4 - 16)/7 = -1.71$

Step 3    Set up a cross products column, $z_x z_y$, by multiplying $z_x$ values with $z_y$ values.
In example, where for student A, the $z_x = -1.75$ and $z_y = -1.71$, the $z_x z_y = (-1.75)(-1.71) = +2.99$

Step 4    Sum the values in the $z_x z_y$ column to obtain $\sum z_x z_y$.
In example, $[(+2.99) + (+1.43) + (.65) + (-.07) + (.14) + (.22) + (-1.43) + (2.99)] = 6.92$

Step 5    Solve using the formula: $r = \dfrac{\sum z_x z_y}{N}$
In example, $6.92/8 = .865$

---

### 10.10.2    Bivariate Scatterplots

Relationships between pairs of variables can also be depicted visually without the computations with the help of bivariate *scatterplots* (also called *scattergrams*). To construct a scatterplot, set up the *x*-axis with score intervals on the first variable ($X$), starting with 0 at the origin. Set up the *y*-axis in the same way for the second variable ($Y$). Then, plot the coordinate points of the two variables for each individual in the group. A scatterplot provides a visual description of both the strength and the direction of a relationship, as shown in Figure 10.8A–E.

Examine carefully the scatterplot for the data presented in Figure 10.8A. One could draw an ellipse around the plotted points and a diagonal line that might pass through the center of the ellipse. The narrower the ellipse, the more concentrated the points are towards the central line, and the stronger the correlation between the two variables. When the correlation has an absolute value of 1.0, all the points fall exactly on the straight line (Figure 10.8B).

The direction of the scatter suggests whether the relationship is positive or negative. When the points move upwards from left to right in a straight line, the relationship is linear and positive. The interpretation is that, in the group studied, as values on $X$ go up, values on $Y$ go up as well; when $X$ values go down, the $Y$ values are correspondingly low. This pattern remains consistent in all the individuals.

If we find that the points in a scatterplot move downwards from right to left, a negative relationship is indicated. Here, as values on $X$ go up, values on $Y$ go down. The reverse tendency now holds across all individuals measured (Figure 10.8C). When there is a random scatter of points that cannot be represented with a straight line in either direction, the correlation is 0 (Figure 10.8D).

Figure 10.8 A–E illustrates different forms of scatterplots which vary with respect to strength and direction. Note that a scatterplot will also reveal if the relationship is *curvilinear* (Figure 10.8E), instead of linear. A curvilinear relationship indicates that the relationship between the two variables is in the positive direction for a certain region of the scale, but changes suddenly to a negative one for the remaining part of the scale. The relationship between age ($X$) and physical strength ($Y$) would very likely yield a curvilinear relationship. Thus, as age increases physical strength increases in most individuals; however, after a certain age, as age increases, we tend to become physically weaker. We should keep in mind that Pearson's $r$ is not an appropriate statistic for assessing nonlinear relationships.

## 10.10.3   What Is a High Correlation Coefficient?

We have already discussed the strength, direction, and general interpretation of correlation coefficients such as $r$. Supposing the $r$ value of .82 represents the correlation between mathematics and science achievement (the $X$ and $Y$ variables) in a group of 8th graders. This tells us that, in the group of interest, as scores in mathematics go up, so do the scores in science. But how do we know if .82 is a low, moderate or a high correlation? Unfortunately, this is a question that cannot be answered in simple terms. Evaluations of correlations really require us to have a command of the existing literature on the variables and the relationships that can be expected in given populations. They are also affected by the units of analysis and the variable scales. Thus the following, *very general,* rules of thumb are provided with the caveat that you interpret the magnitude of correlation coefficients *with caution and in context.* The ranges can be applied irrespective of the sign that precedes them.

.80–1.0          High correlation
.40–.60          Moderate correlation
.20 and less     Low correlation

***Coefficient of Determination***   A further aid to interpreting $r$ is the *coefficient of determination,* $r^2$. While $r$ values cannot be interpreted directly as percentages, if we squared them, the corresponding $r^2$ is interpretable as the *percent of variance in X accounted for by the Y distribution* (also referred to as the percent of overlapping variance in $X$ and $Y$). As you see next, once converted to $r^2$, negative correlations are interpreted in the same way as positive correlations. The greater the $r^2$ value, the stronger the relationship.

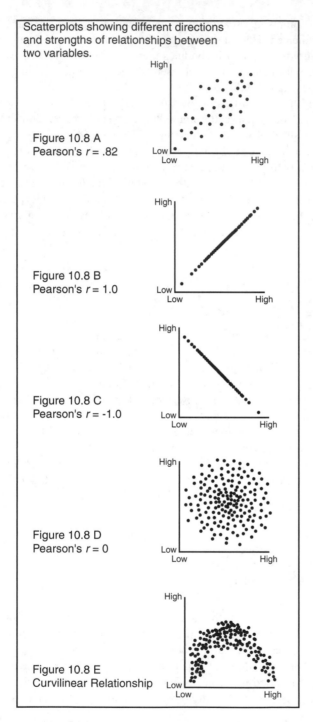

Scatterplots showing different directions and strengths of relationships between two variables.

Figure 10.8 A
Pearson's $r$ = .82

Figure 10.8 B
Pearson's $r$ = 1.0

Figure 10.8 C
Pearson's $r$ = -1.0

Figure 10.8 D
Pearson's $r$ = 0

Figure 10.8 E
Curvilinear Relationship

**FIGURE 10.8A–E   Scatterplots**   Scatterplots showing different directions and strengths of relationships between two variables.

**Interpreting the Coefficient of Determination**

| $r$ | $r^2$ | Interpretation |
|---|---|---|
| .82 | .67 | 67% of the variability in the $X$ distribution is explained by the $Y$ scores. |
| .50 | .25 | 25% of the variability in the $X$ distribution is explained by the $Y$ scores. |
| $-.22$ | .05 | About 5% of the variability in the $X$ distribution is explained by the $Y$ scores. |

## 10.10.4   Correlation and Causation

In interpreting bivariate $r$ values, we should also remind ourselves that correlation is not the same as causation. For example, if the salary earned by sports coaches (Variable $A$) is found to be highly and positively correlated with the performance of players (Variable $B$), we cannot automatically conclude that higher paid coaches are the cause for better players or that better performing players are the cause for higher paid coaches. Often there are other variables that influence both variables in the same direction, causing them to correlate. It could be that the more experienced or qualified coaches (Variable $C$) earn higher salaries (Variable $A$), and also prepare better players (Variable $B$). Thus, with increases in experience or qualifications, salaries of sports coaches increase. Similarly, as coaches become more experienced or qualified, their ability to train players also improves. The positive correlation coefficient between variables $A$ and $B$ is not because one causes the other, but by the influence of the third variable, Variable $C$, on both these constructs.

Alternately, we might have a situation where a variable $X$ causes $Y$ (practice in an area results in proficiency), and $Y$ causes $Z$ (proficiency causes us to make better decisions in that area), but a correlation between $X$ and $Z$ does not mean that one is the cause of the other (practice by itself is not a direct cause for better decision-making). There may also be situations where multiple variables together cause two variables to correlate. The bivariate correlation coefficient will not shed any light on the influence of the other factors or reveal any information on which of the causal explanations is most plausible.

Correlation coefficients simply tell us that the variables are associated, but they are mute as to the explanations of causality. Direct causal inferences, thus, are not warranted based solely on correlational statistics, unless there are additional experimental or statistical controls built into the design of the research.

## 10.10.5    Nonlinear Relationships, Range Restriction, and Statistical Significance of *r* Values

The calculation of Pearson's *r* assumes that we have a linear or straight-line relationship between the two variables. Pearson's *r* works well when the distributions of both variables are unimodal and relatively symmetrical, although not necessarily normal. The statistic does not detect nonlinear relationships well at all. This is a limitation that we should bear in mind when we interpret *r* and related correlational statistics.

Secondly, *r* also assumes that the distributions of both variables have an adequate spread. If the range on either variable is restricted, the statistic will underestimate the actual relationship between the two variables. Thus, prior to computing *r* in a sample, we should ensure that we have the variability that can be reasonably expected in the population on the variables of interest.

Finally, when we read published reports on *r,* we might encounter information such as the following.

$$r_{XY} = .38, p < .05$$

The "$p < .05$." refers to the *statistical significance* of the *r* value obtained ($r_{XY} = .38$). The *X* and *Y* measurements were made in a sample drawn from a larger population. The *p* is an attempt to answer the question: What are the chances that the obtained value of $r = .38$ was caused by *sampling error only* and not a true relationship between *X* and *Y* in the population? The statistical significance results are obtained by performing a test of the *null hypothesis,* a hypothesis of no relationship between the variables in the population. The *p* stands for the "probability that, given the size of the *r* in the sample studied, the population *r* is 0 for *X* and *Y*." If, following an appropriate hypothesis test, the *p* is found to be equal to or less than 5% (.05), most researchers would consider the result to be "statistically significant" (i.e., not caused by sampling error).

The *p* has nothing to do with the *magnitude* of *r* or $r^2$. It might be possible to have an $r_{XY}$ of .14 associated with a $p < .01$, making it a statistically significant result. Literally, such a finding would mean that the chances of the population correlation being 0 was found to be less than 1%. However, the $r_{XY}$ of .14 translates to $r^2_{XY}$ of .02, suggesting a very small amount of overlap in the variables. Thus, even if the relationship might be statistically significant (i.e., hold true in the larger population), the practical significance of the size of the correlation might be questionable!

## 10.10.6    Related Statistics Used in Psychometric Research

Two terms that are related to correlation will be introduced to you in this section because they are used extensively in empirical validation studies examining predictive validity or the internal structure of measured constructs. Empirical estimation of validity is discussed in greater detail in Chapter 13. The concepts introduced here are *regression* and *factor analysis.*

*Regression analysis* enables us to make use of an observed correlation between two (or more) variables, usually represented by a linear equation, for the purposes of making predictions. An understanding of regression is facilitated by thinking of a two-variable relationship represented with a scatterplot. Suppose we know that college GPA (Variable *A*) and scores on the *Scholastic Assessment Test* (SAT, Variable *B*)) have a correlation coefficient of .50, can we predict a person's future GPA if we knew his/her SAT score, starting with a scatterplot of the two variable distributions? Regression analysis attempts to derive a straight "line of best fit" that represents the scatter between the two variables. The origin (where the line starts) and slope (the steepness of that line) are then mathematically represented in a linear equation, which we can then use to make predictions of one variable from the other. The variable in the horizontal axis is called the *predictor,* the variable to be predicted is called the *criterion*. Regression analysis is often reported as a part of predictive or criterion-related validity studies on tests such as the SAT.

*Factor analyses* are multivariate correlational techniques useful in checking the internal structure of data generated by assessment tools. Studies of internal structure are relevant for construct validation. Although the details of mathematical procedures for fac-

## Computer Resources

There are many easy-to-use software packages that will help you compute the statistics described in this chapter. Some people simply enter formulas into a basic spreadsheet program (such as Microsoft Excel) to get the statistics or graphs they want. Here are some other resources that you can investigate.

Statistical Package for the Social Sciences (SPSS)
- for Windows
- for MacIntosh

SPSS Inc.
444 N. Michigan Ave.
Chicago, Illinois 60611
(312) 329-2400

Assessment Systems Corporation for software on:
- Item and test analysis (classical methods)
- Scale and survey analysis
- Analysis of test structure

Assessment Systems Corporation
2233 University Avenue
St. Paul, MN 55114
(612) 647-9220

tor analysis are beyond the scope of this book, as consumers of technical information on tests and assessments, practitioners should be aware of the purposes for conducting factor analysis and when such information is useful.

Suppose we design an assessment intended to measure two underlying constructs: arithmetic operations and geometry knowledge. How can we confirm that the arithmetic items on our assessment call for a *separate* ability in students than the geometry items? Factor analysis is a procedure that we can use to validate the constructs underlying a test (called dimensions). Factor analysis usually starts with a table called a *correlation matrix* (or *covariance matrix*) built with item-level responses made by a group of individuals. The matrix includes correlations of responses to every item with that of others. We use factor analysis to check if the variations and covariations in response distributions to individual items can be explained by one or more mathematically derived dimensions, called *factors* or *latent factors*. There are many different ways to factor-analyze a correlation or covariance matrix, and each might yield a different result. Selection of the factor analytic method must be done judiciously by researchers.

## Summary

Chapter 10 dealt with selected descriptive statistics that can be used in various decision-making contexts or in examining psychometric properties of scores from various assessment tools. Data on constructs we measure can be generated through four measurement scales: nominal, ordinal, interval and ratio. Variables we measure with assessment tools can be distributed in a continuous or discrete form. Before we begin data analysis, we should let the level of scaling and the variable's distribution properties guide our decisions on analytic procedures. For achievement and attitudinal measures, we usually assume continuous, equal-interval scale properties.

Organization of the data set in appropriate ways helps in the computation of various statistics, while simultaneously giving information on the group. The chapter illustrated three methods for organizing data:

- Rank order distributions
- Simple (ungrouped) frequency distributions
- Grouped frequency distributions

Of these, the most useful arrangement was the simple frequency distribution.

Distributions of scores are evaluated with respect to their central tendency and variability. Three measures of central tendency discussed in Chapter 10 were the mean, median, and mode. Two measures of dispersion treated were range and standard deviation. Individually, the different procedures have advantages and disadvantages in particular situations. They should therefore be chosen with the problem context in mind.

Shapes of distributions can be described in terms of their variability, symmetry, modality, skewness, and kurtosis. Graphing of frequency distributions facilitates visual interpretation of group performance. The chapter demonstrated three procedures for plotting frequency distributions: frequency polygon, histogram and the ogive. The properties of the normal distribution were presented with applications in deriving percentile ranks.

Measures of relative position, such as standard scores and percentile ranks, provide a means for "ranking" individuals in a given group. The computation and interpretation of percentile ranks in normal and non-normal distributions vary.

To determine the extent to which two variables are related, we compute correlation coefficients. There is more than one type of correlation coefficient, but they have common properties and are interpreted similarly. Pearson's $r$ was given special attention in Chapter 10. Relationships between pairs of variables can be depicted with bivariate scatterplots. As an aid to interpret the $r$, the coefficient of determination, $r^2$, was introduced. Once converted to $r^2$, negative correlations are interpreted in the same way as positive correlations. The greater the $r^2$ value, the stronger the relationship. The chapter concluded by making mention of regression and factor analysis as correlational techniques that are frequently used in empirical validation research.

# QUESTIONS FOR CLASS DISCUSSION

1. In a corporation with four members, the following distribution of income was observed. Which measure of central tendency, mean, median, or mode, is more suitable for such a distribution?

   |  | $\underline{X}$ |
   |---|---|
   | CEO | $ 250,000 |
   | Manager | $ 40,000 |
   | Employee 1 | $ 30,000 |
   | Employee 2 | $ 20,000 |

   1. What statistical descriptor would be suited to describe the CEO's salary?
   2. What type of data organization is this?
   3. Mean=?
   4. Mdn=?
   5. Mo=?

2. Set up the necessary columns in a frequency table to compute and interpret the following statistics in the two distributions given.

   Mean
   Median
   Mode
   Range
   Standard Deviation

| | BOYS | | | | GIRLS | | |
|---|---|---|---|---|---|---|---|
| X | f | Cum f | Cum % | X | f | Cum f | Cum % |
| 9 | 4 | | | 10 | 1 | | |
| 6 | 2 | | | 9 | 8 | | |
| 5 | 2 | | | 7 | 1 | | |
| 4 | 1 | | | 6 | 3 | | |
| 2 | 1 | | | 3 | 2 | | |
| | N=10 | | | | N=15 | | |

3. Review the data set in Item 2. To evaluate the utility of the *ogive* relative to the *frequency polygon* in comparing the performance of two groups, construct both types of graphs for the two distributions for boys and girls. When would you use one versus the other? Which graphing technique would give you better visual discrimination on the distributional patterns of the two groups? Round your computations to the hundredths place.

4. Examine the test scores for a class (Data Set 1) provided below. Set up a simple frequency table and calculate all the descriptive statistics you will need to answer the questions that follow.

    Data Set 1: 13, 21, 20, 17, 16, 15, 14, 20, 17, 16, 15, 20, 15, 15, 20, 20, 15, 13, 11, 10

    (a)  Find the mean, median, mode, range, and standard deviation of the above data set.
    (b)  Plot the scores in a frequency polygon. Describe the shape of the distribution with respect to its modalility, symmetry, skewness, kurtosis, and variability.
    (c)  Identify two differences between this distribution and a normal distribution.
    (d)  Suppose you obtained the given distribution following the administration of a pre-test. What do your descriptive statistics and the shape of the distribution tell you about your students? Identify two classroom decisions you would make with the results. Explain your answers.
    (e)  What would be the $z$-scores and percentile ranks for students who received scores of 13 and 20? What method did you use to calculate the PRs and why?

5. The following questions deal with measures of relative position in normalized distributions.
    (a)  A student obtained a score of 600 on the GRE verbal test. What is his percentile rank in a normalized distribution with a mean of 500 and a standard deviation of 100?
    (b)  The Wechsler Adult Intelligence Scale (WAIS) scores are normally distributed with a mean of 100 and a standard deviation of 16. John Doe and Jane Doe obtained the following WAIS scores. Find their percentile ranks. What percent of cases lie between John's and Jane's scores?

    John Doe = 116
    Jane Doe = 84

6. The following problems focus on correlations.
    (a)  What is the most likely correlation between the following two sets of scores? Interpret their correlation with respect to strength and direction.

| Student | $X$ | $Y$ |
|---------|-----|-----|
| A       | 16  | 25  |
| B       | 14  | 23  |
| C       | 18  | 21  |
| D       | 10  | 19  |
| E       | 11  | 17  |

(b) In a correlational study relating college grades to class attendance, a researcher found an $r = .78, p < .02$. Make a statement describing what she can conclude about the strength, direction, and statistical and practical significance of the correlation.

(c) A test-maker developed a multiple choice test for undergraduate students in economics. He gathered data to examine whether the test's overall scores and responses to individual items correlated. What kind of a correlation coefficient would he use? Explain your answer.

**NOTE:** Answers to problems are provided in the instructor's manual.

# 11 Decision-Making Applications in Different User Paths

## Overview

Data-based decision-making calls for extended applications of several of the statistical techniques introduced in Chapter 10. The aim of Chapter 11 is to illustrate selected applications in which practitioners in Paths 1–5 are typically required to be proficient.

Decisions with quantitative information from assessments might involve routine tasks of teachers, such as assigning report card marks, or more involved applications for a more diverse group of practitioners, such as preparing classroom, school, or program improvement plans, tracking achievement gains in students, evaluating needs for programs/services, or determining the effectiveness of programs/services. The specific applications in different decision-making paths may vary, and your role could cross from one user path to another. The Process Model provides a way of working when we design/select, validate and eventually, use assessments in particular contexts. The applications described in Chapter 11 would coincide with the areas marked as "Assessment Use" in Chapter 5's Figure 5.1. As outlined in the objectives, five major applications are the focus of this chapter.

## CHAPTER 11 OBJECTIVES

After studying this chapter and completing the structured exercises in the module, you should be able to:

1. Set standards on score continua for decisions on admissions, selection, assigning of marks, or determination of domain mastery (User Paths 1, 3, 5)

2. Describe philosophical and methodological issues related to assigning marks establishing marking schemes (User Path 1)

3. Assign marks in User Path 1 using measures of relative position (norm-referenced marking) or preset standards (criterion-referenced marking)

4. Conduct domain-referenced mastery analyses in User Path 1 with data from classroom or standardized assessments

5. Apply and evaluate methods for tracking changes over time on measured constructs for individuals and groups (User Paths 1–2)

6. Interpret and use aggregated data summaries for needs assessments, planning, or summative evaluations of programs/services (User Paths 2–4, 6)

# 11.1   Setting Standards

In educational measurement, the term "standard" is used in more than one way. In Chapters 6–8, we saw that it could refer to broadly stated learning outcomes in subject area curricula. In this section, we will use the term in another way—to refer to a *performance standard,* or a *cut score* on a continuum of scores obtained through the administration of a test or performance assessment. Standard-setting involves the processes we use to arrive at fair and defensible cut-scores when we need to differentiate between individuals who show different levels of performance on measured constructs. In other words, standard-setting is necessary when we want to make discriminatory decisions that are test-score dependent, such as identification of students with special needs, assigning of report card marks, identifying readiness for admission, or certifying teachers and other professionals for particular positions.

Here is an example. Suppose that you are asked to serve on a committee to select qualified students for admission into a rigorous educational program at your institution. How will you decide who is "qualified"? To assist with this task, you and the members of the committee are provided with student scores from a relevant assessment tool, either standardized or locally developed. In a real setting, the scores from a single test are not all that would be factored into the selection decision. However, test scores could, and usually do, serve as an important piece of information in such deliberations. Given this reality, how would you go about determining a cut-score or criterion that will dependably and meaningfully distinguish qualified students from those who are unqualified for the program? Standards for high stakes decisions cannot be made in an arbitrary fashion. It is thus helpful for us to have some knowledge of methods that have been tested out in the field of educational measurement, even if most were originally applied in large-scale testing programs.

This section presents a few, somewhat formal methods for arriving at standards that could facilitate a wide variety of criterion-referenced interpretations and decisions that teachers and practitioners might make. As will be evident from several citations in this section, most standard-setting procedures we see in practice were developed in the 1970–1980s, an era marked by widespread use of large-scale, minimum competency testing in the United States. Recent reviews on standard-setting procedures mention more current procedures applicable to performance assessments (Hambleton & Plake, 1995); however, such methods have been characterized by their authors as extensions of older methods, such as the Angoff procedure (Angoff, 1971).

In essence, thus, there are three or four methods that continue to dominate standard-setting practices today. They offer ideas that we could adapt fairly easily in classroom and local assessment applications. If you would like to study standard-setting procedures in more depth, consult Berk (1986b), Cizek (1996), Jaeger (1989), Shepard (1984), and Shepard, Glaser, Linn, & Bohrnstedt (1993).

### 11.1.1    What Is a "Standard" in Standard-Setting Applications?

The term "standard" refers to the "cut score" or passing criterion on a continuum of scores that we could employ to discriminate among different levels of proficiency on the construct measured. *Standard(s)* are usually set on a *domain score* scale generated from a single assessment or a *composite score* scale based on compiled assessment results from more than one domain or source.

We could set standards to reflect "minimum competency" on the domain of interest, similar to a C in a marking scheme. Alternately, we could establish standards to identify "excellent performance," comparable to an A in a marking scheme. The same standard-setting methods would generalize to situations where we need to separate examinees into two regions (e.g., mastery versus non-mastery states) or more than two regions of the distribution (minimal proficiency, moderate proficiency, high proficiency levels). The same procedures would also apply whether we are concerned with deriving cut scores for an entire achievement domain or smaller subdomains within some larger construct domain.

To begin the standard-setting process, we must first recognize that all standards are essentially driven by informed *judgments* about what we think is meritorious or acceptable performance by typical examinees in a given domain (Jaeger, 1989). If we set 70% correct as a passing standard on a structured-response test that we design, we have probably selected that score based on our knowledge of the domain, the items representative of that domain, and what we know typical examinees can reasonably do with the material assessed. We could then take the process a step further and empirically verify whether the cut score holds up from semester to semester in new and different groups of examinees. In other words, we can seek an answer to a question like, Does the cut score of 70% consistently separate the "masters" from the "non-masters" in independent classes of students who have the same opportunities to learn the material in the domain? Despite the use of data, professional judgment still plays the most important role in our selection of the dividing "score." Judgment is the main element employed in two of three formal approaches to standard-setting that we find in large-scale testing programs. Three categories of procedures offered in the standard-setting literature are (after Crocker & Algina, 1986):

- The overall item pool
- Content of individual items or groupings of items
- Distributions of typical examinees

---

**Key Concepts**

■ Standard-setting is necessary for decisions involving report card marking, admissions, selection, certification, recognition, and domain mastery.

■ Standard-setting is a procedure requiring judgment.

---

## 11.1.2    Standards Based on Judgment of the Overall Item Pool

In the first method for standard-setting, we ask expert judges to carefully review the overall domain, the content of all the assessment items or tasks in the pool, and answer questions on minimum or excellent levels of performance.

To set a *minimum competency standard* on structured-response tests, the question would be:

> What percent of the items would be answered correctly by students who are *minimally competent* in this domain of skills/knowledge?

With performance assessments, we would ask:

> What would be the rating given to a performance that is *minimally competent,* taking into consideration all the learning outcomes/competencies that will be demonstrated through the task? What would be the defining features of performance at the minimum competency level?

Similarly, to set a *standard of excellence* on structured-response tests, the question would be:

> What percent of the items would be answered correctly by students who have *excellent grasp* of the domain of skills/knowledge?

And on performance assessments, we would ask:

> What would be the rating given to a performance that is *excellent,* taking into consideration all the learning outcomes/competencies that will be demonstrated through the task? What would be the defining features of *excellent* performance?

The judgments of expert judges are then averaged to obtain the cut scores at the requisite levels.

It is obvious that the definition of an "expert judge" would greatly influence the outcomes of this approach to standard-setting. For high stakes testing applications, such as an assessment to certify high school graduates, experts have suggested that judges represent various constituencies of test users, such as teachers, students, parents, members of the larger community, members of the state legislature, and so forth. In a classroom or local context, judges could be certified teachers or specialists in a given content area and grade level. For example, to decide on a standard for admitting students into a high school fine arts program, one could have a panel of the qualified fine arts teachers in a school district who also had teaching experience at the high school level.

### 11.1.3   Standards Based on Individual Items or Classes of Items

*The Angoff and Modified-Angoff Procedures*   In the 1970s, several different methods were in use that essentially asked expert judges to project the proportion of minimally competent examinees who would be likely to answer each item correctly. For example, in the Angoff procedure (1971), judges were asked, What is the probability that an examinee with minimum competence in the domain will answer this item correctly? The sum of the projected proportions (probabilities) for a given judge yielded a minimum passing score. Then judges were asked to arrive at a consensus on the final passing score by considering the range of scores obtained from various judges.

The original Angoff procedure has been modified in practice, has been well researched, and has been pronounced to be functional in a variety of situations, including performance assessment applications (see Cizek, 1996). In the modified-Angoff procedure, the judges are typically provided with two opportunities to provide judgments—that is, at least two rounds of ratings are collected as a part of the deliberation process. Judges are also given data on the actual proportions of examinees who answer the items correctly or perform at particular levels on the rating scale after the first round of judgments is completed. The passing score is derived by averaging the item means across all judges, rather than by consensus. Usually, the second round of ratings is given more importance in deriving the cut score (computing the average), because by then the judges' ratings tend to agree with each other and show less variability.

*The Ebel and Modified-Ebel Procedure*   In a similar procedure, Ebel (1972) used a 3 × 4 table to classify items from a defined domain on their degree of difficulty (from Easy to Difficult), and their level of relevance (from Essential to Questionable), prior to setting minimum passing scores. Each cell in the table was weighted by the number of items it contained. As before, the judges were asked, What percent of the items in each cell would an examinee with minimum competence answer correctly? A minimum passing score would thus be identified by consensus among judges for each cell in the table. Then, the sum of the weighted percents across all cells would yield the minimum passing score for the test.

Ebel's "relevance" dimension has been criticized on the grounds that tests should not be designed to include items that are of questionable relevance. Others have pointed out that judges (who are usually practitioners) might have difficulty separating the "relevance" dimension from the "difficulty" dimension, because the two dimensions tend to be correlated. To combat these potential problems, this book presents a modified procedure similar to Ebel's method, that we could use starting from the Assessment Specifications that we develop in Phase II when using the Process Model for designing/selecting assessment tools (see Chapter 5).

The modified procedure utilizes information we routinely enter in a Table of Specifications when we design structured response tests for classroom or local assessment purposes, and is illustrated in Table 11.1. Assuming we employed the Process Model, we should have this step accomplished before we design/select the assessment tool. In the table of specifications shown, the items are sorted by *cognitive level* of a learning taxonomy, which replaces Ebel's dimension on difficulty; and by the *competency/content dimension,* corresponding to Ebel's dimension on relevance. Once the item groupings and weights are specified in a Table of Specifications, we would ask an expert team of teachers to identify the percent of items in each cell of the table that a minimally qualified examinee should answer correctly. For each cell, we could obtain a weighted percent of items that a minimally qualified examinee would be likely to answer. The sum of these weighted percents would yield the minimum passing score.

The computations are illustrated at the bottom of the Table 11.1. Based on teacher consensus, a minimum passing score on the test could be determined in two steps, by the formulas

**1.** Minimum passing score (Min $X$) =

Sum of (Projected percent of items to be answered correctly per cell × Number of items in the cell) across all the cells in a Table of Specifications.

**2.** Minimum score percent (Min %) = Min $X$ ÷ Total # of items (or maximum possible score).

The above procedure assumes that all items have a weighting of 1. In the event that items in some cells were weighted more (say, two or three times the weight of others), one would have to apply the weighting factor (e.g., × 1, × 2, or × 3) to the number of items in the cell. The formula would alter as follows.

**1.** Minimum Passing Score (Min $X$) =

Sum of (Projected percent of items to be answered correctly per cell × Number of items in the cell × weighting factor) across all the cells in a Table of Specifications.

The standard thus set can be validated and further refined by allowing participating judges to look at actual percents of examinees who answer particular items correctly in given cells of the table.

***Setting Benchmarks: Holistic Models for Performance Assessments***   A lot of the work on setting standards for performance assessments has been done with ratings from writing assessments, such as essay scores. Cut points from rating scales should correspond with "benchmark performances," or "anchor papers" at the selected levels of a rating scale (see Chapter 8). Judges are provided with sample items, the rating scale (rubric), and benchmark papers (sample answers or taped performances in behavior-based assessment). Once the judges are thoroughly familiar with the assessment tasks and the rubric, identi-

**TABLE 11.1   Adapting Ebel's Procedure for Standard-Setting to Classroom Assessments**

| | Cognitive Levels | | | |
| Domain | Factual Knowledge | Application | Higher-Order Thinking | Marginal Total |
| --- | --- | --- | --- | --- |
| **Competencies:** | | | | |
| State definitions. | **10<br>*(80%) | | | 10 |
| Use formulas. | | **8<br>*(60%) | | 8 |
| Evaluate Conclusions. | | | **6<br>*(30%) | 6 |
| **Marginal Total** | 10 | 8 | 6 | 24 |

Weight for each item = 1
Minimum Passing Score on Test = 10 (.80) + 8 (.60) + 6 (.30) = 8 + 4.8 + 1.8 = 14.6 out of 24
Minimum Percent Score = 61%

** No. of items allocated to each cell of Table of Specifications

* Percent of items that should be answered correctly by minimally competent examinees, as determined by consensus among expert teachers.

fying benchmark papers at a particular rating level is done through iterative discussions and consensus among expert judges. Following the review and discussions, judges then select the cut point on the scale that would depict the desired level of performance, such as "excellent" performance.

## 11.1.4   Standards Based on Empirical Distributions of Typical Examinees

A very pragmatic method for both setting cut scores and verifying whether they are realistic is to study actual distributions of scores. Superficially, the practice of using real distributions of typical examinees (or "normative data") to derive cut scores seems to contradict the very principle on which we base criterion-referenced assessment practices. In truth, we cannot escape the fact that when "expert judges" select cut scores, they do so based on their knowledge of real distributions of students taking similar assessment tasks/items. Comparing their subjectively proposed cut-scores against real data distributions helps us verify how consistent the expert judgments were compared to actual examinee performances. If we choose to employ these methods, we should ensure that the composition of the group used for standard-setting purposes closely mimics the population for which the standards are being set, on factors such as grade level, age, demographic characteristics, and exposure to a particular instructional program.

***Method 1: Contrasting Groups Method for Setting Standards*** In the contrasting groups procedure, overlapping frequency polygons of qualified and unqualified groups are used to derive an appropriate cut score at the point where the distributions intersect (see Figure 11.1). The contrasting group method can be attempted with groups that teachers can clearly identify as "masters" versus "non-masters." Alternatively, the same group of students could be used to derive the cut score, using "preinstruction" and "postinstruction" distributions of scores. In employing the one group, pretest–posttest design, we should allow an adequate time gap between the two testing occasions to control for possible practice effects and inflation of student scores associated with prior test exposure. Another design in standard-setting would involve the use of an *instructed group* (IG) to serve as the "masters" and an *uninstructed group* (UG) as the "non-masters." In this last design, we need to be careful that the predominant difference in the two groups is that one is formally trained on the instructional domain while the other is not. If the UG students have previous knowledge of the domain, it will bias our decision on the cut score.

D E M O N S T R A T I O N **11.1**

## Applying a Contrasting Groups Approach to Obtain Cut Scores

***Step 1*** Ask expert judges to identify "master" versus "non-master" groups of examinees in a population that they know well. For example, to set a standard for a 5th-grade writing assessment, ask teachers at that grade level to identify competent and incompetent writers in their classes.

***Step 2*** Administer the assessment for which the standard needs to be set to examinees in both competent and incompetent groups.

***Step 3*** Plot frequency polygons of the competent and incompetent groups on the same *x*-axis.

***Step 4*** Locate the region on the *X* score scale where the "master" and "non-master" distributions intersect to identify the cut score.

***Step 5*** If the judges used a subjective judgment method to initially set a pass score, compare that judgment-based score with the empirically derived cut score. If there is a major discrepancy, arrive at a reasonable compromise for the cut score by consulting judges.

K e y   C o n c e p t s

- The contrasting groups method uses overlapping frequency polygons of qualified and unqualified groups to set a cut score on an assessment score continuum.
- Three possible designs for the Contrasting Groups Method involve:

  1. Master versus non-master group distributions
  2. Preinstruction versus postinstruction distributions
  3. Instructed versus uninstructed group distributions

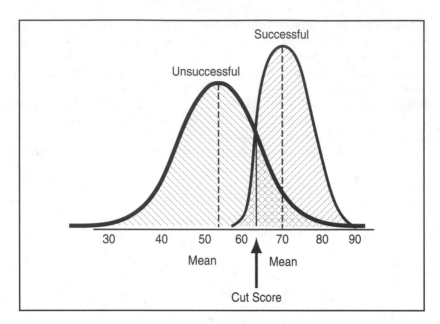

**FIGURE 11.1    Contrasting Group Method for Standard-Setting**

***Method 2: Ogive Method for Setting Standards***    In the second standard-setting procedure involving empirical distributions, we use scores corresponding to particular percentiles, say the 25th percentile, in an instructed group of students, to distinguish between
mastery and non-mastery states. For example, if a score of 100 on the domain score scale,
*X,* corresponds to the 25th percentile, choice of 100 as the passing standard would suggest
that in a typical distribution, 75% of examinees receiving similar instruction would be
likely to reach that cut score and pass. To facilitate application of this method, called the
*ogive method* here, the data collected after assessment administration should be arranged
in a cumulative frequency table accompanied with a plot of an ogive graph.

To bolster the ogive approach for standard-setting purposes, we might prefer to
examine two groups of students, instead of one. In one such design, both groups would be
administered the assessment for which the standard is to be set, at a given time. One group
would have received instruction (instructed group, IG), while the other would be an uninstructed group (UG). To ensure that it was *only the instruction* that had the intended effect,
the two groups would need to have comparable characteristics in other respects (age,
grade level, demographic background). Figure 11.2 illustrates how the ogive procedure
would work with UG and IG design.

As in all standard-setting applications, it is always helpful to have expert judges
review the ogive distributions to make the final decision on an appropriate cut score. For
example, in Figure 11.2, we see that the score of 130 (upper limit 130.5) corresponds to
the 50th percentile in the UG distribution. (Relatively, the score at the 50th percentile in
the IG distribution is 170.) After instruction, we see that 95% of a typical group would be
likely to surpass the score of 130. If knowledgable experts agree that 130 (or an interval

of 129.5–130.5) is a reasonable score that "masters" of the domain are likely to achieve, it can be selected as the passing standard or cut score.

The steps for standard-setting using the two-group (UG–IG) ogive approach are detailed in Demonstration 11.2. The ogive method for standard-setting could also employ designs involving master versus nonmaster group distributions or preinstruction versus postinstruction distributions.

---

DEMONSTRATION **11.2**

## Applying the Ogive Method to Obtain Cut Scores

*Step 1*    Set up two frequency tables with data from the two groups, for example, IG and UG, with $X$, $f$, Cum $f$ and Cum % columns, respectively.

*Step 2*    Using a common $X$ scale, plot ogives of the two groups next to each other. (Smooth the ogives if they are very irregular.)

*Step 3*    Compare the score points in the UG and IG distributions that correspond to particular percentiles, say, the 20th, 25th, and the 50th.

*Step 4*    Based on comparison of the two distributions, select a cut score at the *upper limit of an interval* that a vast majority of students in the IG are likely to reach.

*Step 5*    Let teachers or curriculum experts review and approve the empirically derived cut score.

---

**Key Concept**

■ In the ogive method for standard-setting, scores on the $X$ scale that correspond to cumulative percents of a typical examinee group are used to derive cut scores. Upper limits of score or class intervals are used as the dividing points.

### 11.1.5    Practical Recommendations

Of the methods described, teachers might like to use the modified-Ebel and the benchmark performance procedures for setting standards in the classroom. As data become available through test administrations, they could use the ogive method to check and refine their cut scores. Because standard-setting is driven largely by the values and judgments of participating judges, we need to attend to several issues when establishing procedures for deriving a cut score. To conclude this section, some recommendations are offered for practitioners at large (after Cizek, 1996).

**1.** *Training and background of participants:* As you have probably determined, participating judges should have a strong background in the targeted subject area, the examinee population, and how typical examinees are likely to be instructed on the subject for which the standard will be set. In addition, judges must grasp the details of the particular assess-

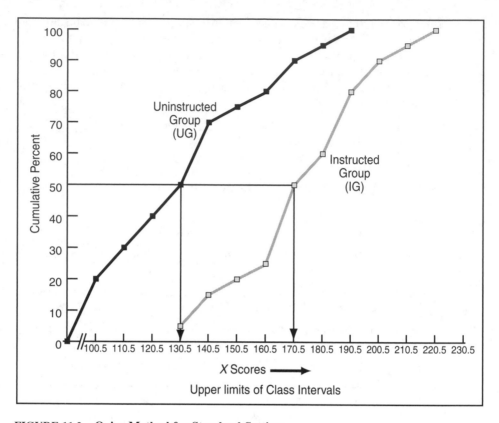

**FIGURE 11.2    Ogive Method for Standard Setting**

ment procedure, the domains tapped, how the scores are derived, the assessment purposes, and how high the stakes are for individual examinees. If the judges are not the assessment designers, such information is best provided through training sessions, where judges have an opportunity to discuss and gain a full understanding of all relevant issues.

There are costs associated with any formal participant-training sessions. While large-scale testing programs might factor such costs into their budgets, standards for local, school, or classroom assessments may be set in less formal meetings where professionals work through standard-setting issues and topics in small groups with a local leader.

**2.** *Extent of interactions among participants:* Discussions on subjective judgments can go on unendingly, or worse, become polarized. To keep the process manageable, a combined judgment-cum-empirical approach to standard-setting could be adopted. Once a procedure is selected, judges could be allowed a certain amount of discussion time to bring their values and opinions to the table. Then they could examine empirical data to finalize their decisions on cut scores. Decisions on the number of times the judges go through iterations of standard-setting and discussion should be guided by the stakes to be tied to the outcomes and the degree of disagreement that surfaces through the discussions.

Not much research exists on what works best; thus, practitioners must use their best judgment in given situations.

**3.** *Validating the standard set:* Once set, the cut score can be further validated, and readjusted, so that it yields consistent classifications of different categories of performance. The standard should work consistently in score distributions of new and different groups of examinees, including ethnic and gender groups. In the end, we should be able to supply evidence that the standard is consistent with the behaviors specified in the construct domain; that the participating judges worked with clear definitions of different levels of examinee performance on the domain, as represented in the scores; and that a systematic procedure was followed for setting the standard.

## 11.2   Report Card Marking

Standards become necessary when we assign *marks* or report card *grades*. (We will use the term "mark" to avoid confusion with grade levels in school.) *Marking* is a responsibility that all classroom instructors must bear, and thus is a pertinent topic for Users in Path 1. Marks also serve as a primary data source for many administrative, educational guidance, and admissions decisions (User Paths 2, 4, 5). In the second section of this chapter, we examine some alternative procedures for deriving report card marks.

In the typical application, marking requires teachers to compile results of multiple assessments to make summative evaluations of student performance. The term "composite score" will be used here to refer to a combined quantitative score based on data from more than one assessment. When a teacher chooses to emphasize one assessment more than another in arriving at a composite, we refer to it as a "weighted composite" score.

### 11.2.1   What Is Marking?

Marks are a means for communicating and reporting individual performance/progress on a range of academic, social, and/or physical domains to appropriate audiences over time. A predominant purpose of marking is to communicate levels of academic achievement to students and their parents/guardians in summary form. Often, marks are awarded over a period of time. Thus, we are used to thinking about quarterly marks, semester marks, annual marks, and so forth. Marks can also be cumulative over several years, as in high school or college Grade Point Averages (GPAs). Recently, we have seen experiments with portfolio-based reporting systems where the mark is based on a collection of work/behavior samples or systems that use one-on-one conferences between teachers and parents/children in conjunction with documentary evidence of achievement (see Arter & Spandel, 1992; Linn & Gronlund, 2000).

A variety of symbol systems are used for marking purposes. The most common one is the A, B, C, D, F system. However, Satisfactory/Unsatisfactory grades, Pass/Fail grades, checklists of performance, and narrative summaries of performance are also not uncommon.

> **Key Concepts**
>
> - Marking involves summative evaluations of student performance or progress.
> - Marks are means for communication of student performance or progress in defined curricular areas to particular audiences.
> - Marking involves the compilation of results of multiple assessments.
> - Marking involves standard-setting.

## 11.2.2   How Should We Assign Marks?

How we assign marks is far from a trivial matter. Marks involve high stakes decision-making by teachers because they affect individual students' futures, particularly in high school and college. In the United States, marks are a matter of public record. Procedures and belief systems that guide us in this task are often subject to controversy, and, thus, approaches we take must be defensible. Some writers have called for abolishing marks altogether (Kohn, 1994)! Others, such as Grant Wiggins (1989) have commented on problems that have plagued high school marking systems for years.

> . . . [T]he school transcript [has become] untrustworthy. An "A" in English means only that some adult thought the student's work was excellent. Compared to what or whom? As determined by what criteria? In reference to what subject area? The high school diploma by remaining tied to no standard other than credit accrual and seat time, provides no useful information about what students have studied and what they can actually do with what was studied (p. 42).

Marking practices tend to vary greatly from classroom to classroom, and from institution to institution (Loyd & Loyd, 1997). This is because procedures for assigning marks are heavily influenced by both teacher beliefs and institutional policies about what a mark should mean. Typically, marks are used for reporting progress in scholastic achievement. However, Canady and Hotchkiss (1989) cite cases that reflect the use of marks to reflect attendance rates, as punishment or motivational devices, for rewarding effort, or for controlling student behaviors.

To be in a position to choose the best procedure for allocating marks, it is important that we consider the most critical issues that affect how marks are derived and what they mean. The following discussion offers some recommendations for practice based on foundational concepts introduced in Chapters 1–5.

***Issue 1: What Attributes Should the Mark Reflect?***   Should the mark be based on achievement only? Should it also include effort, improvement, or aptitude? What about classroom conduct and behaviors such as paying attention, attendance, punctuality, and citizenship?

Ideally, a single mark should provide feedback on achievement in a well-defined subject or behavioral area only, rather than represent performance in a combination of several attributes. This has been the recommendation from the measurement community for years; however, it is a recommendation that is most often forgotten or pushed aside in educational practice. The instant we fully appreciate the challenges in designing construct-valid assessments in qualitatively different domains, we can recognize the fallacy of attempting to lump together performances in different areas with a single mark.

If a mark is assigned for a particular academic subject, such as science, it should reflect a student's academic achievement in science only, based on documentation of performance from the teacher's science assessments. That same mark should not reflect whether or not the student submitted science assignments on time, or whether he/she followed classroom rules while completing the exercises, or whether he/she appeared to "pay attention" and "work harder than others" in class. If particular behavioral areas, such as effort, punctuality, and responsibility, are valued components of the teacher's curriculum, separate marks should be allocated to these areas, based on separate assessment records.

Assignment of marks using concepts like "improvement" or "aptitude" becomes methodologically unwieldy when one acknowledges that individual students enter an educational program with varying degrees of prior knowledge and potential. Tracking student progress one by one can become a practical challenge for teachers, without even beginning to consider the difficulties surrounding the accurate assessment of aptitude or improvement levels. For all the previously listed reasons, the recommendation here is to have marks that focus on single attributes, and to keep marks in different curricular areas separated.

### Issue 2: What Kinds of Assessment Data Should Contribute to a Final Mark?

Should marks be based on results of formal tests/assessments only, or should they utilize homework and classwork exercises as well? Should marks utilize scores from traditional tests only, or can we include results of performance-based or portfolio assessments in the mark?

To address the second issue, this section will adopt the philosophy of the *outcome-driven model* for classroom instruction and assessment (see Chapter 2). The outcome-driven model tells us that if assessments are conducted early in the unit of instruction, as homework and classwork exercises often are, their results should appropriately be incorporated in *formative* decisions only. Results of homework/classwork can be legitimately used by teachers to improve their instruction to better fit the needs of students. They could reteach the material, reassign readings, rearrange the classroom and instructional groups, revise instructional goals and materials, and so forth, using data from preliminary assessments. Such data should not be simultaneously factored into a summative decision, such as a quarter or semester mark.

Premature summative decision-making leads to invalid and unfair conclusions about student achievement before teaching is properly completed. For example, if an early outline of a student's essay is scored and aggregated with the score on the finally submitted product, it might bring a student's overall score down drastically even when the final essay is an outstanding piece of work. All writers go through several revisions of initial outlines, which are often not representative of the quality of their final work. Students can get extremely discouraged and unmotivated by such actions, becoming fearful in taking the risks necessary in future learning conquests. Ideally, the outline should be assessed and formatively evaluated for providing feedback, while the final essay can be subjected to a summative evaluation for a report card mark.

Exercises used for homework and classwork are often informal assessment tools that may lead to erroneous conclusions about achievement. As teachers, we often gather information through informal observations, say, on a student's class participation, to guide our actions. Such procedures are usually adequate for a formative decision (such as assigning students to temporary instructional groups). If, however, we subsequently use the same information for making more critical summative decisions for individual students (as in marking), we would immediately face concerns surrounding the validity of that assessment usage. Did we adequately cover all the material relevant to the lesson prior to and during the "observation" exercise? Did every pupil get an opportunity to demonstrate his/her knowledge during the exercises? Were the conclusions about individual students warranted, given the relatively superficial information-gathering procedure? We must guard against inappropriate uses of assessment methods by separating formative applications of assessment results from summative ones. Once again, marks should communicate our summative judgments of a student's overall proficiency in particular domains.

The recommendation here is that first, teachers design assessments for summative purposes such as marking more formally and carefully than those for formative decisions; and second, that they administer the summative assessments at a time when they are fairly sure that all or most students have received adequate opportunities to learn the targeted goals/objectives.

Does it make a difference whether the assessments are traditional paper and pencil tests or performance assessments? If the assessments are appropriately matched to a teacher's instructional program and yield reasonably reliable results, it really does not matter if they are structured or open-ended, or whether they are written, performance-based, or portfolio-based assessments. The key is that they yield valid and reliable data that can be statistically or qualitatively summarized to generate the marks in a fair manner.

***Issue 3: How Many Assessments Should Contribute to a Mark? How Should the Different Assessments Be Weighted in the Mark?***    The total number of assessments on which teachers choose to base their marks, and the weights allocated to different assessments, are entirely matters of professional judgment. Depending on the disciplines and developmental level of students, teachers may use a variety of data sources for marking—from quizzes, midterm tests, and final examinations, to reports, papers, products, and live performances.

Once the domain for an instructional program is defined, there should be some logical correspondence between our instructional emphases and the weights we assign to particular assessments included within the marking system. Configurations can vary greatly from teacher to teacher. Some teachers might decide to have three unit tests and one paper, all weighted equally; others might choose to have four products in a portfolio, where the last two products carry twice the weight of the first two. To encourage and motivate students towards higher levels of achievement, our weighting plan should be communicated to students in a timely manner.

***Issue 4: Should the Standards Used in the Marking System Be Derived with Norm-Referenced or Criterion-Referenced Methods?***    Marking involves the use of standards. Should we compare students to one another in assigning the marks, or should we use a system that uses previously set performance criteria for assigning the A, B, C, D or F marks (or whatever symbol system that is in use)?

Table 11.2 provides examples of a norm-referenced and a criterion-referenced marking system. Other writers (Terwilliger, 1989) have offered systems that combine a norm- and criterion-referenced approach.

The decision on norm-referencing versus criterion-referencing will inevitably be guided by a teacher's values about what the marks should mean. Marks in a norm-referenced system will signify where students stand in relation to one another, irrespective of their level of domain mastery. Choice of a relative system of marking suggests that the teacher places less value in communicating information relevant to how well a student mastered the domain. This approach is often used when large numbers of students are served in an educational program, as in a college freshman class, and the marks serve to weed out the better-performing students from the weaker ones. "Curving the grades" is an example of a norm-referenced marking scheme, which pays little attention to the actual proficiency levels of students in the curricular area. In the norm-referenced system, irrespective of whether the composite score distribution is on the upper or lower end of the scale, the top 20% of the students, for example, would always receive an A mark.

Where the main function of an educational program is to enhance student achievement, marks should be viewed as devices for providing feedback on important learning outcomes in the achievement domain. Here, the criterion-referenced model would appear to be a better fit. When an educational program and its marking system emphasizes "what students can do with what was studied" (Wiggins, 1989, p. 42) and sets standards of performance tied to subject-area domains, it is founded on a criterion-referenced philosophy.

The criterion-referenced marking approach places some burdens on the teacher, however. A properly designed criterion-based marking system would do at least two things—it would:

1. Differentiate levels of proficiency with defensible criteria to distinguish As from Bs, and Bs from Cs and so forth, with direct reference to a well-defined domain of knowledge/skills.
2. Use domain-referenced assessments that call for students to meet specific performance requirements (e.g., a score of 90% or more to obtain an A), at each level of the marking scheme.

---

**Key Concepts**

Three questions to answer prior to selecting and applying a marking system are:
- What construct(s) will be incorporated in the mark?
- How many assessments will be used for marking and how much weight will each carry?
- Will the standards for the marking system be derived using norm-referenced or criterion-referenced methods?

**TABLE 11.2   Examples of Norm-Referenced and Criterion-Referenced Marking Schemes**

| Marking System | Characteristic | Composite Score Ranges |
|---|---|---|
| Norm-Referenced Marks | Marks are based on where individual students' summary scores are placed compared to the score distribution of the class or grade level. | Norm-Referenced<br>A = top 20% of distribution<br>B = next 20% of distribution<br>C = middle 20% of distribution<br>D = next 20% of distribution<br>F = bottom 20% of distribution |
| Criterion-Referenced Marks | Marks are based on preset summary score ranges that correspond to As, Bs, Cs, etc. | Criterion-Referenced<br>90–100% = A<br>80–89%  = B<br>70–79%  = C<br>60–69%  = D<br><60%    = F |

### 11.2.3   Methods for Combining Assessment Results to Assign Marks

Once the philosophical issues are sorted out in your mind, you will be ready to implement a procedure to combine assessment results to assign marks. There are a number of ways to combine data from assessments to assign report card marks. Three quantitative procedures are described next; two reflect a norm-referenced approach, while one is criterion-referenced.

*System 1: Assigning Norm-Referenced Marks Using* **T-*Scores***   One method for deriving marks is based on $T$-scores. Here, marks are assigned by obtaining a weighted, *composite T-score* across all the assessment scores that a teacher decides to use in the particular semester or quarter. Recall from Chapter 10 that $T$-scores are derived from $z$-scores, with the mean of a distribution fixed at 50 and the standard deviation set at 10. Like $z$-scores, $T$-scores indicate how far a particular student's score deviates from the mean of a distribution in standard deviation units ($s$, or $\sigma$). In a classroom context, the reference distribution consists of students enrolled in a particular teacher's class.

Examine the hypothetical data set given below for one student, Ann, and her class.

Exam: Mean   = 17, $s$ = 2.45   (Maximum possible score 20) Ann's score = 13
Speech: Mean = 12.2, $s$ = 2.48 (Maximum possible score = 15) Ann's score = 8
Paper: Mean   = 78, $s$ = 14.6   (Maximum possible score = 100) Ann's score = 53

All students in the same class would have data from the three teacher-administered assessments shown above. To begin the marking process, a teacher must first make a decision on how to weight each separate assessment in the mark. For example, both the examination and speech could each count for 25% of the mark (weight = .25), and the paper/report could be given a weight of 50% (weight = .50). Next, the teacher should decide on *standards,* or the ranges of *T*-scores that would correspond with different marking categories. A normal distribution would have *T*-scores ranging from 20 to 80 corresponding to +3.0 to −3.0 *z*-units. However, we cannot make the assumption that classroom distributions will have a normal shape or a limited range of *T*-values. Thus, a teacher might decide on a more open system with the following ranges.

**Standards for a T-Score Based Marking System:**

| *Composite T- Score Ranges* | *Mark* |
| --- | --- |
| 60 and above | A |
| 50–59 | B |
| 40–49 | C |
| 30–39 | D |
| 29 and below | F |

To interpret the *T*-score mark, the criterion for obtaining an A is that a student is placed at or above one standard deviation above the mean of the class' distribution of Composite *T*-scores across all the assessments conducted in a given marking period. An F is given to students who were placed two standard deviations or more below the mean. The steps in computing marks with *T*-scores follow in Demonstration 11.3, using Ann's data.

*System 2: Assigning Norm-Referenced Marks Using the Ogive Method*   An alternate way to assign marks using a norm-referenced approach is shown in Figure 11.3 and uses the *ogive*. The ogive method of marking would use the cumulative frequency distribution of weighted composite scores from assessments that an instructor selects. As before, we would have to start the marking process with a prespecified set of standards for the marking scheme that are distribution-dependent, and hence norm-referenced. In Table 11.2 we see a norm-referenced set of composite scores where an A is defined as the top 20% of a distribution, a B is the next 20% of the scores, and so on. Figure 11.3 presents a hypothetical ogive constructed with a large sample of scores based on the norm-referenced grading criteria in Table 11.2, where the top 20% of the distribution (cum % of 80 and above) has scores of 50 and above; the next 20% (cum % of 60 to 80) has scores of about 45 to 50; and so on.

---

**Key Concepts**

■ The standards or cut-score ranges for marks are applied to the composite scores derived from multiple assessments conducted by the instructor.

■ *T*-score based marks are determined based on weighted, composite *T*-score ranges.

DEMONSTRATION **11.3**

## Steps in Computing the T-Score–Based Mark

*Step 1*   Calculate the mean and standard deviation for the distribution of scores on each assessment that will be used to derive a mark.

For example, the mean and standard deviations of the three assessments in the example are:

| | |
|---|---|
| Exam: | Mean = 17, $s$ = 2.45 |
| Speech: | Mean = 12.2, $s$ = 2.48 |
| Paper: | Mean = 78, $s$ = 14.6 |

*Step 2*   Determine the $T$-scores for each student on each separate assessment, using the formulas: $z = (X - \text{mean})/s$; $T = 10z + 50$.

For example, for Ann, the calculations will be:

|  |  | Ann's $T$-scores |
|---|---|---|
| Exam: | $z = (13 - 17)/2.45 = -1.63$ | $T = 10 (-1.63) + 50 = 33.7$ |
| Speech: | $z = (8 - 12.2)/2.48 = -1.69$ | $T = 10 (-1.69) + 50 = 33.1$ |
| Paper: | $z = (53 - 78)/14.6 = -1.69$ | $T = 10 (-1.7) + 50 = 32.9$ |

*Step 3*   Multiply each $T$ by the weight assigned to obtain a weighted $T$-score. Sum the weighted $T$-values for each student across all the assessments.

For example, Ann's weighted $T$-scores

| | |
|---|---|
| Exam: | 33.7 (.25) = 8.43 |
| Speech: | 33.1 (.25) = 8.28 |
| Paper: | 32.9 (.50) = 16.45 |
| Composite $T$ = | 33.16 |

*Step 4*   Apply the marking criteria to the score obtained and determine the marking category. For example, Ann's composite $T$ score is 33, which is in the D category in the marking scheme given.

| *Composite T-Score* | *Mark* |
|---|---|
| 60 and above | A |
| 50–59 | B |
| 40–49 | C |
| 30–39 | D ✓ |
| 29 and below | F |

The interpretation of Ann's performance across the 3 assessments would be as follows. Given the weights assigned, and the means and variabilities of each of the three distributions, Ann tends to be placed about $1\frac{1}{2}$ standard deviations below the average scores of her class' distributions (her absolute $z$-scores ranged from 1.63 to 1.69), giving her a D based on the marking system.

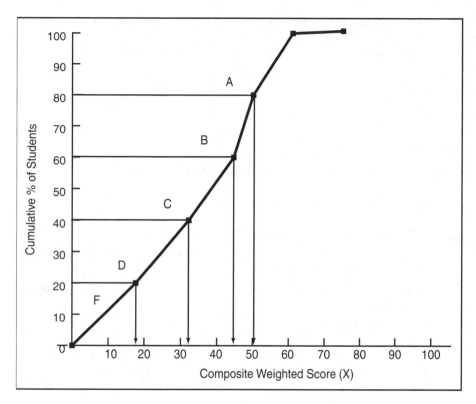

**FIGURE 11.3  Ogive-Based Method for Assigning Marks (Hypothetical Data)**

As was observed in the earlier discussion on standard-setting, the score ranges on the $X$ scale that correspond to A, B, C, D, and F will change as the shapes of different class distributions and maximum and minimum scores vary. Thus, in a low-performing class, "A" students will have a lower range of composite scores than "A students" in a class performing at a higher level. This can be viewed as a limitation of the ogive method of marking and standard-setting.

**Key Concept**

- The ogive-based mark is determined based on composite score ranges that correspond to particular percentile ranks in the cumulative frequency distribution of a group.

***System 3: Assigning Marks Using a Criterion-Referenced Marking Scheme***   If you subscribe to the domain-referenced philosophy of classroom instruction and assessment, you would probably prefer a criterion-based scheme for assigning marks (see Table 11.2). In this method, we use preset ranges of the Composite % Score to determine the marks.

The difference in System 3 is that the ranges for the marks would be set *without considering how the composite scores were distributed*. The computational steps for criterion-referenced marks are summarized in Demonstration 11.4.

---

DEMONSTRATION **11.4**

## Steps in the Criterion-Referenced Marking Process

*Step 1*   To standardize the scale from 0–100, calculate % scores for each student on each assessment.
For example, if Ann has 13 of 20 points, she gets $13/20 \times 100 = 65\%$ on the exam.

*Step 2*   Next, multiply each % score with the weight assigned to the assignment.
E.g., if the weight is .25, Ann's weighted score on the exam is: $65 (.25) = 16.25$.

*Step 3*   Create a sum of the weighted % scores by adding each student's weighted % scores from all the assessments.
Hence, the sum of weighted % = (wt.) (test 1%) + (wt.) (test 2%) + (wt.) (test 3%), etc.
For Ann, the sum of weighted % is $16.25 + 13.33 + 26.5 = 56.08$.

*Step 4*   Apply the criterion-referenced marking scheme to assign marks to students. For example, using the scheme in Table 11.2, Ann would receive an F. Interpret the marks according to the marking scheme.

For Ann: Using the marking criteria based on summed weighted percent scores, Ann receives an F or failing grade. Although Ann received a D in the first exam (65%), its weight of only 25% in the combined mark does not influence the weighted sum enough to bring her overall grade up from an F to a D.

---

*A Comparison of the Marking Results in System 1 and System 3*   To compare the merits and demerits of a norm-referenced and a criterion-referenced marking procedure, examine the results of System 1, using the composite *T*-score, versus System 3, using a composite percent on the five students below (Demonstration 11.5).

We see discrepant outcomes in Systems 1 and 3 for Henry and Ann. Factoring in the assigned weights, Henry gets a score of 94% across all three assignments, clearly an A in System 3. Assuming that the assessments were tightly designed to allow for valid domain-referenced interpretations, his mastery of the domain places him in the same category as Ola. Norm-referencing with System 1, unfortunately, hurts Henry's mark. Relative to the rest of the group, his very high score places him just below the *T*-score criterion of 60, set in System 1, giving him a B mark there.

In Ann's case, norm-referencing works to her advantage. Her composite percent of 56 is clearly below the 60% mastery criterion set by the teacher for a D in System 3, but in

| | Assessment Scores (1–3) | System 1: Norm-Referenced Composite $T$ | Mark | System 3: Criterion-Referenced Composite % | Mark |
|---|---|---|---|---|---|
| Ann | 3, 8, 53 | 33 | D | 56% | F |
| Henry | 19, 14, 94 | 59 | B | 94% | A |
| Ola | 20, 15, 91 | 60 | A | 96% | A |
| Mat | 16, 11, 74 | 46 | C | 75% | C |
| Nell | 17, 13, 78 | 51 | B | 82% | B |

*Note:* The numbers have been rounded. Computation procedures are given in Demonstrations 11.3–11.4.

comparison to the rest of the group in System 1, she is above a $T$ of 30 and thus gets a D. Earlier, we saw that if the reference group performs very poorly, the ogive method could result in awarding As to students with only 50% mastery of the domain (Figure 11.3).

### 11.2.4  Assigning Marks with Qualitative Data

The previous methods for compiling data across several assessments all assume that the data consist of quantitative scores. What if marking systems use assessments with narrative comments describing performance in particular areas? Rather little guidance is available in the literature on how to synthesize large amounts of qualitative data for marking purposes. The recommendation here is to employ a thematic analysis similar to the procedures illustrated for compiling open-ended comments from surveys (see Chapter 9). We could summarize narrative comments that teachers make over time by extracting the major themes that surface with the highest frequency in different areas for individuals. Narrative reporting is common in early childhood or special education programs that emphasize individualized growth and development.

### 11.2.5  Choosing a Marking System

Most marking systems can be classified as either criterion-referenced or norm-referenced in their orientation, including those that depend on qualitative data, such as student- or parent-conference records or narrative reporting. Occasionally, you may find a system that is a combination of both. (Some standardized test-makers provide reports on test performance with percentile ranks and percentage of items answered correctly by skill/topic.)

Which way should you go? The school district or institution in which you work will very likely provide some guidelines for assigning marks. Start by evaluating their policy recommendations and how well they fit with your own beliefs about what marks should represent. Generally, individual instructors have a considerable degree of "wiggle room" within the policy frameworks that institutions provide. Accuracy, fairness, objectivity, and consistency are principles that we apply to design/select assessments; the same principles should carry over when we use assessment results to develop report card statements. Loyd and Loyd (1997) suggest that we use the following four principles in our marking and reporting practices (pp. 482–484).

> *Principle 1*    Marking systems should be clear and understandable to users and stakeholders.
>
> *Principle 2*    Marking systems should be communicated to all stakeholders, students, parents, and other interested users.
>
> *Principle 3*    Marking systems should be fair to all students irrespective of gender, class, race, or socioeconomic status.
>
> *Principle 4*    Marking systems should support, enhance, and inform the instructional program.

We must recognize that our marking schemes and methods will very likely be influenced by our personal values and belief systems, quite apart from the underlying principles of measurement that this text has attempted to communicate. Value conflicts that you face in making decisions on marks must necessarily be resolved in your own work situations, in consultation with colleagues and superiors, with attention to the particular students you serve. In concluding this section, this source of possible conflict must be acknowledged.

## 11.3    Domain-Referenced Mastery Analysis

While marking is essentially a summative evaluation of individual performance based on several assessments over a period of time, *domain-referenced analysis* is geared towards both formative and summative decision-making using results of assessments at a single point in time. These methods, also called *criterion-referenced, objective-referenced,* or *skill-based analysis,* emphasize the use of assessment data to diagnose specific strengths and weaknesses of students at particular junctures of their programs. In the current educational environment that stresses standards-driven curricula and success for all, domain-referenced analysis provides instructors with the tools to evaluate the effectiveness of their instruction and to identify specific instructional needs for different students.

The prerequisites for conducting a domain-referenced analysis are threefold.

- First, the achievement domain for which we wish to make interpretations must be clearly differentiated by topic/skill area, so that it provides a framework for designing or selecting assessment tools to support a domain-referenced analysis. If one starts the assessment design/selection process with a well-specified domain of targeted learning outcomes, this condition should be automatically satisfied (see Chapters 5–8).
- Second, the linkage between particular topics, skills, or competency areas in the domain and particular assessment items/tasks must be clear, with the item/tasks yielding scores that describe how student performance varies in the different topic/skill areas.
- Finally, the teacher must set standards or criteria in the different topic/skill areas to allow for interpretation of mastery.

Given that the above three conditions are met during the *assessment development* phases, a domain-referenced analysis can be done with data from either classroom or standardized achievement tests, or with data from multiple choice or performance assessments.

Performing domain-referenced analysis does not demand any special mathematical skills beyond the aggregation or summarizing of student responses to items or ratings linked to particular learning outcomes. Domain-referenced analysis can be conducted at the individual, classroom, or program levels, and is likely to be of primary interest to Users in Paths 1 and 2. The motivation for conducting a domain-referenced analysis would be to make the types of decisons listed in the next box.

---

**Decisions Based on a Domain-Referenced Analysis**

| Type of Decision | Questions Answered | Time of Decision |
|---|---|---|
| *1. Formative Decision* | Can the assessment results tell me if students are achieving differently in different areas of the domain? If so, how can I tailor my instruction to help all students master the domain more evenly? | Before beginning or in the middle of a unit |
| *2. Formative Decision* | Can the results help me provide targeted feedback and coaching to individual students who are lagging behind in particular areas of the achievement domain? | In the beginning or middle of a unit |
| *3. Summative Decision* | How many students have demonstrated mastery of the domain and subdomains? Was the instruction effective? | At the end of a unit |

---

Key Concepts

■ Domain-referenced analysis is a criterion-referenced analysis that uses assessment data to diagnose specific strengths and weaknesses of students at particular junctures of their programs or to determine mastery.

## 11.3.1    A Domain-Referenced Analysis with Data from a Multiple Choice Test

Let us first examine two applications of a domain-referenced analysis which use data from a structured-response test. The hypothetical scores of a student, Maria, serve to illustrate the logic of a domain-referenced analysis discussed in Example 1 below.

*Example 1: An Individual Student Analysis Using a Structured-Response Assessment*    Suppose a 60-item structured-response assessment of Language Skills is constructed to target the domain shown below. The test has a multiple choice format, with 30 items focusing respectively on language mechanics and 30 on language expression skills. Within each of these subdomains, there are subsets of items tied to specific competency areas. In the area of language mechanics, for example, we see three competencies dealing with punctuation, capitalization, and grammar, with 7 items, 11 items, and 12 items respectively, in each.

The instructor has set passing standards on the overall assessment, for each subdomain as well as each competency area. To show mastery of the competency "Uses/recognizes correct punctuation," for instance, the student must at least get 5 of the 7 items right. Similarly, to demonstrate mastery of the "Uses/recognizes correct grammar" competency, the student is expected to get 7 of the 12 items right. On the overall Language Skills assessment, a student needs to get 50 of 60 items correct.

How does Maria perform based on a domain-referenced analysis? In the report, we see that Maria has a total score of 40 indicating that she answered 67% of the items correctly. This score fails to meet the teacher's mastery criterion for the overall domain, giving Maria an F. The breakdown of Maria's scores by subdomain, however, makes evident that this student's performance varies considerably across different competencies and in the two subdomains when compared against the teacher's mastery standards. Maria fails to show mastery of language mechanics skills (only 15 items correct out of 30, or 50% correct), but has met the teacher's mastery criterion in the language expression area (25 items correct out of 30, or 83% correct). Further, we see that Maria's weakest areas are punctuation and capitalization, but not grammar. Similarly, in the language expression subdomain, Maria needs some assistance in evaluating sentence correctness to meet her teacher's expectations, but appears to be doing satisfactorily in identifying effective sentences. In sum, Maria's domain-referenced profile provides the teacher with adequate diagnostic information to prepare an *individualized educational plan* to help her improve in language skills.

---

**Maria's Domain-Referenced Report from a Structured-Response Test**

| Assessment Domain | *No. of Items* | *Maria's Score/(Status)* | *Mastery Standard* (set by teacher) |
|---|---|---|---|
| Language Skills | 60 | 40 (F) | 50 correct |
| *Language Mechanics* | 30 | 15 (F) | 20 correct |
| Uses/recognizes correct capitalization | 7 | 2 (F) | 5 correct |
| Uses/recognizes correct punctuation. | 11 | 5 (F) | 8 correct |
| Uses/recognizes correct grammar. | 12 | *8 (P)* | 7 correct |
| *Language Expression* | 30 | *25 (P)* | 25 correct |
| Evaluates sentence correctness. | 20 | 15 (F) | 17 correct |
| Identifies effective sentences. | 10 | *10 (P)* | 8 correct |

F = Fails to meet teacher's mastery criterion
P = Passes or meets teacher's mastery criterion

*Example 2: A Group Analysis*   The same procedure can be extended to a class of, say, 10–30 students, using a response matrix generated from a structured-response test. Review the data in Table 11.3 to obtain an understanding of the process for groups.

The illustrative matrix presents the item by item responses given by 10 students, A–J. A dot indicates that a student selected the keyed (or correct) answer. The first five items on the test are linked to the subdomain on language mechanics, where the teacher expects students to obtain at least 60% correct for a demonstration of mastery. The next five items are designed to assess the second subdomain, language expression. The standard of mastery set for the second area is higher, with 80% correct. Using these criteria, we can place (P)ass and (F)ail symbols for each subdomain to identify the number and percent of students who meet the teacher's mastery criterion.

The data on the overall group allow some inferences on whether the teacher's instructional efforts have succeeded thus far. In Table 11.3, we see that 70% of the students met the teacher's passing standard in language mechanics, while only 50% appear to have met the standard in language expression. These differences in mastery levels suggest that the teacher might want to devote considerably more class instruction in the second subdomain, with some attention also to the first subdomain. Summative testing might be deferred until more students show proficiency in the targeted skills in classwork and homework exercises.

For individual students, the total scores based on all 10 items mask the diagnostic information that the domain-referenced analysis of the subdomains reveals. Students I and J, for instance, have identical total scores but completely different areas of strength (or

**TABLE 11.3   Domain-Referenced Mastery Analysis with Data from a 10-Item Structured-Response Test**

| Student | Total Score | | Subdomain Language Mechanics | | | | | Subdomain Language Expression | | | | |
|---|---|---|---|---|---|---|---|---|---|---|---|---|
| | | Correct Answers: | 2 | 3 | 4 | 1 | 3 | 2 | 3 | 2 | 3 | 1 |
| | | Items: | 1 | 2 | 3 | 4 | 5 | 6 | 7 | 8 | 9 | 10 |
| A | 9 | | • | 4 | • | 4 | • | • | • | • | • | • |
| B | 5 | | • | • | 5 | 3 | • | • | 4 | 1 | 2 | • |
| C | 3 | | 3 | 2 | 5 | 2 | • | • | 4 | 1 | 2 | • |
| D | 8 | | • | • | • | • | 4 | • | • | 5 | • | • |
| E | 5 | | • | 4 | 5 | 4 | • | • | • | • | 2 | 5 |
| F | 6 | | • | 5 | • | • | 1 | • | • | 5 | • | 5 |
| G | 10 | | • | • | • | • | • | • | • | • | • | • |
| H | 10 | | • | • | • | • | • | • | • | • | • | • |
| I | 5 | | • | 1 | 5 | 3 | 4 | 4 | • | • | • | • |
| J | 5 | | 3 | 4 | • | • | • | • | • | 4 | 1 | 5 |

Criteria for Mastery:                     3/5 correct                    4/5 correct

Domain-Referenced
Master Analysis:   % Students Passing in Language Mechanics _____
                         % Students Passing in Language Expression _____

Note: • Denotes that student picked keyed (correct) answer.

weakness). Other students, such as C and E, need help in both subdomains. In contrast, students such as A, D, G, and H have met the teacher's standard of mastery on both subdomains and are ready to move on to more advanced goals of instruction.

## 11.3.2    A Domain-Referenced Analysis with Data from Open-Ended Assessments

The procedures for conducting a domain-referenced analysis with data from open-ended, performance assessments are identical to those illustrated structured response tests. A prerequisite, however, is that the assessments are designed with *analytic scoring rubrics* (see Chapter 8).

To better appreciate the necessity for analytic rubrics for domain-referencing, examine Table 11.4 A–B, where we see writing assessment for persuasive essays, and two alternate scoring rubrics, one holistic (Table 11.4A) and the other analytic (Table 11.4B) in structure. Although both rubrics might match the competencies in the domain equally well, only the latter has the structure to allow a differentiated analysis on domain mastery. *Only analytic rubrics yield separate scores in the separate subdomains or skill/topic areas*.

Data from an analytically scored performance assessment can be easily organized into a data matrix for groups. Once standards for mastery are set, it is possible to evaluate summatively the extent to which an individual or class demonstrates mastery on subdomains within a domain. Domain-referenced analysis for the writing assessment in Tables 11.4 A–B is elaborated in Examples 3 and 4 for individuals and groups, respectively.

*Example 3: An Individual Analysis with an Open-Ended Assessment*   In Table 11.4B, we see an analytic checklist for assessing mastery on 16 competencies related to writing persuasive essays. The competencies are organized under three subdomains, labeled "Benchmarks," dealing with *expessing ideas to persuade, using a writing process,* and *organization.* The teacher has set mastery standards in each subdomain. For example, 4/6 competencies need to be checked in the "expessing ideas" subdomain for mastery. Using the teacher-set standards, the student whose essay is examined with the rubric shown in Table 11.4B shows mastery of the "writing process" and "organization," but not in "expessing ideas to persuade." Such data can now be fed back to inform instructional planning decisions for the student.

*Example 4: A Group Analysis with an Open-Ended Assessment*   Table 11.5 illustrates hypothetical data for two students produced using the assessment and similar analytic rubric. Using a 0–1–2 scale for each item on that same rubric, the teacher has set standards of mastery in the different skill/topic areas of the domain for a group analysis. In the examples, a student could achieve a maximum of 12 points in the Expression area, 14 points in Writing Process, and 6 points in Organization (total points = 32). To reach mastery, a student would require 8 of 12 points in Expression, 10 of 14 in Writing Process, and 4 of 6 under Organization.

**TABLE 11.4A   Domain-Referenced Mastery Analysis of a Writing Assessment Using a Holistic Scoring Rubric**

### SAMPLE ASSESSMENT

Instructions:

1. Plan, draft, revise, and compose a <u>persuasive essay</u> on the topic given.
2. You will need 45 minutes to complete the task.
3. Your essay should include a draft, showing editing marks for grammar, punctuation, sentence structure, spelling, and capitalization.
4. Turn in your edited draft and final essay when done.

Topic:
Write a 3–4 paragraph essay to persuade your school principal on the following topic:

*Middle school students should not be required to do homework every day.*

Scoring Rubric:
You will be scored using the following rating scale. Ask your teacher for sample essays at each score level.

| SCORE | DESCRIPTION |
|---|---|
| 1 | No clear position on topic. Arguments lacking or not understandable. Loses focus of topic. Sentences often incompletely constructed. Ideas not well developed or supported. Organization does not show a clear beginning, middle, or end. Transitions are weak. Many errors in capitalization, punctuation, usage, spelling, and/or grammar. |
| 2 | (Falls in between 1 and 3) |
| 3 | A position is taken on the topic. Points are made and argued, but without adequate support, vivid examples, logic, or clarity. Organization weak in some areas but there is a beginning, middle, and end. Sentences are complete. Minor corrections needed in capitalization, punctuation, usage, spelling, and/or grammar. The writing shows the basic elements of persuasive writing but writer does not make the case convincingly. |
| 4 | (Falls in between 3 and 5) |
| 5 | A position is taken and a compelling argument is made. Clear focus in writing. Each idea is well developed and supported with details and vivid examples. Word choice is rich and appropriate for topic, purpose, and audience. All sentences are complete with good use of capitalization, punctuation, usage, spelling, and/or grammar. Well-organized piece with beginning, middle, and end. Transitions from one paragraph to the next are smooth. The writer definitely persuades the reader with the essay. |

**TABLE 11.4B   Domain-Referenced Mastery Analysis of a Writing Assessment Using an Analytic Scoring Rubric**

Analytic Scoring Rubric:
This scoring rubric is provided to help the teacher in conducting formative assessments.

NAME:

| DESCRIPTION OF EXPECTATIONS | YES | NO | Improvements needed in: (Notes) | Standard of mastery |
|---|:---:|:---:|:---:|:---:|
| Benchmark:   Express ideas clearly in persuasive pieces. | | | | |
| 1. Takes a clear position on a topic. | | √ | | |
| 2. Expresses ideas clearly to persuade or convince an audience. | | √ | | 4/6 |
| 3. Makes a compelling and logical case for or against a topic. | | √ | | |
| 4. Provides arguments (reasons) to support points made. | | √ | | |
| 5. Uses vivid examples to illustrate points. | √ | | | |
| 6. Uses vocabulary (words) suitable for topic, purpose, and audience. | √ | | | |
| Benchmarks:   Use the writing process.  Use correct capitalization, spelling, and punctuation.  Use language appropriately in interpersonal and academic contexts. | | | | |
| 7. Outlines essay. | √ | | | |
| 8. Creates a draft of essay. | √ | | | |
| Revises/edited the essay for: | | | | |
| 9. sentence structure | √ | | | |
| 10. capitalization | √ | | | 5/7 |
| 11. punctuation | √ | | | |
| 12. spelling | | √ | | |
| 13. language usage | √ | | | |
| Benchmark:   Use effective techniques of organization. | | | | |
| 14. Organizes essay with a beginning, middle, and end. | √ | | | 3/3 |
| 15. Makes transitions from introduction to body. | √ | | | |
| 16. Makes transitions from body to conclusion. | √ | | | |

**TABLE 11.5 Domain-Referenced Analysis of an Essay-Writing Assessment with 3-Point Rating Scale: Hypothetical Data for Two Students**

| | Subdomain 1 | | Subdomain 2 | | Subdomain 3 | |
|---|---|---|---|---|---|---|
| | **Expressing Ideas** | | **Writing Process** | | **Organization** | |
| **Competency #:** | 1 2 3 4 5 6 | | 7 8 9 10 11 12 13 | | 14 15 16 | |
| **Max. Rating:** | *2 2 2 2 2 2* | *Total* | *2 2 2  2  2  2  2* | *Total* | *2  2  2* | *Total* |
| *Mastery Standard* | 8/12 | | 10/14 | | 4/6 | |
| Ann | | | | | | |
| Scores: | 1 1 0 1 0 2 | *5* | 2 2 1  1  2  2  1 | *12* | 2  1  1 | *4* |
| Decision: | *(F)* | | *(P)* | | *(P)* | |
| Bob | | | | | | |
| Scores: | 2 2 2 1 1 2 | *10* | 2 2 2  2  2  2  2 | *14* | 2  1  1 | *4* |
| Decision: | *(P)* | | *(P)* | | *(P)* | |

The results show that Ann's profile reveals strength in the use of the Writing Process and mastery of Organization skills, but a failure to reach the criterion level of performance in Expression. Bob, on the other hand, demonstrates mastery in all three subdomains.

**Key Concept**

■ Domain-referenced analysis can be conducted with data from structured-response or performance assessments, and can focus on either individuals or groups of examinees.

## 11.4 Mapping Long-Term Trends on Measured Constructs

Students enter school to learn, to develop, to grow, and to change. These changes are presumably caused by the scholastic program offerings, support services, and resources that a school provides. Historically, educational practitioners, policymakers, parents, students, and other stakeholders have wanted to know whether students are making any achievement gains as a result of their experiences in school.

When schools are accountable to the public, as they are in all government-funded educational systems, studies of achievement gains become particularly significant. Federally funded educational programs in the United States, such as Title 1 of the Elementary and Secondary Education Act, make it mandatory for schools to show that their students are making achievement gains. The Title 1 Evaluation and Reporting System (TIERS) asks for the administration of standardized achievement tests in fall and spring to track student progress over time. Recent educational reforms have spawned state accountability programs, such as Tennessee's Value-Added Accountability System (TVAAS), that attempt to measure student achievement gains and their relationship to various school and teacher variables (Sanders & Horn, 1994).

Measurement of achievement changes is neither easy nor straightforward. Formal methods for the measurement of change over time are well beyond the scope of this book. The purpose of this section is to look at a few *descriptive* methods that classroom, school, or other institutional practitioners can use to examine achievement trends in individuals and groups. Issues that we must deal with to properly map gains are briefly discussed in the concluding section. Keep in mind that these procedures are quite different in purpose from assigning marks to individuals based on prior achievement. Marks for students are not the end result in the measurement of change; rather, these analyses are usually pursued for meeting external accountability requirements by Users in Path 2. Teachers in User Path 1 may be involved in data collection but usually not in the use of results. Users in Paths 3 and 4 might find the methods useful in examining longitudinal effects of counseling, clinical interventions, or therapy.

## 11.4.1    Methods for Measuring Long-Term Trends

To evaluate changes over time, we need to measure the same students, on the same variable, on more than one occasion. Frequently, the construct measured is achievement, and the tools we use are standardized or locally made achievement tests. Measurement of change could also focus on psychological, physical, or physiological variables.

A typical data set for tracking gains might provide 2–4 measurements in a particular achievement domain, say, Reading Comprehension, of a group of students. Here is some data from 2 students from a group of 30:

| Student | Reading Scores: | | | |
| --- | --- | --- | --- | --- |
|  | Time 1 | Time 2 | Time 3 | Time 4 |
| Pedro | 205 | 243 | 268 | 302 |
| Anna | 190 | 230 | 250 | 269 |
| Group Mean: | 160.3 | 195.7 | 220.5 | 246.1 |
| SD | 35.28 | 32.25 | 36.32 | 38.62 |

Time 1 might represent scores from an end of grade testing. Measurements from Time 2, 3, and 4 could occur at the end of each quarter when the same students are at the next grade level. The means and standard deviations of the distributions at each point in time could vary as shown. In the first measurement, the mean is 160.3 and the standard deviation, 35.28. Over the course of four measurements, the group mean increases to 246.1, with a standard deviation of close to 39. Such changes over time would suggest that on the first occasion, the scores were more variable than in the second measurement, but less so than in the fourth measure. With such longitudinal data, we could employ one of four alternate methods for mapping achievement trends. These can use two, three or more data points, and focus on individuals or groups. Each method is briefly described next.

---

**Measuring Long-Term Trends**

| Method | How many data points? | Group/individual? |
|---|---|---|
| 1. Difference score | Uses two data points, Time 1 and Time 2 | Group/individual |
| 2. Effect size | Uses two data points, Time 1 and Time 2 | Group |
| 3. Ogives over time | Uses two or more data points, Time 1, 2 . . . t | Group |
| 4. Growth trajectories | Uses two or more data points, Time 1, 2 . . . t | Group/individual |

---

*1. Difference Score (Gain Score)*   This method of measuring change involves just two measurements on a given group of students, one conducted before instruction (or treatment) and the other performed after instruction (or treatment) is completed. In the data shown, a difference score can be calculated with measures taken at Time 1 and Time 4 only, using the formulas displayed below. In both the examples, we see positive gains in achievement based on the two data points, that is, on two occasions of testing. Here the gain is expressed in raw score units.

> *Difference score = (Postinstruction Score − Preinstruction Score)*
>
> Difference score for Pedro = 302 − 205 = +97
>
> Difference score (or gain score) for Group = (postinstruction mean − Preinstruction mean) = 246.1 − 160.3 = +85.8

**Key Concept**

■ The difference score (or gain score) is the difference in raw score points between the preinstruction and postinstruction measurements.

*2. Effect Size.*   The effect size can be thought of as a descriptive measure of the net effect of the instruction (or treatment) on a given group of students. It is the difference between the pre- and postinstruction means, expressed in standard deviation units of the Time 1 distribution. The calculation for the Time 1 and Time 4 data shown is as follows. The interpretation of the effect is that following instruction, the group showed a gain of two and a quarter standard deviation units. A gain that is one standard deviation unit or more is considered a very strong effect (Cohen, 1988).

Key Concept

- Effect size, $\Delta$, is the difference between the pre- and postinstruction means, expressed in standard deviation units of the Time 1 distribution.

  Effect Size, $\Delta$ = (postinstruction mean − Preinstruction mean) ÷ standard deviation of preinstruction distribution.

  $\Delta = (246.1 - 160.3)/35.28 = +2.43$

*3. Comparing Ogives over Time*   Visually, gains can be evaluated by comparing the ogives over time for the same group of students. One could use measurements from Time 1, 2, 3, and 4 to accomplish this graphic display of a group's growth on the same measurement scale. If the ogives gradually shift to the right, and the scores corresponding to the 50th percentile show increases, we can conclude that the group is demonstrating gains.

Key Concept

- Ogives of the Time 1, Time 2, . . . Time $t$ distributions on a given group can be compared to see if the score corresponding to the 50th percentile shows change in the desired direction.

*4. Growth Trajectories of Individuals*   Individual students growth can be plotted graphically in a line graph to show how they progress over time. To construct a graph plotting growth, the *y*-axis is used for the assessment scores, and the *x*-axis is used for the occasions of measurement. If a large number of individual growth trajectories are plotted, we are likely to find that there is a great deal of variability in the slope of each line, and that the spread of scores in the group (measurable with a standard deviation) fluctuates from one measurement occasion to the next. Individuals will also vary with respect to where they start. Both the means and standard deviations at each point of measurement, thus, need to be considered in evaluating gains for a group.

## 11.4.2   Measurement, Research Design, and Statistical Issues

To measure change accurately, we need to be mindful about some measurement, research design, and statistical issues. A brief summary of six major issues follows. New concepts and terms introduced in the list below are elaborated by topic.

Issues to Address when Mapping Trends

1. Validity and Reliability of the construct over time
2. Control for practice effects
3. Control for ceiling effects
4. Need for a vertical metric
5. Accounting for inter-individual and intra-individual differences in growth
6. Choosing the number of data points that will best depict growth
7. Regression towards the mean

***Validity Issues***    The measurement of change involves making multiple measurements of the same people, usually with the same instrument or on parallel instruments that tap the same construct domain. We cannot talk of change if "what" we are measuring also changes over time. For measuring achievement gains in a valid way, we have to make sure that the assessment is matched to the curriculum that will be delivered over time. Thus, if we want to assess reading gains, we should have reading tests that are based on all reading skills and passages that teachers will teach over time as they progress through the curriculum. The items should have both *content relevance* and *representativeness* with respect to the domain. If different tools are used at different times, they should all be "parallel tests" tapping the same construct domain. Other relevant evidence of validity of the scores should exist to support the use of an instrument to map achievement gains (see Chapters 3 and 13).

***Reliability Issues***    We must ensure that the assessment scores are sufficiently free of random error before we evaluate gains with them. Unreliability is usually caused by poor item sampling, test construction problems, poor administration conditions, or rater inconsistencies. Chapters 7–9 addressed techniques for controlling for error during the design process; Chapter 13 provides some methods for evaluating the extent of unreliability in scores after the assessment is administered. In measuring change, we would like the measures to have internal consistency reliability at each time point.

***Scale Properties***    To measure gains over time, we need an equal-interval scale that will yield comparable scores from one time to the next. Assessments that yield ordinal scores, such as percentile ranks, are unsuitable for mapping longitudinal gains. A vertically equated *scale score* is often provided by standardized test-makers for analyzing gains over time (more on vertical scaling and equating in Chapter 14). With locally made instruments, we must ensure that the test is a multi-level test that will be able to measure different students as they follow different growth trajectories.

   Title 1 evaluations use a "standard score" called the Normal Curve Equivalent (NCE) to track student gains. NCE scores are described in Chapter 14. Standard scores, such as the NCE, although equal-interval, are norm-referenced. The composition of the norm group changes from one measurement to the next when the measures are taken in different grades or years. Interpretations of gains based on norm-referenced standard scores should be interpreted with this limitation in mind.

***Ceiling Effects***    A ceiling effect is evident in those students who reach the maximum possible score on the assessment tool the first or second time they are assessed, making it impossible for us to continue measuring their gains using the same tool or procedure. Some advanced students will obtain very high scores to start with; a factor that causes them to hit the "ceiling" on the test before the instructional intervention is begun or fully delivered. Ceiling effects can be addressed by using "vertically equated" longitudinal scales that span grades K–12 in a subject-area curriculum. Standardized achievement test developers provide instruments with such scale properties. (See Chapter 14.)

*Inter-Individual and Intra-Individual Differences in Growth*    As we saw earlier, researchers have documented that individuals grow at different rates and in different ways. The shape and slope of the growth curve can vary from person to person. These are called "inter-individual differences." There are also "intra-individual differences." These reflect the fact that the same individual may grow very fast or very slowly at different points in time. The time at which we begin to measure change for a group or individual is thus crucial in the detection of growth (Willett, 1988).

*How Many Measurements Are Needed to Detect Gains?*    Typically, educators use two measurements, a preinstruction score and a postinstruction score, to calculate a gain score. If we want to account for inter-individual and intra-individual differences in growth patterns, however, we would prefer to use more than two measurements to track gains. Experienced researchers tell us that multiple data points are better for mapping growth than two-wave data (Willet, 1988).

*Regression Towards the Mean*    Lastly, a statistical artifact associated with the measurement of gains is observed in students who get extremely low or extremely high scores in the first measurement. It is called "regression towards the mean." Because of factors such as unreliability in the measures and correlation between the pre- and posttest score distributions, individuals who make very low scores on the pretest will always make a score that moves them upwards towards the mean of the distribution in the second testing. Conversely, individuals who make very high scores in the first testing will drop towards the mean of the distribution in the posttest scores. The movement of these extreme cases will be caused simply due to regression towards the mean, and not an effect of the instructional intervention. This is a problem that we must bear in mind when interpreting gain scores.

## 11.5    Using Assessment Results for Planning, Determining Needs, or Evaluating Programs and Services

Summarization of assessment results in appropriate ways can help us identify needs and develop plans for improving programs and services, as well as evaluate the quality of programs and services summatively. To close, this chapter will illustrate a few planning and evaluation applications that could be pertinent to Users in Paths 1–5.

### 11.5.1    Needs Assessments and Planning for Individuals, Classrooms, Programs, or Services

Needs assessments and planning call for *formative decision-making*. Three tasks are involved in assessing needs and preparing data-based *action plans*. These are:

- Gathering assessment data from suitable sources to identify needs
- Creating data summaries to highlight patterns in the results (see Chapter 10)
- Preparing action plans based on conclusions from the data summaries

Action plans specify long-term goals, short-term measurable objectives, strategies for goal accomplishment, timelines, and criteria for evaluating goal accomplishment.

Data to support planning decisions can be obtained from a variety of sources, such as student assessments, client surveys, program observations, interviews, service logs, or inventory records (see Chapter 2). Program data can deal with *program process* variables, as in assessments of teachers' instructional delivery methods, or with *program outcome* variables, as when we attempt to measure the results of a program or service using student achievement scores or parent satisfaction survey results. Depending on whether we wish to make inferences about needs for individuals, classrooms, schools, or entire programs or services for an institution, the results of our assessments must be aggregated at the appropriate level. These *data summaries* can then be used to develop plans. Depending on the level of aggregation, plans can be of three kinds:

| Type of Plan | Level of Aggregation of Assessment Results |
|---|---|
| Individualized Educational Plans (IEPs) | Individual |
| Classroom Educational Plans (CEPs) | Classroom-level aggregates |
| School/Program Improvement Plans (SIPs) | School or program-level aggregates |

***Individualized Educational Plans***    In Table 11.6 we see an example of an Individualized Educational Plan or IEP. IEPs are mandated by federal law in special education programs in the United States. Students receive special education services only after a comprehensive series of assessments are conducted and evaluated by a multidisciplinary team of clinical specialists and educators. These assessments address intellectual, language, speech, social, emotional, physical, and social functioning levels in children. IEPs identify long-term and short-term goals and objectives for each child, the special education services to be provided, and performance criteria on assessments that will enable an evaluation of the extent to which the goals/objectives are reached at particular points in time. IEPs can also identify areas that might hinder a student's successful participation in typical instructional environments. In short, they are tools that guide the special educators' service delivery and evaluation of programs for individual students.

***Classroom, School, or Program-Level Plans***    To bring about goal-focused improvements in their classes or groups, mainstream educators could employ planning practices similar to the IEPs of special educators. To prepare Classroom Educational Plans (CEPs), we could use data from multiple assessments and indicators, such as:

**TABLE 11.6   An Individualized Educational Plan**

Goal: *The student (name) will demonstrate reading comprehension and vocabulary skills at the targeted grade level.*

| Objectives | Criteria | Assessment Procedure | Date of Review | Code |
|---|---|---|---|---|
| *Complete all reading comprehension assignments in workbook* | *85% accuracy* | *Record of completion and scores on workbook assignments* | *5/4/99* | |
| *Answer detail recall, sequence, and vocabulary questions in literature-based readers.* | *95% accuracy* | *Reading Inventory Scores* | *5/4/99* | |

Goal: *The student (name) will write complete sentences with correct capitalization and punctuation.*

| Objectives | Criteria | Assessment Procedure | Date of Review | Code |
|---|---|---|---|---|
| *Capitalize beginning word of each sentence and proper nouns. Use commas, periods, question marks and exclamation marks.* | *Write 5 sample sentences without any punctuation or capitalization errors* | *Written Sample: Classroom assessments* | *5/4/99* | |

- Demographic data
- Past achievement records
- Attendance, behavioral, and health data
- Results of classroom assessments and standardized tests

Suitable descriptive and graphical summaries can be prepared on groups or subgroups. Results of domain-referenced mastery analysis, effect sizes, pre- to post-gain analyses, or longitudinal growth curve mapping may be used to evaluate needs and develop plans. A sample CEP is shown in Table 11.7(A). Here, the teacher chose to use attendance, classroom assessment, and standardized achievement test data to develop a plan.

Similar plans for schools, programs and other support services can also be developed. Table 11.12(B) shows a staff development plan prepared for elementary teachers in a school district. As noted before, the level of aggregation of the data in the data summaries will vary depending on whether the plan is developed for a school, a program, or a district. For example, a school improvement plan would use school means. In comparison, a CEP would be based on classroom means.

**TABLE 11.7  Sample Classroom and Program Plans**

**A.  Excerpt of a Classroom Educational Plan**

**Grade:**  *9*

**School:** *Lawton Middle School*                           **Teacher:** *Ms. Smith*

| Long-term goals and objectives with performance criteria | Strategies | Timeline for accomplishment |
| --- | --- | --- |
| Goal:  1.0  A majority of the students will show mastery of targeted learning outcomes in 8th- and 9th-grade Math domains. | | |
| Objective:  1.1  Students will complete required content area examinations and projects with 80% proficiency on Outcomes 3, 4, 10. | Reteach material on outcomes 3, 4, and 10 with peer tutoring, homework with individualized feedback, and reinforcement exercises. Teach material for grade 9 after students have mastered 8th-grade outcomes. | Semester 2, grade 9. |
| Objective:  1.2  90% of students will show a scaled score gain on 20 or more units on the CTB math battery from grade 8 to grade 9. | | |
| Goal:  2.0  All students will attend school regularly.<br><br>Objective:  2.1  All students will demonstrate a 90% or better attendance rate. | Set attendance policy for class with minimum requirement of 90% attendance. Show students effects of low attendance on math scores. | Semester 1–2, grade 9. |

**B.  Excerpt of a Staff Development Plan for a District**

**Plan applies to:**        ✔*Teachers/Instructional staff*

**Level:**                        ✔*Elementary*

**Areas of Highest Need:**    *Science Knowledge and New Teaching Methods*

| Long-term goals and objectives | Strategies | Timeline for accomplishment |
| --- | --- | --- |
| Goal:<br>1.0  Elementary teachers will complete a 60 hour training program or 16 week upper level university course in science.<br><br>Objectives:<br>1.1  Complete required content area examinations and projects with 80% proficiency.<br><br>1.2  Pass state certification test in science. | Provide summer stipends and in-service points to teachers lacking adequate training to attend courses/training programs. | 2000–2003 |

## 11.5.2   Evaluating the Quality of Programs and Services

Summative evaluations of programs and services are motivated by a need to judge the effectiveness or worth of a program or service following delivery. Like the preceding applications, summative evaluations call for the use of appropriate kinds of assessments, data sources and analysis. The last illustration in this chapter, presented in the following case study, focuses on a summative evaluation of a parent involvement program. The case should be read in conjunction with the data in Table 11.8.

Evaluation studies should use research designs that fit the complexities of the problem under investigation. The case study uses only descriptive statistics on the measured variables, namely, means, standard deviations, and effect sizes, to support decisions on program adequacy.

## Case Study 11.1
## Summative Evaluation of a Parent Involvement Program

Recent research reported a high correlation between levels of parent involvement in the education of their children and levels of student achievement. Guided by that research, a school district implemented an intensive set of strategies to get their parents involved in their children's education. Following two years of implementation of the program, district officials contracted with external evaluators to determine whether the parent involvement program was having the expected effects on student achievement. Results from a summative evaluation study of the parent involvement program were aggregated at the program level (Table 11.8 presents sample results). On all the student outcomes measured, the study found that students whose parents were more involved showed an advantage over students whose parents were less involved (see Effect Sizes). The largest positive effects were found in the areas of mathematics achievement and discipline. Such results supported the conclusion that the parent involvement program was yielding effects in the desired directions. The district officials decided to expand the program to all schools in the system.

**TABLE 11.8   Illustrative Data:   Evaluating the Effects of a Parent Involvement Training Program on Student Outcomes**

| Student Outcomes | High Parent Involvement | | Low Parent Involvement | | Effect Size |
| --- | --- | --- | --- | --- | --- |
| | Mean | SD | Mean | SD | |
| Math Achievement Test Scores | 250 | 20 | 228 | 18 | +1.15 |
| Language Arts Achievement Test Scores | 213 | 17 | 211 | 16 | +0.12 |
| Attendance Rate/Year (%) | 97 | 9 | 91 | 16 | +0.04 |
| # of Discipline Referrals (rounded) | 5 | 3 | 9 | 3 | −1.33 |

*Note:* Negative effects are desirable with discipline referrals.

# Summary

Chapter 11 illustrated how statistical and graphical summaries can be used in particular decision-making contexts by practitioners in User Paths 1–5. The applications dealt with:

- Standard-setting
- Assigning report card marks
- Conducting domain-referenced analysis
- Evaluating longitudinal trends
- Developing plans
- Conducting summative evaluations of programs/services

In each of these areas, the chapter identified methodological and philosophical issues that affect our decisions, made recommendations for best practices, and presented step-by-step guidelines for selected applications.

Standard-setting is necessary when we need a cut score to discriminate among individuals with varying capabilities on the construct we measure. All standards basically depend on expert judgments on what is meritorious performance by typical examinees in a given domain. Standards set by experts can be empirically validated with real score distributions. This chapter presented methods for setting standards based on judgments about item content, the content of an overall assessment, or score distributions of typical examinees using the contrasting groups method and the ogive method.

Marking requires teachers to compile results from multiple assessments to make summative evaluations of student performance over time. Marks can be assigned using criterion-referenced or norm-referenced methods. For teachers who prefer a norm-referenced approach, the chapter illustrated procedures using $T$-scores and ogives. For those inclined towards a criterion-referenced marking scheme, the chapter presented a procedure using preset criteria based on weighted percent of the maximum possible score.

A domain-referenced analysis uses assessment data to diagnose specific strengths and weaknesses of students during or before instruction, or to make a summative judgment of their level of mastery of the achievement domain. To support a domain-referenced analysis, assessments must initially be designed with clear linkages between particular learning outcomes and assessment items or tasks. The teacher must also set standards or mastery criteria to determine a student's mastery status. Domain-referenced analyses can be performed with data from both structured-response and open-ended assessment tools. The chapter described procedures for individual and group analyses.

To follow achievement changes over time we need to measure the same students on the same variable on more than one occasion. The chapter showed four methods for mapping achievement changes using the difference score (gain score), effect size, graphing growth curves, and examining group means and standard deviations at each point of measurement. Measurement and statistical issues that affect the measurement of change were briefly introduced in the chapter, and a recommendation made to use multiple measurements over pre- to postinstruction gains.

The chapter concluded by illustrating how assessment data can be used to formulate Individualized Educational Plans, Classroom Educational Plans, Program Improvement

Plans (School Improvement Plans), conduct needs assessments, and provide summative evaluations to determine the effectiveness of programs/services.

## QUESTIONS FOR CLASS DISCUSSION

1. Ask four experienced classroom instructors to describe their philosophies and approaches to marking. Classify their systems as criterion-referenced, norm-referenced, or a combination of both. Explain your answers.

2. Use a method of your choice to determine *a standard of minimum competency* and *a standard of excellence* on a score continuum from an assessment of your choice. State why you chose the method(s) that you did.

3. Suppose you are the chair of the school improvement planning committee at your institution. Your charge is to educate various members of the committee on how to conduct needs assessment and prepare data-based plans for the school and grade level programs. Prepare a presentation outlining the following:
   - How many types of assessment data to use
   - Methods of data analysis that might help in creating data summaries
   - Components of the plans

4. Discuss the pros and cons of measuring longitudinal achievement gains of students for summative evaluations of school and district programs.

5. Describe the philosophy and methods of a domain-referenced analysis to a colleague who uses assessments primarily for summative purposes in the classroom. What challenges did you face in communicating the concepts?

# 12 Quantitative Item Analysis

## Overview

Quantitative methods for item analysis, the focus of Chapter 12, enable us to evaluate the quality of individual items with respect to the assessment purposes. Item analysis should be a part of the item development process. In Chapter 5, quantitative item analysis was mentioned as a component of Phase IVB of the Process Model (see Figure 5.1), which deals with the empirical evaluation of assessments.

One could conduct item analysis with methods from classical test theory or item response theory (IRT). This chapter illustrates item analysis applications from a classical perspective only. Item analysis from IRT perspectives lie outside the scope of this book. More detailed presentations of procedures described in this chapter can be found in Berk (1980), Crocker & Algina (1986) and Hopkins (1998). Although the formulas might look formidable at first glance, as soon as you understand what they do, their utility during item development will become apparent. Information on computer software that can facilitate item analysis is provided at the end of the chapter.

Most of the procedures discussed in this chapter apply to multiple choice item development. We could apply item-level descriptive statistics and the homogeneity indices presented here when developing affective scales and questionnaires. Ideally, this chapter should be read in conjunction with sections in Chapters 7 and 9 focusing on the development of structured-response items for measuring achievement, ability, and affective constructs.

## CHAPTER 12 OBJECTIVES

After studying this chapter and completing the structured exercises in the module, you should be able to:

1. Identify the purposes for quantitative item analysis as a component of the assessment design/selection process.

2. Describe commonly used item statistics and their applications (item difficulty, item discrimination, item means, item standard deviations, item-to-total score correlations).

3. Calculate and interpret item difficulty indices, item discrimination indices, and results of distracter analysis for norm-referenced testing applications.

4. Calculate and interpret item difficulty indices, item discrimination indices, and results of distracter analysis for criterion-referenced testing applications.

5. Recognize the limitations of commonly used item statistics.

## 12.1    Purposes for Item Analysis

Quantitative item analysis methods help us select items that function best, given our stated purposes for assessment, in typical groups of examinees. Suppose that we develop a pool of structured-response items to serve our achievement testing needs. Following reviews by experts, we find that most of the items pass the necessary content-validity screenings (see Chapters 7 and 9). Now, we wish to refine the individual items further with empirical try-outs and analyses. Our goal is to arrive at a smaller set of items with maximum validity and reliability for our stated purposes, for example, to make criterion-referenced or norm-referenced interpretations with the assessment results.

Item analysis techniques are useful for diagnosing causes for item malfunctioning and correction of item flaws *before* we formally assemble and use an assessment tool. Ideally, we would conduct item analysis as a component of the assessment design or selection process. In the typical application, we would follow item analysis with the needed item deletions, revisions, and rewriting.

---

**Key Concept**

■ Quantitative item analysis is used for diagnosing causes for poor item functioning in a typical examinee/respondent group, and for improving the item pool before an instrument is finalized.

## 12.2    Item Analysis Indices

The major statistics for multiple choice item analysis are *item difficulty (p)* and *item discrimination (D)* indices. Also useful is a procedure for analyzing the effectiveness of the foils or *distracters* in multiple choice items, referred to as a *distracter analysis*. Assuming a domain-sampling approach to assessment design, descriptive statistics such as item means, standard deviations, and variances yield additional, enlightening information on the characteristics of item response distributions. Measures of the extent to which item response data correlate with the overall domain or subdomain scores, called *item homogeneity* indices, are other useful methods for evaluating item properties. In preparation for the demonstration exercises in item analysis that follow, the next section provides a conceptual introduction to the purposes and logic underlying each item analysis procedure.

## 12.2.1 Item Difficulty Index

The *item difficulty* statistic is useful in evaluating properties of multiple choice items in achievement/ability tests. The item difficulty index (the $p_i$ value) is the proportion (%) of students who get an item right by selecting the keyed response option. Computed $p_i$ values range from 0 to 1.0 (or 0% to 100%). The higher the $p_i$ value, the easier the item. When the calculated $p_i$ value is .95, it indicates that 95% of the examinee group responded correctly to the item. Such an item is considered very easy for a typical student group. On the contrary, if an item performs at or below chance level, then it is considered to be rather difficult. As you will recollect from Chapter 7, whether or not an item is operating at the level of chance can be determined by the number of answer options it offers. In a multiple choice item with four answer options, we would expect examinees to pick the right answer simply "by chance" 25% of the time if they had no systematic information on the domain. If the computed $p_i$ value for a four-option item turns out to be 0.25 or thereabouts, it would appear to have a prohibitive difficulty level for most examinees.

We compute item difficulty to evaluate whether an item is too obscure, ambiguous, or complex for a majority of examinees to identify the correct answer. Item difficulty can be lowered if the content and behavior in the targeted learning outcome is poorly represented in the item, that is, if there is:

- an unclear item presentation format
- use of confusing language in an item
- lack of student exposure to the content or skill tapped by the item

When the computed item difficulty values are too low, the appropriate follow-up action is to reexamine the item closely to determine possible causes for the difficulty value and either revise or delete it.

## 12.2.2 Item Discrimination Index

The *item discrimination index* ($D$ value) is another statistic that applies to structured-response items in achievement/ability tests. When we develop items, we would like them to be sensitive to differences among individuals on the attribute continuum. The item discrimination index ($D$ value) allows us to evaluate this property.

The item discrimination index or $D$ value is the difference in proportions of students who get an item right in two, carefully selected, criterion groups of examinees in the item analysis sample. We compute $D$ values to determine whether the item is able to discriminate between the preselected criterion groups in the desired direction. In the next section, we will see who the best candidates would be for "criterion" groups in item analysis studies for different types of assessments, such as criterion-referenced (CRTs) and norm-referenced tools (NRTs).

$D$ values range from $-1.0$ to $+1.0$. Generally, we like items to discriminate positively. A positive discrimination suggests that the item is discriminating between the criterion groups in the direction desired by the item developer. A negative $D$ value typically carries bad news, indicating that the item is discriminating in a reverse direction from that hypothesized by the item developer. Negative $D$ values are usually caused by confusing item wording or content, and sometimes, the miskeying of items. A negative $D$ value could also indicate that the item fails to fit the targeted domain or subdomain (i.e., the item measures something other than the construct measured by the other items from the same domain). A $D$ value of 0 indicates that the item does not show any difference between the two criterion groups. Depending on the purposes for an assessment, a $D$ of 0 can be a desirable or an undesirable result. (The reasons for this will become evident in the application sections.)

### 12.2.3   Distracter Analysis

A well-written multiple choice item should have effective distracters (see Chapter 7). This means that the correct answer should not be an obvious "giveaway" to examinees, but rather an answer that effectively separates individuals who have a good grasp of the content/skills tested from those who have partial knowledge, no knowledge, or confusions about the material. Good distracters, the wrong answers in a multiple choice item, should attract the latter group. We conduct a *distracter analysis* to evaluate whether individual distracters are drawing the expected proportions of examinees from criterion groups specified by the assessment designer. A distracter analysis involves compiling counts of responses to different distracters or foils in a multiple choice item, and verifying the extent to which the response distributions of the criterion groups are consistent with our predictions about their performance.

### 12.2.4   Item Homogeneity and Descriptive Statistics
of Item Scores

In the domain-sampling approaches to assessment design, we assume that responses to each item contributes to the variability of the total score in typical respondents/examinee groups—assuming the items tap content and behavior that is relevant to and representative of the construct domain. To evaluate the extent to which individual item scores correlate with the summated total scores from the remaining items on the assessment, we use *item homogeneity* statistics. Examinations of the frequency distributions, means, and standard deviations/variances of responses to individual items and descriptive statistics of the total score distributions, help us further understand the meaning of construct scores. While the $p_i$ and $D$ statistics were invented for evaluating structured-response items in assessments of achievement/ability, descriptive item statistics and item homogeneity indices (see section 12.6) are applicable in attitudinal or psychological scale development contexts where structured, Likert-type items are used (see Chapter 9).

We begin the demonstration exercises with item analysis applications for achievement instruments that were intended to serve norm-referencing purposes. Next we will examine procedures for criterion-referenced tools. Finally, we will review applications of item descriptive statistics and item homogeneity indices with data from an attitude scale.

---

**Key Concepts**

■ Item analysis procedures for multiple choice items include the item difficulty index, item discrimination index, and distracter analysis.

■ Item analysis procedures for Likert-scaled items include reviews of item descriptive statistics and homogeneity indices.

■ Item difficulty is the proportion of students who select the keyed correct response.

■ Item discrimination is the difference in proportions of students who select the correct response in two well-defined criterion groups.

---

## 12.3 Differences between NRT and CRT Item Analysis

Before beginning item analysis for achievement/ability tests, we need to be clear as to whether we are designing a norm-referenced tool (NRT) or a criterion-referenced tool (CRT). The selection of item statistics will be different in each case, as will be the selection of criterion groups, methods of derivation, and interpretation of results.

NRT item analysis is conducted to improve tests intended for measuring individual differences on a particular construct or on another construct that the test scores are expected to predict (an external criterion measure). The purpose of a NRT is to maximally discriminate among individuals who are at the upper and lower ends of the achievement/ability continuum—that is, to sort the high- and low-performing individuals. For a test designed to meet norm-referencing needs, the best set of items would be those with the necessary sorting properties, evaluated with NRT item difficulty and item discrimination indices. For an informative NRT item analysis, the criterion groups of examinees should include the highest-performing (H) and lowest-performing (L) individuals in a typical examinee group, as evidenced by the total scores on the assessment tool being investigated.

The CRT difficulty and discrimination indices, although labeled similarly, serve a different purpose altogether and are interpreted quite differently from their NRT counterparts. In designing CRTs, the assumption is that we will use the assessment items as a part of an instructional program with a defined curricular domain. (See Chapter 6 for a refresher of the term "domain" as it applies to User Path 1.) Item properties that we value here are the *instructional sensitivity* of items. Good items on a CRT would satisfactorily discriminate between individuals who have received instruction on the curricular domain versus those who have not. While there may be some overlap, the CRT criterion groups do *not necessarily correspond* with the H and L groups of an NRT analysis.

The criterion groups commonly used to derive the CRT item indices are "master" (M) versus "non-master" groups (NM) or "instructed" (IG) versus "uninstructed" groups (UG). Alternatively, we could compare "preinstruction" (pre) versus "postinstruction" (post) item data on the *same* group of individuals to examine whether the items changed in their difficulty following instruction. We define all these terms here exactly as we did when discussing domain-referenced analysis (Chapter 11). The next two sections illustrate how to conduct item analysis in NRT and CRT contexts, respectively.

---

**Key Concepts**

- NRT and CRT item analysis procedures use different criterion groups.
- NRT item analysis involves the use of (H)igh and (L)ow sub-groups from a typical examinee population.
- CRT item analysis involves the use of (Pre)instruction and (Post)instruction, Instructed and Uninstructed (IG, UG), or Master and Non-Master (M, NM) groups.

---

## 12.4  Application of Item Analysis for NRTs

Suppose that we have the results from a preliminary tryout of 10 multiple choice items from a group of 30 individuals for the purposes of an item analysis. The test is a mathematics test for elementary students. It is being developed to serve norm-referencing and large-scale testing purposes. Two sample items from the test are presented in Figure 12.1. Each of the items on the NRT had five answer options with one correct answer.

Table 12.1 mimics the output from a scanner with the capability of scoring structured-response tests when provided with a key, similar to the NRT under examination in our example. When a student selects the keyed answer, it is represented with a dot on the chart; otherwise the incorrect option number selected by the examinee appears on the printout. Item numbers (1–10) are read across. Students (labeled with letters, A–T in Table 12.1) are listed vertically.

Using the sample data in Table 12.1, the steps in the NRT item analysis are as described next. The two items in Figure 12.1, Items 2 and 3, are used to demonstrate the calculations and interpretations.

---

**DEMONSTRATION 12.1**

### Steps in NRT Item Analysis

**Step 1**   Identify H and L criterion groups for NRT item analysis.

**Step 2**   Set up an item analysis table for each item.

**Step 3**   Calculate the NRT item difficulty ($p_i$) value.

$p_i = (p_H + p_L)/2$

**Step 4**   Calculate the discrimination index, $D$ value.

$D = (p_H - p_L)$

**Step 5**   Conduct a distracter analysis.

**Step 6**   Interpret the NRT item analysis results taking into consideration qualitative characteristics of the item, the examinee group, and assessment purposes.

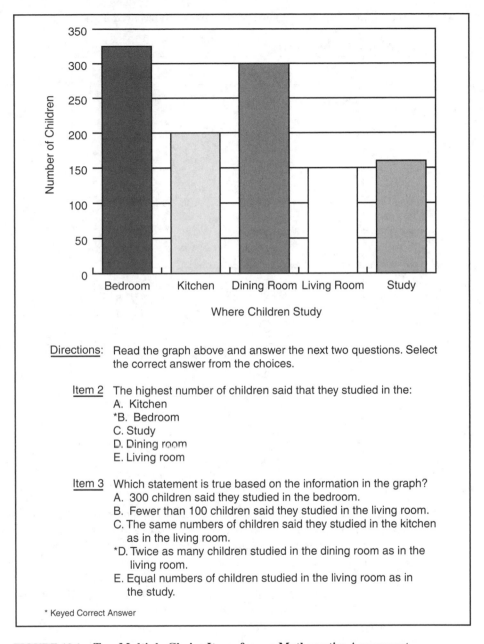

Directions: Read the graph above and answer the next two questions. Select the correct answer from the choices.

Item 2  The highest number of children said that they studied in the:
A. Kitchen
*B. Bedroom
C. Study
D. Dining room
E. Living room

Item 3  Which statement is true based on the information in the graph?
A. 300 children said they studied in the bedroom.
B. Fewer than 100 children said they studied in the living room.
C. The same numbers of children said they studied in the kitchen as in the living room.
*D. Twice as many children studied in the dining room as in the living room.
E. Equal numbers of children studied in the living room as in the study.

* Keyed Correct Answer

**FIGURE 12.1   Two Multiple Choice Items from a Mathematics Assessment**

**TABLE 12.1  Data Matrix for Item Analysis for a Norm-Referenced Tool**

| Keyed Correct Response | | | ② | ② | ④ | ① | ③ | ② | ③ | ② | ③ | ① |
|---|---|---|---|---|---|---|---|---|---|---|---|---|
| | | Item #: | 1 | 2 | 3 | 4 | 5 | 6 | 7 | 8 | 9 | 10 |
| Group | Students | Total Score | | | | | | | | | | |
| High | A | 8 | • | 4 | • | 4 | • | • | • | • | • | • |
| | D | 8 | • | • | • | • | 4 | • | • | 5 | • | • |
| | F | 9 | • | • | • | • | 1 | • | • | • | • | • |
| | G | 10 | • | • | • | • | • | • | • | • | • | • |
| $N_H = 10$ | H | 9 | • | • | 5 | • | • | • | • | • | • | • |
| | K | 9 | • | • | • | • | • | • | • | • | 4 | • |
| | N | 8 | • | • | 5 | • | • | • | • | • | • | 4 |
| | P | 8 | • | • | 5 | • | • | • | 5 | • | • | • |
| | Q | 10 | • | • | • | • | • | • | • | • | • | • |
| | R | 10 | • | • | • | • | • | • | • | • | • | • |
| Low | B | 5 | • | • | 5 | 3 | • | • | 4 | 1 | 2 | • |
| | C | 3 | 3 | 3 | 5 | 2 | • | • | 4 | 1 | 2 | • |
| | E | 5 | • | 4 | 5 | 4 | • | • | • | • | 2 | 5 |
| | I | 5 | • | 1 | 5 | 3 | 4 | 4 | • | • | • | • |
| $N_L = 10$ | J | 2 | 3 | 4 | 1 | • | 4 | • | 4 | 4 | 1 | 5 |
| | L | 5 | • | 4 | 1 | 2 | • | • | • | 5 | 3 | • |
| | M | 3 | • | 4 | 1 | 2 | • | 3 | 2 | 5 | 2 | • |
| | O | 4 | • | • | 2 | 2 | 5 | • | 4 | 5 | 4 | • |
| | S | 5 | 4 | • | • | • | • | • | 1 | 6 | 3 | 4 |
| | T | 5 | • | • | 3 | • | 5 | 3 | 4 | • | • | • |
| Total $N = 30$ | | | | | | | | | | | | |

**Step 1**  H(igh) and L(ow) groups in an NRT item analysis are specified using the top third (33%) and the bottom third (33%) of the examinee sample's scores. Table 12.1 shows only the upper 10 (H group) and lower 10 scores (L group) of the total sample of 30 students, based on their raw scores. To obtain the H and L groups, first obtain a raw score, $X$, for each student by totaling the number of correctly answered items. (For a student who answers 8 of 10 items correctly, $X = 8$.) Then, rank-order the students by their raw scores. Leave the students with the middle scores (6 and 7 in the example) out of the item analysis. The $N$s in the item analysis sample are denoted with $N_H$ in the High group and $N_L$ in the Low group. Table 12.1 shows that $N_H = 10$ and $N_L = 10$ in the illustrative data set.

In a scanned output, raw scores might already have been calculated by the scanner, and it may be possible for you to code your computer software to sort your students by their total scores. In the group shown, the top 33% of students have scores of 8 and above and those in the bottom 33% receive 5 and below.

***Step 2*** Identify the particular item for analysis, say, Item 2, from the item pool. Create an Item Analysis Table for the item as shown in Table 12.2. This will require you to examine the vertical column of responses to an item in the scanned output, and tally the counts of individuals who selected each option in the high and low groups, including the correct answer. For Item 2, we see that nine of the H group selected Option 2, the correct answer, while one chose Option 4. In the L group, four individuals picked Option 2, one chose Option 3, while four chose Option 4. (Note that these option numbers correspond to options A–E in Figure 12.1.)

***Step 3*** The item difficulty, $p_i$, is computed by taking the average of the item difficulties in the high (H) and low (L) performing subgroups of examinees. The formula is:

$p_i = (p_H + p_L)/2$, where
$p_H$ = proportion in the H group who select the correct answer.
$p_L$ = proportion in the L group who select the correct answer.

To obtain the $p_H$ and $p_L$ values one would divide the number selecting the correct response by the number of individuals in the H and L groups, respectively. With Item 2, the values are:

$p_H = 9/10 = .90$, $p_L = 4/10 = .40$, and
$p_i = (.90 + .40)/2 = .65$

***Step 4*** The $D$ (item discrimination index) is computed by subtracting the $p_L$ value from the $p_H$ value. The formula is:

$D = (p_H - p_L)$, where $p_H$ and $p_L$ have the same meanings as before.

With Item 2, the $D$ value is obtained as shown below.

$D = (.90 - .40) = +.50$

**TABLE 12.2  Item Analysis Table for Item 2 from an NRT**

|  | 1 | ② | 3 | 4 | 5 | Omit | $p_i$ | $D$ |
|---|---|---|---|---|---|---|---|---|
| High group |  | ‖‖‖ ‖‖‖‖ |  | / |  |  | .65 | + .50 |
| Low group | / | ‖‖‖‖ | / | ‖‖‖‖ |  |  |  |  |

Item 2 from Math (Graphing) Assessment

Correct Answer

$p_H$ (proportion correct in High) $= 9 \div 10 = .9$
$p_L$ (proportion correct in Low) $= 4 \div 10 = .4$

$p_i = (p_H + p_L)/2 = (.9 + .4)/2 = 1.30 \div 2 = .65$
$D = p_H + p_L = .9 - .4 = +.50$

***Step 5***    To perform a distracter analysis, we must review the distribution of responses to each answer option in the Item Analysis Table, and answer questions such as the following:

- Was the correct (keyed) answer selected by a majority of students who also tended to perform well on the remaining items in the domain (the high scorers)?
- Did each distracter attract expected numbers of the L group, who are assumed to have more misunderstandings and less mastery of the domain?
- Did any distracter attract an inordinately large number of high scorers?
- How many did not respond to the item in the H and L groups?

In Item 2, we see that 90% of the H group were able to select the correct response, relative to only 40% in the L group—an expected and desirable result for a well-functioning NRT item. Option 4 appears to be a very good distracter, as 50% of the L group are drawn to it. Options 1, 3, and 5 are relatively weak distracters and may even have appeared obviously wrong to the L group.

***Step 6***    Table 12.3 provides some general guidelines for interpreting NRT item analysis results in a holistic way. The item developer should carefully consider all possible expla-

**TABLE 12.3   Some Guidelines for Interpretation of NRT Item Analysis**

| Item Characteristics | Interpretation | Action |
| --- | --- | --- |
| $p$ values .49 to .70<br>$D$ values of +.10 to +.40<br>Distracters and correct options show predictable response distributions in H and L groups | Desirable NRT item | Keep item. |
| $p$ values of higher than .70 or approaching .90<br>$D$ values positive | Easy or too-easy item | Keep item. Consider revising distracters to raise difficulty. |
| $p$ values of .40 or lower<br>$D$ values of +.40 or higher<br>Distracters and correct options show some unpredictable patterns | Difficult or too-difficult item | Drop item or consider revising stem and responses to improve difficulty value. |
| $p$ values equal to or close to chance level<br>$D$ values of 0, or negative | Poor item | Drop or consider revising stem, correct response, and distracters to improve clarity.<br>Check for miskeying, lack of student exposure to item content, or item measuring something unrelated to the domain. |

nations for the calculated item statistics by reviewing the qualitative characteristics of the item in conjunction with the results of the quantitative item analysis. When a test is designed for norm-referencing, the $p_i$ values should ideally range from .50 to .70 (the average $p$ should be around .50) and all items should show *positive* discrimination indices. We want moderate levels of item difficulty in NRTs.

If $p_i$ values are found to be below .40, the item is likely to be operating at a fairly high level of difficulty (in a three-option item, chance level is 33%). Irrespective of the $p_i$ value, a $D$ of 0 signals no discriminating ability in an item, which makes it useless as an NRT item.

### 12.4.1 Comparing NRT Item Analysis Results for Two Different Items

To obtain a relative perspective on item characteristics, let us compare the item analysis results for Item 2 with that of Item 3 (see Figure 12.1 with Table 12.2 and Table 12.4). In Item 2, we see the $p_i$ value of .65, accompanied with a $D$ of +.50, making it a very suitable item for an assessment tool intended for sorting individuals into H and L groups.

Item 3 is considerably more difficult than Item 2 and has an extremely high discrimination index ($p_i = .40, D = +.60$). Without examining the response distributions on distracters, Item 3 appears to be an acceptable although far more difficult NRT item. The distracter analysis for Item 3, however, reveals some problems that might call for further investigation and action. Option 4, the correct answer draws 70% of the H group compared to 10% of the L group—a desired and predictable response pattern. Option 5, an incorrect option, however, draws the remaining 30% of the H group. This finding suggests that something in the item or response Option 5 could be problematic, making the latter appear correct to a few members of the H group. As we see in Figure 12.1, the bars at issue in Option 5 (Living Room and Study) are so close in height that they might be mistaken as equal even by knowledgeable examinees. Such item problems call for revisions to the graphics in the item and further attention from item writers.

Options 2 and 3 for Item 3, both incorrect, draw only one respondent each. It could be that these options are perceived as obviously wrong by typical examinees. Taking the

**TABLE 12.4  Item Analysis Table for Item 3 from NRT**

| | | | | | | | | |
|---|---|---|---|---|---|---|---|---|
| | | | Item 3 From Math (Graphing) Assessment | | | | | |
| | | | Correct Answer | | | | | |
| | 1 | 2 | 3 | ④ | 5 | Omit | $P_i$ | $D$ |
| High group | | | | ⫽⫽⫽⫽⫽ ⫽⫽ | ⫽⫽⫽ | | .40 | + .60 |
| Low group | ⫽⫽⫽ | ⫽ | ⫽ | ⫽ | ⫽⫽⫽⫽ | | | |

$p_H = 7 \div 10 = .7$    $p_i = (p_H + p_L)/2 = (.7 + .1)/2 = .8 \div 2 = .40$
$p_L = 1 \div 10 = .1$    $D = p_H - p_L = .7 - .1 = +.60$

results together, therefore, a developer might decide to make revisions to both Options 2, 3, and 5 to help Item 3 function optimally. In the event that the pictorial, language, or content are impossible to modify in an item, one might choose to drop it altogether from the item pool.

## 12.5   Application of Item Analysis for CRTs

Earlier we saw that the goal of a CRT item analysis is to determine whether individual items, constructed to specifically measure a given curricular domain, become *lower* in their difficulty following instruction. In an effective item, the discrimination index, (*D*), would indicate that students made gains on the item following instruction, allowing us to conclude that it had *instructional sensitivity*—a desirable outcome in CRT item design.

### 12.5.1   Item Analysis for CRTs with One Group

To illustrate how a CRT item analysis works, we have item data from a Preinstruction (Pre) and Postinstruction (Post) administration of a structured-response test in Table 12.5. Here, the same group of individuals were tested twice on the same set of items—once before instruction was begun, and then again after the instructional unit was completed. Results of four items are shown with 0s and 1s, where a 0 indicates the choice of an incorrect option by students and a 1 indicates choice of the correct option. The steps in a CRT item analysis are illustrated with computational details for Items 1 and 2 from Table 12.5.

---

D E M O N S T R A T I O N   **12.2**

**Steps in a One-Group Item Analysis for CRTs**

*Step 1*   Organize item response data for each criterion group in quadrant form.

*Step 2*   Calculate and compare $p_i$ values for both criterion groups. So,

$p_i$ (pre) = number of individuals in pretest who select the right answer $\div N$
$p_i$ (post) = number of individuals in posttest who select the right answer $\div N$

*Step 3*   Calculate appropriate *D* values.

$$D_{\text{pre-post}} = p_{i\,(\text{post})} - p_{i\,(\text{pre})}$$
$$D_{\text{igain}} = n_3 \div N$$
$$D_{\text{ngain}} = (n_3 - n_4) \div N$$

*Step 4*   Conduct an item distracter analysis

*Step 5*   Interpret the CRT item analysis results taking into consideration qualitative characteristics of the item, the examinee group, and assessment purposes.

---

**TABLE 12.5  Data Matrix of Item Analysis for a CRT**

| Student | Item #: | Preinstruction Data | | | | Postinstruction Data | | | |
|---------|---------|---|---|---|---|---|---|---|---|
| | | 1 | 2 | 3 | 4 | 1 | 2 | 3 | 4 |
| A | | 0 | 0 | 1 | 1 | 1 | 1 | 1 | 1 |
| B | | 0 | 1 | 1 | 0 | 1 | 1 | 1 | 1 |
| C | | 0 | 1 | 1 | 1 | 1 | 0 | 1 | 1 |
| D | | 0 | 0 | 1 | 1 | 1 | 1 | 1 | 1 |
| E | | 0 | 0 | 1 | 0 | 1 | 0 | 1 | 1 |
| F | | 0 | 1 | 1 | 0 | 1 | 1 | 1 | 1 |
| G | | 0 | 0 | 1 | 1 | 1 | 1 | 1 | 0 |
| H | | 0 | 0 | 1 | 0 | 1 | 0 | 1 | 1 |
| I | | 0 | 0 | 1 | 0 | 1 | 1 | 1 | 0 |
| J | | 0 | 0 | 1 | 0 | 1 | 0 | 1 | 1 |

*Step 1*   We start by organizing the Pre and Post item data in an *item-by-student matrix,* as illustrated in Table 12.5. Then, for each item, we obtain counts of the total number of individuals ($N$) that fall into the following quadrants so that $N = n_1 + n_2 + n_3 + n_4$ (after Berk, 1984). In the quadrants, shown in Table 12.6,

**TABLE 12.6  Item Analysis Quadrants for Item 1 and CRT**

|  | Postinstruction Data (Post) | |  |
|---|---|---|---|
|  | Correct | Incorrect |  |
| Preinstruction Data (Pre) Correct | $n_1 = 0$ | $n_2 = 0$ | $\dfrac{n_1 + n_2}{N} = p_{(Pre)}$ |
| Preinstruction Data (Pre) Incorrect | ~~HH~~  ~~HH~~ <br> $n_3 = 10$ | $n_4 = 0$ |  |

*Note:* $\dfrac{n_1 + n_3}{N} = p_{(Post)}$

Total $N = 10$

$n_1$ = number of students who answer the item correctly in both pre- and posttests

$n_2$ = number of students who answer the item correctly on the pretest but incorrectly on the posttest

$n_3$ = number of students who answer the item correctly on the posttest but incorrectly on the pretest, and

$n_4$ = number of students who miss the item on both occasions.

Once the individual item data are reorganized in quadrants, it becomes easy for us to recognize items that have high instructional sensitivity. For example, with Item 1, we see a stark difference in pre and post measurements, and can conclude that the item demonstrates maximum possible sensitivity to instruction. Compare these results with those for Item 2 in Table 12.7. Here, we see mixed results with only 4 of 10 individuals making clear gains from pre- to posttest.

**Step 2**   The CRT $p_i$ values can be computed from the student by item matrix constructed in Step 1 (Table 12.5) or from the quadrants (Table 12.6). In a CRT analysis, we should calculate $p_i$ values for *both* criterion groups and compare the differences (Berk, 1984). The formula in a pre–post design is:

$p_i$ (pre) = number of individuals in pretest who select the right answer $\div$ N, or ($n_1$ + $n_2$)/N

**TABLE 12.7   Item Analysis Quadrants for Item 2 from CRT**

|  | Postinstruction Data (Post) | |  |
|---|---|---|---|
|  | Correct | Incorrect |  |
| **Preinstruction Data (Pre)** Correct | // $n_1 = 2$ | / $n_2 = 1$ | $\dfrac{n_1 + n_2}{N} = p_{(Pre)}$ |
| Incorrect | //// $n_3 = 4$ | /// $n_4 = 3$ |  |

*Note:* $\dfrac{n_1 + n_3}{N} = p_{(Post)}$

Total N = 10

$p_i$ (post) = number of individuals in posttest who select the right answer $\div$ $N$, or $(n_1 + n_3)/N$

For Item 1 in Table 12.6, the pretest difficulty is: $0/10 = .00$ (Interpretation: *extremely difficult*). The posttest difficulty in Item 1 is: $10/10 = 1.00$ (Interpretation: *extremely easy*). The results for Item 1 fit the idealized expectation for item performance in a CRT context.

Now compare the Item 1 results to the $p_i$ values for Item 2 shown in Table 12.7, where the pretest difficulty is: $3/10 = .30$ (Interpretation: *very difficult*); and the posttest difficulty is: $6/10 = .60$ (Interpretation: *moderately difficult*). The Item 2 results suggest that only a small amount of the desired change in difficulty has been achieved by the instructional intervention.

**Step 3** The true extent of instructional sensitivity of items can be further evaluated with at least three, easy-to-understand $D$ values that apply to CRT analyses. They are:

**i.** $D_{\text{pre-post}} = p_{i \text{ (post)}} - p_{i \text{ (pre)}}$ or the difference between the item difficulty levels from pre- to posttest administration in a single-group design.

**ii.** $D_{\text{igain}} = n_3/N$ or the item discrimination based on individual gains. This index uses the number of students who answer the item correctly on the posttest but not on the pretest $(n_3)$, from the bottom left quadrant (see Table 12.7). The denominator is the total $N$ ($N = n_1 + n_2 + n_3 + n_4$).

**iii.** $D_{\text{ngain}} = (n_3 - n_4)/N$ or the item discrimination based on net gains. This index adjusts the proportion of students who answer the item correctly on the posttest by subtracting from it the proportion that makes no gains at all from pre- to post measurement, before dividing by the total $N$. The $n_3$ and $n_4$ counts are obtained from their respective quadrants. $D_{\text{ngain}}$ is considered to be the most statistically sensitive $D$ value of the three as it takes into account both gains and losses resulting from instruction (Berk, 1984).

With data for Item 2 (see Table 12.7), the three computed $D$ values would be as follows:

$D_{\text{pre-post}} = p_{i \text{ (post)}} - p_{i \text{ (pre)}} = .60 - .30 = +.30$
(Interpretation = Moderate sensitivity)

$D_{\text{igain}} = n_3/N = 4/10 = .40$
(Interpretation = Moderate sensitivity)

$D_{\text{ngain}} = (n_3 - n_4)/N = (4 - 3)/10 = 1/10 = .10$
(Interpretation = Low sensitivity based on net gain. With Item 1 as a benchmark, we see that the maximum possible value of $D_{\text{ngain}}$ for an item can be 1.0.)

**Step 4** To conduct a distracter analysis, set up item analysis tables for each item with the appropriate CRT criterion groups, as shown in Tables 12.8A–B. The logic of a distracter analysis here is the same as that in NRT item analysis. The tables contain counts

**TABLE 12.8A   Illustrative Data for a Distracter Analysis in a Pre- and Posttest Item Analysis**

| Item 15 | 1 | 2 | 3 | Correct answer<br>_4_ | 5 |
|---|---|---|---|---|---|
| **Postinstruction data** | 1 | 5 | 2 | 32 | 0 |
| **Preinstruction data** | 11 | 12 | 7 | 10 | 0 |
| $N = 40$ | | | | | |

of students who select each distracter and the correct option for an item from each criterion group. The primary interest in a CRT distracter analysis is in answering the following types of questions.

- Is the correct answer attracting a majority of students in the postinstruction data?
- Are the distracters attracting expected numbers of students prior to instruction?
- How many students chose to omit the item before and after instruction?
- Are there patterns in the response distributions that point to a confusing/ambiguous item?

Table 12.8A illustrates a pre-post item analysis with desirable shifts in numbers from the Pre to Post assessments. Altogether, 32 postinstruction students select the keyed correct answer in the posttest, compared to only 10 in the pretest, and we see reduced numbers of students in all the distracter cells in the posttest data. (Table 12.8B shows data for distracter analysis from an IG/UG design, discussed later.)

*Step 5*   As before, the item analysis results should be considered as an integrated whole. Table 12.9 provides some general guidelines for CRT item analysis and follow-up actions you could consider (after Berk, 1984).

**TABLE 12.8B   Illustrative Data for a Distracter Analysis in an IG and UG Item Analysis Study**

| Item 25 | 1 | 2 | 3 | Correct answer<br>_4_ | 5 | Omit |
|---|---|---|---|---|---|---|
| **Instructed Group (IG)** | 2 | 3 | 2 | 30 | 3 | 0 |
| **Uninstructed Group (UG)** | 10 | 6 | 7 | 8 | 2 | 7 |
| $N_{IG} = 40$ | | | | | | |
| $N_{UG} = 40$ | | | | | | |

**TABLE 12.9   Guidelines for Interpretation of CRT Item Analysis**

| Item Characteristics | Explanations | Action |
|---|---|---|
| $p$ value in preinstruction, uninstructed, or non-master data unexpectedly high (Expected .25, obtained .50) | Students had prior knowledge of content tested, OR item not dependent on instructional domain. | Reconsider learning outcome; Match of item to learning outcome; Write higher-level item. |
| $p$ value does not show change in criterion groups, $D$ values much lower than expected or *negative* (expected $D = +.50$, obtained $D = +.06$). Response distributions not consistent with predictions in criterion groups. | Instruction was ineffective, or item was too complex, difficult, or ambiguous, OR item was miskeyed. | Write better, cleaner item; Modify instructional methods; check your key. |
| Large numbers who omit item in both criterion groups. | Students cannot get to item in a lengthy test, OR item too complex, difficult, or ambiguous, OR outcome was not taught. | See above. |
| $p$ value of .70 or higher in postinstruction, instructed, or master data. $D$ value is positive and of adequate magnitude ($+.40$ or better). Distracter and keyed response distributions show expected patterns. | Item and instructional program working as expected. | Keep item. |

## 12.5.2   Item Analysis for CRTs with Two Groups

If we were to use a two-group design (either UG/IG or M/NM) instead of the pre-post approach on a single group of students, the same procedures for calculation of item statistics apply, with the understanding that the data were generated by separately administering the same test to two criterion groups, either UG/IG or M/NM. In these latter applications, we have to make sure that the two student groups have equal *N*s and are similar in every respect other than their exposure to instruction or level of domain mastery. Establishing equivalence in the groups can be a sticky challenge. A strategy is to identify some critical variables that could confound interpretations of the results, such as gender, socioeconomic status, prior training on related curricular areas, field experience, and so forth, and include individuals matched on the chosen variables in the item analysis sample.

   With IG/UG or M/NM as the criterion groups, the formulas for a CRT $p_i$ value would be adjusted as follows:

$p_i(IG)$ = Number of individuals in instructed group who select the right answer/$N$

$p_i(UG)$ = Number of individuals in uninstructed group who select the right answer/$N$

$p_i(M)$ = Number of individuals in master group who select the right answer/$N$

$p_i(NM)$ = Number of individuals in non-master group who select the right answer/$N$.

We would make the necessary adjustments to the formulas for the $D$ values using a similar logic, starting with an organization of the data into quadrants with pretest/posttest dimensions replaced by either M/NM or IG/UG labels. For example, the pre-post formula for $D$ would be adjusted as follows:

$$D_{M\text{-}NM} = p_{i\,(M)} - p_{i\,(NM)}$$
$$D_{IG\text{-}UG} = p_{i\,(IG)} - p_{i\,(UG)}.$$

Illustration of a distracter analysis for an item using the IG/UG design is shown in Table 12.8B. Here, the desired differences in distributions of responses to each option in the item are evident in that greater numbers choose the correct answer in IG, no individuals omit the item in the IG, and far more individuals choose the incorrect options in the UG than in the IG.

# 12.6   Item Descriptive Statistics

As mentioned earlier in the chapter, descriptive statistics that help us evaluate item properties include the item-level *mean, standard deviation,* and *item homogeneity* indices. Total or domain score statistics are used for reference in interpreting item data. The illustrative data in this section are shown in Table 12.10, and taken from an attitude scale instead of achievement/ability measures.

## 12.6.1   Item Means and Variances/Standard Deviations

What can the individual item means, standard deviations, and variances tell us about the quality of a scale made up of a group of similar items? The *item mean* tells us where the typical respondent is likely to be found on the response scale. The item standard deviation and variance ($s_i$ and $s_i^2$ respectively) show how much variability there is in a typical group's responses around the item mean. If we create an item with five response options and find that there is *little* or *no variability* in the responses (all the respondents selected only Options 1 and 2), we could conclude that the item is failing to draw the predicted range of responses and needs to be reexamined. This is useful information for the assessment designer. Second, by comparing the item means and variances to the total score mean and variance, we can answer the question, To what extent is this item contributing to the variability of the total score? If an item is a useful addition to the domain or subdomain, we would expect it to increase the variability in the total score (Crocker & Algina, 1986; Nunnally & Bernstein, 1994).

In practice, item means, standard deviations, and variances are calculated with the procedures illustrated in Chapter 10 in items scaled on ordinal or higher levels of measurement (e.g., rating scales with five or more scale points/options, 1–5; 1–10). In cases where an item has a nominal scale (right-wrong), as most structured-response achievement/ability items do, the item mean is represented by the proportion of examinees who pick the right answer, $p_i$. The proportion of examinees who pick the wrong response is $q_i$ or $(1 - p_i)$. As you will recognize, the item mean, $p_i$, is the item difficulty index. If we have 75 of 100 examinees picking the right answer, the item mean is:

$$p_i = 75/100 \text{ or } .75.$$

The item variance is $s_i^2$ given by:

$$s_i^2 = p_i \, q_i \text{ or } (.75)\,(.25) = .188$$

The positive square root of $s_i^2$ is the item standard deviation. Here it is .434.

In Table 12.10 (part A), we see item-level and domain score means and standard deviations from an instrument designed to measure attitudes of college-going students towards the Hepatitis B vaccine (adapted from Ganguly & Banerji, 2000). The items have ordinal scales, with five-point Likert scales ranging from 1 (Strongly Disagree, SD) to 5 (Strongly Agree, SA). A sample item from the instrument is presented in the table.

The results of descriptive item and domain score analysis are shown for four of the 15 items on the overall instrument. The maximum and minimum scores possible on the scale in Table 12.10 are 75 and 15, respectively. The overall domain score mean, with all 15 items included, is 45.8, with a variance of 34.69 on the group assessed. The results show that at the item level, Items 1, 3, and 4 have means and variances that are similar (means are from 3.29 to 3.34, variances are from .302 to .369). However, the mean for Item 2 is lower (2.68), with the item variance somewhat higher than the rest (.608). Such a difference might lead us to ask, Is Item 2, with an apparently different distribution from the other items, as relevant for the overall scale score?

In comparing the item and total score information with that given in the extreme right-hand column, we can see that Items 1, 3, and 4 all appear to be contributing to the domain score variance to some degree. Removal of Item 2 brings the total scale variance down from 34.69 to 29.99, a considerable drop. Such a finding suggests that although the descriptive statistics on Item 2 make it different from the remaining items, it is making the biggest contribution to the variability of the domain score. Similar results on other items are signals for us to retain the items.

## 12.6.2  Item Homogeneity

When we use a statistical index of homogeneity, we are trying to answer the question, Is this item measuring the same attribute as the remaining items in the domain/subdomain? Although we will treat it as different here, *item homogeneity* is conceptually related to

**TABLE 12.10   Descriptive and Homogeneity Statistics from Items on an Attitude Scale:**

**Sample Item from *Hepatitis B Vaccine* — Attitude Scale:**
*I am willing to take the Hepatitis B Vaccine.*      1    2    3    4    5
                                                    SD—D—U—A—SA
Number of Items in the Domain = 15

**A.   Item and Total Score Descriptive Statistics (four items):**

| Item Number | Item Mean | Item Variance | Domain Score Mean | Domain Score Variance | *Domain Score Minus Item* | |
|---|---|---|---|---|---|---|
| | | | | | *Mean* | *Variance* |
| 1. | 3.34 | 0.336 | 45.80 | 34.69 | 42.46 | 31.02 |
| 2. | 2.68 | 0.608 | 45.80 | 34.69 | 43.12 | 29.99 |
| 3. | 3.29 | 0.369 | 45.80 | 34.69 | 42.52 | 30.78 |
| 4. | 3.34 | 0.302 | 45.80 | 34.69 | 42.46 | 32.05 |

**B.   Item-to-Total Score Correlations (four items):**

| Item Number | Adusted Item-Total Score Correlation (*Minus Item*) |
|---|---|
| 1. | .51 |
| 2. | .47 |
| 3. | .50 |
| 4. | .37 |

the *D* index (see Section 12.2), where we ask, Is this item discriminating between my chosen criterion groups in the same way as the total domain/subdomain score? Item homogeneity is also parallel to the notion of internal consistency reliability (Chapters 3 and 13), where we are interested in determining whether an item is consistently measuring the same characteristic as the other items in the domain/subdomain with correlational procedures. In this chapter, we will look at item homogeneity with the statistical technique called *item-to-total score correlation,* using the attitudinal scale items from Table 12.10.

The *item-to-total score correlation* for a structured item is computed using the *point-biserial correlation coefficient* ($r_{pb}$, a variation of Pearson's *r* statistic, see Chapter 10). Basically, it correlates the item response distribution with the domain score (total score) distribution, with the item deleted from the total score calculation. Hence the statistic is labeled the *adjusted item-to-total score correlation* in the table.

The bottom panel of Table 12.10 provides the adjusted item-to-total score correlations for the four attitudinal items of the Hepatitis B scale. As we can see, all four items show moderate positive correlations with the remainder score, ranging from .37 to .51. Such results allow the interpretation that all four items tend to be homogeneous with the remaining domain, with Item 1 showing the highest degree of homogeneity and Item 4 the lowest. When items show adjusted item-to-total score correlations of .40 or better, they are considered a good addition to the domain or subdomain score. Negative or low values suggest item problems.

## 12.7   Limitations of Item Analysis Studies

A few cautionary caveats in the interpretation and use of item analysis results are necessary prior to concluding this chapter.

- Item analysis, in and of itself, cannot correct item flaws. The procedures simply provide us with methods to detect them. Assuming we choose the procedures with care and interpret the results with thoughtful judgment, item analysis findings can help to improve the original item pool.
- The accuracy and utility of the findings of item analysis studies are dependent on appropriate selection of *criterion groups*. If we fail to take this factor into account in designing NRT and CRT item analysis studies, the interpretation of results can be seriously confounded and misleading.
- This chapter attempted to provide guidelines for definition of CRT and NRT criterion groups that are generally consistent with the research literature. Readers should be aware that researchers and textbooks have previously recommended the use of the upper and lower 27% of the test scores for NRTs, and in technical manuals of many current tests, the proportion varies from 24% to 37%. Use of the upper and lower 33% is recommended in this chapter as it does not assume any distributional properties, adequately serves the purposes of NRT item design, and is easy to remember.
- When conducting CRT item analysis studies, we should attempt to control for confounding effects of variables that can distort our conclusions about item characteristics. For example in a single-group, pre–post design, we should allow an adequate time gap between the two measurements so that the effects of exposure to the item in the pretest wear off in the examinee sample. Similarly, when we use two different groups (e.g., IG/UG), the individuals in both groups should be similar in composition in every respect other than their exposure to instruction on the item domain. Otherwise, our conclusions regarding the instructional sensitivity of an item will stray from the mark.
- We should remember that all item analysis studies based on the classical approach are group-dependent. The $p$, $D$, or $r_{pb}$ values could well change in different groups. To improve stability of item statistics, we should use large samples ($N > 30$), and ensure that the group is composed of individuals that are representative of the specified population for which the instrument is intended. If we follow the Process Model (Chapters 5–9), we would refer back to our specifications to ensure that actions taken in selecting the group for item analysis or other empirical validation efforts are consistent with our original plan.

---

### Computer Resources for Item Analysis

Check out the "Conventional Item Analysis" options from Assessment Systems Corporation software on:
- Item and test analysis
- Scale and survey analysis

Assessment Systems Corporation
2233 University Avenue
St. Paul, MN 55114
(612) 647–9220

---

# Summary

Item analysis is an important part of the assessment development process. It allows the designer to refine an item pool and ensure that items retained are good representations of the construct and best serve the assessment purposes. Poor items should either be eliminated or revised before we put together the final instrument.

A variety of statistical and logical procedures can help us in identifying items that fail to function as intended in a typical population. Chapter 12 dealt with four major item analysis procedures/statistics: item difficulty ($p_i$), item discrimination ($D$), distracter analysis, and item homogeneity. It also described how item descriptive statistics can be evaluated in relation to the total score statistics to improve item quality. Of the procedures in Chapter 12, $p_i$, $D$, and distracter analysis are best applied when developing written, structured-response items for achievement/ability tests. Descriptive item statistics and item homogeneity indices are also applicable in attitudinal or psychological scale-development contexts with structured, Likert-scale items.

Before embarking on item analysis for achievement/ability items, the designer should decide on whether the assessment is a norm-referenced tool (NRT) or a criterion-referenced tool (CRT). Item analysis studies will differ for NRTs and CRTs in terms of criterion groups used, formulas for computing item statistics, and the interpretation of results. Item statistics should be reviewed along with the qualitative characteristics of the item. Items for NRTs should have moderate to high difficulty and positive discrimination indices. CRT items should have instructional sensitivity in suitable curricular contexts.

Item homogeneity was illustrated in Chapter 12 with the item-to-total score correlations in an attitude scale made up of Likert-type items. In instruments developed with a domain-sampling procedure, the item-to-total score correlation should be positive, and moderate to high in value.

We should be aware of the possible limitations of item statistics and various data collection designs before applying results of item analysis. The better studies use larger samples ($N > 30$) composed of individuals with the same characteristics as the targeted examinee/respondent group. Classical item statistics are all group-dependent. We should make sure that appropriate criterion groups were used in the studies. We should remind ourselves that conducting an item analysis will not automatically improve an instrument unless we use the results to delete, rewrite, or otherwise alter a flawed item. Follow-up work on items and the overall instrument should be continued until we obtain the desired item properties.

## QUESTIONS FOR CLASS DISCUSSION

1. Using the data in Table 12.1, conduct an item analysis for Items # 4–8. Evaluate which of the items are most suitable for inclusion in a norm-referenced instrument. For each item, comment on the $p$, $D$, and effectiveness of distracters.

   What actions would you take to keep, delete or re-examine/revise the content of the items? Explain your answers.

2. Using the data in Table 12.5, conduct an item analysis for Items # 3–4. Calculate the item difficulty value and all three item discrimination values demonstrated in this section, for each item. Comment on each item's difficulty and instructional sensitivity. What actions would you take to keep, delete or re-examine/revise the content of the items? Explain your answers.

3. Review a technical manual for a published instrument in each of these categories:
   (a) a CRT achievement test
   (b) a NRT achievement test
   (c) a psychological construct measure

   Identify and describe all the item analysis statistics that are reported in the manual that you recognize. Evaluate the quality of items used in each of the instruments based on the item information provided.

4. The following results were obtained for an item from a norm-referenced test, when administered to a group of 270 students. The item analysis study table is shown below.

   *Item 7*

   | | | | *Correct answer* | | | |
   |---|---|---|---|---|---|---|
   | | n | 1 | <u>2</u> | 3 | 4 | Omit |
   | High group | 90 | 2 | 74 | 4 | 10 | 0 |
   | Low group | 90 | 24 | 33 | 15 | 3 | 15 |

   Calculate the $p$ value.
   Calculate the $D$ value.
   Which distracters are functioning as intended?
   What problems do you identify, if any, with the item? What actions would you take to improve the item?

5. Suppose you obtained the results shown below for an item from a CRT.
   Calculate and compare the $p_i$ (pre) and $p_i$ (post) values.
   Calculate the $D_{\text{pre-post}}$ value.
   Which distracters appear to be functioning as intended?
   What problems do you identify, if any, with the item? What actions would you take to improve the item?

   *Item 5*

   |  | n | 1 | 2 | 3 | *Correct answer*<br>*4* | Omit |
   |---|---|---|---|---|---|---|
   | Pre-instruction | 80 | 0 | 45 | 10 | 20 | 5 |
   | Post-instruction | 80 | 10 | 10 | 0 | 45 | 15 |

6. Compare the usefulness of the three $D$ values for CRT item development.
   **i.**  $D_{\text{pre-post}} = p_{i\,(\text{post})} - p_{i\,(\text{pre})}$
   **ii.**  $D_{\text{igain}} = n_3 \div N$
   **iii.**  $D_{\text{ngain}} = (n_3 - n_4) \div N$

   Which one(s) would you prefer to use in your own work and why?
   Which one(s) would you look for when selecting or adopting a commercially developed CRT?

# 13  Quantitative Evaluation of Validity and Reliability

## Overview

In earlier chapters, we started with the assumption that professionals/practitioners often need to develop their own assessment tools. The last two chapters, Chapters 13 and 14, turn their focus to *adoption* and *selection* of preexisting instruments. They deal with issues and factors that you should consider when making decisions on the quality of instruments that were developed by others.

Specifically, Chapter 13 deals with the application and interpretation of information pertinent to score validity and reliability. An examination of validity and reliability is an important first step in evaluating the quality of information provided by assessments. We revisit concepts initially presented in Chapter 3, with a particular focus on empirical methods for the quantitative estimation of errors from different sources. Within the framework of the Process Model introduced in Chapter 5 (see Figure 5.1), this chapter addresses Phase IVB, which deals with empirical evaluation of assessments and the scores they yield. Following brief conceptual presentations of particular procedures, the chapter illustrates hypothetical or real psychometric data excerpted from technical reports or journal articles on selected instruments in a series of case studies. To orient yourself to the statistical procedures employed in this chapter, you may wish to review Chapter 10 again, particularly Sections 10.8 and 10.9.

Although the material will appear more complex than the information in Chapter 3, Chapter 13 provides only a general overview of the validity and reliability statistics that would be most relevant to support particular uses of test scores, how they are derived, and what they mean in applied situations. This information is relevant for practitioners who serve as consumers and/or interpreters of psychometric reports of standardized, externally developed assessments, and more formally developed local tools. It may also serve as a guide for planning validation and reliability studies for instruments you have designed. If you are asked to review psychometric information on particular tests and make recommendations for their selection or adoption for particular purposes, the chapter could prove helpful. Methods described here should be employed by test developers who anticipate widespread use of their instruments, especially when high stakes applications are likely. For more in-depth expositions on topics that interest you, you should consult more advanced textbooks in measurement (for example, Crocker & Algina, 1986; McDonald, 1999; Nunnally & Bernstein, 1994).

## CHAPTER 13 OBJECTIVES

After studying this chapter and completing the structured exercises in the module, you should be able to:

1. Differentiate among methods for obtaining, analyzing, and reporting evidence to support the validity of particular score interpretations

2. Interpret the needed forms of validity evidence in a unified manner in given contexts of assessment use

3. Describe key concepts from classical reliability theory: observed scores, true scores, and standard error of measurement

4. Describe the standard error of measurement and reliability coefficients as two alternate methods for estimation of score reliability

5. Interpret different types of reliability coefficients, errors estimated, and data collection designs for estimating errors of measurement (split-half, K-R 20, Cronbach's alpha, test–retest, interrater, and parallel forms reliability coefficients)

6. Describe decision-theoretic approaches to estimating reliability of cut scores (for criterion-referenced tests)

7. Describe error variance and generalizability as it applies to domain score interpretation

## 13.1   Empirical Validation Methods

The same assessment tool can be, and is often used for fulfilling multiple purposes. Unless we have the evidence to support each different application, however, our inferences from the results (we will refer to the results as "scores" here) will not be valid or defensible. Empirical validation studies are necessary to validate the desired score interpretations in particular contexts of assessment use. Consider the following case of a statewide assessment program (Case Study 13.1).

### Case Study 13.1

### Validity in a Statewide Assessment Program

The *Accountability Update,* Vol. VI, No. 3, published by the Florida Commission of Education Reform and Accountability in summer, 1998, specified the following uses of the recently developed *Florida Comprehensive Assessment Tests* (FCAT) in reading, mathematics, and writing (p. 1):

(1)  as an accountability measure for school performance,
(2)  to identify "critically low" performing schools,
(3)  as the criterion measure for high school graduation of individual students,
(4)  to identify recipients for Florida's Bright Futures Scholarships, and
(5)  as a placement tool for student advising and counseling

Newspaper reports add other purposes to this already formidable list, such as grade retention of elementary and middle school students.

*Validity issues that we could raise:*

- Can the scores of the FCAT tests be used to make valid decisions to fulfill all these different purposes?
- Do the test-makers and users have evidence to support the use of the FCAT scores in a valid and dependable manner for each of the separate applications—such as, criterion-referenced decisions to certify high school graduates, separating effective schools from ineffective ones, and so on? If not, what evidence should they seek?
- How much error can (or should) be tolerated in each of these decisions?

To ascertain validity it is not sufficient for us to ask: Does the assessment tool measure what it was supposed to measure? To ensure valid interpretations of results with respect to purposes, we should also ask, Do the scores have the properties to allow the inferences we would like to make in the desired contexts of use? An assessment tool should measure what it was intended to if we formally determine that it has acceptable content-based validity (such as reading, mathematics, or writing skills in the *FCAT*). However, it can still be used for purposes for which it was not originally designed, in new situations, or with different populations. Varied assessment applications demand that developers and/or users undertake empirical validation studies to justify the different usages of the scores.

### 13.1.1   Assessment Purposes, Contexts of Use, and Validation

*Validation* is a process for gathering, documenting, and evaluating a unified body of evidence to support particular interpretations of an assessment's scores in given user contexts (AERA, APA, & NCME, 1999). Assessment developers in formal settings should start the assessment design process with an explicit statement of the purposes for which the scores are likely to be used. Based on the anticipated uses of the scores, they should then begin systematic research to document the extent to which the scores are indeed valid for their stated purposes. Users of the same assessment tool, who may or may not participate in the assessment design process, should evaluate the body of evidence provided by the developers to determine the extent to which it supports their anticipated interpretations of the assessment results, *before* they put the instrument to use. If users wish to employ an assessment tool for purposes not identified by the original authors, they bear the responsibility to conduct the needed work to validate the scores for the new or different applications (AERA, APA, & NCME, 1985, 1999).

All forms of evidence collected to validate scores can be called *construct validity evidence,* since it improves our understanding of the construct that a tool measures. Validation starts with gathering *content-based validity evidence,* described in Chapters 5–9. We establish content validity by asking experts to conduct a structured review of an assessment tool with respect to its *content relevance* and *content representativeness.* Content validation occurs in Phase IVA of the Process Model for assessment design, selection, and validation. While content-based validity evidence is often adequate to meet the needs of small-scale, local assessment development efforts, empirical evidence is necessary when users are planning to use the assessment results in ways that could have potentially serious consequences for the examinees or other stakeholders.

Generally, empirical validity evidence is gathered in Phase IVB of the Process Model. It also calls for more involved data-gathering and analysis than the content-validation phase, when the instrument we design or choose to adopt is administered to samples of the targeted population. Our approaches to validation can vary. Depending on the purposes specified for an assessment tool and inferences to be made with the scores, such evidence can be obtained from a variety of sources with different methods of data collection and analyses. In Chapter 3, Table 3.3 introduced you to various kinds of validity evidence. In this section, we review six of the most predominant approaches to empirical validation. These deal with gathering:

- Convergent and discriminant validity evidence
- Evidence of predictive validity
- Evidence of concurrent validity
- Evidence of internal structure
- Evidence of group differences
- Evidence of lack of bias in items/test scores

For each approach, we will first consider the assessment purposes and anticipated contexts of use that drive the evidence-gathering efforts, examine the validation procedures involved, and interpret samples of results.

**Key Concepts**

- Validation is a process for gathering, documenting, and evaluating a unified body of evidence to support particular interpretations of an assessment's scores in given contexts.
- We should follow content-validation reviews with appropriate empirical validation studies.
- Depending on the assessment's purposes, contexts in which it is likely to be used, and specific inferences to be made with the results, the empirical validation methods we use can vary.

## 13.1.2   Convergent and Discriminant Validity Evidence

*Assessment Purposes Driving the Evidence-Gathering.*   *Convergent* or *discriminant validity* coefficients help to confirm or disconfirm our hypotheses about the nature of the construct we are attempting to measure on the basis of empirical correlations with scores from other measures of the same and different constructs. We gather evidence of *convergent validity* by observing how well scores from our instrument correlate with other measures of the same construct. We seek evidence of *discriminant validity* when the underlying theory suggests that scores from our tool should be uncorrelated with measures of constructs known to be distinctly different.

***Description of Procedures/Analyses.*** Validation procedures for obtaining convergent and discriminant validity evidence involve the computation of correlation coefficients, such as Pearson's *r* for continuous, interval-scaled variables. We would measure the same group of individuals on a variety of instruments, including the tool for which scores are being validated. Some of the tools would be selected because they are known to tap the same construct as the tool under investigation. Others would be deliberately selected because they measure clearly different attributes. Following test administration and data collection, we would compute bivariate correlation coefficients using paired scores from the various instruments. The *correlation matrix* created thus would enable us to evaluate whether our hypotheses about convergence or divergence of constructs were supported by the data. A comparison of the size of the *r* or $r^2$ values would help a determination of the extent to which data from "like" measures converge, while data from "unlike" measures diverge.

***Interpretation of Validity Evidence.*** Interpretation of convergent and discriminant validity coefficients should be guided by theoretical hypotheses about what the construct represents and the relationships that can be expected based on existing knowledge of all the measures employed in the study. In interpreting all correlation coefficients, we must remember that they are affected by the variability of scores in the group and the sample size. Unless the reported correlation coefficients are accompanied by information on statistical significance of the *r* value, the relationship will apply only to the group studied.

Lastly, we should remember that other construct measures we use to establish convergence or divergence of scores from the instrument under examination will have varying levels of reliability. Reliability in measures can be quantitatively estimated (see next section). If less reliable measures are used, it will attenuate or weaken the correlation coefficients we obtain. There are formulas that can help correct for attenuated correlations (see Crocker & Algina, 1986 or Nunnally & Bernstein, 1994, if interested). In examining various validity coefficients, we should thus also weigh the available information on reliability and corrections for attentuation.

## Case Study 13.2

## Convergent and Discriminant Validity for a Fifth-Grade Achievement Battery

A test development corporation developed an achievement test battery for 5th graders, composed of a series of reading and mathematics subtests made up of multiple choice items. Because of the verbal loading in the domains of the various reading subtests (e.g., reading comprehension, vocabulary, language skills), the developers hypothesized that the reading subtest scores would be strongly intercorrelated with each other, affirming their *convergent* validity. They also hypothesized

*(continued)*

## 13.2  Continued

that the mathematics subtest scores, based on computation, number concepts, and word problem domains, would show high convergent validity with each other because of their shared quantitative elements. In contrast, they expected the mathematics subtest scores to yield lower correlations with the reading scores, providing evidence of *discriminant* validity.

To test the above validation hypotheses empirically, the developers designed a convergent and discriminant validity study where they administered their battery to a representative sample of 5th graders. Table 13.1 presents results of this hypothetical study (adapted from the CTB-4; CTB/McGraw-Hill, 1989). To illustrate the concepts of discriminant and convergent validity, let us focus on the reading vocabulary test.

**TABLE 13.1  Convergent and Discriminant Validity Evidence on Mathematics and Reading Subtests: Case Study 13.2**

| Subtest | Correlation Matrix | | | | | | Subtest # and Description |
|---------|------|------|------|------|------|------|---------------------------|
|         | 1    | 2    | 3    | 4    | 5    | 6    |                           |
|         | 1.00 | .73  | .77  | .49  | .42  | .61  | **1.** Reading Comprehension |
|         |      | 1.00 | .69  | .38  | .35  | .59  | **2.** Reading Vocabulary |
|         |      |      | 1.00 | .39  | .40  | .58  | **3.** Language Skills |
|         |      |      |      | 1.00 | .75  | .60  | **4.** Number Concepts |
|         |      |      |      |      | 1.00 | .65  | **5.** Math Computation |
|         |      |      |      |      |      | 1.00 | **6.** Math Problem Solving |

*Note:*

.73   Convergent validity evidence

.77   Convergent validity evidence

.35   Discriminant validity evidence

.38   Discriminant validity evidence

The correlation matrix shows coefficients of the different subtest scores from the reading and mathematics sections of the CTB achievement battery. To read the table, we would read the subtest number from the vertical column (for example, Subtest number 2) and pick up the Pearson correlation of its scores in the table with the subtest label that corresponds with it horizontally. Thus, we see that Subtest 2 (reading vocabulary) scores correlate in the order of .73 with Subtest 1 (reading comprehension) scores.

The correlations of .73 and .77 between the reading and language subtest scores suggest convergence in the underlying reading constructs, confirming the developers' expectations. Relatively, the correlations of reading vocabulary with number concepts and mathematics computation scores range from .35 to .38, providing evidence of discriminant validity. If we then examine the correlations among scores of the three mathematics subtests, again we find evidence of convergence among the underlying constructs in *r* values of .75 and .60. Overall, thus, the validity coefficients confirm the developers' theory that the mathematics subtests are measuring somewhat different constructs from their reading subtests. Notice, however, that discriminant validity coefficients are relatively weak between mathematics problem-solving scores and reading/language subtests (correlations of .58–.61, see column 6). This may be due to the verbal skills needed by examinees to answer word problems in mathematics.

---

**Key Concept**

■ Discriminant and convergent validity evidence helps to confirm the extent to which scores of an assessment tool overlap, or fail to overlap, with scores of other theoretically relevant measures with empirical correlations.

## 13.1.3   Method Variance and Convergent and Discriminant Validity

Campbell and Fiske (1959), the original proponents of convergent and discriminant validation, recommended that assessment developers control for *method variance* when they gather and analyze convergent and discriminant data from assessments. Method variance has to do with the extent to which scores from two instruments are related because of the use of a common assessment method, as opposed to the commonality in the underlying construct. As we know, different assessment methods, such as multiple choice tests, essays, or behavior-based observations, can be used to measure the same construct. To tease out the effects of assessment methods from the common variance in two measures of the same attribute, they proposed that we employ a *multitrait, multimethod matrix* of correlations. In a multitrait, multimethod matrix, we could compare the magnitude of correlations of like and unlike constructs, when measured with similar and dissimilar assessment methods.

---

## Case Study 13.3
## The Effect of Assessment Method on Validity

Table 13.2 illustrates hypothetical data for evaluating convergent and discriminant validity evidence in a multitrait, multimethod matrix. The assessment being validated is a multiple choice test of mathematical ability (Test $A_1$). To evaluate convergent and discriminant validity of scores from Test $A_1$, the table uses examples of several assessments of two clearly different constructs: mathematics (Tests $A_{11}$, $A_2$, $A_3$), and language arts (Tests $B_1$, $B_2$, $B_3$).

The diagonal of the matrix presents *test–retest reliability coefficients,* based on correlations of the same instrument's scores on a given group of individuals, measured on two occasions. Test-retest reliability coefficients, underlined in Table 13.2, are different from the convergent and discriminant validity coefficients in that they convey the extent to which scores from the same instrument are reproducible over short periods of time (see Section 13.2 for more details on reliability).

*(continued)*

## 13.3    Continued

**TABLE 13.2    Hypothetical Data for Evaluating Convergent and Discriminant Validity Evidence in a Multitrait Multimethod Matrix: Case Study 13.3**

| Domains | Test | Method 1 Multiple Choice | | | Method 2 Interview-based Assessment | | Method 3 Written Open-ended Tasks | |
|---|---|---|---|---|---|---|---|---|
| | | $A_1$ | $A_{11}$ | $B_1$ | $A_2$ | $B_2$ | $A_3$ | $B_3$ |
| Math | $A_1$ | .90 | | | | | | |
| | $A_{11}$ | (.81) | .89 | | | | | |
| Language Arts: | $B_1$ | .50 | .45 | .88 | | | | |
| Math | $A_2$ | (.75) | .71 | | .85 | | | |
| Language Arts: | $B_2$ | .44 | .48 | .60 | [.65] | .82 | | |
| Math: | $A_3$ | .52 | .59 | .62 | .70 | | .78 | |
| Language Arts: | $B_3$ | .26 | .30 | .63 | [.41] | .68 | .56 | .85 |

.81    Convergent validity with same methods

.75    Convergent validity with different methods

[.65]    Discriminant validity with same methods

[.41]    Discriminant validity with different methods

.89    Reliability coefficient (all reliability coefficients underlined)

***Interpretation of Validity Evidence.***    As before, interpretation of validity data is facilitated if we start with some informed hypotheses about the directions and strengths of the relationships. In Table 13.2, we would expect scores from Test $A_1$ to correlate positively and strongly with scores from other tests of the same underlying trait, measured with the same method, such as Test $A_{11}$, thus affirming convergent validity under conditions where same assessment method is employed. Simultaneously, we would also expect $A_1$ scores to correlate reasonably well with other mathematics assessments even when they employ different assessment methods (e.g., Tests $A_2, A_3$), thus providing evidence of convergent validity under conditions of method variance.

To evaluate discriminant validity, we would expect scores from Test $A_1$ to have much lower correlations with an assessment of language ability (Test $B_1$), a qualitatively different construct. Discriminant validity should be evident in the size of the correlation coefficients or $r^2$ values, whether or not the variables are measured with the same assessment method.

In Table 13.2, we have evidence supporting convergent validity of scores from Test $A_1$ in the $rA_1, A_{11}$ of .81, showing that scores from two multiple choice tests of mathematical ability, $A_1$ and $A_{11}$, correlate substantially ($r^2$ value suggests over 64% overlapping variance). Convergence is also evident when the assessment methods vary. For example, the $rA_1, A_2 = .75$ and $rA_1, A_3 = .62$, indicate that the overlapping variance is 56% to 38%, respectively, when different assessment methods are used to measure the same trait.

Do the discriminant validity data support the inference that Test $A_1$ scores are providing information on a clearly distinct trait from the language ability construct measured by Tests $B_1$, $B_2$, and $B_3$? Test $A_1$ scores correlate as follows with the $B_1$, $B_2$, and $B_3$ scores: $rA_1, B_1 = .50$, $rA_1, B_2 = .44$, and $rA_1, B_3 = .26$ (approximately 9–25% overlapping variance). These correlations are considerably lower than those with scores of the mathematics tests. The highest across-trait correlations are found when both traits are measured with nontraditional assessment methods ($rA_2, B_2 = .65$, when both constructs are measured with interviews, and $rA_3, B_3 = .56$, when both measured are with written, open-ended tasks). Such results suggest a "method effect"; however, the general pattern of correlations suggest that Test $A_1$ scores do indeed have the convergent and discriminant validity expected by the developers.

---

**Key Concept**

■ The multitrait multimethod matrix helps us to take into account the effects of assessment methods when interpreting convergent and discriminant validity evidence.

## 13.1.4 Predictive Validity Evidence

***Assessment Purposes Driving the Evidence-Gathering.*** When we expect that the assessment scores/results will predict a future "criterion" behavior in the individuals assessed, we establish validity by gathering evidence of *predictive validity*. Evaluation of predictive validity depends on the selection of a defensible external criterion measure, and falls under the broad umbrella of *criterion-related validity* (see Chapter 3). The assessment tool that generates the scores being checked is called the "predictor," while the instrument yielding measures against which the predictor is validated is called the "criterion." Scores of aptitude tests, which are purported to measure *potential for success* in an area (as opposed to the *current status of proficiency* in an area) require predictive validity evidence to support their use.

***Description of Procedures and Analyses.*** This form of validation involves a longitudinal data collection design and correlation/regression analysis with scores from predictor and criterion measures. We would measure a group on the predictor, follow the individuals to a future time that is appropriate, and then measure them on the criterion measure. The scatterplots, magnitude of the correlation coefficient (usually Pearson's $r$), and the $r^2$ values would provide evidence of the predictive power of scores from the predictor.

Results of the correlation or regression can also be used to set up *expectancy tables,* which present the calculated probabilities of a criterion score, given a predictor score range. Furthermore, the regression line can be used to calculate the *standard errors of estimate* and *confidence bands* around predicted scores on the criterion measure, allowing users to make statements such as the following:

> *Taking into account the random errors of estimation, 95% of the time this student's score on the criterion measure will fall within (this) range.*

Confidence bands are discussed in further detail in Section 13.2 of this chapter.

***Interpretation of Predictive Validity Evidence.***   Like all types of validity evidence, predictive validity evidence should be evaluated in conjunction with pre-existing information about the constructs and population in question. Again, the interpretive guidelines for validity coefficients in Section 13.1.2 would apply here as well. An application scenario follows.

## Case Study 13.4
## Predictive Validity

Advanced Placement (AP) examinations, developed and administered by the College Board, are usually recommended for 12th-grade students. Typically, 12th graders take the AP examinations after they complete AP classes in selected subject areas during their last year in high school. Teachers in a particular high school wanted to offer Science AP classes to selected students in 11th grade, a year ahead of the recommended schedule. They decided to administer a science aptitude test (Test C) to help identify students most likely to succeed in the AP program. To determine whether scores from Test C, the predictor, had adequate validity for predicting future AP performance, they sought *predictive validity evidence.*

The question they wanted answered was, To what extent are scores on Test C useful for identifying 10th graders most likely to receive scores of 3, 4, and 5 on the AP examinations at the end of 11th grade? Two predictive validity studies were reported in the test publisher's manuals that addressed their question. In both studies, scores on Test C were obtained on 10th-grade samples of students. The criterion measure consisted of Science AP test scores measured a year later, when the same students had completed 11th grade. The predictive validity evidence on Test C was reported in two forms: a *predictive validity coefficient* and an *expectancy table.* Table 13.3 presents that data.

The *r* values reported in the studies were in the range of .55 to .60, and indicated that about 30–36% of the variance in the criterion scores was explained by the scores on the predictor. Such results suggested that scores on Test C had modest predictive properties. Based on the correlation between the scores of the AP test and Test C, the cells in the expectancy tables provided the percent of students likely to obtain particular AP scores in 11th grade. The probabilities in the expectancy table can be interpreted as percents. From the moderate correlations reported, one could expect only 15% of the students who scored in the range of 60–79 on Test C to obtain AP scores of 3, 4, or 5. Similarly, 25% of students who obtained scores of 80–100 on Test C would be likely to receive AP scores in the same range; and only 5% of those scoring 59 or below would be likely to get a passing score of 3 on the AP test. The results of both studies seemed close enough to suggest that the test-makers had been able to replicate the predictive validity findings in two different samples of students.

**TABLE 13.3  Predictive Validity Evidence for a Science Aptitude Test: Case Study 13.4**

**Predictor:**  **Test C Scores in Tenth Grade**
**Criterion:**  **Science AP Examination Scores in Eleventh Grade**
$r_{C,AP} = .60$

Expectancy Table

AP Exam Scores

| Test C Scores | 1 | 2 | 3 | 4 | 5 | |
|---|---|---|---|---|---|---|
| 80–100 | | | .10 | .10 | .05 | .25 |
| 60–79 | .10 | .25 | .05 | .05 | .05 | .50 |
| 50 and below | .10 | .10 | .05 | | | .25 |
| | .20 | .35 | .20 | .15 | .10 | 1.00 |

The teachers evaluated the predictive validity data in light of what they knew scientifically inclined 10th graders in their own school could reasonably accomplish within the fraemwork of their AP program. The results seemed credible and consistent enough for them to adopt Test C to meet their decision-making needs at their school.

---

**Key Concept**

■ Predictive validity evidence is gathered to support a developer's claim that the respondents' present status on the predictor can be used to forecast their future performance or behavior on a relevant criterion measure.

*Selection Biases in Prediction Studies.*   The ultimate goal of most prediction studies is to develop instruments that yield scores with sufficient predictive validity to support accurate decisions when selecting or classifying individuals for jobs or special educational interventions. The effectiveness of prediction depends on more than the predictive validity coefficient. We have to consider the cut-scores set on the predictor and criterion distributions. In addition, it requires that we consider the *selection ratio,* or the proportion of candidates that will be selected based on their scores only on the predictor (i.e., those who meet the cut on the predictor); and the *base rate,* or proportion that would be selected based on their scores on the criterion (i.e., those who meet the cut on the criterion). Because of errors in prediction and unreliability, the *success ratio,* or the proportion that is actually selected based on the cut scores, is usually lower. There can be two kinds of prediction errors: *false positive* errors, where we select unqualified candidates, and *false negative* errors, where we fail to select qualified candidates.

The Taylor-Russell Tables (1939) were developed to take into account the interdependencies among predictive validity, the selection ratio, and the proportion that would be successfully selected in the absence of the assessment tool in question. The accuracy of a classification decision (success ratio) can be evaluated for different-sized predictive validity coefficients by consulting the tables, provided we have information available on the base rate and selection ratio. Here is an example. According to the table, when the base rate is .50 (a situation where half the examinees would be selected because they meet the cut on the criterion) and the selection ratio is .10 (and one-tenth meet the cut on the predictor), we would need a predictive validity coefficient of .60 to obtain a .90 success ratio (for 90% candidates to be classified without false positive or false negative errors in our decisions).

### 13.1.5   Concurrent Validity Evidence

*Assessment Purposes Driving the Evidence-Gathering.*   Criterion-related validity evidence can be of two kinds: that which yields *predictive validity coefficients,* needed when our purpose is to predict performance on the criterion at some time in the future (as shown in Section 13.1.3); or that which yields *concurrent validity coefficients,* needed when we wish to determine overlap between scores of the predictor and criterion when they are measured at the *same time.* Concurrent validity evidence is gathered when the developer aims to substitute the use of the criterion scores, usually an older test, with those from the predictor, usually claimed to be a newer and better test.

In terms of the data collection design and correlational procedures employed, concurrent validity is no different from convergent validity. With respect to purpose, however, these two forms of validity evidence differ. Concurrent validity studies are guided by the developer/user's need to replace an existing instrument with another, purported to measure the same construct. In contrast, convergent validity evidence is motivated by a need to better understand the meaning of a construct and construct-based scores.

*Description of Procedures/Analyses.*   This form of validation also involves correlational analysis of scores from a predictor (scores of the test being validated) with scores of a criterion instrument. The distinctiveness of a concurrent validity study lies in the fact that we would collect data on both the predictor and criterion at the same time, using a cross-sectional design. The term "cross-sectional" implies that we would take a sample of the population at a given time, administer both tests to the sample simultaneously or closely following one another, and compute a bivariate correlation coefficient using the score distributions ($r$).

*Interpretation of Concurrent Validity Evidence.*   Concurrent validity evidence should also be evaluated with reference to information about the constructs and population in question. Concurrent validity coefficients are also interpreted like other correlation coefficients (see Section 13.1.2). Consider the application scenario described next.

### Case Study 13.5

### Concurrent Validity Evidence

When the developers of the *Stanford Achievement Test Series* developed the 9th Edition of their battery, the SAT9, they wanted to convince their customers (school districts across the United

States) that the new version of their test would yield scores comparable to those from the older version, the SAT8, which was already in use in most of the districts. To do so, they conducted concurrent validity studies. Their objective was not so much to obtain evidence of the construct meanings of the SAT9 scores, but rather to persuade their clients to buy the new edition of their tests, which they claimed would yield much the same information as the earlier edition, while providing updated norms. (Test publishers generally discontinue older versions of their tests due to technical inadequacies related to the age of a test, such as outdated norms.)

Table 13.4 provides concurrent validity data reported for the Intermediate 2 level of the SAT9 tests. The table presents descriptive statistics on raw score distributions of the total batteries and subtests in reading, mathematics, and language areas. Concurrent validity coefficients are in the far right-hand column of the table. The $r$ values of .89, .82, and .92 suggest considerable overlap in the Total Reading, Total Mathematics, and All Language battery scores of the SAT9 and SAT8. However, we see that the relationships are lower at the subtest level ($r$ values around .70 or below), particularly for subject area tests like Science and Social Studies. In conclusion, the total battery scores of SAT9 appear to have much higher concurrent validity than the subtest scores.

**TABLE 13.4   Raw Score Correlation between Scores of SAT8 and SAT9, Intermediate 2: Case Study 13.5**

| Test/Total | $N$ | SAT 9 (Form S) | | | SAT 9 (Form J) | | | $r$ |
|---|---|---|---|---|---|---|---|---|
| | | Number of Items | Mean | S.D. | Number of Items | Mean | S.D. | |
| Total Reading | 605 | 84 | 47.1 | 17.5 | 94 | 54.3 | 19.2 | 0.89 |
| Reading Vocabulary | 605 | 30 | 18.4 | 6.5 | 40 | 24.5 | 8.9 | 0.78 |
| Reading Comprehension | 605 | 54 | 28.7 | 11.7 | 54 | 29.9 | 11.3 | 0.86 |
| Total Mathematics | 751 | 78 | 47.2 | 14.0 | 118 | 68.0 | 23.7 | 0.82 |
| Problem Solving/Concepts | 751 | 48 | 29.1 | 8.4 | 34 | 18.3 | 7.3 | 0.73 |
| Problem Solving/Applications | 751 | 48 | 29.1 | 8.4 | 40 | 22.4 | 9.2 | 0.75 |
| Math Procedures/Computation | 751 | 30 | 18.1 | 6.4 | 44 | 27.3 | 9.6 | 0.69 |
| All Language | 573 | 108 | 62.0 | 21.2 | 140 | 82.4 | 26.5 | 0.92 |
| Language | 573 | 48 | 26.8 | 10.3 | 60 | 37.2 | 11.9 | 0.82 |
| Language Mechanics | 573 | 24 | 13.6 | 5.3 | 30 | 19.2 | 6.1 | 0.72 |
| Language Expression | 573 | 24 | 13.1 | 5.7 | 30 | 18.0 | 6.7 | 0.76 |
| Spelling | 573 | 30 | 17.6 | 6.3 | 50 | 27.1 | 10.3 | 0.80 |
| Study Skills | 573 | 30 | 17.7 | 6.5 | 30 | 18.1 | 6.7 | 0.83 |
| Science | 584 | 40 | 24.1 | 6.9 | 50 | 26.6 | 10.1 | 0.68 |
| Social Science | 589 | 40 | 19.7 | 7.3 | 50 | 25.1 | 9.3 | 0.68 |
| Listening | 461 | 40 | 25.4 | 6.8 | 45 | 26.9 | 7.6 | 0.72 |

*Source:* Stanford Achievement Test: Ninth Edition Copyright © 1996 by Harcourt, Inc. Reproduced by permission. All rights reserved.

To make a decision on test adoption, school districts (the users) need to consider which score forms, the total battery or the subtest scores, would be of use to them in local decision-

*(continued)*

**13.5     Continued**

making contexts. They also need to consider whether the lack of consistently high correlations (.80 or higher) across various subtest scores might be caused by national curriculum changes that parallel those occurring in their district, or whether differences in population demographics and the sample used in the developer's studies could have contributed to such differences.

---

**Key Concept**

■ Concurrent validity evidence is gathered to support a developer's claim that the respondents' performance on the predictor and criterion overlap to such an extent that the user can use the criterion in place of the predictor.

---

## 13.1.6   Evidence of Internal Structure

*Assessment Purposes Driving the Evidence-Gathering.*   Evidence of internal structure is needed to verify the "dimensionality" of an instrument in applications where the item scores or subscores of an instrument are used to make inferences about the underlying dimensions of a theoretical construct (see Chapter 3). From a classical perspective, the methods and statistical criteria for identifying latent "dimensions" are from an area of work labeled as factor analysis (described in some detail later). Some instruments are composed of sets of items organized in subtests, yielding a series of scores that provide information on the underlying construct. In such a case, the developer might claim that the scores from the different items will interrelate in particular, theory-driven ways; in other words, the developer will postulate that the construct has a given *internal structure*. In such cases, before we use such scores or subscores to make any inferences, we should collect or evaluate empirical evidence of internal structure. In the event that the evidence supports the theoretically specified relationships, we could justify using the scores/subscores to make the interpretations claimed possible by the developers.

*Description of Procedures/Analyses.*   Depending on the complexity of the internal structure proposed by the developer, the analytic procedures can vary greatly. Various methods of factor analysis provide us with the tools to verify a test's internal structure and dimensionality. Methods for examining item homogeneity can also be applied when a unidimensional structure needs to be supported. Procedures from item response theory, outside the scope of this book/module, are also useful methods for investigating scale dimensionality, but the statistical criteria and mathematical models there are very different.

Many test manuals and published validity studies offer factor analysis evidence to justify claims about internal structure. For this reason, it is relevant for prospective test consumers to be familiar with the basic vocabulary and purposes of factor analysis.

*Interpretation of Internal Structure Evidence.*   What is the meaning of the word, "factor" or "dimension," in the classical sense? To answer this question, a few basics of an exploratory factor analysis (EFA) procedure are provided here. Keep in mind that this is one of several factor analytic techniques that assessment designers could use.

Fundamentally, EFA attempts to search for an order and pattern in the correlations among responses to a set of variables, the items on an assessment tool. Factors have to be mathematically derived using computationally intense methods (usually done by a computer). If the factor analysis reveals that one mathematically-derived factor explains most of the variability in response distributions of all the items in a test, we say that the instrument yields unidimensional data (it is a one factor test). If there is more than one factor that explains the variability in the inter-item correlation matrix, we conclude it is a multifactor test. The findings of internal structure analyses must be evaluated with reference to the theoretically-postulated domain structure, the scores or sub-scores that the user intends to employ for interpretive purposes, and the particular technique used to derive the factors. The developer could expect that factors will correlate with each other, or not. Such hypotheses provide opportunities to conduct empirical validity checks.

In an ideal validation outcome, when a set of items is intended by the designer to measure a single underlying trait, they would all be explained by one, mathematically-derived factor after a factor analysis is completed. In a case where the developer had two sets of items that were purported to measure two different traits, the developer could claim validity when the item responses were indeed explained by two uncorrelated factors, and so on. How well the response distributions to different items correlate with the factors extracted are called the *factor loadings;* the overall picture of these item-factor loadings is called the *factor pattern.* When a test is expected to measure two or more distinct traits, the factors derived should be uncorrelated. In other cases, the developer might expect some level of inter-correlations among the factors.

## Case Study 13.6
## Verifying Internal Structure

(Note: The following case study is based on a test that was used on a nationwide scale during the 1980s. Because of its dated norms and other psychometric limitations, very few people use it today.)

The early childhood test, the *Gesell School Readiness Screening Test* (GSRT), is purported to measure a child's "developmental age" (DA). The developers of the GSRT claim that although the GSRT yields an overall score indicating a child's DA, it is actually made up of two underlying traits, Language and Adaptive behaviors, represented by two sets of tasks (consisting of 3 items and 5 items, respectively). To diagnose specific areas of delay, they recommend that users examine the subtest scores separately for each child. They strongly recommend that different types of interventions be planned and delivered for children whose development varies in the two behavioral dimensions. Specifically, they recommend that children identified on the GSRT as developmentally delayed be held back in kindergarten for two years.

In Table 13.5 we see the results of an exploratory factor analysis study that was conducted several years ago by this author at a school district that had adopted the GSRT for administration to their kindergarten students. The purpose of the study was to evaluate whether the internal structure of the GSRT suggested by the test developers (with two factors), was supported with data

*(continued)*

## 13.6     Continued

gathered from 416 kindergartners who were tested on the GSRT locally. The first question to be answered was whether two factors could be derived that explained the variances in the item sets labeled Language and Adaptive behaviors by the developer. The second question was whether the two factors were sufficiently uncorrelated to allow for differential diagnosis of delays in the two behavioral areas.

The results of the factor analysis examining the internal structure of the GSRT are presented in Table 13.5. As the table shows, when two factors were derived from the correlation matrix, the tasks of the Language and Adaptive subdomains loaded separately and heavily on the two factors, exactly as predicted by the developers' theory. The five tasks identified as "adaptive behaviors" by the developers, loaded on the first factor with fairly high loadings of .47 to.77. In comparison, the three "language" items had very low loadings (.08 to .26) on the same factor. Conversely, the "language" items had high loadings of .54 to .73 on the second factor, while the "adaptive" items had much lower loadings of .08 to .31. This factor pattern supported the two-factor internal structure given by the developers. Contrary to the developers' predictions, however, the two factors were found to correlate rather strongly, with an inter-factor correlation of .72 (interpreted just like a Pearson's $r$ value).

**TABLE 13.5  Validity Evidence to Verify Internal Structure: Case Study 13.6**

| Domains | Factor Pattern (Promax-rotated two-factor solution) | GSRT Items (Labels) | Factor Loadings | |
|---|---|---|---|---|
| | | | *Factor 1* | *Factor 2* |
| Adaptive Behaviors | | 1. Writing Numbers | .77 | .08 |
| | | 2. Writing Name | .74 | .13 |
| | | 3. Copy Forms | .74 | .11 |
| | | 4. Incomplete Man | .52 | .31 |
| | | 5. Cubes | .47 | .14 |
| Language Behaviors | | 6. Interview | .08 | .73 |
| | | 7. Animals | .14 | .64 |
| | | 8. Interests | .26 | .54 |

Interfactor correlation = .72

$N = 416$

What could be concluded from the internal structure evidence on the validity of the GSRT scores? The two-factor solution with the high interfactor correlation indicated that although the two subtests were holding up as two separate constructs that contributed to the overall construct of "developmental age" (as theorized by the developers), their overlap was far too high to justify the use of the subtest scores for differential diagnosis—a recommendation of the developer. The internal structure findings were tested again in a second subsample and replicated (Banerji, 1992).

---

**Key Concept**

■ When the use of scores or subscores of an assessment tool are contingent on the developer's assumptions about dimensionality, we need empirical validity evidence to support that internal structure.

---

## 13.1.7 Evidence of Group Differences

***Assessment Purposes Driving the Evidence-Gathering.*** We should seek evidence of group differences when a developer claims that the scores of the assessment will show differences among subpopulations in the specified population, or among other specified groups of individuals (Angoff, 1988).

***Description of Procedures/Analyses.*** Group differences can be investigated by administering the assessment to carefully selected groups of individuals and calculating appropriate descriptive and inferential statistics to evaluate whether the groups do indeed differ on the measured attribute. Other, mutivariate approaches to examining group differences include descriptive discriminant function analysis.

***Interpretation of Evidence on Group Differences.*** Validity evidence on group differences should be evaluated based on the developer or user's hypotheses regarding the magnitude and direction of various group differences on the construct measure. The next application shows how a test that was intended to measure mathematics proficiency at four different age levels held up when it was empirically tested for age-based group differences.

---

## Case Study 13.7
## Validating Age Group Differences

Developmental tests are designed based on the assumption that there will be distinct age-related differences on the attribute being measured that correspond with developmental gains made by individuals tested. In a scholastic program, such tests are made up of progressively more difficult tasks that are expected to correspond with the delivery of a developmentally adaptive curriculum.

A researcher and teachers in a school district designed a series of mathematics tests that were intended for an individualized, developmentally graded program, called "Continuous Progress" (CP). To test the hypothesis that students of different ages would perform differently on the test, the researcher examined group differences in children with different years of birth (B-Y 1982–1986). The results for the total score of the Mathematical Patterns Assessment, are presented in Table 13.6.

In the table, we see the means and standard deviations of each of the four main age groups (top line), and univariate effect sizes ($\Delta$) evaluating the degree to which the score means of the

*(continued)*

## 13.7    Continued

older group differed from the youngest group, in standard deviation units (see Section 1.4.1 in Chapter 11 on how to compute effect sizes). The youngest group's mean served as the baseline and a pooled standard deviation of 9.0 was used to determine effects, as follows.

$$\Delta_{(B\text{-}Y\ 1985,1986)} = (24.34 - 25.20)/9 = -0.09$$
$$\Delta_{(B\text{-}Y\ 1984,1986)} = (31.57 - 25.20)/9 = +0.71$$
$$\Delta_{(B\text{-}Y\ 1983,1986)} = (30.15 - 25.20)/9 = +0.55$$
$$\Delta_{(B\text{-}Y\ 1982,1986)} = (26.30 - 25.20)/9 = +0.12$$

Assuming that the curriculum was developmentally delivered, is the test showing the expected age-related group differences in proficiency? We see that the achievement difference is barely discernible ($-.09$) between the youngest group and the next-youngest group (born in 1985), but clear differences can be seen between each of the groups born in 1984 and 1983 compared to the youngest group (.71 and .55, respectively). The oldest group (born 1982) did little better (.12) than the youngest group, but that may have been due to the presence in the small (5-member) oldest group of children who had already been held back once.

In conclusion, a four-level developmental structure could not be validated with the empirical data on age groups. Rather, the Mathematical Patterns total score appeared to be valid for making inferences about development in two broad age ranges (age 8–10 years and 11–12 years), under the current conditions of instruction. Factor analytic work helped to further validate the two-level structure of the test (Banerji & Ferron, 1998).

**TABLE 13.6    Evidence of Age Group Differences on the Total Scores of the Mathematical Patterns Assessment: Case Study 13.7**

**Skill Area Tested: Identifying Mathematical Patterns**

| Birth Year | 1986 (youngest) | | 1985 | | 1984 | | 1983 | | ≤1982 | |
|---|---|---|---|---|---|---|---|---|---|---|
| | *Mean* | *SD* | *Mean* | *SD* | *Mean* | *SD* | *Mean* | *SD* | *Mean* | *SD* |
| Total Score | 25.20 | 8.57 | 24.34 | 9.68 | 31.57 | 8.26 | 30.15 | 10.07 | 26.30 | 5.77 |
| Age Group Differences in standard deviation units compared to youngest group | | | −0.09 | | +0.71 | | +0.55 | | +0.12 | |

Examples of skills tested at different levels of difficulty:
- Identify, continue, and explain simple repeating patterns involving shapes or numerals (e.g., 123123 123 . . .)    Easy
- Identify, continue, and explain growing patterns involving beginning-level arithmetic operations, number concepts or geometric concepts (e.g., 3 (+2), 5 (+2), 7 (+2), 9, 11, . . . )    More difficult

Key Concept

■ When the use of scores or subscores of an assessment tool are contingent on the developer's claim that particular populations or subpopulations will differ on the measured construct, we need empirical validity evidence on group differences.

## 13.1.8  Evidence of Fairness or Lack of Bias in Items/Test Scores

***Assessment Purposes Driving the Evidence-Gathering.***   Fairness of tests and assessments can be an issue that provokes heated social, ethical, and legal debates. Psychometric definitions of bias can vary depending on whether we focus on items or total scores, and whether we are interested in examining systematic sub-group differences in how well a score predicts some future performance or describes current performance of examinees. Generally, "bias" studies seek evidence that particular subgroups do not obtain significantly lower (or higher) scores that can be associated with a group-related trait rather than the construct of interest. "Biases" that can be linked to differences in gender, culture, or language, a disabling condition in subgroups of respondents within the population specified, can have serious social and political implications. With achievement tests, bias is often caused by contextual factors, such as certain subgroups not having the "opportunity to learn" relevant portions of the curriculum prior to testing.

Usually, assessment designers do not seek to intentionally bias the results of an instrument or items one way or the other. However, circumstantial, language, and test content factors that cause systematic errors in score interpretations must be carefully evaluated. It thus becomes necessary to check for "bias" when assessments are used for high stakes decisions, such as placement, admissions, certification, or graduation.

***Description of Procedures/Analyses.***   Differential Item Functioning (DIF) studies attempt to investigate differences in subgroup response distributions to individual items. To appreciate the importance of "bias" studies, we will look at DIF as one of many possible procedures, and draw on concepts introduced in Chapter 12. DIF is present if we find that an item is more difficult, more discriminating, or more easily guessed by members of a subgroup of test-takers. For example, to check for gender DIF, we could compare item response distributions of girls and boys in an item analysis table, similar to those demonstrated in Chapter 12. Item DIF studies are not technically equivalent to the concept of "item bias"—as other substantive factors need to be considered to determine the cause or source of bias once we establish item DIF.

***Interpretation and Use of Bias Evidence.***   DIF or bias evidence should be evaluated based on our knowledge of the groups concerned and circumstances of assessment. For example, if a vocabulary test uses terms from a game played predominantly by boys (e.g., baseball), we might find evidence of a bias against girls in all the items that use baseball-related terms. Such evidence is best interpreted with advice from professionals who are familiar with the groups or subgroups affected by the bias. Context factors, such as whether or not subgroups of students received adequate exposure to the curriculum tested, or whether other subgroups had greater prior knowledge on the domain tested, can cause group differences not foreseen by the developers or the users. Evidence of bias should be used by developers to revise or delete particular items or portions of tests that perform differentially in particular subgroups.

With structured response items, major causes for differential item-functioning (DIF) were elaborated by Berk (1984) as the following.

1. Flaws resulting from item ambiguities in the stem, correct response, or distracters, including poor test or item instructions that cause particular subgroups to respond differently.
2. Flaws that cause one or more answer options to be differentially attractive to members of different subgroups in the population.
3. Item features that reveal actual trait-related differences in the subgroups assessed.
4. Item features that reveal actual differences in the subgroups assessed, but which are not related to trait of interest.

Of the above factors that could contribute to DIF, # 1 is a more generalized validity/reliability problem that should be addressed through careful content validation work; #s 2 and 4 are directly relevant to what most people consider "bias" and can result from factors like the use of baseball-terms in a vocabulary test for girls; while #3 can be caused by the "lack of opportunity to learn" the material targeted on the achievement test.

## Case Study 13.8

Berk (1984) provided the illustrative data in Table 13.7 on item DIF, showing two, four-option, multiple choice items with different levels of performance in Black versus White subpopulations. DIF evidence is analyzed here by comparing percents of students who select each distracter, following an evaluation of the item difficulties in the two subgroups.

**TABLE 13.7  Illustration of Item Bias Analysis Based on Response Distributions on Distracters: Case Study 13.8**

| Item | Group | Response Choice | | | | DIFF |
|------|-------|-----|-----|-----|-----|------|
|      |       | A | B | C | D[a] | |
| 17 (*unbiased*)[b] | black | 11 | 14 | 75 | — | 45 |
|                    | white | 13 | 7 | 80 | — | 60 |
| 32 (*biased*)[c] | black | 21 | 61 | 18 | — | 33 |
|                  | white | 40 | 57 | 8 | — | 70 |

*Source:* Berk, R.A. (1984) (Ed.). A Guide to Criterion-referenced Test Construction (97–143). Reproduced with permission. All rights reserved.

[a]Correct answer

[b]$\chi^2 = 4.92$ (n.s.)

[c]$\chi^2 = 28.73$ (p $<$ .01)

With the data in Table 13.7, Item #17 was determined to be unbiased. The item was more difficult for blacks (p value = .45) than for whites (p value of .60). However, because the percent responses to the the various response foils was not found to be statistically different in the Black and White subgroups studied, it was not considered to be functioning differentially. Relatively, Item #32 was considerably more difficult for blacks than for whites (p values of .33 and .70, respectively). In addition, however, the response distributions on all three distracters were significantly different for Blacks, as compared to Whites, supporting the conclusion that the item was demonstrating a selective bias. The criterion for determining DIF in this illustration is the statistical significance of the chi-squared value.

**Key Concept**

- To establish construct validity, we need empirical evidence to verify that particular items, or scores from sections of a test or an entire test do not perform differentially in particular subgroups because of factors unrelated to the construct.

### 13.1.9    Unified Interpretation of Validity Evidence

Evidence-gathering to establish validity of assessment results, as dictated by the anticipated score uses, should be an ongoing, integrated, and unified process. Validity of an assessment's results should be the central, most important concern of both the assessment developer and user. The most current *Standards* (AERA, APA, & NCME, 1999) states that all technical aspects of an assessment procedure, including matters pertinent to score reliability (which we examine next), are subsumed under or related to the fundamental property of "validity." The document states:

> A sound validity argument integrates various strands of evidence into a coherent account of the degree to which existing evidence and theory support the intended interpretation of test scores for specific uses. It encompasses evidence gathered from new studies and evidence gathered from earlier reported research. The validity argument may indicate the need for refining the construct definition, may suggest revisions in the test or other aspects of the testing process, and may indicate areas needing further study. . . . Ultimately, the validity of an intended interpretation of test scores relies on all the available evidence relevant to the technical quality of a testing system. This includes evidence of careful test construction, adequate score reliability, appropriate test administration and scoring, accurate score scaling, equating, and standard-setting, and careful attention to fairness for all examinees . . ." (AERA, APA, & NCME, 1999, p. 13).

## 13.2    Empirical Estimation of Reliability

### 13.2.1    Classical Conceptions of Reliability

In estimating errors from different sources, we distinguish between "validity" and "reliability" with the concepts of *systematic* versus *random error* (see Chapter 3; Stanley, 1971). Even under conditions where all relevant systematic errors might be eliminated in an assessment application, random error could affect the consistency of scores we obtain, causing unreliability. Reliability refers to the degree of consistency or reproducibility of an assessment's results under different conditions, assuming that random error always affects scores.

Random error could potentially enter an assessment situation from a variety of sources, such as distractions in the assessment environment, the occasion of testing, the rater, the respondent/examinee's state of mind at the time of testing, and poorly designed items and instructions (see Chapter 3). According to classical reliability theory, the direction in which random errors influence assessment results is unpredictable. However, because of its random nature, we could employ principles of probability theory to estimate the amount of error variability associated with test scores/results.

### 13.2.2   True Scores, Observed Scores, Standard Error of Measurement, and Reliability Coefficients

The concept of reliability, in statistical terms, is based on three assumptions from classical test theory. We start with the assumption that each individual who is assessed has a fixed amount of the construct being measured, referred to as the "true score" for that person (or object), $T$. Second, we assume that on every assessment occasion when we make observations of a person on the trait of interest, there will be some degree of random error associated with the test score. This error is referred to as the "measurement error," $E$. As mentioned earlier, $E$ is unpredictable in its magnitude and direction. Finally, we assume that a person's raw score, called the "observed score," $X$, is made up of two additive components, the *true score* and *error,* as follows:

$$X = T + E$$

If we were to make a set of repeated measurements on the same person, using the same assessment tool (say, 100 or more observations), we would find that a frequency polygon of the observed scores would take the shape of a normal distribution. This is simply because the normal distribution is based on a mathematical function which describes how random variables, such as observed scores ($X$), tend to be distributed. Such a curve, shown in Figure 13.1, represents the degree to which a person's true score is likely to fluctuate on repeated measurements due to the influences of random measurement error.

Based on the definition of the normal distribution function, the mean of a person's distribution of repeated measurements would always be equal to his/her true score *(T),* and the standard deviation of the error distribution would be the *Standard Error of Measurement* (SEM). The SEM is an important indicator of test score reliability and can be mathematically estimated using the assumptions of classical test theory just presented.

Generalizing the previous theoretical concepts to measurements made on several individuals, we see that different persons would have their own observed score distributions, influenced by random errors (i.e., each person's curve of error). For an entire group of individuals, thus, there would be three respective distributions, comprised of the $T$, $X$, and $E$ scores. We refer to the variabilities of these distributions as the *true score variance,*

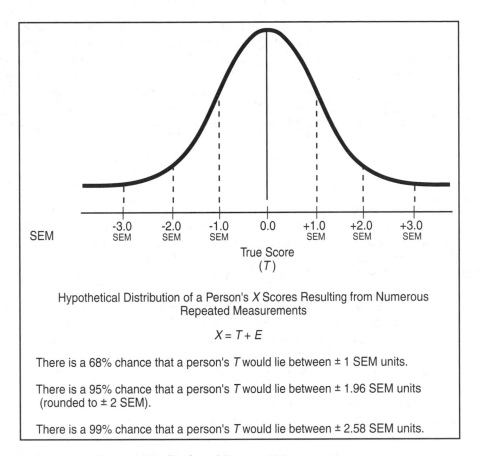

SEM

-3.0 SEM    -2.0 SEM    -1.0 SEM    0.0    +1.0 SEM    +2.0 SEM    +3.0 SEM

True Score
(*T*)

Hypothetical Distribution of a Person's *X* Scores Resulting from Numerous
Repeated Measurements

$$X = T + E$$

There is a 68% chance that a person's *T* would lie between ± 1 SEM units.

There is a 95% chance that a person's *T* would lie between ± 1.96 SEM units
(rounded to ± 2 SEM).

There is a 99% chance that a person's *T* would lie between ± 2.58 SEM units.

**FIGURE 13.1    Normal Distribution of Errors of Measurement**

*observed score variance,* and *error score variance.* Because *E* is random, it follows that
for a population of examinees,

(a) the true score and error score distributions would be uncorrelated or $\rho_{TE} = 0$;
(b) distributions of error scores from two repeated testings of the same individuals on
the same assessment would also be uncorrelated; and
(c) the mean of error scores for a population of examinees is zero.

In theory, the reliability coefficient is $r_{XT}^2$, and a second indicator of reliability. It is
derived from the Index of Reliability, $r_{XT}$ ($r_{XT}$ represents the correlation between observed
scores and true scores in a group). The Reliability Coefficient is the square of the Index of
Reliability. As a statistical index, it provides an estimate of the *proportion of observed
score variance that is the "true" variance rather than "error" variance* in a group of
individuals.

The *T* scores in $r_{XT}^2$ can only be theoretically estimated but not empirically obtained.
Thus, we do not commonly see the above notation to refer to the reliability coefficient, nor

can we derive it in practice using this formula. *Rather, the symbol for the reliability coefficient is $r_{XX'}$.* The $r_{XT}^2$ formula can be mathematically connected to $r_{XX'}$, assuming that two tests are strictly parallel. The $r_{XX'}$ refers to the correlation between observed scores of two parallel forms of an assessment tool with items sampled from the same domain. When tests are strictly parallel, examinees have the same true scores and the error variances are equal. Thus, the reliability coefficient, $r_{XX'}$, is the statistic we find commonly reported in technical manuals and used in testing practice. The SEM is another commonly reported estimate of reliability.

---

**K e y   C o n c e p t s**

■ The usefulness of an assessment's scores depends on the extent to which it reflects "true score" variance in examinees/respondents, rather than "error" variance.
■ Two indices, derived from classical test theory, that help us estimate random measurement error are the Standard Error of Measurement (SEM) and the reliability coefficient, $r_{XX}$.
■ The SEM is a measure of the expected variability in $X$ scores that is due to $E$.

---

The conceptualization of *parallel forms reliability,* then, assumes that parallel and equivalent sets of items are randomly sampled from the same assessment domain. When investigating reliability empirically, we interpret the size of the $r_{XX'}$ value as the extent of overlap in scores from two parallel forms. If the reported $r_{XX'}$ is .98, we conclude that the influence of random error on the scores is $(1.0 - 0.98) = .02$. What are the interpretations allowed for $r_{XX'}$? The reliability coefficient is the *proportion of the X score variance* that is explained by $T$ scores for a group of examinees. Thus, if a $r_{XX'} = .70$ is reported for an assessment, it indicates that 70% of the variability in observed scores is accounted for by the examinees' true scores. The positive square root of $r_{XX'}$, in this case $\sqrt{0.70}$ (=0.84), represents the correlation between observed scores and true scores, referred to as the *index of reliability.*

To generate quantitative estimates of score reliability, the idea of parallel forms reliability can be extended to apply to "parallel" assessment conditions, "parallel" raters, or "parallel" occasions of assessment from a universe containing all possible conditions, raters, or test occasions. Each reliability estimate, described in more detail in the next section, is used for estimating random error from different, but relevant sources in a given assessment situation.

---

**K e y   C o n c e p t s**

■ In theory, the proportion of *observed score* variance that is due to *true score* variance is called the reliability coefficient.
■ In practice, the reliability coefficient we use is $r_{XX'}$, which refers to the correlation between observed scores from two parallel forms (or other parallel conditions) sampled from the same assessment domain.
■ Different reliability estimates, symbolized with the general notation, $r_{XX'}$, are used for estimating random error from different, but relevant sources in a given assessment situation.

### 13.2.3 The Relationship between SEM and $r_{XX'}$

The reliability coefficient, $r_{XX'}$, and the standard error of measurement, SEM, are inversely related. This means that when the reported SEM is high, the $r_{XX'}$ value for the scores will be low. Conversely, when the SEM is low, the $r_{XX'}$ value will be high. The relationship is mathematically represented by the following formula.

$SEM = s_X \sqrt{1 - r_{XX'}}$, where
SEM is the standard error of measurement,
$s_X$ is the standard deviation of the observed scores, and
$r_{XX'}$ is the reliability coefficient.

---

DEMONSTRATION **13.1**

**Calculating the SEM**

Case 1

$r_{XX'} = .60$

$s_X = 5.0$

$$SEM = 5.0 \sqrt{(1 - .60)}$$
$$= 5.0 \sqrt{.40}$$
$$= 3.162 \checkmark \checkmark$$

Case 2

$r_{XX'} = .95$

$s_X = 5.0$

$$SEM = 5.0 \sqrt{(1 - .95)}$$
$$= 5.0 \sqrt{.05}$$
$$= 1.118 \checkmark \checkmark$$

---

Consider the applications shown in Demonstration 13.1, where we see how the SEM can be calculated, starting with two empirically derived reliability coefficients of .60 and .95, respectively, for two assessments. The inverse relationship is evident in the calculated values of SEM. (Note: The correct theoretical notation for the above formula should use population estimates, as shown below.)

$$\sigma_e = \sigma_X \sqrt{1 - \rho_{XX'}}$$

### 13.2.4    Methods for Estimating Reliability

Like the various methods for score validation, empirical data for calculating reliability coefficients can be obtained via different data collection designs and computed using different formulas. In Table 13.8, we see the four major types of reliability coefficients, tied to different sources of random error. These are:

- Test-retest reliability coefficient
- Parallel forms reliability coefficient
- Internal consistency reliability coefficients
- Interrater reliability coefficient

Although they appear superficially different, conceptually, all the reliability coefficients derive from the theoretical notion of randomly sampling "parallel" forms, raters, occasions, or testing conditions from an infinitely large domain of all possible cases. Random errors from each different, but relevant source are estimated with different reliability coefficients, as summarized in Table 13.8. To select the reliability coefficient(s) most appropriate for a given assessment situation, the potential sources of random error, such as forms, raters, or occasions, must be identified by the assessment designer or user as a potential threat.

For example, for a standardized test with multiple choice items and two parallel forms, Forms A and B, we would seek out a *parallel forms reliability coefficient.* This coefficient would indicate the degree of random error that can be expected in the results depending on whether an examinee responds to Form A versus Form B. However, it would not be necessary for us to look for an *interrater reliability coefficient,* as human judges would not be involved in assigning the scores—thus, error variance due to raters would not be a potential factor affecting reliability. When domain and subdomain scores are intended by the developer to behave as homogeneous indices reflecting a larger domain (as is the case with virtually every assessment tool), we should check for internal consistency reliability. Test-retest reliability applies in cases where the users expect the scores to remain stable over short durations of time (this is also a common need). As a rule, the closer the reliability coefficient is to 1.0, the better the reliability—coefficients approaching .90 or above are considered very good for most assessment purposes.

Some factors for us to remember in examining reliability data on assessments are as follows (after Nitko, 1996):

- Different methods for obtaining reliability coefficients will give different results stemming from the different errors that they estimate.
- The predominantly used reliability estimation methods are correlation-based, and thus dependent on the composition and variability of the group used in the estimation procedure.
- The greater the size of the sample of items, behaviors, or products included in the assessment procedure, the better the reliability.
- Objectively scored assessments tend to be more reliable.
- Examinees/respondents at different levels of an attribute can have different amounts of errors related to their scores.

In the following sections, we examine the methods of data collection, estimation, and interpretation for the four major types of reliability coefficients summarized in Table 13.8. Computational demonstrations and sample data from technical reports are inserted in the descriptions.

***Parallel Forms Reliability Coefficient.*** A parallel forms reliability coefficient (also called "alternate forms reliability coefficient") is computed using a Pearson correlation coefficient of two sets of scores generated by administering two alternate, but parallel forms of the same assessment, to the same group of examinees. Symbolically represented as $r_{AB}$, for a test with Forms A and B, it indicates the extent to which users can be confi-

**TABLE 13.8  Sources of Random Error, Reliability Coefficients, and Procedures for Estimating Reliability**

| Source of Random Error | Reliability Coefficients | Procedures for Estimating Reliability |
| --- | --- | --- |
| 1. Error related to occasion or time of assessment<br><br>Q. Would the assessment results stay the same if the assessment was conducted a week or two later, or the occasion was changed? | *Test–retest reliability coefficient* (Also called a *stability coefficient*) | Administer the assessment to the same group of individuals on two occasions, usually with a two-week time delay.<br>Correlate scores from the two occasions of testing to obtain $r_{xx'}$ |
| 2. Error related to use of multiple, parallel forms of an assessment tool (e.g., Form A versus Form B).<br><br>Q. Would the assessment results stay the same if the examinees responded to Form A versus Form B? | *Parallel forms reliability coefficient* (Also called *alternate forms reliability coefficient*) | Administer two or more parallel forms of the assessment to the same group, at the same time.<br>Correlate scores from the parallel forms to obtain $r_{AB}$. |
| 3. Error in sampling items, tasks, or behaviors from the domain OR random errors built into the construction of the assessment.<br><br>Q. Are all the items consistently measuring behaviors from the same domain? | *Internal consistency reliability coefficient*<br><br>Common indices:<br>**(a)** Split-half reliability, $r_{AB}$<br>**(b)** Kuder-Richardson formula 20 ($KR_{20}$)<br>**(c)** Cronbach's alpha reliability ($\alpha$ coefficient) | Administer the assessment to the same group on one occasion. Split the assessment randomly into parts, subparts, or individual items. Intercorrelate scores from each part, subpart, or individual items to check for homogeneity. |
| 4. Error related to different raters who rate or judge a performance assessment.<br><br>Q. Would the scores remain consistent irrespective of the rater? | *Interrater reliability coefficient*<br><br>Common indices:<br>**(a)** Cohen's kappa, $\kappa$<br>**(b)** $r_{AB}$, with raters A and B | Administer the assessment to the same group. Have two or more raters score or judge the performances. Intercorrelate scores from pairs of raters, A and B, to obtain $r_{AB}$. |

**TABLE 13.9  Parallel Forms Reliability Coefficients Reported for the SAT9, Primary 3 Tests and Subtests**

| Subtest/Total | Number of Items | N | Form S | | | Form T | | | $r_{XX'}$ |
|---|---|---|---|---|---|---|---|---|---|
| | | | Mean | S.D. | SEM | Mean | S.D. | SEM | |
| Total Reading | 84 | 605 | 57.0 | 14.4 | 4.8 | 57.2 | 15.2 | 5.0 | .89 |
| Reading Vocabulary | 30 | 605 | 22.0 | 5.1 | 2.3 | 21.8 | 5.4 | 2.4 | .80 |
| Reading Comprehension | 54 | 605 | 35.0 | 10.0 | 3.9 | 35.4 | 10.6 | 4.1 | .85 |
| Total Mathematics | 76 | 639 | 51.9 | 12.4 | 3.9 | 51.3 | 12.2 | 3.9 | .90 |
| Problem Solving | 46 | 639 | 31.5 | 7.4 | 3.0 | 31.0 | 7.1 | 2.8 | .84 |
| Math Procedures | 30 | 639 | 20.4 | 6.0 | 2.5 | 20.2 | 5.9 | 2.5 | .82 |
| All Language | 78 | 594 | 49.2 | 13.0 | 4.5 | 49.8 | 13.1 | 4.5 | .88 |
| Language | 48 | 594 | 29.1 | 9.3 | 3.4 | 30.1 | 9.4 | 3.4 | .87 |
| Spelling | 30 | 594 | 20.1 | 5.2 | 2.5 | 19.8 | 5.3 | 2.6 | .76 |
| Science | 40 | 607 | 25.2 | 7.1 | 3.3 | 24.8 | 7.3 | 6.5 | .78 |
| Social Science | 40 | 600 | 21.0 | 7.0 | 3.4 | 21.6 | 7.2 | 3.5 | .76 |
| Listening | 40 | 594 | 25.3 | 6.0 | 2.9 | 25.2 | 6.8 | 3.3 | .77 |

dent that scores from multiple, parallel forms are interchangeable. The size of a parallel forms coefficient depends on how well an assessment designer was able to construct equivalent forms of the tool.

Acceptable parallel forms reliability coefficients range between .80 to .90 in size. Sample data on parallel forms reliability from the SAT9, as reported by the publishers on Forms S and T of their Primary 3 level tests and subtests are presented in Table 13.9. As is evident, their reliability data on the Total Reading, Total Language, and Total Mathematics batteries are well above the .80 criterion of acceptability.

***Test–Retest Reliability Coefficient.***   A test–retest reliability coefficient is also calculated using a Pearson correlation coefficient. Here, the two sets of scores are obtained from the same group of individuals, using only one form of the assessment, by administering it on two different occasions. The assumption built into the data collection design is that *no systematic factors will affect the scores on the construct measured* between Time 1 and Time 2. Given that this assumption is met (often a challenge in actual settings), the resulting $r_{XX'}$ indicates the extent to which the scores will remain free from the influence of random factors associated with the occasion of testing. Setting up test–retest studies are difficult, because the designer must make every attempt to control for various systematic errors that might affect the interpretation of the results on score reliability. Common obstacles are the maturation of examinees from Time 1 to Time 2 when the time gap is too long; interventions that alter the examinees' standing on the trait (e.g., they learn new things);

or systematic factors in the assessment environment that change from one assessment occasion to the next.

***Internal Consistency Reliability Coefficients.*** When assessments are developed using a domain-sampling approach, designers are not only interested in where the examinees stand on the sample of items included in the tool; they also want to know how consistently the examinees' performance will generalize to the entire domain of all possible items. Estimates of *internal consistency reliability* provide an index of errors inherent in the domain-sampling approach.

Another way to think of internal consistency reliability is as follows. If we assume that we have randomly sampled items from a theoretical domain or subdomain, all the items should be substantively interchangeable, generating within-person consistency in responses. Internal consistency reliability estimates allow designers and users to evaluate the extent to which items from the same domain or subdomain generate consistent patterns of responses for individual respondents/examinees.

All procedures for obtaining internal consistency reliability estimates require a single administration of an assessment, and is thus advantageous from a logistical standpoint. Following administration, the instrument is randomly broken into two or more parts and subparts, each of which is then scored. The intercorrelations among the scores of these "testlets" yields the internal consistency coefficient.

To be acceptable, internal consistency estimates should be at least .70 (Crocker & Algina, 1986). As the different formulas will illustrate, these indices reflect the extent to which the variance of the composite score, obtained by summing scores on all the items, is a consistent reflection of the variability in the "testlets," or individual items. There are three major methods for obtaining internal consistency estimates of reliability, all of which are conceptually and mathematically equivalent: split-half, Kuder-Richardson Formula 20 ($KR_{20}$), and Cronbach's alpha. Let us examine each of these in some detail.

***Split-half Reliability.*** The split-half reliability coefficient can be computed by hand and is easy for practitioners to use. The steps in computation are illustrated in Demonstration 13.2. They are as follows:

1. Split a test in two using the odd-numbered and even-numbered items.
2. Sum the scores of odd-numbered and even-numbered items on the test to obtain total scores for two half-tests, A and B.
3. Calculate a Pearson's correlation of the scores from Forms A and B.
4. Correct the correlation using the *Spearman-Brown Prophecy Formula.*

Use of the above approach assumes that the two forms are strictly parallel. Note that because of shortening of the test's length when it is halved, the reliability is at first underestimated with this procedure (Step 3). Given the calculated reliability for halved tests, we use the Spearman-Brown Prophecy Formula in the final step to estimate what the reliability would have been for a full-length instrument (Step 4).

D E M O N S T R A T I O N  **13.2**

## Corrected Split-Half Reliability

**Split-Half Reliability Examination**                    **Scores**

| Examinee | 1 | 2 | 3 | 4 | 5 | 6 | Odd Items Form A | Even Items Form B |
|---|---|---|---|---|---|---|---|---|
| A | 0 | 1 | 0 | 1 | 0 | 1 | 0 | 3 |
| B | 1 | 0 | 1 | 1 | 1 | 0 | 3 | 1 |
| C | 1 | 1 | 1 | 1 | 1 | 1 | 3 | 3 |
| D | 1 | 1 | 1 | 1 | 0 | 0 | 2 | 2 |
| E | 0 | 1 | 1 | 1 | 1 | 1 | 2 | 3 |
| F | 0 | 1 | 1 | 1 | 1 | 1 | 2 | 3 |
| G | 0 | 0 | 0 | 0 | 0 | 0 | 0 | 0 |
| H | 1 | 1 | 1 | 1 | 1 | 0 | 3 | 2 |

$N = 8$

$$\sum X_A = 15 \quad \sum X_B = 17$$
$$\overline{X}_A = 1.88 \quad \overline{X}_B = 2.13$$
$$s_A = 1.095 \quad s_B = 1.052$$

$$r_{AB} = \frac{\sum z_A z_B}{N} = \frac{2.31}{8} = .29 \checkmark\checkmark$$

Spearman-Brown Prophecy Formula applied to half-tests:

$$r_{XX'} = \frac{2r_{AB}}{1 + r_{AB}}$$

Corrected Split-Half Reliability

$$r_{XX'} = \frac{2(.29)}{1 + .29} = \frac{.58}{1.29} = .45 \checkmark\checkmark$$

---

In the data set shown, we find that the reliability is only .45 after the the Spearman-Brown adjustment. The reasons become obvious once we notice the lack of consistent agreement in paired scores for individual examinees. Such results suggest that items on the A and B forms are flawed either because they are nonhomogeneous in their content or are intrinsically ambiguous, yielding rather inconsistent response patterns from individual examinees. In evaluating reliability results, we should remember that length of a test domain or subdomain, in terms of *number of items,* will affect its estimated reliability. In the example, we have six items, generally considered to be adequate for determining internal consistency. Here, the results point to a test score with an unacceptable level of reliability.

*KR$_{20}$ Reliability.*   The KR$_{20}$ formula, based on the 20 steps that the authors, Kuder and Richardson (1937) needed to derive the formula, applies only to tests composed of selected or structured-response items, yielding dichotomous 0,1 responses. It is computed using the following formula:

$$KR_{20} = \frac{k}{k-1}\left(1 - \frac{\Sigma pq}{\sigma_X^2}\right)$$

The formula compares the sum of the item score variances, $\Sigma pq$, in the numerator, with the variance of the summated total score on an instrument, $\sigma_X^2$, in the denominator, to obtain the reliability estimate. The $KR_{20}$ can be interpreted as another measure of item homogeneity (see Chapter 12). Its computation and interpretations are shown in Demonstration 13.3. In this example, the calculated internal consistency is .89 and lies above the acceptable minimum standard of .70.

DEMONSTRATION **13.3**

## Computing the Kuder-Richardson Formula 20 Reliability

| Item | $p$ | $q$ | $pq$ |
|------|-----|-----|------|
| 1 | .30 | .70 | .21 |
| 2 | .60 | .40 | .24 |
| 3 | .70 | .30 | .21 |
| 4 | .60 | .40 | .24 |
| 5 | .50 | .50 | .25 |
| | | | $\Sigma pq = 1.15$ |

$\overline{X} = 3.0$
$s_X = 2.0$
$s_X^2 = 4.0$

$$KR_{20} = \frac{k}{k-1}\left(1 - \frac{\Sigma pq}{s_X^2}\right)$$

$$KR_{20} = \frac{5}{4}\left(1 - \frac{1.15}{4.00}\right)$$

$$= \frac{5}{4}(1 - .29)$$

$$= 1.25\,(.71)$$

$$KR_{20} = .89\ \checkmark\checkmark$$

Note: The formula using population estimates appears as follows:

$$KR_{20} = \frac{k}{k-1}\left(1 - \frac{\Sigma pq}{\sigma_X^2}\right)$$

***Cronbach's Alpha.*** The Cronbach's alpha coefficient, $\alpha$, developed by Cronbach and his colleagues in 1951, is a more general form of the $KR_{20}$. The alpha coefficient can be applied to instruments having response scales with 2 or more response categories (e.g., a Likert scale). It is computed using the following formula:

$$\alpha = \frac{k}{k-1}\left(1 - \frac{\Sigma\sigma_i^2}{\sigma_X^2}\right)$$

Also an indicator of item homogeneity (see Chapter 12), the alpha coefficient can be obtained with the computational steps shown in Demonstration 13.4. Sample data on internal consistency reliability using $KR_{20}$ coefficients and SEM are shown in Table 13.10 for Forms S and T of the Advanced 2 level of the SAT9. The SEM is reported in raw score

## DEMONSTRATION  **13.4**

## Calculating Cronbach's Alpha Coefficient

| Item | Item Variance, $s_i^2$ |
|------|------------------------|
| 1 | 8 |
| 2 | 5 |
| 3 | 10 |
| 4 | 7.2 |
| 5 | 12.5 |
| | $\Sigma s_i^2 = 42.7$ |

$$\alpha = \frac{k}{k-1}\left(1 - \frac{\Sigma s_i^2}{s_x^2}\right)$$

$s_X = 10.0$
$s_X^2 = 100.0$

$$\alpha = \frac{5}{4}\left(1 - \frac{42.7}{100}\right)$$

$$\alpha = \frac{5}{4}(.573)$$

$$\alpha = 1.25\,(.71)$$

$$\alpha = .72 \checkmark\checkmark$$

*Note:* The formula using population estimates appears as follows:

$$\alpha = \frac{k}{k-1}\left(1 - \frac{\Sigma\sigma_i^2}{\sigma_x^2}\right)$$

**TABLE 13.10   KR$_{20}$ Coefficients and SEM Values Reported for the SAT9, Advanced 2 Level Tests and Subtests**

| Test/Total | Number of Items | Form S | | | | | Form T | | | | |
|---|---|---|---|---|---|---|---|---|---|---|---|
| | | N | Mean | S.D. | SEM | $r_{xx'}$ | N | Mean | S.D. | SEM | $r_{xx'}$ |
| Total Reading | 84 | 1343 | 60.2 | 14.5 | 3.62 | .94 | 279 | 57.3 | 17.3 | 3.63 | .96 |
| Reading Vocabulary | 30 | 1374 | 22.2 | 5.6 | 2.04 | .87 | 279 | 20.6 | 5.7 | 2.14 | .86 |
| Reading Comprehension | 54 | 1391 | 37.8 | 9.8 | 2.97 | .91 | 279 | 36.7 | 12.5 | 2.89 | .95 |
| Total Mathematics | 82 | 1082 | 42.5 | 16.1 | 4.00 | .94 | 418 | 44.7 | 17.5 | 3.91 | .95 |
| Problem Solving | 52 | 1095 | 28.3 | 10.3 | 3.19 | .90 | 425 | 28.3 | 11.0 | 3.14 | .92 |
| Mathematical Procedures | 30 | 1084 | 14.2 | 6.8 | 2.35 | .88 | 418 | 16.2 | 7.1 | 2.32 | .89 |
| Language | 48 | 1394 | 30.3 | 9.7 | 2.95 | .91 | 435 | 30.3 | 10.6 | 2.92 | .92 |
| Spelling | 30 | 1405 | 21.0 | 5.4 | 2.23 | .83 | 435 | 19.6 | 5.5 | 2.29 | .83 |
| Study Skills | 30 | 1394 | 18.5 | 6.0 | 2.33 | .85 | 435 | 20.9 | 6.7 | 2.14 | .90 |
| Science | 40 | 1360 | 24.5 | 7.8 | 2.70 | .88 | 104 | 24.7 | 7.6 | 2.65 | .88 |
| Social Science | 40 | 1351 | 21.1 | 7.1 | 2.84 | .84 | 109 | 22.1 | 8.1 | 2.83 | .88 |
| Listening | 40 | 1367 | 27.4 | 6.7 | 2.66 | .84 | 107 | 26.2 | 6.5 | 2.63 | .83 |
| Using Information (Basic) | 36 | 1082 | 21.7 | 7.0 | 2.59 | .86 | 68 | 23.3 | 7.4 | 2.46 | .89 |
| Using Information (Complete) | 73 | 1070 | 43.3 | 12.8 | 3.72 | .92 | 71 | 43.7 | 14.1 | 3.66 | .93 |
| Thinking Skills (Basic) | 179 | 1046 | 110.6 | 29.9 | 5.75 | .96 | 65 | 117.6 | 30.5 | 5.56 | .97 |
| Thinking Skills (Complete) | 241 | 1045 | 146.0 | 39.5 | 6.72 | .97 | 68 | 152.5 | 41.2 | 6.60 | .97 |

*Source:* Stanford Achievement Test: Ninth Edition Copyright © 1996 by Harcourt, Inc. Reproduced by permission. All rights reserved.

### DEMONSTRATION **13.5**

## Creating Confidence Bands with Standard Errors of Measurement

Raw Score for a Person:

$X_{SAT9} = 80$

Reported KR$_{20}$ = .94

Reported SEM = 3.62

*95% Confidence Band* 1.96 × (3.62) = ±7.10

$$80 + 7.10 = 87.10 \text{ Upper Limit}$$
$$80 - 7.10 = 72.9 \text{ Lower Limit}$$

or (rounded) 2.0 × (3.62) = ±7.24

$$80 + 7.24 = 87.26 \text{ Upper Limit}$$
$$80 - 7.24 = 72.76 \text{ Lower Limit}$$

- What would be the 68% confidence band for the same score?
- What would be the 99% confidence band for the same score?

units. The reported reliabilities of their subtest and total battery scores, ranging from .83 to .97, appear to be from satisfactory to excellent.

***Creating Confidence Bands with Reported SEMs.***   The SEM and the concept of a normal distribution of error around given $X$ scores can be used to set up *confidence bands* around scores of individuals. This procedure, shown in Demonstration 13.5, helps us estimate a person's "true score," $T$, from the obtained $X$ score, using the SEM.

## DEMONSTRATION  **13.6**
## Calculating Absolute Levels of Rater Agreement with Cohen's Kappa

$$K = \frac{P_A - P_C}{1 - P_C}$$

Ratings from Rater A

| | | Satisfactory | Unsatisfactory | |
|---|---|---|---|---|
| Ratings from Rater B | Satisfactory | a (11) | b (4) | a + b |
| | Unsatisfactory | c (1) | d (9) | c + d |
| | | a + c | b + d | $N = a + b + c + d$ |

$P_A$ = Total Percent Agreement

$$P_A = \frac{a}{N} + \frac{d}{N} = \frac{a + d}{N}$$

$P_C$ = Percent Agreement Expected by Chance

$$P_C = \left[ \frac{a + b}{N} \times \frac{a + c}{N} \right] + \left[ \frac{c + d}{N} \times \frac{c + d}{N} \right]$$

$$P_A = \frac{11}{25} + \frac{9}{25} = \frac{11 + 9}{25} = \frac{20}{25} = .80 \checkmark$$

$$P_C = \left[ \frac{15}{25} \times \frac{12}{25} \right] + \left[ \frac{10}{25} \times \frac{13}{25} \right] = .50 \checkmark$$

$$K = \frac{P_A - P_C}{1 - P_C} = \frac{.80 - .50}{1 - .50} = \frac{.30}{.50} = .60 \checkmark\checkmark$$

*Source:* Adapted from *Educational Assessment of Students* (2nd edition), by Nitko, Anthony J., © 1996 with permission. All rights reserved.

Suppose, a student receives a raw score of 80 on the SAT9 Total Reading battery, Form S. The SEM reported in the publisher's manual is 3.62, with a $KR_{20} = .94$. Based on the properties of the normal distribution, we can say that if we add and subtract *two SEM units* to the observed raw score of 80, giving us a range of scores from 72.76 to 87.24, 95% of the time the person's true score, *T*, would lie in that range, if the person were repeatedly tested on the same measure. Thus, we can have "confidence" that the person's score is located somewhere inside the band created with the estimated SEM value. This approach to score interpretation takes into account the inevitable random error associated with the score, preventing us from overinterpreting the results. (In more exact terms, the probability defined by $+/-1.96\sigma$ units in a normal curve is 95%.)

***Interrater Reliability Coefficient.*** As we see in Table 13.8, we seek interrater reliability when we wish to establish that the results from different judges, raters, or observers are not unduly influenced by random factors, and thus, can essentially be treated as interchangeable. Interrater reliability can be investigated by gathering data from two independent observers or raters on the same individuals, using the same tool, and then examining the extent to which the ratings/scores agree. "Agreement" can be evaluated in absolute terms, using indices of percent agreement; or we could look at correlation coefficients of data from two raters which tell us how comparably they rank the same individual on the assessment. Correlation coefficients employed with data from ordinal or interval scales could be Kendall's $\tau$ or Pearson's *r* (see Chapter 10).

In Demonstration 13.6, we see hypothetical data analyzed using *Cohen's kappa* ($\kappa$), an index of absolute agreement adjusted for chance. In practice, absolute agreement between raters is much harder to establish than agreement in ranks based on correlation coefficients. Our choice of approach should depend on whether the relative or absolute score is likely to be used for score interpretation purposes (Nitko, 1996).

### Key Concepts

■ The four predominant reliability coefficients are tied to different sources of random error. They are the parallel forms, test–retest, internal consistency, and interrater reliability coefficients.

■ To select the appropriate reliability coefficient(s), we should identify the potential sources of random error that might affect the reliability of the results.

## 13.3  Reliability in Criterion-Referenced Measurements

All of the reliability coefficients described thus far assume variability in the item response distributions and total scores. When we design assessments for making criterion-referenced interpretations of performance, high levels of variability may not be evidenced in the score distributions. How would we determine that our results are reliable? What are the ways in which we need to think about reliability when considering criterion-referenced instruments? In this section, we will briefly touch on some of these issues. More details are given on all the procedures in Crocker & Algina (1986).

Criterion-referenced test (CRT) items are designed with reference to tightly defined domains of knowledge and skill. Decisions made about examinee performance are in absolute terms, rather than relative terms. Thus, we can say, a person has been correct on 80% of the items from a domain measuring a particular skill. In a CRT context, we think of a person's "true score" *(T)* as the "domain score." The results of criterion-referenced assessment tools are either used in estimating a person's *domain score* or in placing the person in the mastery versus non-mastery category using a pre-set cut score (see Chapters 7–8, 11). If an examinee's raw score exceeds the cut score, we conclude that the individual has mastery of the domain. Two reliability concerns arise out of the use of CRTs. First, how well does the individual's raw score approximate their *domain score*? Second, how consistently and accurately can we place a person in a mastery category, using the cut score—something that we call "decision consistency" and "decision accuracy"?

### 13.3.1    Reliability of the Domain Score Estimate

Reliability theory on domain score estimates is drawn from a specialized area called generalizability theory. A generalizability coefficient is related to the $KR_{20}$ estimate, and addresses the extent to which we can generalize from our observed domain score to the "true" domain score. It is one indicator of the reliability of the domain score. Because generalizability theory is outside the scope of this book, the concept of generalizability of the domain score estimate will not be described in detail here. Conceptually, the generalizability coefficient is calculated by first estimating the error variance in a set of scores, and next, by separating the error variance from the total variance in individual scores, so that we obtain an estimate of their "true variance." The statistical analysis uses ANOVA (analysis of variance) procedures. In general, the higher the generalizability coefficient, the more accurate our estimation of the persons' domain scores. The generalizability coefficient would be a perfect 1.0 when every examinee's observed score is equal to that individual's true domain score. During calculation, it is affected by the variance of the domain scores as well as the accuracy of the variance estimates. Some authors (e.g., Crocker and Algina, 1986) prefer the use of only the error variance estimated through application of generalizability theory as an indicator of domain score accuracy.

### 13.3.2    Reliability of Mastery Classifications

How well students are placed in mastery categories can be examined by looking at results of two statistical procedures, *decision consistency* and *decision accuracy.* Decision consistency deals with how well the same decisions are made with two different sets of measurements on the same group of individuals, using a given cut score. The consistency can concern the agreement in decisions made with two parallel forms of the same test domain, or from two administrations of the same test or assessment tool. There are several methods for obtaining decision consistency estimates, including the use of Cohen's κ (discussed earlier). Our estimate of decision consistency will be affected by the length of the test, location of the cut score on the continuum, the generalizability of the domain score, as well as the similarity of the two distributions that are used in the estimation.

Decision accuracy concerns the extent to which our classification of an examinee as a master versus a non-master is accurate. Four types of decisions can result from criterion-referenced measurement involving a cut score. We would make correct decisions when a master is classified as a master (a true positive) and a non-master is accurately classified as such (a true negative). However, there could be two types of errors: a false positive classification, where we classify a non-master as a master; and a false negative classification, in which we would mistakenly place a master in the non-master category. To evaluate how well the cut score permits accurate classifications, we need to estimate the probabilities of the false positive and false negative classifications occurring. Again, there are many methods that can be used to obtain these probabilities, which we do not look at in this course.

## Summary

In Chapter 5 we saw that empirical validity evidence is gathered in Phase IVB of the Process Model. Chapter 13 provided information on how we would seek and interpret the most commonly reported forms of validity and reliability evidence in particular assessment applications. If we select or adopt assessment tools designed by other test publishers or developers for our own use, we should seek out relevant information on score validity and reliability. If engaged in assessment design efforts for high stakes purposes, all practitioners should carry out appropriate studies to investigate the validity and reliability of the scores they wish to use in their decision-making.

As in Chapter 3, this chapter also made a distinction between "validity" and "reliability" with the concepts of systematic error and random error. The chapter described six different methods for obtaining, analyzing, and reporting evidence to support the validity of particular score interpretations. They include (but are not limited to) the following: convergent validity, discriminant validity, predictive validity, concurrent validity, internal structure, group differences, and lack of bias. The chapter recommended that we interpret different forms of validity evidence in a unified manner in given contexts of assessment use, keeping in mind the interpretations and uses to which the scores would be subjected.

Reliability theory assumes that the scores would be influenced by random factors. Concepts of classical reliability theory, such as true scores, observed scores, and error were presented to show how the two major indices of reliability, standard error of measurement (SEM) and the reliability coefficient, $r_{XX'}$, are derived.

The chapter demonstrated how to obtain and interpret four major types of reliability coefficients, tied to different sources of random error. These were the parallel forms, test–retest, internal consistency, and interrater reliability coefficients. The chapter demonstrated the method for setting confidence bands around scores using the SEM. The chapter reminded practitioners that different methods for obtaining reliability coefficients may yield different results, and that the results are likely to be group-dependent and tied to the number of items, observations, or work samples built into the assessment procedure. Finally, approaches to estimating generalizability of the domain score and decision-theoretic methods for evaluating accuracy and consistency of cut-scores during criterion-referenced measurement, were briefly discussed.

## QUESTIONS FOR CLASS DISCUSSION

The *Graduate Record Examination* (GRE) is used widely to admit students into graduate programs in U.S. universities. It has multiple (parallel) forms that are administered in paper and pencil format, as well as a computerized version (a computer adaptive test). It is made up of verbal, quantitative, and analytic sections. Suppose that your institution is interested determining whether it is worthwhile to continue to use the GRE score as an admission criterion for students entering graduate programs. (You may have seen newspaper articles focusing on a similar discussion currently occurring in the California university system on the use of the SAT.) The following problems are based on validity/reliability of GRE scores.

1. Faculty and administrators of your institution examined the match between the item content of the GRE and the topics in graduate courses to decide how well the GRE would help them select candidates with the potential to succeed in different graduate programs.
   A. What kind of validity evidence were they examining?
   B. Compared to other kinds of validity evidence, how important is this type of evidence in evaluating the validity of GRE scores?
   C. What other types of validity evidence would you seek before you made a recommendation to your institution about continuing or discontinuing the GRE? Explain your answers.

2. The makers of GRE report that the verbal, quantitative, and analytic sections of the GRE have $KR_{20}$ values of .90 or above.
   A. Comment on the meaning and usefulness of this reliability information.
   B. What other reliability data might you look for to support the use of the GRE scores? Justify your answers.

3. A study reports that the GRE scores of 215 students in Psychology programs correlated .32 and .47 with measures of scholarly productivity during their professional life.
   A. What kind of validity evidence do these data provide?
   B. What is the proportion of shared variance in GRE scores and future productivity measures? (Interpret the range.) Would these data convince you to continue using the GRE as an admissions test?

4. The GRE general test scores correlated .30 (in engineering majors) and .37 (in social science majors) with GPA in first year graduate students (n = 1000). When undergraduate GPA is added as a predictor, the multiple correlation coefficient increased to .44. Evaluate these coefficients, keeping in mind the factors that affect the computed values of correlation coefficients (see Chapter 10) and purposes of the GRE. Explain your answers.

# CHAPTER

# 14 Selecting and Using Standardized Assessment Tools

## Overview

When selecting standardized, commercially marketed tools, it is important that we begin with an evaluation of the validity and reliability evidence supplied by the developer (Chapter 13). But that is rarely enough. The meaningfulness of an assessment's results (or scores) for local purposes also depends on several other relevant forms of empirical evidence, such as the appropriateness of the scaling procedures, the quality of standards in criterion-referenced tests, and the quality of the norms for norm-referenced tools. Chapter 14 focuses on different types of published standardized tests, the properties that make them distinct from locally developed or teacher-made assessments, and factors that practitioners should consider when adopting published assessments for local testing purposes.

Standardized test-makers report various types of information, including norm-referenced and criterion-referenced scores. Users need to be informed about how different scores and score scales are derived. Users also need to know how to interpret the various score reports disseminated by publishers.

Finally, practitioners need to know what resources exist to help select the best standardized tests for their needs. National organizations, such as the American Educational Research Association (AERA), the National Council on Measurement in Education (NCME), the American Psychological Association (APA), and the American Federation of Teachers (AFT) have developed ethical guidelines and technical standards of practice that responsible educators and assessment users should follow when appraising or employing published tools.

Chapter 14 is concerned with both Phases IVA and IVB of the Process Model, dealing with procedures for content validation and empirical evaluation of externally developed and/or published assessments that we select for our local needs (Chapter 5, Figure 5.1). As before, descriptions and presentations of particular procedures are reinforced with real reports and score profiles from selected published instruments. Most of the statistical procedures employed are derived from concepts introduced to you in Chapter 10.

## CHAPTER 14 OBJECTIVES

After studying this chapter and completing the structured exercises in the module, you should be able to:

1. Describe the predominant characteristics of standardized tests and their distinguishing properties.

2. Describe the main types of standardized tests used in educational contexts, their users and typical uses.

3. Interpret the main types of norm-referenced scores, scales, and score reports/profiles.

4. Evaluate the technical qualities of standardized achievement tests meant for criterion-referencing versus norm-referencing.

5. Select standardized tools for given purposes and populations based on relevant technical standards and criteria.

6. Identify the major resources for finding and evaluating published assessments.

7. Evaluate the technical standards and ethical guidelines for test practice that apply when using published tests in different decision-making contexts.


# 14.1   Distinguishing Characteristics of Standardized Tools

To determine whether you have ever taken a standardized assessment, ask yourself the following questions.

- Was the assessment administered in a highly structured manner?
- Did the proctors appear to be following a script?
- Did the assessors appear to have been trained?
- Was the test strictly timed?
- Did the proctors or test administrators work to maintain a quiet (or otherwise conducive) atmosphere during the assessment process?
- Did the scoring procedure appear to be structured?

If your answers to one or more of the above questions was in the affirmative, you have probably taken a test that was standardized to some degree. *A standardized instrument is one that is administered and scored under uniform and controlled conditions.* Standardized tools stand apart from most local or teacher-made tests because of the deliberate controls that are imposed by the developers on the respondents, the assessment environment, the proctors or test administrators, and the scorers and scoring procedures employed during testing. They are purposely designed to keep errors down to a minimum and, when norm-referenced, to allow for controlled comparisons of results on particular subtests or a test as a whole, with defined groups of examinees/respondents.

Different standardized tests measure different constructs. Most of us are familiar with standardized aptitude tests, such as the *Graduate Record Examination* (GRE) or the *Scholastic Assessment Test* (SAT, called the *Scholastic Aptitude Test* prior to 1994); or standardized achievement test batteries, such as the *Stanford Achievement Test Series* (Stanford) or the *Iowa Tests of Basic Skills* (ITBS); or with standardized intelligence tests, such as the *Stanford-Binet* Scale (S-B). Standardized tests can be widely different with respect to their item format and content, from highly structured, verbal and quantitative items presented in written format, to non-verbal, interview-based performance assessments—and various combinations of these features. Standardized tests also differ with respect to how they are administered—some are group-administered while others employ an individualized, one-on-one format. Finally, different standardized tests vary with respect to the type of information they report, providing norm-referenced or criterion-referenced scores, or a combination of both score types. Most, although not all, standardized assessment tools are also published and commercially marketed for widespread dissemination and use. Irrespective of their differences, however, a common characteristic that they all share is the deliberate set of constraints imposed on the conditions of administration and scoring by the test-makers.

Just because an instrument is published is no guarantee of its quality. Responsible test developers supply adequate documentation, compiled in technical manuals and reports, that accompany their instruments or batteries. A major technical obligation borne by test publishers toward prospective consumers is the provision of both content-based and empirical documentation to support their tests and use of their test scores in particular contexts. To guard against misuse, developers who publish their tests should clearly delineate the purposes and contexts in which their tools might be appropriately employed, and how the evidence they provide supports particular inferences with the results. To comply with nationally agreed-upon technical standards for educational and psychological testing (AERA, APA, & NCME, 1999), large-scale publishers generally establish programs of research to systematically gather and document evidence on the quality of their instruments and scores. This chapter will provide examples of established instruments that are well documented.

Prior to adopting an instrument, consumers of published tests (such as you or I) bear the responsibility to seek out and appraise the evidence provided by test developers in their technical manuals. Such documentation could include evidence of *all* of the following that apply:

- How the tool was constructed and content-validated
- Empirical validity evidence to support particular uses of scores
- Reliability of scores
- Accuracy and equivalency of scales and score forms (results of what are called "equating" studies)
- Adequacy of standards and standard-setting procedures (for CRTs)
- Fairness for all groups assessed
- Adequacy of norms (for NRTs)

## An Historical Recommendation

In an article published in the *American Psychologist* in 1961, titled "Must all tests be valid?," Professor R. L. Ebel attempted to persuade the psychometric community that it was important to evaluate the "meaningfulness" of an assessment's scores broadly by integrating evidence from several different but relevant sources. Ebel was protesting against the prevalent, but rather narrow understandings of "validity" at the time, based solely on the "correlation of test scores with criterion measures"—what we refer to as criterion-related validity today. The 1999 *Standards for Educational and Psychological Testing* (AERA, APA, & NCME, 1999), published almost four decades later, now echo Ebel's recommendations. In the summary statement of the above article, Ebel had stated:

> . . . [T]he characteristics which we regard as determining the quality of a mental test or measurement procedure . . . are:
> 1. The importance of the inferences that can be made from the test scores.
> 2. The meaningfulness of the test scores, based on
>    a. An operational definition of the measurement procedure
>    b. A knowledge of the relationships of the scores to other measures, from
>       i. validity coefficients, predictive and concurrent
>       ii. Other correlation coefficients or measures of relationships
>    c. A good estimate of reliability of the scores
>    d. Appropriate norms of examinee performance
> 3. The convenience of the test in use. (Ebel, 1961, p. 646)

This book has classified the above characteristics under the broad labels of "validity," "reliability," and "utility."

(*Source:* Ebel, R. L. (1961). Must all tests be valid? *American Psychologist, 16,* 640–647.)

## 14.2   Standardized Tools in Use in Education

Educators in public and private institutions in the United States use five major kinds of standardized or published tests. These are:

- Standardized achievement tests and test batteries
- Intelligence and scholastic aptitude tests
- Career/educational interest inventories
- Attitude scales
- Personality measures

This section discusses the characteristics and examples of instruments in each category, the contexts in which they are typically used, and how we should select them to meet local needs.

### 14.2.1 Standardized Achievement Tests and Test Batteries

*Characteristics.*   Standardized achievement tests, used mostly in K–12 institutions, are intended to measure learning outcomes and skills that are common to curricula in a vast number of schools and school districts across the United States. The achievement domain is developed through consensus among expert panels of curriculum and instructional specialists at particular grade levels. Experts from representative districts, universities, and national and regional organizations are invited by the test developers to participate in the design or review processes required during test development. Usually, the test items are written by content specialists who are trained by the developers to follow very tightly constructed sets of item specifications (see examples in Chapters 7 and 8). The items developed thus are pretested and screened on the basis of item analysis and other studies investigating the frequency of errors in the targeted age groups, independent reviews of other experts, and screenings for the "appearance of bias." As a result of the intensive and often lengthy developmental procedures that test publishers follow, the quality of items in the pool for standardized achievement tests is generally very good.

The procedures for administration and scoring are typically very controlled for achievement tests. Users are provided with detailed and specific instruction booklets to guide them during test administration. The reliability coefficients they report are also generally high for such tests (see examples in Chapter 13). To help appropriate interpretations of results, the manuals accompanying the tests provide information on other correlational properties of scores.

Most standardized achievement tests are accompanied with nationally representative norms. *Norms Tables* and *Norm-referenced Scores* provide a common reference framework against which different school districts can interpret their students' scores. The sample of students used to develop norms and norm-referenced scales is referred to as the *standardization sample.* Making sure that the norming sample is recent and similar in composition to the local population is important for accurate norm-referenced score interpretations at the local level.

As you saw in the examples discussed in Chapter 13, several of the published tests have *parallel* or equivalent forms of their tests, sampled from the same achievement domain, and built to match the same set of specifications. Parallel forms help test users maintain greater security during test administration so that scores are not affected by repeated usage of the same instrument or, in rare instances, by cheating.

*Types of Standardized Achievement Tests.*   The most widely used standardized achievement tests are general measures, referred to as "survey" batteries of reading, mathematics, and language domains. However, specific subject area tests, focusing on areas such as science and social studies, are also found. Published achievement tests are generally of three main kinds:

1. Multilevel achievement batteries
2. Diagnostic achievement batteries
3. Individualized achievement tests

*Multilevel Achievement Batteries*    These batteries consist of a group of several subject area tests, such as reading, mathematics, and language, that are designed to broadly survey achievement domains at consecutive grade levels. Each grade level test is standardized on a *national standardization sample,* allowing for norm-referenced interpretation of an individual's performance in the different subject areas using a common, national reference group. Further, within given subject-area domains, the scores at different test levels corresponding to increasing grade levels are *vertically equated,* or statistically linked to create a common metric. The *scaled scores* derived thus allow users to track student growth over time in particular subject area domains. Multilevel batteries are typically group-administered.

Three test publishers with very widely used multilevel batteries in English are listed in Table 14.1. We should note here that some of the publishers of multilevel batteries, such as CTB/McGraw-Hill, and Harcourt Brace, have designed such tests in Spanish to accommodate students with limited English language skills. To illustrate the breadth of the content domain of such tests with an example, Table 14.2A-B provide the CTB/4 skills outline for two subtests produced for grade levels K–12. Table 14.2B shows two sample items in Language Expression intended for two grade levels.

To meet demands of the market most manufacturers of multilevel achievement batteries include criterion-referenced information in their score reports along with norm-referenced scores and scales. The *Stanford* series, for example, produces scores in both the general domains and specific content clusters; the latter being better suited for criterion-referencing of individual student or group needs. To illustrate, Table 14.3 (top panel) shows an individual student's raw score and norm-referenced report on the broad content domains covered in the Ninth Edition of the Grade 1 test of the *Stanford* series. The bottom panel of Table 14.3, on the other hand, presents the specific content clusters on which the same student's performance can be described. Although the descriptors "above average" and "average" are used in this part of the report, it is easy to see that differences

**TABLE 14.1    Multilevel Achievement Survey Batteries**

| Examples of Multilevel Achievement Survey Batteries | Grade Levels Covered | Publisher |
|---|---|---|
| *Iowa Tests of Basic Skills* | K–9 | Riverside Publishing Co. 425 Spring Lake Drive, Itasca, IL 60143-2079 |
| *TerraNova (Comprehensive Tests of Basic Skills)* | K–12 | CTB/McGraw-Hill 20 Ryan Ranch Rd. Monterey, CA 93940-5703 |
| *Stanford Achievement Test Series* | 1–12 | Harcourt Brace Educational Measurement 555 Academic Court San Antonio, TX 78204-2498 |

**TABLE 14.2A   CTB5 Objectives**

**Reading/Language Arts**

**01   Oral Comprehension**                                                            **10, 11**
Demonstrate both literal and interpretive understanding of passages that are read aloud.

*Use writing or other means to respond to literal and interpretive questions about passages that are read aloud.*

**02   Basic Understanding**                                                           **10–21/22**
Demonstrate understanding of the literal meaning of a passage through identifying stated information, indicating sequence of events, and defining grade-level vocabulary.

*Write responses to questions requiring literal information from passages and documents.*

**03   Analyze Text**                                                                  **11–21/22**
Demonstrate comprehension by drawing conclusions; inferring relationships, such as cause and effect; and identifying theme and story elements, such as plot, climax, character, and setting.

*Write responses that show an understanding of the text that goes beyond surface meaning.*

**04   Evaluate and Extend Meaning**                                                   **11–21/22**
Demonstrate critical understanding by making predictions; distinguishing between fact and opinion, and reality and fantasy; transferring ideas to other situations; and judging author purpose, point of view, and effectiveness.

*Write responses that make connections between texts based on common themes and concepts; evaluate author purpose and effectiveness, and extend meaning to other contexts.*

**05   Identify Reading Strategies**                                                   **11–21/22**
Demonstrate awareness of techniques that enhance comprehension, such as using existing knowledge, summarizing content, comparing information across texts, using graphics and text structure, and formulating questions that deepen understanding.

*Write responses that interpret and extend the use of information from documents and forms, and that demonstrate knowledge and use of strategies.*

**06   Introduction to Print**                                                         **10–12**
Demonstrate knowledge of sound/symbol and structural relationships in letters, words, and signs.

*Write responses that show knowledge of letters and words.*

**07   Sentence Structure**                                                            **11–21/22**
Demonstrate an understanding of conventions for writing complete and effective sentences, including treatment of subject and verb, punctuation, and capitalization.

Demonstrate an understanding of conciseness and clarity of meaning in combining two sentences.

**TABLE 14.2A** (continued)

**Reading/Language Arts (continued)**

08 **Writing Strategies**                                                              11–21/22

Demonstrate knowledge of information sources, outlines, and other prewriting techniques.

Demonstrate an understanding of the use of topic sentences, concluding sentences, connective and transitional words and phrases, supporting statements, sequencing ideas, and relevant information in writing expository prose.

09 **Editing Skills**                                                                  11–21/22

Identify the appropriate use of capitalization, punctuation, nouns, pronouns, verbs, adjectives, and adverbs in existing text.

*Demonstrate knowledge of writing conventions and sentence structure through identifying and correcting errors in existing text and in text written by the student.*

**Mathematics**

10 **Number and Number Relations**                                                     10–21/22

Demonstrate an understanding of number, number sense, and number theory by ordering numbers, representing numbers in equivalent forms, identifying relationships, interpreting numbers in real-world situations, and applying number concepts in real-world situations.

*Communicate, model, or represent an understanding of number and number relationships.*

11 **Computation and Numerical Estimation**                                            10–21/22

Demonstrate proficiency in computation procedures, solve real-world computation problems, apply a variety of estimation strategies, and determine reasonableness of results.

*Explain estimation strategies, compare computation techniques, and evaluate and verify solutions.*

12 **Operation Concepts**                                                              11–21/22

Demonstrate an understanding of the properties and relationships of operations, relate mathematical representations to problem situations, and apply operational processes to solve problems.

*Communicate, model, or represent an understanding of operation concepts.*

13 **Measurement**                                                                     10–21/22

Demonstrate an understanding of measurement systems, units, and tools by describing, calculating, or estimating size, location, and time; by using the concepts of perimeter, area, volume, capacity, weight, and mass; and by identifying appropriate degrees of accuracy.

Solve problems involving principles of measurement, rate, and scale.

*Use manipulatives to explore shapes, area, and perimeter; and to model and represent measurement problems.*

*Describe measurement processes, compare techniques, estimate, and communicate estimation strategies.*

*Source:* CTB/McGraw-Hill (2000). CTBS/5: Preview Materials. Monterey, CA: McGraw-Hill. Reproduced with permission.

**TABLE 14.2B   CTB/4 Sample Items in Language Expression at Two Levels**

## Language Expression

*This item shows how well students can distinguish correct and concise sentences from ineffective sentences.*

Read the underlined sentences. Then read the sentences below the underlined sentences. Choose the sentence that best combines the underlined sentences into one. Mark your answer.

> The old house is big. The old house is yellow.
>
> ○ The old house is big and yellow.
>
> ○ The house is old and big and yellow.
>
> ○ The house is bigger than the old, yellow house.
>
> ○ The old house is a big house and a yellow house.

## Language Expression

*This item shows how well students understand the relationship between the sentences in a paragraph.*

Choose the topic sentence that best fits the paragraph.

> _____. The best type of wood to choose has a dense, even grain, such as oak or walnut. The wood should be seasoned, for green wood tends to crack and split as carving progresses. Select air-dried wood over heat-dried; the latter contains more moisture and will expand, changing the contours of your carving.
>
> A  Hardwoods are the most suitable types of wood for making furniture.
>
> B  Finding the proper piece of wood for carving is essential.
>
> C  Woodcarving is an art that requires patience as well as imagination.
>
> D  The type of wood a sculptor chooses to carve depends on the subject.

*Source:* CTB/McGraw-Hill (1989). CTBS/4: Preview Materials. Monterey, CA: McGraw-Hill. Reproduced with permission. All rights reserved.

in a student's proficiency in different areas can be picked up for instructional use from the skill-referenced section (procedures for conducting a domain-referenced analysis were described in Chapter 11). It must be remembered that diagnostic decisions based on scores from general achievement batteries such as the *Stanford* series will be weaker than those made using tests specifically designed to support diagnosis (see next section). This is simply because general achievement tests are constructed to cover very broad domains of knowledge and skill.

*Diagnostic Achievement Batteries*   These batteries provide in-depth information of individual performance relative to specific skill or content areas within a domain. Such tests are deliberately designed to reveal areas of strength and weakness of a student in very specific areas of skill and knowledge. Thus, there are many items tied to particular subdomains, yielding highly reliable scores in relatively narrow areas. Decisions on individualized instructional programs are supported by data from well-designed diagnostic batteries. For example, reading specialists often need to administer and interpret the results of diagnostic reading inventories to determine a child's reading level prior to an instructional placement. Two examples of published tests useful for diagnostic decisions

**TABLE 14.3   Stanford Achievement Test Series, Ninth Edition with Otis-Lennon School Ability Test, Seventh Edition (Simulated Data)**

| | |
|---|---|
| TEACHER:   HUNT | |
| SCHOOL:   NEWTOWN ELEM | GRADE:   01 |
| DISTRICT:   NEWTOWN DISTRICT | TEST DATE: 04/96 |
| TEST TYPE:   MULTIPLE CHOICE | |

**STUDENT REPORT FOR PAMELA T HUTTON**

Age: 7 yrs 03 Mos
Student No: 0000027123

| SUBTESTS AND TOTALS (A) | No. of Items | Raw Score | Scaled Score | National PR-S | National NCE | Grade Equiv | AAC Range (D) |
|---|---|---|---|---|---|---|---|
| Total Reading | 106 | 69 | 527 | 48-5 | 48.9 | 1.8 | MIDDLE |
| Word Study Skills | 36 | 30 | 582 | 76-6 | 64.9 | 3.0 | HIGH |
| Word Reading | 30 | 22 | 528 | 61-6 | 55.9 | 2.0 | MIDDLE |
| Reading Comp. | 40 | 17 | 485 | 19-3 | 31.5 | 1.4 | LOW |
| Total Mathematics | 69 | 46 | 532 | 53-5 | 51.6 | 1.8 | MIDDLE |
| Problem Solving (B) | 44 | 29 | 543 | 45-5 | 47.4 | 1.7 | MIDDLE |
| Procedures | 25 | 17 | 515 | 61-6 | 55.9 | 2.0 | MIDDLE |
| Language | 44 | 31 | 577 | 72-6 | 62.3 | 2.5 | HIGH |
| Spelling | 30 | 18 | 507 | 48-5 | 48.9 | 1.8 | MIDDLE |
| Environment | 40 | 30 | 590 | 82-7 | 69.3 | 3.2 | HIGH |
| Listening | 40 | 34 | 622 | 87-7 | 73.7 | 3.6 | HIGH |
| Basic Battery | 289 | 198 | NA | 59-5 | 55.1 | 2.0 | MIDDLE |
| Complete Battery | 329 | 228 | NA | 62-6 | 56.6 | 2.0 | MIDDLE |

| OTIS-LENNON SCHOOL ABILITY TEST (C) | Raw Score | SAI | Age PR-S | Age NCE | Scaled Score | Natl Grade PR-S | Natl Grade NCE |
|---|---|---|---|---|---|---|---|
| Total | 60 | 33 | 96 | 40-5 | 44.7 | 549 | 42-5 | 45.7 |
| Verbal | 30 | 19 | 105 | 62-6 | 56.4 | 567 | 64-6 | 57.5 |
| Nonverbal | 30 | 14 | 87 | 21-3 | 33.0 | 533 | 26-4 | 36.5 |

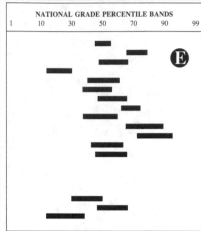

**NATIONAL GRADE PERCENTILE BANDS**
1   10   30   50   70   90   99   (E)

| CONTENT CLUSTERS (F) | RS/ | NP/ | NA | Below Average | Average | Above Average |
|---|---|---|---|---|---|---|
| **Word Study Skills** | 30/ | 36/ | 36 | | ✓ | |
| Structural Analysis | 10/ | 12/ | 12 | | ✓ | |
| Phonetic Analysis-Consonants | 11/ | 12/ | 12 | | | ✓ |
| Phonetic Analysis-Vowels | 9/ | 12/ | 12 | | | ✓ |
| **Word Reading** | 22/ | 30/ | 30 | | ✓ | |
| **Reading Comprehension** | 17/ | 40/ | 39 | ✓ | | |
| Two-Sentence Stories (Riddles) | 5/ | 5/ | 5 | | | ✓ |
| Short Passages (Cloze) | 9/ | 15/ | 14 | | ✓ | |
| Short Passages w/Questions | 3/ | 20/ | 20 | ✓ | | |
| Recreational | 1/ | 10/ | 10 | ✓ | | |
| Textual | 1/ | 5/ | 5 | ✓ | | |
| Functional | 1/ | 5/ | 5 | ✓ | | |
| Initial Understanding | 0/ | 9/ | 9 | ✓ | | |
| Interpretation | 3/ | 11/ | 11 | ✓ | | |
| **Mathematics: Problem Solving** | 29/ | 44/ | 43 | | ✓ | |
| Concepts/Whole No. Comput. | 1/ | 3/ | 3 | | ✓ | |
| Number Sense and Numeration | 10/ | 12/ | 12 | | | ✓ |
| Geometry and Spatial Sense | 2/ | 5/ | 5 | ✓ | | |
| Measurement | 4/ | 8/ | 7 | ✓ | | |
| Statistics and Probability | 5/ | 5/ | 5 | | | ✓ |
| Fraction and Decimal Concepts | 3/ | 3/ | 3 | | | ✓ |
| Patterns & Relationships | 2/ | 5/ | 5 | ✓ | | |
| Problem-Solving Strategies | 2/ | 3/ | 3 | | ✓ | |
| **Mathematics: Procedures** | 17/ | 25/ | 25 | | ✓ | |
| Number Facts | 6/ | 8/ | 8 | | ✓ | |
| Computation, Symbolic Notation | 6/ | 11/ | 11 | | ✓ | |
| Computation in Context | 5/ | 6/ | 6 | | | ✓ |

| CONTENT CLUSTERS | RS/ | NP/ | NA | Below Average | Average | Above Average |
|---|---|---|---|---|---|---|
| **Language** | 31/ | 44/ | 44 | | ✓ | |
| Capitalization | 4/ | 7/ | 7 | | ✓ | |
| Punctuation | 3/ | 7/ | 7 | | ✓ | |
| Usage | 6/ | 6/ | 6 | | | ✓ |
| Sentence Structure | 8/ | 10/ | 10 | | ✓ | |
| Content and Organization | 7/ | 10/ | 10 | | | ✓ |
| Study Skills | 3/ | 4/ | 4 | | ✓ | |
| **Spelling** | 18/ | 30/ | 30 | | ✓ | |
| Sight Words | 5/ | 5/ | 5 | | | ✓ |
| Phonetic Principles | 10/ | 18/ | 18 | | ✓ | |
| Structure Principles | 3/ | 7/ | 7 | | ✓ | |
| **Environment** | 30/ | 40/ | 40 | | | ✓ |
| Earth & Space Science | 4/ | 5/ | 5 | | | ✓ |
| Physical Science | 4/ | 5/ | 5 | | | ✓ |
| Life Science | 7/ | 10/ | 10 | | ✓ | |
| History | 4/ | 5/ | 5 | | ✓ | |
| Geography | 5/ | 5/ | 5 | | | ✓ |
| Civics & Government | 2/ | 5/ | 5 | | ✓ | |
| Economics | 4/ | 5/ | 5 | | ✓ | |
| **Listening** | 34/ | 40/ | 40 | | | ✓ |
| Vocabulary | 8/ | 10/ | 20 | | | ✓ |
| Comprehension | 26/ | 30/ | 30 | | | ✓ |
| Recreational | 12/ | 14/ | 14 | | ✓ | |
| Informational | 8/ | 8/ | 8 | | | ✓ |
| Functional | 6/ | 8/ | 8 | | ✓ | |
| Initial Understanding | 11/ | 14/ | 14 | | ✓ | |
| Interpretation | 15/ | 16/ | 16 | | | ✓ |

*Source:* Harcourt Brace Educational Measurement (1997b). *Stanford Achievement Test Series,* ninth edition. All rights reserved. Reproduced with permission.

in the mathematics and reading areas are the *DMI Mathematics System* and the *PRI Reading Systems,* respectively. The *KeyMath Diagnostic Arithmetic Test—Revised* (Levels: Grade K-6), and the *Woodcock Reading Mastery Tests—Revised,* are other examples.

*Individualized Achievement Tests*    These instruments are designed for special needs populations. They can be administered individually to students by their teachers, and require little or no writing. Most use a one-on-one, interview-based or a behavior-based format. Two examples of individualized achievement tests (also used for diagnostic purposes) are the *KeyMath* and the *Woodcock,* mentioned in the previous paragraph.

### Applications of Standardized Achievement Tests and their Results.

Results of standardized achievement tests are used both within and outside the classroom to support instructional, program evaluation, and accountability decisions. Individual score reports (similar to that shown in Table 14.3) and aggregated summaries for classrooms can be used by teachers to:

- Describe where individual students or groups of students at particular grade levels stand on general educational areas when compared to national norms
- Identify specific strengths and weaknesses that students may have in particular curricular areas for instructional planning or individual student placement, movement, or remediation within the educational program
- Communicate curricular expectations and provide feedback on educational progress to students and parents

The multilevel standardized achievement test batteries are often annually administered at school districts for creating systemwide reports describing how students in regions, schools, or grade levels across a system are performing. Such aggregated reports can be used by school officials and superintendents for making decisions on the quality of their instructional programs, and make improvements and modifications that might be warranted based on results. Educational evaluators and researchers routinely use standardized test data as one indicator for examining the effectiveness of educational innovations and schools as a whole.

### Selecting and Using Achievement Tests.

Guided by the context of use, criteria that we could use for selecting a standardized achievement test or battery at the local level are summarized below.

We should make sure that multi-level batteries focus on the major basic skill and curricular areas that are emphasized locally. Remember that the match might vary at different grade levels, with scores providing only a limited picture of student achievement levels. Note the date of test construction and publication, as curriculum objectives that define the domain for the test may become outdated or irrelevant from time to time. Compared to general batteries, diagnostic test batteries should contain enough items in each specific skill area. Remember to examine the available empirical documentation on validity and reliability of scores, item analysis, data on test score and item bias, and other studies pertinent to the different score types and scales that will be used in the decision-making context. Norms should be evaluated when a test provides norm-referenced scores, such as percentile ranks. Utility should not be overlooked in making a final judgment on the value of the assessment tool, with particular attention to cost of tests themselves versus costs of score reports and other services needed by users.

Two important guiding criteria for achievement test selection are content relevance and content representativeness. Prior to selecting a test, users should carefully review all the documents provided by the publisher that are pertinent to evaluating content-based validity in the local context, similar to those shown in Table 14.2 and 14.3. Multilevel batteries pose a challenge with respect to content validity, as the tests at some grade levels might be a better match for the local curriculum than others. Achievement batteries are usually better matched at the elementary level than secondary levels, since students tend to branch out into specialized subject-area tracks in middle and high school. When interpreting results, a key factor to keep in mind is the *instructional validity* of the test in question—that is, whether most teachers in the school district or organization are likely to have delivered adequate instruction on the content domain by the projected time of testing. We should also be careful that the content outline presented by the developers is not outdated or unaligned to the local curriculum in other respects.

We should look for adequate reliability in scores that we intend to use for decision-making. Thus, if the total raw score or a transformed version of the same are to be used, we should ensure that it has both adequate internal consistency reliability and stability over time. If we intend to use total scores from parallel forms of a given standardized test, we should examine the reported parallel forms reliability coefficient. If our intent is to use subtest scores (subdomain scores) instead of the total scores, it would then be relevant for us to evaluate reliability information for the appropriate subtest.

For criterion-referenced tests, we would require that item sets are linked to clearly defined domains of knowledge or skill, rather than the more general domains commonly tapped by norm-referenced tests. Further, reliability information must not only support internal consistency reliability of the domains tested, but also the generalizability of the domain score. In the event that cut scores are provided by the test developers, we should look for empirical and judgment-based studies that support the validity of the recommended standards. Studies of decision consistency and decision accuracy are crucial for tests intended for making high stakes decisions for individual examinees.

Item analysis data for norm-referenced and criterion-referenced tests should likewise be based on studies with different criterion groups (Chapter 12). Systematic biases in item or score functioning should have been investigated by test developers.

*Norm-referenced achievement tests* must be evaluated based on different criteria. Factors to consider in evaluating norms are discussed later in this chapter, in Section 14.3.1.

Guarding against misuses is important because of the numerous controversies surrounding standardized test score uses and a lack of attention to their limitations (see Chapter 2). Some serious—and unfortunately common—misuses of standardized achievement tests and test scores are the following.

*Misuse* 1.   Promotion or retention of individual students at a particular grade level.
*Reason:*   Test-makers *rarely or never* provide validity evidence supporting the

long-term effectiveness of grade retention practices on the basis of their scores. In the absence of supporting data, retaining students is an inappropriate practice.

*Misuse* 2. Assignment of report card marks.
*Reason:* General survey batteries lack the needed content-based validity and specificity to match an individual teacher's classroom curriculum. They are also single point measurements lacking the comprehensiveness of an array of multiple assessments on which "valid" marks should be based.

*Misuse* 3. Teacher performance evaluations.
*Reason:* Such applications are guided by the beliefs that first, student learning is accurately reflected in the achievement test score, irrespective of technical limitations of the test; and second, that scholastic learning is influenced by a single factor only—the performance of the teacher. Both research and common sense tell us that learning is the result of the interaction of a complex array of variables, only one of which is the teacher's influence. More importantly, test-makers *rarely or never* provide validity evidence showing correlations between student achievement scores on their tests and other reliable indicators of teacher effectiveness.

In Section 14.5, we examine technical standards and guidelines that we should follow to control for misapplications of standardized achievement tests and their scores.

## 14.2.2   Intelligence and Scholastic Aptitude Tests

***Characteristics of Intelligence and Aptitude Tests.*** The conceptualizations of *intelligence* have evolved over time. Serious work on intelligence theory and test development began in the early nineteenth century with the work of Sir Francis Galton in Britain, Binet and Simon in France, and the work of Terman at Stanford University in the United States. Today, the theoretical and empirical work of cognitive psychologists such as Sternberg (1981) and neurobiologists such as Pedersen, Plomin, and McLearns (1994) and Reed and Jensen (1992) are continually redefining our understandings of intelligence. The procedures for operationalizing intelligence has been influenced by the manner in which the construct of intelligence was understood at particular times in history. Based predominantly on the work of psychologists, Walsh and Betz (2000) recently provided the following summary on the meaning of human intelligence.

> . . . Intelligence is a combination of (1) a general, or *g,* component, reflecting overall reasoning and problem-solving abilities, judgment, and learning ability; and (2) subcomponents reflecting school ability and more specific group factors of ability representing various content areas or types of mental operations. The existence of *g* is inferred from the positive correlations among tests of mental ability *varying* in content and type of intellectual processes involved . . . The existence of separate components of *g* is inferred from factor analytic studies . . . (from *Tests and Assessment* by Walsh & Betz, © 2000, p. 156).

*Aptitude* is closely related to intelligence but is treated as a different construct in education and psychology. Aptitude indicates a person's future *capacity to learn or be successfully trained* in a specified domain of skills, behaviors, or knowledge. For example, scholastic aptitude refers to the capacity to be successful in a school-related curriculum; musical aptitude indicates the potential to successfully learn musical skills and knowledge; clerical aptitude denotes the likelihood of success in acquiring clerical skills (Walsh and Betz, 2000). As a construct, aptitude probably has greater practical value than its relative, intelligence.

### Examples of Intelligence and Aptitude Tests.    In public education settings, *intelligence* and *aptitude* tests that are widely used are the following.

*Individual Intelligence Tests: The Stanford-Binet Intelligence Scale (S-B)*    The *Stanford-Binet Intelligence Scale* test is one of the best-known intelligence tests in the world. It descended from the original developed by Terman in 1905. The Fourth Edition (S-B IV) is an extensively revised version (Thorndike, Hagen, & Sattler, 1986) consisting of 15 subtests, including six core areas administered to examinees of all age groups. The S-B IV includes vocabulary, quantitative, memory, pattern analysis, copying, paper folding and cutting, verbal relations, and equation-building tasks. The S-B IV is used for assessing people of all ages, from children of age 4 to adults. It is administered by psychological examiners who are trained to determine the basal and ceiling levels of individual examinees (the entry and stopping points). The administration process for the test is adaptive, which means that examiners must estimate the examinee's ability level to decide where to begin the testing process for a person. The examiners use chronological age to determine entry levels for the first test, focusing on vocabulary. They then estimate the examinee's ability level using performance on the vocabulary section and his/her chronological age, and decide on the entry point for the remaining subtests. The ceiling level is set based on the number of items that an examinee fails at two consecutive levels. The raw score of the S-B IV is converted to a Standard Age Score (SAS) based on norms that correspond to chronological age ranges. The S-B IV yields a composite score, purported to be a general index of intellectual performance. The report also provides raw scores and SAS for each subtest, grouped under four major "factors": Verbal Reasoning, Abstract/Visual Reasoning, Quantitative Reasoning, and Short-term Memory.

*Individual intelligence tests: The Wechsler Intelligence Scale for Children (WISC)*    The WISC, authored by David Wechsler, is another individually administered test that serves as a major alternative to the S-B in public school applications. It is applicable to individuals between ages 6–16 years and is comprised of 10 basic subtests along with 3 supplementary tests, organized under a Verbal Scale and a Performance Scale. The subtest labels suggest the nature of the construct domain: Information, Similarities, Arithmetic, Vocabulary, Comprehension (Verbal Scale); Picture Completion, Picture Arrangement, Block Design, Object Assembly, Coding (Performance Scale). The third edition of the test, WISC-III, was published in 1991 by Psychological Corporation. The WISC-III and its counterparts for very young children, the *Wechsler Preschool and Primary Scale of Intelligence-Revised* (WPPSI-R), and for adults, *Wechsler Adult Intelligence Scale* (WAIS-III) must be administered by trained psychologists. Together, they provide a comprehensive set of well-researched instruments for assessing a wide range of age groups.

*Group-Administered, Multilevel Cognitive Ability Tests: The Cognitive Abilities Test (CogAT)*   Like multilevel achievement batteries, multilevel mental ability tests are deliberately designed for large group administration. Their intent is to measure general intellectual abilities across a range of grade levels. They measure comparable domains of ability which overlap in difficulty at adjacent grade levels. At the same time, the content varies enough to portray growth in the cognitive areas progressively from grade K through 12. The *CogAT,* published by the Riverside Publishing Company, is an example of a group-administered mental test. It is based on the original Lorge-Thorndike Intelligence Tests (Lorge, Thorndike, & Hagen, 1964) and was developed by Thorndike & Hagen (1978). The test has three sections focusing primarily on reasoning tasks presented through verbal (using words), quantitative (using numbers) and nonverbal (using geometric shapes and figures) formats.

*Group-Administered, General Scholastic Aptitude Tests: The Scholastic Aptitude Test (SAT), the American College Testing (ACT) Assessment, and the Graduate Record Examination (GRE).*   The *Scholastic Aptitude Test,* now called the *Scholastic Assessment Test* (SAT-I and SAT-II) are administered for the College Board by the Educational Testing Service (ETS) of Princeton, New Jersey, and intended for the selection and placement of students who are moving out of high school into college. The SAT-I is a group-administered, general aptitude test focusing on verbal and mathematical reasoning tasks, including items dealing with verbal analogies, sentence completion, critical reading of passages, mathematics, and quantitative comparisons. The SAT-I scores are reported to have high internal consistency reliability (.90s), parallel forms reliability (.80s) and "strong" predictive validity when used with high school rank data (Walsh & Betz, 2000).

## An Interesting Statistic

The SAT-I, combined with the Preliminary Scholastic Aptitude Test/National Merit Scholarship Qualifying Test (PSAT/NMSQT) and the Advanced Placement (AP) program tests, are all parts of the College Entrance Examination Board's (CEEB) assessment program for helping students make the transition from high school to college. Combined, these tests were administered to nearly six million students in 1997–98 (Walsh & Betz, 2000).

The *ACT Assessment,* another measure of scholastic aptitude, was originally developed as a part of the Iowa Testing Program by E.F. Lindquist and his colleagues at the University of Iowa. With the SAT, this assessment serves as a major component of the national testing program designed for helping institutions select students who are ready for college-level work, and in assisting students select an appropriate undergraduate school or major area of study. The assessment focuses on a student's ability to solve problems, grasp implied meanings, draw inferences, evaluate ideas, and make judgments. The items are delivered using four subject areas as the medium, English, Mathematics, Science and Reading. The ACT score reliabilities range from .84 (Subtest level) to .96 (Composite). The predictive validity of scores using college GPA as the criterion is .43; when high school grades are added to the prediction equation, the multiple correlation coefficient increases to .53 (Walsh & Betz, 2000).

The general form of the *Graduate Record Examination* (GRE) test, also developed and administered by the Educational Testing Service (ETS), is widely used in U.S. universities for decisions on graduate school admissions. It contains verbal, quantitative, and analytical reasoning sections with high K-R 20 reliabilities and modest predictive validity coefficients (usually from the low to high .30s across several graduate departments (Briel, O'Niell, & Schueneman, 1993). Much discussion and debate have surrounded the possible underestimation of the predictive power of GRE scores due to the range restriction problems associated with criterion measures, such as graduate school GPAs. Other criteria for graduate school success, such as faculty ratings, grades, course examination scores, and completion rates for Ph.D programs, should thus be considered as external criteria.

*Applications of Intelligence and Aptitude Tests.*   Intelligence tests are typically employed in public institutions to identify mental retardation, learning disabilities, or giftedness, so that students can be placed in suitable intervention and treatment programs at school. Aptitude tests, on the other hand, are used for admissions, selection, and placement of students in future educational programs or in the workplace.

*Selecting and Using Intelligence and Aptitude Tests.*   Selection of *intelligence* tests must be supported by an array of construct validity evidence, including data on predictive accuracy when the test results are likely to be used for classifying individuals as "gifted" or "mentally retarded." Misclassification rates should be reported by test developers. Compelling evidence that scores differentiate among groups of regular, gifted, mentally retarded, and learning disabled students is absolutely vital. Depending on the construct definitions, scores should show high to moderate convergent validity with scores from other intelligence measures. High reliabilities are also a must.

*Aptitude* tests should be accompanied by convincing predictive validity coefficients using appropriate criterion indices. Expectancy tables make it possible to interpret raw scores with respect to the expected level of performance on another measure. High reliability of scores is also necessary, with an emphasis on internal consistency and test–retest reliabilities. In instances where parallel forms are used, one would examine the parallel forms reliability as well. The illustrative examples given in this section are of norm-referenced tests. All such tests would require to be supported with norms that are recent, relevant, and representative. Last, but not least, we should make sure that the developers report the results of fairness and bias studies in particular legislative and policy environments. Sound intelligence and aptitude tests should not yield scores that have biases against particular subgroups of the population.

In different applications, one should consider the procedural, legislative, and policy constraints that affect decisions with test scores. Most uses with intelligence and aptitude tests involve very high stakes decisions for individuals tested. Measurement of intelligence, interpretation of results, and preparation of reports are tasks performed by school psychologists in public schools (User Path 3). If prescribed, intelligence test administration and scoring should be conducted by appropriately trained and certified specialists. Procedures delineated in technical and policy manuals should be followed. Legislation at the state or national level might require that particular procedures be followed for decision-making on long-term placement and intervention, involving classroom teachers, parents, students, and broad-based staffing committees.

## 14.2.3   Career and Educational Interest Inventories

*Characteristics*   Career and educational interest measures focus on preferences individuals have towards particular types of activities when not forced to engage in them. Studies of interest were pioneered by Strong (1927) who empirically investigated how individual likes and dislikes for particular activities correlated with reported likes and dislikes of individuals in particular occupational areas. Soon after, Kuder (1934) introduced a series of content scales called the *Kuder Preference Record,* where individuals indicated their preferences for outdoor activities, mechanical activities, social tasks, and so on.

Most of the current instruments of interest are self-report questionnaires that pose questions such as the following.

| | |
|---|---|
| **Response options:** | I would dislike doing this activity................................... D |
| | I am indifferent (I don't care one way or the other)....... I |
| | I would like doing this activity........................................ L |
| **Items:** | Explore a science museum. |
| | Play jazz in a combo. |
| | Help settle an argument between friends. |

*Source:* The *ACT Interest Inventory* (excerpted with permission). All rights reserved.

In sum, interest inventories aim to measure motivations of individuals that influence major life decisions such as choosing an educational or career path. Research on assessing interests suggests that interest scores *do not* correlate highly with cognitive abilities or aptitudes. They predict better how likely it is that a person will stay in his or her chosen area of liking. Measurement and interpretation of interest measures usually fall within the job functions of school guidance or career counselors (User Path 4).

*Types and Examples of Interest Inventories.*   Researchers of interest measures distinguish among four different assessment approaches.

| | |
|---|---|
| **1.** Measuring *expressed interests:* | Where the respondents are asked to make a verbal statement of the extent to which they like or dislike particular activities or occupations. |
| **2.** Measuring *manifest interests:* | Where the respondents' likes and dislikes are identified based on activities or lines of work in which they are already engaged. |
| **3.** Measuring *tested interests:* | Where interests are inferred based on specific knowledge that individuals possess in particular areas using objective-type, information based tests. |
| **4.** Measuring *inventoried interests:* | Where interests are inferred based on preferences reported by individuals when provided with a long list of activities and occupations (an inventory of activities/occupations). |

Of the above approaches, measuring inventoried interests is the most utilitarian and popular. It allows for a bigger sampling of activities and occupational areas in relatively little time. It yields quantitative, objectively derived scores that have been used for comparative interpretations.

*The Strong Interest Inventory (SII)*    Of the large number of interest inventories found in the market (some authors report that there are over 200), this section will provide a brief description of one example, the *Strong Interest Inventory* (SII). The SII evolved from its original precursor, the *Strong Vocational Interest Blank for Men* (SVIB) and the most recent revised editions were published in 1985 and 1994 (Hansen & Campbell, 1985; Harmon, Hansen, Borgen, & Hammer, 1994). The most current version is a re-normed, updated inventory for men and women, with areas of interest grouped under Holland's (1997) theoretical framework of personality types and social environments. The latter theory holds that people tend to be of six personality types: realistic, artistic, investigative, social, enterprising, and conventional, and that individual likes and dislikes are determined by their personality. Empirical work on the Strong inventory has supported the above organizational and interpretive framework. The SII profile consists of 317 items under six general occupational themes based on Holland's framework, 25 basic interest scales, 211 personality scales, and 4 personal style scales. The results for individuals are computer-scored and the profile presents scores with interpretive information. The interest scale scores are standard scores, where a higher score indicates a stronger liking towards an area. The SII has high test–retest reliability over long periods of time (median $r = .87$ to $.92$). Longitudinal research shows that SII scores will not predict a person's future success in a job area; however, they do predict how likely a person is to enter their chosen area of interest and remain in that occupational area (Walsh & Betz, 2000). The SII can be administered to students of age 14 to adults.

***Applications of Interest Measures.***    The main application of interest inventories is in educational and career planning and advancement. Interest measures are useful for communicating to high school students the options available to them in the world of work and education, to guide them in areas where they have made tentative choices, and to help resolve conflicting areas of interest/choice. These tools could also be useful for employers in selecting employees with particular inclinations.

***Selecting and Using Interest Measures.***    Use of interest inventories in high school is rarely a high stakes endeavor for subjects assessed. However, guidance counselors should be aware of the technical characteristics that make results of an interest inventory valid, reliable, and useful, with particular attention to male and female differences in interests. Currency of the inventory of educational areas/jobs is important to accommodate global changes occurring in occupations for men and women; this factor affects the content validity of interest inventories. Norms should also be current. Ease of interpretation of results is another key factor to consider in choosing an interest inventory.

## 14.2.4   Attitude Scales

***Characteristics.***    While interests have to do with a person's likes and dislikes, attitudes deal with feelings, values, and beliefs that people have towards objects, situations, institutions, services, or other people. We should remember that attitudes and values are learned and can change over time.

Attitudinal instruments are affective measures. An individual's attitudes can be both positive and negative. With secondary school populations, we often attempt to measure attitudinal constructs such as: "attitude toward school," "attitude toward high school graduation," or "attitude toward teachers." Other affective measures include instruments of self-concept and motivation.

***Types of Attitude Scales.*** Construction of attitude scales is a challenge because of their affective emphasis. In Chapter 9, we reviewed in detail the different methods of measuring attitudes using Likert scales, Thurstone scales, Guttman scales, and the Semantic Differential Scales. All of these are different kinds of self-report measures, vulnerable to faking and ambiguous interpretations—thus lowering both the validity and reliability of results. Other than self-report inventories, attitudes can also be measured via interviews or parent and teacher rating scales. Details and several examples of attitude scales were provided in Chapter 9.

***Applications of Attitude Scales.*** Attitudinal instruments are useful measures of school and student outcomes when affective development forms a significant part of the curriculum offered by institutions. In dropout prevention programs, for example, teachers and instructional staff often set explicit goals to alter students' attitudes toward school, particularly, their attitudes toward school completion. In such circumstances, measurement of attitudes is necessary along with the measurement of academic outcomes to better evaluate the effectiveness of the programs.

Teachers and counselors might also wish to assess attitudes formatively, prior to providing services or specific instructional strategies in given areas. When planning to offer programs for prevention of drug use among adolescents, for example, instructional staff might be interested in conducting a needs assessment survey of "attitudes toward drug usage" in their school's population.

***Selecting and Using Attitudinal Instruments.*** Selection of attitudinal measures should be guided by the purposes for use and the theoretical framework for the particular attitudinal construct. Most published attitude scales yield norm-referenced information. Construct validity and reliability evidence should be evaluated holistically, along with standardization data on samples used by the developers.

## 14.2.5 Personality Measures

***Characteristics.*** In the fields of psychology and counseling, "personality" is not a construct with an agreed-upon definition. Some define personality as a series of characteristics, including abilities, interests, attitudes and values, that indicate the patterns of behavior of an individual. Others define personality as an individual's actual behavior in social situations. Published personality tests have been derived based on a variety of theoretical models and reflect a variety of techniques.

***Types of Personality Tests.*** The study of the psychology of human personality has followed five major but different conceptual models. Each model has yielded different techniques for measuring personality. Each model is described briefly next with examples of available tools of each type (for more details, see Walsh & Betz, 2000).

1. *The Trait Model:* This model assumes that human behavior can be characterized along dimensions of four defined traits of dominance, achievement, affiliation, and responsibility. Accordingly, individuals can be measured and ordered along these trait continua. The trait model is one of the productive models for personality assessment. Self-report inventories built on the trait model are the *Minnesota Multiphasic Personality Inventory* (MMPI) and the *California Psychological Inventory* (CPI).

2. *The Phenomenological Model:* This model derives from a person's subjective perceptions and experiences of the world. A person's self-concept is considered to be the main determinant of human behavior, predicting consistent behaviors across a range of situations. The *Tennessee Self-Concept Scale* was constructed based on this model.

3. *The Psychodynamic Model:* This approach is based on the Freudian model that personality is made up of the id, the ego, and the superego. The motivations for behavior are motivated by these constructs, which are believed to be relatively stable. Projective tests were constructed based on this theory. Examples include the *Rorschach Test* and the *Thematic Apperception Test* (TAT).

4. *The Situational Model:* The situational model defines human personality on the basis of a person's overt behavior. Personality measurement is based on the pattern of behavioral responses that an individual demonstrates stably across a set of situations. Operational methods of measurement are currently gaining popularity with direct observations, naturalistic observations, and behavioral questionnaires.

5. *The Interactional Model:* This theory holds that person-environment interactions determine personality. The approach emphasizes the person-situation interactions. Instruments built on this model are still undergoing developmental research and employ both questionnaires and observational methods.

***Applications of Personality Tests.***    Personality tests have limited applications in education (Thorndike, Cunningham, Thorndike, & Hagen, 1991). Typically, they call for administration and interpretation by psychologists and counselors with graduate-level training. Teachers and administrators participating in a student's planning program might occasionally have to participate in interpretation and use of scores from personality measures.

***Selecting and Using Personality Tests.***    Personality tests should be carefully selected by psychologists and counselors. We should evaluate their theoretical orientation, validity, reliability, norms, and interpretability of the scales and scores for the purposes at hand.

## 14.3    Norms, Norm-Referenced Scores, and Score Profiles

As is evident from the preceding overview of major types of standardized assessment tools that are published and/or widely used, most are normative in the orientation. To evaluate the quality of norm-referenced information, it is important for us to be knowledgeable about norming procedures and norms tables provided by the developers. In this section, we look at how norms tables are developed by publishers and how the major types of norm-referenced scores are derived from these.

## 14.3.1 Quality of Norms

When we administer educational and psychological assessments to targeted groups, the results are first generated in the form of *raw scores*. Raw scores become more meaningful when we have some sort of controlled framework against which to compare and interpret them. *Norms* (also called *norm groups* or the *standardization sample*) are the carefully selected, well-defined samples of individuals from the targeted population that provide a structured framework for us to make *norm-referenced interpretations* of raw scores.

With published, standardized tools intended for norm-referencing, *norming* is a part of the test development process. Typically, norming is conducted soon after the content validation and item analysis studies. The standardization sample is deliberately selected to have a certain demographic breakdown by the developers. Norming is often carefully stratified with respect to region, socioeconomic status, urban-rural-suburban location, ethnicity, and age of subjects. To make valid norm-referenced interpretations, all the individuals in the standardization sample should have been administered the instrument under the *same conditions,* with the same directions, timing constraints, scoring procedures, and supporting materials, as applicable to members of the target population.

The quality of norms should be evaluated by users based on their recency, representativeness, and local relevance (Hopkins, 1998). *Recency* has to do with whether or not the standardization of a test was done by the publishers within the last 5–10 years. Because demographic shifts and other dynamics of society affect test performance in populations, norms should be continually updated. The date of norming should be clearly communicated to users in the technical manuals accompanying a test. Achievement test norms should be updated more frequently, because of the documented problems of the "Lake Wobegon Effect," resulting from a combination of teaching to high stakes tests and outdated norms (Cannell, 1988).

Technical manuals should provide information on the demographic composition of the norm group to help users evaluate its *representativeness* with respect to the local population. In Table 14.3, we see an example of such a table, provided by Harcourt Brace Educational Measurement, for their *Stanford 9* achievement test series. Here, the publisher is selling a test with national norms. Thus, they provide information on the total U.S. school enrollment figures against which users can compare the composition of the standardization sample.

A similar table is also provided in the technical manual of the *Wechsler Preschool and Primary Scale of Intelligence-Revised* (WPPSI-R), as shown in Table 14.5. Because the WPPSI yields age-referenced test scores, the developer provides information on the ethnic composition of the norms organized by the nine age groups targeted by the test. Simultaneously, the table compares the breakdowns in the standardization sample by age with that of the U.S. population in 1986. To support use of the test scores in the U.S. contexts, the table provides us with adequate information to judge the representativeness of the norms in terms of ethnicity by geographic region.

*Relevance* is judged based on whether separate norms are provided for the different subgroups against which the users wish to compare results. For achievement tests, both national and local district norms could be relevant to the user's needs. With interest inventories, different norm groups would be needed according to major occupational areas, for example, in correspondence with Holland's (1997) six themes.

---

**Key Concepts**

■ Norms consist of well-defined samples of individuals from the targeted population that are used to make norm-referenced interpretations of scores.
■ For published tests, the norm group is called the standardization sample.
■ A high-quality standardization sample is recent, relevant, and representative.

---

## 14.3.2    Types of Norm-Referenced Scores

*Norms Tables.*    Test-makers use the standardization sample to derive a variety of norm-referenced scores intended to facilitate interpretation of performance. Norm-referenced scores are also referred to as *derived scores,* as they are derived from the norm group's raw score distribution. The basic procedure involves the administration of a test to the norming sample, followed by the derivation of $z$-scores using the means and standard deviations of the score and subscore distributions. Starting from the $z$-scores, other transformed scores are derived next, such as the $T$-score and percentile rank. These scores are then set up in Norms tables. *Norms tables* enable us to simply read off a person's standard score or percentile rank, given that we know his/her raw score on the test or subtest.

*Normalized Distributions.*    A characteristic of norm distributions employed by test publishers is that they are often *normalized.* The process of normalizing involves transformation of the raw scores into a new set of scores that are forced to take on the shape of the *normal distribution.* Do not confuse "norming" and "normalizing." As we saw in Table 14.4, norming samples are typically very large (thousands of examinees are tested). Even so, the original distributions of scores can be non-normal. Test-makers prefer to forcibly normalize non-normal distributions by stretching or scrunching the scales so that they mimic the properties of the normal curve. Once normalized, standard scores, percentile ranks, and other forms of derived scores have certain interpretive advantages. Table 14.6 reproduces data provided by Nitko (1996) showing how non-normal, linear $z$-scores, produced using statistics from a sample distribution (Mean = 26.75 and Standard Deviation = 3.8) can be normalized with reference to the normal curve table.

There are five major types of derived scores reported by different test publishers. They are:

■ Percentile ranks and percentile bands
■ Standard scores
■ Stanines
■ Grade-equivalent scores
■ Age-equivalent scores

**TABLE 14.4 Demographic Characteristics of SAT9 Standardization Sample**

| | Percentage of Total U.S. School Enrollment* | Percentage of Students in Spring Standardization |
|---|---|---|
| Geographic Region | | |
| Northwest | 19.6 | 21.3 |
| Midwest | 23.8 | 22.1 |
| South | 24.1 | 22.7 |
| West | 32.4 | 33.8 |
| SES Status | | |
| Low | 31.3 | 30.0 |
| Middle | 35.9 | 32.6 |
| High | 32.8 | 37.4 |
| Urbanicity | | |
| Urban | 26.8 | 24.5 |
| Suburban | 48.0 | 47.0 |
| Rural | 25.2 | 28.5 |
| Ethnicity (89.7% Reporting) | | |
| African American | 16.1 | 16.4 |
| Hispanic | 12.7 | 11.5 |
| White | 66.6 | 65.9 |
| Asian | 3.6 | 4.1 |
| Native American | 1.1 | 2.1 |
| Handicapping Condition | | |
| Emotionally Disturbed | — | 0.3 |
| Learning Disabled | — | 2.5 |
| Mentally Handicapped | — | 0.1 |
| Hearing Impaired | — | 0.2 |
| Visually Impaired | — | 0.1 |
| Orthopedically Impaired | — | 0.1 |
| Limited English Proficiency | — | 2.4 |
| Other | — | 0.6 |
| Nonpublic Schools | | |
| Catholic | 5.4 | 4.1 |
| Private | 4.9 | 6.9 |

*National Center for Education Statistics, United States Department of Education, 1992–1993.

*Source:* Stanford Achievement Test: Ninth Edition Copyright © 1996 by Harcourt, Inc. Reproduced by permission. All rights reserved.

**TABLE 14.5  Standardization Sample for the Wechsler Preschool and Primary Scale of Intelligence–Revised (WPPSI-R)**

**Comparison of Target Sample and Standardization Sample by Geographic Region and Ethnicity**

| Geographic Region | Ethnicity | Percentage in U.S. Population (1986) | Percentage in WPPSI-R Sample by Age Group | | | | | | | | | Total Sample |
|---|---|---|---|---|---|---|---|---|---|---|---|---|
| | | | 3 | 3.5 | 4 | 4.5 | 5 | 5.5 | 6 | 6.5 | 7 | |
| Northeast | White | 14.5 | 14.0 | 14.0 | 14.5 | 15.5 | 15.0 | 14.5 | 14.0 | 15.0 | 15.0 | 14.6 |
| | Black | 2.2 | 2.5 | 2.0 | 2.0 | 2.0 | 2.0 | 1.5 | 2.0 | 2.0 | 2.0 | 2.0 |
| | Hispanic | 1.9 | 2.5 | 2.5 | 1.0 | 2.0 | 1.5 | 2.0 | 2.0 | 0.5 | 0.0 | 1.6 |
| | Other | 0.4 | 0.5 | 0.5 | 0.5 | 0.5 | 0.5 | 0.5 | 0.5 | 0.0 | 0.0 | 0.4 |
| | Total | 19.0 | 19.5 | 19.0 | 18.0 | 20.0 | 19.0 | 18.5 | 18.5 | 17.5 | 17.0 | 18.6 |
| North Central | White | 22.1 | 25.0 | 21.5 | 21.5 | 21.0 | 22.0 | 21.5 | 22.0 | 21.5 | 22.0 | 22.0 |
| | Black | 3.0 | 3.0 | 2.5 | 3.5 | 3.0 | 3.0 | 3.0 | 3.5 | 3.0 | 3.0 | 3.1 |
| | Hispanic | 0.8 | 1.0 | 0.5 | 1.5 | 1.5 | 0.5 | 1.5 | 1.5 | 1.0 | 0.0 | 1.1 |
| | Other | 0.6 | 0.5 | 1.0 | 0.5 | 1.0 | 1.0 | 0.5 | 0.5 | 1.0 | 2.0 | 0.8 |
| | Total | 26.4 | 29.5 | 25.5 | 27.0 | 26.5 | 26.5 | 26.5 | 27.5 | 26.5 | 27.0 | 26.9 |
| South | White | 20.3 | 20.5 | 21.5 | 20.0 | 20.0 | 20.5 | 20.0 | 20.5 | 21.0 | 19.0 | 20.4 |
| | Black | 8.8 | 9.0 | 10.0 | 9.0 | 9.5 | 9.0 | 9.0 | 9.0 | 9.0 | 9.0 | 9.2 |
| | Hispanic | 3.4 | 3.5 | 4.0 | 3.5 | 3.0 | 3.5 | 3.5 | 2.5 | 3.5 | 5.0 | 3.5 |
| | Other | 0.6 | 0.5 | 0.5 | 1.0 | 0.5 | 0.5 | 0.5 | 0.5 | 0.5 | 1.0 | 0.6 |
| | Total | 33.0 | 33.5 | 36.0 | 33.5 | 33.0 | 33.5 | 33.0 | 32.5 | 34.0 | 34.0 | 33.6 |
| West | White | 13.4 | 11.5 | 12.0 | 13.5 | 13.5 | 13.5 | 13.5 | 13.5 | 13.5 | 14.0 | 13.1 |
| | Black | 1.2 | 1.0 | 1.0 | 1.0 | 0.5 | 1.0 | 1.5 | 1.0 | 1.5 | 1.0 | 1.1 |
| | Hispanic | 5.0 | 4.0 | 5.0 | 5.0 | 5.0 | 5.0 | 5.0 | 5.0 | 5.5 | 6.0 | 5.0 |
| | Other | 1.9 | 1.0 | 1.5 | 2.0 | 1.5 | 1.5 | 2.0 | 2.0 | 1.5 | 1.0 | 1.6 |
| | Total | 2.15 | 17.5 | 19.5 | 21.5 | 20.5 | 21.0 | 22.0 | 21.5 | 22.0 | 22.0 | 20.8 |
| Total Sample | White | 70.3 | 71.0 | 69.0 | 69.5 | 70.0 | 71.0 | 69.5 | 70.0 | 71.0 | 70.0 | 70.1 |
| | Black | 15.1 | 15.5 | 15.5 | 15.5 | 15.0 | 15.0 | 15.0 | 15.5 | 15.5 | 15.0 | 15.3 |
| | Hispanic | 11.0 | 11.0 | 12.0 | 11.0 | 11.5 | 10.5 | 12.0 | 11.0 | 10.5 | 11.0 | 11.2 |
| | Other | 3.5 | 2.5 | 3.5 | 4.0 | 3.5 | 3.5 | 3.5 | 3.5 | 3.0 | 4.0 | 3.4 |

*Note:* The cell values reflect rounded values; the total values are the sums of the cell values before rounding and therefore, in some cases will not equal the sum of the rounded cell values.

*Source:* D. Wechsler (1989). *Wechsler Preschool and Primary Scale of Intelligence—Revised: Manual.* San Antonio, TX: The Psychological Corporation.

**TABLE 14.6  Illustration of Normalized $z$-Scores and Actual $z$-Scores in a Distribution**

| Raw Score | Percentile Rank | Normalized $z$-Score | Linear[a] $z$-Score |
|---|---|---|---|
| 36 | 98 | 2.05 | 2.43 |
| 33 | 96 | 1.75 | 1.64 |
| 32 | 94 | 1.55 | 1.38 |
| 31 | 90 | 1.28 | 1.12 |
| 30 | 88 | 1.18 | 0.86 |
| 29 | 84 | 0.99 | 0.59 |
| 28 | 72 | 0.58 | 0.33 |
| 27 | 54 | 0.10 | 0.07 |
| 26 | 32 | −0.47 | −0.20 |
| 25 | 16 | −0.99 | −0.46 |
| 24 | 10 | −1.28 | −0.72 |
| 22 | 8 | −1.41 | −1.25 |
| 21 | 6 | −1.55 | −1.51 |
| 15 | 4 | −1.75 | −3.09 |
| 14 | 2 | −2.05 | −3.36 |

[a]$z$-values based on the actual distribution and using the equation:

$$z = \frac{X - M}{SD} \text{ where M} = 26.75 \text{ and SD} = 3.80$$

*Source:* Adapted from Educational Assessment of Students (2nd edition), by Nitko, Anthony J., © 1996 with permission. All rights reserved.

Some of these derived scores are variants of the basic $z$-score or involve completely different approaches to scaling. In the following section, each score and its method of derivation is briefly described. Allowable interpretations for each are also presented. We will be drawing on information presented in Chapter 10 here. To elaborate on how to correctly interpret these scores, this section will refer back to Table 14.3, showing a norm-referenced and criterion-referenced report of a first-grade student, Pamela, on the *Stanford 9*.

***Percentile Ranks.***  The *percentile rank* denotes the *percent of students in the norm group who scored below a person's raw score.*

*Method of Derivation*  The method of derivation of percentile ranks was described in detail in Chapter 10 for normalized and non-normalized distributions. The formula is:

$$PR = 100 \left[ \frac{\dfrac{f(X - \text{Lower limit of interval of } X)}{\text{interval size, } i} + \text{Cum} f_{\text{in interval below}}}{N} \right]$$

where, $X$ = raw score for which PR needs to be calculated,
$f$ = frequency,
$i$ = size of class or score interval (In a simple frequency distribution, this value is always 1),
Cum $f$ is cumulative frequency, and
$N$ is total number of cases.

*Interpretation*    Let us say that a student, such as Pamela in Table 14.3, receives a raw score of 69 out of 106 items on the Total Reading Section of a standardized achievement test. In the Norm-referenced Score Report provided by the test publisher, the reported *National Percentile Rank* is 48. The correct interpretation of that student's performance would be: The student's raw score of 69 places her above 48% of similar students in the national norm group.

**Percentile Bands.**    With a *percentile band,* test-makers construct a confidence band around the raw score by adding and subtracting the Standard Error of Measurement (SEM) in raw score units. Then, the percentile ranks corresponding with the upper and lower limits of the raw score band are read off the norms table. This gives us greater confidence in interpreting the score, taking into account the errors of measurement.

*Method of Derivation*    Let us say the raw score for a student is 86 in Total Reading, and the reported SEM for that test is 1.5 SEM units. Construction of a 95% confidence band using errors of measurement would occur as follows.

1.  Create upper and lower limits of band in raw score units.
    86 + (2)SEM = 86 + 3 = 89 (Upper Limit of Band)
    86 − (2)SEM = 86 − 3 = 83 (Lower Limit of Band)

2.  Look up norms tables to find percentile ranks that correspond to raw scores at Upper and Lower Limits. For example, in Pamela's report, we see the percentile bands for the various subtest scores on the extreme right hand side of Table 14.3 (top panel). In Total Reading the Percentile Band ranges approximately from a PR of 44 to 53.

*Interpretation*    The interpretation of Pamela's Percentile Band would go as follows: Assuming errors of measurement at the time of testing, we can have 95% confidence that Pamela's percentile rank would fluctuate between 44 and 53.

**Standard Scores**    Standard scores (SS) describe *how far away a score is located from the mean of the norm group in standard deviation units.* The fundamental form of the standard score is the *z*-score, developed by test developers using the norm group's mean ($M_{\text{norm group}}$) and standard deviation ($SD_{\text{norm group}}$) with the formula shown next.

$$z = (X - M_{\text{norm group}}) \div SD_{\text{norm group}}$$

*Method of Derivation*    Standard scores (SS) that standardized test developers report are normalized. Several different linear transformations of the basic *z*-score have been used by publishers by multiplying the standard deviation and the mean of the *z*-score scale with constants, to produce standard score scales similar to the *T*-score scale (Chapter 10). Different testing companies use different values for the constants S and M, in the formula SS = z(S) + M, for obtaining linear transformation of z-scores. The computations are illustrated for the *T*-score, normal curve equivalent (NCE) scores, GRE, and S-B standard scores in the demonstration box that follows.

Figure 14.1 illustrates a normalized distribution of z-scores, percentile ranks, and the transformed standard scores for some popular published tests. NCEs were developed for tracking growth of students in Title 1 Programs funded by the federal government. The NCE units, with a mean of 50 and standard deviation of 21.06, are on an equal-interval scale (like all standard scores) but they are designed to correspond with percentile ranks 1–99 in a normalized distribution. The computation procedures for the different standard scores illustrated in Figure 14.1 are shown in Demonstration 14.1.

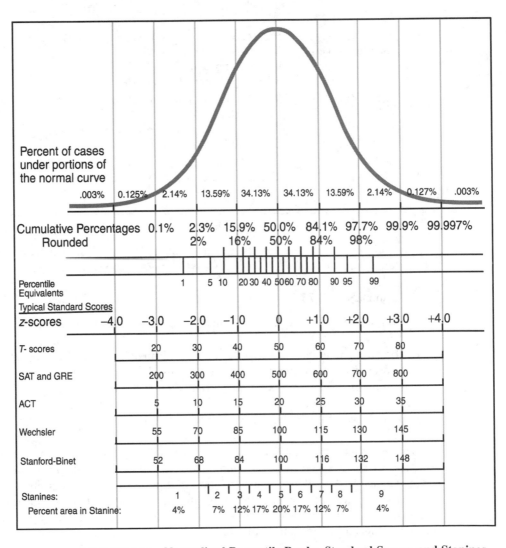

**FIGURE 14.1   Normalized Percentile Ranks, Standard Scores, and Stanines**

DEMONSTRATION **14.1**

## Deriving Standard Scores from z-scores.

**Standard Score (SS) = z (S) + M**

*T*-score:
S = 10; M = 50 (mean); SS = z (S) + M
$T = 10z + 50$
If a student obtains a z = +1.5, his *T* is:
$T = 10 (1.5) + 50 = 65.$ ✓

NCE:
S = 21.06; M = 50 (mean); SS = z (S)+ M
$NCE = 21.06z + 50$
If a student obtains a z = +1.5, his NCE is:
$NCE = 21.06 (1.5) + 50 = 81.59.$ ✓

S-B:
(Stanford-Binet)
S = 16; M = 100 (mean); SS = z (S)+ M
$S\text{-}B = 16z + 100$
If a student obtains a z = +1.5, his S-B is:
$S\text{-}B = 16 (1.5) + 100 = 124$ ✓

GRE-(V)
S = 100; M = 500 (mean); SS = z (S)+ M
$GRE = 100z + 500$
If a student obtains a z = +1.5, his GRE-(V) score is:
$GRE = 100 (1.5) + 500 = 650$ ✓

WISC:
(Wechsler)
If a student obtains a z = +1.5, his WISC score is?
(Refer to Figure 14.1 for M and S values)
✓ Denotes answer.

---

*Interpretation of Standard Scores*    Let us examine Pamela's National NCE in Listening for interpretation purposes. She receives a NCE = 73.7, shown in Table 14.3 (top panel).

Pamela's NCE *73.7 = 21.06 (z) + 50*

By solving for *z*, we see that Pamela's *z* is +1.12 units.

The correct interpretation of her performance is: Pamela's is placed a little more than one standard deviation unit above (exactly 1.12 units above) the average score of the norm group in the Listening area. Another interpretation of the NCE (or any of the normalized standard scores) can be done by referring back to the percentile ranks. Here, Pamela has a high NCE score which places her at the 87th percentile.

***Stanines.***    Stanines (*St*andard-*nine*) are closely related to standard scores. If we divide the *z*-score scale in a normal distribution into nine parts with standard deviation units, we would create bands called "stanines." Figure 14.2 presents a stanine distribution. Stanines are rank-ordered bands ranging from 1 to 9 that denote placement of a student's score relative to that of the norm group. An advantage of the stanines is that they are fairly stable bands, allowing for fluctuations of scores due to measurement error. On repeated testings,

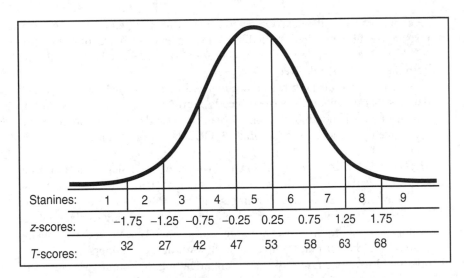

| Stanines: | 1 | 2 | 3 | 4 | 5 | 6 | 7 | 8 | 9 |
|---|---|---|---|---|---|---|---|---|---|
| z-scores: | | −1.75 | −1.25 | −0.75 | −0.25 | 0.25 | 0.75 | 1.25 | 1.75 |
| T-scores: | | 32 | 27 | 42 | 47 | 53 | 58 | 63 | 68 |

**FIGURE 14.2    The Stanine Scale in a Normal Distribution**

the chances are higher that students would receive the same stanine, even when their point scores might vary.

*Method of Derivation*    In a normalized distribution, stanines 1 through 9 are defined by fixed *z*-units and upper and lower percentile ranks, as shown in Figure 14.1. The percents of individuals scoring within particular stanines are thereby also fixed. For example, we will always find the highest 4% in a normal distribution in the 9th stanine. The stanine scale is constructed starting from the mean, by marking off a quarter of a standard deviation unit on either side. This defines the middle stanine of 5, which is exactly half a standard deviation unit in width. Next, we mark off similar bands on either side of the 5th stanine, each exactly half a standard deviation unit in width until we reach the two extreme bands of 1 (the lowest stanine) and 9 (the highest stanine). Because the width of the two extreme bands are undefined, the stanine scale is ordinal.

*Interpretation*    Stanines of 1, 2, and 3 are considered *below average;* values of 4, 5, and 6 are considered *average;* while values of 7, 8, and 9 indicate *above average* performance. With Pamela's performance in Total Reading, we see that her national stanine, reported next to her PR, is 5 (see under NATL PR-S column). We would correctly interpret her performance as follows: Pamela's stanine of 5 indicates average performance relative to the norm group in Total Reading. Her score falls within the middle range of scores in the norm group.

**Grade- and Age-Equivalent Scores.**    Unlike the previously described scores, which are derived from a cross-sectional, standardization sample at a single grade level, *grade-equivalent* (GE) and *age-equivalent* (AE) score scales are developed deliberately to compare performance along a developmental continuum—as a child moves from one grade level or age level to the next. Grade-equivalents are reported for standardized achievement tests; age equivalents are reported in the measurement of psychological attributes such as IQ. Here, we will closely examine the *grade equivalent* (GE) score to understand how both these scales are derived.

GE scores are reported as decimalized numbers, such as 3.9. A GE score of 3.9 denotes that the student's performance is equivalent to the average performance of a 3rd grader in the 9th month of the school year. Because there are ten months in a school year, for a given grade level, such as grade 3, GE scores would range from 3.0–3.9.

*Method of Derivation (Figure 14.3)*   To derive a GE scale, the publishers develop a series of overlapping, multilevel tests in an area such as reading. They then administer each individual test to large norming samples at 2–3 grade levels closest to the level to be tested. The norming is typically done in the fall or spring of a school year. The dates of norming are the *empirical norming dates*. The GE scale is derived using the median scores from the norming samples at each level of the overlapping tests, as shown in the horizontal axis of Figure 14.3. The empirically-based points are linked to construct a developmental scale (see horizontal axis in Figure 14.3). These points are ordinal, represented by the median scores at grade 1, grade 2, grade 3, grade 4, and so on, all the way up to grade 12. The intermediate points between the median scores at consecutive grades are interpolated. Points falling outside the empirical markers are extrapolated.

Let us say that first graders in the norm group are tested in spring, or the fifth month of the school year. If they receive a median score of 25 on the first grade test, the score of 25 would be marked on the GE scale as a score of 1.5, denoting the average score of a first grader on the test, taken in the fifth month of the school year (see Figure 14.3). In Figure 14.3, the GE points 1.5, 2.5, 3.5, and 4.5 are empirically-derived; points between 1.5 and 2.5 are interpolated points. A GE score of 1.0 is an extrapolation from the empirical 1.5 point. As we see, the scale score differences between GEs of 1.5 and 2.5 are much greater than the differences between GEs of 3.5 and 4.5, showing the ordinality of the GE scale. AGE score of 5.5 is also extrapolated.

*Interpretation*   The GE scale is a popular but an oft misinterpreted scale. The areas of the GE scale that allow for the most valid interpretations at each level are the empirically-based points. The interpolated and extrapolated regions can easily mislead both laypersons and professionals. It is easy to see that if a first grader receives a GE score of 6.4, the common interpretation would be that the child is reading at the sixth-grade level. In reality, the student neither received a sixth-grade curriculum, nor took a sixth-grade test. The score is an estimate for a first grader, and the most conservative and accurate interpretation would be that the child is reading well above the median score for his or her grade level. Interpretations of curriculum mastery cannot be made with any certainty with a GE score. The utility of the GE scale is that it allows us to see whether the child is developing along on the vertically linked scale from year to year. Nitko (1996), however, warns that we should see GEs only as "coarse indicators" of growth and that we should always report them in conjunction with percentile ranks of individuals on particular tests or subtests. The GE scale has been criticized by measurement specialists because of its limitations.

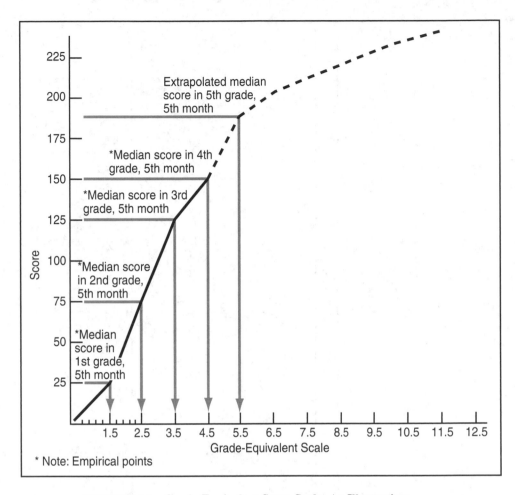

**FIGURE 14.3   Grade-Equivalent Score Scale: An Illustration**

*Source:* Adapted from Educational Assessment of Students (2nd edition), by Nitko, Anthony J., © 1996 with permission. All rights reserved.

***Scaled Scores.*** An important property of a multilevel achievement battery is that it offers a continuous score scale that facilitates the interpretation of individual student growth across levels. The *scaled-score*, obtained using Item Response Theory (IRT) techniques, are a technically more defensible alternative to the GE or AE scales. The *Stanford Achievement Test Series* employs an overlapping test administration design, as shown in Figure 14.4 for the SAT9, to collect data to construct a vertically equated scale for their scaled scores. The technicalities of this type of scale development are beyond the scope of this textbook. Practitioners should be aware that IRT-based scaled scores have equal interval properties and are unidimensional. If we look at Pamela's report in Table 14.3 again, we see that she receives a scaled score of 527 on the Total Reading test. We could compare this score to her previous year's scaled score on the same test to make a determination of how well she has developed in reading.

| Grade | Battery Level |
|---|---|
| K | SESAT 1 - SESAT 2 |
| 1 | SESAT 2 - Primary 1 |
| 2 | Primary 1 - Primary 2 |
| 3 | Primary 2 - Primary 3 |
| 4 | Primary 3 - Intermediate 1 |
| 5 | Intermediate 1 - Intermediate 2 |
| 6 | Intermediate 2 - Intermediate 3 |
| 7 | Intermediate 3 - Advance   Advanced 2 |
| 9 | Advanced 2 - TASK 1 |
| 10 | TASK 1 - TASK 2 |
| 11 | TASK 2 - TASK 3 |

**FIGURE 14.4   Design for Collecting Data on Overlapping Forms of the Stanford-9 Series: Scale Score Development**

*Source:* Standard Achievement Test: Ninth Edition Copyright © 1996 by Harcourt, Inc. Reproduced by permission. All rights reserved.

### 14.3.3 Criterion-Referenced Interpretation of Pamela's Report

As you may have noticed during the review of norm-referenced information in Pamela's report (Table 14.3), the bottom section provides detailed information on Pamela's performance on the content clusters targeted by the test. The content clusters provide us with insights into the content present in the specific learning outcomes in the test domain, allowing for a skill-referenced analysis (see Chapter 11). For example, the Word Study Skills subtest has 36 items (see top panel). In the bottom panel, we see that there are three content breakdowns within the vocabulary test: structural analysis, phonetic analysis (vowels), and phonetic analysis (consonants). Pamela misses 6 items out of the 36 on the Word Skills test, giving her a score of 30. However, the content breakdowns make clear that the missed items are distributed evenly from the three sections of the test. This information can be picked up by a discerning teacher to provide targeted instruction to the student in particular knowledge/skill areas. In fact, students can be trained to conduct such analyses themselves so that they identify areas in which they would like to improve. Overall, Pamela's weakest areas appear to be various skill areas under Reading Comprehension and mathematics, based on a skill-referenced analysis. As you may recall from Chapter 11, such analyses can be conducted by setting mastery criteria for each test or subtest.

### 14.3.4 Different Types of Score Reports and Profiles

The type of standardized score report shown for Pamela is called an *Individual Score Report* or *Profile*. Most publishers provide an array of reports and profiles, including customized reporting services for individual institutions. Aggregate reports, summarizing performance for a class of students, individual schools, districts, or regions are also commonly provided.

A sample of a *Class Record Summary Sheet* for the CTB/4 (updated summaries may appear different from the illustration) is presented in Table 14.7. Note that the report in Table 14.7 provides information on the "Mean NCE," "Mean National Stanine," and so on, because the norm-referenced scores are derived from the average raw score for the 27 students tested from the class. The interpretations of group mean scores are the same as those for the individual case, as long as we understand how the group mean is obtained. One should also clarify whether the publisher did the norm-referencing against individual student norms (a distribution of individual student test scores) or group norms (a distribution of class means), as the results can vary depending on the spread of the distributions.

## 14.4 Evaluating Standards-Based Assessments

Despite the fact that standardized tests were originally designed to provide users with norm-referenced information, they often offer criterion-referenced information as well (similar to the previous SAT9 report). Currently, standardized achievement test developers are also creating *standards-based assessments* linked to particular subjects that at once

TABLE 14.7 CTB/4 Class Record Summary

# Comprehensive Test of Basic Skills, Fourth Edition

**CTBS/4**

## CLASS RECORD SUMMARY SHEET

Class _____ Pole _____  Grade: _____

**A** Number of Students **B** Scores

| | Number of Students | MSS | GME | MNCE | MNS | MDNP |
|---|---|---|---|---|---|---|
| Reading | | | | | | |
| Vocabulary | 27 | 701.8 | 5.0 | 51.9 | 5.1 | 52.0 |
| Comprehension | 27 | 701.0 | 5.2 | 54.7 | 5.4 | 61.0 |
| Total Reading | 27 | 701.7 | 5.2 | 53.3 | 5.3 | 56.7 |
| Language | | | | | | |
| Language Mechanics | 27 | 682.6 | 4.8 | 50.4 | 5.0 | 50.0 |
| Language Expression | 27 | 688.1 | 4.7 | 50.4 | 5.0 | 44.0 |
| Total Language | 27 | 685.6 | 4.7 | 50.2 | 5.0 | 49.0 |
| Mathematics | | | | | | |
| Math Computation | 27 | 711.2 | 4.5 | 48.1 | 4.7 | 46.0 |
| Math Concepts & Applications | 27 | 697.5 | 5.0 | 51.9 | 5.2 | 46.0 |
| Total Mathematics | 27 | 704.6 | 4.8 | 49.9 | 5.0 | 52.0 |
| Total Battery | 27 | 697.1 | 4.8 | 50.6 | 5.0 | 49.0 |
| Spelling | 27 | 698.7 | 5.0 | 52.8 | 5.1 | 55.0 |
| Study Skills | 26 | 703.5 | 5.0 | 52.0 | 5.1 | 56.5 |
| Science | 27 | 644.0 | 5.0 | 52.3 | 5.3 | 52.7 |
| Social Studies | 27 | 669.4 | 5.1 | 52.6 | 5.1 | 55.0 |

**C** MEDIAN NATIONAL PERCENTILE

1  2  5  10  20  30  39  45  50  55  60  68  72  80  90  95  98  99

**D** NORMAL CURVE EQUIVALENT

1  2  15  23  32  39  45  50  55  60  68  72  85  93  99

— Obtained Achievement

**E**
MSS: Mean Scale Score
GME: Grade Mean Equivalent
MNCE: Mean Normal Curve Equivalent

MNS: Mean National Stanine
MDNP: Median National Percentile

**F** NARRATIVE SUMMARY

The Median Percentile Ranks indicate that the average student is highest in Comprehension 61st Percentile and Study Skills 57th Percentile. The average student is lowest in Language Expression 44th Percentile and Word Analysis 45th Percentile. Overall, the Total Battery Score places the class higher than 493 of the students in the National Norm Group. This report is a summary only. For a complete description of the performance, individual scores should be examined.

**G**
| | | |
|---|---|---|
| SCHOOL: | TAFT | |
| DISTRICT: | WINFIELD | |
| CITY: | WINFIELD | |
| STATE: | ANYSTATE | |

FORM/LEVEL: R/14/R15
TEST DATE: 4/ 8/89
PATTERN (IRT): **H**
QUARTER MONTH: 29

Source: CTB/McGraw-Hill (1989). CTBS/4: Preview Materials. Monterey, CA: McGraw-Hill. Reproduced with permission. All rights reserved.

provide both norm-referenced and criterion-referenced information to users. When the tests are structured-response tools, a percent correct score in a defined test domain such as "reducing fractions," would yield criterion-referenced information. Because standards-based assessments are a kind of CRT, they would yield a meaningful domain score only when tasks are systematically designed to match a tight domain of cognitive skills or knowledge. In addition, when test developers provide performance standards that will permit users to distinguish between "highly proficient," "proficient," and "not proficient" categories of performance, they should also provide information on the validity of their cut-scores.

Linn and Gronlund (2000) suggest that expectancy tables can be useful for examining how well standards-based assessments help us make criterion-referenced interpretations of results. For example, to evaluate the quality of a standards-based writing assessment that separates "highly proficient," "proficient," and "not proficient" writers, we could check how well the test-based classifications agree with teacher-given marks, such as A–F. A high level of agreement in the categories would support the quality of the assessments, independent of the quality of the norms or norm-referenced scores.

## A Suggested Guide for Reviewing Information on a Standardized Assessment Tool

The following checklist is to help you gather information and make judgments about the quality of an assessment tool prior to adoption. As desired, you can alter the list for a more or less detailed review of an instrument.

✓ Who is the test publisher?
✓ In what year was the test published?
✓ What are the purposes for the test, as described by the publisher?
✓ What is the targeted population for the test?
✓ What are the costs of the test per examinee/respondent?
✓ What types of norm-referenced scores does the publisher provide?
✓ What types of criterion-referenced information does the publisher provide?
✓ Does the publisher provide a clear and detailed description of the domain and subdomains and sources for the same?
✓ Are the items/tasks clear and presented in a usable format?
✓ Are the items current?
✓ Are the items content-valid, given the local context?
✓ What is the quality of the tool based on information the publisher has provided in the technical manual?

- Item analysis statistics
- Recency, relevance, and representativeness of norms
- How norm-referenced scores were derived
- How criterion-referenced scores and cut scores were derived
- Validity evidence to support the stated purposes (Were all the needed validity data gathered? Does the evidence support the use of the test scores in the ways intended?)

*A Suggested Guide continued*

■ Reliability evidence to support different scores reported (Are all the needed reliability coefficients provided? Are the reliability coefficients sufficiently high?)

■ How equating and scaling studies were done (Are scores from different forms or levels of the test comparable?)

■ How fairness and bias studies were done (Will use of the assessment adversely affect some groups?)

✓ Does the publisher provide easy-to-use manuals and guides for users?

✓ What is the quality and cost of the scoring services?

✓ Do formal reviews of the test by psychometric researchers suggest that the tool is a high quality instrument?

## 14.5    Resources for Finding Published Assessment Tools

Several resources are available to help you locate and evaluate published instruments. This section will briefly summarize the major resources that you might find helpful.

*Buros Institute of Mental Measurements.*    The Buros Institute of Mental Measurements at the University of Nebraska–Lincoln publishes documents containing listings of published tools, descriptions of instruments, critical reviews of tests in print, bibliographies for particular tests, and listings of measurement books and book reviews. The Institute periodically produces two companion documents called the *Mental Measurements Yearbooks* (MMY), and *Tests in Print*. The *MMY* and *Tests in Print* together serve as key resources to practitioners searching for published tests.

*Tests in Print* is an indexed guide to all published tests and instruments out in the market. The reviews included in the *Mental Measurements Yearbooks* (MMY) should be of particular interest to users. Reviews for individual instruments are done by at least two independent testing experts. The reviewers alert users about possible problems inherent in the instruments as well as developer's claims that might not be well supported by the available information in the technical manuals or existing research on the test. There is no schedule for publication for the MMY. New editions are published every few years.

An on-line database service of the Buros Institute is available at http://www.unl.edu/buros/sp.html website. Users can access the database by subscribing to the SilverPlatter's internet service. This service is updated every six months and includes reviews of all tests published in the tenth, eleventh, and twelfth *MMY*s.

*Other Sources, Reviews and Test Publisher's Catalogs.*    The Educational Testing Service in Princeton, New Jersey, also has a Test Collection database with information on more than 10,000 instruments. The ETS Test Collection was compiled jointly with the

ERIC Clearinghouse on Assessment and Evaluation. Each entry provides an abstract describing the tool, its purposes and development, title, author, and date of publication. You can reach them on the Web (http://ericae.net/testcol.htm#ETSTF).

Another source of information is a publication from PRO-ED, Inc., called *Tests: A Comprehensive Reference for Assessments in Psychology, Education, and Business*. It includes an index and descriptions of about 3000 tests written in English. Most commercial test publishers, such as the ETS, Psychological Corporation, Psychological Assessment Resources, PRO-ED, CTB/McGraw-Hill, and Riverside Publishing provide test consumers with informative catalogs that help in selecting assessments. Journals on measurement and technical articles on printed tests are another key source of information on assessments.

***Standards for Educational and Psychological Testing.*** Published periodically by joint committees of the American Educational Research Association (AERA), the National Council on Measurement in Education (NCME) and the American Psychological Association (APA), the *Standards* are recommendations and technical guidelines that should be followed by both assessment designers and users.

The most recent *Standards* document was published in 1999. This document is organized with an Introduction and three sections, Parts I–III. The introduction provides a general overview of the testing process and how the *Standards* should be used. The purposes for the *Standards* are:

> . . . to provide criteria for the evaluation of tests, testing practices, and the effects of test use. Although the evaluation of the appropriateness of a test and testing application depend heavily on professional judgment, the *Standards* provides a frame of reference to assure that relevant issues are addressed. It is hoped that all professional test developers, sponsors, publishers, and users will adopt the Standards and encourage others to do so (AERA, APA, & NCME, 1999, p. 2).

Part I of the *Standards* provides guidelines for test construction, evaluation, and documentation. Part II deals with fairness in testing and test use, with particular attention to the rights and responsibilities of test takers, and fairness of tests for LEP and special populations. Part III deals with applications of assessments in educational and psychological testing, program evaluation and policymaking, and for employment and credentialing purposes. Responsibilities of users are also elaborated in the third section.

Table 14.9 shows you a sampling of a few of the guidelines pertinent to classroom and large-scale assessment programs, testing for credentialing or psychological purposes, and fair assessment of special needs populations. To obtain a sense of how the *Standards* can help during test adoption, examine the excerpted standards with reference to the variety of purposes listed (purposes are identified as I–V in Table 14.8). For classroom assessment of achievement, Standard 13.3—dealing with local-level content validity—is crucial. For program evaluation purposes, Standards 13.2, 13.4, 13.7, and 13.10 would help us guard against test score misuse in local contexts. If tests are to be used for licensure-type decisions, Standards 14.4 and 14.5 would guide us in searching for information on predictive and content validity relevant to professional credentialing needs. For psychological diagnoses, Standards 12.6, 12.8, and 12.11 would remind us of the neces-

**TABLE 14.8   Excerpted *Standards* for Assessment Development and Use and Fair Testing Practices**

---

### I. Assessment Purposes and Inferences to Be Made with Results

Adopting assessment tools from textbooks or other published sources for classroom assessment purposes.

Inferences about achievement in specified domains.

#### Standard 13.3 (excerpted)

*When a test is used as an indicator of achievement in an instructional domain or with respect to specified curriculum standards, evidence of the extent to which the test samples the range of knowledge and elicits the processes reflected in the target domain should be provided. Both tested and target domains should be described in sufficient detail so that their relationship can be evaluated.*

---

### II. Assessment Purposes and Inferences to Be Made with Results

Using results of assessments for institutional, school district, state and other systemwide evaluation and accountability decisions.

#### Standard 13.2 (excerpted)

*In educational settings, when a test is designed or used for multiple purposes, evidence of the test's technical quality should be provided for each purpose.*

#### Standard 13.4 (excerpted)

*Local norms should be developed when necessary to support test users' intended interpretations.*

#### Standard 13.7 (excerpted)

*In educational settings, a decision or characterization that will have major impact on a student should not be made on the basis of a single score.*

#### Standard 13.10 (excerpted)

*Those responsible for educational testing programs should ensure that the individuals who administer and score the test(s) are proficient in the appropriate test administration and scoring procedures and they understand the importance of adhering to the directions provided by the test developer.*

---

### III. Assessment Purposes and Inferences to Be Made with Results

Using results of assessments for employment, licensure, certification, admission, and/or merit recognition.

#### Standard 14.5 (excerpted)

*Individuals conducting and interpreting empirical studies of predictor-criterion relationships should identify contaminants and artifacts that may have influenced the study findings, such as error of measurement, range restriction, and the effects of missing data.*

#### Standard 14.4 (excerpted)

*The content domain to be covered by a credentialing test should be defined clearly and justified in terms of the importance of the content of credential-worthy performance in an occupation or profession.*

**TABLE 14.8    Continued**

**IV.  Assessment Purposes and Inferences to Be Made with Results**

Using results of assessments for psychological testing, screening and diagnoses.

**Standard 12.6 (excerpted)**

*When differential diagnosis is needed, the professional should choose, if possible, a test for which there is evidence of a test's ability to distinguish between the two or more diagnostic groups of concern.*

**Standard 12.8 (excerpted)**

*Professionals should ensure that persons under supervision, who administer and score tests, are adequately trained in the settings in which testing occurs and with the populations served.*

**Standard 12.11 (excerpted)**

*Professionals and others who have access to test materials and test results should ensure the confidentiality of the test results and testing materials consistent with legal and professional ethics requirements.*

**V.  Assessment Purposes and Inferences to Be Made with Results**

Using results of assessments to make decisions on members of special populations or linguistic minorities.

**Standard 9.2 (excerpted)**

*When credible research evidence reports that test scores differ in meaning across subgroups of linguistically diverse test-takers, then . . . test developers should collect for each subgroup, the same form of validity evidence collected for the examinee population as a whole.*

**Standard 10.1 (excerpted)**

*In testing individuals with disabilities, test developers, test administrators, and test users should take steps to ensure that test score inferences accurately reflect the intended construct.*

sity for trained psychologists to administer, score and interpret tests/scores. Finally, Standard 9.2 would inform decisions on the need for data from group bias studies.

The 1999 *Standards* has been referenced repeatedly in various chapters of this book. It is a critical resource that should guide practitioners in decisions on sound assessment practices. Copies of the latest *Standards* can be purchased directly from the AERA and NCME offices at 1230, 17th St. NW, Washington, D.C. 20036-3078.

***Code of Professional Responsibilities in Educational Measurement.***    Another document prepared and disseminated by NCME in 1995 is the *Code of Professional Responsibilities in Educational Measurement,* prepared by the NCME Ad Hoc Committee on the Development of a Code of Ethics. This documents outlines the roles and responsibilities of a wide range of educational professionals who work with assessments. Copies of the

Code can be obtained from the NCME offices at 1230, 17th St. NW, Washington, D.C. 20036–3078.

***Standards for Teacher Competence in Educational Assessment of Students.***     Another collaborative effort by the American Federation of Teachers, the National Council on Measurement in Education, and the National Education Association (AFT, NCME, & NEA; 1990), resulted in the production of an important document that delineates standards for teacher competence in the educational assessment of students. These standards are intended to guide teacher education institutions in developing curricula for preservice and in-service educators, and to establish certification requirements for classroom teachers in the area of assessment. This document, too, can be obtained by writing to NCME at the above address.

# Summary

The purpose of Chapter 14 was to make you familiar with types of published standardized tests and factors to consider when selecting, administering, or using published assessments locally. Responsible standardized test developers supply documentation on content-based validity and empirical validity evidence to support their tests and test scores for various assessment purposes. Test consumers shoulder the responsibility of reviewing the technical manuals and evaluating the documented evidence provided by test developers, before they put a standardized test to use.

Five different kinds of standardized or published tests described were: multilevel achievement tests and test batteries, intelligence and scholastic aptitude tests, career/educational interest inventories, attitude scales, and personality measures. The chapter provided examples of widely used, published instruments in each category, the contexts in which they are typically used, and how we should select them to meet local needs.

Next the chapter provided an overview of how norms and norm-referenced scores are derived by standardized testmakers. Norms provide a structured framework for us to make norm-referenced interpretations of raw scores. The chapter outlined how standardization samples are obtained by developers to create norms tables. Five major types of *derived scores* were described, starting with normalized *z*-scores and moving to other transformed scores, such as the T-score, NCE, other standard scores, percentile ranks, percentile bands, stanines, grade-equivalents and scaled scores. Interpretative guidelines for these scores were given.

The chapter concluded by presenting the resources available to users for locating and evaluating published instruments. Among others, documents suggested were the *Mental Measurements Yearbooks* (MMY), *Tests in Print,* the Educational Testing Service's *Test Collection* database, and PRO-ED's *Tests: A Comprehensive Reference for Assessments in Psychology, Education, and Business.*

The chapter emphasized that users and practitioners consult the 1999 Standards for educational and psychological testing when engaging in assessment practices. Excerpted standards were presented to illustrate the importance of following the *Standards,* which show typical guidelines provided for users and developers. The chapter also described the *Code of Professional Responsibilities in Educational Measurement,* prepared by an NCME Ad Hoc Committee, and briefly mentioned a document that sets standards for teacher competence in educational assessment.

## QUESTIONS FOR CLASS DISCUSSION

1. Suppose that you are chairing a committee charged with the selection of a standardized, published test to meet large-scale achievement testing and program evaluation needs in a school system. Suppose further that the school system officials wish to use the test results to examine how many students are meeting certain standards of performance as well as how well they compare with a national comparison group.
   (a) What resources would you gather to help the committee begin their search and evaluation of instruments?
   (b) How would you guide the committee members in developing a set of specifications to select an instrument to meet your needs?
   (c) What kinds of evidential information would you emphasize when evaluating available instruments?

2. Now assume that you are interested in selecting a norm-referenced general aptitude battery for selecting able students for an advanced program.
   (a) What resources would you gather to help the committee begin their search and evaluation of instruments?
   (b) How would you guide the committee members in developing a set of specifications to select an instrument to meet your needs?
   (c) What kinds of evidential information would you emphasize when evaluating available instruments?

3. Review the guidelines in the *1999 Standards* as they apply to screening and diagnostic applications of tests. If you were a consultant to an organization on the proper use of tests for screening and diagnoses of special needs, how would you summarize the main guidelines to encourage sound testing practices?

4. Find an individual score profile of a student tested on a standardized achievement test (e.g., the Stanford 9 or CTB/4). Pretend you are speaking with a parent during a one-on-one conference. Interpret the following scores in terms that a layperson can understand, attending to accuracy of interpretation.
   (a) standard score
   (b) percentile rank
   (c) percentile band
   (d) grade-equivalent score
   (e) raw score
   (f) stanine
   (g) scaled score
   (h) domain score
   (i) mastery/non-mastery with a standard (cut score).

# BIBLIOGRAPHY

Airasian, P. W. (1991). *Classroom Assessment*. New York, NY: McGraw-Hill, Inc.

American Association for the Advancement of Science (AAAS) (1993). *Benchmarks for Science Literacy* (Project 2061). New York, NY: Oxford University Press.

American Educational Research Association, American Psychological Association, & National Council on Measurement in Education (1985). *Standards for Educational and Psychological Testing*. Washington, DC: AERA, APA, & NCME.

American Educational Research Association, American Psychological Association, & National Council on Measurement in Education (1999). *Standards for Educational and Psychological Testing*. Washington, DC: AERA, APA, & NCME.

American Federation of Teachers, National Council on Measurement in Education, & National Education Association (AFT, NCME, NEA) (1990). *Standards for Teacher Competence in Educational Assessment of Students*. Washington, DC: Author.

Andrews, F. M., & Robinson, J. P. (1991). Measures of subjective well-being. In J. P. Robinson, P. R. Shaver, & L. S. Wrightsman (Eds.), *Measures of Personality and Psychological Attitudes* (61–114). San Diego, CA: Academic Press, Inc.

Angoff, W. H. (1971). Scales, norms, and equivalent scores. In R. L. Thorndike (Ed.), *Educational Measurement* (2nd edition, 508–600). Washington, DC: American Council on Education.

Angoff, W. H. (1988). Validity: An evolving concept. In H. Wainer and H. I. Braun (Eds.), *Test Validity* (pp. 19–32). Hillsdale, NJ: Lawrence Erlbaum Associates, Publishers.

Arter, J. A., & Spandel, V. (1992). Using portfolios of student work in instruction and assessment. *Educational Measurement: Issues and Practice, 11* (1), 36–44.

Babbie, E. (1990). *Survey Research Methods* (2nd edition). Belmont, CA: Wadsworth, Inc.

Banerji, M. (1992). Factor structure of the Gesell School Readiness Screening Test. *Journal of Psychoeducational Assessment, 10*, 342–354.

Banerji, M., & Ferron, J. (1998). Construct validity of scores on a developmental assessment with mathematical patterns tasks. *Educational and Psychological Measurement, 58* (4), 634–660.

Bender, T. A. (1997). Assessment of subjective well-being during childhood and adolescence. In G. D. Phye (Ed.), *Handbook of Classroom Assessment: Learning, Adjustment, and Achievement* (199–225). San Diego, CA: Academic Press.

Berk, R. A. (1984). Conducting the item analysis. In R. A. Berk (Ed.), *A Guide to Criterion-referenced Test Construction* (97–143). Baltimore: Johns Hopkins University Press.

Berk, R. A. (1986a). *Performance Assessment: Methods and Applications*. Baltimore, MD: Johns Hopkins University Press.

Berk, R. A. (1986b). A consumer's guide to setting performance standards on criterion-referenced tests. *Review of Educational Research, 56*, 137–172.

Bloom, B. S., Englehart, M. D., Furst, E. J., Hill, W. H., & Krathwohl, D. R. (1956). *Taxonomy of Educational Objectives: The Classification of Educational Goals: Handbook 1. Cognitive Domain*. White Plains, NY: Longman.

Bracey, G. W. (1996). International comparisons and the condition of American education. *Educational Researcher, 25* (1), 5–11.

Brennan, R. L. (1998). A perspective on the history of generalizability theory. *Educational Measurement: Issues and Practice, 19* (4), 14–20.

Briel, J. B., O'Neill, K. A., & Schueneman, J. D. (1993). *GRE Technical Manual*. Princeton, NJ: Educational Testing Service.

Byrne, B. M. (1984). The general/academic self-concept nomological network: A review of construct validation research. *Review of Educational Research, 54*, 427–456.

Byrne, B. M. (1986). Self-concept/academic achievement relations: An investigation of dimensionality, stability and causality. *Canadian Journal of Behavioral Science, 18*, 173–186.

Calfee, R. C. (1994). *Implications of Cognitive Psychology for Authentic Assessment and Instruction.* (Tech. Report No. 69). Berkeley, CA: National Center for the Study of Writing, University of California.

Campbell, D. T., & Fiske, D. W. (1959). Convergent and discriminant validation by the multi-trait multi-method matrix. *Psychological Bulletin, 56,* 81–105.

Canady, R. L., & Hotchkiss, P. R. (1989). It's a good score! Just a bad grade. *Phi Delta Kappan, 70,* 68–75.

Cannell, J. J. (1987). *Nationally Normed Elementary Achievement Testing in America's Public Schools: How All 50 States Are Above the National Average.* Daniels, WV: Friends for Education.

Cannell, J. J. (1988). Nationally normed elementary achievement testing in America's public schools: How all 50 states are testing above the national average. *Educational Measurement: Issues and Practice, 7* (2), 5–9.

Cizek, G. J. (1996). An NCME module on setting passing scores. *Educational Measurement: Issues and Practice, 15* (2), 20–31.

Cizek, G. J. (1997). Learning, achievement, and assessment: Constructs at a cross-roads. In G. D. Phye (Ed.), *Handbook of Classroom Assessment: Learning, Adjustment, and Achievement* (1–32). San Diego, CA: Academic Press.

Cohen, J. (1988). *Statistical Power Analysis for the Behavioral Sciences* (2nd Edition). Hillsdale, NJ: Lawrence Erlbaum Associates.

Crocker, L., & Algina, J. (1986). *Introduction to Classical and Modern Test Theory.* New York, NY: CBS College Publishing.

Cronbach, L. J. (1970). *Essentials of Psychological Testing* (3rd edition). New York, NY: Harper & Row.

Cronbach, L. J., & Meehl, P. (1955). Construct validity in psychological tests. *Psychological Bulletin, 52,* 281–302.

Cronbach, L. J., & Suppes, P. (Eds.) (1969). *Research for Tomorrow's Schools: Disciplined Inquiry for Education.* New York, NY: Macmillan Publishing Co.

CTB/McGraw-Hill (1989). *CTBS/4: Preliminary Technical Information.* Monterey, CA: McGraw-Hill.

CTB/McGraw-Hill (1989). *CTBS/4: Preview Materials.* Monterey, CA: McGraw-Hill.

Dake, D. M., & Weinkein, J. L. (1997). Assessment in visual arts. In Phye, G. D. (Ed.), *Handbook of Classroom Assessment: Learning, Adjustment, and Achievement.* San Diego, CA: Academic Press.

Darling-Hammond, L. (1998). Teachers and teaching: Testing policy hypotheses from a national commission report. *Educational Researcher, 27* (1), 5–15.

Deiner, E. (1994). Assessing subjective well-being: Progress and opportunities. *Social Indicators Research, 31,* 103–157.

Ebel, R. L. (1961). Must all tests be valid? *American Psychologist, 16,* 640–647.

Ebel, R. L. (1971). How to write true-false items. *Educational and Psychological Measurement, 31,* 417–426.

Ebel, R. L. (1972). *Essentials in Educational Measurement* (2nd edition). Englewood Cliffs, NJ: Prentice-Hall.

Edwards, A. L. (1957). *The Social Desirability Variability in Personality Assessment and Research.* New York, NY: Dryden Press.

Fink, A. (1995). *How to Ask Survey Questions.* Thousand Oaks, CA: Sage Publications, Inc.

Florida Commission on Education Reform and Accountability (1998). *Accountability Update, 6* (3). Tallahassee, FL: Author.

Florida Department of Education, Department of Curriculum, Instruction, and Assessment (1997). *A Guide for Teaching and Assessing with the Goal 3 Standards: Level 1 Guide.* Tallahassee, FL: Author.

Florida Department of Education, Student Assessment Services (1997a). *Florida Comprehensive Assessment Test: Mathematics Test Item and Performance Task Specifications (Grades 4, 8, 10).* Tallahassee, FL: Author.

Florida Department of Education, Student Assessment Services (1997b). *Florida Comprehensive Assessment Test: Reading Test Item and Performance Task Specifications (Grades 5, 8, 10).* Tallahassee, FL: Author.

Freijo, T. D., & Freijo, K. K. (1980). *A Guide to Writing Items for Local Criterion-Referenced Tests.* Tampa, FL: PDE Associates, Inc.

Ganguly, R., & Banerji, M. (2000). Hepatitis B virus infection and vaccine acceptance among university students. *American Journal of Health Behavior, 24* (2), 96–107.

Gifford, B. R., & O'Connor, M. C. (Eds.) (1992). *Changing Assessments: Alternative Views of Aptitude, Achievement, and Instruction.* Boston, MA: Kluwer.

Glaser, R., Lesgold, A., & Lajoie, S. (1987). Towards a cognitive theory for the measurement of achievement. In R. Ronning, J. Glover, J. C. Conoley, & J. Witt (Eds.), *The Influence of Cognitive Psychology on Testing and Measurement* (96–131). Hillsdale, NJ: Erlbaum.

Glass, G. V., & Hopkins, K. D. (1984). *Statistical Methods in Education and Psychology.* Englewood Cliffs, NJ: Prentice Hall, Inc.

Good, C. V. (Ed.) (1973). *Dictionary of Education* (3rd edition). New York, NY: McGraw-Hill.

Good, T. L., & Brophy, G. E. (1986). *Educational Psychology* (3rd edition). New York, NY: Longman.

Greeno, J. G. (1976). Cognitive objectives of instruction: Theory of knowledge for solving problems and answering questions, in Klahr, D. (Ed.), *Cognition and Instruction.* Hillsdale, NJ: Lawrence Erlbaum.

Gronlund, N. E. (1981). *Measurement and Evaluation in Teaching* (5th edition). New York, NY: Macmillan Publishing Co.

Gronlund, N. E. (2000). *Stating Objectives for Classroom Instruction* (6th edition). Upper Saddle River, NJ: Merrill, an imprint of Prentice Hall, Inc.

Hales, L. W., & Tokar, E. (1975). The effect of the quality of preceding responses on the grades assigned to subsequent responses to an essay question. *Journal of Educational Measurement, 12,* 231–240.

Hambleton, R. K., & Plake, B. S. (1995). Using an extended Angoff procedure to set standards on complex performance assessments. *Applied Measurement in Education, 8* (1), 41–55.

Hambleton, R. K., & Traub, R. E. (1974). The effects of item order on test performance and stress. *Journal of Experimental Education, 43,* 40–46.

Hansen, J. C., & Campbell, D. P. (1985). *Manual for the SVIB-SCII* (4th edition). Palo Alto, CA: Consulting Psychologists Press.

Harmon, L. W. (1989). Counseling. In R. L. Linn (Ed.), *Educational Measurement* (13–103). New York: American Council on Education.

Harmon, L. W., Hansen, J. C., Borgen, F. H., & Hammer, A. L. (1994). *Strong interest inventory applications and technical guide.* Stanford, CA: Stanford University Press.

Harcourt Brace Educational Measurement (1996a). *Stanford achievement test series, Ninth edition: Preliminary technical report.* San Antonio, TX: Author.

Harcourt Brace Educational Measurement (1996b). *Stanford achievement test series, Ninth edition: Preliminary technical tables.* San Antonio, TX: Author.

Harcourt Brace Educational Measurement (1997a). *Stanford achievement test series, Ninth edition: Parent preview manual.* San Antonio, TX: Author.

Harcourt Brace Educational Measurement (1997b). *Stanford achievement test series, Ninth edition: Technical Data Report.* San Antonio, TX: Author.

Hegerty, Stephen (1999, May 9). Pressure on schools could test teachers' honesty. *St. Petersburg Times,* pp. A1, A21.

Herman, J. L., Aschbacher, P. R., & Winters, L. (1992). *A Practical Guide to Alternative Assessment.* Alexandria, VA: Association for Supervision and Curriculum Development.

Holland, J. L. (1997). *Making vocational choices: A theory of vocational personalities and work environments* (3rd edition). Odessa, FL: Psychological Assessment Resources.

Hopkins, K. D. (1998). *Educational and Psychological Measurement and Evaluation* (8th edition). Boston, MA: Allyn & Bacon.

Hopkins, K. D., Kretke, G., & Averill, M. (1983–84). *District Testing Report.* Boulder, CO: Boulder Valley School District.

Hopkins, K. D., & Stanley, J. C. (1981). *Educational and psychological measurement in education* (6th edition). Englewood Cliffs, NJ: Prentice Hall.

Hopkins, K. D., Stanley, J. C., & Hopkins, B. R. (1990). *Educational and psychological measurement and evaluation* (7th edition). Englewood Cliffs, NJ: Prentice Hall.

Hughes, D. C., Keeling, B., & Tuck, B. F. (1980). The effect of context position and scoring method on essay scoring. *Journal of Educational Measurement, 17,* 131–136.

Impara, J. C., & Plake, B. S. (1996). Professional development in student assessment for educational administrators: An instructional framework. *Educational Measurement: Issues and Practice, 15* (2), 14–19.

Jaeger, R. M. (1989). Certification of student competence. In R. L. Linn (Ed.), *Educational Measurement* (3rd edition, 485–514). Washington, DC: American Council on Education and Macmillan Publishing Co.

Jaeger, R. M. (1997). *Complementary Methods for Research in Education* (2nd edition). Washington, DC: American Educational Research Association.

Jones, L. V. (1997). A history of the National Assessment of Educational Progress and some questions about its future. *Educational Researcher, 25* (7), 15–22.

Kohn, A. (1994). Grading: The issue is not how but why. *Educational Leadership, 52* (2), 38–41.

Krathwohl, D. R., et al. (1964). *Taxonomy of Educational Objectives: Handbook II, Affective Domain.* New York, NY: D. McKay.

Kubisyn, T., & Borich, G. (1996). *Educational Testing and Measurement: Classroom Application and Practice* (5th edition). New York, NY: HarperCollins College Publishers.

Kuder, G. F. (1934). *Kuder General Interest Survey.* Chicago, IL: Science Research Associates.

Kuder, G. F., & Richardson, M. W. (1937). The theory of the estimation of test reliability. *Psychometrika, 2*, 151–160. Chicago, IL: Science Research Associates.

Lewinsohn, P. M., Redner, J. E., & Seeley, J. R. (1991). The relationship between life satisfaction and psychosocial variables: New perspectives. In F. Strack, M. Argyle, & N. Schwarz (Eds.), *Subjective Well-Being: An Interdisciplinary Perspective* (141–169). Oxford: Permagon.

Likert, R. A. (1934). A technique for the measurement of attitudes. *Archives of Psychology.* No. 140.

Linn, R. L. (1989). *Educational Measurement* (3rd edition). New York, NY: American Council on Education/Macmillan Publishing Company.

Linn, R. L., & Gronlund, N. E. (2000). *Measurement and Assessment in Teaching* (8th edition). Upper Saddle River, NJ: Merrill, an imprint of Prentice Hall, Inc.

Lorge, I., Thorndike, R. L., & Hagen, E. P. (1964). *Lorge-Thorndike Intelligence Test: Multi-level Edition.* Lombard, IL: Riverside Publishing Co.

Loyd, B. H., & Loyd, D. E. (1997). Kindergarten through grade 12 standards: A philosophy of grading. In G. D. Phye (Ed.), *Handbook of Classroom Assessment: Learning, Adjustment, and Achievement.* San Diego, CA: Academic Press, Inc.

Marsh, H. W., Byrne, B. M., & Shavelson, R. (1988). A multifaceted academic self-concept: Its hierarchical structure and its relationship to academic achievement. *Journal of Educational Psychology, 80*, 366–380.

Marsh, H. W., & Craven, R. G. (1997). Academic self-concept: Beyond the dustbowl. In G. D. Phye (Ed.), *Handbook of Classroom Assessment: Learning, Adjustment, and Achievement* (199–225). San Diego, CA: Academic Press.

Marzano, R. J., & Kendall, J. S. (1996). *Designing Standards-Based Districts, Schools, and Classrooms.* Alexandria, VA: Association for Supervision and Curriculum Development (ASCD) and the Mid-Continental Regional Educational Laboratory (MCREL).

Marzano, R. J., Pickering, D. J., & McTighe, J. (1993). *Assessing Student Outcomes: Performance Assessment Using the Dimensions of Learning Model.* Alexandria, VA: Association for Supervision and Curriculum Development (ASCD).

McDonald, R. P. (1999). Test theory: A unified treatment. Mahwah, NJ: Lawrence Erlbaum Associates.

McTighe, J., & Ferrarra, S. (1996). Performance-based assessment in the classroom: A planning framework. In R. E. Blum & J. A. Arter (Eds.), *A Handbook of Student Performance Assessment in an Era of Restructuring* (I–5, 1–9). Alexandria, VA: Association for Supervision and Curriculum Development.

Mehrens, W. A. (1992). Using performance assessment for accountability purposes. *Educational Measurement: Issues and Practice (1)*, 3–20.

Mehrens, W. A., & Lehman, I. J. (1984). *Measurement and Evaluation in Education and Psychology.* NY: Holt, Reinhart, & Winston.

Mehrens, W. A., & Lehman, I. J. (1991). *Measurement and Evaluation in Education and Psychology* (4th edition). Chicago, IL: Holt, Reinhart, & Winston.

Messick, S. (1989). Validity. In R. L. Linn (Ed.), *Educational Measurement* (13–103). New York: American Council on Education.

Messick, S. (1994). The interplay of evidence and consequences in the validation of performance assessments. *Educational Researcher, 23* (2), 13–23.

Miles, M. B., & Huberman, A. M. (1994). *Qualitative Data Analysis*. Newbury Park, CA: Sage Publications, Inc.

Miller, R. D. (1988). Foreword. In M. Lazarus (Au.), *Evaluating Educational Programs*. Arlington, VA: American Association of School Administrators.

Millman, J. (1992). Standards for tests and ethical test use. In Marvin C. Alkin (Editor in Chief), *Encyclopedia of Educational Research* (6th edition, 1259–1262). New York, NY: Macmillan Publishing Co.

Millman, J., & Greene, J. (1989). The specification and development of tests of achievement and ability. In R. L. Linn (Ed.), *Educational Measurement* (13–103). New York: American Council on Education.

Mitchell, R. (1992). *Testing for Learning: How New Approaches to Evaluation Can Improve American Schools*. New York: The Free Press.

Myford, C., & Mislevey, R. J. (1995). *Monitoring and Improving a Portfolio Assessment System*. Princeton, NJ: Educational Testing Service.

National Center for History in Schools (1994). *National Standards for United States History: Exploring the American Experience*. Los Angeles, CA: Author.

National Commission for Excellence in Education (1983). *A Nation at Risk: The Imperative for Educational Reform*. Washington, DC: Government Printing Office.

National Council for the Accreditation of Teacher Education (NCATE) (2000). *Professional Standards for the Accreditation of Schools, Colleges, and Departments of Education*. Washington, DC: Author.

National Council for Teachers of English (1996) and the International Reading Association (IRA) (1996). *Standards for the English Language Arts*. Urbana, IL: Author.

National Council for Teachers of Mathematics (NCTM) (1989). *Curriculum and Evaluation Standards for School Mathematics*. Reston, VA: Author.

National Council for Teachers of Mathematics (NCTM) (1995). *Assessment Standards for School Mathematics*. Reston, VA: Author.

National Educational Goals Panel (1993). *The National Educational Goals Report: Building a Nation of Learners*. Washington, DC: National Education Goals Panel.

National Research Council (1996). *National Science Education Standards*. Washington, DC: National Academy Press.

Nitko, A. J. (1989). Designing tests that are integrated with instruction. In R. L. Linn (Ed.), *Educational Measurement* (13–103). New York: American Council on Education.

Nitko, A. J. (1996). *Educational Assessment of Students* (2nd edition). Englewood Cliffs, NJ: Merrill, an imprint of Prentice-Hall.

Noddings, N. (1996). Teachers and subject matter knowledge. *Teacher Education Quarterly* (Fall Issue), 86–89.

Norris, S. P., & Ennis, R. H. (1989). *Evaluating Critical Thinking*. Pacific Grove, CA: Midwest Publications, Critical Thinking Press.

Nunnally, J. C. (1978). *Psychometric Theory* (2nd edition). New York, NY: McGraw-Hill Book Co.

Nunnally, J. C., & Bernstein, I. H. (1994). *Psychometric Theory* (3rd edition). New York, NY: McGraw-Hill Book Co.

Oosterhof, A. (1999). *Developing and Using Classroom Assessments*. Upper Saddle River, NJ: Prentice Hall.

Osgood, C. E., Suci, G. J., & Tanner, P. H. (1957). *The Measurement of Meaning*. Urbana, IL: University of Illinois.

Patton, M. Q. (1986). *Utilization-Focused Evaluation*. Newbury Park, CA: Sage Publications.

Pedersen, N. L., Plomin, R., & McLearns, G. E. (1994). Is there G beyond g? *Intelligence, 18,* 133–143.

Pellegrino, J. W., Chudowski, N., & Glaser, R. (Eds.) (2001). *Knowing what students know: The science and design of educational assessment*. Washington, DC: National Academy Press (National Research Council).

Phye, G. D. (Ed.) (1997). *Handbook of Classroom Assessment: Learning, Adjustment, and Achievement.* San Diego, CA: Academic Press.

Plake, B. S., Impara, J. C., & Fager, J. J. (1993). Assessment competencies of teachers: A national survey. *Educational Measurement: Issues and Practice, 12* (4), 10–13.

Popham, W. J. (1984). Specifying the domain of content or behaviors. In R. A. Berk (Ed.), *A Guide to Criterion-Referenced Test Construction* (29–48). Baltimore: Johns Hopkins University Press.

Reed, T. E., & Jensen, A. R. (1992). Conduction velocity in brain nerve pathway of normal adults correlates with intelligence level. *Intelligence, 16,* 259–272.

Resnick, L. B., & Resnick, D. P. (1992). Assessing the thinking curriculum: New tools for educational reform. In B. R. Gifford & M. C. O'Connor (Eds.), *Changing Assessments: Alternative Views of Aptitude, Achievement, and Instruction* (37–75). Boston, MA: Kluwer.

Runyon, R. P., & Haber, A. (1977). *Fundamentals of Behavioral Statistics.* Reading, MA: Addison-Wesley Publishing Co.

Salvia, J., & Ysseldyke, J. E. (1981). *Assessment in Special and Remedial Education.* Dallas, TX: Houghton Mifflin Co.

Sanders, W. L., & Horn, S. P. (1994). The Tennessee value-added assessment system (TVAAS): Mixed model methodology in educational assessment. *Journal of Personnel Evaluation in Education, 8,* 299–311.

Sattler, J. M. (1988). *Assessment of Children.* San Diego, CA: Jerome M. Sattler, Publisher.

Sax, G., & Carr, A. (1962). An investigation of response set on altered parallel forms. *Educational and Psychological Measurement, 22,* 371–376.

Scheuneman, J. D. (1982). A posteriori analysis of biased items. In R. A. Berk (Ed.), *Handbook of Methods for Detecting Test Bias.* Baltimore, MD: Johns Hopkins University Press.

Schmidt, W. H., McKnight, C. C., & Raizen, S. A. (1996). *A Splintered Vision: An Investigation of U.S. Science and Mathematics Education.* Norwell, MA: Kluwer Academic Publishers.

Schumann, H., & Presser, S. (1996). *Questions and Answers in Attitude Surveys: Experiments on Question Form, Wording, and Content.* Newbury Park, CA: Sage Publications, Inc.

Scriven, M. (1967). The methodology of evaluation. In R. E. Stake (Ed.), *Curriculum Evaluation. American Educational Research Association Monograph Series on Evaluation, No. 1.* Chicago: Rand McNally.

Secretary's Commission on Achieving Necessary Skills (SCANS) (1991). *What Work Requires of Schools: A SCANS Report for America 2000.* Washington, DC: U.S. Department of Labor.

Shavelson, R., & Baxter, G. (1992). What we've learned about hands-on science. *Educational Leadership, 49* (8), 20–25.

Shepard, L., Glaser, R., Linn. R., & Bohrnstedt, G. (1993). *Setting Performance Standards for Student Achievement.* Stanford, CA: National Academy of Education.

Shepard, L. A. (1984). Setting performance standards. In R. A. Berk (Ed.), *A Guide to Criterion-Referenced Test Construction* (169–198). Baltimore, MD: Johns Hopkins University Press.

Shepard, L. A. (1989a). Why we need better assessments. *Educational Leadership, 46* (7), 1–9.

Shepard, L. A. (1989b). Identification of mild handicaps. In R. L. Linn (Ed.), *Educational Measurement* (13–103). New York, NY: American Council on Education.

Shepard, L. A. (1993). Evaluating test validity. *Review of Research in Education, 19,* 405–450.

Shulman, L. (1987). Knowledge and teaching: Foundations of the new reform. *Harvard Educational Review, 57,* 1–22.

Shulman, L. (1997). Disciplines of inquiry in education: A new overview. In R. M. Jaeger (Ed.), *Complementary Methods for Research in Education* (3–29). Washington, DC: American Educational Research Association.

Stanley, J. C. (1971). Reliability. In R. L. Thorndike (Ed.), *Educational Measurement* (2nd edition, 359–442). Washington, DC: American Council on Education.

Sternberg, R. J. (1981). Testing and cognitive psychology. *American Psychologist, 36,* 1181–1189.

Stevens, S. S. (1946). On the theory of scales of measurement. *Science, 103,* 677–680.

Stiggins, R. J. (1991). Challenges of a new era in assessment. *Applied Measurement in Education, 4* (4), 263–273.

Stiggins, R. J. (1996). *Student-Centered Classroom Assessment.* Upper Saddle River, NJ: Merrill, an imprint of Prentice Hall, Inc.

Stiggins, R. J. (2001). The unfulfilled promise of classroom assessments. *Educational Measurement: Issues and Practice, 20* (3), 5–15.

Stiggins, R. J., & Conklin, N. F. (1992). *In Teachers' Hands: Investigating the Practices of Classroom Assessment.* Albany, NY: SUNY Press.

Strong, E. K. (1927). Vocational interest test. *Educational Record, 8,* 107–121.

Taylor, W. L. (1953). Cloze procedure: A new tool for measuring readability. *Journalism Quarterly, 30,* 415–433.

Taylor, H. C., & Russell, J. T. (1939). The relationships of validity coefficients to the practical effectiveness of tests in selection: Discussion and tables. *Journal of Applied Psychology, 23,* 565–578.

Terwilliger, J. S. (1989). Classroom standard-setting and grading practices. *Educational Measurement: Issues and Practice, 8* (2), 15–19.

Thorndike, E. L. (1904). *An Introduction to the Theory of Mental and Social Measurements.* New York: Science Press.

Thorndike, E. L. (1918). The nature, purposes, and general methods of measurement of educational products. *The Seventeenth Yearbook of the National Society for the Study of Education, Part II.* Bloomington, IL: Public School Publishing Company.

Thorndike, R. L., & Hagen, E. P. (1978). *The Cognitive Abilities Test.* Lombard, IL: Riverside Publishing Co.

Thorndike, R. L., Hagen, E. P., & Sattler, J. M. (1986). *Guide for Administering and Scoring the Fourth Edition Stanford-Binet Intelligence Scale.* Chicago, IL: Riverside Publishing Co.

Thorndike, R. L., Hagen, E. P., & Sattler, J. M. (1986). *Technical Manual for the Stanford-Binet: Fourth Edition.* Chicago, IL: Riverside Publishing Co.

Thorndike, R. M., Cunningham, G. K., Thorndike, R. L., & Hagen, E. P. (1991). *Measurement and Evaluation in Psychology and Education* (5th edition). New York, NY: Macmillan Publishing.

Thurstone, L. L. (1959). *The Measurement of Values.* Chicago, IL: University of Chicago Press.

Turney, B. I., & Robb, G. P. (1973). *Statistical Methods for Behavioral Science.* New York, NY: Intext Educational Publishers.

Tyler, R. W. (1951). The functions of measurement in improving instruction. In E. F. Lindquist (Ed.), *Educational Measurement.* Washington, DC: American Council on Education.

Valencia, S. P., Paerson, P. D., Peters, C. W., & Wixson, K. K. (1989). Theory and practice in statewide reading assessment: Closing the gap. *Educational Leadership, 46,* (7), 57–63.

Walsh, W. B., & Betz, N. E. (2000). *Tests and Assessment* (4th edition). Upper Saddle River, NJ: Prentice Hall.

Wechsler, D. (1989). *Wechsler Preschool and Primary Scale of Intelligence—Revised: Manual.* San Antonio, TX: The Psychological Corporation.

Wesman, A. G. (1971). Writing the test item. In R. L. Thorndike (Ed.), *Educational Measurement* (2nd edition) (81–129). Washington, DC: American Council on Education.

Whitney, D. R. (1989). Educational Admissions and Placement. In R. L. Linn (Ed.), *Educational Measurement* (13–103). New York: American Council on Education.

Wiggins, G. (1989). Teaching to the (authentic) test. *Educational Leadership, 46* (1), 41–47.

Wiggins, G. (1998). Research news and comments: Response to Terwilliger. *Educational Researcher, 27* (6), 20–21.

Willett, J. B. (1988). Questions and answers in the measurement of change. In E. Z. Rothkopf (Ed.), *Review of Research in Education* (1988–89, 345–422). Washington, DC: AERA.

Williams, P. L. (1988). The time-bound nature of norms: Understandings and misunderstandings. *Educational Measurement: Issues and Practice, 7* (2), 5–9.

Wolf, D., Bixby, J., Glenn, J., & Gardner, H. (1991). To use their minds well: New forms of student assessment. *Review of Research in Education, 17,* 31–74.

Woolfolk, A. E. (1995). *Educational Psychology* (6th edition). Boston, MA: Allyn & Bacon.

Worthen, B. R., Sanders, J. R., & Fitzpatrick, J. R. (1997). *Program Evaluation: Alternative Approaches and Practical Guidelines.* White Plains, NY: Longman

# INDEX

Accountability, 35, 49
Achievement, 27, 122–123
Achievement domains, 124–135
  language arts, 135–136
  mathematics, 10, 130, 134, 135
  specifying, 128–135
Achievement tests, 23–25, 38, 80, 84,
  449–457
Action plans, 376–377
Adjusted item-to-total score correlation,
  402–403
Admissions, assessment for, 26, 46–48
*Advanced Placement* (AP) tests, 47, 416–417
Affective assessments, 80, 84, 250–287,
  263–287
Affective domains, 137
Age-equivalent scores, 473–475
Airasian, P. W., 26, 27
Algina, J., 344, 383, 400–401, 407, 411,
  435, 441–442
Alternative assessment, 79–83
*America 2000*, 15–16
American College Testing Program (ACT),
  46, 459–460
American Educational Research Associa-
  tion (AERA), xii, 9, 18, 20, 38, 54,
  58, 104, 109, 149, 409, 427, 445,
  447, 448, 481, 483
American Federation of Teachers (AFT),
  445, 484
American Psychological Association (APA),
  xii, 9, 18, 20, 38, 54, 58, 104, 109,
  149, 409, 427, 445, 447, 448, 481
Analytic rubrics, 206, 234–235, 368, 370
Andrews, F. M., 148, 258
Anecdotal observation, 91, 279–282
Angoff, W. H., 64, 343, 346, 423
Angoff procedure, 346
Anonymity, 276
Answer key, 193
Arter, J. A., 79, 93–94, 229, 353
Aschbacher, P. R., 79, 123, 202
Assessment process, 12
Assessment specifications, 108, 161–163
Attitude scales, 3, 5, 462–463
Attitudes toward subject area, 27
Attributes, 9–10
Authentic assessment, 18, 79, 82, 83
Averill, M., 276
Awards, assessment for, 26, 46–48

Babbie, E., 271–273
Back-to-basics movement, 14–15
Banerji, M., 98, 401, 422, 424
Base rate, 417
Behavior-based assessments, 80, 84, 90–91,
  96, 99–100, 219–223, 250–287

Benchmark performance, 347–348,
  368–371
Bender, T. A., 147–148, 257, 258
Berk, R. A., 82, 344, 395–398, 426
Bernstein, I. H., 400–401, 407, 411
Betz, N. E., 457–460, 462–464
Bias, 55, 57
  in assessment design, 195–196, 273–276
  evidence of, 425–427
  lack of, in items/test scores, 425–427
  in scoring, 244–247
  selection, 47, 417–418
  in structured observation forms, 278–279
Bimodal distributions, 302
Bivariate correlation, 330, 332–333
Bixby, J., 16, 123
Bloom, B. S., 135, 137–138, 139
Bloom's taxonomy, 135, 137–138, 139–
  142, 190–191
Borgen, F. H., 462
Borhnstedt, G., 344
Bracey, G. W., 17
Brennan, R. L., 7–8
Briel, J. B., 460
Brophy, G. E., 123
Buros Institute of Mental Measurements,
  480
Byrne, B. M., 284, 286

Calfee, R. C., 12
*California Psychological Inventory* (CPI),
  464
Campbell, D. P., 462
Campbell, D. T., 63–64, 413
Canady, R. L., 31, 32, 51, 354
Cannell, J. J., 23–24, 465
Carr, A., 193
Causation, 335
Ceiling effects, 375
Central tendency, 297, 301–308
Checklists, 236, 243
Chudowski, N., xi
Cizek, G. J., 12, 122, 123, 344, 346, 351
Classification of assessments
  advantages and disadvantages of, 95–
  100
  methods of, 80–81, 83–94
Class intervals, 298–301
Classroom assessments, 80
Classroom conduct and behavior, 27
Classroom Educational Plans (CEPs),
  377–379
Clinicians, 39–43
Cloze test, 89, 175–176
Clues, 190
*Code of Professional Responsibilities in
  Educational Measurement*, 483–484

Coefficient of determination, 333–335
*Cognitive Abilities Test* (CogAT), 459
Cognitive domains, 137–138
Cohen, J., 373
Cohen's kappa, 433, 440, 441, 442–443
College Board, 46
Comparison group, 323
Competency/content dimensions, 347
Completion exercises, 171–176
Complex interpretive exercises, 187–190
Composite scores, 344
*Comprehensive Tests of Basic Skills*
  (CTBS), 80, 477
Computer-based assessment, 86
Concept-mapping, 136
Concrete language, 266–268
Concurrent validity, 64–65, 418–420
Conditions
  bias due to, 246
  in classification of assessment, 80–81,
  84–85
Confidence bands, 415–416, 439, 440–
  441
Confidentiality, 276
Conklin, N. F., 19, 145, 146, 253
Constants, 11
Construct domain, 107
  in Process Model, 121–151, 155–157,
  211
  in User Path 1, 122–142
  in User Path 2–6, 142–149, 262
Constructs, 2, 6–11, 55
  in classification of assessment, 80, 84
  in Process Model, 107
  in User Paths 2–6, 262
Construct validity, 409
Content relevance, 60–61, 109, 161, 375,
  409–410, 466
Content representativeness, 60, 109, 161,
  409–410
Content validity, 58–61, 65–66, 109,
  118, 158, 193–195, 242, 243, 284,
  409–410
Continuous variables, 294–295
Contrasting groups method, 349
Convergent validity, 59, 63–64, 410–415
Correlation coefficients, 328–338
Correlation matrix, 338, 411
Covariance matrix, 338
Craven, R. G., 284, 286
Criterion-referenced tests (CRTs), 81, 85,
  87, 111, 157–158, 192, 214–215, 356–
  357, 358, 361–363, 364, 456, 477
  item analysis for, 385, 387, 394–400,
  403
  reliability in, 441–442
Criterion-related validity, 59, 64–65, 415

Critical incident technique, 147, 280
Critical thinking skills, 111
Crocker, L., 344, 383, 400–401, 407, 411, 435, 441–442
Cronbach, L. J., 4, 276
Cronbach's alpha coefficient, 433, 438
Cunningham, G. K., 464
Curriculum-based assessment. *See* Performance assessment and Written structured response assessments.
Cut-scores, 47–48, 85, 343

Dake, D. M., 2
*Daniel Hoffman v. the Board of Education of the City of New York,* 43
Darling-Hammond, L., 145, 146, 253
Data summaries, 377
Deiner, E., 257
Descriptive statistics, 289–339
  central tendency measures, 297, 301–308
  continuous and discontinuous variables, 294–295
  correlation coefficients, 328–338
  graphic displays of distributions, 312–322
  item, 386, 400–403
  organizing data, 295–301
  relative position measures, 322–328
  scales of measurement, 290–294
  variability measures, 309–312
Developer, in classification of assessment, 81, 86
Diagnostic achievement batteries, 453–455
Difference score (gain score), 373
Differential item functioning (DIF), 57, 425–426
Disciplined inquiry, 4–5
Discontinuous variables, 294–295
Discriminant validity, 59, 63–64, 410–415
Distractor analysis, 384, 386
Domain-referenced mastery analysis, 364–371
  for multiple choice test, 365–368
  for open-ended assessments, 368–371
Domains, 58
  achievement, in User Path 1, 124–135
  construct, 2–6, 107, 121–151, 155–157, 211, 262
Domain-sampling method, 284
Domain scores, 344, 442

Ebel, R. L., 176, 346–347, 448
Ebel procedure, 346–347, 348
Educational assessment
  defined, 2
  educator responsibilities, 18–19
  elements of useful procedure, 6–8
  international, 17
  methods of. *See* Tools for assessment
  nature of, 2–5
  process of, 12
  purposes for, 22–50

recent and historical trends in, 14–17, 371–376
  as term, 1
Educational measurement. *See* Educational assessment
Educational research and development, assessment for, 26, 48
Educational Testing Service (ETS), 46, 246–247, 460, 480–481
Education for All Handicapped Children Act (1974), 41
Edwards, A. L., 276
Effect size, 373
Elementary and Secondary Education Act, 371–372
Empirical evidence, 58
Empirical norming dates, 474
Empirical validation, 110
End-of-unit assessment, 31
Englehart, M. D., 135, 137–138
Ennis, R. H., 111
Error score variance, 428–431
Essays. *See* Written open-ended assessment
Ethics, 483–484
Expectancy tables, 415
Exploratory factor analysis (EFA), 420–423

Factor analysis, 337–338
Factor loadings, 421
Factor patterns, 421
Factors, 338
Factual knowledge, 181–183, 190–191
Fager, J. J., 19
Faking, 273
False positive errors, 417
False prediction errors, 417
Ferron, J., 424
Fill-in-the-blank exercises, 171–176
Fink, A., 269, 271, 272, 282
Fiske, D. W., 63–64, 413
Fitzpatrick, J. R., 35
Florida, 14, 239–241, 408–409
Florida Department of Education, 36
Formative decisions, 27, 28, 32, 33–35, 227, 355, 376–379
Frequency, 296–297
Frequency distributions, 298–301, 311, 313
Frequency polygon, 313–314
Full inclusion, 49
Functional taxonomies, 137, 139–142, 159
Furst, E. J., 135, 137–138

Gain score, 373
Ganguly, R., 401
Gardner, H., 16, 123
Gauss, K. F., 320
*Gesell School Readiness Screening Test* (GSRT), 421–422
Glaser, R., xi, 344
Glenn, J., 16, 123
Goal-setting, 30
Good, C. V., 122

Good, T. L., 123
"Gotcha" teaching, 32
Grade-equivalent scores, 473–475
Grade Point Averages (GPAs), 353
Gradient, 269
Grading. *See* Report card marking
*Graduate Management Admissions Test* (GMAT), 47
*Graduate Record Examination* (GRE), 46–48, 64, 80, 81, 85, 447, 459, 460
Greene, J., 26
Greeno, J. G., 136
Gronlund, N. E., 12, 70–71, 137, 167, 173, 187–190, 280, 353, 479
Group differences, 423–424
Grouped frequency distributions, 298–301, 311, 313
Guidance and counseling, assessment for, 26, 43–46

Hagen, E. P., 458, 459, 464
Hales, L. W., 245
Halo effect, 244
Hambleton, R. K., 193, 343
Hammer, A. L., 462
Hansen, J. C., 462
Harmon, L. W., 43–45, 462
Hawthorne effect, 279
Herman, J. L., 79, 123, 202
*High School Competency Test,* 81
High-stakes decisions, 29, 37, 38
Hill, W. H., 135, 137–138
Histograms, 314–315
Holistic rubrics, 206, 235, 369
Holland, J. L., 462, 466
Homogeneous item structure, 264–265, 384, 386
Hopkins, B. R., 8
Hopkins, K. D., 8, 12, 23, 95, 138, 170–171, 193, 244, 270, 276, 286, 383, 465
Horn, S. P., 372
Hotchkiss, P. R., 31, 32, 51, 354
Huberman, A. M., 273
Hughes, D. C., 245

Impara, J. C., 19, 38–39
Implementation, 31
Index of reliability, 430
Individualized achievement tests, 455
Individualized Educational Plans (IEPs), 38, 366, 377, 378
Inferential statistics, 289
Inflammatory bias, 196, 246
Informed consent, 276
Instructed group (IG), 349, 350–351
Instructional sensitivity, 387
Instructional validity, 456
Instruments, 2
Intelligence and aptitude tests, 80, 84, 457–461
Interest inventories, 80, 461–462
Inter-individual differences, 376

Internal consistency reliability, 433, 435, 442–443
Internal structure, validity of, 59, 62–63, 420–423
International assessment, 17
International Reading Association (IRA), 125–127
Interrater reliability, 432, 433, 440, 441
Interval scales, 291–294
Interview-based assessments, 92–93, 97, 226–228
Intra-individual differences, 376
*Iowa Tests of Basic Skills* (ITBS), 80, 86–87, 447
Ipsative approach, 85
IQ tests, 42
Item analysis, 383–405
    for criterion-referenced tests (CRTs), 385, 387, 394–400, 403
    descriptive statistics in, 386, 400–403
    distractor analysis, 384, 386
    item difficulty, 384, 385
    item discrimination, 384, 385–386
    item homogeneity, 264–265, 384, 386, 401–403
    limitations of, 403
    for norm-referenced tests (NRTs), 388–394
    purposes for, 384
Item carry-over effects, 245
Item construction, 165–186
    choosing best format, 190–191
    completion exercises, 171–176
    fill-in-the-blank exercises, 171–176
    matching exercises, 165–171
    for performance assessment, 215–234
    true/false items, 176–180
Item difficulty index, 384, 385
Item discrimination index, 384, 385–386
Item-level specifications, 163–165
Item Response Theory (IRT), 383, 475
Item-to-total score correlation, 402–403

Jaeger, R. M., 266, 344
Jensen, A. R., 457
Jones, L. V., 72

Keeling, B., 245
Kendall, J. S., 125–127
Kentucky, 16
Kiellor, G., 24
Kohn, A., 354
Krathwohl, D. R., 135, 137–138
Kretke, G., 276
Kuder, G. F., 436–437, 461
*Kuder Preference Record*, 461
Kuder-Richardson Formula 20, 433, 436–437, 439
Kurtosis, 321–322

Lake Wobegon effect, 23–25, 38, 465
Language arts achievement, 135–136
Language mechanics effects, 245–246

Large-scale assessments, 36
Latent factors, 338
*Law Schools Admissions Test* (LSAT), 46, 47
Learning outcomes
    achievement versus, 122–123
    dimensions of learning, 138–139
    process, 123–124
    product, 124
    taxonomies of, 135, 137–141
Lehman, I. J., 91
Lewinsohn, P. M., 148, 258
Licensure, assessment for, 26, 46–48
Likert, R., 89, 284
Likert scales, 401
Linn, R. L., 12, 173, 187–190, 280, 344, 353, 479
Locally-made tests, 80, 81
Locus of control, 93
Logical evidence, 58
Lorge, I., 459
Low-stakes decisions, 29
Loyd, B. H., 354, 364
Loyd, D. E., 354, 364

Maine, 16
Marking. *See* Report card marking
Marsh, H. W., 284, 286
Maryland, 16
Marzano, R. J., 15, 16, 123, 125–127, 138–139, 142, 201–202
Mastery classifications, reliability of, 442–443
Matching exercises, 165–171
Mathematics achievement, 10, 130, 134, 135
McDonald, R. P., 407
McLearns, G. E., 457
McTighe, J., 15, 16, 123, 138–139, 142, 201–202
Mean, 303–305
    item, 400–401
    regression toward, 376
Measurement, 6, 8, 12. *See also* Educational assessment
Median, 305–308
Mehrens, W. A., 16, 91, 95
Mental constructs, 9
Messick, S., 49–50, 58
Metacognition, 202
Miles, M. B., 273
Millman, J., 18, 26
Minimum competency standards, 344, 345
Minnesota, 16
*Minnesota Multiphasic Personality Inventory* (MMPI), 147, 464
*Minnesota Teacher Attitude Inventory* (MTAI), 80
Mislevy, R. J., 246
Mitchell, R., 83, 95, 201–202
Mode, 296–297, 302
Modified-Angoff procedure, 346

Modified-Ebel procedure, 346–347, 351
Multilevel achievement batteries, 450–453, 456, 459
Multimethod matrix, 413–415
Multimodal distributions, 302
Multiple choice items, 180–186, 365–368
Multiple correlation, 330
Multitrait matrix, 413–415
Myford, C., 246

National Assessment of Educational Progress (NAEP), 72–73, 74
National Center for Education Statistics, 467
National Center for History in Schools (NCHS), 125, 127
National Commission for Excellence in Education (NCEE), 15
National Council for the Accreditation of Teacher Education (NCATE), 253
National Council of Teachers of English (NCTE), 125–127, 201–202
National Council of Teachers of Mathematics (NCTM), 16, 125, 134, 201–202
National Council on Measurement in Education (NCME), xii, 9, 18, 20, 38, 54, 58, 104, 109, 149, 409, 427, 445, 447, 448, 481, 483–485
National Education Association (NEA), 484
National Research Council, xi
National Research Council (NRC), 125, 127
National standardization sample, 450
*National Standards for United States History,* 125–127
*Nation at Risk, A,* 15
Naturalistic observation, 279–282
Negative errors, 417
Nitko, A. J., 26, 29, 111, 171, 173, 176, 202, 432, 440, 441, 466, 474, 475
Noddings, N., 145, 146, 253
Nominal scales, 291, 292
Nonstandardized tests, 80, 84
Normal Curve Equivalent (NCE), 375, 471
Normal distributions, 318–320, 466–469
Norm groups, 85, 323, 465
Norm-referenced interpretations, 465
Norm-referenced tests (NRTs), 25, 81, 85, 87, 157–158, 193, 356–357, 358, 363, 449, 456–457, 464–477
    item analysis for, 385, 388–394, 403
    quality of norms, 465–466
    types of norm-referenced scores, 466–476
Norms tables, 449, 466
Norris, S. P., 111
Null hypothesis, 336
Nunnally, J. C., 400–401, 407, 411

Objective-referenced tests, 364
Observed scores, 428–430

Ogives, 315–318, 350–351, 352, 359, 361
O'Neill, K. A., 460
Oosterhof, A., 190
Open-ended assessment, 89, 96, 99, 112, 215–219, 268–271, 275, 368–371
Operational definitions, 9–10
Opportunity-to-learn bias, 196, 246
Order effects, 245
Ordinal scales, 291, 292
Osgood, C. E., 284–286
Outcome-driven model, 29–32, 355
Outliers, 304–305, 313

Paerson, P. D., 136
Parallel forms reliability, 430, 432, 433–434
Parent involvement programs, 380
Participant-observer, 280
Patton, M. Q., 35
Pearson product moment correlation, 330–332, 336, 411
Pederson, N. L., 457
Pellegrino, J. W., xi
Percentile bands, 470
Percentile ranks, 85, 317–318, 325–328, 469–470
Percentiles, 308
Performance assessment, 79, 82–83, 104, 200–248
  assessment specifications for, 239–243
  bias in design, 244–247
  item construction guidelines for, 215–234
  justifying methods in, 202–205
  Process Model with, 206–215
  reasons for using, 201–202
  scoring rubrics for, 206, 234–238, 244–247
  test assembly, 243
Performance carry-over effects, 245
Performance criterion, 135
Performance standards, 343
Personality assessments, 80, 84, 250–287, 463–464
Peters, C. W., 136
Pickering, D. J., 15, 16, 123, 138–139, 142, 201–202
Plake, B. S., 19, 38–39, 343
Planning, 30–31
Plomin, R., 457
Point-biserial correlation coefficient, 402–403
Popham, W. J., 163
Populations, 6–7, 55
  in Process Model, 107, 155, 206
Portfolio-based assessment, 93–94, 98, 229–234
Power tests, 80
*Praxis I and II,* 46, 47
Prediction, 328–329
Predictive validity, 42, 47, 64, 415–418
Presentation mode, in classification of assessment, 81, 86
Presser, S., 272
Privacy, 276

Probes, 226
Process Model, xii, xiii, 103–120
  case study using, 111–117
  components of, 105–110
  importance of systematic process, 117–119
  need for, 104–105
  for performance assessments, 206–215
  Phase I, 106–107, 155–157, 206–211, 252–253, 257
  Phase II, 108, 157, 211–212, 253–255, 257–258
  Phase III, 108–109, 157, 212, 255, 258
  Phase IV, 109–110, 157–158, 213–215, 255, 258–262
  for User Path 1, 111–117
  for User Path 2–6, 251–262
  for written structured-response assessments, 155–158
Process outcomes, 123–124, 135
Product-based assessments, 2, 4, 91–92, 97, 223–225
Product moment correlation, 330–332, 336, 411
Product outcomes, 124
PRO-ED, Inc., 481
Program-level assessments, 33–39
Program outcomes, 377
Program Plans, 377–379
Program process variables, 377
Psychometrics, 18
Psychomotor domain, 137
Purposes for educational assessment, 22–50
  crossover across user groups, 48–49
  need for clear, 22–25
  in Process Model, 107, 155, 206–211
  responsibilities for appropriate use, 49–50
  typology of assessment uses, 25–26
  User Path 5: Admissions, Certification, Recognitions, and Awards, 26, 46–48
  User Path 4: Guidance and Counseling, 26, 43–46
  User Path 2: Program Planning, Evaluation, and Policy Contexts, 26, 33–39
  User Path 6: Research and Development, 26, 48
  User Path 3: Screening and Diagnosis of Exceptionalities, 26, 39–43
  User Path 1: Teaching and Learning, 26, 27–32

Qualitative data, in assigning marks, 363
Quality control, 36–37

Random error, 67–70, 244–247, 427–428, 433
Range, 296–297, 309–310
Rank-ordered distributions, 296–297, 303–305, 311
Rating scales, 2, 236–237
Ratio scales, 293, 294

Raw scores, 322–323, 465
Readability bias, 195–196, 246
Readiness for learning, 27
Recency of norms, 465
Redner, J. E., 148, 258
Reed, T. E., 457
Regression analysis, 337, 376
Relative position measures, 322–328
Relevance of norms, 60–61, 109, 161, 375, 409–410, 466
Reliability, 67–70, 71, 375, 427–443
  classical conceptions of, 427–428
  Cohen's kappa, 433, 440, 441, 442–443
  confidence bands, 415–416, 439, 440–441
  in criterion-related measurements, 441–442
  Cronbach's alpha coefficient, 433, 438
  in domain score estimates, 442
  internal consistency, 433, 435, 442–443
  interrater, 432, 433, 440, 441
  Kuder-Richardson Formula 20, 433, 436–437, 439
  of mastery classifications, 442–443
  methods of estimating, 432–441
  observed scores, 428–430
  parallel forms, 430, 432, 433–434
  priorities and, 73–74
  quantitative estimates of, 70
  random error and, 67–70
  Reliability Coefficient, 70, 429–431
  split-half, 433, 435–436
  standard error of measurement (SEM), 70, 428–431, 439, 440–441, 470
  test-retest, 413–415, 433, 434–435
  true scores, 428–430
Reliability Coefficient, 70, 429–431
Report card marking, 353
  choosing a system for, 363–364
  combining assessment results for, 358–363
  method of, 354–357
  nature of, 353
  with qualitative data, 363
Representativeness of norms, 375, 465
Resnick, D. P., 16, 123, 202
Resnick, L. B., 16, 123, 202
Response mode, in classification of assessment, 81, 86
Response process, validity of, 59, 61–62
Response sets, 276
Richardson, M. W., 436–437
Robinson, J. P., 148, 258
*Rorschach Test,* 464
Rubrics
  analytic, 206, 234–235, 368, 370
  scoring, 79–82, 206, 234–238, 244–247
Rules, 8
Russell, J. T., 417–418

Salvia, J., 40
Sampling error, 336
Sanders, J. R., 35

Sanders, W. L., 372
Sattler, J. M., 39, 43, 458
Sax, G., 193
Scaled scores, 450, 475
Scale points, 271, 285
Scale scores, 375
Scales of measurement, 290–294
Scaling constructs, 7–8
Scattergrams, 332–333
Scholarships, assessment for, 26, 46–48
*Scholastic Assessment Test* (SAT), 46, 80, 337, 447, 459
Schueneman, J. D., 460
Schumann, H., 272
Scores, in classification of assessment, 81, 85
Scoring process, validity of, 59, 61–62, 71, 244–247
Scoring rubrics, 79–82
  for performance assessment, 206, 234–238, 244–247
Scriven, M., 33
Second International Assessment of Educational Progress (IAEP-2), 17
*Second International Mathematics and Science Study* (SIMSS), 17, 18–19
Secretary's Commission for Achieving Necessary Skills (SCANS), 16
Seeley, J. R., 148, 258
Selection biases, 47, 417–418
Selection ratio, 417
Self-concept measures, 286
Self-Description Questionnaire (SDQ), 286
Self-report instruments, 263–276
  assembly of, 272–273
  problems with, 273–276
  rules for designing, 263–272
  scoring, 273
Semantic ambiguity, 276
Semantic differential scales, 285–286
Shavelson, R., 284, 286
Shepard, L. A., 12, 16, 24, 38, 41–42, 79, 344
Short response tasks. *See* Written open-ended assessment
Shulman, L., 4, 145–146, 253
Simple frequency distributions, 298, 303–305, 306–307
Skewness, 320–321
Skill-based analysis, 364
Social desirability, 274
Social maladjustment, 280
Spandel, V., 79, 93–94, 229, 353
Spearman-Brown Prophecy Formula, 435–436
Speed tests, 80
Split-half reliability, 433, 435–436
Stakeholders, 35
Standard deviation, 310–312
  item, 400–401
Standard error of estimate, 415–416
Standard error of measurement (SEM), 70, 428–431, 439, 440–441, 470

Standardization sample, 449, 450
Standardized tests, 23–25, 80, 84, 445–485
  distinguishing characteristics of, 446–448
  evaluating, 477–480
  norms in, 464–477
  resources for finding, 480–484
  use in education, 448–464
Standards, 343–353
  based on empirical distributions of typical examinees, 348–353
  based on individual items or classes of items, 346–348
  based on judgment of overall item pool, 345–346
  in standard-setting applications, 344
Standard scores, 470–472
*Standards for Educational and Psychological Testing* (AERA, APA, and NCME), xii, 9, 13, 18, 20, 38, 54, 58, 104, 109, 149, 409, 427, 447, 448, 481–483
*Standards for English Language Arts*, 125–127
Standards of excellence, 345–346
*Stanford Achievement Test Series* (STA), 2, 3, 80, 81, 86–87, 418–420, 447, 450–453, 465, 467, 469, 475, 476
*Stanford-Binet Scale*, 447, 458
Stanines, 472–473
Stanley, J. C., 8, 67, 427
Statistical significance, 336
Sternberg, R. J., 457
Stevens, S. S., 6, 8, 290–291
Stiggins, R. J., xi, 16, 19, 79, 145, 146, 201–202, 253
Strong, E. K., 461
*Strong-Campbell Interest Inventory* (S-CII), 80
*Strong Interest Inventory* (SII), 462
Structured observation forms, 277–279
  problems with, 278–279
  rules for designing, 278
Structured-response assessment, 87–89, 95–99, 112, 152–197, 201–202, 268–271, 365–368
Students with special needs, 26, 39–43
Subjective well-being, 147–149
Success ratio, 417
Suci, G. J., 284–286
Summative decisions, 27–29, 32, 33–35, 37, 38, 355–356
Summative evaluation, 380
Suppes, P., 4
Symmetrical distributions, 313, 318
Systematic error, 54–57, 244–247, 427–428
Systematic rater bias, 246–247

Table of specifications, 159–161
Tanner, P. H., 284–286
Targeted content domain, 245–246
Task carry-over effects, 245

Taylor, H. C., 417–418
Taylor, W. L., 175
Teacher-made tests, 81
Tennessee, 372
*Tennessee Self-Concept Scale*, 464
Terwilliger, J. S., 18, 357
Test carry-over effects, 245
*Test of Spoken English*, 92–93
Test-retest reliability, 413–415, 433, 434–435
Tests, 2, 4
*Thematic Apperception Test*, 464
*Third International Mathematics and Science Study* (TIMSS), 17, 18
Thorndike, E. L., 2, 6
Thorndike, R. L., 458, 459, 464
Thorndike, R. M., 464
Thurstone, L. L., 284, 285
Title 1 Evaluation and Reporting System (TIERS), 371–372
Tokar, E., 245
Tools for assessment, 78–101
  advantages and disadvantages of, 95–100
  alternative assessment, 79–83
  authentic assessment, 18, 79, 82, 83
  classification methods, 80–81, 83–94
  performance assessment, 79, 82–83, 104, 200–248
  traditional assessment, 79
Traditional assessment, 79
Traub, R. E., 193
Tree diagrams, 127, 134
True/false items, 176–180
True scores, 428–430
True score variance, 428–430
True zero, 294
T-scores, 325, 358–359, 360, 362–363, 429–430
Tuck, B. F., 245
Tyler, R. W., 25–26, 29

Ungrouped frequency distributions, 301
Unidimensionality, 264–265
Unimodal distributions, 313, 318
Uninstructed group (UG), 349, 350–351
U.S. Department of Labor, 16
User Path 5: Admissions, Certification, Recognitions, and Awards, 26, 46–48
  construct domain in, 142–147, 262
  instrument design in, 284–286
  nature of constructs in, 262
  Process Model in, 251–262
  selecting assessment tools in, 282–284
User Path 4: Guidance and Counseling, 26, 43–46
  construct domain in, 142–149, 262
  instrument design in, 284–286
  nature of constructs in, 262
  Process Model in, 257–262
  selecting assessment tools in, 282–284

User Path 2: Program Planning, Evaluation, and Policy Contexts, 26, 33–39
construct domain in, 142–147, 262
instrument design in, 284–286
nature of constructs in, 262
Process Model in, 252–256
selecting assessment tools in, 282–284
User Path 6: Research and Development, 26, 48
construct domain in, 142–147, 262
instrument design in, 284–286
nature of constructs in, 262
Process Model in, 251–262
selecting assessment tools in, 282–284
user domain in, 142–147
User Path 3: Screening and Diagnosis of Exceptionalities, 26, 39–43
construct domain in, 142–149, 262
instrument design in, 284–286
nature of constructs in, 262
Process Model in, 257–262
selecting assessment tools in, 282–284
User Path 1: Teaching and Learning, 26, 27–32
construct domain in, 122–142
Process Model in, 111–117
Utility, 70–73
administration conditions for, 71
ease of interpretation and use, 72–73
human and material costs of, 71
priorities and, 73–74
scoring procedures for, 71

Valencia, S. P., 136
Validation, 42, 58–66, 408–427
Validity, 54–66, 71, 375, 408–427
concurrent, 64–65, 418–420
construct, 409

content, 58–61, 65–66, 109, 118, 158, 193–195, 242, 243, 284, 409–410
convergent, 59, 63–64, 410–415
criterion-related, 59, 64–65, 415
differential item functioning (DIF), 57, 425–426
discriminant, 59, 63–64, 410–415
group differences and, 423–424
instructional, 456
of internal structure, 59, 62–63, 420–423
predictive, 42, 47, 64, 415–418
priorities and, 73–74
process, 59, 61–62
in response, scoring, and administration processes, 59–62
of scoring methods, 425–427
systematic error and, 54–57, 244–247, 427–428
Variability measures, 309–312
Variables, 11
continuous and discontinuous, 294–295
program outcome, 377
program process, 377
Variance, 310–312
error score, 428–431
item, 400–401
Vermont, 16
*Vineland Adaptive Behavior Scales* (VABS), 64–65, 80

Walsh, W. B., 457–460, 462–464
Wechsler, D., 458
*Wechsler Adult Intelligence Scale* (WAIS), 80, 81, 458
*Wechsler Intelligence Scale for Children* (WISC), 458
*Wechsler Preschool and Primary Scale of*

*Intelligence-Revised* (WPPSI-R), 84, 458, 465, 468
Weighting constant, 163
Weinkein, J. L., 2
Wesman, A. G., 190
Whitney, D. R., 46
Wiggins, G., 16, 18, 79, 82, 101, 201–202, 354, 357
Willett, J. B., 376
Williams, P. L., 24
Winters, L., 79, 123, 202
Wixson, K. K., 136
Wolf, D., 16, 123
Woolfolk, A. E., 111
Work samples, 223–225
World-class standards, 17
Worthen, B. R., 35
Writing mechanics effects, 245–246
Written open-ended assessment, 89, 96, 99, 112, 215–219
Written structured-response (W-SR) assessments, 87–89, 95–99, 112, 152–197, 201–202
assessment specifications for, 158–165
bias in design, 195–196
clues in, 190
complex interpretive exercises in, 187–190
content validation, 193–195
item construction guidelines for, 165–186
item format for, 190–191
Process Model for, 155–158
reasons for using, 153–154
test assembly, 191–193

Ysseldyke, J. E., 40

z-scores, 323–324, 469, 472